UNDERSTANDING DYING, DEATH, AND BEREAVEMENT

Third Edition

Michael R. Leming
St. Olaf College

George E. Dickinson
College of Charleston

HARCOURT BRACE COLLEGE PUBLISHERS

Fort Worth   Philadelphia   San Diego   New York   Orlando   Austin   San Antonio
Toronto   Montreal   London   Sydney   Tokyo

Publisher	Ted Buchholz
Senior Acquisitions Editor	Christopher P. Klein
Developmental Editor	Linda Wiley
Project Editor	Kelly Riche
Production Manager	Kathleen Ferguson
Art Director	Peggy Young
Picture Development Editor	Greg Meadors

Cover & Text design: John Odom Design, Del Mar, Ca.

Address for editorial correspondence
Harcourt Brace College Publishers
301 Commerce Street, Suite 3700
Fort Worth, Texas 76102

Address for orders
Harcourt Brace & Company
6277 Sea Harbor Drive
Orlando, Florida 32887
1-800-782-4479; in Florida 1-800-433-0001

Copyrights and Acknowledgments continue on p. 527, which constitutes a continuation of the copyright page.

ISBN: 0-15-500632-0

Library of Congress Catalog Card Number: 93-77913

Printed in the United States of America

7 8 9 0 1 2   090   9 8 7 6 5

MICHAEL R. LEMING

Michael R. Leming is Professor of Sociology and Anthropology at St. Olaf College. He holds degrees from Westmont College (B.A.), Marquette University (M.A.), and the University of Utah (Ph.D.) and has completed additional graduate study at the University of California in Santa Barbara. He is co-author with George E. Dickinson of *Understanding Dying, Death, and Bereavement* (Holt, Rinehart and Winston, 1985 and 1990) and *Understanding Families: Diversity, Continuity, and Change* (Allyn and Bacon, 1990). He is also co-editor of *The Sociological Perspective: A Value-Committed Introduction* (Zondervan, 1989) and *Annual Editions: Dying, Death, and Bereavement* (Dushkin, 1993).

Dr. Leming is founder and former director of the St. Olaf College Social Research Center, former member of the board of directors of the Minnesota Coalition on Terminal Care, steering committee member of the Northfield AIDS Response, and a hospice educator, volunteer, and grief counselor.

GEORGE E. DICKINSON

George E. Dickinson is Professor and Chair of the Department of Sociology and Anthropology at the College of Charleston in Charleston, South Carolina. He holds degrees from Baylor University (B.A. in biology and M.A. in sociology), and Louisiana State University (Ph.D. in sociology). He has completed graduate work in gerontology at Pennsylvania State University, in thanatology at the University of Kentucky School of Medicine, and in medical sociology at the University of Connecticut. Dickinson is co-author with Michael R. Leming of *Understanding Families: Diversity, Continuity, and Change* and co-editor of *Annual Editions: Dying, Death, and Bereavement.* He has published more than forty articles in journals such as *Omega, Death Studies, Academic Medicine, Medical Care, Family Practice Research, Journal of the American Medical Women's Association, Loss, Grief and Care, Journal of Dental Education, Journal of Nursing Education, Journal for the Scientific Study of Religion, Journal of Marriage and the Family, Youth and Society,* and *Journal of Family Issues.*

Dr. Dickinson has been teaching courses on death and dying for more than twenty years, as well as conducting research on thanatology offerings in the health professions and on the attitudes of physicians and other medical personnel toward terminally ill patients. He is also actively involved with Hospice of Charleston.

Preface

Since publication of the earlier editions of *Understanding Dying, Death, and Bereavement,* we have received many helpful comments from students, faculty, and clinical practitioners, with suggestions for improvements and additions to be incorporated into the third edition. These suggestions proved to be a tremendous resource for us in our task of producing this new version of our textbook. The input of numerous individuals has been both encouraging and valuable to us. The third edition includes more than cosmetic changes. At least 30 percent of the manuscript has been rewritten or is entirely new.

Our goal has been to produce a book that is informative, practical, and multidisciplinary in orientation, inclusive of the major foci of the interdisciplinary subject of social thanatology, and yet humanistic. We have tried to equip the reader with the necessary information to both *understand* and *cope* with the social processes of dying, death, and bereavement. Because both of us have taught courses on this subject for twenty years, we realize that *every* student comes with both academic and personal agendas when approaching the topic of thanatology.

In our first edition, we brought together nine national authorities who had extensive academic experience and personal involvement in the topical areas on which they wrote. However, we discovered that differences in writing styles and levels of treatment created some problems for our readers. Therefore, with the exception of Chapter 11, we have rewritten the chapters previously contributed by our professional colleagues (see Acknowledgements).

Though collaboration occurred throughout the writing of this third edition, a division of labor was established from the outset. Chapters 2, 5, 7, 8, 12, and 13 were primarily the responsibility of Michael Leming. George Dickinson was responsible for writing Chapters 1, 3, 4, 6, 9, and 10. Thus, if you occasionally encounter a reference to "I" in a chapter, the first person singular refers to the primary author of that particular chapter. It is our hope that these personal accounts throughout the text will give a more personal touch to the chapters and make the reading seem less "textbookish."

We believe that *Understanding Dying, Death, and Bereavement,* third edition, will make a significant contribution to your class. It is comprehensive and deals with the full range of topics in social thanatology; is scholarly and academically sound; represents a unified effort informed by forty years of experience; and is practical for the student since it is concerned with personal issues relating to an individual's ability to cope with the social and psychological processes of dying, death, and bereavement.

This book is intended primarily for undergraduate students, though it would be appropriate for professional courses in medicine, nursing, mortuary science, social work, and pastoral counseling. *Understanding Dying, Death, and Bereavement,* third edition, could be used in sociology, psychology, nursing, social work, physical education, religion, health science, family studies, and education courses. It could also be used as a primary or supplementary text in courses on gerontology, health, human development, counseling, and medical sociology. We believe that this edition will appeal to a vast audience, not only because of its wide adaptability on college and university campuses, but also because of its practical implications for all persons who must cope with this topic.

The following features have been included in this edition to make it interesting and personally relevant to the student: (1) boxed inserts present timely readings and articles that illustrate issues covered in the text; (2) chapter summaries serve as study aids to outline the important points of each chapter; (3) discussion questions highlight important issues in each chapter; (4) annotated bibliographies provide information on suggested readings for students who desire further research; and (5) glossaries of unfamiliar terms can be found at the end of each chapter. There is also an instructor's manual available from Harcourt Brace that recommends audiovisual materials and provides a test bank of more than 800 true-false, multiple-choice, and essay questions.

We welcome suggestions and feedback from readers that might improve future editions of this book. We would also appreciate correspondence from instructors concerning pedagogy related to the teaching of this subject.

ACKNOWLEDGMENTS

Looking back over the past ten years, we are struck by the degree to which this book is the result of a very large team effort. We are indebted to the work of the contributing authors for the first edition. We continue to be grateful for the original contributions of Professors Robert Bendiksen of the Department of Sociology at the University of Wisconsin at La Crosse; Nils C. Fribert of Bethel Theological Seminary in St. Paul, MN; Ann L. Overbeck of the School of Social Work at Western Michigan University; Glenn M. Vernon (deceased), former sociologist at the University of Utah; John W. Abbott of Connecticut Hospice; and Robert C. Slater (retired from the Department of Mortuary Science at the University of Minnesota). Chapter 11 is entirely the work of Professor James J. Farrell of the History Department at

St. Olaf College in Minnesota. We could not have produced a book of this quality without the earlier contributions of these individuals.

We are also indebted to Chris Klein, Linda Wiley, Kelly Riche, Kathy Ferguson, and Peggy Young at Harcourt Brace for their work in producing this manuscript and for the confidence and encouragement they invested in this project.

We also acknowledge the support of our families during the writing of this book. We appreciate their sharing in our struggle as we "walked in the valley of the shadow of death." They know how much strength we have gained from reflecting upon our death-related experiences. They have also been able to observe "our mourning changed into dancing." We hope that our readers will experience a renewed appreciation for life as they begin to understand more fully, intellectually and emotionally, the social-psychological processes of dying, death, and bereavement. Indeed, this book is on dying and death, but it is really about living and life. May your reading of this book help to make life more meaningful.

Contents

Preface   iv

PART ONE:
UNDERSTANDING DYING AND DEATH   1

CHAPTER 1:
THE AMERICAN WAY OF DYING   2

    Current Interest in Thanatology   4
      Why the Increased Interest?   4
      The Media and Death   6
      The Discipline of Thanatology   8
      Thanatology for Health Professionals   11
    Defining Death   11
      International Definitions of Death   12
      American Definitions of Death   13
    Denying Death   16
    Fearing Death   20
      Content of Death Fears   21
      Death Fears and Gender   22
      Death Fear Scale   24
    Mortality Statistics   27
      Death Etiology and Life Expectancy   28
      Gender Differences in Mortality Rates   30
    Coping with the American Way of Dying   34

Conclusion 36
Summary 38
Discussion Questions 39
Glossary 39
References 40
Suggested Readings 42

CHAPTER 2:
UNDERSTANDING THE SOCIAL MEANING OF DYING AND DEATH 44

The Social Nature of Meaning 48
Creating and Changing Meaning 49
A Social Science Understanding of Dying and Death 50
The Sociological Approach to Understanding Dying and Death 50
The Social Factist Paradigm 53
The Social Definitionist Paradigm 61
Conclusion 72
Summary 73
Discussion Questions 75
Glossary 76
References 76
Suggested Readings 77

PART TWO:
UNDERSTANDING DEATH ATTITUDES 79

CHAPTER 3:
CHILDREN AND DEATH 80

The Dying Child 85
Knowledge Is Kindness 85

The Child Needs Support   86

Parents of the Dying Child   89

Siblings of the Dying Child   91

Explaining Death to Children   93

    Be Honest and Open   94

    Avoid Euphemisms   95

    Show Emotion   97

Children's Understanding of Death   99

    Birth to Age 3   100

    Ages 3 to 5   101

    Ages 6 to 10   103

Sudden Infant Death Syndrome (SIDS)   108

    The Etiology of SIDS   109

    Parents of SIDS Children   112

Conclusion   113

Summary   114

Discussion Questions   115

Glossary   115

References   115

Suggested Readings   118

CHAPTER 4:
DEVELOPMENTAL PERSPECTIVE ON DYING AND DEATH:
ADOLESCENCE THROUGH OLDER ADULTHOOD   120

Adolescence   123

    An Identity Crisis   124

    Socialization to Death Fears   126

    Helping Adolescents Cope with Death   128

Introduction to Adulthood   129

Young Adulthood   131

    Remember Death   131

    The Novice Phase   132

    Acquired Immunodeficiency Syndrome (AIDS)   132

Middle-Aged Adulthood   134

    The Panic Begins   134

    A More Philosophical Outlook Develops   136

    Personal Growth Continues   136

Older Adulthood   137

    Erikson's Final Stage of Life   140

    Death Taboo and the Elderly   140

    Death Fears   141

    The Place of Death   144

Conclusion   146
Summary   147
Discussion Questions   148
Glossary   148
References   150
Suggested Readings   152

CHAPTER 5:
RELIGION AND DEATH ATTITUDES   154

Death and the Origin of Religion   156
Religion as a Means of Providing Understanding of Death   159
Religious Interpretations of Death   164
    Judaism   166
    Christianity   169
    Islam   172
    Hinduism   175
    Buddhism   179
Temporal Interpretations of Death   184
    Symbolic Immortality   185
    Relative Death Meanings in Society   187
    Society's Heroes   189
Afterlife Experiences by the Clinically Dead   191
    Empirical Evidence for Afterlife Beliefs?   191
Conclusion   196
Summary   197
Discussion Questions   198
Glossary   198
References   199
Suggested Readings   201

PART THREE:
UNDERSTANDING THE DYING PROCESS   203

CHAPTER 6:
THE DYING PROCESS   204

Death Meanings and Their Effects Upon the Dying Process   206
    Time Meanings   206
    Space Meanings   209
    Norm and Role Meanings   211
    Value Meanings   213
    Object and Self Meanings   213
    Social Situation Meanings   218
Physicians and the Dying Patient   218
    Death Education in Medical Schools   220
    More Death Education Needed in Medical Schools   222
Relating to Dying Patients   223
    Gender versus Professional Role   224
    Awareness Contexts of Dying   225
Dying as Deviance in the Medical Setting   228
    Labeling Theory   228

Deviance Results in Punishment   229
The Autopsy   230
Conclusion   236
Summary   237
Discussion Questions   237
Glossary   238
References   239
Suggested Readings   · 242

CHAPTER 7:
THE HOSPICE APPROACH: ALTERNATIVE CARE FOR THE DYING   244

The History of the Hospice Movement   246
The Nature of the Contemporary Hospice   249
   Pain Management   249
   Home and Inpatient Care   250
   The Hospice Team   250
   Patient-Centered Care   256
   Bereavement Care   258
   Persons Served by the Hospice   259
   Special Aspects of Home Care   259
   Special Aspects of Inpatient Care   261
Models of Inpatient Hospice Care   266
Hospice Issues   268
   Quality of Life   268
   The Patient-Family as the Unit of Care   270
   Cost of Hospice Care   272
   Training Professionals   273
   Public Attitudes   273
Evaluation of Hospice Programs   274
AIDS: Hospice Challenge for the 1990s   278
Conclusion   281
Summary   281
Discussion Questions   282
Glossary   283
References   283
Suggested Readings   284

CHAPTER 8:
EUTHANASIA AND BIOMEDICAL ISSUES   286

 Sanctity and Quality of Life   288
 Passive and Active Euthanasia   291
  Living Wills   293
  The Legalization of Mercy Killing: The Dutch Experiment 300
  The Slippery-Slope Argument   303
 Organ Donations   309
 Public Policy   313
 Conclusion   317
 Summary   318
 Discussion Questions   319
 Glossary   320
 References   321
 Suggested Readings   322

CHAPTER 9:
SUICIDE   324

 Theoretical Perspectives on Suicide   330
  Sociological Perspective   330
  Dramaturgical Perspective   332
  Existentialist Perspective   333
  Alienation   334
 Social Factors, Signs, and Methods of Suicide   335
  Social Factors of Suicide   335
  Signs of Suicide   336
  Methods of Committing Suicide   337
  Childhood Suicidal Behavior   338
 Adolescent Suicidal Behavior   339
 The Media and Suicide Clusters   343
 Suicide and the Elderly   345
  Gender and Suicide in the Elderly   345
  Danger Signals and Methods of Suicide   346
 Rational Suicide   347
 Conclusion   353

Summary	*355*
Discussion Questions	*356*
Glossary	*356*
References	*357*
Suggested Readings	*360*

PART FOUR:
UNDERSTANDING THE BEREAVEMENT PROCESS

363

CHAPTER 10:
THE ANTHROPOLOGY OF DEATH RITUAL

364

Societal Management of Death-Related Emotions	*367*
Why Study Cross-Cultural Death Rituals?	*369*
Death as a Rite of Passage	*371*
The Ritual of Mourning at Death	*372*
The Display of Emotions	*374*
Types of Weeping	*376*
Attitudes Toward Death	*377*
Customs at Death	*382*
Norms Prior to Death	*382*
Handling the Corpse	*383*
Burial Rites	*388*
Functions	*389*
Variations	*392*
Conclusion	*395*
Summary	*396*
Discussion Questions	*397*

Glossary	*398*
References	*399*
Suggested Readings	*402*

CHAPTER 11:
THE HISTORY OF BEREAVEMENT AND BURIAL PRACTICES IN AMERICAN CULTURE   *404*

Living Death, 1600–1830	*407*
The Reformed Tradition	*407*
Reforming the Reformed Tradition	*410*
The Dying of Death, 1830–1945	*413*
The Rise of the Middle Class	*413*
Intellectual Influences	*414*
Institutional Influences	*421*
The Resurrection of Death, 1945 to the Present	*434*
The Atomic Age	*434*
Conclusion	*441*
Summary	*442*
Discussion Questions	*442*
Glossary	*443*
References	*444*
Suggested Readings	*446*

CHAPTER 12:
THE FUNERAL: EXPRESSION OF CONTEMPORARY AMERICAN BEREAVEMENT   *448*

Social and Cultural Roots of American Funeral Traditions	*450*
Early American Funeral Practices	*454*
The Contemporary American Funeral	*458*
How the Funeral Meets the Needs of the Bereaved	*459*
The Needs of Children and Their Attendance at Funerals	*461*
The American Practice of Funeral Service	*463*
Education and Licensure	*463*
The Role of the Funeral Director	*467*
Body Preparation	*467*
Final Disposition	*469*
Alternatives to the Funeral	*472*
Funeral, Final Disposition, and Related Expenses	*474*
New Trends in Funeral Service	*479*
Preneed Funerals: A "New" Trend in Planning Funerals	*479*
After-Care: The Future Business Is to Be Found in Today's Customers	*482*

Conclusion   483
Summary   483
Discussion Questions   484
Glossary   484
References   485
Suggested Readings   487

CHAPTER 13:
THE BEREAVEMENT PROCESS   488

The Bereavement Role   490
Disenfranchised Grief   494
• The Grieving Process   495
Coping with Grief   497
    Shock and Denial   497
    Disorganization   498
    Volatile Reactions   498
    Guilt   499
    Loss and Loneliness   499
    Relief   501
    Reestablishment   501
The Four Tasks of Mourning   503
    Accept the Reality of the Loss   504
    Experience the Pain of Grief   504
    Adjust to an Environment in Which the Deceased Is Missing   505
    Withdraw Emotional Energy and Reinvest It in Another Relationship   505
Assisting the Bereaved   506
Support Groups for the Bereaved   509
Grieving Parents and the Loss of an Infant   510
    Support from Health-Care Professionals   511
    Parental Involvement with Professional Helpers: Perinatal Deaths   512
The Death of Pets: A Special Kind of Grieving   514
    Pets in the Lives of the Elderly   516
    Having a Pet "Put to Sleep"   517
    Disposal of Pets after Death   517
Conclusion   520
Summary   521
Discussion Questions   522
Glossary   523
References   523
Suggested Readings   525

Index   528

Part One

Understanding Dying and Death

Chapter

1

The American
Way of Dying

I mourn not those who lose their vital breath
But those who, living, live in fear of death.

The Ancient Greek Anthology

PEOPLE WHO RELATE to any aspect of dying and death are thought by many to be "weird" or "morbid." Note the reactions of others when you tell them you are taking a course on death and dying! The startled reactions of others when told that we teach courses on death and dying are rather interesting, to say the least. One woman, when informed that we offer courses on death and dying, reacted by saying, "How could you do such a thing?"

Imagine the responses to persons who are funeral directors or who work in a nursing home or on a cancer ward of a hospital. From the reactions that most people have to these death-related issues, it appears that discussions of death are considered in bad taste and something to be avoided. **Elderhostel** programs, for example, can present any topic of interest to older persons *except death and dying.*

Dying in the United States today occurs "offstage," away from the arena of familiar surroundings of kin and friends. Seventy percent of current deaths in the United States occur in institutional settings—hospitals and nursing homes. Today, Grandfather seldom dies at home, where he has spent most of his life, but in a rather impersonal institutional setting. The removal of death from the usual setting prompted Richard Dumont and Dennis Foss (1972:2) to raise the question: "How is the modern American able to cope with his own death when the deaths he experiences are infrequent, highly impersonal, and viewed as virtually abnormal?"

CURRENT INTEREST IN THANATOLOGY

Today's thanatology student is bombarded with pressing issues of the day that involve death and death-related matters: the AIDS crisis, the prolongation of dying from cancer, the growing incidence of chronic illnesses with uncertain courses, murder, ecological disasters, fetal transplants, and abortion. The topic of death is "alive and well" in contemporary society. Let's look at some of the reasons why dying and death as topics of discussion have come into their own in recent years.

Why the Increased Interest?

This increased interest in **thanatology** (the study of dying, death, and bereavement) was due to several reasons. *First*, with the majority of Americans dying in hospitals and nursing homes—not the case at the turn of the century—an aura of mystery developed. One is taken to the hospital or nursing home and is brought back dead. Often small children are not allowed to go into certain parts of a hospital; thus the taboo nature of a hospital setting makes one wonder what is going on in there. A desire to examine this mysterious thing called death has contributed to a growing interest in thanatology.

Second, with individuals living longer today because of life-support equipment, organ transplants, penicillin and other antibiotics, an interest has developed in the topic of dying and death. Such prolongation of life has raised ethical issues (e.g., Karen Ann Quinlan and Baby Jane Doe) involving the right to die, causing a furor in philosophy, law, and medicine. With the media highly publicizing these cases, the public was alerted to moral and legal questions on death not previously posed. Whether or not to "pull the plug" and disconnect life-supporting equipment presented questions for which ready answers were not found.

The whole issue of when death occurs evolves from these medical developments. The question of who determines when one is alive or dead has been addressed by physicians, lawyers, philosophers, and theologians. These questions, along with the controversy over abortion rights, were a few of the significant ethical issues of the 1970s that provided an open forum for discussion and debate concerning the topic of dying and death.

Third, fewer individuals are raised on farms today than at the turn of the century. Being brought up in a rural environment gave one direct exposure to birth and death as an everyday event. Children were surrounded by the alpha and omega of the life cycle. Kittens, puppies, piglets, calves, chicks, and colts were born—and also died. Thus, it was commonplace to observe death and to deal with these situations accordingly. With less than 10 percent of the United States population living on farms today, these birth and death scenes have largely been removed from the personal observations of most individuals.

Fourth, the space shuttle disaster in 1986 certainly brought death to the attention of millions of school children around the country. And in drawing attention of children to this topic, it forced adults to deal with the issue. Though the astronauts and the teacher were not visible to television viewers, their spaceship was in sight. The live television coverage revealed sudden death on the tube. Death was discussed in the media for weeks following this event.

Fifth, the topic of dying and death continues to maintain a high profile in the 1990s. Extensive media coverage followed Dr. Jack Kevorkian's "suicide machine" in the self-assisted death of a terminally ill Alzheimer's patient in Michigan in 1990. Subsequent "suicide machine" deaths have sparked the fire of this controversy.

Operation Desert Storm, involving the invasion of American troops into Iraq in 1991, brought reminders of the Vietnam conflict to the American public. Though different in many ways from Vietnam, nonetheless, dying and death were brought to us live through the media. For several weeks this war was the primary focus of the news.

NBA star Earvin "Magic" Johnson's announcement in late 1991 that he had tested positive for the human immunodeficiency virus (HIV) reverberated throughout this country and beyond. This revelation brought the topic of AIDS and death into living rooms and coffee shops everywhere. Because of Johnson's prominence as an athlete, the topic of dying and death was particularly discussed among children and young adults.

Following the failure in 1992 to indict the Los Angeles policemen involved in the beating of motorist Rodney King, riots broke out in Los Angeles and resulted in over 50 deaths. Death and destruction continue to maintain a high profile.

While dying and death have now become issues of intellectual concern and occasional topics of controversy in the media, our society has done little toward formal **socialization** of its members to deal with death on the personal and emotional levels. Hospitals have traditionally excluded visitors under the age of 14. Parents have often tried to shield their "innocent" children from death scenes. Medical and theological schools, which train persons who will work with the dying, have not had significant curricular offerings to prepare their students for this death-related work. Overall, our socialization to dying and death situations has been unsystematic and ineffective.

The Media and Death

As a child growing up in Texas, I have fond memories of spending the night with my grandparents on Fridays and going to the movies with my grandfather. The movie was always a Western with basically the same theme—the "good guys" (the cowboys) wore white hats and the "bad guys" were the Indians. Though toward the end of each movie it appeared that the "good guys" were going to be

THE WIZARD OF ID   Brant parker and Johnny hart

BY PERMISSION OF JOHNNY HART AND CREATORS SYNDICATE, INC.

wiped out, military reinforcements would *always* come to the rescue just at the last minute! The guys in the white hats would be rescued, and the "bad guys" would receive their just reward of death!

In the early 1970s, however, Hollywood began to produce films revolving around the theme of death where the "good guy" died. For example, in *Love Story* one of the two main characters is dying throughout much of the film, and does die during the film. Since that time numerous films have been produced with death as a principal theme. Certainly, Woody Allen films are filled with references to death.

Many situational comedies on prime time television in the 1970s, 1980s, and 1990s have addressed the topic of death. Some viewed death in a serious vein, while others took a humorous approach. Both death and sex are topics about which we joke. They are somewhat uneasy topics; thus to laugh about them is a way of coping.

Numerous television specials in the early 1970s discussed dying and death in one- and two-hour programs viewed at prime times. "Living with Death" presented various death-related situations observed through the eyes of a CBS reporter. ABC's "The Right to Die" addressed moral questions of mercy killing and suicide.

The National Endowment for the Humanities sponsored a program called "Dying" in the mid 1970s. For two hours this program very sensitively portrayed four cancer patients, ranging in age from the late twenties to the early seventies, interacting with others. Each died during the course of the filming. A PBS documentary in 1979 showed the last three years of Joan Robinson's life. This three-hour film revealed the experience of a woman and her husband as they tried to live with her cancer of the breast and uterus.

Death appears to be more abstract for those growing up today than for previous generations. Some media experts say that by the age of 15 the average American has seen 13,000 murders on television and has been exposed to an endless stream of war, famine, and holocaust in the daily news (Bordewich, 1988:34). Since we are unlikely to know the deceased individuals, however, the effect of this "death news" upon us is minimal.

Robert Fulton and Greg Owen (1988:381) note that for the baby boom generation, which constitutes nearly one-third of the American population, the television experience with death revolved around three messages. The first was one of entertainment. Shows such as "Tom and Jerry" and "Popeye" presented cartoon characters who systematically annihilated each other in a variety of ways, only to reappear in the next frame or after the commercial break as alive and ready for the next event. The second message was that life was brutal and often lethal. On shows such as "The Untouchables" and "Miami Vice" young males killed and were killed. This tradition of associating violence and death with the young American male continues in the real world today. The third message was that death, when it actually occurred, occurred elsewhere and mostly to people alien to ourselves. "Real" death as depicted on television news programs usually happened outside the continental limits of the United States, and it was death by violence.

How have the media in the 1980s and 1990s handled acquired immunodeficiency syndrome (AIDS)? Edward Albert (1986) notes that the media portrayals of AIDS reflect the confusion and ambiguity experienced by society at large. He found that media coverage tended to reaffirm the stigmatized status of those at high risk: intravenous drug users and gay men. Reports emphasized deviant lifestyles. For that reason the normally rather private tennis great Arthur Ashe had not revealed that he had AIDS, acquired through a blood transfusion, yet he was forced to make the announcement because the media threatened to leak the information. Prior to his death in 1993, Ashe spent his last months of life working toward reducing this stigma. Indeed, Albert (1987) notes that as the media begin associating the disease with other groups such as college students, heterosexuals, and children, the stigma should diminish to the point that those considered at significant risk belong increasingly to "socially valued" groups. Thus, through his death, Arthur Ashe has contributed to this diminished stigma.

Peter Nardi (1990) analyzed how the media handle AIDS and obituaries. He noted that one of the main issues raised by obituary reporting is personal privacy versus journalistic ethics. Unlike other diseases often unreported in earlier generations, such as tuberculosis and cancer, AIDS raises questions of both medical and sexual ethics. The dilemmas faced by the media in AIDS cases draw attention to the continuing stigma attached to AIDS.

Thus with a flurry of events involving dying and death in recent years and with the tremendous impact of prime time television in disseminating information, our focus on dying and death has been highlighted. As Fulton and Owen (1988:383) note, however, television only superficially portrays grief and the ruptured lives that death can leave in its wake. Certainly a need for death education seems apparent in today's society.

The Discipline of Thanatology

The topic of dying and death did not come into its own in recent times until the 1970s. Death, like sex, was not a new event, but both rarely had been discussed openly. Sex, as a subject of discussion, came "out of the closet" in the 1960s, followed by death in the 1970s.

Thanatology flourished in the academic world in the 1970s and continues on today. Literally hundreds of courses on dying and death are offered in high schools

and colleges. According to Dan Leviton (1977), the number of death-education college courses back in the 1970s increased from 20 in 1970 to 1100 in 1974. However, thanatology offerings at the secondary school level seem to have declined in
recent years, perhaps because of the pressure to return to the basics (Pine, 1986).
V. A. Cummins (1978) in a survey of 1251 colleges and universities found that 75
percent were offering courses in dying and death and that these courses were
offered in many different departments. The majority of courses were housed in
sociology and social-work departments followed by psychology, religious studies,
philosophy, and health education.

Fergus Bordewich (1988) observes that a generation ago death was a subject
less likely to be found in the curricula of American public schools than sex. If death
was acknowledged at all, it was usually discussed within the context of literary classics. In the past decade courses treating dying and death far more explicitly have
appeared in schools across the country. Though the actual number is not known,
thousands of schools are involved, according to groups that either oppose or support death education. Many secondary schools have blended some of the philoso-
phies and techniques of death education into health, social studies, literature, and
home economics courses. Others have introduced suicide-prevention programs.

An argument for death education noted by Bordewich (1988:31) from *The
School Counselor* in 1977 read:

> An underlying, but seldom spoken, assumption of much of the death-educa-
> tion movement is that Americans handle death and dying poorly and that we
> ought to be doing better at it. As in the case of many other problems, many Amer-
> icans believe that education can initiate change. Change is evident, and death edu-
> cation will play as important a part in changing attitudes toward death as sex
> education played in changing attitudes toward sex information and wider accep-
> tance of various sexual practices.

Death education provides an opportunity to familiarize students and professionals with the needs and issues surrounding dying and death. This is important because of the pervasiveness of formal death institutions, media exposure to
death, and haphazard experiences with death professionals, notes Vanderlyn Pine
(1986:212). One of the goals of death and dying courses for all age groups is to
increase knowledge about death and about the professions involved with death—
funeral directors, medical personnel, and governmental organizations, for example
(Gordon and Klass, 1979). Another goal is to help students learn to cope with the
death of significant others, deal with their own mortality, and be more sensitive to
the needs of others. A more abstract goal is to understand the social and ethical
issues concerning death with the value judgments involved with these issues.

What effects do courses on dying and death have on students? As noted in pre- and post-tests of the attitudes of 184 students enrolled in a college course on dying and death (Dickinson, 1986), the majority of responses revealed less fear of death and death-related events at the end of the course. These students had higher death anxieties on entering the course than did four similar studies of other populations, including one of coal miners just prior to entering the mines (Dickinson, 1986). After the course, these students revealed death anxieties much lower than the other four populations. Perhaps students coming into an elective course in thanatology have a high fear for the topic anyway and enter the course to alleviate their concerns. Nonetheless, this study did reveal less anxiety in the students of death and dying after discussions, readings, films, and visits to a funeral home and cemetery. Results of a similar high-school study of pre/post comparisons of adolescents (Rosenthal, 1980) also showed that their level of anxiety decreased as a result of an 18-week death education course.

In the 1970s Michel Vovelle (1976) published an article entitled "The Rediscovery of Death" in which he documented the sudden flurry of publications on the subject of death that appeared in the Western world from the 1950s on. Geoffrey Gorer's 1955 essay "The Pornography of Death" seemed to open the door as far as publications on the subject of "death" were concerned. Vovelle argued that the focus of attention represented by these texts amounted to nothing less than the "displacement of a deeply seated taboo on a subject which had lain hidden in the shadows of the Western psyche since some unspecified point in the 19th century" (Prior, 1989:4).

One of the early texts for thanatology, published in 1959, was an anthology by psychologist Herman Feifel titled *The Meaning of Death*. Feifel's work was an interdisciplinary attempt to restore death to cultural consciousness. In 1963 Jessica Mitford's *The American Way of Death* was very critical of the funeral industry. Elisabeth Kübler-Ross's *On Death and Dying*, published in 1969, advised Americans that they can play a significant role in the lives of the dying. It was Kübler-Ross, a physician, who was a real catalyst in making the medical profession realize that a terminally ill patient is more than just the cancer patient in Room 713; he or she is a warm, living human being with personal needs. Ernest Becker's *The Denial of Death*, published in 1973, and Kübler-Ross's book both became best sellers, alerting the public to the issue of dying in America.

Three professional journals in thanatology emerged in the 1970s. One did not survive into the 1980s; the two existing journals are called *Death Studies* (formerly *Death Education*) and *Omega: The Journal of Death and Dying*. The number of articles on death also expanded considerably in education, medicine, health, nursing, psychology, social work, and sociology journals.

Thanatology for Health Professionals

The emotional conflicts related to dying and death are particularly acute for primary health professionals. While limited emphasis has historically been placed on death education in schools for health professionals in the United States, the current status of death education offerings in nursing, medicine, pharmacy, dentistry, and social work is somewhat encouraging (Dickinson, Sumner, and Frederick, 1992). Though few offer a full course in death education, the majority (with the exception of dentistry) have some emphasis in their curricula on this topic. Most have begun their offerings since 1975.

As more emphasis in the health professions is placed on relating to terminally ill patients and their families, we would hope that more positive attitudes toward treatment of the dying patient will emerge when these students become practitioners. Helping students deal with their own anxieties about death at the time they actually face terminally ill patients would seem to be an appropriate time for intervention. Such anxieties are expressed by Dawn McGuire (1988:341), a fourth-year medical student at Columbia Presbyterian Medical Center in New York City:

> I think the proper role for a physician with a dying patient is to enter into a partnership where there is a sense that that partnership is not going to end with the end of medical therapy. But we're not trained for that. Most of us feel totally inadequate and have found our own defenses, including abandoning the patient. It's been confusing to me and a constant source of frustration.

In the end, the young professional, the patient, and the patient's family should all benefit from this emphasis on death education.

Death education should not only prove useful in coping with dying and death situations, but can actually improve the quality of our living. As Kübler-Ross (1969) notes, relating to the dying does not depress her but makes her both appreciate each day of life and be thankful each morning she awakes for the potential of another day. Learning more about dying and death should make one strive to make each day count in a positive way. It tends to make one "look for the good in others and dwell on it," as the late Alex Haley suggested on his letterhead stationery.

DEFINING DEATH

The "Wizard of Id" defines death as a "once in a lifetime experience." While one cannot refute the Wizard's answer, such a response would not suffice in the medical or legal professions.

A recent headline in a newspaper (*News and Courier*, September 22, 1988) read "Doctors 'Kill' Patient to Save Her Life." The article went on to say that surgeons

THE WIZARD OF ID   by Brant parker and Johnny hart

REPRINTED BY PERMISSION OF JOHNNY HART AND NAS, INC.

had put the patient in a coma, stopped her heart, chilled her by 40 degrees, and drained her body of blood for 40 minutes to save her from the aneurysm pressing on her brain. She was placed in a sort of suspended animation which allowed surgeons to cure a hard-to-reach, high-risk aneurysm once considered inoperable. As one surgeon noted, "It may be the surgery of the future in cases where bleeding poses the greatest risk to the operation." Thus, the headline said the physicians "killed" in order to "save" the patient. Defining death is indeed a confusing issue!

The definition of death has changed significantly from the strictly physical criteria of the 1960s to a debate about the value of life and the essence of human qualities (Prior, 1989:12). That debate relocated the origin of death to the brain rather than the respiratory system, and the first test of death became one that questioned the receptivity and awareness of the dying patient (Gervais, 1987). Death, once so clearly defined as a physical fact, became entangled in a discussion about the value of life.

International Definitions of Death

Defining death is a difficult assignment. In the 1950s the United Nations and the World Health Organization proposed the following definition of death: "Death is the permanent disappearance of all evidence of life at any time after birth has taken place" (United Nations, 1953). Thus, as death can take place only after a birth has occurred, any deaths prior to a (live) birth cannot be included in this definition. The latter is called a fetal death and is defined as (Stockwell, 1976):

> Death (disappearance of life) prior to the complete expulsion or extraction from its mother or a product of conception irrespective of the duration of pregnancy; the death is indicated by the fact that after such separation the fetus does not breathe or show any other evidence of life, such as beating of the heart, pulsating of the umbilical cord, or definite movement of voluntary muscles.

Not all countries follow the definition of death recommended by the United Nations. In some countries, infants dying within 24 hours after birth are classified

---

"DEAD" CANCER PATIENT AWAKENS IN MORTUARY

HARARE, ZIMBABWE—After being pronounced dead in the hospital, a cancer patient later awoke in a mortuary. She said her superstitious relatives were afraid to visit her.

The family of Beauty Shitto had made funeral arrangements to bury her, after doctors at the hospital in Gweru had declared her dead and sent her body to the mortuary.

Adapted from the *News and Courier*, Charleston, SC, June 22, 1988, p. 9A.

---

as stillbirths rather than deaths, or are disregarded altogether. In some other countries infants born alive, who die before the end of the registration period (which may last several months), are considered stillbirths or are excluded from all tabulations. Thus, one is not "alive" until officially registered, and one cannot be legally "dead" if never alive!

For the Kaliai of Papua, New Guinea (Counts and Counts, 1991:193), dying is almost complete "if the breath smells of death, if the person stares without blinking or shame at another person's face, is restless and must be moved frequently, or loses bladder or bowel control." Dying is complete "when breathing stops, when the heart ceases to beat, and when the eyes and mouth hang open." The Kaliai also believe that persons dying or dead may return to life at any time after the dying process begins. The Kaliai have no generic term for "life." Thus, the whole question of life and death is more complicated than might initially appear on the surface.

American Definitions of Death

By traditional definitions, death is when heartbeat and breathing stop. But medical advances have made this heartbeat definition of death obsolete. Under this definition many people living today would have once died since their hearts stopped beating and breathing stopped as a result of heart attacks. With respirators to breathe artificially for a patient, along with other life-support equipment, many lives are saved. A diagnosis of **brain death** allows respirators to be turned off when the brain is "totally and irreversibly" dead (Cope, 1978).

Leon Kass (1971:699) simply defines death as "the transition from the state of being alive to the state of being dead." Simple enough, yet the issue is clouded by many factors. Traditionally, death has clinically meant "the irreparable cessation of spontaneous cardiac activity and spontaneous respiratory activity" (Ramsey, 1970:59). The functions of heart and lungs must cease before one is pronounced dead by this definition.

In 1968 a committee of the Harvard Medical School (Beecher, 1968) claimed that the ultimate criterion for death is brain activity rather than the functioning of heart and lungs. The Harvard Report notes that death should be understood in terms of "a permanently nonfunctioning brain" for which there are many tests. With brain death the body would not be able to breathe on its own because breathing is controlled in the brain. If the brain is dead, any artificially induced heartbeat is merely pumping blood through a dead body.

In 1981 President Ronald Reagan created the President's Commission for the Study of Ethical Problems in Medicine and Biomedical and Behavioral Research to study the ethical and legal implications of the matter of defining death (Crandall, 1991:565). The commission examined three possible ways of determining death: death of part of the brain, death of the whole brain, or other nonbrain ways to determine death, such as absence of heartbeat. They decided on a definition of death that included the traditional nonbrain signs of death and a "whole brain" definition. Their proposal to determine death, which was accepted by both the American Bar Association and the American Medical Association, was as follows (Crandall, 1991:565):

> An individual who has sustained either (1) irreversible cessation of circulatory and respiratory functions, or (2) irreversible cessation of all functions of the entire brain, including the brain stem, is dead. A determination of death must be made in accordance with accepted medical standards.

The majority of states have adopted the proposal or one similar in content.

A recent case in Florida (*New York Times*, 1992) involved a baby girl, Theresa Ann Campo Pearson, born without a fully formed brain. She had only a partially formed brain stem, which controls breathing and the heartbeat, and no brain cortex, the largest part of the brain. Her parents asked the courts to declare their daughter brain dead, but to no avail. The Florida Supreme Court said it did not have the constitutional authority to hear the case. Theresa Ann did not have an "entire brain" and thus did not fit the legal definition of declaring one dead: "irreversible cessation of all functions of the entire brain, including the brain stem." The parents had wanted to donate their daughter's organs, but by the time the 10-day-old girl died, her organs had deteriorated so much that they could not be transplanted. (Note: The Pearson case is discussed further in Chapter 8.)

Various tests can be given to detect any signs of brain activity (Cope, 1978). The determination can be made reliably by competent physicians. They search for any hint of normal brain-controlled reflexes. They turn the head, and even put cold water in the ear, to look for any sign of movement. They search for any sign of the eye pupils responding to light. One test is to touch the cornea of the eye and see whether this triggers a blink. The respirator is also stopped briefly to look for any sign of spontaneous breathing. Absence of brain activity as signified by a flat elec-troencephalogram (EEG) is another criteria for brain death. The tests can be repeated 24 hours later to make certain that the absence of these life signs is not temporary. The brain death prognosis is totally predictable and uniform: Brain-dead people never regain consciousness, much less any recovery, and suffer cardiovascu-lar failure within a short time (Jasper, Lee, and Miller, 1991:34).

According to one neurologist (Cope, 1978), when death is declared on the basis of cessation of breathing and heartbeat, the brain is deprived of blood supply and dies within a matter of minutes. Death of the brain is what is final and absolute. On the other hand, one may lose all brain function, but not irreversibly. For exam-ple, a person who takes an overdose of barbiturates may have a temporary absence of any signs of brain activity, but this is not brain death because it is reversible.

Perhaps as a result of President Reagan's commission, there has come to be increasing acceptance of a brain-oriented criterion for determining death as the "irreversible loss of all brain function" (Youngner et al., 1989:2205). Nonetheless, Raanan Gillon (1990) argues that the criteria for brain death are a compromise between extreme versions of two concerns. On the one hand, death is thought of as complete disintegration of the human organism's biological functioning, with all living components dead or at least totally disintegrated and dissociated from each other. On the other hand, brain death criteria also take into account the concept of death understood as cessation of personal existence, for brain death criteria will

MAN REVIVED AFTER OBITUARY PUBLISHED

CINCINNATI—A man whose obituary was published after doctors declared him "brain dead" revived and was returned to intensive care in critical condi-tion. Physicians at the University of Cincinnati Hospital declared John Birck-head, 41, of Cincinnati brain dead Wednesday morning.

Funeral arrangements had been made by that evening, and a death notice was purchased for Birckhead, who had been hospitalized in a coma after being found hanging by his T-shirt at a jail. Meanwhile, breathing was detected during a final medical evaluation and Birckhead was returned to intensive care at the hospital.

A misunderstanding between hospital officials and members of Birckhead's family resulted in the publication of John Birckhead's obituary Thursday morn-ing in the Cincinnati Enquirer. The family was told that before a legal declaration of death, a second medical evaluation had to be performed.

Adapted from the News and Courier, Charleston, SC, September 28, 1985, p. 17A. Copyright Associ-ated Press, used by permission.

classify as alive some humans who are dead as persons. A clinical example is permanent vegetative state, which involves permanent loss of consciousness and of the capacity and potential for consciousness. Since a capacity for consciousness is a necessary condition for being a person, an individual in a permanent vegetative state cannot be a person, yet according to brain death criteria (whether brain-stem death criteria or whole brain criteria) that same human being is unequivocally alive.

DENYING DEATH

Though some evidence exists to suggest that Americans accept death (the majority have life insurance policies and many have wills), it has been suggested that we are a death-denying society (Dumont and Foss, 1972). Such evidence of death-denying in the United States includes the following.

First, we tend to use **euphemisms** for death rather than the words "dying," "dead," and "death." Examples of these euphemisms are: succumbed, passed away, was taken, went to heaven, departed this life, bit the dust, kicked the bucket, croaked, passed on, was laid to rest, cashed in, expired, ended his/her days, is no more, checked out, signed off, breathed his/her last breath, returned to dust, went out like a light, ran out of time, brought down the curtain, went on to glory, is pushing up daisies, was taken by the Grim Reaper, heard the trumpet call, and is six feet under. It is easier to use euphemisms as buffers, rather than use the stark words dying, dead, and death.

Second, we have a taboo on death conversation. A friend recently wrote a two-page letter describing her family's summer activities. She noted that she and her husband were on vacation, and he became ill. He was taken to the hospital for surgery. She said, "He had the best of care. I lov*ed* him so." She never said that her husband had died, but it was obvious. It is difficult to say those words—dying, dead, and death.

Third, **cryonics** (body freezing) suggests a denial of death. The person's body is frozen in dry ice and liquid nitrogen. Being a very expensive process initially, with additional high annual costs, cryonics has not caught on. Cryonics is based on the idea that someday a "cure" will be found for the "deceased," and that he or she can then be treated with the "cure" and thawed out. Thus, one does not die; he or she is put in the cooler and brought back at a later date.

As many as 40 people have had their bodies frozen after death in hopes that new technology would someday be able to restore them to health (Adams, 1988:332). The first was James Bedford, a 73-year-old psychologist from Glendale, California, who was frozen in 1967. Many of the 40 were thawed after their estates ran out of money, and allegedly only 11 are still in cryonic suspension.

The creation of the Vietnam Memorial in Washington, D.C., was the result of a popular movement to recognize the many men and women who lost their lives in a highly unpopular war. This social movement ran contrary to the death denial sentiment typically found in American society.

Out of 13 cryonics centers in operation a few years ago, only three remain open today (Selvin, 1990). Alcor Foundation in Riverside, California, is the largest of the three facilities. Options at Alcor include whole-body preservation for $100,000 or just a head for $35,000.

Fourth, we do not die in America, we simply take a long nap. Caskets have built-in mattresses, some straw-like and others innerspring, and the head of the deceased person rests on a pillow in the casket. The room in the funeral home where the body is "laid out" is referred to by some as the "slumber room." Certainly, no one ever heard of having a pet *killed* by the veterinarian; we have them "put to

CHILLING ANSWER TO LIFE AFTER DEATH

Katherine Bishop

SAN FRANCISCO—Everyone knows that you can't take it with you. But if members of the American Cryonics Society Inc. have their way, they are going to come back and get it.

Last week the organization, which is dedicated to the proposition that death is an imposition on life and ought to be eliminated, celebrated its 20th anniversary here with a $100-a-plate dinner attended by 65 people. The Speaker of the State Assembly, Willie Brown, showed up at the Fairmont Hotel to cut the cake, and Angela Alioto, a newly elected member of the San Francisco Board of Supervisors, made an appearance, testifying to the fact that no group is too eccentric to be ignored here.

Since the term was coined in 1965, cryonics has taken some small steps from the realm of science fiction and has even come up with its own independent religion known as Venturism. Cryonics (derived from the Greek word for cold) refers to the practice of freezing the body of a person after death to preserve it for possible revival in some distant future after a cure has been found for whatever killed the poor soul. Adherents make arrangements to have their bodies placed in cryonic suspension, meaning preservation at extremely low temperatures using liquid nitrogen in stainless steel capsules.

As it turns out, members are planning to come back to a body vastly better than the one they left in. "Usually the body is shot and they don't want to come back in that kind of shape," said H. Jackson Zinn, a San Francisco lawyer who is the organization's president.

Many members believe science will be able to restore their body and build a better one as long as the basic "information" of the person remains properly stored. Thus one popular choice is the "neuro only" option, in which only the head is preserved.

Such practices are not without problems. Last year, six people from Alcor Life Extension Foundation in Riverside, a nonprofit cryonics storage center independent of the Cryonics Society, were handcuffed and taken away for questioning on suspicion of homicide after they removed and froze the head of one client after her heart stopped beating but without having a doctor present at Alcor to pronounce her legally dead.

While criminal charges have not been filed, a grand jury investigation is continuing and Alcor has sued the State Department of Health Services, which believes that cryonics does not qualify as a "scientific" use of human remains and refuses to issue required forms. The lawsuit's outcome will affect the work of all existing storage centers, said Alcor's Manager, Michael Federowicz, who goes by the name Mike Darwin.

Should cryonics prove to work, it might lead to a host of social issues, including what is to be done about overpopulation if people continue to be born while others refuse to stay dead. The organization believes that space will be colonized, opening up vast new adventures in living for millions of humans, new or reconstituted.

"To think that we must be confined to this planet is, come on, too parochial," said Jerry White, a founder of the Cryonics Society.

Another problem is where to store all the stainless steel capsules holding the "suspension members," as the frozen bodies are called. Thus far, there are fewer than a half dozen storage centers in the country, with two of them in this state.

Mr. White suggested that there are a number of existing structures that could be adapted for such use, including an abandoned Titan missile site the group has toured in Northern California.

"I was envisioning these big silos just full of liquid nitrogen, the liquid nitrogen generators busy 24 hours a day just spewing stuff in there," he said. "And you could see thousands of patients in there, see them bobbing around."

Cryonics also involves a host of moral and philosophical problems that have not been addressed by society. The most immediate one might be faced by the survivors of the suspended, who might not agree with their loved ones' choice of body preservation and might bring legal challenges to them.

"If I'm frozen, will my wife say, 'Gee, I should have gotten that insurance money,'" mused Irving Rand, a New York City insurance salesman. Mr. Rand is president of Cryonics Coordinators of America, which helps people obtain insurance to cover the cost of freezing and storage.

A more weighty issue to ponder grows out of the fact that if future technology makes it possible to duplicate a person from those parts that have been frozen, it follows that a frozen person could not only be restored, but could also have complete copies made of himself as a sort of human floppy disk.

As Mr. Darwin states the issue, "If you duplicate and store yourself as a backup copy, is that copy you?"

And there is also the question of what the state of the world will have become over time. As Mr. Rand said, "Who knows what the world is going to be like 100 years from now; if it's even worth coming back."

But Mr. Zinn is more upbeat about the prospects. "One hundred years from now, anything that's fun, I don't want to miss it."

New York Times, January 20, 1989, p. 6. Copyright © 1989 by the New York Times Company. Reprinted by permission.

sleep." Cemetery markers sometimes say "rest in peace" or make other references to sleeping. Indeed, some markers for burials from the 19th and early 20th centuries have a crib or bed effect—headboard, footboard, and sideboards, sometimes with a "double bed" for a married couple. Dying does not occur in America, one just goes to sleep.

Fifth, unlike nonliterate societies, we call in a professional when someone dies. The funeral director takes the body away, and we do not see it again until it is ready for viewing. When we see the body again, the cosmetic job is such that the person looks as alive as possible under the circumstances. When viewing a body at a funeral home, I have heard people make the comment that the person "looks better than I have seen him/her look for years!" This is the dying of death that is discussed in Chapter 11.

Sixth, in many places in the United States, the casket is not lowered into the ground until after the family and friends have left the cemetery. It is not easy to watch a casket lowered into the ground because this reminds the viewers of the finality of death. There are several "bad trips" when a significant other dies—initially being told of the death, seeing the body for the first time, seeing the casket closed for the last time, and seeing the casket lowered into the ground. One can avoid the last "trip" by leaving the cemetery.

Thus, numerous examples of denial of death can be found in the United States. We are not suggesting that this is all bad. It is a way of coping and simply seems to be evident in the American way of dying.

FEARING DEATH

Lord, If I have to die, Let me die;
But please, Take away this fear.

Ken Walsh
Sometimes I Weep

A point that will be made often in this book is that death *per se* has no meaning other than that which people give it. If this is true, why is it that most of us believe that death is something that intrinsically engenders fear? Not everyone, however, seems to have **death anxiety** (used synonymously with death fear). For example, B. F. Skinner, the psychologist who popularized behavior modification, approached his death from leukemia with apparently no regrets. The 86-year-old Skinner, just a few weeks before he died, said with a laugh (1990), "I will be dead in a few months, but it hasn't given me the slightest anxiety or worry or anything. I always knew I was going to die."

Anthropologists would be quick to respond that not all cultures in the world hold that death is necessarily something to be feared. There seem to be a large number of cultures, including our own, however, that attach fearful meanings to death and death-related situations. Why is it that so many people have less-than-positive views of death?

Death in the United States is viewed as fearful because Americans have been taught systematically to fear it. Horror movies portray death, ghosts, skeletons, goblins, bogeymen, and ghoulish morticians as things to be feared. Sesame Street tries to create for children a more positive view of monsters as children are befriended by Grover, Oscar, and Cookie Monster. With the possible exception of Casper "the Friendly Ghost," death-related fantasy figures have not received the same positive images. Instead of providing positive images, our culture has chosen to reinforce fearful meanings of death. Cemeteries are portrayed as eerie, funeral homes are to be avoided, and morgues are scary places where you "wouldn't be caught dead."

One of the reasons death and dying classes often incorporate field trips to funeral homes and cemeteries is to confront negative death meanings and fantasies with first-hand, objective observations. The preparation room at the mortuary is a good example. If you have never been to one, think about the mental image that comes to your mind. For many, the preparation room is a place one approaches with fear and caution—something like Dr. Frankenstein's laboratory, complete with bats, strange lighting, body parts, and naked dead bodies. The great disappointment for most students as they walk through the door is that they find a room that looks somewhat like a physician's examination room. "Is that all there is?" is a comment often heard after visiting the embalming room.

Sociologist Erving Goffman (1959) observed that first impressions are unlikely to change and tend to dominate the meanings related to subsequent social interaction patterns and experiences. Some of us want to retain untrue fearful meanings of death, even when confronted by positive images. On a recent field trip to a funeral home, one student refused to enter the preparation room. While other students were hearing a description of embalming procedures, she discovered a bottle labeled "skin texturizer" and became nauseated. Other students had a difficult time understanding her problem because they had had positive experiences.

Another reason for fearful meanings being ascribed to death can be attributed to a traumatic death-related experience. Being a witness to a fatal auto accident, discovering someone who has committed suicide, or attending a funeral where emotional outbursts create an uncomfortable environment for mourners can increase death anxiety for individuals. However, such occurrences are rather uncommon for most people and do not account for the prevalence of America's preoccupation with death fears.

Content of Death Fears

When one speaks of death fear or death anxiety, it is assumed that the concept is unidimensional and that consensus exists about its meaning. Such is not the case, however, since two persons may say that they fear death and yet the content of their fears may not be shared. Death anxiety is a multidimensional concept and is based upon the following four concerns: (1) the death of self; (2) the deaths of significant others; (3) the process of dying; and (4) the state of being dead. This model's more elaborated form (Leming, 1979–1980) shows eight types of death fears that can be applied to the death of self and the death of others:

1. dependency
2. the pain in the dying process
3. the indignity in the dying process
4. the isolation, separation, and rejection that can be part of the dying process
5. leaving loved ones
6. afterlife concerns
7. the finality of death
8. the fate of the body

From Table 1.1 we can see that the content of fear will be influenced by whose death the individual is considering. From a personal death perspective, one may have anxiety over the effect that one's dying (or being dead) will have on others. There might also be private worries about how one might be treated by others. From the perspective of the survivor, the individual may be concerned about the financial, emotional, and social problems related to the death of a significant other.

Since there are many factors related to the experience of death and death-related situations that can engender fear, we would expect to find individual differences in type and intensity of death fear, including social circumstance and past experiences. However, with all of the potential sources for differences, repeated administrations of the Leming Death Fear Scale yield consistently high scores for the fears of dependency and pain related to the process of dying, and relatively low anxiety scores for the fears related to the afterlife and the fate of the body. Approximately 65 percent of the more than 1000 individuals surveyed had high anxiety concerning dependency and pain, and only 15 percent experienced the same level of anxiety relative to concerns about the afterlife and the fate of the body (Leming, 1979–1980). Thus it is the *process of dying*—not the *event of death*—that causes the most concern.

Death Fears and Gender

Is there a difference in death fear between males and females? Gender differences in death fear is one of the most frequently noted and poorly understood findings in thanatology (Dattel and Neimeyer, 1990). In a survey of research studies on death fear by sex, Pollack (1979) reported that the majority of findings concluded

Table 1.1   The Eight Dimensions of Death Anxiety as They Relate to the Deaths of Self and Others

SELF	OTHERS
PROCESS OF DYING	
1. Fear of dependency	Fear of financial burdens
2. Fear of pain in dying process	Fear of going through the painful experience of others
3. Fear of indignity in dying process	Fear of being unable to cope with physical problems of others
4. Fear of loneliness, rejection, and isolation	Fear of being unable to cope emotionally with problems of others
5. Fear of leaving loved ones	Fear of losing loved ones
STATE OF BEING DEAD	
6. Afterlife concerns: Fear of divine judgment	Afterlife concerns: Fear of the judgment of others—"What are they thinking?"
Fear of the spirit world	Fear of ghosts, spirits, devils, etc.
Fear of nothingness	Fear of never seeing the person again
7. Fear of the finality of death	Fear of the end of a relationship
Fear of not being able to achieve one's goals	Guilt related to not having done enough for the deceased
Fear of the possible end of physical and symbolic identity	Fear of not seeing the person again
Fear of the end of all social relationships	Fear of losing the social relationship
8. Fear of the fate of the body Fear of body decomposition Fear of being buried Fear of not being treated with respect	Fear of death objects Fear of dead bodies Fear of being in cemeteries Fear of not knowing how to act in death-related situations

that women reveal more death fear than men, yet other studies find virtually no differences between the sexes. Judith Stillion (1985) suggests that the discrepancy in these findings simply reflects the greater tendency of women to admit troubling feelings than men.

In summary, death fears are not instinctive; they exist because our culture has created and perpetuated fearful meanings and ascribed them to death. They are also a function of the fact that death is not an ordinary experience challenging the order of everyday life in society. They are a function of occasional first-hand encounters with deaths so unusual that they become traumatic.

Death Fear Scale

We have been discussing the concept of death anxiety and factors that influence it. We have suggested that death anxiety is a multidimensional concept with at least eight areas of potential fear for the individual as he or she contemplates the deaths of loved ones and the death of self. We have also suggested that death fear may vary by gender. Now, having read about death fear, you can assess your own death fear by following the Leming Fear of Death Scale (1979–1980) below.

Read the following 26 statements. Decide whether you strongly agree (SA), agree (A), tend to agree (TA), tend to disagree (TD), disagree (D), or strongly disagree (SD) with each statement. Give your first impression. There are no right or wrong answers.

After you have responded to the statements, add the numbers below each section and divide by the number of questions in the section to get the fear score for each area. Finally, add up all eight sections to get your total Death Fear Score (maximum score is 48; minimum score is 8).

I. Fear of Dependency

1. I expect other people to care for me while I die.

SA	A	TA	TD	D	SD
1	2	3	4	5	6

2. I am fearful of becoming dependent on others for my physical needs.

SA	A	TA	TD	D	SD
6	5	4	3	2	1

3. While dying, I dread the possibility of being a financial burden.

SA	A	TA	TD	D	SD
6	5	4	3	2	1

4. Losing my independence due to a fatal illness makes me apprehensive.

SA	A	TA	TD	D	SD
6	5	4	3	2	1

(Total of 4 scores) _____ divided by 4 = _____

II. Fear of Pain

5. I fear dying a painful death.

SA	A	TA	TD	D	SD
6	5	4	3	2	1

6. I am afraid of a long, slow death.

SA	A	TA	TD	D	SD
6	5	4	3	2	1

(Total of 2 scores) _____ divided by 2 = _____

III. Fear of Indignity

7. The loss of physical attractiveness that accompanies dying is distressing to me.

SA	A	TA	TD	D	SD
6	5	4	3	2	1

8. I dread the helplessness of dying.

SA	A	TA	TD	D	SD
6	5	4	3	2	1

(Total of 2 scores) _____ divided by 2 = _____

IV. Fear of Isolation/Separation/Loneliness

9. The isolation of death does not concern me.

SA	A	TA	TD	D	SD
1	2	3	4	5	6

10. I do not have any qualms about being alone after I die.

SA	A	TA	TD	D	SD
1	2	3	4	5	6

11. Being separated from my loved ones at death makes me anxious.

SA	A	TA	TD	D	SD
6	5	4	3	2	1

(Total of 3 scores) _____ divided by 3 = _____

V. Fear of Afterlife Concerns

12. Not knowing what it feels like to be dead makes me uneasy.

SA	A	TA	TD	D	SD
6	5	4	3	2	1

13. The subject of life after death troubles me.

SA	A	TA	TD	D	SD
6	5	4	3	2	1

14. Thoughts of punishment after death are a source of apprehension for me.

SA	A	TA	TD	D	SD
6	5	4	3	2	1

(Total of 3 scores) _____ divided by 3 = _____

VI. Fear of the Finality of Death

15. The idea of never thinking after I die frightens me.

SA	A	TA	TD	D	SD
6	5	4	3	2	1

16. I have misgivings about the fact that I might die before achieving my goals.

SA	A	TA	TD	D	SD
6	5	4	3	2	1

17. I am often distressed by the way time flies so rapidly.

SA	A	TA	TD	D	SD
6	5	4	3	2	1

18. The idea that I may die young does not bother me.

SA	A	TA	TD	D	SD
1	2	3	4	5	6

19. The loss of my identity at death alarms me.

SA	A	TA	TD	D	SD
6	5	4	3	2	1

(Total of 5 scores) _____ divided by 5 = _____

VII. Fear of Leaving Loved Ones

20. The effect of my death on others does not trouble me.

SA	A	TA	TD	D	SD
1	2	3	4	5	6

21. I am afraid that my loved ones are emotionally unprepared to accept my death.

SA	A	TA	TD	D	SD
6	5	4	3	2	1

22. It worries me to think of the financial situation of my survivors.

SA	A	TA	TD	D	SD
6	5	4	3	2	1

(Total of 3 scores) _____ divided by 3 = _____

VIII. Fear of the Fate of the Body

23. The thought of my own body decomposing does not bother me.

SA	A	TA	TD	D	SD
1	2	3	4	5	6

24. The sight of a dead body makes me uneasy.

SA	A	TA	TD	D	SD
6	5	4	3	2	1

25. I am not bothered by the idea that I may be placed in a casket when I die.

SA	A	TA	TD	D	SD
1	2	3	4	5	6

26. The idea of being buried frightens me.

SA	A	TA	TD	D	SD
6	5	4	3	2	1

(Total of 4 scores) _____ divided by 4 = _____

Total Death Fear Score (addition of all 8 areas of death concern) _____

(In any given subscale, a score of 3.5 or higher means slightly fearful of death.)

MORTALITY STATISTICS

Ask an individual how he or she wishes to die. With the exception of the comical reply, "When I am ninety-two and at the hands of a jealous lover," most people will respond, "When I am very old, at home, unexpectedly, in my own bed, while sleeping—and with my full mental and physical capabilities." Unfortunately for most of us, we will not die as we would like. For some, this may be a source of apprehension and anxiety.

PLEASE NOTIFY

A lecturer was about to address a business association in Los Angeles when the association director reminded its members: "Every week we pay return postage for mail that goes to our members and is not deliverable because you have moved, changed your post office box number, or died without letting us know."

Mountaineer, Waynesville, NC, April 11, 1980.

As noted earlier, most Americans die in institutionalized settings and not at home. According to the insert above, we should be more considerate about our dying, whether at home or away.

Death Etiology and Life Expectancy

As noted in Table 1.2, the cause of death (**etiology**) for most of us (65 percent) will be from one of two **chronic diseases**—heart disease and cancer. With these chronic diseases, death is usually prolonged, not sudden and unexpected as most people would desire.

Life expectancy has increased considerably in the past 50 years. Life expectancy for males in the United States has increased from 54 years to nearly 70 years over the past half century. Females' life expectancy during this same period has increased from 55 to 77 years. Whites live nearly 6 years longer than blacks in the United States. According to a recent study reported in the *New York Times* (1990), however, there may be a limit on how long our bodies can hold out. The study concluded that science and medicine have pushed human life expectancy to its natural limit of about 85 years. The researchers note that even if a cure were found for most fatal

THE WIZARD OF ID   by Brant parker and Johnny hart

REPRINTED BY PERMISSION OF JOHNNY HART AND NAS, INC.

Table 1.2   Ten Leading Causes of Death in the United States/1900 and 1990
(in death rates per 100,000 population)

CAUSES OF DEATH	DEATH RATES PER 100,000 POPULATION	% OF ALL DEATHS
	1900*	
1. Pneumonia	191.9	12.5
2. Consumption(Tuberculosis)	190.5	12.5
3. Heart Disease	134.0	8.3
4. Diarrheal Diseases	85.1	5.6
5. Diseases of the Kidneys	83.7	5.5
6. All Accidents	72.3	4.7
7. Apoplexy (Stroke)	66.6	4.3
8. Cancer	60.0	3.9
9. Old Age	54.0	3.5
10. Bronchitis	48.3	3.2
All Other Causes		36.0
	1990	
1. Major Cardiovascular Diseases	366.9	41.8
2. Malignancies (Cancer)	201.7	23.4
3. Accidents	37.3	4.2
4. Pulmonary Diseases	35.5	4.1
5. Pneumonia and Influenza	31.3	3.6
6. Diabetes	19.5	2.2
7. Infective Diseases (includes AIDS)	12.3	1.4
8. Suicide	12.8	1.5
9. Chronic Liver Disease	10.2	1.2
10. Homicide	10.2	1.2
All Other Causes		15.4

*These data are limited to the registration area that included 10 registration states and all cities having at least 8000 inhabitants. In 1900 this composed 38 percent of the entire population of the continental United States. Since accidents were not reported in the 1900 census, this rate was taken from Monroe Lerner, "When, Why and Where People Die." In *The Dying Patient,* O.G. Brim, H.E. Freeman, and N.A. Scotch (Eds.). New York: Russel Sage Foundation, 1970, p. 14.

Sources: *Abstract of the Twelfth Census of the United States, 1900.* Table 93. Washington, DC: U.S. Government Printing Office, 1902. And *Statistical Abstract of the United States, 1992.* 112th edition. Table 114. Washington, DC: U.S. Government Printing Office, 1992.

diseases such as heart disease and cancer, the natural degeneration of the body puts a cap of about 85 years on the average age of death.

Though medical and scientific breakthroughs have obviously contributed to an increased life expectancy, the American public has also changed its lifestyle in recent years. Priorities for health promotion are smoking cessation, physical exercise, nutrition and weight control, stress management, and appropriate use of alcohol and other drugs (Hyner and Melby, 1987). With the increasing number of AIDS cases, safe sex is also being promoted. While one cannot change his/her heredity, an individual can have an impact on life expectancy through exercise, nutrition, and patterns of living. Expectation of life by race, age, and sex is shown in Table 1.3.

Gender Differences in Mortality Rates

Why females outlive males is a long-debated topic. This pattern tends to exist in most parts of the world except for a few nonliterate societies where a high maternal mortality rate exists. The suggestion that females have traditionally engaged in less strenuous work and have not historically been allowed to work in occupations with high accident rates, such as coal mines and steel mills, actually does not explain this greater longevity of females. Traditional housework involves lifting many pounds of laundry, daily picking up and keeping up with small children, handling foodstuffs, and walking several miles within the house performing daily chores. No, housework is not a plush job.

Perhaps it would be correct to suggest that females historically have watched their diet more carefully than males due to their traditional knowledge about food and a special cultural emphasis on weight maintenance. With more current emphasis on diet and exercise for both genders, however, this argument may no longer be completely accurate.

Anthropologist Ashley Montagu (1968) suggests that women have a superior use of emotions because they are more likely to cry than men. Since it is not "macho" to cry, men generally refrain from such behavior, resulting in more psychosomatic disorders such as peptic ulcers. Montagu asks, "Is this a superior use of emotions?" Perhaps being freer to express themselves through the release of emotional feelings contributes to a decrease of stress for women.

Males have traditionally been involved in more risk-taking activities through "macho" behaviors like smoking (the rugged Marlboro man, for example) and drinking. Indeed, accidents cause more deaths among males than females (Cockerham, 1992:40). Males have, for example, been historically more inclined to drive fast cars and live the James Dean devil-may-care type of life.

On the biological side of the argument, the conception ratio (projected to be higher than 120 males per 100 females) favors males, as does the **sex ratio** at birth

Table 1.3   *Expectation of Life by Race, Age, and Sex/1988*

| | | EXPECTATION OF LIFE IN YEARS | | | |
| | | WHITE | | BLACK AND OTHER | |
AGE (IN YEARS)	TOTAL	MALE	FEMALE	MALE	FEMALE
At birth	74.9	72.3	78.9	64.9	73.4
1	74.7	72.0	78.5	65.2	73.6
2	73.8	71.0	77.5	64.3	72.7
3	72.8	70.1	76.6	63.3	71.7
4	71.8	69.1	75.6	62.4	70.8
5	70.8	68.1	74.6	61.4	69.8
6	69.9	67.1	73.6	60.4	68.8
7	68.9	66.2	72.7	59.5	67.8
8	67.9	65.2	71.7	58.5	66.9
9	66.9	64.2	70.7	57.5	65.9
10	65.9	63.2	69.7	56.5	64.9
11	64.9	62.2	68.7	55.5	63.9
12	64.0	61.2	67.7	54.5	62.9
13	63.0	60.2	66.7	53.6	61.9
14	62.0	59.3	65.7	52.6	61.0
15	61.0	58.3	64.8	51.6	60.0
16	60.1	57.3	63.8	50.7	59.0
17	59.1	56.4	62.8	49.8	58.0
18	58.2	55.5	61.8	48.8	57.1
19	57.2	54.6	60.9	47.9	56.1
20	56.3	53.6	59.9	47.0	55.1
21	55.3	52.7	58.9	46.2	54.2
22	54.4	51.8	58.0	45.3	53.2
23	53.5	50.9	57.0	44.4	52.3
24	52.5	50.0	56.0	43.5	51.3
25	51.6	49.0	55.0	42.7	50.4
26	50.6	48.1	54.1	41.8	49.4
27	49.7	47.2	53.1	41.0	48.5
28	48.8	46.3	52.1	40.1	47.5
29	47.8	45.3	51.2	39.2	46.6

(continued)

30	46.9	44.4	50.2	38.4	45.7
31	45.9	43.5	49.2	37.5	44.7
32	45.0	42.6	48.3	36.7	43.8
33	44.1	41.6	47.3	35.9	42.9
34	43.1	40.7	46.3	35.1	42.0
35	42.2	39.8	45.4	34.3	41.1
36	41.3	38.9	44.4	33.5	40.2
37	40.4	37.9	43.4	32.7	39.3
38	39.4	37.0	42.5	31.9	38.4
39	38.5	36.1	41.5	31.1	37.5
40	37.6	35.2	40.6	30.3	36.6
41	36.7	34.3	39.6	29.6	35.7
42	35.8	33.4	38.7	28.8	34.8
43	34.9	32.5	37.7	28.0	33.9
44	33.9	31.6	36.8	27.2	33.1
45	33.3	30.7	35.8	26.5	32.2
46	32.1	29.8	34.9	25.7	31.4
47	31.3	28.9	34.0	25.0	30.5
48	30.4	28.0	33.1	24.3	29.7
49	29.5	27.2	32.1	23.5	28.8
50	28.6	26.3	31.2	22.8	28.0
51	27.8	25.5	30.3	22.1	27.2
52	26.9	24.6	29.5	21.4	26.3
53	26.1	23.8	28.6	20.8	25.5
54	25.3	23.0	27.7	20.1	24.8
55	24.4	22.2	26.8	19.4	24.0
56	23.6	21.4	26.0	18.8	23.2
57	22.8	20.6	25.1	18.1	22.5
58	22.0	19.8	24.3	17.5	21.7
59	21.3	19.1	23.5	16.8	21.0
60	20.5	18.4	22.6	16.2	20.3
61	19.8	17.6	21.8	15.6	19.6
62	19.0	16.9	21.0	15.0	18.9
63	18.3	16.3	20.2	14.5	18.2
64	17.6	15.6	19.5	13.9	17.6
65	16.9	14.9	18.7	13.4	16.9

70	13.6	11.8	15.0	10.9	13.8
75	10.7	9.1	11.7	8.6	10.9
80	8.1	6.8	8.7	6.8	8.4
85 and over	6.0	5.1	6.3	5.5	6.6

Source: Statistical Abstract of the United States, 1991. 111th edition. Table 107. Washington, DC: U.S. Government Printing Office, 1991.

(105 males per 100 females). In the early teens the sex ratio levels off, and after age 80, the ratio is less than 50 males per 100 females. Perhaps females simply have better-built bodies. Their bodies must be capable of carrying and supporting a fetus/embryo. Thus, they are the "Porsche" model, whereas males are the more "thrown-together" model.

The debate goes on. Whether females outlive males in the United States because of biological or cultural reasons, we will not settle here. The fact is females outlive males. As sex roles continue to change and females are found in greater numbers and in a greater variety of nontraditional occupations, as males share more in domestic tasks, and as the sexes come together in more unisex behaviors (more

Differences in life expectancies for males and females create a situation where there are twice as many females as males at age 80. Is America ready for polygyny as a reward (or punishment) for octogenarians?

women smoking and drinking, for example, and living the "fast" life), stresses and strains of life should be more equally distributed between the genders. The argument of biology versus culture as influencing life expectancy by sex can then be better addressed.

COPING WITH THE AMERICAN WAY OF DYING

Human beings do not respond to all deaths in the same manner. As noted in Chapter 2, humans ascribe meanings to death and then respond to these meanings. The American way of dying places higher values on some causes of deaths and ascribes less status to other causes. Likewise, coping with the death of a significant other will be influenced by the cause of the death.

While there are some special problems associated with deaths caused by a chronic disease such as a heart disease or cancer, there are some real advantages also. The following is a partial list of the opportunities provided by a slow death caused by a chronic disease:

1. The dying person is given an opportunity to attend to unfinished business—make out a will, complete incomplete projects.
2. The dying person and his or her family can attempt to heal broken family relationships, can say their final farewells, and can all participate in constructing a meaningful and dignified death.
3. Funerals and other arrangements can be made with the consent and participation of the dying person.
4. Anticipatory grief on the part of the survivors and dying patient can take place.

Deaths due to **acute diseases** (such as pneumonia), accidents, and suicide also provide special problems and advantages to survivors. For all quick deaths there is the problem of being unprepared for the death. The survivors did not have a support group in place and did not have the advantage of having experienced anticipatory grief. Some of the grieving that has preceded the death due to a chronic disease cannot be expressed in deaths of this type. Consequently, grief is usually more intense when the dying takes place in a short period of time. Survivors may also experience more intense guilt—"If only I had done something, she wouldn't have died." Suicide creates special problems for survivors because they can become stigmatized by having a relative commit suicide—"They drove him to it." Finally, when people die without warning, survivors often are troubled because they did not have a chance to mend a broken relationship or say good-bye.

On the other hand, survivors of deaths due to acute diseases, accidents, and suicide are spared the following problems associated with chronic diseases:

INDIVIDUAL LIFE EXPECTANCY

The following method for calculating longevity not only points to the inevitability of dying but identifies specific ways of increasing one's chances for longer living. The base number of years of computing life span in the United States is 75.

If you are male, subtract 4; if you are female, add 4: _____

If you plan to live in an urban area for most of your life, subtract 2; if a town or a rural area is planned, add 2: _____

If you anticipate having a desk job for most of your life, subtract 3; if the work requires regular physical labor, add 3; if you anticipate working after 65, add 3: _____

If you anticipate earning over $50,000 or under $10,000 a year, subtract 2: _____

If you exercise vigorously several times weekly, add 3: _____

If you anticipate living with a spouse or friend for most of your life, add 4; if not, subtract 1 for each decade alone after reaching age 30: _____

If you are an extrovert, enjoying the society of others, add 2; if you are an introvert, preferring to be by yourself, subtract 2: _____

If you are intense, aggressive, and easily angered, subtract 3; if you are relaxed, easygoing, and worry little, add 3: _____

If you have been given a ticket for speeding in recent years, subtract 2; if you regularly wear a seat belt while traveling, add 2: _____

If you anticipate finishing, or have finished, college, add 1; for a graduate degree, add 2: _____

If any grandparent lived to 85, add 2; if all four grandparents lived to 73, or are now living, add 3: _____

If either parent died of heart failure before 50, subtract 5; if any parent, brother, or sister under 50 has (or had) a heart condition, or has diabetes, subtract 3: _____

If you get intoxicated at least once a month, subtract 2; if a chronic alcoholic, subtract 8: _____

If you are overweight by more than 50 pounds, subtract 8; by 30-50 pounds, subtract 4; by 10-30, subtract 2: _____

If you smoke more than 2 packs a day, subtract 8; 1 or 2 packs, subtract 6; 1/2 to 1, subtract 3: _____

If you are over 30 make this adjustment: 31-40, add 2; 41-50, add 3; 51-70, add 4; over 70, add 5.   _____

Reprinted from William E. Phipps, *Death: Confronting the Reality*. Atlanta, GA: John Knox Press, 1987.

1. Dying persons may not be willing to accept death, and when learning of their fates, may act in unacceptable ways.
2. Families may be unwilling to accept the death.
3. The dying process may be a long and painful process, not only for the dying patient, but for the family as well.
4. The cost of dying from a chronic disease can be, and usually is, very expensive. The entire assets of a family can be wiped out by the medical bills of a chronically ill patient.

Thus, there seem to be advantages and disadvantages of dying a sudden death and of dying a lingering death. Since we have limited choices in the matter (unless one intervenes), we will simply have to take whatever comes along. Who knows? Perhaps death will come "while sleeping in one's own bed at home at night in old age and with full mental and physical capabilities."

CONCLUSION

While the American way of dying is being discussed and researched more today than in previous decades, discussion often poses as many questions as answers. Aristotle (1941: 975) observed long ago that "death is the most terrible of all things," yet it will not go away and, thus, we must learn to cope with it. The following questions do not have simple and straightforward answers: When does death take place? Who should determine the timing of a particular death? Who in society should be responsible for defining the meaning of life and death? When is a death an accident and when is it a suicide?

PUTTING A PRICE ON HUMAN LIFE

Putting a price on human life is a common activity among life insurance companies, airlines, courts, industries, and agencies. Being required by law (Executive Order 12291 issued by President Ronald Reagan in February of 1981), the federal government routinely calculates the value of a life. Ordinary citizens make much the same determination when they choose small cars over larger, take jobs hundreds of feet below the ground for higher pay, or buy inexpensive houses in a flood plain instead of more expensive ones in safer areas.

People have been calculating the worth of their lives and the lives of others for as long as archaeologists, anthropologists, and historians can document human existence. The Aztecs in the 15th century and the Code of Hammurabi of ancient Babylonia created elaborate systems of compensation for injuries and deaths. In both ancient and medieval law a sum of money was paid by a guilty party to satisfy the family of the person injured or killed.

A fundamental difference exists, however, between calculating the value of a life to compensate for its loss, a common practice throughout the centuries, and determining whether it is worth saving, a practice growing more common today. Some philosophers argue that the value of human life is infinite or incalculable. However, insurance agents, economists, legal experts, scientists, and agency administrators are assigning life values ranging from a few dollars to many millions of dollars, depending on the formulas used.

One way of figuring value is to break down the body into chemical elements—5 pounds calcium, 1½ pounds phosphorus, 9 ounces potassium, 6 ounces sulfur, 6 ounces sodium, a little more than 1 ounce magnesium, and less than an ounce each of iron, copper, and iodine. On that basis a human life today is worth $8.37, up $1.09 in six years because of inflation.

Another approach is to look at the going price of contract murder. Andreas Santiago Hernandez, 22, recently told the Los Angeles Police Department that he was paid $5,000 to kill Lorraine Keifer, the 67-year-old widow of a San Fernando Valley executive. Lt. Fahey says that in New York City a murder contract can cost nothing, if it is "for practice," or $10,000 and up.

The life insurance industry determines what people would have earned had they lived. It is their earning power over the course of their working life.

Adapted from William R. Greer, "Putting a Price on Human Life Is Being Questioned." *The Courier-Journal*, Louisville, KY, June 30, 1985, p. 1D.

Americans have developed a paradoxical relationship with death—we know more about the causes and conditions surrounding death, but we have not equipped ourselves emotionally to cope with dying and death. The American way of dying is such that avoiding direct confrontation with dying and death is a real possibility for many persons. What we need is the ability to both understand and cope with dying and death. The purpose of this book is to provide an understanding of dying, death, and bereavement that will assist individuals to better cope with their own deaths and with the deaths of others.

SUMMARY

1. The American way of dying is typically confined to institutional settings and removed from usual patterns of social interaction.
2. American society has done little to socialize formally its members to deal with dying and death on the personal and emotional levels.
3. The "thanatology movement" was a concerted effort in the 1970s to bring about an open discussion and awareness of behaviors and emotions related to dying, death, and bereavement. The movement continues in the 1990s.
4. An increased emphasis on dying and death is reflected in today's media.
5. The issue of when death occurs is a difficult one to resolve because consensus does not exist in America regarding the definitions of life and death.
6. The American way of dying has changed considerably since 1900. Relative to earlier times, Americans are less likely to die of acute diseases. Currently more than 75 percent of the deaths taking place in the United States can be attributed to chronic diseases.
7. In the past 50 years, life expectancy has increased 20 years. With the increase in life expectancy, there have been many effects upon Americans' understanding and ability to cope with dying and death.
8. The manner in which an individual dies will influence the way in which his or her survivors cope with the death. Chronic and acute diseases have advantages and disadvantages for the coping abilities of dying patients and their families.
9. Death anxiety is a multidimensional concept.
10. The United States is basically a death-denying society.
11. The "value" of human life can be "calculated" in various ways.

12. Death in the United States is feared because we have been taught systematically to fear it.

DISCUSSION QUESTIONS

1. Why did death "come out of the closet" in the 1970s? What events related to the thanatology movement helped change the American awareness of dying and death?
2. What factors have contributed to the American avoidance of death and dying?
3. Discuss whether you think the United States is basically a death-denying or a death-accepting society.
4. How has the definition of death changed over the years? What complications has this created for the American way of dying?
5. Compare and contrast the relative advantages and disadvantages of dying from acute and chronic diseases. What effects do each of these causes have on the abilities of families to cope with the death of a family member?
6. Discuss why women outlive men in the United States and most countries of the world.
7. What is meant by this statement: Death anxiety is a multidimensional concept?

GLOSSARY

Acute Disease: A communicable disease caused by a number of microorganisms including viruses, fungi, and bacteria. Acute disease lasts for a relatively short period of time and results either in a cure or death. Examples of acute disease include: smallpox, malaria, cholera, influenza, and pneumonia.

Brain Death: The brain is totally and irreversibly dead. Sometimes referred to as the Harvard definition of death.

Chronic Disease: A noncommunicable self-limiting disease from which the individual rarely recovers, even though the symptoms of the disease can often be alleviated. Chronic disease usually results in deterioration of organs and tissues, making the individual vulnerable to other diseases, often leading to serious impairment and even death. Examples of chronic disease include: cancer, heart disease, arthritis, emphysema, and asthma.

Cryonics: A method of subjecting a corpse to extremely low temperatures through the use of dry ice and liquid nitrogen.

Death Anxiety: A learned emotional response to death-related phenomena characterized by extreme apprehension. Used synonymously with death fear.

Elderhostel: Inexpensive short courses, usually five days in duration, for older persons on college campuses. Over 160,000 individuals participate annually in a wide variety of courses offered by over 1000 colleges in the United States and some foreign countries.

Etiology: The cause of death.

Euphemism: A word or phrase that is considered less distasteful than other words or phrases.

Life Expectancy: The number of years that the average newborn in a particular population can expect to live.

Sex Ratio: The number of males per 100 females.

Socialization: The process by which individuals are integrated into a social group by learning its values, goals, norms, and roles. This is a lifelong process that is never completed.

Thanatology: The interdisciplinary study of death-related behavior including actions and emotions concerned with dying, death, and bereavement.

REFERENCES

Adams, Cecil. 1988. *More of the Straight Dope.* New York: Ballentine Books.

Albert, Edward. 1986. "Illness and Deviance: The Response of the Press to AIDS." In *The Social Dimensions of AIDS: Method and Theory,* Douglas A. Feldman and Thomas M. Johnson (Eds.). New York: Praeger.

Albert, Edward. 1987. "AIDS and the Press: The Creation and Transformation of a Social Problem." Unpublished paper presented at the annual meeting of the Society for the Study of Social Problems. Chicago.

Aristotle. 1941. "Nicomachean Ethics III." In *The Basic Works of Aristotle,* R. McKeon (Ed.). New York: Random House.

Beecher, Henry K. 1968. "A Definition of Irreversible Coma." *Journal of the American Medical Association,* 205(August 5):85–88.

Bordewich, Fergus M. 1988. "Mortal Fears: Courses in 'Death Education' Get Mixed Reviews." *Atlantic Monthly,* February 261: 30–34.

Cockerham, William C. 1992. *Medical Sociology,* 5th ed. Englewood Cliffs, NJ: Prentice-Hall.

Cope, Lewis. 1978. "Is Death, like Pregnancy, an All-or-Nothing Thing?" *Minneapolis Tribune,* June 22, pp. 1 and 6A.

Counts, Dorothy A., and David R. Counts. 1991. "Loss and Anger: Death and the Expression of Grief in Kaliai." In *Coping with the Final Tragedy: Cultural Variation in Dying and Grieving,* David R. Counts and Dorothy A. Counts (Eds.). Amityville, NY: Baywood Publishing Company.

Crandall, Richard C. 1991. *Gerontology: A Behavioral Science Approach,* 2nd ed. New York: McGraw-Hill.

Cummins, V. A. 1978. "Death Education in Four-Year Colleges and Universities in the U.S." Paper presented at the First National Conference on the Forum for Death Education and Counseling (September).

Dattel, Andrew R., and Robert A. Neimeyer. 1990. "Sex Differences in Death Anxiety: Testing the Emotional Expressiveness Hypothesis." *Death Studies,* 14:1–11.

Dickinson, George E., Edward D. Sumner, and Lynn M. Frederick. 1992. "Death Education in Selected Health Professions." *Death Studies,* 16(May–June):281–289.

Dickinson, George E. 1986. "Effects of Death Education on College Students' Death Anxiety." Unpublished paper presented at the Forum for Death Education and Counseling. Atlanta, GA (April 18–20).

Dumont, Richard G., and Dennis C. Foss. 1972. *The American View of Death: Acceptance or Denial?* Cambridge, MA: Schenkman.

Fulton, Robert, and Greg Owen. 1988. "Death and Society in Twentieth Century America." *Omega,* 18:379–394.

Gervais, K. G. 1987. *Redefining Death.* New Haven: Yale University Press.

Gillon, Raanan. 1990. "Editorial: Death." *Journal of Medical Ethics,* 16:3–4.

Goffman, Erving. 1959. *The Presentation of Self in Everyday Life.* New York: Doubleday.

Gorer, Geoffrey. 1955. "The Pornography of Death." *Encounter,* 5(October):49–53.

Gordon, A. K., and D. Klass. 1979. *The Need to Know: How to Teach Children about Death.* Englewood Cliffs, NJ: Prentice-Hall.

Hyner, Gerald C., and Christopher L. Melby. 1987. *Priorities for Health Promotion and Disease Prevention.* Dubuque, IA: Eddie Bowers.

Jasper, Jackson H., Brian C. Lee, and Kyle E. Miller. 1991. "Organ Donation Terminology: Are We Communicating Life or Death?" *Health Psychology,* 10:34–41.

Kass, Leon R. 1971. "Death as an Event: A Commentary on Robert Morison." *Science,* 173:698–702.

Kübler-Ross, Elisabeth. 1969. *On Death and Dying.* New York: Macmillan.

Leming, Michael R. 1979–1980. "Religion and Death: A Test of Homans' Thesis." *Omega,* 10(4), 347–364.

Leviton, Dan. 1977. "The Scope of Death Education." *Death Education,* 1:41–56.

McGuire, Dawn. 1988. "Medical Student, Fourth Year." In *Life and Death: The Story of a Hospital,* Ina Yalof (Ed.). New York: Random House.

Montagu, Ashley. 1968. *The Natural Superiority of Women,* rev. ed. New York: Collier Books.

Nardi, Peter. 1990. "Aids and Obituaries: The Perpetuation of Stigma in the Press." In *Culture and Aids,* Douglas A. Feldman (Ed.). New York: Praeger.

New York Times. 1990. "Is Life Expectancy Now Stretched to Its Limit?" November 2, p. A-13.

New York Times. 1992. "Baby Born Without Brain Dies, but Legal Struggle Will Continue." March 31, p. A-8.

News and Courier, 1988. "Doctors 'Kill' Patient to Save Her Life." Charleston, SC, September 22, p. 1-A.

Pine, Vanderlyn R. 1986. "The Age of Maturity for Death Education: A Socio-Historical Portrait of the Era 1976–1985." *Death Studies,* 10:209-231.

Pollak, J. M. 1979. "Correlates of Death Anxiety: A Review of Empirical Studies." *Omega,* 10:97–121.

Prior, Lindsay. 1989. *The Social Organization of Death: Medical Discourse and Social Practices in Belfast.* New York: St. Martin's Press.

Ramsey, Paul. 1970. *The Patient as Person: Explorations in Medical Ethics.* New Haven: Yale University Press.

Rosenthal, Nina R. 1980. "Adolescent Death Anxiety: The Effect of Death Education." *Education,* 101(Fall):95–101.

Selvin, Paul. 1990. "Cryonics Goes Cold: People Just Aren't Dying to Be Frozen." *News and Courier,* Charleston, SC, July 17, p. 5C.

Skinner, B. F. 1990. "Skinner to Have Last Word." *Harvest Personnel,* Associated Press, August 7.

Stillion, Judith M. 1985. *Death and the Sexes.* Washington, DC: Hemisphere/McGraw-Hill.

Stockwell, Edward G. 1976. *The Methods and Materials of Demography,* cond. ed. New York: Academic Press.

United Nations. 1953. *Principles for a Vital Statistics System.* Statistical Papers, series M, no. 19 (August):6.

Vovelle, Michel. 1976. "La redecouverte de la mort." *Pensee,* 189:3–18.

Walsh, Ken. 1974. *Sometimes I Weep.* Valley Forge, PA: Judson Press.

Youngner, S. J., C. S. Landefeld, C. J. Coulton, B. W. Juknialis, and M. Leary. 1989. "'Brain Death' and Organ Retrieval: A Cross-sectional Survey of Knowledge and Concepts Among Health Professionals." *Journal of the American Medical Association,* 261:2206–2210.

SUGGESTED READINGS

Buckman, Robert. 1992. *I Don't Know What to Say: How to Help and Support Someone Who Is Dying.* New York: Viking Press. *From his own clinical experiences as an oncologist, the author discusses many issues that evolve in the process of watching someone die, including the topic of how to communicate with a dying person.*

Feldman, Douglas A. 1990. *Culture and AIDS.* New York: Praeger. *An anthology on AIDS as related to different cultures, obituaries, language, and politics.*

Oaks, Judy, and Gene Ezell. 1993. *Dying and Death: Coping, Caring, Understanding,* 2nd ed. Scottsdale, AZ: Gorsuch Scarisbrick, Publishers. *A helpful book for teachers, counselors, and health professionals in better understanding dying and death.*

Rosenberg, Jay F. 1983. *Thinking Clearly About Death.* Englewood Cliffs, NJ: Prentice-Hall. *A philosophical treatise of death and dying.*

Sloan, David Charles. 1991. *The Last Great Necessity: Cemeteries in American History.* Baltimore: The Johns Hopkins University Press. *Changing attitudes and changing landscapes from churchyards to urban cemeteries to suburban parks in the United States are explored in this excellent historical account.*

Stine, Gerald J. 1993. *Acquired Immune Deficiency Syndrome: Biological, Medical, Social, and Legal Issues.* Englewood Cliffs, NJ: Prentice-Hall. *An up-to-date account of AIDS from numerous academic perspectives.*

Waitzkin, Howard. 1991. *The Politics of Medical Encounters: How Patients and Doctors Deal With Social Problems.* New Haven: Yale University Press. *The micropolitics of medicine, medical micropolitics and social change, and medicine mediating social problems are presented here.*

Wolinsky, Fredric. D. 1988. *The Sociology of Health: Principles, Practitioners, and Issues,* 2nd ed. Belmont, CA: Wadsworth. *Presents the sociology of health and the health care delivery system.*

Chapter

2

Understanding the Social Meaning of Dying and Death

The symbols of death say what life is and those of life define what death must be. The meanings of our fate are forever what we make them.

W. Lloyd Warner
The Living and the Dead

THIS CHAPTER FOCUSES on one of the basic themes of this book—the social meaning of dying, death, and bereavement. Social meaning is the most important component of every aspect of dying and death considered in this text. If dying is perceived to be primarily a biological process, then defining dying and death simply as a biological or physical process would seem to be appropriate. Most people would likely agree with the "biology-is-primary, social meaning-is-secondary" interpretation. *We do not.*

Dying, in fact, is much more than a biological process. It is truly one of the most individual things that can happen to the body, and what happens takes place exclusively within the skin of the one person. However, with reference to the *meaning of dying,* the dying process is one of the most social experiences one can have— all human bodies exist within a social and cultural context. When a person dies, many things other than internal biological changes take place. For nearly all human beings, every act of dying influences others. Consequently, the act of dying is a social or shared event.

The sociological perspective emphasizes the social-symbolic nature of human interaction. The key factor that unites biological entities into a social group entity is shared meaning: Many of the goals one person wants to achieve, and many of the experiences a person wants to have, require shared and coordinated cultural meanings. Symbols are the means by which socially created meaning is shared in the process of human interaction. Symbols are words or gestures that stand for something else by reason of association.

A specific death has distinct meanings wherever the deceased had meaningful relationships, and the death of one person has extensive social consequences. With a death in a husband–wife **dyad,** half of that entity dies. If the couple has two children, one fourth of the family dies. One thirty-thousandth of the community dies, and one two-hundred fifty-millionth of a nation dies.

If a person is identified with many social roles or positions, and that death creates a situation where many roles or positions are vacated, then many persons or role occupants die in a single death. Furthermore, we may agree that while one biological body dies, ownership of that body is difficult to determine. "Who owns my

THE FREE FALL

When I die, my husband loses his wife, his lover, his confidante. My children lose their mother. Each friend loses me as a friend. But I lose all human relationships. That's the meaning of the free fall. That's the meaning of being alone.

JoAnn Kelley Smith (a dying person), *Free Fall*. Valley Forge, PA: Judson Press, 1975, p.36.

body?" is a question often posed by people who are dying. Related to the basic ownership question are "Who is qualified to make decisions about *my* body?" and "If I am the one who is dying, what right do any others have to tell me what to do with my body?" Because humans are social animals, ownership is a creation of symbol-using people. Joint ownership patterns are created and exist for most people. Therefore, body ownership might be considered shared and the decisions related to it would be joint decisions.

The elimination or departure of a person from the ranks of "the living" leaves a hole in the midst of the living. Certain meaning is lost, while new meaning is added—behavior that previously involved the dead is literally no longer possible for it also has ceased to exist. Established interaction or behavior patterns are disrupted, an event that demands attention. The funeral process involves activities, rites, and rituals associated with the final disposition of the dead. This process usually reduces the social disruption caused by death insofar as the rituals are acceptable to those involved and are performed according to societal norms. The living are not only concerned with the death of a person, but also with what happens to the living as a result of that death. While the biological person may be gone, the meaning remains just so long as the living grant the "symboled immortality" or "meaning immortality" to the deceased (Lifton and Olson, 1974).

The granting or creating of such immortality is one of the things symbol-using beings can do. In fact, a given person may even take on more significance after dying than before. For the bereaved, changing the meaning of lost relationships is essential and may be done with varying degrees of ease, depending upon the nature of the relationship (see Chapter 5 for further treatment of this subject).

This book will try to counter the widespread tendency to interpret dying as primarily a biological process—something the body does to the person. We are concerned, rather, with what people *do* about these processes. For example, biologists and medical personnel (or anyone else, including social scientists) respond to the meaning of the biology rather than to the biology per se. The physician's decisions are made on the basis of what the biological condition means to that physician. Making a medical diagnosis is the process by which the physician decides the meaning of the biological factors. This diagnosis, then, represents the process of transposing biological factors into meaning factors.

Death-related meaning has changed extensively since the early 1970s. With reference to past knowledge about death, much of what was known was either untrue or incompatible with contemporary knowledge. While ignorance may cause problems, greater harm stems from people's convictions. The sociological statement made popular by W. I. Thomas illustrates this principle—whatever is *defined* as being real to the physician will *become* real in its consequences for diagnoses. Thus, the "biology-is-primary" perspective creates a **self-fulfilling prophecy.**

A recurring dramatic illustration of the fact that the behavior of the physician and others stems from the meaning rather than from the biology per se can be seen each time the news media reports that a corpse in the morgue has come back to life after wrongly being pronounced dead by the experts. The physician's belief that a body is dead does not guarantee that it is. Behavior follows from the meaning, not from the biological factors per se—a *living* body was sent to the morgue.

Finally, the dying process almost always occurs in a social situation to which meanings are ascribed. Physically, everyone dies in some place, and that place is given symbolic meanings by those involved. Therefore, in this book we will focus on the fact that dying is more than a biological or physical event because it is shared, symboled, and situated.

THE SOCIAL NATURE OF MEANING

To understand the role of meaning in death-related behavior, it is necessary to understand the influence of meaning in all human behavior. We use words to tell ourselves and each other what something means. This book consists of words about dying and death. Words consist of configurations of symbols. The words or symbols are not inherently embedded in the things named—we do not somehow extract words or meaning from the things we see as meaningful. Rather, we create symbols or words to represent the things named. In fact, the symbols re-present (present in a different way) the phenomena of concern. For example, currently the symbol C-A-S-K-E-T represents the container into which a dead body is deposited before burial. However, prior to 1850 the primary meaning of C-A-S-K-E-T was a case for storing valuable jewelry.

The fact that all symbols are **empirical** means that they can potentially be shared or understood by more than one person. The meaning of a CASKET can be shared by many—the CASKET per se cannot. Meaning is created from symbols that are socially constructed, transmitted, and used. However, we must also remember that meaning is always challengeable and changeable because it depends upon group consensus or agreement.

Some symbols have empirical referents. These are the symbols—especially names or labels—that people use to identify, talk, or think about the aspects of the empirical world. Some symbols, however, do not refer to anything empirical. These types of symbols would include beauty, humor, indignity, and evil. Such nonempirically referenced words have an exceptionally meaningful impact upon behavior because they are involved in the human process of making choices. To engage in social behavior, we employ both types of symbols or meanings.

Thus, we have attempted to recognize distinct differences between the empirical world and the meaning world. We have attempted to emancipate the words (symbols or meaning) from the world. Most people do just the reverse: They enslave the words by joining, locking, or laminating them to the empirical world so strongly that their separate identity is lost or hardly recognized.

Most discussions of words (symbols or meaning) involve people who think primarily in terms of the world. They have an empirical-world bias, even though they are talking to each other about things that are not physically present and that have no empirical existence. They effectively execute a symbol bypass.

CREATING AND CHANGING MEANING

Biological bodies are created, live, and die. Bodies of meaning are also created, live, and die. Biological continuity occurs through a process of biological transmission or transference. Meaning (culture) continuity occurs through a process of social-symboled transmission. The socialization process occurs as biological bodies are transformed into social beings and as we teach our children how to behave in what our society considers to be a human way.

Creation of new meaning is always possible. Death-related meaning is no different from any other type of meaning. It is important to remember that this meaning is created by humans, not discovered in the world. All meanings are subject to change. However, well-established meaning is difficult to change. Meaning, for example, is frequently defined as sacred and, therefore, more likely to be protected and perpetuated than changed. Crises or traumatic conditions may be necessary for change in death-related meaning. As noted in Chapter 11, many of the contemporary death-related meanings, including the rituals involved in adjustment, were created by ancestors who experienced dying in quite different social circumstances than those found today. Furthermore, considering the dramatic changes in health, longevity, and health care, our ancestors experienced death in somewhat different biological bodies. Therefore, it is not surprising that discontinuities have developed in American death-related meanings and experiences.

Any aspect of death-related behavior can be changed if there is enough societal (or subsocietal) support. One person can change death-related meaning for himself or herself, but it is difficult to maintain and sustain the new vision if **significant others** do not support, legitimate, or validate this meaning system.

As in the ripples caused by dropping a stone into the lake, changes in death-related meaning will inevitably have consequences that move into and penetrate other areas of living. Change in the sacred components of dying and death may come in through the back door, so to speak. Cremation may gain increased acceptance, not as a direct result of changes in religion, but as a result of the unavailability of space for earth burials. Likewise, changes in life-prolonging, or dying-prolonging, procedures may result more from availability of technological devices than from changes in religion or **mores.**

A SOCIAL SCIENCE UNDERSTANDING OF DYING AND DEATH

In this book we will present many research findings produced in the social sciences to help provide an understanding for death-related experiences. We will also provide sociological, psychological, religious, historical, and anthropological perspectives for interpreting contemporary American customs dealing with dying, death, and bereavement. Finally, in providing an awareness of the many ways in which humans deal with death-related phenomena, we hope to give the perspective that different does not necessarily mean bad or good but simply different, and that death-related behavior can only be evaluated in reference to its social context.

It is our goal to provide multidisciplinary perspectives on dying, death, and bereavement from the bodies of knowledge developed in the social sciences. Chapters 3 and 4 will emphasize a psychological viewpoint to understanding death awareness and meanings; Chapters 5 and 10 utilize an anthropological or comparative approach in providing a cross-cultural perspective on death rituals; and Chapters 11 and 12 review the history of American bereavement and funeral customs. In the remainder of this chapter we will focus on the sociological approach in providing a conceptual understanding of dying and death.

The Sociological Approach to Understanding Dying and Death

Sociology has been defined in many ways. We define sociology as *the scientific study of human interaction.* There are two parts of this definition that we will explore—sociology as (1) a scientific endeavor, with (2) human interaction as the subject of investigation. George C. Homans (1967:7) in *The Nature of Social Science*

This picture is much more than a hole in the ground. Consider the emotional response you have to this photograph: your society has helped produce this response.

claims that any science has two basic jobs to do: discovery and explanation. By the first we judge whether it is a science, and by the second, how successful a science it is. The first job is to state and test more or less general relationships between empirical events of nature. The second task is to explain these relationships within a theoretical context. A scientific explanation will tell us why, under a given set of conditions, a particular phenomenon will occur (Homans, 1967:22). In the process of discovery, the scientist is attempting to formulate general statements concerning empirical variables that can be verified by systematic observation.

Even though the claim has often been made that sociology and the other social sciences differ from the natural sciences because they use a radically different technique for doing research, Richard Rudner (1966:5) contends that the differences between the natural and social sciences are much less fundamental than a difference in methodology. Both the natural and social sciences use the same empirical methodology. This empirical methodology is based on observation and reasoning, not on supernatural revelation, intuition, appeals to authority, or personal speculation.

Sociology, as a science, aims at both discovering empirical regularities and explaining these regularities by referring to an interrelated set of empirical **propositions.** The goal of sociology is to produce a body of knowledge that will not only provide an understanding of the causal processes influencing human interaction, but will enable the sociologist to predict future social behaviors.

This is the basis for Homans's contention that sociology is scientific.

> What makes a science are its aims, not its results. If it aims at establishing more or less general relationships between properties of nature, when the test of the truth of a relationship lies finally in the data themselves, and the data are not wholly manufactured—when nature, however stretched out on the rack, still has a chance to say "No!"—then the subject is a science. By these standards all the social sciences qualify. (1967:4)

Sociology shares with the other social sciences the scientific epistemology (study of knowledge) and a concern for understanding human interaction. The success of sociology, like any other science, is judged by the explanatory power and predictive ability of the body of knowledge produced by the research efforts within the discipline.

A body of scientific knowledge is a collection of those statements of relationship (or propositions) for which there is empirical evidence. It is organized in two ways. The first is the unsystematic collection of all research studies dealing with a particular content area published in research periodicals. For example, one might expect to find all social science research investigations concerned with death-related behavior to be published in a broad range of sociological and psychological journals. However, one would be more likely to find them in one of the following periodicals: *Omega: The Journal of Death and Dying, Death Studies, The Gerontologist, The American Sociological Review, The American Psychological Review, Human Organization, The Journal of Social Psychology,* and *The Journal of Abnormal and Social Psychology.* The only organization of these findings would be found in the theoretical frameworks of other research investigations and textbooks citing these studies.

The second method by which a body of knowledge is organized is through a theoretical **paradigm.** Research studies sharing general commitments to methodological techniques, research assumptions, and levels of analysis are brought together to form theoretical paradigms. According to George Ritzer:

> A paradigm is a fundamental image of the subject matter within a science. It serves to define what should be studied, what questions should be asked, how they should be asked, and what rules should be followed in interpreting the answers obtained. The paradigm is the broadest unit of consensus within a science and serves to differentiate one scientific community (or sub-community) from another. It subsumes, defines, and interrelates the examples, theories, methods, and instruments that exist within it. (1975:7)

Sociology, like most other scientific disciplines, is a multiparadigm science. There is much debate over the number of paradigms existing within the field of sociology, yet sociologists would agree that no single paradigm is dominant within the discipline. Paradigms are further divided into subparadigms or theoretical orientations. Examples of these theoretical traditions (discussed later in this chapter) would include structural-functional theory, conflict theory, social exchange theory, and symbolic interaction theory.

Ritzer divides sociological knowledge into three basic paradigms—social factist, social definitionist, and social behavioralist. The social factist and definitionist approaches are the two central paradigms within the discipline of sociology and serve to organize contemporary sociological knowledge related to death and dying issues. The social behavioralist paradigm is more concerned with psychological issues, influenced by the work of B. F. Skinner, and will not be discussed here.

The social factist paradigm is generally concerned with group actions and societal structures, and the social definitionist paradigm focuses on analysis of the behavior, attitudes, meanings, and values of individuals. For the purpose of simplicity, we will discuss these two general paradigms and the following four subparadigms: structural-functional theory, conflict theory, social exchange theory, and symbolic interaction theory.

The Social Factist Paradigm

Emile Durkheim's work served as the primary foundation for the social factist paradigm. In attempting to differentiate sociology from social philosophy, Durkheim defined the discipline as the study of social facts. For Durkheim (1964) social facts are "any way of doing things (fixed or not) which are capable of exercising restraint upon the individual." He advocated that sociologists study social facts *as if* they were things. To accomplish this end, Durkheim formulated the following four guidelines in his *Rules of the Sociological Method* (1964, originally published in 1895):

1. All preconceptions must be eradicated.
2. The subject matter for sociological research must be social facts directly observed.
3. Social facts must be viewed as a product of group experiences and not individual actions.
4. The cause of any given social fact must be sought in its preceding social facts.

The social factist paradigm is primarily concerned with group actions and societal structures. This point is exemplified in Durkheim's claim that "society is a social system which is composed of parts which, without losing their identity and individuality, constitute a whole which transcends its parts." From the social factist point of view, social groups or collectivities (e.g., a particular nuclear family) cannot be reduced to merely a collection of individuals. From the social factist point of view social phenomena have a reality of their own that transcends the constituting parts.

Therefore, sociological research from this perspective will study group-related phenomena (e.g., death rituals, structures that provide care for dying patients, and professional groups of funeral functionaries) rather than behaviors of particular individuals.

Durkheim advocated the use of historical and comparative methods in sociological research. An example of this type of death-related research might be comparison of the size, structure, and function of colonial funerals in Concord, Massachusetts, with a similar contemporary analysis of funerals in the same city.

Unlike Durkheim, however, many contemporary social factists employ the survey research design. The use of the latter technique creates a problem for some; as Ritzer (1975:27) says, "How can one study social facts (cultural patterns) by asking individuals questions?" This issue might be more clearly understood by considering the analogy of the relationship between forests and trees. One can study forests in the United States and describe their sizes and distribution, their rates of reproduction, morbidity, and mortality, and the impact of acid rain upon them. However, to adequately understand a forest one must look at a few trees. The same may be true of cultural and social patterns and the behaviors of individuals.

Subsumed under the social factist paradigm are the subparadigms of structural-functional theory and conflict theory. The former is concerned with explaining the persistence of social facts, social institutions and structures, and the stability of society. Conflict theory focuses on the competition between the various parts, institutions, and/or structures within a given society and the coercive forces that allow societies to perpetuate themselves at times and change at others.

Structural-Functionalist Theory

Structural-functionalists view society as a social system of interacting parts in which death-related behavior is analyzed from two perspectives:

1. How do death-related meaning systems and death institutions contribute to the maintenance of the larger social system?
2. In what ways are death-related meaning systems and death institutions affected by their relationships to the larger social system?

Functionalists are interested in positive (eufunctional) and negative (dysfunctional) results of social interaction as well as the intended (manifest) and unintended (latent) consequences of death-related behavior. When family members commit themselves to care for a dying family member, it can be eufunctional for emotional ties within the family; however, this behavior (especially if family members must interrupt their employment) may be dysfunctional for the security of family financial resources. A manifest function of attending a funeral is to support the bereaved as they attempt to adapt to the loss of a loved one, but a latent function is to strengthen the relationships that exist within social groups.

If structural-functionalist theorists were interested in the funeral rites and rituals, they might investigate one or more of the following research questions:

1. How do funerals help to celebrate and maintain society's most salient social values?
2. How do funerals help to promote relationships within kinship groups (grandparents, parents, aunts and uncles, cousins, brothers, sisters, etc.)?
3. How do funerals contribute to and/or affect the relationships between bereaved families and the larger society?
4. How do funerals facilitate the grieving process as one mourns the death of a loved one?
5. How do death-related rituals help return bereaved persons to their normal social responsibilities?
6. How do differing methods of body disposition and funeral rituals socially differentiate families regarding social status?

The following research example, written by Kathy Charmaz (1980:183–187), describes the strategies employed by coroners' deputies in maintaining the routine character of their work as they attempt to get surviving family members to take over the responsibility for the care of the dead body and the financial obligations related to final disposition. In this description we can observe that if each party performs his or her socially prescribed role (or social function), the social system runs efficiently and social equilibrium is maintained.

THE ANNOUNCEMENT OF DEATH BY THE CORONER'S DEPUTY

Kathy Charmaz

In these coroners' departments, the ways in which deaths are announced to heretofore unsuspecting relatives are strategically constructed with an eye toward accomplishing the objectives of getting the relatives to quietly accept both the burial costs and the death without the deputy's personal involvement.

(continued)

Burial costs are likely to be the "real" issue in countries without access to inexpensive burials. Then, the deputies feel constrained to handle the notification of death strategically in order for the family to readily assume the costs of disposal of the body.

Consequently, the strategies employed in announcing the death to relatives differ according to the necessity of getting them to pay for burial costs. When this is necessary, and therefore an important part of the deputy's work, special techniques are likely to be employed. Notable, strategic control of the encounter is enhanced by making the announcement in person. The deputies then lay the grounds for ensuring that an uneventful and speedy disposition of the body is made at the expense of the family.

The other objective, to induce the relative to accept the death as real, coincides with the deputy's interest in making the announcement of death efficiently without eliciting a subsequent fuss from the bereaved or becoming involved themselves. Part of doing that means constructing situations in which the deputy's sense of self is protected, in addition to his or her control over the encounter in which he or she is engaged. Self-protection strategies are employed to maintain the routine character of the work and to keep the deputies from feeling personally involved in the ongoing scene. Part of the self-protection strategy consists of the effort to remain the polite, sincere, authoritative, but basically disinterested, official.

The strategies for making the announcement help the deputies remain in control of the situation and handle the special problems that emerge in the course of interaction. Not the least of these problems is the necessity of deputies to construct the contextual properties of the announcing scene, besides constructing the announcement itself. In other words, they must create the kind of ambience and interactional circumstances wherein the announcement logically fits so that it is effective and believable; they have no ready-made scene to serve as an official backdrop for their proclamation.

Compared to physicians who announce "bad news" to the relative, deputies have a weighty problem. Besides their much lesser amount of authority and prestige, deputies lack the advantages typically possessed by physicians of a prior relationship with the relative, a fitting organizational setting for giving the news, and a series of prior interactional cues that serve to prepare the relative.

Since deputies have neither the structural supports provided by the hospital situation nor the physician's status, they must devise tactics to get their work done without incident. Typically, their objectives are to announce quickly, to turn the responsibility of the body and its subsequent burial expense over to the family, and to determine that the person who received the news is holding up well or is with someone. But all these tasks may be embellishments to their main task of the disposition of the body and getting the family to assume the expenses, when this is their real objective.

Deputies try to create an authoritative context by rapidly supplying one meaningful cue after another that brings the relatives into interaction as they prepare to move into the announcement. Compared to the medical scene, the cues come much more rapidly and sharply. Thus, the cues cannot be easily dismissed, although the survivor has little time to think about them.

Skillful deputies can be expected to handle the situation in such a way that cues will neither be missed or misinterpreted. The relatives are not permitted enough time to disattend to them and, should they attempt to, the deputies will alter their presentation accordingly. For example, a deputy stated, "Sometimes I'm stern, sometimes I'm sympathetic, sometimes I even shout a little bit louder than they can."

The deputies who telephone find they get a better response when they successively lead the relative into questioning them. By doing so, the officials set the conditions wherein they can impart progressively unpromising news. For example:

> I tell them that he collapsed today while at work. They asked if he is all right now. I say slowly, "Well, no, but they took him to the hospital." . . . They ask if he is there now. I say, "They did all they could do—the doctors tried very hard." They say, "He is dead at the hospital?" Then I tell them he's at the coroner's office.

Most deputies expressly avoid the word "dead" when first imparting the news, since they feel it is too harsh. Substitutes are used, such as "fatally injured" and "passed away," if they must refer directly to it at all. A preferred technique is to control the interaction so that the relative refers to the person as "dead." Those making telephone announcements attempt to manipulate the conversation so that the relative says the word "dead." Several deputies remarked that having the survivors themselves say it made the announcement more meaningful to them and the death more "real." Describing a close family member as "dead" becomes symbolic and sets the stage for treating the deceased as such. The deputies then reaffirm the survivor's statements and elaborate on them. Consequently, when the deputies' strategies work, the transition from perceiving one's relative from alive to dead can be made rapidly. The symbolic shift is likely to occur so quickly during the encounter that the relative may remain unaware of how the interaction was managed. Indeed, in an encounter deputies deem successful, the relative is likely to express appreciation for their "sensitivity."

Deputies state that the relatives always ask about the circumstances of dying. The coroners give them what information they have and can release, then turn the situation around by asking about funeral and burial arrangements. To illustrate: "They always ask what happened. Then we reverse it and ask what type of arrangements they are going to make."

Or in the case of the telephone notification, the relative typically inquires, "What can I do [to help]?" The deputies simply state, "All you need to do now is call your family funeral director, and he'll direct you." In both situations, this

(continued)

approach gets the relatives down to business and usually results in their agreement to "help" while in the midst of the initial encounter with the deputies.
Likely, the relatives have unwittingly volunteered to underwrite the expenditures before they have any conception of the implications or expense. Simultaneously, the deputies have played the role of officials who cut through the
survivor's grief and shock by pointing to the work that has to be done. Moreover, the deputies have strategically managed the situation in ways that foster
the relatives' acceptance of their directives.

Urban Life, (4:3) pp. 296-316, copyright 1975. Reprinted by permission of McGraw-Hill Publishing
Company

Conflict Theory

While structural-functional theory focuses upon the issue of societal maintenance and social equilibrium, conflict theory is primarily concerned with issues
related to social change and disequilibrium. Conflict theorists focus upon competition, conflict, and dissension resulting from individuals and groups competing over
limited societal resources.

In emphasizing social competition over limited scarce resources, conflict theorists interested in death-related behavior would point out the inequality in the
availability and quality of medical care and the differential death rates. For example,
the poor are deprived of optimal care, in general, and of lifesaving procedures, in
particular (Charmaz, 1980:37). Relying on the work of Herbert Marcuse, Allan
Kellehear argues that those who control life are the same as those who control
death. According to Kellehear (1990:13):

> The power elite in any society and that society's politico-economic arrange-
> ments—that is class arrangements—determine one's Life and Death chances. Soci-
> ety determines not only what types of death will occur, but when they occur and to
> whom and the chances, if any, of doing anything about it.

From a conflict theoretical perspective, Charmaz argues that American society,
which has an individualistic perspective on death (as it does on most other social
issues), abdicates most of its social responsibilities to the dying and their family
members. She asserts that in America we are assured of an inequitable distribution
of health care and a lack of social concern for the dying precisely because Americans value individualism and privacy.

> Beliefs in individualism, self-reliance, privatism, and stoicism are ideological
> and justify the ways in which dying is handled. The ideological view of dying as a
> private affair, something that *should* be the responsibility of the family, relieves
> other social institutions, notably health and welfare organizations, from the neces-
> sity of providing comprehensive services. Such beliefs are justified by ideological

THE WIZARD OF ID   **Brant parker and Johnny hart**

views that human beings deserve privacy in their problems, and in order to maintain self-respect, they wish to rely on themselves to handle them whenever possible. When it is not possible, failure may be conferred upon those unable to handle their situations.

If conflict theorists were interested in funeral rites and rituals, they might investigate one or more of the following research questions:

1. What are the dysfunctional consequences of attending funerals?
2. What role conflicts and family disputes arise as a result of planning a funeral for family members?
3. How does not attending a funeral create conflicts between adults in neighborhood, friendship, and occupational groups?
4. What are the problems created by the presence of children at funerals?
5. How do particular family relationships contribute to increased competition for status among family members as they participate in the funeral of a family member?
6. How do methods of planning a funeral and the related expenditures contribute to increased family conflict and competition for scarce financial resources within the family?
7. In what ways might members of the clergy and funeral directors engage in social conflict due to the fact that family members allocate each functionary with differing amounts of authority and social rewards (money) for conducting the funeral?
8. How does the death of a parent create sibling rivalry among the children, and how does the death of a child create marital problems for the parents?

The following reading is an example of conflict theory's approach applied to family behavior related to the division of family property and the reading of the will.

WHAT'S FAIR IS FAIR

Even where a will or the law of intestacy calls for equal division of a bequest among a group of beneficiaries and the beneficiaries accept the principle of equal division, conflict may occur. Some possessions are indivisible but desirable to more than one person, such as a prized antique clock. Problems may arise in the attempt to divide valuables equally. Under what circumstances can a treasured rocking chair and a family Bible be divided equally between two or more family members?

If all beneficiaries want fair treatment and a will attempts fair treatment, conflict may occur because beneficiaries have different perceptions of what is fair. Fairness can mean that something is divided equally, but fairness also takes into account various principles of deservingness or right; a division of an estate can be fair without being equal. Because fairness can be determined on many different bases, there may be many competing interpretations on what is fair. The following list, derived from the work of Marvin Sussman et al. (1970) and from interviews carried out during our research, indicates some of the competing principles for determining if the outcome in inheritance is fair.

1. Long residence in a house confers some right to it.
2. Last name identity with the deceased confers some rights to the property of the deceased.
3. Blood relationship confers some rights.
4. High frequency of contact with the deceased confers some rights.
5. Material support of the deceased confers some rights.
6. Coresidence with the deceased confers some rights.
7. Having given the deceased a thing confers rights to its return.
8. Need arising from relative poverty, handicap, minorhood, orphan status, or infirmity confers rights.
9. Contribution in building the deceased's estate increases rights.
10. Kinship closeness confers rights.
11. Previous perceived underinheritance increases rights.
12. Overinheritance reduces rights.
13. Hostile relationship with the deceased reduces rights.
14. Congenial relationship increases rights.

In addition to people having discrepant interpretations of what is equal or what is fair, there will be instances where equality and fairness may be competing principles. Some individuals will believe that the estate should be divided equally, while other individuals will believe that it should be divided on the basis of what is fair, though fairness may be perceived differently by different persons.

Because there are so many possible interpretations of what is fair or what is equal and because people often seek fairness or equality, a dispute may not be resolved easily. Disputes over inheritance may be one of the major reasons for adult siblings to break off relationships with each other. In some cases the inheritance dispute may be the final battle between competitive siblings, and in that sense it resembles the "last straw" reported in breakups in other close relationships (Hill, Rubin, and Peplau, 1976; Nevaldine, 1978).

Sandra L. Titus, Paul C. Rosenblatt, and Roxanne M. Anderson, "Family Conflict over Inheritance of Property." *The Family Coordinator,* July 1979, pp. 337–338. Copyright 1979 by the National Council on Family Relations, 3989 Central Ave. NE, Suite 550, Minneapolis, MN 55421. Reprinted by permission.

The Social Definitionist Paradigm

The social definitionist paradigm differs from the social factist paradigm at two crucial points: the first is that the definitionist would contend that the essential feature of society is its subjective character. Social facts do not have any inherent meaning other than that which humans attribute to them. W. I. Thomas argues that if people define situations as real, they will be real in their consequences. This argument is a basic premise of the social definitionist paradigm. The social definitionist would contend that all social facts are either intrasubjective or intersubjective.

The second distinguishing feature of the social definitionist paradigm is the methodological unit of analysis—the individual. The social definitionist will emphasize individual behavior over group actions and societal structures.

George Ritzer (1975:85–86) rightly credits the writings of Max Weber as the exemplar of the social definitionist paradigm. The essence of Weber's analysis of social action was the *meaningful action of individuals.* Weber (1966:88) defines social action as human behavior to which the acting individual attaches subjective meaning and that takes into account the behaviors of others.

Weber advocated "interpretative understanding" (*Verstehen*) as the research methodology for investigating social action. The interpretative understanding approach requires the researcher to develop an empathy for the subjects he or she studies. At times this will require the investigator to enter the subjective world of the subject by participating in this person's life experience. A Native American proverb encourages us not to judge the behavior of others until we have walked a mile in their moccasins. In this context, interpretative understanding attempts to describe and explain social behavior from the perspective of the subjective meanings of the actors' intentions for their behavior. Today, contemporary sociologists utilize the *Verstehen* approach as they employ participant observation research techniques.

WORDS AND MEANINGS

Blood,
and Pus . . .
Entrails,
Vomit,
Dung, Spit and Afterbirth.
Disgusting words.

Love,
And Soft.
Mother.
Kiss, Mood, and Friendship.
Tender words.

Spring,
And Smile.
Dance,
Play,
Fun, Sing, and Beachball.
Happy Words.

Death,
And Fire.
Pain,
War,
Divorce, Poverty, Hospital.
Sad Words.

No. That's not right at all. You cannot
String words together
And say They're bad
Or good.

Where are the verbs?
Who are we talking about?
What are the circumstances?

Vomit is beautiful to a mother whose child
Had just swallowed a pin.
Love is pain if you are a third party,
Outside, looking in.

Death is very nice for someone very old,
Very ill, and ready.

And surely you've danced with a clod.
Or had a sad spring.

No, Words aren't sad
Or glad.
You are.
Or I am.
Or he is.

Reprinted from W. A. Armbruster, *A Bag of Noodles.* St. Louis: Concordia, 1972, p. 8. Copyright 1973 Concordia Publishing House. Reprinted by permission.

We will now consider social exchange theory and symbolic interaction theory as two theoretical traditions that might be implied by the social definitionist paradigm.

Social Exchange Theory

There are two traditions followed by social exchange theorists. The first is consistent with principles of behavioral psychology and stresses psychological reductionism and behavioral reinforcement techniques. The second type of social exchange theory has been influenced by the work of Peter Blau (1964) and is committed to many of the assumptions held by symbolic interactionists and the social definitionist paradigm. Social exchange theories of this type would contend that human behavior involves a subjective and interpretative interaction with others that attempts to exchange symbolic and nonsymbolic rewards. It is important that such social exchange involves reciprocity so that each interacting individual receives something *perceived* as equivalent to what is given.

From this perspective, individuals will continue to participate in social situations so long as they perceive that they derive equal benefits from their participation. For example, the social exchange theorist would contend that individuals will attend funerals (even though they tend to feel uncomfortable in such situations and find body viewing distasteful and anxiety-producing) because they perceive social benefit in being supportive of bereaved friends.

REPRINTED BY PERMISSION OF JOHNNY HART AND NAS, INC.

RELIGIOUS RITUAL OBSERVANCE AND ANXIETY

George C. Homans (1965:87–88) concludes his synthesis of the theories of Malinowski and Radcliffe-Brown by citing seven elements related to the study of religious ritual and anxiety.

1. *Primary anxiety.* Whenever individuals desire the accomplishment of certain results and do not possess the techniques which will make for success, they feel sentiments which we call anxiety.

2. *Primary ritual.* Under these circumstances, they tend to perform actions which have no practical result and which we call ritual. But these persons are not simply individuals—they are members of a society with definite traditions. Among other things society determines the form of rituals and expects individuals to perform the rituals on appropriate occasions.

3. *Secondary anxiety.* When these people follow the technical procedures and perform the traditional rituals, their primary anxiety remains latent. We say that the rites give them confidence. Under these circumstances, they will feel anxiety only when the rites themselves are not properly performed. In fact, this attitude becomes generalized, and anxiety is felt whenever any of the traditions of society are not observed. This anxiety may be called secondary or displaced anxiety.

4. *Secondary ritual.* This is the ritual of the purification and expiation which has the function of dispelling secondary anxiety. Its form and performance, like those of primary ritual, may or may not be socially determined.

5. *Rationalization.* This element includes a system of beliefs which are associated with the rituals. They may be very simple: such statements as that the performance of a certain magic does ensure the catching of fish, or that if an Andaman mother and father do not observe the food taboos they will be sick. The statements may be very elaborate. Such are the statements which accompany the fundamental rituals of any society: the equivalents of the Mass of the Catholic Church.

6. *Symbolization.* Since the form of the ritual is not determined by the nature of a practical result to be accomplished, it can be determined by other factors. We say that it is symbolic, and each society has its own vocabulary of symbols. Some of the symbolism is relatively simple; for example, the symbolism of sympathies and antipathies. Some are complicated. In particular, certain of the rituals of a society, and those the most important, make symbolic reference to the fundamental myths of that

society just as surely as the Mass makes reference to Christ's
sacrifice on Calvary.

7. *Function.* Ritual actions do not produce a practical result on the
external world—that is one reason why we call them ritual. But
to make this statement is not to say that ritual has no function.
Its function is not related to the world external to the society but
to the internal constitution of the society. It gives the members
of the society confidence; it dispels their anxieties; it disciplines
the social organization.

In this seven-step conclusion, we can see that Homans has carefully
brought together the major points of both Malinowski and Radcliffe-Brown. His
basic contention is that when individuals experience anxiety in life crisis events,
such as death, ritual will be instrumental in making sentiment latent. However,
the fear of violating ritual obligations will again make anxiety manifest. This
new anxiety will call for institutionalized ritual. Once individuals have fulfilled
these religious magical ceremonies required by society, they will experience a
reduction of anxiety.

Having discussed Homans's explicit theory of anxiety and ritual, we shall
now turn to his implicit theory of these phenomena. In elaborating upon an
implicit theory we must extrapolate Homans's position from his earlier theoretical treatises found in *The Human Group* (1950) and *Social Behavior: Its Elementary Forms* (1961). While any exegesis adds to the substantive writings of the
author, it is believed that our elaboration will not distort Homans's exchange
theory (in the tradition of psychological behaviorism) which is predicated upon
belief in utilitarian self-interest. Abstracting Skinnerian behaviorism, the basic
principle of Homans's theory is that if the individuals have needs they will
manifest behaviors which have in the past satisfied these needs. To this basic
theorem Homans (cited by Turner, 1974:233) adds the following corollaries:

1. Individuals will avoid unpleasant experiences, but will endure
    limited amounts of them as the cost of emitting these behaviors
    satisfies overriding needs.
2. Individuals will continue to perform activities as long as they
    continue to produce desired and expected effects.
3. As needs are satisfied by particular behaviors, individuals are
    less likely to emit these behaviors until the needs are again
    present.

Applying this theorem and its corollaries and Homans's explicit theory to
the study of religion and anxiety, we have the following analysis. If individuals
encounter an anxiety-producing situation, such as a death of a significant other,
and they have utilized religious symbolizing in the past to define death and dis-

(continued)

pel anxiety, they will engage in religious activity to meet their psychological needs in the present situation. Assuming that their sentiment of anxiety was latent before this present encounter with death, they may have been inactive in religious ritual behavior. The return to religious experience may cause anxiety due to the non-observance of religious obligations. While anxiety may be increased at this time (as Radcliffe-Brown would suggest) individuals will continue to perform religious rituals as long as they perceive them as having a potential for anxiety reduction. When the requirements for proper religious observance have been met (as determined by the group), death anxiety will again become latent.

In conclusion, Homans's social exchange theory states that religion functions to relieve anxiety associated with life-crisis situations. Death anxiety calls forth religious activity which serves to make anxiety latent. However, in order to maintain the external system of religious activity (which eventually becomes institutionalized), the group must continually reaffirm the potential threat of anxiety to unite individuals through a "common concern." This secondary anxiety may be effectively relieved through the group rituals of purification and expiation. However, primary reduction of anxiety is operative within the internal system of individual religion.

Michael R. Leming. 1977. "Social Exchange: Providing an Understanding of Religion and Its Function." In *A Time to Die*, Glenn Vernon (Ed.). Washington, DC: University Press of America.

The preceding research summary of George C. Homans's work, written by Michael Leming, provides an analysis of human behavior that draws on both types of theoretical traditions found in the social exchange paradigm.

If exchange theorists were interested in funeral rites and rituals, they might investigate one or more of the following research questions:

1. Why do individuals attend funerals—what are the social rewards acquired by attending?
2. Why do some individuals not attend funerals—what are the social punishments or sanctions acquired by not attending?
3. What are the social and personal costs and benefits for families when they provide wakes, funerals, and other death-related rites of passage?
4. What are the social and personal costs for families when they do not provide wakes, funerals, and other death-related rites of passage?
5. Why would the average American family spend approximately $4000 in burying their dead, when they could accomplish the same purpose at a fraction of the cost?

Symbolic Interaction Theory

The foundation of symbolic interaction theory is that **symbols** (meaning) are a basic component of human behavior. People interact with each other based on their understanding of the meanings of social situations and their perceptions of what others expect of them within these situations. Stressing the symbolic nature of social interaction, Jonathan Turner (1985:32) says: "Symbols are the medium of our adjustment to the environment, of our interaction with others, of our interpretation of experiences, and of our organizing ourselves into groups."

From the symbolic interactionist perspective, human beings are autonomous agents whose actions are based upon their subjective understanding of society as socially constructed reality. Randall Collins (1985:200) makes this point in the following statements:

> Each individual projects himself or herself into various future possibilities; each one takes the role of the other in order to see what kind of reaction there will be to this action; as a result each aligns his or her own action in terms of the consequences he or she foresees in the other person's reactions. Society is not a structure, but a process. Definitions of situations emerge from this continuous negotiation of perspectives. Reality is socially constructed. If it takes on the same form over and over again, it is only because the parties to the negotiation have worked out the same resolution and because there is no guarantee that they cannot do it differently next time.

The symbolic interactionist perspective can be summarized in what some have called the **ISAS** paradigm statement—*Individual*-level behavior is in response to *Symbols*, relative to the *Audience*, and relative to the *Situation*. "ISAS" stands for the four basic components (see Vernon and Cardwell, 1981). Death-related behavior of the one dying, and of those who care about that person, is in response to meaning, relative to the audience and to the situation. Death-related behavior is shared, symboled (given meaning), and situated. It is socially created and not biologically predetermined.

Symbols   Interaction is a dynamic, flexible, and socially created phenomenon. Meaning is socially created and socially perpetuated; it is preserved in symbols or words. However, preserved words have to be rediscovered and reinterpreted if they are to be continually used in human interaction. Generation after generation repeats the process with a somewhat different content—no book means the same to every reader. Similarly death-related behavior and meanings are dynamic phenomena.

Audience-Related Behavior   As we relate to each other in normal social relationships, talking is the most common form of interaction. Even if we do not

CONFLICTING DEATH-RELATED MEANINGS

Glenn M. Vernon

Some believe:

They are dying when they are not.
They are not dying when they are.

They should refuse to let some people die who want to die.
They, or maybe the state, should kill some people who want to live.

It would be good for a specific person to die.
It would be wrong for that specific person to die.

Dying is caused by the moral condition of the person dying.
Dying has nothing to do with the moral condition of a person.

God causes particular deaths.
God created universal death (thus everyone dies at some time) but
    does not influence particular deaths.

Wishing another person to die caused that death.
Wishing it were so cannot make it so.

Death is terminal—there is nothing beyond death.
Death is transition—it involves movement to another type of
    existence. There is nothing for the person beyond death.

An individual's dying time is predestined—a person dies when his
    or her time is up.
An individual's dying time is emergent—a person's time is up when
    death occurs.

Every person should fight to stay alive.
You should not fight that which is inevitable.

Dying is the worst thing that can happen to a person.
Certain types of living, such as living in an incapacitated and
    dependent state, are worse than dying.

Keeping the biological body alive is the greatest value.
Humans in fact have a God-given instinct for such preservation.
    The well-being of the person is of greater value than just
    keeping the body alive.

Quantity of biological life is an overriding value.
Quality of life is an overriding value.

Nothing is of greater value than preserving one's life.
All have something for which they would give their life.

They can help the dying most by telling them the "real" meaning
    of death—"Let me tell you what dying should mean to you."
They can help the dying most by helping them decide what dying
    means to them—"Let me help you live fully while you are
    dying."

Dying is inherently fearful.
Dying can be welcomed and may be beautiful.

If death could be eliminated from our society, it would be
    wonderful—a step toward the creation of heaven on earth.
If death could be (and were) eliminated from our society it would
    be awful—a step toward the creation of a hell on earth.

A genuine concern with the dying person qualifies one as an
    effective care-giver.
Good intentions alone do not automatically qualify one as an
    effective care-giver.

Death would be welcomed—they want to die.
Death would be undesirable—they do not want to die.

Glenn M. Vernon, former Professor of Sociology, University of Utah.

convey meaning to others with words, other people understand our meanings with their own words. In making decisions about the meaning of death, one can, in effect, consult established words, other people, the self, or situational conditions. If one is dying, one can make decisions about dying behavior by observing the treatment by others. The audience involved may be family, physicians, clergy, nurses, peers, or even strangers walking down the hall of the hospital. How the patient is treated by these people reveals something about the patient. This treatment includes, but is not limited to, the following:

1. What people are willing to talk about with me—and what they avoid.
2. Whether they are willing to touch me, and how they touch me when they do.
3. Where I am, or maybe where others have located me—hospital, nursing home, intensive care unit, isolation unit, my room at home.
4. Tangible and verbal gifts others give me.

5. What people will let me do, or expect me to do, or will not let me do.
6. The tone of voice people use when they talk to me.
7. Frequency and length of visits from others.
8. Excuses these people make for not visiting.
9. The reactions of others to my prognosis.

Dying with dignity or self-respect does not always happen. Self-meaning can be created and sustained with the help of others. Dying as an unsupported or unloved person, however, makes the dying an extremely difficult experience. How you treat another also influences how that person will treat you. If another thinks you are leveling with him or her, he or she will treat you one way. If one thinks you want to engage in a game of let's pretend, one may be willing to play, as a favor to you. In death-related behavior, as in all behavior, one watches others for cues in deciding how to act.

The audience to which the dying person relates may also be supernatural. Symbol users are not restricted to the natural-empirical world. Neither are they restricted to the world of the living. If believers realize that those who have died have an existence in another realm, or that there is a life after death, this belief is real to them and has consequences for their behavior.

People who are approaching death may involve themselves in a gradual replacement of a living audience with a supernatural, or other-world audience. As we have demonstrated, the dying relate to many audiences.

The Situation   Where a person dies is also given meaning. As patients come to grips with the terminal condition, the manner in which they define the situation

WHAT CAREGIVERS SHOULD NOT ASSUME ABOUT THE DYING

Glenn M. Vernon

For the terminally ill person, the significant meaning that is taken into account in decision-making concerning self and others is the meaning she or he realizes. It is suggested that priority attention be given to meaning in any confrontation with death. Likewise the caregiver's behavior is influenced by the meaning the caregiver realizes. The same is also true of all people who are in social situations where dying and death occur.

Working from this perspective, it may be helpful to identify some frequently accepted assumptions that need to be questioned. It is accordingly suggested that those working with the dying and the bereaved **should *not* assume that**:

1. Those with whom you work necessarily share your meaning of death.
2. Meanings that were helpful to earlier generations are equally functional today.
3. Meaning remains constant and does not change.
4. Dying biologically is all that is happening.
5. Knowing about the biological aspects of dying will in and of itself provide knowledge about how humans expect to behave in death-related situations.
6. Pretension or deception, which you believe will help you cope with those who are dying, will help those with whom you are working.
7. The terminal patient is the only person who has death adjustment problems.
8. Persons facing bereavement have to wait until the death actually occurs before they can start working on their bereavement— meaning adjustment.
9. The person who is dying has somehow stopped meaningful living during the terminal period.
10. A death that is defined as meaningless, from the perspective of the person dying, cannot be given meaning in the last stages.
11. The terminal period without an extended future is necessarily one of no hope.
12. Talking is the only way for the caregiver to communicate "I care."

Glenn M. Vernon, former Professor of Sociology, University of Utah.

(and respond to it) will have a tremendous impact upon their dying. Dying in a nursing home or hospital is different from dying in the home, in bed, surrounded by a loving family and feelings of belonging. If patients view the institutional death setting as a supportive environment, their coping behavior may be helped. On the other hand, if they feel all alone, and if they have defined the place of dying as a foreign environment, adjustment will not be facilitated (Leming et al., 1977).

Like other meanings, the definition of the situation is an attempt by the individual to bring meaning to the world. Since the situational definition always involves selective perception, the terminal patient will assign meaning to the environment and will respond to this symbolic reality. The thing to which the patient responds does not have existence independent of his or her definition. Therefore, each terminal patient will interpret the dying environment differently. This accounts for the different experiences of dying patients (Leming et al., 1977). This point will be elaborated upon further in Chapter 6.

If symbolic interactionists were interested in funeral rites and rituals, they might investigate one or more of the following research questions:

1. What are the social meanings that give rise to the attendance of funerals?
2. How are death-related behaviors influenced by the social audiences of the American funeral?
3. In what ways do families utilize the funeral service to project an image of family value commitments and group cohesiveness?
4. How do families use the funeral in order to demonstrate status differentiation?
5. What is the influence of location of the funeral upon the meaning of the funeralization process?
6. How does the size of the funeral audience convey meaning to the bereaved and attribute social importance to the life of the deceased?

CONCLUSION

Why study death from a sociological perspective? The answers are many. While the primary goal of this book is *not* to prepare you for your own death or the deaths of loved ones, you may still learn many things that will be personally beneficial. Given the fact that you will have death-related experiences, it might be useful for you to employ a sociological perspective to acquire valuable insights into your own life and the lives of people about whom you care.

Secondly, as you read about the history of death-related customs in the United States and elsewhere, and comprehend social class and ethnic variations in bereavement customs, the sociological perspective may provide you with a new appreciation for your own life experiences and family traditions as they relate to issues of dying, death, and bereavement.

Thirdly, as you consider the ways the family socializes its members to develop death conceptualizations, attitudes, and feelings, the sociological perspective may help you to understand more fully how your own abilities to cope are a function of your upbringing. Furthermore, as you study the material in this book, you may attain a more objective perspective on some of the decisions that may confront you and your family as, one day, you attempt to deal with death-related situations. The sociological perspective, then, can make you more aware of the many options available to you regarding death-related decisions.

Finally, the study of dying, death, and bereavement is an important and interesting area of study to which social and behavioral scientists have much to contribute. A good reason to study death and dying from a sociological perspective is to learn more about the discipline of sociology. Social thanatology provides the student with an opportunity to investigate the meaning and application of many concepts developed in sociology and the other behavioral sciences.

SUMMARY

1. The goal of this chapter is to emphasize the extensive involvement of meaning in what many consider to be primarily a biological process—that is, dying.

2. Meaning consists of symbols that are socially created and socially used. Some symbols refer to something else or have an empirical referent. Some do not. The major function of both types of symbols is to permit humans to relate to each other and thus create shared behavior and meaning.

3. Death-related meaning permits sharing death-related behavior. The death-related behavior of the dying individual and those who are significant to that person is in response to meaning, relative to the audience and to the situation. It is a phenomenon that is socially created, not biologically predetermined.

4. Since most people participate in various social groups, they are involved in many different interaction patterns. Consequently, even though it is but one biological body that dies, many "role holes" or

vacancies are left with the death of a single individual. Bodies die—so do social relationships and social networks.

5. Death meaning includes evaluations of whatever those involved decide to evaluate. Evaluators may include values believed to be absolute, abstract, and situational. Defining values such as "living is always preferable to dying" as abstract rather than absolute helps explain the relativity of situational values and is likely to lead to fewer adjustment problems when confronting dying.

6. Dying is a social process. The person who is dying is living and is involved in living experiences with others.

7. Evolving death meanings are part of the general cultural changes taking place in contemporary society. Much of this change is centered around a discounting of biological influences upon social behavior.

8. Research studies that share general commitments to methodological techniques, research assumptions, and levels of analysis are brought together to form theoretical paradigms.

9. Sociology, like most other scientific disciplines, is a multiparadigm science.

10. The social factist paradigm is primarily concerned with group actions and societal structures. From the social factist point of view, society cannot be reduced to a collection of individuals—social phenomena have a reality of their own. Sociological research from this perspective will study group-related phenomena (social institutions and structures) rather than behaviors of particular individuals.

11. Structural-functionalists view society as a social system of interacting parts. Structural-functional theory focuses upon the issue of societal maintenance and social equilibrium.

12. Conflict theory is primarily concerned with issues related to social change and disequilibrium. Conflict theorists focus upon competition, conflict, and dissension resulting from individuals and groups competing over limited societal resources.

13. The social definitionist paradigm would contend that the essential feature of society is its subjective character. The social definitionist will emphasize individual behavior over group actions and societal structures.

14. Social exchange theory contends that human behavior involves a subjective and interpretative interaction with others that attempts to exchange symbolic and nonsymbolic rewards. Social exchange will always involve reciprocity so that each individual involved in the

interaction receives something perceived as equivalent to what is given.

15. From the symbolic interactionist perspective, human beings are autonomous agents whose actions are based on their subjective understanding of society as socially constructed reality.

DISCUSSION QUESTIONS

1. Discuss the differences between biological and symbolic death.
2. What arguments are offered in the rejection of the premise: In death, biology is primary, meaning is peripheral? Evaluate and discuss.
3. Each act of dying has three interconnected characteristics: shared, symboled, and situated. How does this relate to the statement that more dies than a biological body?
4. Answer the question "Who or what dies?"
5. Discuss the implications of the following quote: "Even though it is but one biological body that dies, many 'role holes' or vacancies are left with the death of that one person."
6. In making decisions about the death meaning, how does the treatment of the dying patient affect that patient's understanding of death and his or her role in the dying process?
7. As one faces imminent death, one becomes increasingly aware of the social nature of life. This change in awareness can lead to a life review where the individual realizes how extensively he or she lives with, through, and for others. Speculate as to why this change in perspective takes place.
8. Discuss the implications of the following quote: "I die for whatever it was for which I lived."
9. What are some of the meanings of "not dying"?
10. What are paradigms, and what are their functions for social science research?
11. Compare and contrast the social factist and social definitionist paradigms within the field of sociology.
12. Compare and contrast the structural-functional and conflict orientations in death-related research.
13. Compare and contrast the symbolic interactionist and exchange orientations in death-related research.

GLOSSARY

Dyad: Two units regarded as a pair (e.g., a husband and wife).

Empirical: Based on experience, sensory observation, or experimentation.

ISAS: A shorthand presentation of the symbolic interactionist's paradigm statement: Behavior of the Individual is in response to Symbols, relative to the Audience, and relative to the Situation.

Mores: Ways of society felt to be for the good of society. "Must" behaviors that have stronger sanctions than a folkway (e.g., eating three meals per day) but not as severe as a law.

Paradigm: A set of shared general commitments to methodological techniques, research assumptions, and levels of analysis that unify bodies of knowledge produced by empirical research.

Proposition: A statement of relationship between two or more empirical variables.

Self-fulfilling Prophecy: When a situation is defined as real, it becomes real in its consequences when individuals act to make it so.

Significant Other: A person to whom special significance is given in the process of reaching decisions.

Symbol: Anything to which socially created meaning is given.

REFERENCES

Blau, Peter M. 1964. *Exchange and Power in Social Life*. New York: Wiley.

Charmaz, Kathy. 1980. *The Social Reality of Death*. Reading, MA: Addison-Wesley.

Collins, Randall. 1985. *Three Sociological Traditions*. New York: Oxford University Press.

Durkheim, Emile. 1964. *The Rules of the Sociological Method*. New York: The Free Press.

Hill, C. T., Z. Rubin, and L. A. Peplau. 1976. "Breakups Before Marriage: The End of 103 Affairs." *Journal of Social Issues*, 32:147-168.

Homans, George C. 1950. *The Human Group*. New York: Harcourt Brace Jovanovich.

Homans, George C. 1961. *Social Behavior: Its Elementary Forms*. New York: Harcourt Brace Jovanovich.

Homans, George C. 1965. "Anxiety and Ritual: The Theories of Malinowski and Radcliffe-Brown." In *Reader in Comparative Religion: An Anthropological Approach*, William A. Lessa and Evon Z. Vogt (Eds.). New York: Harper and Row.

Homans, George C. 1967. *The Nature of Social Science*. New York: Harcourt Brace and World.

Kellehear, Allan. 1990. *Dying of Cancer: The Final Year of Life*. Chur, Switzerland: Harwood Academic Publishers.

Leming, Michael R., Glenn M. Vernon, and Robert M. Gray. 1977. "The Dying Patient: A Symbolic Analysis." *International Journal of Symbology*, 8(July):77–86.

Lifton, Robert J., and E. Olson. 1974. *Living and Dying*. New York: Praeger.

Nevaldine, A. 1978. *Divorce: The Leaver and the Left*. Unpublished doctoral dissertation, University of Minnesota.

Ritzer, George. 1975. *Sociology: A Multiple Paradigm Science*. Boston: Allyn and Bacon.

Rudner, Richard S. 1966. *Philosophy of Social Science*. Englewood Cliffs, NJ: Prentice-Hall.

Sussman, M. B., J. N. Cates, and D. T. Smith. 1970. *The Family and Inheritance*. New York: Sage.

Turner, Jonathan H. 1974. *The Structure of Sociological Theory*. Homewood, IL: Dorsey.

Turner, Jonathan H. 1985. *Sociology: A Student Handbook*. New York: Random House.

Vernon, Glenn M., and Jerry D. Cardwell. 1981. *Social Psychology: Shared, Symboled, and Situated Behavior*. Washington, DC: University Press of America.

Weber, Max. 1966. *The Theory of Social and Economic Organization*. New York: The Free Press.

SUGGESTED READINGS

Charmaz, Kathy. 1980. *The Social Reality of Death*. Reading, MA: Addison-Wesley. *An important book that provides phenomenological, interactionist, conflict, and Marxist interpretations of death-related behavior.*

Collins, Randall. 1985. *Three Sociological Traditions*. New York: Oxford University Press. And Ritzer, George. 1975. *Sociology: A Multiple Paradigm Science*. Boston: Allyn and Bacon. *Two books on sociological theories that will provide more information and analysis on the four theoretical perspectives discussed in this chapter.*

Dickinson, George E., Michael R. Leming, and Alan C. Mermann (Eds.). 1993. *Annual Editions: Dying, Death, and Bereavement*. Guilford, Connecticut: Dushkin Publishing Group. *Forty-eight articles emphasizing the meaning of a wide variety of various aspects of death-related behavior.*

Frankl, Viktor. 1959. *Man's Search for Meaning*. Boston: Beacon Press. *An outstanding book examining the human desire to find meaning in both life and death.*

Kellehear, Allan. 1990. *Dying of Cancer: The Final Year of Life*. Chur, Switzerland: Harwood Academic Publishers. *Provides a sociological analyis of the process of dying with cancer.*

Vernon, Glenn M., and Jerry D. Cardwell. 1981. *Social Psychology: Shared, Symboled, and Situated Behavior*. Washington, DC: University Press of America. *Explores the symbolic nature of social life and provides a detailed analysis of the symbolic interactionist perspective.*

Part Two
Understanding
Death Attitudes

Chapter

3

Children
and Death

The way I see it, we die in the same order we were born.
It's the only fair way of working it!

Charles Schulz and Kenneth F. Hall
Two-by-Fours

D ESPITE A NEW openness to death in the United States, as discussed in
Chapter 1, children are generally not encouraged to express themselves
on the topic of dying and death. As Jane Sahler (1978:XV), in writing
about children and death notes, "One of the fascinating things about children is the
naive, simplistic way in which they approach the unknown. Yet it is this very
naiveté that makes their questions the most difficult to answer." Children usually
have no prior experience on which to base their reactions; thus, their earliest experiences are unique to each of them.

Children most often confront death at an early age. Their vivid recollections
confirm the impact death has had on them (Hall, 1922; Tobin, 1972; Kastenbaum,
1991). George Dickinson (1992) found in analyzing 440 essays of college students
(average age of 24) about their first childhood death experiences that the average
age at first experience was 8 years and that their recollections were quite clear.

A child's first experience with death is often the death of an animal. Dickinson
found that 28 percent of his subjects' first death experiences involved a pet. From
stepping on an ant to seeing a dead animal lying beside the road to the death of a
pet, animals are generally involved in the early experiences of children with death.

Israel Orbach and associates' study (1985) of 6- to 11-year-old children's concepts of death in humans and animals showed that death in humans is easier to
comprehend than death in animals. They conclude the comprehension of animal
death is acquired chronologically later than that of death in humans. Apparently
animal death is a more difficult concept than human death. Since animals are
known to be a favorite identification object of young children, the death of a pet
may be more meaningful and more personal to a child than that of a generalized
other human being. Thus, children may erect more defenses against death in animals. Another explanation noted by Orbach is that human and animal deaths can
be regarded as two specific examples of the complicated concept of life and death.
While a child may comprehend the meaning of death to a specific example of life,
such as among humans, he/she may not comprehend it in another sphere of life,
such as plants and animals. This reflects a lack of understanding of the broader
concepts of life, birth, death, and animate and inanimate objects.

In a thorough review of literature on children's death concepts, Cotton and Range (1990) conclude that several factors have been shown to influence the development of death concepts. They note that children's death concepts change with age—older children are considered to have more accurate death concepts; are affected by cognitive level—those more cognitively mature have relatively more accurate death concepts; and are affected by experience—those having more experience with death are more likely to believe in personal mortality.

There is a need to look more carefully at the dynamics of the young and their families relating to the concept of death. This chapter will discuss dying children and their parents and siblings and how to explain death to children. In trying to understand children's concepts of death and of their dying, we must also include significant others involved in this relationship. This chapter will also address children's understanding of death from a developmental perspective and focus on age groups. As with any life-cycle approach, the division lines between ages often overlap rather than serve as clear-cut absolute divisions. However, this is a way to understand children's conceptions of death at various ages. In addition, a puzzling cause of death in children called Sudden Infant Death Syndrome (SIDS) will be presented in this chapter.

A BURDEN IN BURYING THE BABIES

Douglas Martin

A cold wind whistled across Hart Island the other morning. It bent the leafless trees and swamp grass, and sent whitecaps dancing on Long Island Sound.

Inmates in orange jumpsuits moved briskly, spoke little and didn't smile. In armfuls of three, they unloaded 53 foot-long pine boxes from the rear of a Ford dumptruck onto the muddy ground. For 50 cents an hour, they were burying New York City's poorest infants.

"It's good they're getting buried and not thrown in a garbage pail," said an inmate who is the father of eight children.

"It takes some getting used to," said another inmate. "It takes some getting used to."

Bruce Leggard, a correction officer who lost his daughter when she was 13 years old, groped for meaning. "Everybody dies; you're born to die," he said. "But these babies never had a shot. Whether they would have been strong or weak, they never got much of a chance to be either."

The little coffins had pink labels pasted on them. Some had names. There was a Liz, an Eileen, a Sam. Some were F/C or M/C for female child or male

(continued)

child.Each slip recorded the lifetime of these former residents of Planet Earth—two hours, newborn, five days. On this day, all were from Brooklyn, the biggest source of babies for New York City's potter's field.

Burials of indigent infants are increasing considerably faster than those of poor adults, also on an upswing. Last year 1,606 babies were buried on Hart Island; in 1986, the number was 1,128.

"There is no question that it is directly linked to the drug epidemic," said Suzanne Halpin, a spokeswoman for the Health and Hospitals Corporation, which first freezes the bodies then delivers them unembalmed to the island off the Bronx.

Infant mortality here has leaped in the last four years, after steadily declining for two decades. The increase coincides with the rise of crack, which causes premature births. Of mothers in the city whose babies died, nearly 32 per 1,000 admitted drug use, up from 7 per 1,000 in 1978, according to city health records.

And Elizabeth Graham, an assistant health commissioner, said the real incidence of narcotics abuse among those mothers might be three times worse because many are reluctant to admit it even on confidential forms.

Further, poor people often don't receive prenatal care. And it doesn't help that the city-owned hospitals are terribly strained: Some neonatal intensive care units are operating at 180 percent of capacity.

A few years ago B.C.—before crack—a study by the Coalition for the Homeless showed that 47 percent of children below the poverty level who died before age one were buried on Hart Island. That hasn't declined.

And their parents, who can't afford what they were brought up to consider proper burial, face yet another indignity. They fill out a form to reserve a small space on a truck to potter's field. Years later, a tiny handful make arrangements to take a Department of Transportation ferry from City Island to Hart Island to stare at a mass grave.

The potter's field comes from the Bible, Matthew 27:6-7. The chief priests of Jerusalem said that it was wrong to put the 30 pieces of silver that Judas had received for betraying Jesus into the general treasury. So the money was used to buy a field from a potter "to bury strangers in."

Hart Island has had a potter's field since the city bought it from a Bronx family in 1869. Over the years, it has had a variety of uses—as a Civil War prison camp, an amusement park, a nuclear missile launching pad and a final repository for some Ebbets Field bleachers. Its only present residents are 80 inmates who would otherwise be on Rikers Island.

The bodies of New York's poor have never stopped coming. There are now 750,000, making this by far the city's largest cemetery, according to a Correction Department official.

"It's like a never-ending sea," said Al Saunders, who operates a backhoe. "It just keeps going and going."

The holes he digs, about 30 feet across, are extended outward to a final length of 100 feet over a period of several weeks. As the shipments arrive, the coffins are placed length-wise along the width of the hole and stacked four or five high.

A Catholic priest sometimes comes to bless God's little children, en masse. A crumbling monument donated by a tombstone company squats by a derelict road. "Cry not for us," it says. "We are at peace."

The wind blew harder. Inmates moved faster. Some boxes contained twins. A few were broken. An inmate cradled one in his arms, much as if things were different.

"This is a heavy little baby," he said.

New York Times, March 28, 1990, p. A–14.

THE DYING CHILD

According to Robert Kavanaugh (1972:139), a psychologist and former priest, little people enjoy the same human rights as their bigger counterparts. They have a right to know if they have a fatal condition. When kept in ignorance, children, like adults, will rarely grow beyond the initial stage of denial and isolation. Not telling denies children of the peace and dignity that can be theirs in the final stage of acceptance and resignation.

Knowledge Is Kindness

The diagnosis of impending death should be made known to children as soon as the decision is clear and final (Kavanaugh, 1972:139–140). Physicians, nurses, and family members obviously need delay-time to bring their own emotions under control. It is now known how to treat the dying child kindly. Knowledge is kindness, ignorance is cruel. The child is the patient whose life is being lost and whose concerns are preeminent. Kavanaugh (1972:143) notes that when children have known the truth about their condition, and were allowed to talk about it openly, they have been as brave as any adult.

Reasons for the advice given above by Kavanaugh (1972:140–143) are based on the following observations. First, the dying child is no ordinary child. The ordinary process of maturing quickens through lengthy illness with confinement, suffering, and deprivation. Children ill for a long time usually exhibit a maturity beyond their calendar years.

Secondly, children's consciences are more tender and concerned than most adults are in a position to know. Deathbed children uninformed of their fate will often feel guilt for the sadness and poorly veiled tears they witness around their bed. They can sense the phoniness around them, and they may tend to believe they are being punished for something evil they have done. Their isolation is heightened in their heavy concerns. Nothing is sadder than for a dying child to learn of his or her fate from playmates.

Finally, moderately aware and normally alert children know what is predicted for them in the signs they see—recognizing their plight in memories of dying scenes on television. They may ponder why the physician comes so often, why everyone is so nice to them, and why they receive all the gifts. As anthropologist Myra Bluebond-Langner (1989) observes from her work with dying children, *all* terminally ill children become aware of the fact that they are dying before death is imminent. Yet Bluebond-Langner notes that for these children the acquisition and assimilation of information is a prolonged process. Either a child shares what he or she knows about his or her dying, or the final weeks and months become a lonely vigil, a sentence to fear and guilt, confinement, and confusion.

How do we tell a child about his or her dying condition? Kavanaugh (1972:142–143) notes that for adults brave enough to listen, this is not a valid question. The child will do the telling, if we create an atmosphere where the child can make all appropriate deductions. The child's talk will flit in and out of the awful revelation.

The Child Needs Support

Who should do the telling or serve as a catalyst for it? Kavanaugh says that anyone strong enough to take the consequences by being a regular visitor, a trusted confidant, and a patient listener can be the catalyst. Many adults cannot qualify.

From her research with hospitalized terminally ill children between the ages of 6 and 10, Eugenia Waechter (1985) agrees with Kavanaugh's conclusions. Her findings indicate that, despite efforts to shield a child from knowledge of the seriousness of his or her illness, the anxiety of those close to the child is likely to alter the emotional climate in the family. The emotional climate may change to such a degree that the child will develop suspicions and fears about his or her condition. Often they will feel that they are not supposed to be aware of their condition, so the silence of those nearby isolates children from needed support.

The question of whether a child should be told is meaningless, notes Waechter. No curtain of silence should exist around the child's most intense fears. Support must especially be made available during and following actual encounters with death on pediatric wards. Support is needed to allow introspective examination of attitudes and fears related to death in general and to the death of children in particular.

In working with children with cancer, Yehuda Nir (1987:64) concludes that children's ability to cope with the stress of cancer is important in the way they deal

WOMAN SENDS "LOVE LETTERS" TO 465 SERIOUSLY ILL CHILDREN

A woman whose 7-year-old son died of cancer four years ago now offers cheer to hundreds of ailing children in a monthly newsletter packed with jokes, puzzles and stories.

"I can't cure them, but I know how to make them smile while they're here," said Linda Bremner, 40.

Her 10-page newsletters, called Love Letters, go to 465 children with terminal or long-term illnesses in 35 states and four other countries. Ms. Bremner said she began writing to seriously ill children in 1984, after the death of her only child, Andy.

"After my son died, I was cleaning out his drawers and I found his address book with the addresses of about 20 children who, like himself, had cancer.

"Remembering how important mail was to Andy, I wrote to them," she said. "What I didn't expect was that they wrote me back and that lit a fire under me," she said.

Stephen Lopez said the newsletter made his three-week hospital stay "much funner." "I like the dot-to dots and the mazes most," said the 12-year-old, who suffers from a behavior disorder.

"It's the passion of my life. Nothing has ever made me feel this good," said Ms. Bremner.

"When I lose one of my kids I grieve," she said. "But it gives me a fervor, and I sit down and write some more letters."

The newsletters carry games, puzzles, jokes and "witty and whimsical" stories, said Ms. Bremner, who has made it a rule never to mention diseases or symptoms.

But sometimes her correspondents address serious topics when they write back, and she draws on her experiences with Andy. One 13-year-old girl wrote that she was being teased by classmates because her hair was falling out. "Andy had lost his hair five times and it grew back, so I wrote her and told her it would grow back, too," Ms. Bremner said. When the girl's hair finally grew back, she sent a little lock of blond hair with a note that read, "You were right—it grew back," Ms. Bremner recalled.

In the beginning, she was sending handwritten letters, she said. Now her pen pals get the newsletter, which is drafted on a computer. About a dozen volunteers help design and mail them.

Adapted from the News and Courier, Charleston, SC, July 30, 1988, p. 3A.

with the illness itself and with the treatment. Feelings of helplessness and vulnerability dominate, often leading to regressive behavior. Withdrawal and refusal to participate in the treatment are seen almost immediately at the onset of the disease in young children. Because these types of behavior interfere with the medical manage-ment of the illness, resistance to treatment is circumvented by such methods as the use of general anesthesia and hypnotic relaxation techniques. While these interven-tions are medically justified, they intensify the child's feelings of passivity and help-lessness.

Nir further notes that regression can take the form of acute separation anxiety. When the parents are unable to stay overnight in the hospital, they often speak with the child by phone. After talking with their parents, young children sometimes fall asleep with the telephone receiver in their laps, as if to maintain contact with what has become elusive.

Families that seem best equipped to cope are those who develop a therapeutic alliance with the **pediatric oncologist** (Nir, 1987:65). This alliance buffers and protects the child from much of the pain and stress of the daily treatment routines. Another group of parents who seem successful in reducing stress are those with strong religious beliefs, notes Nir.

Through observing and talking to leukemic children ages 3 to 9 in a hospital, anthropologist Myra Bluebond-Langner (1978) concluded that most of them knew not only that they were dying, but that this was a final and irreversible process. Children may wish and need to be open about their condition, but adults are often traumatized by a child's openness and honesty. Bluebond-Langner notes that the age of the children is not as important in their self-awareness of their dying as their experience with the disease and its treatment.

The founder and executive director of Children's Hospice International, Ann A. Dailey, says (Gamarekian, 1987:19):

> Kids intuitively know when they are dying and they tend not to have the fears that adults have. But they want to know what it is going to feel like. Will someone be with them to hold their hand? Will a grandmother who died last year be there to greet him? Families need to cry together, to tell how much they are going to miss each other.

Though one may not know what to say to a dying child or feel "skilled" in this area, it is imperative that we show support to them and let them know that we care. Support of others is important throughout life, whether relating to a terminally ill person or otherwise. This point is illustrated in the following story told by Rabbi Harold Kushner (1985).

> A little boy had gone to the store, but was late in returning home. His mother asked, "Where were you?" He said, "I found a little boy whose bicycle was broken, and I stopped to help him." "But what do you know about fixing bicycles?" his mother asked. "Nothing," the little boy replied, "I sat down and cried with him."

Many times, we may not know how to "fix the bicycle," but like the little boy in the story above, we can give support to the individual in other ways.

PARENTS OF THE DYING CHILD

Although there are many problematic aspects of parenting, none is as devastating to the parent as the death of a child. This was observed by Ronald Knapp (1986:13), based on his interviews with 155 families suffering the loss of a child ranging in age from 1 to 28. Likewise, C.M. Sanders (1980) notes that the death of a child is one of the most grievous of losses, significantly greater, on average, than that of a parent or spouse. The death of a child represents the death of the self. Symbolically, a parent will die along with the child, only to survive in a damaged state with little or no desire to live today or plan for tomorrow. In addition to losing part of themselves, parents lose some of their hope for the future, concludes Reiko Schwab (1992) from a study of 20 couples who had lost children.

Since children are "not supposed to die," especially before their parents, the death of a child seems more tragic and traumatic than the death of an older person. We often take our children for granted. While one can *imagine* the loss of a child, how often does one have such thoughts? Even so, such thoughts bear little resemblance to reality. For parents who have lost a child through death, however, the reality of the situation lingers forever. A friend whose son had recently died told me that the stark reality hit him in the face every morning when he woke up and realized that this was not just a bad dream—his son was really dead.

Four years after the death of his son, Eric Wolterstorff said (Buursma, 1987:6):

> We took him too much for granted. Perhaps we all take each other too much for granted. The routines of life distract us; our own pursuits make us oblivious; our anxieties and sorrows, unmindful. The beauties of the familiar go unremarked. We do not treasure each other enough. He was a gift to us. . . . When the gift was finally snatched away, I realized how great it was. Then I could not tell him. . . . The pain of the no more outweighs the gratitude of the once was. Will it always be so?

Though the parent can never be really prepared for the end, as the dying child continues to lose ground, one reaches a point where resignation begins to replace hope for survival, and the inevitable end slowly comes into focus (Knapp, 1986:62). The character of hope changes from hoping for survival to hoping for a full range of living in the time available and for a comfortable, pain-free death. When parents consciously accept the fact that death is imminent, they become totally absorbed in the life of that child and try to make each day a memorable occasion.

Ronald Knapp (1986:67) notes that parents "live" the child's death over and over in their imaginations, as the end is near. This imaginary scenario takes them from the moment of death through the funeral of the child. Parents may wish to keep the child at home so that he or she will not die in strange surroundings. When one is able to make the decision to terminate all further treatment and let the disease take its course, a sense of tranquility results, and parents are ready to release their hold. Sometimes parents must take on the painfully hard task of telling the child that it is alright to let go, it is alright to stop fighting, it is alright to die! Giving permission to die is difficult. Sometimes it only takes gentle encouragement from parents, gentle persuasion that all has been done, and that nothing more remains.

Available literature (Schwab, 1992), based on research and clinical observations, indicates that the death of a child strains the parents' marital relationship,

THE ART OF CONSOLING

Joe Ward

As anyone knows who has ever tried, it is difficult to talk to a parent who has lost a child. Julie McGee, coordinator of the Louisville chapter of The Compassionate Friends—an organization of bereaved parents—says no one who has not lost a child can really understand how it feels.

She says bereaved parents themselves recognize how misguided were their past efforts to console a friend or relative in the same situation. So the organization has compiled the following list of do's and don't's.

DO

Be available to listen, to run errands and to help with housework and other children.

Say you are sorry about what happened to their child and about their pain.

Allow them to express grief without holding back. Listen if they want to talk about the child, as much and as often as they want to.

Encourage them to be patient with themselves, not to expect too much of themselves and not to impose any "shoulds" on themselves.

Talk to them about the special endearing qualities of the child who has died.

Give special attention to the child's brothers and sisters at the funeral and later.

Reassure parents about the care their child received, but be careful not to say anything that is obviously not true.

DON'T

Avoid them because you are uncomfortable.

Say you know how they feel unless you have lost a child yourself.

Tell them they've grieved long enough and "ought to be feeling better by now." Your guess at an appropriate timetable probably is short. Avoid telling them, in general, what they "should" feel and do.

Change the subject when they mention their dead child.

Worry about mentioning their child's name. You won't make them think of him or her; they probably are doing that anyway.

Try to point out some bright side. They don't want to hear, "At least you have your other children," or "At least you can have another child," or, "At least you had the child for a while."

Try to commiserate with them by saying the child's case was bungled by the doctors or the hospital or someone else involved. They will be plagued by guilt and feelings of inadequacy without any help from you.

"When Death Takes Your Child." *The Louisville Courier-Journal,* Louisville, KY, July 27, 1980. Copyright © 1980. Courier-Journal and Louisville Times Co. Reprinted with permission.

sometimes resulting in separation and divorce. One study (Klass, 1987) concluded, however, that marriages did not end because of a child's death but because after the child's death the parents felt that their struggle with marital problems was no longer worth the effort. In a study of 145 bereaved parents, J. A. Cook (1983) concluded that because fathers find it difficult to grieve openly, and thus keep their grief to themselves, a barrier is created to their wives' attempts to communicate about the loss. In another article, Cook (1988) noted that men are given little comfort and support in bereavement and are expected to be strong and provide a source of support for others, yet their nonexpressiveness comes into conflict with their wives' needs for expression. Reiko Schwab (1992) concluded in a study of 20 couples who had lost children that they appeared generally irritable and less tolerant of their spouses. On the other hand, Schwab noted that couples with a good marital relationship prior to a child's death appeared to have come closer together through the tragedy. Thus, a weak marriage may tend to collapse with the death of a child, and a strong marital relationship may indeed be strengthened. Whatever the result, the strain of the death of a child is certainly a test of the marital relationship.

SIBLINGS OF THE DYING CHILD

When a newborn comes into the family, siblings of the baby often feel neglected. Most of the attention seems to go to the baby; therefore the young siblings often have a "pity party" for themselves. Presents are given to the baby, and adults carry on about how cute the baby is. All this time the siblings may be jealous because they do not seem "special."

A similar situation to the newborn in the family may occur when a sibling is dying. The energies of parents, grandparents, and significant others seem to be directed toward the dying child. The dying sibling seems to be receiving all of the attention. In her studies of siblings of children dying with cancer and cystic fibrosis, Myra Bluebond-Langner (1989) states that the well siblings live in houses of chronic sorrow. The signs of sorrow, illness, and death are everywhere, whether spoken of or not. Some well siblings see themselves as the less-favored child in the family, and they often feel confused and rejected. Many of the well siblings felt that they could not express their feelings to their parents because their parents were already too upset, and they did not want to upset them any more.

A study of siblings of children with cancer (Sourkes, 1981) notes that parents tend to provide them with less attention, causing them to feel lonely and neglected. Siblings are also distressed by the visibility of the illness and their tendency to identify with it. They are distressed by the treatment process and may feel guilty about being healthy.

Even during remission, siblings are neglected by parents who must catch up on the instrumental tasks of daily living (Spinetta, 1981). Sibling anger begins to surface most clearly during remission when their loss of parental attention becomes even more prominent than at diagnosis.

In a study of 65 children (between the ages of 4 to 16 years) who were the siblings of deceased children, McCown and Pratt (1985) confirmed previous studies indicating that 30 to 50 percent of surviving children demonstrate increased behavior problems following the death of a sibling. Their studies showed that children in the middle age group, 6 to 11 years, developed more behavior problems than other age groups. Reasons cited for more problems in this age group are that the loss of a sibling at this phase may lead to a sense of self-vulnerability and inferiority, and for the child in this age group who is making the transition to concrete thought, the event and cause of sibling death may evoke confusion. The increased behavior problems may be a reflection of that confusion and concern.

David Adams and Eleanor Deveau (1987:284) note that after a child's death, many siblings fear minor physical symptoms and worry about death occurring at the same age. Siblings resent parents for their preoccupation with the dead child and blame them for their inability to protect these children during illness. Parents are often so consumed by their own grief that they have little energy left to help surviving children. Problems also develop when parents expect surviving siblings to surpass or equal the achievements of a deceased child or to replace the deceased brother or sister.

DID I REALLY LOVE MY BROTHER?

"Everybody told me to be strong for my parents and to be quiet because I might make them more upset. Everyone told me to put my feelings aside, like my feelings weren't as important as my parents'. I never cried until about a year later, when it hit me that my sister Sandy wasn't around." That's how 18-year-old Lisa describes her own grieving for an older sister who was murdered.

"When I was told my brother had died, I just left the room. I couldn't even cry. My father cried, although he had never cried in his life. Because I couldn't cry, I began to wonder if there was something wrong with me. Did I really love my brother?" That is the way 18-year-old Sharon reacted to her little brother's dying of a brain tumor.

Children are not supposed to die—or so we like to think. But, of course, they do. When a child dies, it means not only the loss of a young life but also the death of parents' hopes and dreams.

Many professionals believe that schools need to do more to comfort surviving children. Too often, when survivors return to school, there is no acknowledgement of the death of a brother or sister.

Sandra Fox, director of the Good Grief Program at Judge Baker Guidance Center in Boston, says, "Teachers want to avoid the subject of death. It's not malicious. It's just they are afraid to say the wrong things. They tend to err on the side of being supercautious."

Psychologist Gerald Koocher believes that death education classes could be useful in giving young people a chance to think about the issues of dying and death before being confronted with personal loss. We obviously cannot just pat siblings on the head and tell them everything will be okay.

Adapted from Elizabeth Richter, *U.S. News and World Report,* August 4, 1986.

Due to limited resources and energies in the home, peer support and special attention for the siblings of dying children are needed. Teachers in particular need to be alert to the special concerns and needs of these individuals. The personal worth of surviving siblings needs to be reinforced. As with siblings of a newborn coming into the family, siblings of a dying child have special needs. They too wish to be noticed and given some love and care.

EXPLAINING DEATH TO CHILDREN

Robert Kavanaugh (1972:126) refers to children as "little people." He sees them as "compact cars instead of Cadillacs," traveling the same roads of life and going the same places as big cars. While they are more vulnerable and fragile, they have all the parts and purposes of big people. They are ready and capable to talk about anything within the framework of their own experience. Little people can handle any situation adults can handle comfortably and should do anything big people should do, as long as they are physically able, notes Kavanaugh (1972:137).

Too often we "big people" fail to give "little people" credit and try to shield them from information. Rather than children not "being able to take it," could it not be that we "big people" feel uncomfortable in talking to children about dying and death, and thus avoid the topic altogether? Avoidance is not the best solution, as noted in this example of needless worry and frustration (Dickinson, 1992:174):

> A four-year-old girl was not told about her puppy's traumatic death by a mowing machine for two or three weeks afterwards. She was allowed to search for him "frantically" every day. She even put out food and would worry at night that he was cold or hungry.

John Bowlby (1980) argues that young children can mourn in a similar way to healthy adults. For this to happen the child should participate fully in the awareness of what is taking place in the time during and after the death. Rather than withhold information, questions should be asked and answered. Robert Kavanaugh (1972:132) suggests that we allow the children to talk freely and ask their own questions, without any adult speeches or philosophic nonanswers, let them ramble, talk crudely if they wish, change the subject, or present unanswerable questions without being squelched. The child should always be supported in a comforting way with an assurance of a continued relationship.

Be Honest and Open

Being honest and straightforward with children in talking about dying and death is a good rule of thumb to follow. To give concrete answers, rather than abstract ones, is a realistic way to handle the topic of death. Answer the child's questions as they are asked. If your answer is unsatisfactory, the child will likely ask a follow-up question in a few seconds or a few hours. If the child asks something you cannot answer, be honest and say you do not know. If you cannot explain something, find someone who can.

Answer directly, but do not be too detailed with your responses. When a small child asks where they came from, you do not go into minute detail about the sperm and the ovum forming a zygote. You state that you came from your mother. If the child is not satisfied, the next question may then be, "How did I get in my Mommy?" At this point, I refer the question to the mother!

The same is true if the child asks, "Daddy, what makes the car run?" I tell him that the car has an engine. If he or she then asks a follow-up question as to what makes the engine run, I refer the child to our local mechanic, since my technical skills are severely limited. The point is that the child's questions should be answered *as they occur,* not postponed hoping they will be forgotten.

If parents are open to discussing death, opportunities will present themselves, such as seeing dead flies, mosquitoes, birds, and animals beside the road. When the explanation is postponed until the death of someone or something deeply loved by the child, either the emotional turmoil will complicate the acceptance of the reality of death or the concept of death may preclude for that occasion the appropriate emotional response.

To bury a deceased pet is a positive learning exercise in relating to death. The animal is cold, still, and not alive—it is dead. That is reality. For parents *and* children to conduct the burial together can be a very meaningful experience.

Avoid Euphemisms

Try to avoid **euphemisms** when talking to a child about death. Use words like *dead, stopped working,* and *wore out*—simple words to establish the fact that the body is biologically dead (Schaefer and Lyons, 1986:31). One child was told that Grandfather's heart was bad and stopped working. This seemed to satisfy the child. Couched in a different way, however, another child was told, "Grandfather can

THE FAMILY CIRCUS
by Bil Keane

"Well, yes — we'll see Granddad someday when we go to heaven."

"Could I just wait in the car?"

REPRINTED WITH SPECIAL PERMISSION OF KING FEATURES SYNDICATE, INC.

breathe easier now," implying that Grandfather is still breathing. This child wanted to join his grandfather because he had asthma and would welcome the chance to "breathe easier." He was told, however, that he was too young to join Grandfather (Dickinson, 1992:173–174).

"Dead" is a difficult word to say, but a euphemism like "went to sleep" may confuse a child: If Grandad "went to sleep" and then was buried in a box underground or destroyed through cremation, the child may fearfully decide that it is best to stay awake and not ever go to sleep again. (And parents wonder why the child is still awake at 10 p.m., having been put to bed at 8!)

To use euphemisms like "went away" or "departed this life" or "passed away" may cause the child to expect the deceased to return, as if he or she is simply on a trip! Even to suggest that "he's gone to heaven and will live forever" is confusing to a child when this is said through heavy tears and upset emotional feelings.

The death of a 4-year-old's younger sister was explained to her as "being too sick to live with us so she went to visit Grandmother in heaven and would never come home again." She was frightened for months afterward because "whenever anyone did not feel well, I thought they would go away forever too" (Dickinson, 1992:173). The father of one 4-year-old girl told her that her kitten "went to heaven to be with God." She responded, "Why does God want a dead kitten?"

In recalling childhood memories of death, however, being told that the deceased had "gone to heaven" had been a comforting feeling for many respondents in Dickinson's study. They had been told that "heaven was a happy place," thus all was well in the world of fantasy of these children.

Rabbi Harold Kushner (1981) cautions, however, that to try to make a child feel better by stating how beautiful heaven is and how happy the deceased is to be with God may deprive the child of a chance to grieve. By doing such, we ask a child to deny and mistrust his or her own feelings, to be happy when sadness is desired. Kushner notes that the child's right to feel upset and angry should be recognized. One should also be cautious that the child not feel that the deceased *chose* to leave and "go to heaven." It should be made clear that the person did not wish to leave or "desert," as the child may feel.

Anthropologist Colin Turnbull (1983) describes death as being like it was before birth—a state of nothingness. Ask someone to describe what it was like prior to birth, and you will probably not receive much of an answer. To suggest that after death there is "no place" to describe—a nothing—would deny children a defined place to imagine. But then with the vast imagination of children, perhaps this might be more creative for them than a vague description of a "big house in the sky."

After you have made an effort to avoid euphemisms and gotten across the fact that the person is dead, the next step is to explain what is going to happen next. Tell the child about the body being moved from the hospital to the funeral home.

Alert the child that funeral arrangements will be made (if that is the case) and a funeral will follow. Outline the format of a funeral itself, then talk about going to the cemetery (if this is the case) and burying the body in the ground. As the following poem by Edna St. Vincent Millay indicates, however, explaining death (even for "big people") is not always easy.

Lament

Listen, children: To save in his bank;
Your father is dead.   Anne shall have the keys
From his old coats   To make a pretty noise with.
I'll make you little jackets;   Life must go on,
I'll make you little trousers   And the dead be forgotten;
From his old pants.   Life must go on,
There'll be in his pockets   Though good men die;
Things he used to put there,   Anne, eat your breakfast;
Keys and pennies   Dan, take your medicine;
Covered with tobacco;   Life must go on;
Dan shall have the pennies   I forget just why.

Show Emotion

It is important that the child knows it is okay to show emotion when someone dies. Because it is a very sad time, the child should be told that everyone is upset and that many may be crying. If the child feels like crying, he or she should be assured that crying is okay. Crying is normal. It should also be explained that because some people do not show emotion does not mean that they did not love the dead person (Schaefer and Lyons, 1986:33).

You probably cannot "overhug" a child during these times. It is important to always reassure the child that you care for him or her. Hugs and tears are very compatible expressions. Do not apologize for crying. Your crying in front of the child gives assurance that crying is okay.

Rabbi Earl Grollman (1967) defines crying as the sound of anguish at losing a part of oneself in the death of one whom he or she loves. Since children often cry when they get hurt, would it not follow that it would be natural to cry when "losing a part of oneself?" Grollman observes that tears and sorrowful words help the child feel relieved. Displaying emotions makes the dead person or pet seem more worthy. Tears are a natural tribute paid to the deceased. The child misses the one who is gone and wishes the person were still around.

In recalling their first childhood experiences with death, some individuals indicated that crying was not acceptable and even had negative consequences (Dickinson, 1992:175). A 15-year-old was spanked with a hairbrush for crying over the

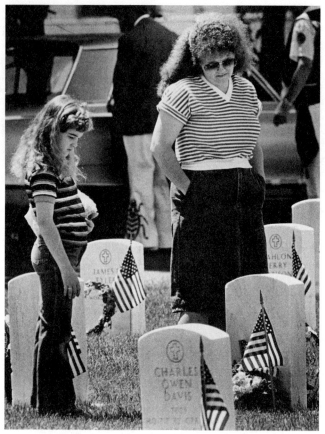

Adults model appropriate bereavement behavior for their children. The best thing adults can do for children is be well-adjusted, secure, and loving people.

death of her puppy. A 10-year-old was "smacked" by her uncle to "make her stop crying at the funeral." Some were told that it was not "grown-up" to cry. For many, their first childhood memories of death included recalling that it was the first time they had seen their fathers cry. No one commented that it was the first time they remembered seeing their mothers cry!

Several college students, in recalling their first childhood experiences with death (Dickinson, 1992:178), noted that they watched others' reactions, then responded accordingly. Since children are watching adults, a parental role model who expresses feelings in front of children might be very beneficial to the socialization of children. Children then would not feel a need to hide in the closet to cry or cry in their pillow at night, as some reported. One child noted the positive experience of his parents and sibling sitting down together to have a good cry at the death of his pet—this pointed out to him the warmth of the family in sharing this common event. It was not a burden he carried alone; his family grieved with him. It is comforting to know that others care.

According to former professional football player Rosie Greer, it is okay to cry. He sings a song where he notes it is all right for women, men, girls, *and* boys to cry. For little boys to cry is *not* "sissy." Anthropologist Ashley Montagu (1968) agrees with Rosie Greer when he states that women have a superior use of their emotions because of their ability to express themselves through crying.

Some men feel that "real men" do not cry because it is not macho to cry. Such men will wear dark shades on the cloudiest of days if they fear they may cry at a funeral. Several years ago, our teenage daughter attended a funeral of a friend with me. After leaving the cemetery on a very cloudy day, she said to me, "Dad, you were right." I said, "About what?" She said, "Nearly all the men at the graveside services were wearing dark sunglasses to hide the fact that they may be crying." Males hold back the tears and develop psychosomatic disorders like peptic ulcers. "Is this a superior use of emotions?" Montagu would ask.

What favors are we doing our children by teaching them that it is not okay to cry? It is okay to laugh; why should it not also be okay to express feelings through crying?

CHILDREN'S UNDERSTANDING OF DEATH

A child growing up in the United States today seldom experiences many aspects of the life cycle. Rather than live on the farm next to grandparents and other extended family, as was the case earlier in the century, urbanization and mobility have contributed to a separation from this older generation and other extended family. Thus, the child today is often removed from dying grandparents because of distance or their dying in the impersonal setting of a hospital or nursing home.

Largely gone are the days when the child lives in the household with a dying grandparent. Death has been removed from the home to more institutionalized settings. This is summed up by the statement of the little boy who said, "I don't want to go to the hospital because that is where you go to die." That is where grandfather was taken the last time the little boy saw him alive. After going to the hospital, grandfather turned into a cold, stiff corpse. The process of the grandfather's dying was not part of the daily routine in the family's home.

As was pointed out in Chapter 1, gone are the days when the majority of children were reared on farms experiencing the life cycle daily—animals were born and animals died. Birth and death were commonplace to the socialization of children raised on farms. Gone are the days when siblings and relatives were born at home and died at home.

The media exposes children to dying and death, but often on television death is viewed as reversible. An individual "dies" on a program this week and reappears in another show the next week. Thus, if the media is the source of death education, a child can acquire the idea that death is only temporary. Another shortcoming of television serving as the "death educator" for children is its inability to respond to questions children may have. One cannot call into the set and receive an answer. One little boy, raised in the television era, expressed his confusion with this question, "Dad, are we alive or on tape?" Another boy, upon being told that his grandfather had died asked, "Who shot him?" He was so accustomed to seeing people die on television via the gun that this was his concept of death.

Not being exposed to dying and death today makes this process and event very removed and foreign to children. This underscores the natural tendency to deny the facts of death. Just how do children conceptualize death? The following discussion breaks children down into age groups, but one must remember that ages and stages are in no way absolute. Each individual child must be interpreted with an understanding of his or her experience and the family's cultural heritage.

Birth to Age 3

By 6 months an infant perceives differences in caregivers and the degree to which physical and emotional needs are being met. One cannot have a concept of death until the beginning of thought, as evidenced by the emergence of symbolic function between 18 and 24 months. It has been suggested that the origin of death anxiety is in the traumatic separation from mother at the time of birth (Hostler, 1978:7). The delight of peek-a-boo lies in the relief of the intermittent terror of separation. Under age 5, death is perceived as separation, but separation from one's caregiver is a terrifying thought.

Erik Erikson (1963) observed that an infant "decides" early in life whether the universe is a warm and loving place to be. Upon this primitive, yet momentous, subconscious conclusion is based to a large degree the ability to deal with threats and difficulties of later life. We must not assume that the small child has no concept or grasp at all of death, and we must be concerned about the effects of a given death upon his or her life.

A toddler recognizes that a pet is alive and a table is not. The toddler's vocabulary normally includes "to die" by age 2½ and "to live" by age 3 (Hostler, 1978:7). While the 2-year-old child dying in a hospital has no real concept of his or her death, the child has a real appreciation of the altered patterns of care and the separation from usual caregivers.

Psychologist Jean Piaget concluded that children progress in stages of **cognitive development** with each qualitatively better than the preceding one (Ginsburg and Opper, 1979). Such an assertion brought about discoveries that small children can grieve over the loss of something only at the point that they have realized that things (and people) are not permanent. This quality, which he called "object constancy," would have to precede any sense of loss. Piaget observed that this happens somewhere around one year to 18 months of age.

A critical analysis of the literature concerning the development of the concept of death in early childhood by Stambrook and Parker (1987:137) suggests that some children, under certain conditions (e.g., experiencing a loss through death), can understand death to be final much earlier than is typically suggested. It has even been hypothesized (Yalom, 1980) that children under 3 years of age "know about but deny death." Perhaps the lack of research consensus found here simply confirms that we cannot depend solely on age categories regarding children's conceptions of death but must also consider individual experiences of the child.

Ages 3 to 5

The clearest and most consistent observation from the literature on death concepts of children is that children as young as 3 have very definite ideas of what death means, though there is considerable disagreement as to the nature of those ideas, according to Stambrook and Parker (1987:138). Most children 3 to 5 years old lack an appreciation that death is a universal phenomenon and is a final and complete cessation of bodily functions. Though death is seen as temporary and/or partial, Stambrook and Parker note that the child is very curious to know and understand the practical and concrete aspects of all that surrounds death. For some children, death is believed to be life under changed circumstances. For example, they might think the dead in caskets can still sense what is happening in the environment but cannot move.

Maria Nagy (1948) interviewed 378 Hungarian children from 3 to 10 years of age, ranging across a broad spectrum intellectually and from various religious backgrounds. She asked the younger children to draw pictures concerning death and those over 7 to write down everything they could think of about death. Children aged 3 to 5 found death to be reversible and not final. Separation and abandonment were seen as equivalent to death.

Since Nagy's research was conducted in the 1930s in Hungary, one could surmise that many children had heard much about death from relatives and neighbors

Regardless of how much adults may wish to protect their children from death, it will always be a part of a child's experience.

who had gone through World War I in Europe. Children's deaths were much more common than in the current era.

The permanency of death is not clear in early childhood as evidenced by this story told to the author about a 3¹/₂-year-old whose father had been killed 6 months earlier in an auto accident. One day the little boy's mother came in and said, "I have a surprise for you." The little boy anxiously replied, "Is Daddy coming home?" On another occasion this same little boy was playing with his Legos and built a house. He placed a person inside the house and was asked to identify the individual. He replied, "Oh, that is Daddy. He is asleep for 100 years." Daddy is not dead; he is simply away on a trip or engaged in a deep sleep. Death is not permanent to young children.

When our daughter was 5 years old, she attended the funeral of an elderly friend of ours. After the service and the final viewing, the casket was closed and sealed. At this point Cindy tugged on my coat, and I bent down on my knees to have horizontal eye contact with her (life is a world of knees to small children). She said to me, "But, Daddy, how is Mrs. Kirby going to breathe in there?" Again, for a 5-year-old it is difficult to grasp a concept of death. Death is not permanent, since one still needs to breathe.

The practicality of young children is apparent in this story of a 5-year-old whose mother had died. While waiting in the airport to travel from Kentucky to Texas to bury the child's mother, she looked up at her father and said, "Daddy, can you cook?" This was a traditional family where the father brought home the bacon, and the mother cooked it. The child's concern was whether or not the father could fill the lost role.

Ages 6 to 10

At this age the child has such motor mastery that he or she can ride a bicycle without holding the handles and can sing a song at the same time (true of better coordinated children, that is). The child begins to view the world from an external point of view, and language skills are becoming communicative and less egocentric. The first major separation from home occurs, and the child enters the world of school where teachers and adults, other than parents, become the models for identification. While magical thinking persists, the child gains in the ability to test reality (Hostler, 1978:11).

A sense of moral judgment continues to develop in this age group. The child attains an understanding that rules are of human origin and he or she can participate in their origin and modification. The child is mastering school and social skills and has an interpretation of that experience based on an external point of view—schoolmates, teachers, other adults, readings, and the media.

Between the ages of 6 and 10, the evolution of the concept of death as a permanent cessation of life begins. However, the cognitive obstacles to abstract thought—the persistence of egocentrism, animism, and magical thinking—prevent its completion. Psychosocial experiences at home and in one's community influence the development of the death concept (Hostler, 1978:16). Death is linked to forces in the outside world and becomes (Lonetto, 1980):

> scary, frightening, disturbing, dangerous, unfeeling, unhearing, or silent. Death can be invisible as a ghost, or ugly like a monster, or it can be a skeleton. Death can be a person, a companion of the devil, a giver of illness, or even an angel.

Nagy's research (1948) in Hungary concluded that children aged 5 to 9 personified death, representing death as a live person or some variation such as an angel, a

Calvin and Hobbes   by Bill Watterson

REPRINTED BY SPECIAL PERMISSION OF UNIVERSAL PRESS SYNDICATE

skeleton, or a circus clown. Death is viewed as a *taker,* something violent that comes and gets you like a burglar or a ghost. These children felt that they could outmaneuver death so that its universality is supposedly not yet acceptable to them. The children over age 9, however, saw death not only as final but inevitable and universal. Yet there is a fear that death is contagious, something that can be caught like a cold (Schaefer and Lyons, 1986:20–21).

MOTHER GOOSE: TEACHER OF DEATH

Richard Gibson

Childhood, a famous poet once wrote, is "the kingdom where nobody dies."

A University of Minnesota psychologist would take issue with that. To illustrate his thesis, Dr. John Brantner tells this story:

A young couple was determined to shield their children from the facts of death. They took extraordinary precautions never to mention the word, or allude to the eventual fate of all men. One day they were at a rented beach house, about ready to romp down to the ocean for a day in the sun, when the father glanced out the window and saw a dead dog in the road they would have to cross. Quickly he drew the blinds and, while his wife distracted the children, called the proper authorities and told them to come and get the carcass.

Within the hour the victim of a speeding motorist had been removed and the father, peeking through the blinds, told his wife it was all right to go to the beach. The family got outside and was about to cross the road separating the beach house from the shore when the little girl looked up at her father and asked, "Daddy, what happened to the dead dog?"

Brantner believes that, by the time children are able to speak, they have some awareness of the reality of death. How do they learn about it?

One way is TV. Brantner cites a recent study which found that, on the average, a child who watches the tube for ten years will see no fewer than 13,500 violent deaths. "And the odds are great that he doesn't see a single natural death," the psychologist adds.

Another, surprising teacher of death is that nice little old lady, Mother Goose. Brantner pulls out the comprehensive *Oxford Dictionary of Nursery Rhymes* as evidence. Consider "The Death and Burial of Poor Cock Robin."

Who killed Cock Robin?
"I," said the sparrow,
"With my little bow and arrow,
I killed Cock Robin."

Who saw him die?
"I," said the fly,
"With my little eye,
I saw him die."

And on it goes, through the funeral, grave digging, burial and final tolling of the bell.

Consider this little ditty:

There was an old woman who had three sons,
*   Jerry and James and John,*
Jerry was hanged, James was drowned,
*   John was lost and never was found;*
And here was an end of her three sons,
*   Jerry and James and John!*

Rhymes were a common conveyance of such grim news, Brantner believes, because, back when the classic children's verse came to be, death was much more of an immediate reality for those who recited them. "Until 1900," the professor said, "67 percent of everyone who died was under the age of 15. It was a common part of growing up that you had younger brothers and sisters who died."

Verses not only described peaceful passings. They also were not hesitant to speak of murder, drownings, hangings and other violent ends, all in light couplet. And death became the ultimate punishment.

Barnaby Bright was a sharp cur,
He always would bark if a mouse did but stir,
But now he's grown old, and can no longer bark,
He's condemned by the parson to be hanged by the clerk.

Or this one. . . :

Little Dicky Dilver
Had a wife of silver;
He took a stick and broke her back

(continued)

And sold her to the miller;
The miller wouldn't have her
So he threw her in the river.

Death was to be mourned, the rhymes told their reciters:

Grandfa' Grig had a pig
*   In a field of clover;*
Piggie died, Grandfa' cried
*   And all the fun was over.*

Fatalism? That can be found, too, as in:

Now I lay me down to sleep,
I pray the Lord my soul to keep;
And if I die before I wake,
I pray the Lord my soul to take.

Nature's destruction of the body comes across grotesquely in this bit of verse:

On looking up, on looking down
She saw a dead man on the ground;
And from his nose unto his chin,
The worms crawled out, the worms crawled in.

Then she unto the parson said,
Shall I be so when I am dead?
O yes, O yes, the parson said,
You will be so when you are dead.

Even pitiful but benign Old Mother Hubbard recounts death, with a magical twist. The second stanza goes like this:

She went to the bakers
*   To buy him some bread;*
But when she came back
*   The poor dog was dead.*
She went to the undertaker's
*   To buy him a coffin;*
But when she came back
*   The poor dog was laughing.*

What's a child to make of that?
There's little doubt about life's brevity, however, in this well-known rhyme:

Solomon Grundy,
Born on a Monday,
Christened on Tuesday,

Married on Wednesday,
Took ill on Thursday,
Worse on Friday,
Died on Saturday,
Buried on Sunday,
This is the end
Of Solomon Grundy.

Your kids don't hear nursery verse? What about fairy tales? Again, the classics are rife with violence and death.

Remember what the giant in *Jack and the Beanstalk* repeated with lust?

Fee–fi–fo–fum,
I smell the blood of an Englishman.
Be he alive, or be he dead,
I'll grind his bones to make my bread.

Hansel and Gretel roast the witch in her own oven. Dorothy is trapped in Oz until the wicked witch of the west could be liquidated.

And Henny-Penny, the paranoid little chick who thought the sky was falling down, leads four friends, Turkey-Lurkey, Goosey-Poosey, Duckey-Daddles, and Cocky-Locky, to decapitation by the fox.

Bluebeard, a misogynist turned mass murderer, began as a children's story.

Some tales have been changed. In the first version of *The Three Little Bears* there is no Goldilocks, but a little old woman who plays the intruder. Upon being discovered by the Bears she jumps out the window to an uncertain fate. The narrator speculates that she possibly broke her neck.

Before Walt Disney got hold of them, the Three Little Pigs were a morbid bunch. The wolf consumed the first two for lunch, but the third, who declined his invitations to dinner, boiled the beast and ate him for supper. And lived happily ever after.

The Minneapolis Star, April 11, 1973, p. 1C.

The sample of Mother Goose nursery rhymes noted above is perhaps cause for concern for childhood readings. In 1937 Allen Abbott urged nursery rhyme reform, as did Geoffrey Hall in 1949. In 1952 Geoffrey Handley-Taylor (Baring-Gould, 1967:20) published a brief biography of the literature of nursery rhyme reform and noted that the average collection of 200 traditional nursery rhymes contains approximately 100 rhymes which "personify all that is glorious and ideal for the child." He noted, however, that the remaining 100 rhymes "harbour unsavory elements." Following is a partial list of Handley-Taylor's findings from Mother Goose:

2 cases of choking to death
1 case of death by devouring

1 case of cutting a human being in half
1 case of decapitation
1 case of death by squeezing
1 case of death by shrivelling
1 case of death by starvation
1 case of boiling to death
1 case of death by hanging
1 case of death by drowning
4 cases of killing domestic animals
1 case of body snatching
7 cases relating to the severing of limbs
1 case of the desire to have a limb severed
2 cases of self-inflicted injury
4 cases relating to the breaking of limbs
1 case of devouring human flesh
12 cases of torment and cruelty to human beings and animals
8 cases of whipping and lashing
15 allusions to maimed human beings and animals

SUDDEN INFANT DEATH SYNDROME (SIDS)

Despite a continuing decline in the rate of infant mortality in the United States, the cause of death known as **Sudden Infant Death Syndrome** (SIDS) has not been declining and, in fact, has been increasing in many populations. In highly advanced countries, SIDS is now the most common single cause of death after the perinatal period and often is more common than all other causes of death combined at the age of 3 months (Nam, Eberstein and Deeb, 1989).

Sudden, unexpected infant death is a major cause of death for infants between the ages of 1 week and 1 year in the United States—an estimated 10,000 deaths per year. Sudden infant death is usually defined as the sudden unexplained death of an infant where no cause is found through a postmortem examination (DeFrain, Taylor, and Ernst, 1982:11-12). According to a study by the Foundation for the Study of Infant Deaths, these babies do not cry out as if in pain, but simply die quietly in their sleep after becoming unconscious.

Historically, unexpected, unexplainable deaths of infants were routinely attributed to the mother's lying on the infant, since mothers often slept with their children. If they woke and found the baby dead, they assumed that they had lain on the child, smothering or crushing it. Perhaps the earliest recorded such death is in the Bible in 1 Kings 3:19: "And this woman's child died in the night, because she overlaid it." It is believed that SIDS was occurring long before it was recognized and accepted as a diagnostic label (Beckwith, 1978).

The Etiology of SIDS

SIDS is a distinct medical entity and not just a category of unexplained infant deaths attributed to different causes. Yet, SIDS is difficult to predict or prevent. SIDS is not hereditary and is not suffocation or regurgitation. Though a minor illness such as a common cold may have been present at the time of death and autopsies reveal inflammation in windpipes in a high number of cases, many SIDS victims are apparently very healthy (DeFrain, Jakub, and Mendoza, 1992).

The **etiology** of SIDS shows that it occurs more often in winter and spring when respiratory illnesses are frequent. The peak age for death is between 2 and 4 months of age. There is a higher incidence among blacks, poor families, and babies born to teenage mothers. Deaths are more frequent in infants with low alertness scores at birth and in infants born to mothers using drugs or who smoke and have premature babies (Cope, 1980; Nam, Eberstein, and Deeb, 1989).

A Swedish study by Haglund and Cnattinguius (1990) highlights the correlation between SIDS and the mother's smoking during pregnancy. They note that smoking is probably the most important preventable risk factor for fetal death. Their findings suggest that if maternal smoking could be eliminated, infants delivered by mothers who gave up smoking would face the same mortality risk as those born to nonsmoking mothers, and SIDS death rates would be reduced by 27 percent.

Support for the above findings was found by Southall and associates (1987) who monitored breathing movements of 301 infants who had a sibling die of SIDS and compared them to a control group of 170 infants, matched by postnatal age. They found that the mothers of the SIDS siblings smoked and consumed alcohol more often during pregnancy than the mothers of control babies. The siblings had lower Apgar (alertness) scores and were more often breast fed than controls.

Most SIDS deaths occur when the baby is sleeping, usually between midnight and 9 a.m., and occur very rapidly with apparently no suffering for the baby. The child turns blue and limp, apparently from lack of oxygen. Clues to SIDS are present in the brain, which should alert the infant to breathe harder, but research is inconclusive on any link to brain dysfunction (Cope, 1980).

J.B. Beckwith (1978) by the late 1970s had catalogued 73 different theories for the cause of SIDS and noted that new ideas were being published almost on a weekly basis. By 1983 over 2000 references on the subject of SIDS were reported in medical journals (Knight, 1983). **Viral infections** have been viewed as a link to SIDS (Valdes-Dapena, 1980). Viral infections are evident in autopsies of some

RESEARCHER LINKS HEART DEFECT WITH NEARLY HALF OF CRIB DEATHS

A newly discovered defect in the hearts of some babies may be responsible for half of all cases of sudden infant death syndrome. The new evidence suggests that these babies' hearts frequently have a defect in their electrical stimulation. The malfunction could make their hearts stall when they begin to speed up for any reason.

While the discovery does not provide immediate new ways to prevent crib deaths, the researchers say it may someday help identify babies who are at high risk so they could be treated with drugs. Dr. Daniel C. Shannon, co-author of the study at Massachusetts General Hospital, speculated the defect could result from immaturity or from damage triggered by an infection or toxin encountered as a fetus.

Adapted from the *News and Courier,* Charleston, SC, December 10, 1987, p. 1A.

CRIB DEATH TIED TO COMMON BEDDING

A study suggests that ordinary bedding materials, not just the beanbag cushions already recalled by the government, may have suffocated many babies whose deaths were reported as "crib death," scientists said today.

"Perhaps one in four of sudden, unexplained infant deaths may be explained by exhaled carbon dioxide being trapped around the baby's face by bedding such as pillows, comforters and foam beds," said Dr. James Kemp, a pediatrician at Washington University School of Medicine in St. Louis.

Babies whose deaths were ascribed to the mysterious Sudden Infant Death Syndrome, called SIDS or crib death, should be investigated as possible suffocation victims if they were found face down, said Dr. Bradley Thach, a Washington University pediatrician who conducted the study with Dr. Kemp. Many possible causes have been proposed for SIDS; none has been proved. At least a quarter of victims are found face down.

In their study, Dr. Kemp and Dr. Thach made rabbits breathe through a model of an infant airway pressed against bedding materials on which infants died. That test and a new mechanical test suggested five types of bedding can suffocate infants by trapping exhaled carbon dioxide, allowing children to rebreathe the gas without getting enough oxygen. The types were a synthetic-filled adult pillow, a three-and-a-half-inch-thick foam couch cushion, a three-inch-thick foam pad covered with a comforter, a sheepskin sold as an infant bed and a soft bassinet cushion covered by a blanket.

Dr. Henry Krous, a pediatrician-pathologist at the University of California at San Diego, said some of the conclusions were premature, but said the researchers were "highly reputable, capable investigators" whose "interesting and provocative" study suggested that bedding might lead to crib death for babies with an inborn vulnerability.

Adapted from an Associated Press article, *New York Times*, April 8, 1992, p. B-9.

babies, but not all. Evidence from postmortem studies showed elevated levels of a thyroid hormone triiodothyronine (T-3) in 44 out of 50 victims (Rowley, 1981). This may be an important step in determining the cause, and hopefully, the cure for SIDS. It is not clear, however, when the elevation of T-3 occurred—prior to birth or after the death.

If T-3 has an influence on breathing and heart beat, an infant with an elevated level of T-3 should perhaps be put on a monitor (DeFrain, Taylor, and Ernst, 1982:14). Apparently, all infants experience numerous short periods of not breathing (apnea). A home **apnea monitor** is frequently used in the management of infants at increased risk for SIDS and helps detect the infant's breathing irregularities by sounding an alarm when breathing stops. Home apnea monitoring remains unproven, however, since some infants have died despite evaluation by infant apnea programs (Ward et al., 1986).

Death-scene investigations (Bass, Kravath, and Glass, 1986) of 26 cases of infants brought into an emergency room, with presumptive diagnoses of SIDS, revealed strong circumstantial evidence of accidental death in six cases and found various *possible* causes of death, other than SIDS, in 18 other cases. These researchers suggest that many sudden deaths of infants may have a definable "cause" other than SIDS. They question the extremely high rate of SIDS reported in the population of low socioeconomic status served by their hospital.

Parents of SIDS Children

The majority of SIDS parents see SIDS as the most devastating crisis they have ever experienced. Approximately one-fourth of SIDS parents move from their homes and to other communities in an effort to escape the pain of the baby's death (DeFrain, Jakub, and Mendoza 1992). Parents generally tend to "recover" from the death in approximately 3 years or more.

When an infant dies suddenly and unexpectedly, the sense of loss and grief may be overwhelming. When that sudden death is due to a known cause, the concrete character of the event can be incorporated into the normal rationalization of mourning. When death is due to an unknown mechanism, however, as in SIDS, feelings of inadequacy in caring for the child are reinforced for the medical staff and the parents (Mandell, McClain, and Reece, 1987).

Since there are still many unanswered questions about SIDS, parents have a tremendous guilt feeling and shoulder the responsibility for the infant's death. Marital conflict, difficulties with surviving children, and anxiety about future children becoming victims of SIDS are often experienced. With the cause of death in a SIDS case being questionable, the parents are likely to undergo a police interrogation, in addition to the stress of having lost their infant. In an era when child abuse has received much attention, the parents may be suspected of smothering the child. Being questioned by the police is difficult enough, yet the perceived inability of others including friends and relatives to understand the depth of their despair is also very frustrating to these parents (DeFrain, Jakub, and Mendoza, 1992).

Young parents whose baby dies of SIDS have not likely experienced the death of a close relative, thus they are not familiar with the social and emotional aspects of grief and mourning. The death of one's baby is traumatic under any conditions, but the sense of not knowing how to mourn adds to the difficulties of socially adjusting to the loss. The parents and siblings are experiencing "anomic grief," a grief without the traditional supports of family, church, and community.

A survey of newly trained local SIDS counselors in North Carolina (Kotch and Cohen, 1985) reported that sharing the autopsy report with bereaved parents was a valuable part of the counseling process and removed some of the mystery surrounding the diagnosis of SIDS. The autopsy report, by documenting that the child died a natural death, may relieve some families of the feeling that they were somehow responsible for the death.

My own discussions with parents who have lost a child through SIDS suggest that friends may turn on them as if they are criminals. Parents tend to "blame" each other for the death—"if only you had. . . ." Parents become "victims" because SIDS is both personally traumatic and socially complicated. The uncertainty of the cause of death is frustrating to the parents and medical staff and clouds the whole issue from a societal perspective. A SIDS death must be one of the more traumatic experiences a parent can have in a lifetime.

CONCLUSION

Rather than trying to "protect the young from death talk," we need more open communication channels with children on this topic. Children from an early age have a concept of death, and terminally ill children seem to know that they are dying. We need to stop pretending that children cannot handle this topic. It is okay for children (and adults!) to show emotions or cry when they feel so inclined. It is okay to feel the way one feels—moral judgments should not be attached to feelings. We should not try to be judgmental of others' feelings.

We "big people" must be alert to the questions of children on dying and death. In speaking to a group of fourth graders a few years ago on the topic of dying and death, my frustration was trying to decide whom to call on when a dozen or more hands at a time were up from these 40 children wanting to ask questions. Each had his or her own concerns, and they were sincere, legitimate interests. I remember one little boy asking if it were true that one would die from getting embalming fluid on the skin. I tried to assure him that this would not likely be a cause of death, but this was a genuine concern of his. When our son was 6, he asked, "Daddy, do we eat dead people?" Since we eat dead cows and pigs, why not people? We certainly do not eat live cows and pigs! The questions are there from these "little people," and we "big people" must respond by answering.

Dying children and significant others surrounding these children need a strong support system. It is important to let the child and family know that others care. Though one may not know what to say in such situations, this should not keep one away from the death environs. Go and visit to show that you care. Parents who lose a child through SIDS not only have lost their child, but face a suspicious public questioning the real "cause" of death. Thus, a double slap for the parents of a SIDS death.

SUMMARY

1. Due in part to an urbanized and industrialized society, children have been removed from death, other than through the rather artificial means of the media.
2. The permanency of death is unclear to young children who tend to see death as reversible.
3. Children can take about anything adults can dish out to them, including the topics of dying and death.
4. Honesty and openness in relating to children about death is very important.
5. Avoid euphemisms when talking to children about death.
6. It is okay to express emotions through crying. Adults can sanction this behavior by not hiding their own tears when they are sorrowful. By seeing big people cry, children can know that crying is normal behavior.
7. Dying children should be told their diagnosis and kept informed of their prognosis. Knowledge is kindness.
8. Dying children and parents and siblings of dying children need the support of others.
9. Research on Sudden Infant Death Syndrome has included the causes of SIDS deaths, though recent research suggests that a defect in the electrical stimulation of the heart may be correlated with SIDS.

DISCUSSION QUESTIONS

1. Discuss your first childhood memory of death. How old were you? Who or what died? What do you remember about this event?
2. As a child growing up, how was death talked about in your family?
3. Discuss the various perceptions of death as one goes from birth to age 10. What shortcomings do you find with a life cycle approach?
4. Analyze the Mother Goose stories in the chapter. What are some of the themes in these "kiddie" rhymes?
5. Put yourself in the place of a parent with a terminally ill child. How do you think you would relate to this child?
6. List as many euphemisms as you can to identify dying and death. Why do you think euphemisms are used with death?
7. Why is knowledge "kindness" in relating to a dying child?
8. What is SIDS? Is this a new or an old phenomenon?
9. Discuss why adults tend to avoid talking about death with children.

GLOSSARY

Apnea Monitor: A device to detect the temporary stopping of breathing in infants.

Cognitive Development: Development of processes of knowing, including imagining, perceiving, reasoning, and problem solving.

Etiology: The science of causes or origins.

Euphemisms: The use of a word or phrase that is less expressive or direct but considered less distasteful or less offensive than another word or phrase.

Pediatric Oncology: A field of medicine related to children with tumors (often malignant).

Sudden Infant Death Syndrome (SIDS): The sudden unexplained death of an infant where no cause is found through a postmortem examination.

Viral Infection: An invasion of the body by viruses (any of a large group of submicroscopic agents capable of infecting animals).

REFERENCES

Adams, David W., and Eleanor J. Deveau. 1987. "When a Brother or Sister is Dying of Cancer: The Vulnerability of the Adolescent Sibling." *Death Studies,* 11:279–295.

Baring-Gould, William S., and Ceil Baring-Gould. 1967. *The Annotated Mother Goose.* New York: World Publishing Company.

Bass, M., R. E. Kravath, and L. Glass, 1986. "Death-scene Investigation in Sudden Infant Death." *New England Journal of Medicine,* 315(July 10):100–105.

Beckwith, J. B. 1978. *The Sudden Infant Death Syndrome.* DHEW Publication No. HSA 75–5137. Washington, DC: U.S. Government Printing Office.

Bluebond-Langner, Myra. 1978. *The Private Worlds of Dying Children.* Princeton, NJ: Princeton University Press.

Bluebond-Langner, Myra. 1989. "Worlds of Dying Children and Their Well Siblings." *Death Studies,* 13:1–16.

Bowlby, John. 1980. *Attachment and Loss,* vol. 3. New York: Basic Books.

Buursma, Bruce. 1987. "Scholar Wrestles with Son's Death." *News and Courier,* Charleston, SC, August 2, p. 6–D.

Cook, J. A. 1983. "A Death in the Family: Parental Bereavement in the First Year." *Suicide and Life-Threatening Behavior,* 13:42–61.

Cook, J. A. 1988. "Dad's Double Binds: Rethinking Fathers' Bereavement from a Men's Studies Perspective." *Journal of Contemporary Ethnography,* 17:285–308.

Cope, L. 1980. "Research Finding Clues to Crib Deaths." *Minneapolis Tribune,* June 4.

Cotton, C. Randy, and Lillian M. Range. 1990. "Children's Death Concepts: Relationship to Cognitive Functioning, Age, Experience with Death, Fear of Death, and Hopelessness." *Journal of Clinical Child Psychology,* 19:123–127.

DeFrain, John D., Deanne K. Jakub, and Betty L. Mendoza. 1992. "The Psychological Effects of Sudden Infant Death on Grandmothers and Grandfathers." *Omega,* 24:165–182.

DeFrain, John, Jacque Taylor, and Linda Ernst. 1982. *Coping with Sudden Infant Death.* Lexington, MA: Lexington Books.

Dickinson, George E. 1992. "First Childhood Death Experiences." *Omega,* 25:169–182.

Erikson, Erik. 1963. *Childhood and Society.* New York: Norton.

Gamarekian, Barbara. 1987. "A Support Network for Dying Children." *New York Times,* June 25, pp. 19–20.

Ginsberg, Herbert, and Sylvia Opper. 1979. *Piaget's Theory of Intellectual Development,* 2nd ed. Englewood Cliffs, NJ: Prentice-Hall.

Grollman, Earl. 1967. *Explaining Death to Children.* Boston: Beacon Press.

Haglund, Bengt, and Sven Cnattinguius. 1990. "Cigarette Smoking as a Risk Factor for Sudden Infant Death Syndrome: A Population-Based Study." *American Journal of Public Health,* 80:29–33.

Hall, G. S. 1922. *Youth: Its Education, Regimen and Hygiene.* New York: D. Appleton and Company.

Hostler, Sharon L. 1978. "The Development of the Child's Concept of Death." In *The Child and Death,* Olle Jane Z. Sahler (Ed.). St. Louis: C. V. Mosby Company.

Kastenbaum, R. J. 1991. *Death, Society, and Human Experience,* 4th ed. New York: Macmillan Publishing Company.

Kavanaugh, Robert E. 1972. *Facing Death.* Baltimore, MD: Penguin Books.

Klass, D. 1987. "Marriage and Divorce Among Bereaved Parents in a Self-Help Group." *Omega,* 17:237–249.

Knapp, Ronald J. 1986. *Beyond Endurance: When a Child Dies*. New York: Schocken Books.

Knight, Bernard. 1983. *Sudden Death in Infancy: The Cot Death Syndrome*. London: Faber and Faber.

Kotch, Jonathan B., and Susan R. Cohen. 1985. "SIDS Counselors' Reports of Own and Parents' Reactions to Reviewing the Autopsy Report." *Omega*, 16:129–139.

Kushner, Harold S. 1981. *When Bad Things Happen to Good People*. New York: Schocken Books.

Kushner, Harold S. 1985. Lecture in Charleston, SC, October 20.

Lonetto, Richard. 1980. *Children's Conceptions of Death*. New York: Springer Publishing Company.

Mandell, F., M. McClain, and R. M. Reece. 1987. "Sudden and Unexpected Death." *American Journal of Diseases of Children*, 141(July):748–750.

McCown, Darlene E., and Clara Pratt. 1985. "Impact of Sibling Death on Children's Behavior." *Death Studies*, 9: 323–335.

Millay, Edna St. Vincent. "Lament." In *Poems and Poets*, 1965, David Aloian (Ed.). New York: Webster Division, McGraw-Hill.

Montagu, Ashley. 1968. *The Natural Superiority of Women*, rev. ed. New York: Collier Books.

Nagy, Maria. 1948. "The Child's Theories Concerning Death." *Journal of Genetic Psychology*, 73:3–27.

Nam, Charles B., Issac W. Eberstein, and Larry C. Deeb. 1989. "Sudden Infant Death Syndrome as a Socially Determined Cause of Death." *Social Biology*, 36:1–9.

Nir, Yehuda. 1987. "Post-Traumatic Stress Disorder in Children with Cancer." In *Children and Death: Perspectives from Birth Through Adolescence*, John E. Schowalter et al. (Eds.). New York: Praeger Publishers.

Orbach, Israel, Yigal Gross, Hananyah Glaubman, and Devora Berman. 1985. "Children's Perception of Death in Humans and Animals as a Function of Age, Anxiety and Cognitive Ability." *Journal of Child Psychology and Psychiatry*, 26:453–463.

Rowley, J. 1981. "Crib Death Discovery May Lead to Simple Test for the Disease." *Minneapolis Tribune*, November 6.

Sahler, Olle Jane Z. 1978. *The Child and Death*. St. Louis: C. V. Mosby.

Sanders, C. M. 1980. "A Comparison of Adult Bereavement in the Death of a Spouse, Child, and Parent." *Omega*, 10:303–322.

Schaefer, Dan, and Christine Lyons. 1986. *How Do We Tell the Children? A Parents' Guide to Helping Children Understand and Cope When Someone Dies*. New York: Newmarket Press.

Schulz, Charles, and Kenneth F. Hall. 1965. *Two-by-Fours: A Sort of Serious Book About Children*. Anderson, IN: Warner.

Schwab, Reiko. 1992. "Effects of a Child's Death on the Marital Relationship: A Preliminary Study." *Death Studies*, 16:141–154.

Sourkes, B. 1981. In *Psychological Aspects of Childhood Cancer*, J. Kellerman (Ed.). Springfield, IL: C. C. Thomas.

Southall, D. P., J. R. Alexander, V. A. Stebbens, V. G. Taylor, and R. E. Jancaynski. 1987. "Cardiorespiratory Patterns in Siblings of Babies with Sudden Infant Death Syndrome." *Archives of Disease in Childhood*, 62 (July):721–726.

Spinetta, J. J. 1981. "The Siblings of the Child with Cancer." In *Living With Childhood Cancer,* J. J. Spinetta and P. Deasy-Spinetta (Eds.). St. Louis: C. V. Mosby Company.

Stambrook, Michael, and Kevin C. H. Parker. 1987. "The Development of the Concept of Death in Childhood: A Review of the Literature." *Merrill-Palmer Quarterly,* 33: (April)133–157.

Tobin, S. 1972. "The Earliest Memory as Data for Research in Aging." In *Research, Planning and Action for the Elderly,* D. P. Kent, R. Kastenbaum, and S. Sherwood (Eds.). New York: Behavioral Publications, Inc.

Turnbull, Colin M. 1983. *The Human Cycle.* New York: Simon and Schuster.

Valdes-Dapena, Maria A. 1980. "Sudden Infant Death Syndrome: A Review of the Medical Literature, 1974–1979." *Pediatrics,* 66:597–613.

Waechter, Eugenia H. 1985. "Children's Awareness of Fatal Illness." In *Understanding Death and Dying,* 3rd ed., Sandra G. Wilcox and Marilyn Sutton (Eds.). Palo Alto: Mayfield Publishing Company.

Ward, S. L., T. G. Keens, L. S. Chan, B. E., Chipps, S. H. Carson, and D. D. Deming. 1986. "Sudden Infant Death Syndrome in Infants Evaluated by Apnea Programs in California." *Pediatrics,* 77 (April):451–458.

Yalom, I. 1980. *Existential Psychotherapy.* New York: Basic Books.

SUGGESTED READINGS

Edelstein, Linda. 1984. *Maternal Bereavement: Coping With the Unexpected Death of a Child.* New York: Praeger. *Deals with women and the loss of a child, with special emphasis on mourning and bereavement, the mother/child relationship, putting one's life back in order, and emotional and social supports.*

Ekert, Henry. 1989. *Childhood Cancer: Understanding and Coping.* New York: Gordon and Breach Science Publishers. *This practical book was written to provide information for parents, relatives, and friends of children and adolescents with cancer.*

Gaffney, Donna A. 1988. *The Seasons of Grief: Helping Children Grow Through Loss.* New York: Plume Books. *Written by a psychiatric nurse, this helpful guide for relating to children about dying and death should be useful for professionals and laypersons.*

Johnson, Sherry E. 1987. *After a Child Dies: Counseling Bereaved Families.* New York: Springer Publishing Company. *Though written for practitioners counseling survivors of families who have experienced the death of a child, this book could be read by anyone experiencing bereavement following the death of a child.*

Knapp, Ronald. 1986. *Beyond Endurance: When a Child Dies.* New York: Schocken Books. *An excellent book based on in-depth interviews with 155 families who have lost a child through death.*

Rosen, Elliott J. 1990. *Families Facing Death: Family Dynamics of Terminal Illness.* New York: Lexington Books. *The author blends the fields of family therapy and death and dying.*

Schaefer, Dan, and Christine Lyons. 1986. *How Do We Tell the Children? A Parents' Guide to Helping Children Understand and Cope When Someone Dies.* New York: Newmarket Press. *Children's thoughts about death, explaining death to children, grief and healing, and children and funerals.*

Schowalter, John E., Penelope Buschman, Paul R. Patterson, Austin H. Kutscher, Margot Tallmer, and Robert G. Stevenson. 1987. *Children and Death*. New York: Praeger. *An anthology on children's concepts of death, the emotional impact of disease, and coping with childhood death.*

Chapter 4

Developmental Perspective on Dying and Death: *Adolescence through Older Adulthood*

I, too, am trying to find some answers.
I, too, am troubled and sad. Did you know that?
Are you surprised that I don't know all the answers
about death?
Don't be.

Even though no one really understands it,
death is something we must accept.
We can talk about it.
You can learn something from me.
I can learn something from you.

We can help each other.

Earl A. Grollman
Talking About Death

I
N THE VERSE above, Rabbi Grollman suggests that, even though no one really understands death, it is something we must accept. We can talk about death, can learn from each other, and can help each other. In this chapter we will talk about death with the hope that we can "help each other" better understand death conceptualizations at different stages of the life cycle. This chapter will discuss death conceptualizations from adolescence through old age.

Sigmund Freud traced our conceptions of death to our earliest feelings concerning sexuality and fears of being punished for them. Alfred Adler had several brushes with death himself and suffered seriously from a debilitating disease as a child. When Adler formulated his theories concerning the human psyche and its development, he attributed our need to strive and overcome to our early sensitivity to weakness and death.

The **ego psychologists** later departed somewhat from Freud and credited the individual with a greater ability to manage the stresses and problems of life. Yet they recognized that humans raise a whole set of defenses against the idea of death. Both children and adults have the power to distort their perceptions according to their needs. For example, individuals have ways of denying harsh or painful thoughts, and people often believe and see what they want to believe and see, thus transforming images of their imaginations into reality.

In his Pulitzer Prize-winning book entitled *The Denial of Death,* Ernest Becker (1973) argued that fear and denial of death are basic dynamics for everyone.

He asserted that we struggle to find meaning in life through heroic efforts. If we discover that heroic efforts are not possible, the dilemma is avoided by building elaborate systems to explain the problem away. Some even flee into neurosis or a psychotic break. Becker felt that the fear of death was a basic problem of meaning with which we all struggle.

Though the subject of death was not a major concern in his writings, Swiss developmental psychologist Jean Piaget was probably instrumental in nudging psychologists to employ better methods of research in the developmental approach to understanding concepts of death (see Ginsburg and Opper, 1979). Through keen observations of his children and others, Piaget postulated that it is not until the early teen years that one is capable of genuinely abstract thought processes.

Since the publishing of Herman Feifel's *The Meaning of Death* in 1959, interest and research on the conceptualization of death has grown. Representing **psychoanalytic, behavioristic, humanistic,** and other points of view, much has now been written on a **developmental approach** to death attitudes and awareness.

It is not the intent of this chapter to suggest that age should be seen as the sole determiner of one's death concept. Many other factors influence cognitive development such as level of intelligence, physical and mental well-being, previous emotional reactions to various life experiences, religious background, other social and cultural forces, personal identity and self-worth appraisals, and exposure to death or threats of death. Though an age-based approach is followed in this chapter, other important factors should not be ignored.

ADOLESCENCE

Adolescence is the "training period" between childhood and adulthood in the life experience of humans. Adolescence, from ages 12 to 19, is composed of two significant periods (Gordon, 1986:17–18). The period from 12 to 15 (with 11 as the threshold) encompasses the acquiring of formal logical thought, the onset of biological sexuality, the growth of the physical structure, and a myriad of psychosocial tasks. The second period, from 16 to 19, with transition around 15, is characterized by the completion of physical maturation, increasing intimacy with the opposite sex, continued acquisition of adult social skills, clarification of ethics and values, and the ability to make long-term commitments to persons and goals. Adolescence is often a time fraught with anxiety, rebellion, and indecision.

Adolescents generally do not think in terms of the distant future in relation to their own lives. Their struggle with present life experiences evidently occupies such mental energy, especially the concern with their own identity and anxiety about

For adolescents, death is an unlikely event. Consequently, when a young person is dying, it is disturbing for all concerned. Death becomes real and must be taken into account.

successes during the immediate future, that thinking about what life will be like at age 45 or 70 is nearly impossible for them.

According to Jean Piaget (1958) and his followers, at about 11 or 12 years of age people are able to move from the use of language and ideation that is concretely oriented to an abstract level of thought. The adolescent can use conditional statements like "if-then." Ideas can be taken apart and put back together again in new ways.

An Identity Crisis

Being gripped by questions such as "Who am I?" and "How do I fit into the scheme of things?", the adolescent struggles with good and evil, love and hate, belonging and loneliness, and thoughts of life and death. These can be disturbing issues to the adolescent who is not sure if he or she is a child or an adult, since identity signals come from all directions, adding to the confusion of one's self-concept.

The adolescent has a vivid awareness of the dialectic between being and not being, according to psychologist Robert Kastenbaum (1986:11). Daily experience provides occasions for assertions of a new self, of "dyings" of the old self, and

BLACK ADOLESCENTS AND DEATH

The black community generally keeps its dying family members at home far more frequently than does the white community, perhaps a reflection of socio-economic variables as well as a strong tradition of family and religious networking. Thus, black adolescents are typically more socialized at an earlier age to the rituals surrounding death and dying than are most white adolescents. Young black children are routinely taken to funerals and encouraged to interact with family members who are dying in the home. Also, the strong religious background of most black families helps to develop a belief about survival after death that makes death less threatening than it is for the more secularized white middle class.

This is not to suggest that the black culture does not have its fears and superstitions about death. On the whole, however, dying and death are not taboo subjects among black adolescents.

Adapted from Audrey K. Gordon, "The Tattered Cloak of Immortality." In *Adolescence and Death*, Charles A. Corr and Joan N. McNeil (Eds.). New York: Springer Publishing Company, 1986, pp. 16–31. Used by permission.

apparent abortions of the new self, notes Kastenbaum. Thus, it is precisely when the adolescent is most endangered by the polarities of being and not being that the concept of self emerges with singular force. The perception of a self under reconstruction is granted most keenly as one experiences the possibility of failure, loss, catastrophe, and death.

One research study (Koocher et al., 1976) demonstrated that high school students experience much more anxiety, depression, and death fear than either junior high students or adults. They propose that it is the "identity crisis" of the adolescent years that could be largely responsible for this. Psychiatrist Robert Lifton (1976) also notes that adolescence is the time when a sense of great potential for disintegration, separation, and instability occupies the mind and brings about greater death anxiety.

Sherry Schachter (1991) states that a high percentage of adolescents must adjust to the death of a peer, and this might contribute to the frustration of the teen years. The death of a peer emphasizes the adolescent's own vulnerability and mortality. Since society does not acknowledge the bereaved adolescent in the same manner the bereaved family is acknowledged, Schachter observes that this experience is compounded for teenagers by isolation, and the adolescent becomes the forgotten mourner. Since adolescents' identity shifts away from parents and family as they tend to see themselves as members of the peer group, the loss of a peer can upset identity formation, which may already be unstable (O'Brien, Goodenow, and Espin, 1991).

Socialization to Death Fears

Like masturbation, adolescent **death fears** are universally experienced and discussed with equally uninformed peers, notes Audrey Gordon (1986:20–21). One of the tasks of adolescence is to begin to grapple with the meaning of life and death and to emerge with a philosophical stance that promotes optimism for the future. This is not an easy assignment, especially since one's attitude toward the future may involve pessimism more than optimism.

Our society's discomfort with the process of aging, illness, and death does not contribute positively toward the adolescent's image of a future (Gordon, 1986:22). Because youth is envied and growing old is feared in America, "growing old along with me" may *not* entail "the best is yet to be" in the minds of adolescents. Consequently, a callousness toward physical deterioration and death often develops in adolescence. When the death of a significant other occurs, previous experience has likely not prepared the adolescent for the feelings of rage, loneliness, guilt, and disbelief that accompany a personal loss. If peers have not experienced a similar loss, they may have difficulty being supportive.

Adolescents often see death and dying depicted in the media as excessively "violent, macabre, distant, or unnaturally beautiful" (Gordon, 1986:22). Brutal death results from chain saws (*The Texas Chain Saw Massacre*, 1974), power tools (*The Toolbox Murders*, 1978), or blenders and microwave ovens (*Gremlins*, 1984). *The Big Chill* (1983) opens with the dressing of a body for a funeral as the titles flash past. Rambo movies of the 1980s are filled with violence and death. *The Faces of Death* (I, II, and III), allegedly depicting actual human decapitation, autopsies, and executions by injection and electrocution, overflows with bizarre death scenes.

There seems to be a fascination with death among adolescents. One perhaps builds up a sense of invulnerability by seeing other people dead or dying, notes psychologist Fred Hinker (*El Dorado Times*, 1985). Hinker says that watching these movies is like teenagers riding motorcycles at extremely high speeds. They are saying, "It can't happen to me. I'm proving it by flirting with death."

"What prepares the adolescent for an embalmed, cosmeticized body, and how does the teenager learn what to do at the time he or she is gripped by powerful emotions that threaten self-control?" asks Audrey Gordon (1986:24). How embarrassing to lose emotional control and perceive yourself as a child again, rather than a maturing young adult.

The following shows that destructive themes in rock music are not unlike many movies viewed by adolescents. According to Wass, Miller, and Redditt

DEATH THEMES IN ADOLESCENT MUSIC

One key to understanding adolescents is cultivating an understanding of the music that occupies a central place in their lives. Music provides adolescents with mirrors of who they and society are and intimations of what they and society might become.

The stark aversion to old age in some of the music is startling. The lead singer of The Who in "My Generation" (1970) repeatedly asserts a wish to die before becoming old seemingly in part because of a repugnance that is attached to old age itself. Some songs, by contrast, express wonder about what it is like to be old and to see life from its end. The Beatles, for example, in "When I'm Sixty-Four" (1967) wonder about connections with others in old age when they ask whether they will still be needed and cared for as elderly people. Paul Simon in "Old Friends" (1968) sketches a lonely scene of two old friends sitting on a park bench, "winter companions . . . waiting for the sunset."

A theme with the need for continuity is found in Paul Simon's "Flowers Never Bend with the Rainfall" (1966). He offers a song that gives testimony to the extreme difficulty of thinking of oneself as anything but immortal. In "Eleanor Rigby" (1966) the Beatles paint a stark portrait of alienation and meaningless life. The concept of survival after death is treated in Joan Baez' rendition of the folk hymn (1969) "Will the Circle Be Unbroken?" The singer anticipates being reunited with her dead mother in a life to come.

Though a desire for symbolic immortality is noted in Neil Diamond's "Morningside" (1972), apparently the wish was not fulfilled by the survivors. After an account of how an old man spent his last days lovingly making a table so his children would remember him, the song reports that when he did die, no one wept and no one claimed the legacy that he had left behind.

The theme of loss and grief is prominent in adolescent music. Songs of tribute are among the best known: countless songs about Elvis Presley have been written and Dion's "Abraham, Martin and John" (1975) refers to Abraham Lincoln, Martin Luther King, Jr., and John F. Kennedy. Also noteworthy is Don McLean's "American Pie" (1972) which views the death of Buddy Holly and other early rockers as a turning point in rock's loss of innocence.

Many songs express alarm over the potentially, sometimes all too real, lethal results of drug use. Lynyrd Skynyrd's "The Smell" (1977) describes the smell of death in the air in the aftermath of the deaths from drug overdoses of many prominent performers including Janis Joplin, Jimi Hendrix, and Jim Morrison. Paul Simon's "Save the Life of My Child" (1968) depicts a scene in which a crowd is gathered beneath a young man perched on a ledge and under the influence of drugs.

Pornographic rock, where fantasy has taken over and death is dehumanized and distorted, is equivalent to the "slasher" movies. Warren Zevon's

(continued)

"Excitable Boy" (1968) describes the rape and killing of "Susie" after a junior prom date and cynically explains that the boy was just "excitable." The Rolling Stones' "The Midnight Rambler" (1969) salutes the Boston Strangler, and Thin Lizzy pays tribute to Jack the Ripper with "Killer on the Loose" (1980).

Death themes in adolescent music afford an opportunity for identification with cultural heroes, values and ideals, hopes and aspirations. It provides communication currency and social connection with peers and provides an alternative frame of reference within which their concerns can be and are addressed.

Adapted from Thomas Attig, "Death Themes in Adolescent Music: The Classic Years." In *Adolescence and Death*, Charles A. Corr and Joan N. McNeil (Eds.). New York: Springer Publishing Company, 1986, pp. 32–56. Used by permission.

(1991:204), however, death themes in rock music might possibly be therapeutic. The themes should be understood metaphorically rather than literally. Rock lyrics may sometimes provide the means for dealing with issues of death and for managing the anxieties created by these themes.

Society is created and held together by **rituals**—morning wake-up rituals, going to school/work rituals, eating rituals, religious rituals, political rituals, and others (Gordon, 1986:23). Ritualization provides sanctioned boundaries within which the self can be safely expressed. Dying, death, and grief are all ritualized by society as a way of containing and giving meaning to feelings of loss. The granting of adult responsibility and privilege to adolescents varies from culture to culture and group to group. Since elders all too often do not teach children the adult rituals for handling dying, death, and grief, it becomes one of the personal tasks of adolescence to acquire this knowledge.

Helping Adolescents Cope with Death

Whenever an individual is going through an unstable or trying period—especially when the stress has to do with basic feelings about self-worth, identity, and capability—the thought of death is particularly difficult to manage. Crucial to positive outcomes is the manner in which parents, friends, peers, teachers, and others enable the adolescent to process positively the ideas of the overwhelming threats of death to self and significant others.

Audrey Gordon (1986:23) notes that adolescents need not stumble around in a darkness that adults have helped to create. With proper preparation and support, young adolescents can be helped to become aware of death in manageable ways, and older adolescents can be helped in imparting a meaning to death and life that transcends everyday events and infuses the future with hope.

Here are some suggestions from Joan N. McNeil (1986:197–198) about improving family communication about death:

1. Adults must usually take the lead, at least in heightened awareness of the teenager's concerns about death and in openness to discussion of anything the adolescent feels like exploring.
2. Listen actively and perceptively, keeping your attention on the other person and the apparent feelings underlying his or her words.
3. Accept the other's feelings as real, important, and "normal."
4. Use supportive responses that reflect your acceptance and understanding of what the teenager is trying to say.
5. Project a belief in the other person's worth by indicating that you are not attempting to solve his or her problems, but instead are trying to help the adolescent find his or her own solutions.
6. Be willing to take time to enjoy each other's company and to provide frequent opportunities for talking together.

INTRODUCTION TO ADULTHOOD

We have already observed that one of the main problems with following a developmental scheme in the explanation of how people think, feel, and integrate life's experiences is that there are so many possible combinations of factors in any given life. The longer one lives, the more complex the picture becomes as the probability of additional factors influencing a particular person increases.

Caution also is needed when attempting to generalize about what is true concerning any stage of life and especially when looking at people beyond the adolescent stage of life. The premise behind this caution is that research findings describing a particular population, age group, or cross-section of people should not be seen as more than a description of that particular sample of people. Research findings are influenced by the theoretical approach of the researcher and limitations of present knowledge, methodologies, and conclusions.

Another implication of this attitude toward understanding adulthood is that accurate conclusions would be drawn concerning any one person at any stage of life if more attention were paid to the many forces and features of that particular person's life history. Other limitations to studying adults' concepts of death include the lack of a satisfactory definition of "maturity" in relation to the concepts of death. There is no way to know when one has arrived in terms of a "mature" view of death.

Developmental psychologists also are limited in that they have not researched enough in the area of adulthood to draw firm conclusions about the changes in death conceptualization that might develop within an age category. For example,

Freud concentrated on infancy and childhood. Erik Erikson was able to move far beyond Freud in describing theoretically how the person develops over the entire life span. Some **longitudinal studies** of men have been published, but few of women. The relationship between these studies and ways of conceiving death is seldom discussed, except in gerontological research. It seems to be assumed that we only need to pay attention to the death concepts of children and the elderly. Research is not taking place in as proportionately great a scale concerning the period of young adult to later middle age as the periods of childhood and old age. The major exceptions to this rule are found in studies of mentally and terminally ill populations.

Finally, a limitation is faced in determining what *adult* actually means. Biologically, though we may stop growing any taller at a certain age, great changes continue in the human body. Psychologically, it is even more difficult to arrive at any definition of adulthood that may be generalized to a significant percentage of the population. One must conclude that the word "developmental" takes on a more individualistic character. Thus, one should expect that age will be less influential in explaining death conceptualizations for adult populations than other age groups.

ECCLESIASTES 3:1–8

For everything there is a season,
and a time for every matter under the heaven:
a time to be born, and a time to die;
a time to plant, and a time to pluck up what is planted;
a time to kill, and a time to heal;
a time to break down, and a time to build up;
a time to weep, and a time to laugh;
a time to mourn, and a time to dance;
a time to cast away stones, and a time to gather stones together;
a time to embrace, and a time to refrain from embracing;
a time to seek, and a time to lose;
a time to keep, and a time to cast away;
a time to rend, and a time to sew;
a time to keep silence, and a time to speak;
a time to love, and a time to hate;
a time for war, and a time for peace.

The Holy Bible, Revised Standard Version. New York; Oxford University Press, 1962.

YOUNG ADULTHOOD

From the discussion of the development of the adolescent's intellectual understanding of death, one could expect the young adult (someone in the 20s or 30s) to have a good grasp of the universality, inevitability, and finality of death. The young adult should know, at least intellectually, that death is an entirely possible event for anyone at any moment. Unless forced to do so, however, one should not expect that every adult person would normally think of death constantly nor take it into consideration with each decision of importance.

Remember Death

In his book *Man's Concern with Death,* historian Arnold Toynbee (1968) wrote:

> From the moment of birth there is the constant possibility that a human being may die at any moment, and inevitably this possibility is going to become an accomplished fact sooner or later. Ideally, every human being ought to live each passing moment of his life as if the next moment were going to be his last. He ought to be able to live in the constant expectation of immediate death and to live like this, not morbidly, but serenely. Perhaps this may be too much to ask of any being.

There have existed certain monastic Christian orders that practiced greeting each other daily with the words, "Remember death!" The fact that one tends to recoil from such a practice, however, is evidence that one would rather not take this advice.

The young adult would appear to especially reject the admonition to remember death. At this stage of life, one is just entering the arena of a somewhat independent life where capabilities and skills can be tested and pride can be taken in positive results. Hopes, aspirations, challenges, and preparation for success in life are the focus at this age. This means that dealing with dying or death would mean to face rage, disappointment, frustration, and despair (Pattison, 1977).

Young adults struck with serious disability or life-threatening disease have demonstrated that an almost universal sense of injustice and resultant anger exist when the young person is forced to "remember death." Along with all the international political issues involved, the protests against the Vietnam conflict in the 60s and 70s probably contained a good deal of repugnance to the idea of risking one's personal future at this stage of life. A walk through the wards of any major veterans' hospital or pediatric oncology floor would soon convince the most stubborn observer that significant physical and mental losses, and death itself, seem most abhorrent when suffered by adolescents or young adults.

The Novice Phase

Daniel Levinson (1978) labeled the young adult stage the "novice phase" since there is a strong sense of the need to learn, practice, and train oneself in the art of reaching one's fullest potential as a person and contributor to self-fulfillment, family, and society. Achieving something worthwhile would be devastatingly contradicted by any thought of serious limitation, sickness, or death.

Lowenthal, Thurnher, and Chiriboga (1975) evaluated 216 people grouped in four stages of the life cycle: high school seniors, young newlyweds, middle-aged parents, and an older group about ready to retire. Each person was asked specific questions concerning concepts and thoughts about death. Older people thought of death mainly in connection with specific and personal circumstances such as the death of a friend, while younger people were likely to have death thoughts in response to general events such as accidents, earthquakes, or war.

Again, it is evident that though age may have some influence over the way one thinks, individual circumstances and external forces have a more powerful effect upon an individual's thoughts about death. The older one grows, the more apparent it becomes that one needs to reflect on life as much as one needs to engage in it. Such a practice can provide the individual with greater life satisfaction. As one moves into middle adulthood, however, it can have both positive and negative results.

Acquired Immunodeficiency Syndrome (AIDS)

AIDS is rapidly becoming a major cause of death in the young adult age group. Though far more deaths in the Third World are due to diseases of childhood (respiratory disease, diarrhea, and measles), AIDS kills young adults at a high rate (see Table 4.1). These are the people whom a developing economy most needs and for whose training it will have already paid (*The Economist,* 1991:22). It is sometimes said that AIDS is a disease of the poor, and in the developed world this is becoming the case. In the United States, it is in the inner cities that AIDS is spreading fastest. In poor countries, however, AIDS is often a disease of the relatively rich.

As noted in Table 4.1, AIDS is now affecting blacks and Hispanics proportionally more than it is affecting whites. Andrew Sullivan (1990:22) noted in talking to minority men with AIDS that it was hard to avoid the impression that the level of denial is measurably greater, the pain more intense, and the isolation more complete than among whites. One gay black man said, "By being black, I'm separated from the white gay community, and being gay, I'm separated from the African American community."

Not only is AIDS a devastating disease, but for individuals in the gay community, their support group is literally dying out. I was recently on a panel at a regional

Table 4.1   *Acquired Immunodeficiency Syndrome (AIDS)*
(deaths in the United States by age, sex, and ethnicity/1982–1989
and by selected years/1982 and 1989)

CHARACTERISTIC	NUMBER OF DEATHS		
	1982–1989	1982	1989
TOTAL	77,350	444	21,675
Age (in years)			
Under 5	976	12	235
5–12	182	1	52
13–29	15,044	88	4039
30–39	34,790	208	9865
40–49	17,001	85	4967
50–59	6393	42	1764
60+	2964	8	753
Sex			
Male	69,929	401	19,499
Female	7421	43	2176
Race/ethnicity			
White, non-Hispanic	43,895	217	12,251
Black, non-Hispanic	22,493	153	6438
Hispanic	10,254	73	2747

Source: U.S. Centers for Disease Control, Atlanta, GA. Taken from U.S. Bureau of the Census *Statistical Abstract of the United States: 1991,* 111th ed. Washington, DC: U.S. Government Printing Office, 1991.

sociology meeting discussing AIDS. One of the other panelists, who happened to be gay and HIV-positive, noted that of his immediate group of 40 friends, all but 6 had died within a short span of time of AIDS. Not only was he saddened, but he had few friends left with whom to share his grief. A similar account is noted in a recent study of the psychosocial impact of multiple deaths from AIDS (Viney et al. 1992:152) by one of the participants:

> I've been counting them up. You know, I've lost 50 people, friends and acquaintances, since this AIDS epidemic started. I've been to that number of funerals in the past few years. And now my lover is ill.

The psychosocial functioning of people dealing with these problems is similar to those of individuals coping with any severe illness: higher than average levels of anxiety, depression, directly and indirectly expressed anger, and helplessness (Viney et al. 1992:153). Thus, for some young adults today, AIDS is a reckoning force bringing death into focus through personal experience.

Middle-Aged Adulthood

While there appears to be no agreement among social scientists as to the exact beginning of middle age, most seem to suggest that this period of life starts between ages 40 and 45. The U.S. Census Bureau defines middle age as ages 45 to 64, while Vera in the Broadway play "Mame" describes middle age as being "somewhere between 40 and death." Middle-aged individuals are sometimes referred to as the "sandwich generation" since they may be supporting and/or caring for their own children as well as their parents. They are "caught between" these two groups.

Carl Jung (1971) believed that middle adulthood is the time of greatest growth for most people—a time of integration of undeveloped dimensions of personality. He described the major task of the middle years as a reassessing and relinquishing the fantasy of immortality and omnipotence that carries us through earlier years when our own death is incomprehensible. Through the increasing awareness of body changes, loss of significant others, and children moving toward independence, we shift from a future-oriented perspective to an inescapable confrontation—a conscious awareness of death and mortality (Douglas, 1991). Erik Erikson's theory of ego development (1963) in these years suggests a concern for the next generation and an acknowledgment of mortality.

For the person who has lived 40 or 50 years, life brings with it the advantages of experience. Promotion to supervisor, foreman, or analogous status rankings in one's work or social milieu demonstrates that one gains greater political and social power during middle age. Everyone is not promoted, however, and even those who are, as well as their less fortunate colleagues, become gradually aware that physical vitality has now begun to wane.

Robert Fulton and Greg Owen (1988:380) describe this group born after World War II as primarily experiencing death at a distance. Unlike earlier generations, they were likely born in hospitals and no longer likely to die from infectious diseases. Unlike their parents and grandparents, this Baby-Boom generation experienced the maximum benefits of an urbanized and technologically advanced society. Fulton and Owen further note that as the commercial meat processing industry removed the slaughtering of animals from the home, so did modern health care institutions shield this group from general exposure to illness and death. Death became invisible and abstract. This generation was the first in which a person could reach adulthood with only a 5 percent chance that an immediate family member would die.

The Panic Begins

The "panic" begins once one realizes that the idealized self, with its accomplishments and fulfillments dreamed of for so many years, may not actually come to pass. Those whose job or self-concept depends upon youthful physical vigor especially suffer from this recognition. No amount of jogging reverses the effects of time. No patent medicine can undo the damage from wear and tear. The only hope is to make the best of what energies and experience remain and to focus on what one does best.

Those whose strengths lie in intellectual and social skills will be less threatened, since there is a cultural–social time clock that one is able to impose over the biological time clock (Neugarten, 1968). This seems to make more actual difference in the way one lives and how much satisfaction one is able to derive from life. Jack Riley (1968) found a stronger correlation between education and more positive views concerning death than between age and positive death views. Stated negatively, people with less education appear more often to have more negative views concerning death. One must remember, however, that a correlation does not prove a *causal* connection.

According to developmental theorists, death is a salient issue for mid-life adults. Failing health, deaths of parents, loss of close friends, and changes in physical appearance contribute to a heightened awareness of death. As long as one's parents are living, there is a buffer between the person and death—one's parents are "supposed" to die first. When one's parents die, however, this buffer is gone and one's own generation becomes the genealogical line of descent to die.

The death of a parent can have a profound effect on the ways adult siblings deal with each other, observes Lawrence Kutner (1990). Adult siblings may experience intense emotions as they re-evaluate the meaning of family and their roles within it. The death of a parent, especially the second parent, often accentuates a pattern already existing—as siblings grow older, good relationships become better and rotten relationships tend to grow worse. The death of a second parent often changes the focal point of family rituals such as organizing Thanksgiving or other significant holiday celebrations, notes Kutner. While the parents are alive, the relationships between siblings tend to be balanced as compared to the unbalanced parent–child relationship; yet when parents die, one sibling tends to break out of this balanced relationship. (Kutner, 1990).

Joan Douglas (1991:135), in studying reactions of middle-aged persons to the death of their parents, concluded that for many, the integration of the loss of a parent involves confronting the loss of parental power and the reality of one's own mortality as part of the developmental process. The tension created by the need to both sever and maintain the parent–child bond and to face one's own death without giving way to despair forced many to move to a new perspective—a new level of integration.

In analyzing the relationships between death anxiety, age, developmental concerns, and socio-economic status in a sample of 74 middle-aged women, Richardson and Sands (1987) found that developmental factors were the salient issues with death concern, death as interpersonal loss, and death as a dimension of time. Age was the sole predictor of death anticipation, and death denial and income were significant with death as physical. No variable predicted death as depressing. These results revealed the multidimensionality of death attitudes and the significance of considering both developmental and socio-economic influences in predicting death attitudes.

A More Philosophical Outlook Develops

Elliott Jacques (1965) observed that awareness of death changes people's lives in middle age, causing them to become more philosophical about their lives and to reevaluate values and priorities. In the process of confronting their own mortality, people deepen their capacities for love and enjoyment and ultimately acquire more meaning in their lives. Carl Jung (1933) also believed that adults become more introspective and concerned with meaning during mid-life and concluded that they experience an inner transformation after recognizing previously suppressed aspects of their personality. He maintained that those who successfully resolve these conflicts become more androgenous and more individuated.

Age differences in types of death concerns were observed by Stricherz and Cunnington (1982). The middle-aged emphasized the pain of dying and dying before being ready. Young adults focused on losing persons they cared for, and the elderly worried about being helpless, taking a long time to die, and having to depend on others. This study found that all age groups consider death, but they do so in different ways and contexts.

Middle-aged adults are aware of getting closer to the "day of reckoning" and will need to evaluate values, meanings, and sense of self-worth in the face of finitude. The individual becomes increasingly conscious of thoughts of painful death, the dying process, and of ceasing to be as a person. An awareness develops of the meaning of absence to significant others—spouse, children, and others.

Thus, death at this point in life often carries with it some of the same sense of injustice and anger that the younger adult experiences with thoughts of death. Now, however, these thoughts are tempered with the recognition that many more forces exist which could bring death "home" to the individual.

Personal Growth Continues

While the mature adult needs to give up fantasies of immortality, omnipotence, and grandiosity, there still needs to be a sense of accomplishment—a fulfilling of oneself and one's plans for family and personal enterprises. Consciousness of time and death, therefore, makes little difference for the middle-aged adult. One strives to put all one's skills and experiences to the best possible use.

Once into the decade of the 50s, a turning point is reached in which one's finitude becomes even more evident. There tends to increase a consciousness that one no longer measures time from birth as much as one measures time until death or until the end of one's most productive years. Focusing upon what one wants most to do before retirement or death causes one to avoid those things considered extraneous and/or uninteresting. All of this is not to say that increase in age means cessation of personal growth. To the contrary, as long as there is life, growth can occur for the individual who has the will to live and the will to give of self to others.

All is not lost in middle age, however. Bernice Neugarten (1968) points to evidence that people in their 40s see the world in a more positive way than those in their 60s. Possibilities for the 60-year-old are more likely to be faced in passive modes of coping than in active modes. She suggests that women tend to cope increasingly in affective and expressive terms, while men at this stage will increasingly employ abstract and cognitive modes of coping.

OLDER ADULTHOOD

Old age and natural death are often linked together. Death is expected for the elderly person, note Kastenbaum and Aisenberg (1972). Indeed, in contemporary American society, death is primarily something that happens in old age. Seventy percent of all deaths occur among those 65 years of age or older, and 30 to 50 percent of all deaths occur among those 80 years of age or older (Brody, 1989). Sweeting and Gilhooly (1991) state that death is seen as appropriate for the very elderly who have lived their allotted span of life. They also note that the elderly are more likely than other members of society to be living alone and are unlikely to be working.

While some have observed that "growing old is hell," others look forward to the autumn of their lives. As Goethe stated, "To grow old is in itself to enter upon a new venture." An aging professional athlete noted that growing old is really mind over matter—as long as you do not mind, it does not matter.

Another division regarding old age has appeared in recent years—a division between the young-old and the old-old (Neugarten, 1974). The young-old come from the age group between 55 and 75; the old-old are 75 and over. Neugarten pictures the young-old as possessing relatively good health, education, purchasing power, and free time, and being politically involved.

The young-old are distinguished from the middle-aged primarily by the fact of retirement. While 65 has been the marker of old age since the beginning of the

Social Security system, age 55 is becoming a meaningful lower age limit for the young-old because of the decreasing age of retirement. Obviously, employment and health status have a tremendous effect upon placement in either older category.

Life can be compared to a train traveling through a tunnel. There is a point at which the train is leaving the tunnel rather than entering it. As older relatives and friends die, one cannot help but become aware that he or she is not immune from death. As noted earlier, when no older generation exists, and the members of one's own generation die with increasing frequency, the awareness of the scarcity of time becomes a reality. Therefore, for the person over the age of 60, the end of the tunnel is in sight.

The letter below, sent to the author and his wife from their friend Lucie Reid, suggests that the "end of the tunnel is in sight" for her. She seems accepting of the fact and ready to die.

The majority of individuals in this age group born near the beginning of the twentieth century were reared on farms or in nonurban environments. For those who lived through the Depression, they often had cause to wonder where

---

After living next door to Lucie Reid for two years in western Pennsylvania, we moved away. For several years after that, my wife and I received a beautiful hand-decorated Christmas ball from her. The ball usually arrived in mid-December. One year, however, the ball arrived in mid-July. The note below was enclosed in the package. Lucie Reid died before "another Christmas."

My Dear Children,

This seems a strange *gift* for this time of the year. This lovely ball was given me by the friend who made it, and I want it to hang for many years on your happy tree. If I live until another Christmas, I would be 97 which is too long to stay in this devastated world which my generation has made. I am ready to depart any time. God has been wonderfully good to me. I have had all anyone could ask for—love and care and now every comfort in this shadowing time. I say with Cardinal Newman, "So long thy hand hath led me, sure it will lead me on."

I know that you are leading lives full of meaning, and my blessings go with this bright ball. I believe a circle has no beginning and no end.

Sincerely your friend,

Lucie Reid

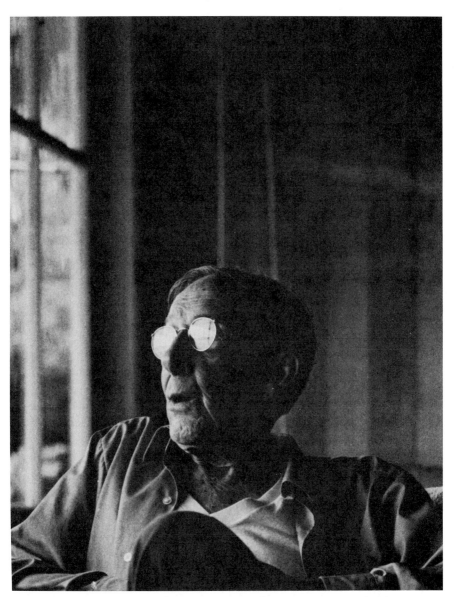

People can and do manage much of what happens within their own minds. The life review is triggered by the realization that one has reached the end of life and death is near. The life review serves to prepare a person for dying—preparation which may decrease fear of death. At any stage of the life cycle, one can be helped to face both life and death more positively.

tomorrow's meal would come from. Robert Fulton and Greg Owen (1988:380) note that illness, dying, and death took place at home and were observed by children and adults alike. Animals were slaughtered for food. Death was visible, immediate, and real. Fulton and Owen observe that to an extent, these individuals had lived in terms of the simple round of life known historically to humankind: birth, copulation, and death.

Erikson's Final Stage of Life

Erik Erikson's theory of human development (1959) divides the life cycle into eight stages from infancy to old age. Each stage of development presents a crisis in understanding of oneself, of one's purposes, and of relationships with others. The developmental task at each stage is to resolve the crisis successfully, then the person can progress to the next stage of maturity. The eight stages are infancy, early childhood, play age, school age, adolescence, young adulthood, adulthood, and **senescence**. Erikson argues that a person must have been successful to some degree in solving the seven crises that come before in order to resolve the eighth stage of senescence. The task of the final stage of life is to achieve integrity—a conviction that one's life has meaning and purpose and that having lived has made a difference.

Hannelore Wass (1979:186) observed that the **life review**, a concept advanced by Robert Butler, is in close harmony with Erikson's eighth stage of the life cycle. The life review is triggered by the realization that one has reached the end of life and that death is near. The life review serves to prepare a person for dying—preparation that may decrease the fear of death.

Death Taboo and the Elderly

The death taboo is still in practice with respect to the elderly in the United States (Wass, 1979:190). There seems to be such reluctance on the part of many to talk about death with the elderly. As noted in Chapter 1, the one taboo topic for elderhostel programs in the United States is death and dying. Since the elderly are nearing the end of their life cycle and dying is in the near future, it is commonly thought that older adults would not want to talk about death. I can remember an undergraduate student of mine in the early 1970s wanting to do a research project on the elderly's attitudes toward dying. I even thought at the time that the elderly might not wish to talk about death. Was I ever wrong! She had a 100 percent response from those she interviewed.

Even the experts on aging largely avoid the subject of death. Wass and Scott (1977) found in a survey that 90 percent of the scholarly and textual books examined on aging devote less than 5 percent of their space to a discussion of death, about 65 percent of the books give less than 1 percent, and nearly 20 percent of the books with a total of 3476 pages (average of 386 pages per book) make no mention of death whatsoever.

Hannelore Wass (1979:190) speculates as to why the topic of death is avoided with the elderly. Some believe that younger adults avoid the topic because it reminds them too chillingly of their own eventual demise. Others believe the topic is avoided so as not to upset an older person unduly. Others think that death is not brought up with the elderly because of some kind of embarrassment, particularly when an inheritance is involved.

To show how the topic of death is still somewhat elusive to many in our society, several years ago, I was invited to speak on death and dying at the annual spring banquet of the local American Association for Retired Persons. As we were sitting at the head table overlooking the 150 members of the local chapter of AARP, the moderator for the banquet turned to me just moments before he was to introduce me and said, "I told them you were going to speak on the aging process. Would you mind introducing your topic of death and dying to them?" Apparently, the person in charge, who invited me to speak on death and dying, could not bring himself to disclose the topic beforehand. So he had previously announced the topic to be the aging process.

Death Fears

Like their younger contemporaries, older adults will have some anxieties and concerns as they approach death. They fear a long, painful, and disfiguring death, or death in a vegetative state hooked to sophisticated machines while hospital bills devour their insurance and savings. They fear that their families will be overburdened by their prolonged care and the expense it involves. And they dread losing control of their lives by consignment to nursing homes (McCarthy, 1991:505–506). There is empirical evidence that suggests older persons think of death more often than younger adults, but the elderly appear to have less fear and anxiety concerning death (Kalish, 1976; Leming, 1980; Lund and Leming, 1975; Kastenbaum, 1969; Kalish and Reynolds, 1976).

According to Richard Kalish (1976), several factors account for the lower death anxiety levels found in older adults: (1) older adults see their lives as having less prospects for the future and less value; (2) older adults who live past what they expected have a sense of living on "borrowed time;" and (3) dealing with the deaths of friends can help socialize older adults toward acceptance of their own death.

Richard Dumont and Dennis Foss (1972) suggest that, since older people are more likely to have fulfilled their goals in life, they are less fearful of death—for others, this might threaten personal achievement. Elderly people who have not attained their goals are more likely to have either made their goals more modest or somehow rationalized their lack of achievement. It is also possible that older people come from an age cohort that was better socialized as children to deal with death. They are more likely to come from rural backgrounds and to have had earlier encounters with deaths of siblings, family members, and friends.

SOCRATES ON THE FEAR OF DEATH

To fear death is nothing other than to think oneself wise when one is not; for it is to think one knows what one does not know. No man knows whether death may not even turn out to be the greatest of blessings for a human being; and yet people fear it as if they knew for certain that it is the greatest of evil.

"The Apology (The Defense of Socrates)." In *Great Dialogues of Plato*, trans. W.H.D. Rouse. " Bergenfield, NJ: Mentor Books, 1971, p. 435.

While the elderly tend to have less fear of death than younger groups, they have had more experience with death (Moss and Moss, 1989:216). They have probably known more people who have died, have been to more funerals, and have visited more cemeteries than have younger persons. Thus, they may have become somewhat more able to imagine a world without them in it, as they experience the death of others and consider what they will leave behind them. Many older persons have, therefore, in some ways come to terms with their own finitude.

Hannelore Wass (1979:193) reports that few studies have examined sex differences in the fear of death among the elderly. The available studies show no sex differences in noninstitutionalized, in institutionalized, and in acute **geriatric** patients. A study by Wass and Sisler (1978) of noninstitutionalized older persons, however, showed significant sex differences that indicated that women have more fear of death than males. Compared to older men, however, older women are less negative about death (Keith, 1979). As Judith Stillion (1985) suggested in Chapter 1, the discrepancy in such findings may simply reflect the greater tendency of women to admit troubling feelings than men are willing to share. When only institutionalized versus noninstitutionalized elderly have been studied to determine if death fears vary with these two populations, Wass (1979:193) cites studies showing that the institutionalized elderly in nursing homes tend to be more fearful than those living out in the community in an apartment or house.

Wass (1979:193–194) further reports that some evidence exists that the widowed tend to be more fearful of death than are the elderly married or remarried. Persons living alone have greater fear of death than those living with a family. As noted earlier in this chapter, education seems to have an impact on views of death: The elderly with a grade school education have a greater fear of death than those elderly who are college graduates. The elderly with low incomes (less than $5000 annually) exhibit a greater fear of death than those with higher incomes (above $15,000 annually). High levels of death anxiety for the elderly seem to be associated with poor physical and mental health.

In a study of terminal cancer patients, Lund and Leming (1975) found that older patients had less anxiety concerning their diseases and terminal conditions than did younger persons. Older patients tended to experience greater depression, however.

There is evidence (Leming, 1980; McKenzie, 1980; Norman and Scaramelli, 1980; Kalish, 1976) that differences in death anxiety and fear appear to be more a function of religiosity than age. Since older persons are more likely to be religious, a sense of comfort should be provided as they approach death. The older person is more likely to believe in an afterlife and rely on a faith in God as a coping strategy in dealing with death.

Despite various concerns of the elderly noted above, the fact is that many elderly Americans die peaceful and relatively painless deaths. A National Institute of Aging study (McCarthy, 1991:506) of 1000 persons over age 65 who had died concluded that their health did not deteriorate until fairly near the end in most cases. Over half were in good or excellent health a year before they died. Ten percent were in good health the day before. About one-third knew death was approaching.

Though Robert Kastenbaum (1992) highlights the diversity of attitudes toward dying and death found in the elderly, he notes certain themes and characteristics found in three studies: Munnichs (1966) in the Netherlands, Weisman and Kastenbaum (1970) in the United States, and Kellehear (1990) in Australia. Munnichs's interviews with 100 men and women over age 70 revealed that fear did not dominate, relatively few were apprehensive about dying, and fewer were obsessed by the idea of death and finitude. Munnichs found that most had worked out some kind of accepting orientation toward death. Death was no longer a threatening stranger or mysterious external force. Kastenbaum (1992:9) notes that these individuals in Munnichs's study had become "philosophical" about death.

Likewise, in the study of hospitalized geriatric patients in the United States (Weisman and Kastenbaum), anxiety was not the predominant response to the prospect of dying and death. The ego integration hypothesis of Erikson and the life review theory of Butler were consistent with the pattern of findings. In the Australian study of 100 dying individuals, Kellehear found that most of the terminally ill people engaged in some form of personal preparation for death (funeral arrangements, for example) and seemed to have an implicit conception of the "good death" that emphasized looking after the needs of the survivors in a practical way.

The Place of Death

Death for the older person becomes a normal and expectable event. The crisis for the elderly is not so much death, but how and where the death will take place. The prospect of dying in a foreign place in a dependent and undignified state is a very distressing thought for the older adult. They do not wish to be a financial or physical burden on anyone, yet the options of care may be limited.

The question of physically relocating the elderly to another place is a sensitive issue among **gerontologists** (Crandall, 1991:561). Those favoring relocation believe that the relocation of older persons is often less detrimental than leaving them where they currently live. To move older persons from substandard facilities, for example, they believe will be beneficial. Those opposed to relocation of the elderly argue that relocating is traumatic and will generally increase their risk of death.

While most elderly individuals would prefer to die in their homes in familiar surroundings, the majority continue to die in hospitals and nursing homes

A coroner's office investigator gathers routine information following a nursing home death. Approximately 70 percent of all deaths take place in institutional settings.

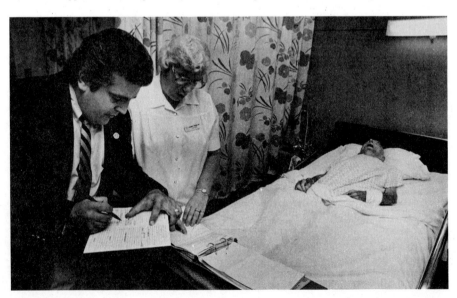

WARNING

Jenny Joseph

When I am an old woman I shall wear purple
With a red hat which doesn't go, and doesn't suit me.
And I shall spend my pension on brandy and summer gloves
And satin sandals, and say we've no money for butter.
I shall sit down on the pavement when I'm tired
And gobble up samples in shops and press alarm bells
And run my stick along the public railings
And make up for the sobriety of my youth.
I shall go out in my slippers in the rain
And pick the flowers in other people's gardens
And learn to spit.

You can wear terrible shirts and grow more fat
And eat three pounds of sausages at a go
Or only bread and pickles for a week
And hoard pens and pencils and beermats and things in boxes.

But now we must have clothes that keep us dry
And pay our rent and not swear in the street
And set a good example for the children.
We must have friends to dinner and read the papers.

But maybe I ought to practise a little now?
So people who know me are not too shocked and surprised
When suddenly I am old, and start to wear purple.

From *When I Am An Old Woman I Shall Wear Purple: An Anthology of Short Stories and Poetry,* Sandra
Martz (Ed.). Watsonville, CA: Papier-Mâché Press, 1987.

(Amenta, 1985). Richard Kalish (1965) notes that these institutionalized settings are better equipped to handle dying individuals, and the family is removed from the considerable strain of caring for a dying family member in the home. Thus, while the elderly might prefer to die at home, they are not likely to be allowed to do so.

The elderly are more likely to be separated from family and friends as they die. For them, the dying process may involve a fear of isolation and loneliness. Younger terminally ill patients are usually more concerned about the fears of pain, indignity, and dependency in the dying process, the fear of leaving loved ones, and the fear of not accomplishing their goals (Leming, 1980).

In preparing to grow old, perhaps the words of Jenny Joseph's poem on p. 145 provide inspiration.

CONCLUSION

Psychosocial studies of developmental concepts of death are themselves in a stage of infancy. Significant progress is being made, however, in an understanding of how children and adolescents experience loss at various stages of their development. Adolescence is a particularly vulnerable period with regard to facing death. A strong sense of injustice is not uncommon when the one who dies has not seemed to reach the fullest potential and opportunity to experience life.

Thinking about death is powerfully influenced by experience with death or threats of death. Mental health, managing anxiety well, and meaningfulness in life are the most powerful factors discovered in relation to developmental concepts of death. Broad cultural-religious influences also enter significantly into each of these features.

People can and do manage much of what happens within their minds. One gathers information and insights, helps self to cope, and gives aid to others in need. At whatever stage of the life cycle, one can be helped to face both life and death more positively.

More research is needed to explore the relationships between death conceptualizations, gender-differentiation, and place within the adult life cycle. Some stereotypes are beginning to fall concerning older men and women, but our conclusions are tentative, and more empirical research is needed.

Growing older pushes one to depend more upon educational, intellectual, and social skills than upon physical prowess. Feeling that one is useful and that one contributes to the well-being of others, as well as having a healthy understanding of death, significantly aids meaningful living and dying. As Robert Kavanaugh (1972:226) wrote:

> I am ashamed how little I know about death and dying, but never have I enjoyed life more, dreamed more beautiful dreams each night, than when I began having courage to begin facing death.

Some pessimism can be found in older people, but disengagement from life is not necessarily a universal trait. The fear of death lessens with age, but the thought of death increases. The way time is used changes, as does the meaning one finds in life's experiences. Yet living a happy and meaningful life is one of the ways to develop a positive and healthy view of death. Perhaps Alex Keaton of the television show "Family Ties" best sums up the developmental approach to death when he said, "Children die with opportunities and dreams; old people die with achievements and memories."

SUMMARY

1. An overall psychosocial theory acceptable to a majority of researchers is still lacking.
2. The older the person the more complex is the task of understanding just what causes one to think about death in a particular way.
3. During adolescence the sense of personal identity is most vulnerable, and concepts and feelings of death are powerfully influenced by that vulnerability.
4. The young adult stage has been labeled the "novice phase" since a strong sense of need to train oneself in the art of reaching one's fullest potential is contradicted by any thought of death.
5. Not only is AIDS rapidly becoming a major cause of death in the young adult age group, but for same-sex oriented HIV-positive individuals, their support group is also literally dying out.
6. The "panic phase" begins during the middle years when one realizes that the idealized self longed for may not actually develop.
7. Research concerning the conceptualization of death in middle adulthood is difficult to find.
8. Most people are capable of thinking of death more often and more profoundly than they do, but psychological defenses sometimes prevent this from happening.

9. According to Erik Erikson, the task of the final stage of life, senescence, is to achieve integrity.

10. In the United States a taboo exists with respect to discussing death-related topics with the elderly.

11. The crisis for the elderly is not so much death, but how and where the death will take place.

DISCUSSION QUESTIONS

1. What are some of the factors, other than age, that influence death conceptualizations? Why are these factors important in understanding the ways people conceptualize death?

2. Why do high school and college-aged students have a higher level of death anxiety than junior high school students?

3. Both death and sex education are viewed by many as problems. Cite any current trends that may suggest that death and sex education are more in vogue in institutional settings today.

4. In your opinion, have death conceptualizations changed much in the past few decades? Do you see death conceptualizations changing much in the next few decades?

5. What are some of the limitations of the developmental approach to the understanding of death conceptualizations?

6. What are some death themes in contemporary adolescent music? How do you explain death themes in music?

7. How do you explain the popularity of some of the movies depicting brutal death scenes?

8. Why would young adults appear to reject the admonition to remember death?

9. Why would education tend to reduce one's anxiety about death?

10. Why does the death taboo exist with respect to the elderly in the United States?

GLOSSARY

Adolescence: Stage of life commonly defined as the onset of puberty when sexual maturity or the ability to reproduce is attained.

AIDS: Acronym for acquired immunodeficiency syndrome, a lethal syndrome caused by a virus that damages the immune system and weakens the body's ability to fight bacteria.

Behaviorists: A school of psychology that focuses chiefly on overt behavior rather than upon inner psychological dynamics that cannot be clearly identified or measured.

Death Anxiety/Death Fear: A learned emotional response to death-related phenomena that is characterized by extreme apprehension.

Developmental Approach: Branch of social sciences concerned with interaction between physical, psychological, and social processes and with stages of growth from birth to old age.

Ego Psychologists: A school of theorists and therapists who moved away from Freud in the direction of making more emphasis fall in therapy upon the coping strategies and strengths of the person rather than upon the more elusive dynamics of the libido and the unconscious.

Geriatrics: The study of the medical aspects of old age.

Gerontology: The study of the biological, psychological, and social aspects of aging.

Humanistic Approach: Psychological model that emphasizes an individual's phenomenal world and inherent capacity for making rational choices and developing to maximum potential.

Life Review: A term of Robert Butler's suggesting a reverence for what one was and a time for judgment; looking back over one's life and perhaps tracing back one's steps in earlier years; a review of one's life, as death draws near; a therapeutic technique in helping the elderly.

Longitudinal Study: Method of scientific investigation in which selected measurements and observations are taken repeatedly over time in order to determine change, growth, or stability.

Psychoanalysis: A school of theory and therapy that concentrates upon the unconscious forces behind overt behavior, dealing principally with instinctual drives and their dynamics in the individual's inner psyche; uses interplay of transference and resistance between psychoanalyst and client as principal foci.

Ritual: The symbolic affirmation of values by means of culturally standardized utterances and actions.

Senescence: Erik Erikson's last stage of the life cycle; the task is to achieve integrity, a conviction that one's life has meaning and purpose and that having lived has made a difference.

REFERENCES

Amenta, M. 1985. "Hospice in the United States: Multiple Models and Varied Programs." *Nursing Clinics of North America,* 20:269–279.

Becker, Ernest. 1973. *The Denial of Death.* New York: The Free Press.

Brody, J. A. 1989. "Toward Quantifying the Health of the Elderly." *American Journal of Public Health,* 79:685–686.

Crandall, Richard C. 1991. *Gerontology: A Behavioral Science Approach,* 2nd ed. New York: McGraw-Hill.

Douglas, Joan D. 1991. "Patterns of Change Following Parent Death in Midlife Adults." *Omega,* 22:123–137.

Dumont, Richard G., and Dennis C. Foss. 1972. *The American View of Death: Acceptance or Denial?* Cambridge, MA: Schenkman Publishing Company, Inc.

The Economist. 1991. "Poor Man's Plague." 320(September 21):21–23.

El Dorado Times. 1985. "Death Films Popular, Store Manager Says." El Dorado, AR, December 13, p. 16.

Erikson, Erik. 1959. "Identity and the Life Cycle: Selected Papers." *Psychological Issues,* 1:1-171.

Erikson, Erik. 1963. *Childhood and Society.* New York: Norton.

Feifel, Herman. 1959. *The Meaning of Death.* New York: McGraw-Hill.

Fulton, Robert, and Greg Owen. 1988. "Death and Society in Twentieth-Century America." *Omega,* 18:379–394.

Ginsburg, Herbert, and Sylvia Opper. 1979. *Piaget's Theory of Intellectual Development,* 2nd ed. Englewood Cliffs, NJ: Prentice-Hall.

Gordon, Audrey. 1986. "The Tattered Cloak of Immortality." In *Adolescence and Death,* Charles A. Corr and Joan N. McNeil (Eds.). New York: Springer Publishing Company.

Grollman, Earl A. 1970. *Talking About Death: A Dialogue Between Parent and Child.* Boston: Beacon Press.

Jacques, Elliott. 1965. "Death and the Mid-Life Crisis." *International Journal of Psycho-analysis,* 46:502–514.

Jung, Carl. 1933. *Modern Man in Search of a Soul.* New York: Harcourt Brace Jovanovich.

Jung, Carl. 1971. "The Stages of Life." In *The Portable Jung,* J. Campbell (Ed.). New York: Viking Press.

Kalish, Richard A. 1965. "The Aged and the Dying Process: The Inevitable Decisions." *Journal of Social Issues,* 21:87–96.

Kalish, Richard A. 1976. "Death and Dying in a Social Context." In *Handbook of Aging and Social Sciences,* Robert Binstock and Ethel Shanas (Eds.). New York: Van Nostrand-Reinhold.

Kalish, Richard A., and D.K. Reynolds. 1976. *Death and Ethnicity: A Psycho-Cultural Investigation.* Los Angeles: University of Southern California Press.

Kastenbaum, Robert. 1969. "Death and Bereavement in Later Life." In *Death and Bereavement,* Austin H. Kutscher (Ed.). Springfield, IL: Thomas.

Kastenbaum, Robert. 1986. "Death in the World of Adolescence." In *Adolescence and Death,* Charles A. Corr and Joan N. McNeil (Eds.). New York: Springer Publishing Company.

Kastenbaum, Robert. 1992. "Death, Suicide and the Older Adult." *Suicide and Life-Threatening Behavior,* 22(Spring):1–14.

Kastenbaum, Robert, and R. Aisenberg. 1972. *The Psychology of Death.* New York: Springer Publishing Company.

Kavanaugh, Robert E. 1972. *Facing Death.* Baltimore: Penguin Books.

Keith, P. 1979. "Life Changes and Perceptions of Life and Death Among Older Men and Women." *Journal of Gerontology,* 34:870–878.

Kellehear, Allan. 1990. *Dying of Cancer: The Final Year of Life.* Chur Switzerland: Harwood Academic Publishers.

Koocher, Gerald P., John E. O'Malley, Diane Foster, and Janis L. Gogan. 1976. "Death Anxiety in Normal Children and Adolescents." *Psychiatric Clinics,* 9:220–229.

Kutner, Lawrence. 1990. "The Death of a Parent Can Profoundly Alter the Relationships of Adult Siblings." *New York Times,* December 6, p. B-7.

Leming, Michael R. 1980. "Religion and Death: A Test of Homans's Thesis." *Omega,* 10:347–364.

Levinson, Daniel J. 1978. *The Seasons of a Man's Life.* New York: Alfred A. Knopf.

Lifton, Robert J. 1976. "The Sense of Immortality: On Death and the Continuity of Life." In *Death and Identity,* rev. ed., Robert Fulton and Robert Bendiksen (Eds.). Bowie, MD: Charles Press Publishers.

Lowenthal, Marjorie F., Majda Thurnher, and David Chiriboga. 1975. *Four Stages of Life.* San Francisco: Jossey-Bass Publishers.

Lund, Dale A., and Michael R. Leming. 1975. "Relationship Between Age and Fear of Death: A Study of Cancer Patients." Paper presented at the Annual Scientific Meeting of the Gerontological Society." Louisville, KY (October).

McCarthy, Abigail. 1991. "The Country of the Old." *Commonweal,* 118 (September 13):505–506.

McKenzie, Sheila C. 1980. *Aging and Old Age.* Glenview, IL: Scott, Foresman, and Company

McNeil, Joan N. 1986. In *Talking About Death: Adolescents, Parents, and Peers,* Charles A. Corr and Joan N. McNeil (Eds.). New York: Springer Publishing Company.

Moss, Miriam S., and Sidney Z. Moss. 1989. "Death of the Very Old." In *Disenfranchised Grief: Recognizing Hidden Sorrow,* Kenneth J. Koka (Ed.). Lexington, MA: Lexington Books.

Munnichs, J.A.A. 1966. *Old Age and Finitude.* New York: S. Karger.

Neugarten, Bernice L. 1968. *Middle Age and Aging: A Reader in Social Psychology.* Chicago: The University of Chicago Press.

Neugarten, Bernice L. 1974. "Age Groups in American Society and the Rise of the Young–Old." *Annals of the American Academy of Political and Social Science,* 415:187–198.

Norman, William H., and Thomas J. Scaramelli. 1980. *Mid-Life: Developmental and Clinical Issues.* New York: Branner/Mazel Publishers.

O'Brien, John M., Carol Goodenow, and Oliva Espin. 1991. "Adolescents' Reactions to the Death of a Peer." *Adolescence,* 26(Summer):431–440.

Pattison, E. Marshall. 1977. *The Experience of Dying.* Englewood Cliffs, NJ: Prentice-Hall.

Piaget, Jean. 1958. *The Growth of Logical Thinking from Childhood to Adolescence.* New York: Basic Books.

Richardson, Virginia, and Roberta Sands. 1987. "Death Attitudes Among Mid-Life Women." *Omega*, 17:327–341.

Riley, Jack W. 1968. "Attitudes Toward Aging." In *Aging and Society: An Inventory of Research Findings*, M.W. Riley et al. (Eds.). New York: Russell Sage Foundation.

Schachter, Sherry. 1991. "Adolescent Experiences with the Death of a Peer." *Omega*, 24:1–11.

Stillion, Judith M. 1985. *Death and the Sexes*. Washington, DC: Hemisphere/McGraw-Hill.

Stricherz, M., and L. Cunnington. 1982. *"Death Concerns of Students, Employed Persons, and Retired Persons." Omega*, 12:373-379.

Sullivan, Andrew. 1990. "Gay Life, Gay Death." *The New Republic*, (December 17):19–25.

Sweeting, Helen N., and Mary L. M. Gilhooly. 1991. "Doctor, Am I Dead? A Review of Social Death in Modern Societies." *Omega*, 24:251–269.

Toynbee, Arnold. 1968. *Man's Concern with Death*. London: Hodder and Stoughton.

Viney, Linda L., Rachel M. Henry, Beverly M. Walker, and Levinia Crooks. 1992. "The Psychosocial Impact of Multiple Deaths from AIDS." *Omega*, 24:151–163.

Wass, Hannelore. 1979. "Death and the Elderly." In *Dying: Facing the Facts*, Hannelore Wass (Ed.). Washington, DC: Hemisphere.

Wass, Hannelore., M. David Miller, and Carol A. Redditt. 1991. "Adolescents and Destructive Themes in Rock Music: A Follow-Up." *Omega*, 23:199–206.

Wass, Hannelore, and M. Scott. 1977. "Aging Without Death." *The Gerontologist*, (August)17:377–390.

Wass, Hannelore, and H. Sisler. 1978. "Death Concern and Views on Various Aspects of Dying Among Elderly Persons." Paper presented at the International Symposium on the Dying Human. Tel Aviv, Israel (January).

Weisman, A.D., and R. Kastenbaum. 1970. *The Psychological Autopsy: A Study of the Terminal Phase of Life*. New York: Behavioral Publications.

SUGGESTED READINGS

Corr, Charles A., and Joan N. McNeil. 1986. *Adolescence and Death*. New York: Springer Publishing Company. *An anthology composed of 17 chapters ranging from contemporary interactions of adolescents and death; coping with dying, grief, and bereavement; suicide and adolescents; prevention, intervention, and postvention; and annotated resources.*

Crandall, Richard C. 1991. *Gerontology: A Behavioral Science Approach*, 2nd ed. New York: McGraw-Hill. *An orientation to the field of gerontology. Such topics as physical, societal, and psychological aspects of aging, work and leisure pursuits of the elderly, and nursing homes are covered.*

Doka, Kenneth J. 1989. *Disenfranchised Grief: Recognizing Hidden Sorrow.* Lexington, MA: Lexington Books. *This edited volume covers death in various stages of the life cycle and is written to help individuals recognize losses and to better understand the pain that accompanies the loss of a significant other.*

Kastenbaum, Robert, and Ruth Aisenberg. 1976. *The Psychology of Death*. New York: Springer Publishing Company. *Though somewhat technical in scope, this book discusses developmental concepts of death.*

LeShan, Edna. 1978. *Learning to Say Good-by: When a Parent Dies.* New York: Macmillan Company. *Aimed at a teen audience, yet helpful for young adults and parents as a model for explaining death to teenagers.*

Lund, Dale A. 1989. *Older Bereaved Spouses: Research with Practical Applications.* New York: Hemisphere. *Summarizes and integrates the findings from the most recent studies in the United States on how older adults cope with the death of a spouse.*

Solomon, David H., Elyse Salend, Anna Nolen Rahman, Marie B. Liston, and David B. Reuben. 1992. *A Consumer's Guide to Aging.* Baltimore: The Johns Hopkins University Press. *A practical work to assist the elderly with keeping healthy, maintaining an emotional balance, planning a financial future, changing family roles, and living in the leisure lane.*

Szinovacz, Maximiliane, David J. Ekerdt, and Barbara H. Vinick. 1992. *Families and Retirement.* Newbury Park, CA: Sage Publications. *This edited work covers such issues as marital relationships in retirement, extended kin relationships in retirement, and the timing of retirement.*

5

Religion and Death Attitudes

Religion provided me with answers to problems I didn't even know I had.

St. Olaf college student, 1977

*Death radically challenges all socially objectivated definitions of reality—
of the world, of others, and of self. . . . Death radically puts in question
the taken-for-granted, "business-as-usual" attitude in which one exists
in everyday life. . . . Religion maintains the socially defined reality by
legitimating marginal situations in terms of an all-encompassing sacred
reality.*

Peter Berger
Sacred Canopy

W HEN ONE THINKS of **religion** as a cultural system of meaning, an important question becomes relevant: Why did religion come into existence? Since this question attempts to discover the **etiology** of religious behavior and since we have no scientific record of the first religious activity, any answers must be speculative in nature. They are based on an *ex post facto* analysis of universal human needs that find fulfillment in a transcendent frame of reference. Such answers are also predicated on the assumption that humans have a need for religious expression. Saint Augustine said, "Thou hast made us for thyself, O God, and our hearts are restless until they find their rest in thee." This idea is also reflected in the following statement by Pascal, the 17th-century French mathematician-philosopher: "There is a God-shaped vacuum in the heart of each man, which cannot be satisfied by any created thing but only by God, the creator, made known through Jesus Christ." Such answers, however, raise another, more fundamental question of why humans have this need.

DEATH AND THE ORIGIN OF RELIGION

From a symbolic interactionist perspective (Chapter 2), meanings are created and reproduced by humans. These meanings supply a base for activities and actions (behavior is in response to meanings) and provide order for the people who share a given culture. Peter Berger (1969) suggests that the human world has no order other than that created by humans. To live in a world without the order contributed by one's culture would force one to experience a meaningless existence. Sociologists refer to this condition as **anomie**—a term that literally means "without order."

There are many situations in life that challenge the order on which social life is based. Most of these situations are related to what Thomas O'Dea (1966) refers to as the three fundamental characteristics of human existence: uncertainty, powerlessness, and scarcity.

Uncertainty refers to the fact that human activity does not always lead to predictable outcomes. Even after careful planning, most people recognize that they will not be able to achieve all of their goals. Less optimistically, the 20th century's Murphy's Law states "Anything that can go wrong, will go wrong." The human condition is also characterized by *powerlessness*. We recognize that there are many situations in life, and events in the universe, over which humans have no control— among them are death, suffering, coercion, and natural disasters. Finally, in *scarcity*, humans experience inequality with regard to the distribution of wealth, power, prestige, and other things that make a satisfying life. This inequality is the basis for the human experience of relative deprivation and frustration. The three experiences of uncertainty, powerlessness, and scarcity are situations that challenge the order of everyday life, and are, therefore, marginal to ordinary experiences. According to O'Dea (1966:5), such experiences "raise questions which can find an answer only in some kind of 'beyond' itself." Therefore, **marginal situations,** which are characteristic of the human condition, force individuals to the realm of the transcendent in their search for meaningful answers.

Peter Berger (1969:23, 43–44) claims that death is the marginal situation *par excellence:*

> Witnessing the death of others and anticipating his own death, the individual is strongly propelled to question the *ad hoc* cognitive and normative operating procedures of "normal" life in society. Death presents society with a formidable problem not only because of its obvious threat to the continuity of human relationships, but because it threatens the basic assumptions of order on which society rests. Death radically puts in question the taken-for-granted, "business-as-usual" attitude in which one exists in everyday life. . . . Insofar as knowledge of death cannot be avoided in any society, legitimations of the reality of the social world *in the face of death* are decisive requirements in any society. The importance of religion in such legitimations is obvious.

It is religion, or a transcendent reference, that helps individuals remain reality-oriented when the order of everyday life is challenged. Contemplating death, we are faced with the fact that we will not be able to accomplish all our goals in life. We also realize that we are unable to extend the length of our lives and/or control the circumstances surrounding the experience and cause for our deaths. We are troubled by the fact that some must endure painful, degrading, and meaningless deaths, while others find *more* meaning and purpose in the last days of their lives than they experienced in the years preceding "the terminal period." Finally, the relative deprivation created by differential life spans raises questions that are unanswerable from a "this world" perspective.

Religious-meaning systems provide answers to these problems of uncertainty, powerlessness, and scarcity created by death. O'Dea (1966:6–7) illustrates this function of religion:

> Religion, by its reference to a beyond and its beliefs concerning man's relationship to that beyond, provides a supraempirical view of a larger total reality. In the context of this reality, the disappointments and frustrations inflicted on mankind by uncertainty and impossibility, and by the institutionalized order of human society, may be seen as meaningful in some ultimate sense, and this makes acceptance of and adjustment to them possible. Moreover, by showing the norms and rules of society to be part of a larger supraempirical ethical order, ordained and sanctified by religious belief and practice, religion contributes to their enforcement when adherence to them contradicts the wishes or interests of those affected. Religion answers the problem of meaning. It sanctifies the norms of the established

Religious-meaning systems help provide individuals with a transcendent point of reference whereby loss created by death is compensated by a system of other-worldly gains.

social order at what we have called the "breaking points," by providing a grounding for the beliefs and orientations of men in a view of reality that transcends the empirical here-and-now of daily experience. Thus not only is cognitive frustration overcome, which is involved in the problem of meaning, but the emotional adjustments to frustrations and deprivations inherent in human life and human society are facilitated.

RELIGION AS A MEANS OF PROVIDING UNDERSTANDING OF DEATH

Twenty years ago, while on a class field trip to a funeral home, I complimented the funeral director on the beautiful pastoral scene hanging on a wall there. He said it was a very unusual wall hanging and took it down to show me the framed, velvet, reverse side that could also be displayed. He then took out a box containing a cross, a crucifix, and a Star of David that could be hung on the velvet backing. The funeral director told the class that he changed the hanging as the religious affiliation of the deceased varied. Since the time of that field trip, I have become very conscious of the way funeral homes extensively employ religious symbols in attempting to create a religious ambiance. Consider the following:

1. Within the funeral home, "chapel" is the name given to the room where the funeral is held.
2. Most memorial cards have the 23rd Psalm on them.
3. The music one hears on the sound systems within most funeral homes is religious in nature.
4. Wall hangings found in most funeral homes usually have religious content.
5. Funeral homes often provide Christmas calendars, complete with Bible verses and religious scenes, for religious groups and other interested members of the community.

Religious systems provide a means to reestablish the social order challenged by death. Our society has institutionalized the continued importance of religion by creating funeral **rituals** that have a religious quality about them.

There have been many attempts to explain the methods by which religion influences death meanings. Most discussion in this area has been strongly influenced by the theoretical writings of Malinowski, Radcliffe-Brown, and Homans.

Stated briefly, anthropologist Bronislaw Malinowski held that religion functioned to relieve the anxiety caused by the crisis experiences that people encounter in their lifetimes. Religion has its origin in the crisis experience in death because it provides individuals with a means of dealing with extraordinary phenomena. Religion functions to bring about a restoration of normalcy for the individual.

Malinowski (1965:70) says:

> Every important crisis of human life implies a strong emotional upheaval, mental conflict and possible disintegration. Religion in its ethics sanctifies human life and conduct and becomes perhaps the most powerful force of social control. In its dogmatics it supplies man with strong cohesive forces.

In elaborating on his theory that religion is the "great anxiety reliever," Malinowski (1965:71) claims that "death, which of all human events is the most upsetting and disorganizing to man's calculations, is perhaps the main source of religious belief." From Malinowski's perspective, death is not only the greatest source of anxiety, it is also the primary crisis event that calls forth religious behavior. Such theorizing leads us to ask the empirical question: Does religion provide humans with a solace in their attempts to cope with death? From the pragmatic perspective of the funeral industry, the question becomes: Are attempts on the part of the funeral home to merge religious and death meanings necessary and effective in assisting the bereaved?

Anthropologist A. R. Radcliffe-Brown (1965) disagrees with Malinowski's contention that religion functions primarily as an anxiety reliever, and claims, rather, that religion gives people fears and anxieties from which they would otherwise be free—the fear of spirits, God's judgment, the devil, hell. From Radcliffe-Brown's perspective, we would be led to expect that the nonreligious individual would have relatively less **death anxiety** and would cope better with his or her death and the deaths of others. We might also be led to the conclusion that from the point of reference of personal death anxiety, religious beliefs have **dysfunctional** consequences. George Homans has attempted to resolve this problem by declaring that both Malinowski and Radcliffe-Brown are correct in their theorizing about the role of religion in death anxiety. Rather than pitting Radcliffe-Brown against Malinowski, he argues that Radcliffe-Brown's hypothesis is a supplement to Malinowski's theory. According to Homans (1965), Malinowski is looking at the individual, Radcliffe-Brown at the community. While Malinowski says that the individual tends to feel anxiety on certain occasions, Radcliffe-Brown says that society *expects* the individual to feel anxiety on certain occasions.

If we start with a psychological frame of reference (as does Malinowski), we focus our attention on the function of religion for the individual. From this perspective, patterns of social integration are contingent upon psychological processes—what works for the individual is functional for society. Therefore, since religious actions and rituals may help some individuals find meaning for death, and consequently dispel anomie in death-related situations, the social function of religion must be anxiety reduction. This point of view is illustrated in the following statement by Malinowski (1965:72):

> Religion in its ethics sanctifies human life and conduct and becomes perhaps the most powerful force of social control. In its dogmatics it supplies man with strong cohesive forces. It grows out of every culture, because life-long bonds of cooperation and mutual interest create sentiments, and sentiments rebel against death and dissolution. The cultural call for religion is highly derived and indirect but is finally rooted in the way in which the primary needs of man are satisfied in culture.

Turning to the perspective of Radcliffe-Brown, we find the following statement, which poses an alternative to Malinowski's reasoning (Radcliffe-Brown, 1965:81):

> I think that for certain rites it would be easy to maintain with equal plausibility an exactly contrary theory, namely, that if it were not for the existence of the rite and the beliefs associated with it the individual would feel no anxiety, and that the psychological effect of the rite is to create in the individual a sense of insecurity and danger.

In this quotation, Radcliffe-Brown argues that religion might serve to increase anxiety for the individual rather than reduce it as Malinowski would contend. Radcliffe-Brown begins with a societal perspective and declares that the function of religion is to create a sense of anxiety that will maintain the social structure of the society:

> Actually in our fears or anxieties, as well as in our hopes, we are conditioned by the community in which we live. And it is largely by the sharing of hopes and fears, by what I have called *common concern* in events or eventualities, that human beings are linked together in temporary or permanent associations.

George Homans's (1965) thesis is that when individuals encounter death, the anxiety they experience is basically socially ascribed, or learned. Death fears can be likened to the fears of other things—snakes, electricity, communism, or whatever. If we believe we are in a dangerous setting, we react accordingly. Religion, with its emphasis on immortality of the soul and its belief in a coming judgment, increases the level of death anxiety for individuals who follow the teachings of the religion. However, once individuals have fulfilled the requisite religious or magical ceremonies, they experience only a moderate amount of anxiety.

Homans brings both the perspectives of Malinowski and Radcliffe-Brown together by making four conclusions:

1. Religion functions to relieve anxiety associated with death-related situations.

2. Death anxiety calls forth religious activities and rituals.
3. In order to stabilize the group of individuals who perform these rituals, group activities and beliefs provide a potential threat of anxiety in
   order to unite group members through a "common concern."
4. This secondary anxiety may be effectively removed through the group
   rituals of purification and expiation.

Summarizing the relationship between **religiosity** and death anxiety, we can
arrive at the following theoretical assumptions:

1. The meanings of death are socially ascribed—death *per se* is neither
   fearful nor nonfearful.
2. The meanings that are ascribed to death in a given culture are transmitted to individuals in the society through the socialization process.
3. Anxiety reduction may be accomplished through social cooperation
   and institutional participation.
4. Institutional cohesiveness in religious institutions is fostered by giving
   participants a sense of anxiety concerning death and uniting them
   through a common concern.
5. If the religious institutions are to remain viable, they must also provide a means for anxiety reduction.
6. Through its promise of a reward in the afterlife, and its redefinition of
   the negative effects of death upon the **temporal** life of the individual,
   religion diminishes the fear that it has ascribed to death and reduces
   anxieties ascribed to death by secular society.

In order to test the empirical validity of these assumptions, Michael Leming
(1979–1980) surveyed 372 randomly selected residents in Northfield, Minnesota,
concerning death anxiety and religious activities, beliefs, and experiences. Subjects
were divided into four groups based on a religious commitment scale developed by
Charles Glock and Rodney Stark (1966) and Joseph Faulkner and Gordon DeJong
(1966). Approximately 25 percent of the respondents were placed in each category—the first group consisted of those persons who were the least religious and
the fourth group contained the people who were the most religious.

The graph shown here gives the mean fear of death scores for each of the levels
of religious commitment. The relationship between the variables of religiosity and
death anxiety is **curvilinear**—persons with a moderate commitment to religion
have added to the general anxiety that has been socially ascribed to death from secular sources. The person with a moderate commitment receives only the negative
consequences of religion—what Radcliffe-Brown calls a "common concern." These
persons acquire only the anxiety, which religion is capable of producing, and none

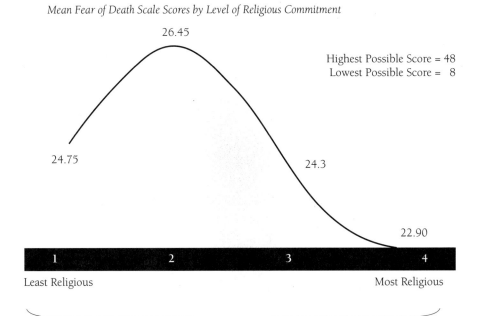

Mean Fear of Death Scale Scores by Level of Religious Commitment

26.45

Highest Possible Score = 48
Lowest Possible Score = 8

24.75

24.3

22.90

| 1 | 2 | 3 | 4 |

Least Religious   Most Religious

Level of Religious Commitment

of the consolation. On the other hand, the highly committed individual has the least anxiety concerning death. Religion, as Malinowski predicts, provides individuals with a solace when they attempt to cope with death attitudes.

In conclusion, religiosity seems to serve the dual function of "afflicting the comforted" and "comforting the afflicted." We have discovered that religion, when

RELIGION AND DYING

Robert E. Kavanaugh

My conclusion is that religious faith of itself does little to affect man's peace near death. Worry warts are worry warts no matter their theology. It is not the substance or content of a man's creed that brings peace. It is the *firmness* and the quality of his act of believing. Firm believers, true believers, will find more peace on their deathbeds than all others, whatever the religious or secular label we place on their creed. *The believer, not the belief,* brings peace.

Facing Death. Baltimore: Penguin Books, 1972, p. 14.

accompanied with a high degree of commitment, not only relieves the dread it engendered, but dispels much of the anxiety caused by the social effects of death.

At this point we might wonder how religious commitment affects the eight types of death fears discussed earlier in Chapter 1. Consistent with what we have seen in the graph, the theoretical model in this chapter suggests a curvilinear relationship between the two variables—those persons with moderate religious commitment experience the greatest amount of anxiety in each of the eight areas. In attempting to empirically evaluate this relationship, Leming (1979–1980) found that the theoretical model was supported with only 2 curvilinear trend deviations (see Table 5.1). The deviations were found among people who were the least religious for the fear of dependency in the dying process. It may be that nonreligious individuals are more concerned about being self-sufficient and independent of others, and that they find dependency even more distressing than persons who are more religious. In terms of the fear of isolation, there does not seem to be a relationship between death fear and religious commitment.

Upon further investigation, Leming found that factors of education, age, and even religious preference did not affect the curvilinear relationship. With the exception of the fear of isolation, persons who had the strongest religious commitment were the least fearful with regard to the various areas of death concern. Furthermore, in each of the eight death fear areas the strength of commitment was the most significant variable in explaining the relationship between religion and the fear of death. Robert Kavanaugh (1972:14) seems to have empirical support for his statement, "The believer, not the belief, brings peace."

Religious Interpretations of Death

Until this point, we have provided a functional perspective on religion—we have defined religion in terms of what religion does *for* the individual and society. This approach focuses on the *consequences* of religion rather than on the *content* of religious belief and practice. In this section we will attempt to provide substantive perspectives on religion and death. The substantive approach to religion attempts to establish what religion *is*. Substantive definitions of religion endeavor to distinguish religious activities from nonreligious behaviors by providing necessary criteria for inclusion as religious phenomena. The substantive definition of religion that has been used most frequently by sociologists is the one formulated by Emile Durkheim in his *Elementary Forms of Religious Life,* first published in 1915.

> A religion is a unified system of beliefs and practices relative to sacred things, that is to say, things set apart and forbidden—beliefs and practices which unite into one single moral community called a Church, all those who adhere to them.

Table 5.1   Mean Scores for the Various Types of Death Fears
by Level of Religious Commitment

| TYPE OF DEATH FEAR* | LEVEL OF RELIGIOUS COMMITMENT | | | |
| | LEAST RELIGIOUS | | | MOST RELIGIOUS |
	1	2	3	4
Fear of dependency in dying process				
Total Mean = 3.9	4.2**	4.1	3.85	3.75
Fear of pain				
Total Mean = 3.7	3.8	4.0	3.65	3.5
Fear of isolation				
Total Mean = 3.0	2.8	3.0	2.95	3.0**
Fear of the finality of death				
Total Mean = 2.9	3.05	3.25	2.8	2.75
Fear of leaving loved ones				
Total Mean = 2.8	3.05	3.25	2.65	2.60
Fear of the indignity in dying process				
Total Mean = 2.75	2.55	2.9	2.85	2.55
Fear of afterlife				
Total Mean = 2.55	2.5	2.95	2.6	2.3
Fear of the fate of the body				
Total Mean = 2.55	2.5	2.7	2.6	2.4
COMBINED LEMING* DEATH FEAR SCORE	24.75	26.45	24.3	22.9
Total Mean = 24.3				

*The possible range for the subscale scores is 1 through 6, with the values of one and six indicating low and high anxiety respectively. For the combined death fear score the potential minimum score is 8 and the highest maximum score is 48.

**Curvilinear Trend Deviation

In this definition, Durkheim designates four essential ingredients of religion—a system of beliefs, a set of religious practices or rituals, the sacred or supernatural as the object of worship, and a community or social base. Most substantive definitions of religion employed by contemporary sociologists will incorporate these four key elements. However, some sociologists have argued that in order to be inclusive of phenomena that most people consider religious, it might be proper to exclude the necessity of having a sacred point of reference. Buddhism, for example, does not have a supernatural being to which beliefs and rituals are oriented. We will now consider five religious traditions and explain how each tradition attempts to interpret the meaning of death-related experiences and provides funeral rites and rituals for the bereaved. The five religious traditions considered are Judaism, Christianity, Islam, Hinduism, and Buddhism.

Judaism

Death in the Jewish tradition came into being as a result of Adam and Eve's sin, which caused them to be expelled from the Garden of Eden. When Adam and Eve ate the fruit from the "Tree of Conscience," they received the curse of pain in childbirth, the burden of work, and the loss of physical immortality. According to the Biblical account in Genesis (2:4–3:24), while death was a punishment, it also brought the ability to distinguish between good and evil as well as the power and responsibility to make decisions that have a future consequence. According to J. Carse (1981:221):

> Adam and Eve lost their immortality, but acquired consciousness instead. God drove them out of paradise into death, but also into history. God's design for the people of Israel is not to save them from death, but to save them from their enemies in order that their history might continue.

In this description we gain an understanding of the importance of God's covenant with Abraham—that Abraham would become the father of many nations, and God would have a special relationship with his descendants forever (Genesis 17). Consequently, immortality was to be found in one's identity with the group.

Among contemporary Jews, including those who consider themselves religious, opinion differs regarding personal immortality. Some contend that there is no after*life*, only an after*death*—the dead go to *Sheol*, where nothing happens, and the soul eventually slides into oblivion. Other Jews believe in a resurrection of the soul, when individuals are brought to a final judgment (Carse, 1981:221). Still, for others there is a real ambivalence regarding the immortality of the soul. Carse cites the writings of Rabbi Leona Modena (1571–1648), who states:

> It is frightening that we fail to find in all the words of Moses a single indication pointing to man's spiritual immortality after his physical death. Nonetheless, reason compels us to believe that the soul continues.

Regardless of the content of Jewish beliefs regarding the immortality of the soul, Jewish funeral customs and rituals emphasize the point that "God does not save us, as individuals, from death, but saves Israel for history, regardless of death" (Carse, 1981:221).

According to Knobel (1987:396), traditional Jewish burial customs require that the body be cleansed by members of the Jewish burial society (*hevra'qaddisha'*, "holy society") in a washing process called *tahorah,* or "purification." Custom forbids embalming, cremation, and autopsy unless local laws require these procedures. The body is then dressed in plain linen shrouds (*takhrikhim*); men are

JEWISH GROUP BURIES ITS OWN

When a Jewish congregation here first began the practice of offering simple, inexpensive burials for its dead, some members were upset. But they now increasingly condone it.

Back in 1977, some people had felt it was barbaric when the body of a devout member, Al Sudit, 75, was lowered into his grave in a plain wooden box, with mourners themselves shoveling on the dirt. But recently, when another respected member, Morris Weiner, 81, was given the same sort of elemental funeral, relatives say they neither sensed nor heard any criticism.

Rabbi Arnold M. Goodman, spiritual leader of Adath Jeshurun Congregation, says volunteers of its society to honor the dead—*Chevra Kevod Hamet*—now handle about half the funerals of members.

Goodman, recently elected president of the Rabbinical Assembly, representing the nation's 1,200 Conservative rabbis, regards his congregation as a pioneer in setting up a model for traditional, simplified funerals.

He says congregations in Highland Park, Illinois, Portland, Oregon, and Washington, D.C., have adapted the method for their own use. But some other rabbis remain dubious.

The Chevra was formed in 1976 after Goodman, in a sermon, dealt with the impact of American values upon the funeral practices of Jewry. He suggested a committee study the requirements of the *Halacha*, or Jewish law, for responding to death.

Months of study convinced committee members that a simple wood coffin should be used, the body should be washed in a ritual process called *tahara* and, because dust is to return to dust as quickly as possible, there should be no formaldehyde in the veins, no nails on the coffin. The society decided to offer traditional funerals free to Adath Jeshurun members. The congregation provided seed money. Memorial donations and voluntary contributions from the bereaved are accepted.

Here's how the Chevra functions: A congregation member signs a revokable agreement, asking for the *Chevra's* service when needed. When death occurs, *chaverim* (friends) call on the family, aid in writing the obituary, explain death benefits, aid in other ways and remain available for help.

Chevra Kadisha (sacred society), people of the same sex as the deceased and usually five in number, wash the body at the mortuary while saying prayers. The body is dressed in a shroud sewn by Chevra members and placed in a wooden coffin.

Shomrin (guards) watch over the body, in blocks of two hours, until burial. The coffin with rope handles is light enough to be borne by pallbearers, including women. Spurning mechanical contrivances, the pallbearers lower the coffin into the grave. Chaverim, the rabbi and cantor shovel in dirt. Family members may participate.

(continued)

> Judaism historically insists that the greatest commandment is to take personal involvement in burying the dead, Goodman says, but affluence enables people to pay surrogates to do it.
>
> Goodman says a funeral costs the Chevra less than $500. A comparable no-frills funeral handled by professionals would cost about $1,500, says Elliot Pinck, a local funeral home director.

Associated Press, *Rocky Mountain News*, Denver, CO, June 25, 1982.

usually buried with their prayer shawls (*tallit*). The body is then placed in a plain wooden casket and buried before sunset on the day of death, if at all possible. Reform Judaism allows for cremation and entombment, but burial is the most frequent form of body disposition. Throughout this process, it is considered inappropriate to use the funeral as a means for displaying one's social position and wealth.

For the bereaved, the Jewish mourning ritual begins by the rending (tearing) of garments. For some, the ripping of a black ribbon, which is then attached to the clothing, has symbolically replaced the process of rending garments. From the death until burial, mourners are exempt from normal religious obligations (e.g., morning prayers) and must *not* engage in the following activities: drinking wine, eating meat, attending parties, and engaging in sexual intercourse (Knobel, 1987:396).

The liturgy for the funeral will consist of the recitation of psalms, a eulogy, and the following *El Male' Rahamin* memorial prayer (Knobel, 1987:396):

> *O God full of compassion, You who dwell on high! Grant perfect rest beneath the sheltering wings of Your presence, among the holy and pure who shine as the brightness of the heavens, unto the soul of [the deceased] who has entered eternity and in whose memory charity is offered. May his/her repose be in the Garden of Eden. May the Lord of Mercy bring him/her under the cover of His wings forever and may his/her soul be bound up in the bond of eternal life. May the Lord be his/her possession and may he/she rest in peace. Amen.*

During the interment service the body is lowered into the grave and covered with earth. The interment service consists of an acclamation of God's justice, a memorial prayer, and the recitation of *Qaddish*—a doxology reaffirming the mourner's faith in God despite the fact of death. After the burial service, the people in attendance form two lines between which the primary mourners pass. Those present comfort the mourners as they pass saying, "May God comfort you among the rest of the mourners of Zion and Jerusalem" (Knobel, 1987:397).

The *shiv'ah* is a period of seven days following the death in which the mourners act as if they were themselves dead. During this period they are forbidden to engage in work, have sexual intercourse, read the Bible, bathe, shave, or have their hair cut. It is expected that during the *shiv'ah* expressions of emotion and grief are to be of lesser intensity than during the funeral and burial rituals.

After the *shiv'ah*, mourners continue to avoid social gatherings until 30 days after the death. When one is mourning the death of a parent, the restrictions are observed for one year. After one year, all ritual expressions of grief cease with the exception of the *Yahrzeit*—the yearly commemoration of the person's death. *Yahrzeit* is observed by lighting a memorial light, performing memorial acts of charity, and attending religious services to recite the *Qaddish* prayer (Carse, 1981:221; Knobel, 1987:397).

Christianity

While Christianity shares much of the historical and mythical foundations found in Judaism, there are many distinct differences in the Christian approach to death, afterlife, and funeral rituals. For the Christian, death is viewed as the entrance to eternal life and, therefore, preferable to physical life. There is a strong belief in the immortality of the soul, the resurrection of the body, and a divine judgment of one's earthly life after death resulting in the eternal rewards of heaven or the punishments of hell. For the Roman Catholic there are four potential dispositions of the soul after death—heaven, hell, limbo, and purgatory. According to McBrien (1987:443), "some will join God forever in heaven; some may be separated eternally from God in hell; others may find themselves in a state of merely natural happiness in limbo; and others will suffer in purgatory some temporary 'punishment' still required of sins that have already been forgiven."

For the Christian, the teachings of Jesus and the Apostle Paul are the most important sources in arriving at a theology of life after death. Jesus declares to his followers:

> *"I am the resurrection and the life, he who believes in me, though he die, yet shall he live, and whoever lives and believes in me shall never die."* (John 11:25 RSV)

In the fifteenth chapter of the first letter to the Corinthians, the Apostle Paul discusses the significance of Jesus's resurrection for the Christian believer. In this chapter Jesus is portrayed as the "first born from the dead" and as "the one who has destroyed death" (I Cor. 15:26 RSV). Paul declares (I Cor. 15:52–58 RSV) that at the end of history,

> *The dead will be raised imperishable, and we shall be changed. For this perishable nature must put on the imperishable, and this mortal nature must put on immortality. When the perishable puts on the imperishable, and the mortal puts on immortality, then shall come to pass the saying that is written:*

Death is swallowed up in victory.
O death, where is thy victory?
O death, where is thy sting?

> *The sting of death is sin, and the power of sin is the law. But thanks be to God, who gives us the victory through our Lord Jesus Christ.*

There are two basic, and somewhat paradoxical, perspectives that are employed by Christian people when facing death. The first has been described above—that through faith in Jesus Christ, the Christian has victory over death and gains eternal life with God. The following passage (Rom. 3:31–39 RSV) provides us with an example of this orientation.

> *What then shall we say to this? If God is for us, who is against us? He who did not spare his own Son but gave him up for us all, will he not also give us all things with him? Who shall bring any charge against God's elect? It is God who justifies; who is to condemn? Is it Christ Jesus, who died, yes, who was raised from the dead, who is at the right hand of God, who indeed intercedes for us? Who shall separate us from the love of Christ? Shall tribulation, or distress, or persecution, or famine, or nakedness, or peril, or sword? As it is written,*
> *"For thy sake we are being killed all the day long; we are regarded as sheep to be slaughtered."*
> *No, in all these things we are more than conquerors through him who loved us. For I am sure that neither death, nor life, nor angels, nor principalities, nor things present, nor things to come, nor powers, nor height, nor depth, nor anything else in all creation, will be able to separate us from the love of God in Christ Jesus our Lord.*

The second approach to death employed by Christians emphasizes the experience of true human loss. This approach is exemplified by Jesus as he responds to the death of his friend Lazarus.

> *Then Mary, when she came where Jesus was and saw him, fell at his feet, saying to him, "Lord, if you had been here, my brother would not have died." When Jesus saw her weeping, and the Jews who came with her also weeping, he was deeply moved in spirit and troubled; and he said, "Where have you laid him?" They said to him, "Lord, come and see." Jesus wept. So the Jews said, "See how he loved him!" (John 11:32–36 RSV)*

C. S. Lewis, in his book *A Grief Observed* (1961:24), illustrates how Christians utilize this paradoxical double approach.

> What St. Paul says can comfort only those who love God better than the dead, and the dead better than themselves. If a mother is mourning not for what she has lost but for what her dead child has lost, it is a comfort to believe that the child has not lost the end for which it was created. And it is a comfort to believe that she herself, in losing her chief or only natural happiness, has not lost a greater thing, that she may still hope to "glorify God and enjoy Him forever." A comfort to the God-aimed, eternal spirit within her. But not to her motherhood. The specifically

"At that time the disciples came to Jesus, saying, 'Who is the greatest in the kingdom of heaven?' And calling to him a child, he put him in the midst of them, and said, 'Truly, I say to you, unless you turn and become like children you will never enter the kingdom of heaven. Whoever humbles himself like this child, he is the greatest in the kingdom of heaven.'" (Matthew 18:1–4)

maternal happiness must be written off. Never, in any place or time, will she have her son on her knees, or bathe him, or tell him a story, or plan for his future, or see her grandchild.

The Christian funeral process reflects these themes of victory and loss. The funeral service is primarily a worship service or mass of Christian burial. During the service, hymns are sung and scriptural passages are read that emphasize the resurrection of the dead and provide consolation for the bereaved. Occasionally a eulogy or biographical statement concerning the deceased is read.

In the United States, Christian teaching does not discourage the process of embalming, nor does it prohibit the autopsy, cremation, or any other form of final disposition (as is the case among Jews)—provided that such practices do not indicate a rejection of a belief in the resurrection of the body. American Christian funerals are conducted by members of the clergy and funeral directors in either a church, funeral chapel, and/or cemetery. Memorial services—religious services in which the dead body is not present—are becoming increasingly popular in many Protestant churches. At the occasion of death, the family of the deceased is expected to disengage from most normal social functioning until after the funeral is completed. Funeral arrangements are typically made with the professional assistance of a funeral director and/or member of the clergy. For most Roman Catholics and many Protestants, on the day before the funeral, a wake or visitation service will be held in the funeral home. During this time (approximately 5 hours in duration), friends may view the body and visit with the family of the deceased. Roman Catholic families may also have a rosary service and/or prayer service during the wake.

The funeral is typically held 2 to 4 days after the death. Occasionally, the funeral is delayed if family members are unable to make travel arrangements on such short notice (this would not be the case for the Jewish funeral). If final disposition involves cremation, the cremation can take place either after the funeral or before the memorial service. Burial and entombment dispositions are usually accompanied by rites of committal. On those occasions where there is no graveside service, words of committal will be read at the conclusion of the funeral service. At the conclusion of the funeral process, family members and others who have attended the services are often invited to share a meal together. This becomes a community rite of reincorporation.

Islam

As in Christianity, life after death is also an important focus within the Islamic tradition. Earthly life and the realm of the dead are separated by a bridge that souls must cross on the day of judgment. After death, all people face a divine judgment. Then they are assigned eternal dwelling places where they will receive either eternal rewards or punishments determined by the strengths of their faith in God and the moral quality of their earthly lives. According to the Qur'an, there are seven layers of heaven and seven layers of *alnar* ("Fire of Hell"), and each layer is separated from the layer above by receiving fewer rewards or greater punishments. The fundamental reason why persons might be condemned to a life of torment in the Fire of Hell is a lack of belief in God and in the message of his prophet Muhammad. Other reasons include lying, corruption, blasphemy, denial of the advent of the judgment day and the reality of the Fire, lack of charity, and leading a life of luxury (Long, 1987:132).

Like Jews and Christians, followers of Islam believe that God is fundamentally compassionate, but also place a similar emphasis on God as just. Therefore, persons are held accountable for moral integrity at the time of their death. The primary expression of the Islamic concern for justice and accountability is found in the belief in the assigning to paradise or damnation. Accordingly, the Qur'an provides very vivid sketches of both paradise and hell. However, many Islamic theologians also stress that God's judgment is also tempered with mercy, that the angel Gabriel will intercede on behalf of those condemned to punishment, and that they will eventually be pardoned.

The following prayer (the opening of the Surah of the Qur'an) illustrates the Islamic perspective on divine justice and mercy.

> In the name of God, the Merciful, the Compassionate. Praise belongs to God, the Lord of all Being, the All-merciful, the All-compassionate, the Master of the Day of Doom. Thee only we serve; to Thee alone we pray for succour, Guide us in the straight path, the path of those whom Thou has blessed, not of those against whom Thou art wrathful, nor of those who are astray.

When death comes to the Muslim, it is expected that he or she will be attended by relatives and close friends. Just prior to death the dying person will recite the following Islamic confession of faith: "There is no god but God, and Muhammad is his messenger." The dying person is also encouraged to request forgiveness from anyone he or she may have offended because, according to the tradition of Islam, "God will not forgive violation of human rights unless those wronged have forgiven" (Rahman, 1987:128). Islamic tradition forbids embalming and, consequently, it is expected that burial should take place as soon as possible—preferably before sundown. Occasionally, burial is delayed one or two days to provide out-of-town family members an opportunity to attend the burial. In preparation for burial, the family will call into their home or the hospital a person of the same gender as the deceased who knows the prescribed ritual for washing and preparing the body. The eyes and mouth of the deceased will be closed, the arms straightened alongside the body, and the body will be washed and wrapped in a white seamless cloth (shroud) similar to that worn for the pilgrimage to Mecca (Eickelman, 1987:401).

When the body has been fully prepared according to the prescribed ritual, it will be placed in a simple wooden coffin. (Occasionally, Muslims will be covered only by the white shroud when they are buried.) During this preparation, prayers and passages from the Qur'an will be recited by a *hoca*—a lay holy man, not a priest—and care will be taken that the body always faces Mecca.

Islamic tradition requires that the funeral service take place without unnecessary delay and that burial rights be simple and austere (Rahman, 1987:128). When it is time for the funeral, the body will be transported from the home or hospital to the mosque on the shoulders of the pallbearers. At the mosque the body will be placed on a stone bier *(musalla)* in the outer courtyard. The funeral service will be a part of one of the five regular daily religious services (usually the noon service). Because Muslims consider burying the dead a good deed, when worshippers leave the mosque and see the coffin in the courtyard, they will participate in the procession to the cemetery even though they were not acquainted with the deceased (Habenstein and Lamers, 1974:162).

The body is now transported from the mosque to the cemetery on the shoulders of those male mourners in the procession. According to Habenstein and Lamers (1974:163),

> It is customary for every man in good health to carry the coffin on his shoulders for seven steps at least, and for passers-by to accompany the procession for at least seven steps. When a new bearer pushes under the coffin, another steps away so that eight or ten people are always under the load. These customs insure that the remains will have an escort, even though the dead person may have no living relatives. At a prearranged spot, hearse and funeral cars await the procession. Where distances to the cemetery are short, the body will be borne to the grave totally on foot.

At the cemetery the body is placed into the grave, and mourners place handfuls of dirt on top of it. The sexton then fills the remainder of the grave using a shovel. At the gravesite, rather than place cut flowers, Muslim mourners plant flowers because they believe that every living plant utters the name of God. During this process prayers are recited and the service concludes with the preaching of a sermon (Habenstein and Lamers, 1974:163). After returning from the cemetery, all of the participants will partake in a meal that is served at the home of the deceased. Occasionally, some food from this meal is placed over the grave for the first three days after the death. Mourning continues for another three days, while family members receive social support and consolation from friends and members of the community.

While Islamic women are allowed to openly express emotion in the bereavement process, men are encouraged to retain their composure as a sign that they are able to accept the will of Allah. A widow is required by the Qur'an to go into seclusion for 4 months and 10 days before she is allowed to remarry (Eickelman, 1987:401–402).

Hinduism

Unlike the religious traditions we have previously discussed, Hinduism does not have a single religious founder nor a single sacred text. Although the *Vedas* are recognized by almost all Hindus as an authoritative source of spiritual knowledge, Hinduism is not dogmatic. Many different theologies and religious approaches exist within the Hindu tradition. Many gods also exist, with each viewed as an aspect or manifestation of a single ultimate reality, but it is *not* essential to believe in the existence of God in order to be a Hindu (Srinivas and Shah, 1968:358). Essentially, Hinduism is a system of social customs embued with religious significance.

The body of this Hindu woman is prepared by mourning female family members and friends in her home.

Three key concepts are central to an understanding of Hinduism—*karma, dharma,* and *moksha*. *Karma* refers to a moral law of causation; it suggests that human actions produce results for which the individual is responsible. *Karma* also refers to the balance of good and bad deeds performed in previous existences. *Dharma* are the religious duties, requirements, and/or prescriptions. The extent to which one fulfills one's *dharma* determines one's *karma*. In turn, *moksha* is the reward for living a saintly life. The main ways of achieving *moksha* are by acquiring true knowledge, performing good deeds, and living a life of love and devotion toward God (Srinivas and Shah, 1968:359).

The central doctrine affecting death-related attitudes and behavior in the Hindu religion is reincarnation and the transmigration of souls (*samsara*). For the Hindu, one's present life is determined by one's actions in a previous life. Furthermore, one's present behavior will shape the future. According to Habenstein and Lamers (1974:116), "The ultimate goal of the soul is liberation from the wheel of rebirth, through reabsorption into or identity with the Oversoul (*Brahma*)—the essence of the universe, immaterial, uncreated, limitless, and timeless."

By way of comparison, while Jews, Christians, and Muslims believe in the immortality of the soul and hope for an afterlife, Hindus hope that their soul will be absorbed at death. For the Hindu, the goal is *not* to experience life after death, but to have one's soul united with the Oversoul. Punishment for the devout Hindu might be to *have* "everlasting spiritual rebirth."

Within the Hindu tradition, death brings two possibilities—liberation and transmigration of the soul. Neither option is inherently fearful, even though separation from one's friends and loved ones may cause sadness and personal loss. Somewhat analogous to the dual perspectives of Christianity, death for the individual

UNDERSTANDING DEATH IN HINDUISM

Anant Rambachan

Death and birth are seen by us Hindus as gateways of exit and entry to the stage of this world. This process is described in one of the most striking and famous analogies in the entire *Bhagavadgita*. It is a verse which we movingly recite when the body is being cremated, and it has given comfort and solace to the grieving Hindu heart for centuries.

Just as a person casts off worn-out garments and puts on others that are new, even so does the embodied-soul cast off worn-out bodies and take on others that are new.

This analogy is full of suggestions, but I can only briefly draw your attention to a few of these. First, a suit of clothing is not identical with the wearer. Similarly, the body, which is likened here to worn-out garments, is not the true being or identity of the human person. Second, there is the similarity of a continuity of being. When a worn-out suit of clothing is cast off, the wearer continues to be. Similarly, with the disintegration of the physical body, the indweller, that is, the Self, continues to be. Finally, there is the parallel with the timing of the change. A suit of clothing is changed when it no longer serves the purpose for which it was intended. Similarly, the physical body is cast off when it no longer serves the purpose for which it came into existence.

This does not mean that the Hindu is not saddened by death or does not lament the loss it brings. There is a mysterious element in death which will always sadden and hurt. While we ache and long for the beauty, tenderness, and companionship of a dear one, we are deeply comforted in the knowledge that all that is good and true and real in him or her continues to be. What has passed away is what has always been limited by time.

Since death is a necessary condition for rebirth, Hindus also understand it to be a gateway for fresh opportunities. When we look at death from the limited perspective of a single and short life experience, we often see only its tragic side. We must admit, however, that the perspective is different for God—whose vision spans the boundless past and the unending future. Where we only see end and loss, there will be new beginnings and opportunities for a loved one. We need a selfless faith to trust his wisdom and judgment.

Hinduism conceives of life as a continuous chain of existence. In the Hindu view, the word of life is not restricted to describing the span of time between birth and death. While there are some variations in views among the many traditions of Hinduism, we agree that life is a journey toward God—the reality of all that exists. Life is a quest for that which is true and real in the midst of an existence which is so changeful and finite. For Hindus, God, the true and the real, has the highest value and is the source of all joy. We are all seekers and pilgrims, and the sacred journey of life will continue as long as it takes us to discover this final truth of ourselves and the world. As long as we cling to the finite and changeful, and seek comfort and solace in these, our journeys will be never-ending. The mortal and the finite will never satisfy us. The attainment of God is the fulfillment of our pilgrimage. This is *moksha*, liberation, our home and destination. The longing for it is captured in our daily prayer:

> *Lead us from untruth to truth*
> *From ignorance to knowledge*
> *From death to immortality.*

Anant Rambachan, Department of Religion, St. Olaf College. By permission of the author.

brings hope of something better but also the human loss of being separated from a dead loved one.

When a death takes place in Hindu society, the body is prepared for viewing by laying it out with the hands across the chest, closing the eyelids, anointing the body with oil, and placing flower garlands around it. This is done by persons of the same gender as the deceased, and this process will be presided over in the home of the deceased by the dead person's successor and heir (Habenstein and Lamers, 1974:119–120).

Because Hindus believe that cremation is an act of sacrifice, whereby one's body is offered to God through the funeral pyre, cremation is the preferred method of body disposal. In preparation for cremation, family members will construct a bier, consisting of a mat of woven coconut fronds stretched between two poles and supported by pieces of bamboo. The uncasketed body of the deceased will be borne on the bier from the deceased's home to the place of cremation by close relatives. This funeral procession will be led by the chief mourner—usually the eldest son— and will include musicians, drum players, and other mourners. The widow of the deceased will always remain behind in the home (Habenstein and Lamers, 1974:121).

According to Habenstein and Lamers, when the body reaches the place of cremation, usually a platform (*ghat*) located on the banks of a sacred river, the body will be removed from the bier and immersed in the holy waters of the river. During this process a priest will perform a brief disposal ceremony. The body will then be smeared liberally with *ghi* (clarified butter) and placed on the pyre for burning. At this point, the chief mourner, who has brought burning coals from the house of the deceased, lights the pyre, and a priest recites an invocation similar to the following:

> *Fire, you were lighted by him, so may he be lighted from you, that he may gain the regions of celestial bliss. May this offering prove auspicious.* (Habenstein and Lamers, 1974:123)

After the body has been consumed by the fire and only fragments of bones remain, the mourners will ritually wash themselves in the river in a rite of purification. They will then make offerings to the ancestral spirits of the deceased. Upon completion of this duty they will recite passages from the sacred texts.

Three days after this ritual, a few relatives of the deceased will return to the cremation site in order to gather the bones. A priest will again read from the sacred texts and sprinkle water on the *ghat*, while any remains of the deceased will be placed in a vase and given to the chief mourner. It is then the obligation of the chief mourner to cast these remains in the Ganges or another sacred river (Habenstein and Lamers, 1974:124).

Between 10 and 31 days after the cremation, a *Shraddha* (elaborate ritual feast) is prepared for all mourners and priests who have taken part in the funeral rituals. During the *Shraddha,* gifts are given to the *Guru* (religious teacher), the *Purohita* (officiating priest), and other *Brahmins* (religious functionaries). The social status of the family will determine how elaborate the *Shraddha* will be—for the poor this ritual will last 8 to 10 hours, and the wealthy may give a *Shraddha* lasting several days. At the close of the *Shraddha,* the mourning period officially ends even though later *Shraddhas* may be given as memorial remembrances (Habenstein and Lamers, 1974:125–126). While it is believed that these ritual meals provide nourishment to the spirit of the deceased in its celestial abode, from a sociological perspective, they serve as rites of family reincorporation and also differentiate the family regarding social status.

According to Habenstein and Lamers (1974:126), next to Hindu wedding ceremonies, funerals are the most important religious ceremonies. While the funeral process is very costly to families, often resulting in their impoverishment, not providing the *Shraddha* creates more social problems for families than do the financial consequences of these rituals.

Buddhism

There are many types of Buddhism, but the most popular are *Theravada, Mahayana,* and *Tantrayana.* According to Peter Pardue (1968:165), Theravada Buddhism is the dominant religion in Southeast Asia (Burma, Thailand, Laos, Vietnam, Cambodia, and Sri Lanka). Mahayana Buddhism is primarily practiced in Korea, China, Japan, and Nepal. Tantranyana has traditionally been the dominant form of Buddhism in Tibet, Mongolia, and parts of Siberia. While there are differences in each of these sects and in many others found throughout the world, in general, all Buddhists find a common heritage in the life of Siddhartha Gautama ("The Enlightened One" or "Buddha"). Buddha was born in 563 B.C. as a prince in northern India. As a child his thoughts were preoccupied with the finitude of human existence. Unsuccessfully, his family tried to shelter him from human suffering and death. At the age of 29 he left his life of privilege and began to search for personal salvation. After rejecting physical asceticism and abstract philosophy, he attained a state of enlightenment through the process of intense meditation. For the remaining 50 years of life, he served as a missionary and preached his message of salvation to all people regardless of social position and gender (Pardue, 1968:168).

The Buddhist message of salvation, taught by Buddha in his first sermon, is "The Four Noble Truths." The first truth is that all human existence is characterized by pain and suffering in an endless cycle of death and rebirth. The second truth is that the cause of the agony of the human condition is desire for personal satisfaction, which is impossible to obtain. The third truth is that salvation comes by destroying these desires. By completely destroying ignorance, one experiences enlightenment and the cycle of transmigration of the soul is broken. Finally, in the fourth truth, one can experience perfect peace through the eightfold path to enlightenment. In the words of Pardue (1968:168):

> For this purpose the proper [meditation] is the "eightfold path," an integral combination of ethics (*sila*) and meditation (*samadhi*), which jointly purify the motivations and mind. This leads to the attainment of wisdom (*prajna*), to enlightenment (*bodhi*), and to the ineffable Nirvana ("blowing out"), the final release from the incarnational cycle and mystical transcendence beyond all conceptualization.

Like the Hindu, the goal for the Buddhist is *not* to experience life after death, but to experience *nirvana*—which has neither the property of existence nor nonexistence. According to Margaret Ayer (1964:52), nirvana is the "state of peace and freedom from the miseries of the constantly changing illusion which is existence."

The location of nirvana is to be found in the image of the flame when a candle is "blown out"—it is in a place beyond human understanding. According to Ayer (1964:53), whenever anyone achieves nirvana "they 'will be seen no more.' It is through loss of desire, selfishness, evil, and illusion that this state of wisdom, holiness, and peace is reached." Buddhism contends that while physical death causes one to experience life again in a transmigrated form, "death to this world" (via nirvana) provides the gateway for ultimate happiness, peace, and fulfillment. Unlike Hinduism and the other religious traditions we have considered, the ultimate goal of Buddhism is a state of consciousness and *not* a symbolic location for the disembodied soul.

As the religious teachings of Buddha were disseminated throughout Asia, the beliefs and practices were adapted to indigenous cultural traditions dealing with death. Consequently, it is not possible to discuss Buddhist funeral rituals *per se*. Rather, there are Japanese, Korean, Chinese, and Thai funeral customs practiced within a Buddhist context.

THE THAI BUDDHIST FUNERAL

There are three parts of the Thai Buddhist funeral: ceremonies at the wat, procession to the site of cremation, and the cremation. When a common person dies the body is cleaned and dressed and placed within a casket. The casket is kept either within the home or at the wat (temple) for a period of three days. During this period monks will come every evening to chant the Buddhist scriptures

(Abhidhamma). Friends will attend these services and will offer as gifts floral tributes. Some of these wreaths will be rented and financial contributions will be made to charitable causes selected by the family of the deceased. On the fourth day the body will be taken to the charnel-ground (cremation site) which is usually a distance from the wat. When a charismatic monk, high governmental official, member of the royalty, or another noble person of high prestige dies, the body will be kept for a longer period of time before final disposition is made. This period of time can vary from a few weeks to a period of many years determined by the status of the deceased. The fourth lunar month (corresponding to the month of March) is the preferred time for funeral ceremonies.

Bodies of high status people are embalmed and then bathed and dressed with new clothes. The entire face of the deceased (notably monks) is covered with gold leaves and then placed within a casket. Visitors will come to pay respect by offering floral tributes and pouring water on the deceased (*aab nam sob*).

The ceremony prior to cremation will last for several days and will typically be held at the big *vihara* at the wat compound. The casketed body will be placed within a larger gilded teak coffin called a *long tong* or outer coffin. The *long tong* will be placed on the right side of the *vihara* and surrounded by many items associated with the deceased (in the case of monks, e.g., bronze statues, certificates of title, the deceased's picture decorated with flowers, the honorific fan called a *kruang soong*, and the three-tailed flag which is purported to be the refuge of the dead while traveling in the cycle of death and rebirth).

During these ceremonies held in the *vihara,* monks will chant important sutras from the *Tripitaka*—Buddhist scriptures. At the conclusion of the final service at the *vihara,* there will be a final tribute of flowers and three lighted candles presented to the deceased. The casket will then be removed from the golden case or *long tong* and removed from the *vihara.*

The procession is a significant rite in the Thai Buddhist funeral. The casket is put on a carriage and taken from the wat compound to the cremation site. During the procession a long white cotton cord is attached to the casket and eight (the number is flexible) monks together with lay devotees will carry the cord. In the urban areas the carriage will be motorized, while traditional funerals and/or funerals in rural areas the carriage will be pulled by walking members of the procession.

The procession is headed by the three-tail flag and followed by the monk's fan, the title certificate, the set of three yellow monk's robes, the deceased's picture, the bronze statue of the deceased, and the coffin, respectively. Upon arriving at the site of the cremation, the casket is carried around the crematorium three times which symbolizes the traveling in the cycle of death and rebirth. After the casket is then placed in front of the crematorium, the relatives will pose for pictures by the casket. After which they will walk around the casket three times.

(continued)

When the funeral is performed under royal patronage the *fai phra rajthaan* or the "Royal Fire" is brought to be used to light the cremation pyre. The royal fire is carried by a group of government officials dressed in the white official uniform, while the orchestra plays the Royal Anthem in salutation to the King of Thailand. During this time all mourners, dressed in black or white, will stand in respect to the King and royal fire.

As a final merit-making rite, five or ten important persons will come forward (one by one) and place a set of yellow robes on the long white cotton cord which is linked to the coffin, and then high-ranking monks will be invited to come forward and receive the robes. The final act is when the most important person in the ceremony (e.g., Prime Minister) will place the last set of yellow robes on the cotton cord. The most senior monk will collect the robes after "contemplating symbolically the dead." According to religious practice in Buddhism, the contemplation of the corpse by Buddhist monks will bring merit to those who provide such opportunity for the monk to do so. And the merit earned can be dedicated further to the dead as well.

The stage is now set for the actual cremation. Just prior to the lighting of the fire, the biography of the deceased is read while *dok mai chan* is distributed to all in attendance. The *dok mai chan* is a sandalwood flower with one incense-stick and two small candles attached. The mourners are all invited to come forward and deposit the *dok mai chan* before the casket. By so doing, mourners are deemed participating in the actual cremation.

The chairman of the ceremony then ignites the fire and the casket is consumed. The next morning the ashes (several pieces of bones) are gathered and made into a shape of a human being with the head facing east. Four monks will attend this ritual which will culminate when the ashes are placed into a receptacle. Afterward the ashes will be enshrined in a reliquary built in the compound of the monastery.

Throughout the funeral ceremony sorrow or lamentation is not emphasized. Rather the focus is upon impermanence of all things. The funeral is primarily a social event that affirms community values and group cohesiveness. Furthermore, it is a time where people are expected to enjoy the fellowship surrounding the rituals. Typically there is entertainment (dancing and musical performances) associated with funeral rituals in order that sorrow and loneliness be dissipated. It is believed that this assists the bereaved to conceptualize the happy and pleasant paradise where the deceased will reside.

Michael R. Leming and Sommai Premchit, "Funeral Customs in Thailand." In *Personal Care in an Impersonal World,* John D. Morgan (Ed.). New York: Baywood Publishing Company, 1993, pp. 231–235.

In general, there are some similarities in all Buddhist funeral ceremonies. At the Buddhist temple, priests assist families as they engage in this important rite of passage. Prayers of the priests illustrate the "lesson of death"—that life is vanity. At

After arriving at the site of cremation the relatives pose for pictures by the casket, walk around the casket three times, and then place the casket in front of the crematorium. Many times young male family members will be ordained as monks for a period of a few days during the funeral ceremonies. The merit earned by these young men can be dedicated to benefit the dead, as well.

funerals, Buddhist priests often read the following words from Buddha (cited by Habenstein and Lamers, 1974:97):

> *The body from which the soul has fled has no worth. Soon it will encumber the earth as a useless thing, like the trunk of a withered tree. Life lasts only for a moment. Birth and death follow one another in inescapable sequence. All that live must die. That man indeed is fortunate who achieves the nothingness of being. All animal creation is dying, or dead, or merits to be dead. All of us are dying. We cannot escape death.*

For most Buddhists, cremation is the preferred form of body disposition, but earth burial is also frequently practiced. In Buddhism, unlike Hinduism, there is no "soul"—both the body and the ideas of a soul distract from the proper meditation and attainment of nirvana. Cremation serves the function of promoting the process of liberation of the individual from the illusion of the present world. As a reflection of this orientation, Buddhist priests will recite these words prior to the final disposition of the body (cited by Habenstein and Lamers, 1974:97–98):

O dead one, pursue your destiny. Flee to paradise. You will know rebirth into a bet-
ter life. Do not linger to haunt those who remain here, and to share this life of invisible
darkness which is the lot of the living. Those whom you leave behind reckon accurately
your good fortune in your liberation. With happy impatience they await their own turn.
You neither want nor need them, and they are happy without you. Now follow your
destiny.

During and after the funeral, family members will make offerings through the priest to the spirit of the deceased. They will also give ritual feasts for the priests and other mourners. As in other religious traditions, all of these funeral activities will emphasize the importance of the religious world view, promote community cohesiveness, and reincorporate chief mourners into routine patterns of social life.

RELIGIOUS AND SECULAR ORIENTATIONS

Robert E. Kavanaugh

Faith or belief are not the sole privileges of religious people as I once thought. Faith is simply that total commitment of the entire person to an ideal, a way of life, a set of values, to anything or anyone beyond the narrow limitations of myself: God, mankind, the poor, science, human relations, growth and development, anything capable of bringing meaning and purpose to life. . . .

The true believer, after I sort out my personal feelings toward the tenets in his creed, reflects to me a sense of inner worth, a spirit of mission and purpose, a confident conviction and a tranquil assurance. Near death the true believer knows why he lived and can face the unfinished tasks of his life with his vision in clear focus. Because true belief brought perspective into life, so will it endow death with a more satisfying point of view. And no matter how wonderful religion may be for many, it is only one of the many ways to gain this stature of true belief.

Facing Death. Baltimore: Penguin Books, 1972, pp. 221 and 224.

TEMPORAL INTERPRETATIONS OF DEATH

Even though the funeral industry and most people in the United States tend to merge religious and death meanings, temporal interpretations of death also provide a means for protecting social order in the face of death. Such interpretations tend to emphasize the empirical, natural, and "this world" view of death.

According to Glenn M. Vernon (1970:33), "when death is given a temporal interpretation and is seen as the loss of consciousness, self-control, and identity, the individual may conclude that he or she can avoid social isolation in eternity by identifying him or herself with specific values, including religious ones." If we define religion as a system of beliefs and practices related to high-intensity value meanings and/or meanings of the supernatural (Vernon, 1970), then it is possible for individuals with temporal orientations to be "religious" in their outlook without affirming an afterlife. Furthermore, since any death has many consequences for the persons on whose life it impinges, we would expect that even religious persons would assign some temporal meanings to death.

Vernon has pointed out that individuals whose interpretations are primarily temporal share the following beliefs and attitudes:

1. They tend to reject or de-emphasize a belief in the afterlife.
2. They tend to believe that death is the end of the individual.
3. They tend to focus upon the needs and concerns of the survivors.
4. They tend to be present-oriented for themselves, but present- and future-oriented for those who will continue after them.
5. Any belief in immortality is related to the activities and accomplishments of the individual during his or her lifetime—including biological offspring and social relationships the individual has created.

There is a strong temptation to view the person with a temporal orientation as being very different from the person who finds comfort in a religious interpretation of death. In fact, both will attempt to restore the order in their personal lives, and that found in society, by placing death in the context of a "higher" order.

For the individual with religious commitments, protection from anomie and comfort for anxiety are to be found by being in relationship with the supernatural. For the person with a secular or temporal orientation, these same benefits are found in becoming involved with other people, projects, and causes. These involvements, while not pertaining to the supernatural, still provide a frame of reference that transcends the finite individual—a person may die but his or her concerns will continue after they die.

Symbolic Immortality

Symbolic immortality (Lifton and Olson, 1974) refers to the belief that the meaning of the person can continue after he or she has died. For the religious, symbolic immortality is often related to the concept of soul, which either returns to its preexistent state, goes to an afterlife, is reincarnated in another body, or is united with the Cosmos. For the person whose primary orientation is temporal, symbolic immortality is achieved by being remembered by others, creating something that remains useful or interesting to others, or by being part of a cause or social movement that continues after the individual's death.

> I am assured of immortality, not by anything I do, but by not dying.
>
> —Woody Allen

One of the reasons many parents give for deciding to have children is the need for an heir—someone to carry on the family name. Research has demonstrated that in the United States, families with only female children are more likely to continue having children (in hopes of producing a male offspring) than are families with only male children. For the ancient Hebrews, the cultural institution of the **levirate marriage** required that a relative of the deceased husband have sexual intercourse with his kinsman's widow in order to provide a male heir. If it is possible to pass on something of oneself to one's children, then children are one method to provide symbolic immortality.

Investing oneself in relationships with others also insures that one will be remembered after death. Damon Runyon said as he was dying, "You can keep your things of bronze and stone, just give me one person who will remember me once a year." Some will argue that if we have influenced the lives of others, something of us will continue in their lives after we die. Organ donations supply a tangible method for providing this type of symbolic immortality. In this way, one can even insure that a part of his or her *physical* self can continue in another person. Currently there is an increasing tendency for individuals to donate their organs and tissues upon death to the living (see Chapter 8). In many urban areas, kidney foundations, eye banks, and transplant centers will supply donor cards and, when death occurs, will arrange for transplants. Currently, there are many kinds of tissues or organs used for transplantation including eye, skin, bone, tendon, bone marrow, kidney, liver, pancreas, blood vessel, lung, and heart.

One of the reasons people write books, especially death and dying books, is to promote their own symbolic immortality. As long as their books can be read, their influence will outlive their biological body. The same is true for television and motion picture stars. Each year the youthful Judy Garland is resurrected from the dead as *The Wizard of Oz* is shown on television.

Great inventors, political leaders, and athletic "hall of famers" are also given immortality when we use their products, remember their accomplishments, and celebrate their achievements. In the case of medical practitioners and bionic inventors, not only do the living remember their accomplishments, but these efforts extend the lives of those who provide the dead with immortality.

TRANSPLANT OR DONOR SON'S FUNERAL? THIS FATHER FOLLOWED HIS HEART

Ed Reid passed up the chance to have his diseased heart replaced with his son's because the transplant surgery would have meant missing his son's funeral.

So, the heart of 23-year-old Eric Reid, who died Friday of head injuries suffered in a July 4 fall from a golf cart, went to someone else.

"I know he had a strong heart, and it would have been a good heart for me, but I just didn't feel like my family and I could deal with it at that particular time," Reid said Wednesday in an interview from his home. His son was buried Monday.

Being with family and friends during such a difficult time was more important, said Reid, 47. "And I also thought that each time his heart beat in me, I would have been thinking back as to how special he was to me and his family, and I didn't know how well I could deal with that."

Reid, whose heart is functioning at 15 percent of capacity, said he hopes the heart "went to someone that may need it worse than I do at the present."

Reid said he is on a waiting list for a transplant and believes another donor heart will be available soon.

Bill Faircloth, of Charlotte-based LifeShare of the Carolinas, said he couldn't recall another person needing a transplant turning down a donor organ. Generally, organ transplants involving relatives are a better match and have a greater success rate.

Associated Press, *Minneapolis Star-Tribune*, July 18, 1991, p. 1A.

Relative Death Meanings in Society

One of the most feared, distressing, and anxiety-producing deaths is a death that is perceived as being relatively meaningless. A lifetime is spent searching for and creating meaning. The search for meaning is a task that all people share. Furthermore, significant others are involved in the process attempted by individuals in creating meaning for themselves. In many respects, the meaning created turns out to be meaning for the group or society.

As the dying of martyrs dramatically illustrates, a death may be willingly entered into if it is meaningful. Given the right configuration of meaning components (see Chapter 2), *not* to die would be more difficult. For example, dying may be preferable to defining oneself, and being defined by others, as a coward or a traitor.

Dying is acceptable if it furthers "the cause." People may, in fact, literally work themselves to death in order to obtain a promotion, an artistic achievement, or public recognition. Whatever the specific content, the key factor of concern is the meaning involved. If the meaning is right, dying may be evaluated as a worthwhile thing.

Within a given society there are high-status types of death, as well as low-status types. Giving one's life in defense of family or country is generally conceived as being in the high-status category. In times past, dying in childbirth was considered to be a high-status death for females.

OZYMANDIAS

Percy Bysshe Shelley

I met a traveler from an antique land
Who said: Two vast and trunkless legs of stone
Stand in the desert . . . Near them, on the sand,
Half sunk, a shattered visage lies, whose frown,

And wrinkled lip, and sneer of cold command,
Tell that its sculptor well those passions read
Which yet survive, stamped on these lifeless things,
The hand that mocked them, and the heart that fed;
And on the pedestal these words appear:

"My name is Ozymandias, king of kings:
Look on my works, ye Mighty, and despair!"

Nothing beside remains. Round the decay
Of that colossal wreck, boundless and bare
The lone and level sands stretch far away.

The person's finite identity is protected by the group's permanence. Just as Standard Oil is the legacy of John D. Rockefeller, John H. Leming and Son's Insurance Agency will remain even after John H. Leming and his sons are dead (providing that the new owners feel that it is in their business interest not to change the name of the company).

The same can be said for people who give themselves to political movements and causes. Marx, Lenin, Stalin, and Mao—as leaders of communism—will be remembered by future communists, despite the efforts by present officials to accomplish the contrary. We even provide infamous immortality to villains, murderers, and traitors. It seems ironic that most of us spend a lifetime working for immortality, when the guns of John Wilkes Booth, Lee Harvey Oswald, Sirhan Sirhan, and James Earl Ray supply their owners with our everlasting remembrance.

Society's Heroes

The death of an individual brings about a change in influence over the members of his or her group or society. Heroes are more likely to come from the ranks of the dead than the living.

Hero meaning is a symboled-meaning component. One cannot become a hero by oneself. Society bestows the rank of hero only upon certain members, one type of symboled immortality. A death may be part of the process by which heroes are born. When something dies, something else is born or created. The death of a Jesus Christ has had consequences that have expanded in significance over the years. It is likely that Christ's death has had greater impact upon humanity than his life. The Roman Catholic Church only grants sainthood to persons who have been dead for many years. Conversely, a government may grant pardons to convicted persons who died many years ago. Meaning is a flexible, yet powerful thing.

A number of interesting speculative questions arise. If there is an afterlife (in which those who are dead are "alive"), and if all of the heroes will become our contemporaries (assuming we make it, too), what would this do to their hero status? In such a situation, would the hero category be retained? Would this person have to

THE FADING OF IMMORTALITY

In quantitative terms, the twentieth century seems more death ridden than any other. Yet mass death is strangely impersonal; an eighteenth-century hanging at Tyburn probably had more immediate impact on the watching crowd than the almost incomprehensible statistics of modern war and calculated terror have today. In the last century, Byron, Shelley, Keats, and a whole generation of young poets haunted by romanticism and tuberculosis could be "half in love with easeful Death," wooing it as they would woo a woman. Even before World War I, German poet Rainer Maria Rilke could still yearn for "the great death" for which a man prepares himself, rather than the "little" death for which he is unprepared.

In today's literature there are few "great deaths." Tolstoy, Thomas Mann, and Conrad gave death a tragic dimension. Hemingway was among the last to try; his heroes died stoically, with style, like matadors. Nowadays, death tends to be presented as a banal accident in an indifferent universe. Much of the Theater of the Absurd ridicules both death and modern man's inability to cope with

(continued)

it. In Ionesco's *Amedee,* or *How to Get Rid of It,* the plot concerns a corpse that grows and grows until it floats away in the shape of a balloon—a balloon, that is, on the way to nowhere.

"If there is no immortality, I shall hurl myself into the sea," wrote Tennyson. Bismarck was calmer. "Without the hope of an afterlife," he said, "this life is not even worth the effort of getting dressed in the morning." Freud called the belief that death is the door to a better life "the oldest, strongest, and most insistent wish of mankind." But now death is steadily becoming more of a wall and less of a door. . . . The Christian view of eternity is not merely endless time, and it need not involve the old physical concept of heaven and hell. It does involve the survival of some essence of self and an encounter with God. "Life after death," said theologian Karl Barth, "should not be regarded like a butterfly"—he might have said a balloon—"that flutters away above the grave and is preserved somewhere. Resurrection means not the continuation of life, but life's completion. The Christian hope is the conquest of death, not a flight into the Beyond."

The Fear of Nothingness

Admittedly, this hope so stated is more abstract than the fading pictures of sky-born glory, of hallelujah choruses and throngs of waiting loved ones. "People today could be described as more realistic about death," says one psychiatrist. "But inside I think they are more afraid. Those old religious assurances that there would be a gathering-in some day have largely been discarded, and I see examples all the time of neuroses caused by the fear of death." Harvard theologian Krister Stendahl agrees. "Socrates," he points out, "died in good cheer and in control, unlike the agony of Jesus with his deep human cry of desertion and loneliness. Americans tend to behave as Socrates did. But there is more of what Jesus stands for lurking in our unconsciousness."

Alone with his elemental fear of death, modern man is especially troubled by the prospect of a meaningless death and a meaningless life—the bleak offering of existentialism. "There is but one truly serious philosophical problem," wrote Albert Camus, "and that is suicide." In other words, why stay alive in a meaningless universe? The existentialist replies that man must live for the sake of living, for the things he is free to accomplish. But despite volumes of argumentation, existentialism never seems quite able to justify this conviction on the brink of a death that is only a trap door to nothingness.

There are surrogate forms of immortality: the continuity of history, the permanence of art, the biological force of sex. These can serve well enough to give life a purpose and a sense of fulfillment. But they cannot outwit death, and they are hardly satisfactory substitutes for the still persistent human hope that what happens here in three score years and ten is not the whole story.

meet new hero qualifications? Would everyone in that "kingdom" be a hero? What would a society of heroes be like? Would the hero category be meaningful?

In conclusion, symbolic immortality is something that only the living can give the dead. Yet people live with the faith that their survivors will remember them and perpetuate the meaning of their lives after they die. Like religious interpretations of death, temporal meanings enable individuals to protect themselves and their social order from death. One problem remains, however, for those whose immortality depends upon others: What would happen if a nuclear holocaust were to occur and there were no survivors?

AFTERLIFE EXPERIENCES BY THE CLINICALLY DEAD

Empirical Evidence for Afterlife Beliefs?

In the past, one of the assumptions most people made about the field of thanatology was that the real "experts" were not among us—they were dead. With the publication of Raymond Moody's Life after Life (1975), many people have stepped forward to challenge this assumption. Having been near death, or having been declared clinically dead by medical authorities, a number of survivors from these experiences have "returned from the dead" to tell us that they now know what it is like to be dead and that they possess empirical evidence to support a rational belief in the afterlife.

A 1981 Gallup Poll reported that 8 million (1 in 19) Americans had experienced the near-death phenomenon (Peay, 1991). If one were to apply this ratio to today's population there would be approximately 13 million people in the United States with the near-death experiences (NDE). Barbara Walker (1989) claims that one adult in five within the United States has undergone a near-death experience. It is not surprising that scholars have organized the International Association for Near-Death Studies (IANDS) that publishes the Journal of Near-Death Studies.

The description in "Life after Life" (page 193), developed by Raymond Moody, is a composite of the many accounts by individuals who have survived the experience of being near death or being declared clinically dead. This ideal model was constructed by interviewing more than 150 people who had had these experiences. Moody reports, and other scientists support (Noyes and Kletti, 1977; Rawlings, 1978; Ring, 1980, Flynn, 1986; Johnson, 1990), the similarity of most of these "life after death" accounts where nine traits (Perry, 1988) define the near-death experience (even though it is rare for anyone to experience all nine). According to Moody (cited by Perry, 1988), at least one of the following nine symptoms is enough to constitute a near-death experience.

1. *A sense of being dead.* At first many people don't realize that the experience they are having has anything to do with being near death. They find themselves floating above their body and feeling confused. They wonder, " How can I be up here, looking at myself down there?"

2. *Peace and painlessness.* An illness or accident is frequently accompanied by intense pain, but suddenly during a near-death experience the pain vanishes. According to research by psychologist Kenneth Ring, 60 percent of people who have had a near-death experience report peace and painlessness.

3. *Out-of-body experience.* Frequently people feel themselves rising up and viewing their own bodies below. Most say they are not simply a point of consciousness but seem to be in some kind of body. Ring says 37 percent have out-of-body experiences.

4. *The tunnel experience.* This generally occurs after an out-of-body experience. For many a portal or tunnel opens and they are propelled into darkness. Some hear a "whoosh" as they go into the tunnel, or they hear an electric vibration or humming sound. The descriptions are many, but the sense of heading toward an intense light is common to almost all tunnel experiences. Twenty-three percent of Ring's subjects reported entering darkness, which some described as entering a tunnel.

5. *People of light.* Once people pass through the tunnel, they usually meet beings of intense light which permeates everything as it fills them with feelings of love. As one person said, "I could describe this as 'light' or 'love' and it would mean the same thing." They frequently meet up with friends and relatives who have died, though the glowing beings can't always be identified. In Ring's research, 16 percent saw the light.

6. *Being of Light.* After meeting several beings of light, there is usually a meeting with a Supreme Being of Light. To some this is God or Allah, to others simply a holy presence. Most want to stay with him forever.

7. *The life review.* The Being of Light frequently takes the person on a life review, during which life is viewed from a third-person perspective, almost as though watching a movie. An important difference from cinema, however, is that the person not only sees every action but also its effect on people in his or her life. The Being of Light helps put the events on life in perspective.

8. *Rising rapidly into the heavens.* Some people report a "floating experience," in which they rise rapidly into the heavens, seeing the universe from a perspective reserved for satellites and astronauts.

9. *Reluctance to return.* Many find their unearthly surroundings so pleasant they don't want to return. Some even express anger at their doctors for bringing them back.

As we consider the near-death experience, the following three questions become relevant as we contemplate the relationship between these experiences and other material presented in this chapter.

LIFE AFTER LIFE

Raymond A. Moody, Jr.

A man is dying and, as he reaches the point of greatest physical distress, he hears himself pronounced dead by his doctor. He begins to hear an uncomfortable noise, a loud ringing or buzzing, and at the same time feels himself moving very rapidly through a long dark tunnel. After this he suddenly finds himself outside of his own physical body, but still in the immediate physical environment, and he sees his own body from a distance, as though he is a spectator. He watches the resuscitation attempt from his unusual vantage point and is in a state of emotional upheaval.

After a while, he collects himself and becomes more accustomed to his body with very different powers from the physical body he has left behind. Soon other things begin to happen. Others come to meet and to help him. He glimpses the spirits of relatives and friends who have already died, and a loving, warm spirit of a kind he has never encountered before—a being of light—appears before him. This being asks him a question, nonverbally, to make him evaluate his life and helps him along by showing him a panoramic, instantaneous playback of the major events of his life. At some point he finds himself approaching some sort of barrier or border, apparently representing the limit between earthly life and the next life. Yet, he finds that he must go back to earth, that the time for his death has not yet come. At this point he resists, for by now he is taken up with his experiences in the afterlife and does not want to return. He is overwhelmed by intense feelings of joy, love, and peace. Despite his attitude, though, he somehow reunites with his physical body and lives.

Later he tries to tell others, but he has trouble doing so. In the first place, he can find no human words adequate to describe these unearthly episodes. He also finds that others scoff, so he stops telling other people. Still, the experience affects his life profoundly, especially his views about death and its relationship to life.

Life after Life: The Investigation of a Phenomenon—Survival of Bodily Death. Reprinted by permission of LAL, Inc.

1. Are NDEs real, and what do they tell us about the dying process and/or being dead?
2. Can afterlife beliefs be empirically supported by these NDE accounts?
3. How do religious beliefs affect the content of near-death or clinical death experiences?

To all of our questions, we must temper our responses by saying that if not real, these experiences are **very** real to those who have experienced them. Not unlike being in love, NDE phenomena are extremely subjective and do not lend themselves to verification by others. Research by Stevenson, Cook, and McClean-Rice (1989) has discovered that of those claiming the near-death experience only 45 percent were judged by medical experts to have had serious, life-threatening illnesses or injuries, the rest were judged to have had no life-threatening condition. It

While on the operating table my heart stopped beating and I died. At that moment, Merv, I learned that there was a life after life and a chance for a best selling book based on this discovery, and a hit movie based on the book, and TV guest shots to plug the movie, and commercials generated by TV appearances and...

TV GUIDE, NOVEMBER 11, 1978. USED BY PERMISSION OF HENRY MARTIN.

is difficult to doubt that the individual has experienced *something*; however, we are unable to prove, or disprove, that the person has died. All we can say scientifically is that the person claims to have had the experience of "being dead."

Returning to our analogy of being in love, all that can be known is that the person says that he or she is in love. Whether or not the person really is cannot be determined empirically. From the perspective of the individual, it does not really matter, because a situation, which has been defined as real, will have very real behavioral consequences.

Barbara Walker claims that many NDE experients have post-NDE depression due to the fact that health-care providers and family members often deny the validity of the NDE experience. It is not uncommon for the NDE experient to tell a nurse or psychiatrist about their near-death event, only to find that they are told that they were hallucinating (Walker, 1989:64). Ring (cited by Walker, 1989:64) has noted a considerable number of divorces resulting from a spouse's inability to relate to the NDE.

If we try to determine the validity of a belief in an afterlife, we are confronted with similar problems as those encountered in the near-death experience. What can science say about beliefs in the afterlife? Scientifically, afterlife beliefs cannot be proved, or disproved, with NDE evidence. **Science** is based upon the principle of **intersubjectivity.** This means that independent observers, with different subjective orientations, must agree that something is "true" based upon their separate investigations. Unfortunately, the opportunity to experience the afterlife (and return) is not uniformly available to all observers. Research by Tillman Rodabough (1985) gives many metaphysical, physiological, and social psychological alternative explanations to account for the near-death experience. Therefore, while those who have had these experiences may feel rationally justified in their beliefs, the evidence they use is not scientifically based. Science, at this point, can neither verify, nor falsify afterlife beliefs.

In responding to our last question concerning the effects of religious beliefs on the content of near-death or clinical death experiences, there is some scientific evidence that can provide limited answers. According to Moody (1975) and Canning (1965), the content of afterlife experiences is largely a function of the religious background, training, and beliefs of the individuals involved. Only Roman Catholics see the Virgin Mary and the host of Catholic saints, while encounters with Joseph Smith are reserved for Mormon believers. Like dreams, continuity exists between experiences in "this world" and experiences in the "afterlife." For example, personages in the afterlife are dressed in an attire that would conform to the individual's cultural customs and beliefs. Also, relatives appear to be at the same age as they were when they were last seen. In fact, there is so much continuity between this world and the "other world" that persons with afterlife experiences report few, if any surprises. In response to this evidence, Kathy Charmaz (1980) raises the following question: Is the consciousness reported in these near-death experiences a *reflection* of a shared myth or *evidence* for it?

What we do know is that most NDE experients have profound affects upon their lives following the encounter. According to P. M. Atwater (Johnson, 1990), 65 percent of NDE experients make significant changes in their lives and 10 percent make radical changes. According to Skip Johnson (1990) people with a near-death experience have the following aftereffects as a result of the phenomenon.

Loss of fear of death. People report they no longer fear the obliteration of consciousness of self.

Sense of the importance of love. A near-death experience can radically change peoples' value structure. They see the importance of brotherly [sic] love.

Sense of cosmic connection. Feeling that everything in the universe is connected. Many have a new-found respect for nature and the world around them.

An appreciation of learning. People gain a newfound respect for knowledge, but not self-gain. Many often will embark on new careers or take up serious courses of study.

A new feeling of control. People feel they have more responsibility for the course of their lives.

A sense of urgency. Some realize the shortness and fragility of their lives.

Better developed spiritual side. This leads to spiritual curiosity and abandoning of religious doctrine purely for sake of doctrine.

Reduction in worries. Some people feel more in control of life's stresses and are able to be more forgiving and patient.

Re-entry syndrome. Some difficulty in adjusting to normal life, especially for those who undergo intensive changes in values that disrupt their former lifestyle. Some people report developing psychic abilities that can be scary to them and/or family and friends.

Finally, there is evidence that individuals (even attempted suicides) do not try to bring about an end to their lives in order to return to the "life beyond." In fact, most individuals find new reasons for living as a result of these experiences (Flynn, 1986).

CONCLUSION

Religion is a system of beliefs and practices related to the sacred—that which is considered to be of ultimate significance. The cultural practice of religion continues because it meets basic social needs of individuals within a given society. A major function of religion, in this regard, is to explain the unexplainable.

For most "primitive," or less complex societies, events are explained by a supernatural rather than rational or empirical means. Thus, an eclipse of the sun or moon was said to be a sign that the gods had a message for humankind. These supernatural explanations were needed, in part, because there were no competing rational or scientific explanations. Technologically and scientifically advanced societies tend to be less dependent upon supernatural explanations. Yet such explanations are still important, especially when scientific explanations are incomplete. It is not uncommon to hear a physician say, "Medical science is unable to cure this patient; it's now in God's hands." Or, a physician might say, "It's a miracle that the patient survived this illness; I can't explain the recovery." Thus, one might suggest that religion takes over where science and rationality leave off. We depend less on religious or supernatural explanations than nonliterate societies, but nonetheless rely on them when knowledge is incomplete.

Religion plays a significant role in societies by helping individuals cope with extraordinary events—especially death. Not only does religion help restore the normative order challenged by death, but strong religious commitments can enable individuals to cope better with their own dying and the deaths of their loved ones. For others, strong commitments to a temporal orientation may fulfill many of the functions provided by a religious world view.

SUMMARY

1. Religion helps individuals, when the order of everyday life is challenged, by providing answers to problems of uncertainty, powerlessness, and scarcity created by death.

2. Religious systems provide a means to reestablish the social order challenged by death.

3. When one encounters death, the anxiety experienced is basically socially ascribed.

4. Religion provides individuals with solace when they attempt to cope with death.

5. Temporal interpretations of death provide a means for protecting the social order by emphasizing the empirical, natural, and "this worldly" view of death.

6. Symbolic immortality is evidenced by offspring carrying on the family name, by donating body organs, and by having accomplishments or achievements (positive and negative) remembered by others.

7. Near-death or afterlife experiences are influenced by the individual's religious background, cultural beliefs, and prior social experiences.

8. The strength of one's religious commitment is a significant variable in explaining the relationship between religion and the fear of death.

Discussion Questions

1. How does religion function to provide a restoration of the order challenged by the event of death?
2. What is the relationship between religious commitment and death fear?
3. Explain the following statement: "Religion afflicts the comforted and comforts the afflicted."
4. With regard to death anxiety, why does the believer, not the belief, bring peace?
5. How can symbolic immortality and temporal interpretations of death provide a source of anxiety reduction for those who face death?
6. How can organ donations provide symbolic immortality for donors and their loved ones?
7. Do accounts of near-death experiences provide empirical evidence for afterlife beliefs? Why or why not?
8. What are the similarities and differences in Jewish, Christian, Islamic, Hindu, and Buddhist beliefs about death and funeral practices?

Glossary

Anomie: A condition characterized by the relative absence or confusion of values within a group or society.

Curvilinear: Referring to a type of nonlinear relationship between two variables where at a certain point, associated with the increasing values in the independent variable, the relationship with the dependent variable changes. A scattergram graph of this relationship will either look like a U or an inverted U.

Death Anxiety: A learned emotional response to death-related phenomena that is characterized by extreme apprehension. In this chapter, death anxiety is used synonymously with death fear.

Dysfunctional: Referring to any consequence of a social system that is judged to be a disturbance to the adjustment, stability, or integration of the group or the members of that group.

Etiology: The study of causal relationships that attempts to delineate those factors responsible for a given occurrence.

Intersubjectivity: A property of science whereby two or more scientists, studying the same phenomenon, can reach the same conclusion.

Levirate Marriage: An institution typified by the Hebrew requirement that a relative of the deceased husband must have sexual intercourse with his kinsman's widow in order to provide a male heir.

Marginal Situations: Unusual events or social circumstances that do not occur in normal patterns of social interaction.

Religion: A system of beliefs and practices related to the sacred, the supernatural, and/or a set of values to which the individual is very committed.

Religiosity: The extent of interest, commitment, or participation in religious values, beliefs, and activities.

Rituals: A set of culturally prescribed actions or behaviors.

Science: A body of knowledge based upon sensory evidence or empirical observations.

Symbolic Immortality: The ascription of immortality to the individual by perpetuating the meaning of the person (the self).

Temporal: Referring to a "here and now" or "this worldly" orientation that does not take into account the afterlife or a supernatural existence.

REFERENCES

Ayer, Margaret. 1964. *Made in Thailand.* New York: Knopf.

Berger, Peter L. 1969. *Sacred Canopy: Elements of a Sociological Theory of Religion.* New York: Doubleday.

Canning, Ray R. 1965. "Mormon Return-from-the-Dead Stories: Fact or Folklore?" *Utah Academy Proceedings, 42,* I.

Carse, J. 1981. "Death." In *Abingdon Dictionary of Living Religions,* Keith Crim, Roger A. Bullard, and Larry D. Shinn (Eds.). Nashville: Abingdon Press.

Charmaz, Kathy. 1980. *The Social Reality of Death.* Reading, MA: Addison-Wesley.

Durkheim, Emile. 1915. *Elementary Forms of Religious Life.* New York: George Allen and Unwin.

Eickelman, Dale F. 1987. "Rites of Passage: Muslim Rites." In *The Encyclopedia of Religion,* 12th ed., Mircea Eliade (Ed.). New York: Macmillan.

Faulkner, Joseph, and Gordon F. DeJong. 1966. "Religiosity in 5-D: An Empirical Analysis." *Social Forces,* 45:246–254.

Flynn, Charles P. 1986. *After the Beyond: Human Transformation and the Near-Death Experience.* Englewood Cliffs, NJ.: Prentice-Hall.

Glock, Charles, and Rodney Stark. 1966. *Christian Beliefs and Anti-Semitism.* New York: Harper and Row.

Habenstein, Robert W., and William M. Lamers. 1974. *Funeral Customs the World Over.* Milwaukee: Bulfin Printers.

The Holy Bible. 1962. Revised Standard Version. New York: Oxford University Press.

Homans, George C. 1965. "Anxiety and Ritual: The Theories of Malinowski and Radcliffe-Brown." In *Reader in Comparative Religion: An Anthropological Approach,* W. A. Lessa and E. Z. Vogt (Eds.). New York: Harper and Row.

Johnson, Skip. 1990. "Near-Death Experiences Almost Always Change Lives." *News and Courier/The Evening Post,* Charleston, SC, August 26, p. 13-I.

Kavanaugh, Robert E. 1972. *Facing Death.* Baltimore: Penguin Books.

Knobel, Peter S. 1987. "Rites of Passage: Jewish Rites." In *The Encyclopedia of Religion,* 12th ed., Mircea Eliade (Ed.). New York: Macmillan.

Leming, Michael R. 1979–1980. "Religion and Death: A Test of Homans's Thesis." *Omega,* 10 (4):347–364.

Lewis, C. S. 1961. *A Grief Observed.* London: Faber and Faber.

Lifton, Robert, and E. Olson. 1974. *Living and Dying.* New York: Praeger.

Long, J. Bruce. 1987. "Underworld." In *The Encyclopedia of Religion,* 12th ed., Mircea Eliade (Ed.). New York: Macmillan.

Malinowski, Bronislaw. 1965. "The Role of Magic and Religion." In *Reader in Comparative Religion: An Anthropological Approach,* W. A. Lessa and E. Z. Vogt (Eds.). New York: Harper and Row.

McBrien, Richard P. 1987. "Roman Catholicism." In *The Encyclopedia of Religion,* 12th ed., Mircea Eliade (Ed.), New York: Macmillan.

Moody, Raymond A., Jr. 1975. *Life after Life: The Investigation of a Phenomenon—Survival of Bodily Death.* Boston: G. K. Hall.

Noyes, Russell, Jr., and Ray Kletti. 1977. "Panoramic Memory." *Omega,* 8:181–193.

O'Dea, Thomas. 1966. *The Sociology of Religion.* Englewood Cliffs, NJ: Prentice-Hall.

Pardue, Peter. 1968. "Buddhism." In *International Encyclopedia of the Social Sciences,* 2nd ed., New York: Macmillan, pp. 165–184.

Peay, Pythia. 1991. "Back From the Grave." *Utne Reader,* (September–October):72–73.

Perry, Paul. 1988. "Brushes with Death." *Psychology Today,* 22 (September):14–17.

Radcliffe-Brown, A. R. 1965. "Taboo." In *Reader in Comparative Religion: An Anthropological Approach,* W. A. Lessa and E. Z. Vogt (Eds.). New York: Harper and Row.

Rahman, Fazlur. 1987. *Health and Medicine in the Islamic Tradition.* New York: Crossroad Press.

Rawlings, Maurice. 1978. *Beyond Death's Door.* Nashville: Thomas Nelson.

Ring, Kenneth. 1980. *Life at Death: A Scientific Investigation of the Near-Death Experience.* New York: Coward, McCann and Geoghegan.

Rodabough, Tillman. 1985. "Near-Death Experiences: An Examination of the Supporting Data and Alternative Explanations." *Death Studies,* 9:95–113.

Srinivas, M. N., and A. M. Shah. 1968. "Hinduism." In *International Encyclopedia of the Social Sciences,* Volume 6. New York: Macmillan, pp. 358–366.

Stevenson, Ian, Emily Williams Cook, and Nicholas McClean-Rice. 1989. "Are Persons Reporting 'Near-Death Experiences' Really Near Death? A Study of Medical Records." *Omega,* 20(4):45–54.

Vernon, Glenn M. 1970. *Sociology of Death: An Analysis of Death-Related Behavior.* New York: Ronald Press.

Walker, Barbara A. 1989. "Health Care Professionals and the Near-Death Experience." *Death Studies,* 13:63–71.

SUGGESTED READINGS

Berger, Peter L. 1969. *Sacred Canopy: Elements of a Sociological Theory of Religion.* New York: Doubleday. *Excellent treatment of the role of religious world views as they relate to life crises. Death is discussed as the ultimate marginal situation to normal social functioning that calls forth religious meaning systems.*

Eliade, Mircea. 1987. *The Encyclopedia of Religion.* New York: Macmillan. *Tremendous academic resource on religious rites, beliefs, and traditions. This reference tool is written from an interdisciplinary perspective by international scholars of religion.*

Flynn, Charles P. 1986. *After the Beyond: Human Transformation and the Near-Death Experience.* Englewood Cliffs, NJ: Prentice-Hall. / Rodabough, Tillman. 1985. "Near-Death Experiences: An Examination of the Supporting Data and Alternative Explanations." *Death Studies,* 9:95–113. / Walker, Barbara A. 1989. "Health Care Professionals and the Near-Death Experience." *Death Studies,* 13:63–71. *A book and two articles that provide a background for dealing with persons who claim to have had the near-death experience.*

Homans, George C. 1965. "Anxiety and Ritual: The Theories of Malinowski and Radcliffe-Brown." In *Reader in Comparative Religion: An Anthropological Approach,* W. A. Lessa and E. Z. Vogt (Eds.). New York: Harper and Row, pp. 83–88. / Leming, Michael R. 1979–1980. "Religion and Death: A Test of Homans' Thesis." *Omega,* 10(4), 347–364. *Two articles that review the theoretical and empirical evidence regarding the relation between religion and death anxiety.*

Kavanaugh, Robert E. 1972. *Facing Death.* Baltimore: Penguin Books. *A former Roman Catholic priest, Kavanaugh reflects on his experiences with death in the context of his religious background. He discusses the role of religion in the adjustment process to dying and death.*

Moody, Raymond A., Jr. 1975. *Life after Life: The Investigation of a Phenomenon—Survival of Bodily Death.* Boston: G. K. Hall. / Ring, Kenneth. 1980. *Life at Death: A Scientific Investigation of the Near-Death Experience.* New York: Coward, McCann and Geoghegan. *Two books that provide an understanding of the Near Death Experience (NDE).*

Part Three
Understanding
the Dying Process

6

The Dying
Process

I'm not afraid of dying. I just don't want to be there when it happens.

Woody Allen

OF ALL EVENTS in life, dying can be the most stressful. As discussed in Chapter 1, people tend to fear the process of dying more than the event of death. Many factors will contribute to and alleviate stress related to the dying process. Primarily, we are concerned with the physical and social factors.

Among other things, dying is a process that happens to the physical body of the individual. Although the determination of the timing of death is problematic, there is a qualitative difference between a live and a dead human being. For the most part, the cause of death is ultimately attributed to physiological factors. However, the biological aspect of dying means less to us than the meaning we place upon the events that take place during the dying process.

Death Meanings and Their Effects Upon the Dying Process

The meaning of our dying will depend to a great extent upon the social context in which the dying takes place. As discussed in Chapter 2, meanings are the basic component of human behavior because individuals respond to the meanings of phenomena rather than to the phenomena themselves. Meanings are both socially created and socially perpetuated. (For further discussion of death meanings see Leming, Vernon, and Gray, 1977.)

The major types of meanings to which individuals respond in death-related situations are the following: time meanings, space meanings, norm and role meanings, value meanings, object and self meanings, and social situation meanings (Vernon, 1972). We will now look at each of these types of meanings and their effects upon the dying process.

Time Meanings

As anthropologist Colin Turnbull told the author, "Americans want to live forever. If you ask someone how long they wish to live, they will probably say somewhere in the upper 90s because they do not suspect they will reach 100. But if they reach 100, then they will aim for 101, 102, etc." Turnbull says African groups know when it is time to die, and they accept this. Perhaps Richard Pryor summed it up well when he said, "Even if I live for 100 years, I'll be dead a lot longer."

In thinking about the dying process, the first thing that comes to our awareness is the concept of time. We are confronted with the fact that time, for the terminal patient, is running out. Yet when does the dying process begin? Are we not all dying, with some reaching the state of being dead before others? From the moment of our births, we are approaching the end of our lives. We assume that terminal patients will experience death before other individuals, but this is not always the case.

GUEST LECTURER

Joan M. Boyle

I invited to class a woman who had been diagnosed as a terminal cancer patient. Deeply impressed by the visitor's positive outlook on the time left to her, one student on the following day noted, "When I came into the session I expected to meet someone who was dying. Instead, I realize that woman is more alive than I am. The discussion wasn't about dying at all, it was about living."

"Dialectic on Dying." In *The Role of the Volunteer in the Care of the Terminal Patient and the Family,* M. M. Newell et al. (Eds.). New York: The Foundation of Thanatology/Arno Press, 1981, pp. 182–189.

Since it is possible to diagnose a disease from which most people die, we can assume that patients with these diseases are "more terminal" than individuals without them. The terminal patient is very much concerned with the time dimension of his or her physical existence. Many surveys (see Glaser and Strauss, 1965) have demonstrated that as many as 80 percent of patients want to be told if their illness is terminal. However, physicians are not always prepared to tell their patients of a terminal diagnosis.

With more emphasis on consumer rights today, physicians are more likely to tell the patient of his or her diagnosis than was the case in the early 1960s. In a 1961 survey of physicians (Oken, 1961), only 10 percent favored telling a cancer patient his/her diagnosis, while in the 1980s telling the patient had become a widespread tendency (Klenow and Youngs, 1987). This change could reflect the American Medical Association's shift in policy in 1980 of encouraging physicians to tell the patient his/her prognosis. Previously, the AMA had left the decision to tell to the discretion of the physician.

A recent study by Dickinson and Tournier (1993a) of physicians' attitudes toward terminally ill patients revealed more of an openness toward informing the patient of his/her prognosis after 10 years of practicing medicine than soon after graduation from medical school. A study by Seale (1991) in England suggests a general preference for more openness between physicians, dying patients, and their families about illness and death. This openness should be tempered by two considerations. Bad news needs to be broken slowly in a context of support, and not everyone wishes to know all.

Though many physicians in the past have not favored telling their patients, Elisabeth Kübler-Ross (1969) claims that it is not a question of whether the patient should be told, but of how the patient is told. Should patients be told the amount of time they have left? Specifying an amount of time dispels hope and serves no more function than telling the patient that the condition is very serious and life-threatening, advises Kübler-Ross. If the patient presses for time specificity, a range of time should be given such as: "Sixty percent of the patients with your disease live as long as 3 to 5 years." This statement provides hope without deluding the patient. Also, it is honest. Medical science cannot say with any certainty that a

When a patient is told that the disease is terminal, the information must be communicated in a manner that is honest, but that does not rob the patient of a sense of hopefulness.

person will live 1 year—some die sooner and others live longer (some even outlive the physician!).

Space Meanings

Even when the patient has not been told of a terminal condition, he or she will eventually become aware of it. Many times factors related to social space will give the patient clues that the condition is terminal. As E. P. Seravalli (1988:1729) notes, "The dying usually come to know when the end is near by observing themselves and the people around them." Within the hospital, there are areas where the very ill are treated. When one is placed in the intensive care unit or on an oncology ward, it becomes obvious that all is not well and that death is a real possibility. When moved from a double room to a single-patient room, 17-year-old Tom Nelson, who was dying of cancer (as seen on CBS' "Living With Death"), said, "Isn't this what they do to you when you are about to die?"

Confinement to a health care institution conveys a tremendous amount of meaning to the patient. For the most part, the patient is alone. Through spatial meanings the individual is "informed" that he or she is removed from those things that give life meaning and purpose—family, friends, and job. For the terminally ill patient this is the first stage of **societal disengagement**—the process by which society withdraws from, or no longer seeks, the individual's efforts.

The following statement (Hale, 1971) demonstrates the significance of space when applied to the dying patient:

As for the patient himself, he faces his life's ultimate crisis in a foreign place—the hospital. Usually, he dies alone, not in the presence of anyone who cares. Often the family is allowed to visit even the dying only during the hours set by the hospital. And since hospital visits usually lack privacy, they are of little comfort either to the patient or to the relatives who are entering the period of "anticipatory grief." There is little room or opportunity for sharing that most poignant moment of a lifetime—death! There is little opportunity for dignity in those settings.

Though many institutional settings have liberalized their visitation policies somewhat since the early 1970s, unfortunately the above statements by Hale still basically hold.

Within any health care setting, the patient's confinement serves to diminish his or her social and personal power. According to Rodney Coe (1970), three processes occur within the institution to accomplish this—"stripping," control of resources, and restrictions on mobility. The process of *stripping* takes place when the patient is issued a hospital gown and stripped of any valuables for safekeeping. In doing this the patient's identity is also stripped. Most factors that differentiate patients with regard to status in the larger society are taken from the patient and create the primary status of a patient—all patients look alike. According to Coe (1970:300), "Every distinctly personalizing symbol, material or otherwise, is taken away, thus reducing the patient to the status of just one of many." Perhaps this helps to explain why physicians are known to be such bad patients—they are forced to relinquish their physician status when they are admitted to the hospital.

The second process is the *control of resources*. When the patient is denied access to medical records and important information about the events of the hospital, personal power is greatly diminished. Personal power is the ability to make decisions that determine the direction of one's own life. Without all the information concerning one's situation and the place of one's confinement, it may not be possible to make important decisions. One method used by hospitals in controlling resources is to deny all patients and their families access to medical charts and records—"ignorance is bliss" mentality.

The third process is the *restriction on mobility*. Not being able to leave one's room or bed further reduces the patient's personal power. The patient is put in a position of dependency upon others. Confinement of this type greatly affects the patient's autonomy. It also makes it possible for others to withdraw from the patient.

Social space is very important in the process of patient disengagement. This disengagement can be accomplished by two methods—the patient can withdraw from others, and others can withdraw from the patient. If the patient is debilitated by illness, he may not have energy enough to continue normal patterns of social interaction. The loss of physical attractiveness can also cause the patient to withdraw. Some patients, knowing that their condition is terminal, may disengage as a coping strategy to avoid having to see all that their death will take from them. They may disengage as a sign of their acceptance of social death—"I'm as good as dead" (anticipatory death).

When significant others withdraw from the patient, patient disengagement will take place. In this situation the process of disengagement is something beyond the patient's control. Family members and friends can refrain from visiting the patient as a sign of their acceptance of social death. The terminal label can stigmatize the patient, and others may treat the individual differently.

Orville Kelly, founder of "Make Each Day Count" (a support group for persons with cancer), tells the story of being invited by a friend to dinner. The table was set with the finest china and silverware—with one exception. His place setting consisted of a paper plate and plastic fork, spoon, and knife. He was the guest with cancer!

Randall Wagner, an active volunteer with the American Cancer Society, recalls a situation at a high school football game when his leukemia was in a state of remission. A friend had a thermos of hot chocolate, but had only two cups. The first cup was given to Randall. After he had finished, he returned the cup to be filled for someone else. Nobody would drink out of Randall's cup, however. He was told to "just keep it."

Many individuals are afraid of "catching" cancer. One does not "catch" cancer. Likewise, many are afraid to be physically near someone with AIDS for fear of acquiring the disease. Since AIDS is primarily passed through sexual intercourse, intravenous drug needles, blood transfusions, and from the mother to the fetus/embryo, one is not going to acquire AIDS by sitting next to someone or physically being in the room with an AIDS victim. Since many do not know how to relate to persons with cancer or AIDS or to the terminally ill in general, they withdraw as a method of coping with their inadequacy.

Norm and Role Meanings

Norms are defined as plans of action or expected behavior patterns felt to be appropriate for a particular situation. **Roles** are plans of action or expected behavior patterns specifying what should be done by persons who occupy particular social positions. Applied to the death-related behavior of the dying patient, norm definitions would involve the general expectation that the dying patient should be brave and accept the fact that life will soon end. The patient is not supposed to cry or become verbal in regard to feelings about his or her death. Nurses often sanction such behavior by giving less attention to patients who deviate from this norm. Elisabeth Kübler-Ross (1969:56–57) gives the following example of one such deviant:

The patient would stand in front of the nurses' desk and demand attention for herself and other terminally ill patients, which the nurses resented as interference and inappropriate behavior. Since she was quite sick, they did not confront her with her unacceptable behavior, but expressed their resentment by making shorter visits to her room, by avoiding contact, and by the briefness of their encounters.

Role meanings differ from norm meanings in that they specify, in a detailed fashion, what behavior is expected for persons who occupy specific social positions. For example, if a wife/mother who is a principal provider in the family is dying, it is expected that she do all that she can before death to provide for the financial needs of her family. It would probably be expected that she make arrangements for her funeral, insure that her bills are paid, finalize her will, and establish a trust fund for her children.

One of the important aspects of norm and role meanings is their relationship to the process of societal disengagement where society withdraws from the individual (Atchley, 1977). The individual can also withdraw from societal participation and choose not to perform the roles he or she performed before the terminal diagnosis. This type of disengagement goes beyond withdrawing from interaction patterns with others and refers to a withdrawal from the social structure (such as quitting one's job and taking a trip around the world).

Role disengagement has many consequences for the patient and his or her family members. N. J. Gaspard (1970:78) notes the following about a family with traditional gender roles:

> If the father is ill, the mother must generally become the breadwinner, and children who are able often must take over household tasks sooner than they otherwise might. Each person in such a situation may feel both guilt and resentment at such a change whereby they can no longer adequately fulfill the expectations they have had of themselves. Conversely, if the mother is ill, household help may be hired, and problems may arise with regard to the mother's maintaining, in so far as is possible, her self-image in relation to caring for her family.

In addition to the disengagement process, patients are expected to acquire the **sick role** (Parsons, 1951). They are expected to want to get better and to want to seek more treatment even though everyone realizes that such treatment only prolongs death and not life. This role disengagement can create conflict within the family, especially when the patient has accepted his or her death (and even longs for it), while family members are unwilling to let the patient go. As Kübler-Ross (1969) documents, families many times cannot comprehend that a patient reaches a point when death comes as a great relief, and that patients die easier if they are allowed and helped to detach themselves slowly from all the responsibilities and meaningful relationships in their lives. Oftentimes, we the survivors are the stumbling blocks for dying persons. We do not want the dying person to die, thus we will not "let go" and allow her/him to say goodbye and break away.

Value Meanings

Values, like all other meaning systems, are socially created. They are not inherent in any phenomena, but they are applied by humans to the phenomena. Death per se is neither good nor evil. Humans do ascribe value, however, to the different types of deaths. Each of these value meanings has important behavioral consequences.

Most people in our society view death as being intrinsically evil and, therefore, something to fear. We tend to see death as an intruder—the spoiler of our best plans. Thus, in the past, the medical profession has attempted to delay death in favor of life. People are kept on machines to prolong life, even if death is inevitable. We assume that people wishing to die are mentally ill or irrational because death is seen as something to be avoided. Yet the terminally ill eventually come to view death as a great blessing, when they have finally accepted the fact that they are going to die. This is possible because humans are able to create hierarchies of values where value meanings take on relative meanings. To the terminally ill patient, dignity is more highly valued than is life with pain, indignity, and suffering. Consequently, death may be ascribed positive value for the dying patient who has accepted the inevitability of his or her death.

Recent research (Goleman, 1989) shows that confronting individuals with the fact that they will die makes them cling tenaciously to their deepest moral values. They tend to become more moralistic and judgmental. They are harsher toward those who violate their moral standards and kinder toward those who uphold them. Open-minded persons, however, even become more tolerant of those whose values differ from theirs. Researchers (Goleman, 1989) note that these findings give the fear of death a central role in psychological life and that a culture's model of "the good life" and its moral codes are all intended to protect people from the terror of death. Cultures prescribe what an individual must do to lead a "good life," and if one leads a "good life," he/she will be protected from tragic fate at death.

Object and Self Meanings

The previous discussion focused on meanings that have been applied to an object—the dying patient. From a biological perspective the person is a living organism—a physical object. From a social-psychological perspective, the patient is a social object—a self.

Many patients defined as having a terminal condition begin to view themselves as being "as good as dead." As discussed in Chapter 4, perhaps the dying person

Dying with dignity or self-respect does not always happen. Positive self-meanings can be created and sustained with the help of others. These others, who become the social audience for dying-related behaviors of the patient, include family, physicians, clergy, nurses, peers, or even strangers walking down the hall of the hospital. How the patient is treated by these people reveals something about the patient.

has reached Erik Erikson's eighth stage of the life cycle—senescence. This feeling of integrity that one's life has meaning and purpose and that having lived made a difference is a final stage of life from which the person is ready to break away. Life is over, and the dying patient is accepting of that. The patient has accepted the terminal label, applied it to his understanding of who he is, and experienced anticipatory death. Families tend to see their loved ones as being in bereavement. This symbolic definition of the patient is reinforced by the role disengagement process, the spatial isolation of the dying patient, and the terminal label placed upon the patient by the physician and other medical personnel. The patient seems to take on a status somewhere between the living and the dead.

The dying person needs to feel that he/she has not lost meaning for significant others. With death close, dying patients may still want to express what they experience and to convey their fantasies about death (Seravalli, 1988). The presence of the physician in this last phase of life may be crucial for a peaceful death. Such a presence may allow the patient not only to die with self-respect but also to feel less lonely. Arthur Frank (1991:4), who himself had two serious illnesses by the age of 40, believes that too many ill individuals are deprived of conversation. He notes that too many believe they cannot talk about their illness—they simply repeat what they know from the medical staff. When ill persons try to talk in medical language, they deny themselves the drama of their personal experience. Frank notes that sick persons need to talk about their hopes and fears and the prospect of death. But because such talk embarrasses us, we do not have practice with it, and lacking practice, we find such talk difficult.

DON'T ABANDON THE PATIENT

When I say I feel as comfortable with a dying patient as with any other, and that I do not find treating a dying patient unpleasant, I do not mean that I am anaesthetized to the fact that they are dying, and do not have feelings about the patient which are different from my feelings about a patient whom I know will get well. Anaesthesia of feeling is the method which we physicians employ initially in dealing with the pain—ours and theirs—involved in treating a dying patient. But this passes, and when one accepts the patient as part of life, and not someone who is no longer a real part of the world (or a frightening part of the world), then caring for the dying patient becomes (though often sad) neither unpleasant nor something one wishes to avoid. To abandon the dying patient is the worst thing that can be done—both for the patient and the doctor.

A physician's comment from a survey of 1093 physicians by Dickinson and Pearson, 1976.

Kübler-Ross (1969:116) states that in the end the terminally ill have a need to detach themselves from the living to make dying easier.

She asked to be allowed to die in peace, wished to be left alone—even asked for less involvement on the part of her husband. She said that the only reason that kept her still alive was her husband's inability to accept the fact that she had to die. She was angry at him for not facing it and for so desperately clinging on to something that she was willing and ready to give up. I translated to her that she wished to detach herself from this world, and she nodded gratefully as I left her alone.

When an individual's condition has been defined by self and others as terminal, all other self-meanings take on less importance. While a given patient may be an attorney, a Democrat, mother, wife, or Presbyterian, she tends to think of herself primarily as a terminal patient. The terminal label becomes her **master status** because it dominates all other status indicators. Consequently, most of the symbolic meanings previously discussed become incorporated into the individual's self-meaning.

Acquiring the terminal label as part of the self-definition is not an easy task for the individual. In her best-selling book *On Death and Dying* (1969), Elisabeth Kübler-Ross delineated the following five stages patients go through in accepting their terminal self meaning: denial, anger, bargaining, depression, and acceptance.

In the first stage, *denial,* the patient attempts to deny that his or her condition is fatal. This is a period of shock and disbelief. The patient wants to believe that a mistake has been made (for example, the physician must have read the wrong X-ray). One may seek additional medical advice, hoping the terminal diagnosis will be proven false. When the diagnosis is verified, the patient may often retreat into self-imposed isolation.

The second stage, *anger,* is a natural reaction for most patients. The patient may vent anger at a number of individuals—at the physician for not doing enough, at relatives for outliving the patient, at other patients for not having a terminal condition, at God for allowing the patient to die. In other words, a scapegoat is sought—the patient seeks someone or something on which the blame can be placed.

When one has incorporated the terminal label into self meaning, an attempt to bargain for a little more time may result. This third stage, *bargaining,* may include promises to God in exchange for an extension of life, followed by the wish for a few days without pain or physical discomfort. For example, in the movie *The End,* Burt Reynolds decides to commit suicide by drowning. He swims far out into the ocean, but begins to change his mind about wanting to die. He bargains with God and prays to God to make him the best swimmer in the world so that he can swim **back** to shore. In return for God's granting his wish, Reynolds promises to give most of his income for the rest of his life to the church. As he draws nearer to shore and realizes that he is going to survive, his "promises" to God are reduced significantly down to 50 percent of his income, then 40, and downward, until he reaches the shoreline and reduces his promise to almost nothing. Bargaining generally includes an implicit promise that the patient will not ask for more if the request to postpone death is granted. The promise is rarely kept, however, notes Kübler-Ross (1969:84).

In the fourth stage, *depression,* the patient begins to realize that a mistake was not made, the X-rays were correctly read, and the prognosis is not good. The patient realizes that meaningful things of life—family, physical appearance, personal accomplishments, and often a sense of dignity—will be lost as death approaches. This is a time to "get one's house in order" and begin breaking away.

In the fifth stage, *acceptance,* the patient accepts death as a sure outcome. While not happy, this acceptance is not terribly sad either. The patient is able to say, "I have said all the words I have to say and am ready to go."

The above stages of dying are not without their critics (see Kellehear, 1990; Charmaz, 1980; Garfield, 1978; Pattison, 1977). Some reject the developmental nature of the sequential stage approach because it lacks universality—not all patients manifest all five behaviors. Others have noted that the stages are not mutually exclusive—some patients may bargain, be depressed, and express anger at the same time. Finally, others have observed that the order of the stages is more arbitrary than Kübler-Ross would have us believe—dying patients may go from denial to acceptance, followed by depression and anger.

Kathy Charmaz (1980:153) argues that the stages emanate from preconceived psychiatric categories imposed upon the experiences rather than emerging from the data. She notes that what originated as *description* of a reality often becomes *prescription* for reality.

The stages also do not take adequately into consideration the perspective of the patient. Anger, for example, may be vented at others because they have withdrawn from the patient as their attempt to cope with the loss of someone for whom they care. The bargaining behavior of the patient may be motivated by a need for moral and social support from caregivers, rather than a hope for an extension of time (Gustafson, 1972). Depression may be a function of the severity of the physical condition of the patient rather than an emotional response to the terminal condition (Charmaz, 1980). As the disease progresses, the strength of the patient will diminish and be evaluated by others as psychological depression. In actuality, the patient may be depressed not by dying, but by the physical effects of the illness.

THE CARE OF THE DYING PATIENT

Robert E. Kavanaugh

No matter how we measure his worth, a dying human being deserves more than efficient care from strangers, more than machines and septic hands, more than a mouth full of pills, arms full of tubes and a rump full of needles. His simple dignity as man should merit more than furtive eyes, reluctant hugs, medical jargon, ritual sacraments or tired Bible quotes, more than all the phony promises for a tomorrow that will never come. Man has become lost in the jungle of ritual surrounding death.

Facing Death. Baltimore: Penguin Books, 1972, p. 6.

With regard to the stages of dying, we must conclude that dying behavior is more complex than five universal, mutually exclusive, and linear stages. Kübler-Ross has helped us, however, in understanding that each of the five behaviors is a "normal" coping strategy employed by dying patients. It may be that it is the social situation that accounts for the similar coping strategies of dying patients, and that in other cultural settings different patterns of behavior will be found.

Social Situation Meanings

As the dying person comes to grips with a terminal condition, the way in which the social situation is defined will have a tremendous impact upon the process of dying. If the hospital is viewed as a supportive environment, patient coping may be facilitated. However, if the patient feels all alone in the place of confinement, and if the hospital is defined as a foreign place, personal adjustment to dying and death will be hindered.

Like all other meaning systems, the definition of the social situation is an attempt by the individual to bring order to one's world. Since situational meaning always involves selective perception, the terminal patient will create the meaning for the social environment and will respond to this meaning and not to the environment itself. Each terminal patient will not only experience death in a different environment, but will have a unique interpretation of the social situation. This accounts for the different experiences of dying patients. The hospice movement (see Chapter 7) is an attempt to create a more positive and supportive social situation in which dying can take place.

PHYSICIANS AND THE DYING PATIENT

Physicians may have a greater need than others to reject death, and some may compensate for their unconscious personal fear of illness and death by using distancing tactics in attempts to protect themselves through a process of mastery (Black, Hardoff, and Nelki, 1989). The death of a patient may be viewed as a professional failure and thus generate guilt for the doctor. Therefore, it is important for medical students to develop technical skills necessary to deal efficiently with terminally ill patients and their families.

Americans are poorly socialized with regard to issues of dying and death, as noted in Chapter 1. One might expect that the early socialization experiences of physicians would be similar to other members of society. This is exemplified by the following story told to the author by Dr. Charles Huggins, Nobel recipient and professor at the University of Chicago School of Medicine, about his first day as a student in medical school:

After the gross anatomy professor finished the initial lecture, the class went to the laboratory to begin work on the cadavers. My cadaver was a female. After taking one look at the body (having never seen either a dead woman or a naked woman), I said to myself, "I should have gone to law school after all."

Even though this Nobel recipient entered medical school many decades ago, many first-year medical students today have had similar experiences and feelings and find that their first exposure to death is an impersonal experience in an anatomy lab. Entry into medical school involves movement from a largely lay to a largely medical culture, notes Frederic Hafferty (1991:178) in his study of the **socialization** of first-year medical students. Experiences such as the dissection of human **cadavers** in anatomy lab provide students with opportunities to internalize a variety of attitudes, values, motives, and rationales with respect to both their current role as student and their future role as physician. These experiences give students an opportunity to assess their progress in identity transformation and skill-building (Hafferty, 1991).

In a day in the United States long before Dr. Huggins's time, acquiring a corpse to dissect for medical purposes was apparently not an easy task. Corpse snatching and grave robbing were known to occur among students desiring to learn human anatomy. Medical societies, formed in the late 1700s and early 1800s, became active in attempting to force legislation to permit legal dissection for medical study (Coffin, 1976:194). In 1824 Connecticut passed a law allowing medical schools to take possession of unclaimed corpses from its prisons, and in 1831 a Massachusetts law made human dissection legal. These pioneer acts served as models for other states, and soon there was no reason for grave snatching in the name of science.

The student entering the medical profession comes with certain attitudes and feelings toward patients that will be shaped and continually processed until his or her attitudes comply with those of the medical profession itself. Howard Becker (1964:44–46) refers to this "molding" as **situational adjustment.** As one moves in and out of social situations, one learns the requirements for success in that situation. With a strong desire to deliver the required performance, the individual becomes the kind of person the situation demands. Thus, the medical student is "molded" into the medical profession by learning what is expected and then doing it. Becker notes that much of the change in an individual is a function of the interpretive response made by the entire group—the consensus the group reaches with respect to its problems.

The process of situational adjustment accounts for changes people undergo, but people also exhibit some consistency as they move from situation to situation. Becker refers to this consistent line of activity in a sequence of varied situations as commitment. A variety of commitments constrains one to follow a consistent pattern of behavior in many areas of life.

Whether one's medical socialization took place many decades ago, as for Dr. Huggins, or in the 1990s, medical training is a pathway by which lay persons are transformed into something else—physicians (Hafferty, 1991). Merton, Reader, and Kendall (1957:287) noted that socialization is the collection of "processes by which people acquire the values and attitudes, the interests, skills, and knowledge—in short, the culture—current in the groups of which they are, or seek to become, a member." When we speak of socialization (Hafferty, 1991:3), we are talking about the structure, the method, and the route by which initiates move from one status to another and acquire the technical skills, knowledge, values, and attitudes associated with the new position or group. Thus, one must attain a new cultural base but must also facilitate movement away from the old status.

Death Education in Medical Schools

As noted in Chapter 1, medical education has historically offered only limited assistance to the medical student encountering death for the first time (Dickinson, 1985). From 1975 to 1985 the number of full-term death and dying courses in medical school in the United States increased from only 7 to 14 (out of total of 113 and 128 medical schools, respectively). By 1990, the number of courses had increased to 18 (Mermann, Gunn, and Dickinson, 1991:36). Eighty percent of the medical schools in 1975, 1985, and 1990 offered death education in the form of an occasional lecture or minicourse. The average number of years of these offerings in 1985 was 8. Thus, a death and dying emphasis in medical schools has a brief history and remains somewhat limited today.

The dilemma faced by Dr. Huggins on his first day in gross anatomy lab would have been addressed by the current offering at the University of Massachusetts Medical School. According to S. C. Marks and S. L. Bertman (1980), sessions on death and dying are integrated into the anatomy course before dissection begins. Some of the objectives are to identify and articulate feelings about death in general and to assist students in identifying and talking about their death and dissection feelings. Unfortunately, this course is unique, and most medical schools today are like that experienced by Dr. Huggins decades ago.

Perhaps physicians are expected to be all things to all people. Certainly the death of a patient runs counter to what medicine is all about, since the graduate of medical school takes an oath to "prolong life." From the point of view that the physician is the defender of life, sworn to use his or her best judgment in protecting the patient, death is the enemy, and the dying patient is a lost cause from the beginning.

The medical training of most physicians historically seems to be primarily concerned with the patient's physical state rather than social-psychological needs. Some changes are occurring though, as noted by Dartmouth Medical School's interest in "facilitating the medical students' understanding of the patient as a bio-social-psychological being" (Nelson, 1980). The medical students are to learn from the terminally ill patients what it is like to be dying. Thus, the patient is used as teacher. The inclusion of a humanistic emphasis in death education should help both the dying patients and the medical students.

Alan Mermann (Mermann, Gunn, and Dickinson, 1991) offers a seminar for first- and second-year medical students at the Yale School of Medicine on problems in communicating with dying and seriously ill patients. Professor Mermann also uses very sick patients as teachers of the students. Approximately one-third of the first-year students take this elective course. Goals for students in the course are to: (1) learn to talk with, and listen to, sick persons; (2) learn to establish a professional relationship without the intrusion of friendship; (3) ascertain the meaning of compassion without sentimentality and the need for humility before the physician's ignorance; (4) learn of our common frailty as human beings, the finality of death, and the need we all have for companionship when death is near; and (5) enrich the students' understanding of those in their care.

Professor Mermann's goals do not differ significantly from those of Black, Hardoff, and Nelki (1989:752) in teaching medical students to better relate to dying patients and their families. They recommend that each course have the following objectives:

1. to identify the dying patient's needs and wishes
2. to understand the family's needs
3. to recognize the phases of normal grief and mourning
4. to be aware of cultural and religious aspects with regard to death and the roles of other people, such as chaplains, in caring for the person and the family
5. to clear away the barriers that have been erected around the subject
6. to make the student appreciate his or her own death, thus contributing to his or her emotional development
7. to appreciate the need to relieve the physical and emotional distress of the dying patient
8. to consider ethical issues such as euthanasia, abortion, organ transplantation, and so on

The care of the dying is an art that should have its fullest expression in helping patients cope with the technologically complicated medical environment surrounding them at the end of life, note Sidney Wanzer and his medical colleagues (1989:846). The concept of a good death requires the art of deliberately creating a medical milieu that allows a peaceful death. The physician must seek a level of care that optimizes comfort and dignity and needs to formulate a flexible care plan, tailoring treatment to the patient's changing needs as the disease progresses. Pain control must be a top priority of physicians, observe Wanzer and associates, since one of the major causes of anxiety among patients and their families is the perception that physicians' efforts to relieve pain are badly deficient. As sickness progresses toward death, dying patients may require **palliative care** of an intensity that rivals even that of curative efforts. Indeed, death education in medical schools must strive to help the physician make the dying patient's last few days more comfortable.

More Death Education Needed in Medical Schools

A survey of over 600 physicians (Dickinson, 1988) in 1986 revealed that the majority (78 percent) agree that more emphasis in medical school should be placed on communication skills with terminally ill patients and their families. A study of medical students in England (Field and Howells, 1986) found that, of the 77 percent of students expressing worries about the prospect of interacting with dying patients, communicating with such patients was their most frequent concern. Results from another study of 350 family physicians in South Carolina (Dickinson, 1988) in 1987 reveal that the majority felt their medical education was inadequate in helping them relate to terminally ill patients and their families.

In a recent Harris survey (Richardson, 1992), 91 percent of 1501 practicing dentists, nurses, pharmacists, physicians, and veterinarians said that teaching students how to communicate effectively with patients and their families was very important, yet 36 percent gave their schools a poor rating in this area. Seeing the need for better communication skills with their patients, the Association of American Medical Colleges in 1991 added two 30-minute essays to the admission test to help medical schools evaluate communication skills (Altman, 1989).

In a study of 441 family medicine practitioners in South Carolina (Durand, Dickinson, Sumner, and Lancaster, 1990), those who reported having been taught concepts concerning terminally ill patients and their families while in medical school had a more "positive" attitude toward death than those who received no instruction. Other studies (Bugen, 1980; Dickinson and Pearson, 1980–1981; Leviton, 1977; and Miles, 1980) have reported more favorable, less fearful, and less avoiding attitudes with respect to death and dying as a result of death education.

Good rapport with dying patients might be an intrinsic quality of certain medical students that is reinforced by experience, or it might be something medical students learn through instruction. Though values, ethics, and communication skills may be presented and "learned" in medical school, there is no guarantee that they will be carried over into clinical practice. Perhaps the results would be known if only the majority of medical schools in the United States offered a course on relating to terminally ill patients and their families. With the current curricula trend since 1975, however, this is not likely to occur in the near future.

RELATING TO DYING PATIENTS

Richard Kalish's study of college students' attitudes toward the dying (1966) perhaps reflects society's reactions to the dying in general. He found that one-third of the respondents would not willingly allow a dying person to "live within a few doors" of them. Only half of the sample would willingly become close friends with a dying person. Kalish notes that if these college students' reactions are in any way typical, then most people would avoid the dying, as they do the grieving, often noting that they do not know what to say.

Physicians likely are no better off than others in the population in their attitudes toward the dying. Physicians' unwillingness to deal with death and terminally ill patients is cited frequently in the literature (see Kane and Hogan, 1986:12). Physicians as a group tend to express more conscious death anxiety than groups of individuals who are physically ill. Anne Kane and John Hogan note that death anxiety is significantly linked with both age and experience for physicians as a whole. The older a physician becomes, the lower the death anxiety. Likewise, the longer one has practiced medicine, the less death anxiety he or she reports. As noted earlier in this chapter, similar findings were noted by Dickinson and Tournier (1993a) in a 10-year follow-up of a study of physicians who had just graduated from medical school. The younger, less-experienced physicians report higher levels of death anxiety and feel less comfortable with dying patients.

In a study of 1012 physicians, Dickinson and Pearson (1979a) concluded that those with a high probability of dealing with dying patients (such as oncologists) were more open with their patients than physicians in areas with a low probability of dealing with death (for example, obstetricians and gynecologists). Since this study suggests that differences exist among medical specialties in relating to dying patients, it is possible that one factor influencing the selection of a medical specialty is the medical student's personal understanding and feelings concerning dying and death issues.

Gender versus Professional Role

Physicians and nurses are intricately entwined in dealing with dying patients (Pine, 1975). It is the physician who defines when the patient is "dying" or "dead," and the nurse must wait for this official message. The patient may then be treated as if there were little chance for recovery. This alteration in treatment is predicated by the physician's decision, but is not carried out until he or she communicates it.

AM I DEAD?

Once upon a time a patient died and went to heaven, but was not certain where he was. Puzzled, he asked a nurse who was standing nearby, "Nurse, am I dead?" The answer she gave was, "Have you asked your doctor?"

Anonymous (c. 1961)

A study by Thomas Campbell and colleagues (1984) comparing the attitudes of physicians and nurses toward death found differences that were tied to professional roles, not to gender. Nurses tended to see a more positive meaning in death than did physicians—death as rebirth rather than abandonment and as tranquil rather than frightening. Since physicians make the crucial decisions while nurses carry out the orders, the implication of patient death as professional failure is reduced for nurses.

Howard Becker's emphasis on situational adjustment (1964), followed by a commitment to consistency, seems to suggest that socialization to occupational role overcomes earlier gender role socialization. This is the conclusion of Dickinson and Ashley-Cameron (1986) in explaining the different attitudes of female nurses and physicians regarding dying patients. Even if women have traditionally been socialized to be the more nurturant gender, more sensitive and responsive to the needs of others, female physicians tend to be less sensitive and responsive than female nurses. Thus, the differences between physicians and nurses regarding death and terminally ill patients tend to be more a function of the role expectations of the particular medical occupation than of gender.

Jack Kamerman (1988:62) cautions, however, that as nurses are given greater responsibility in diagnosis and treatment, their attitudes toward death may move closer to those of physicians. In addition, as nurses become more susceptible to the strain that physicians experience when a patient dies, it is possible they will retreat farther behind the shield of professional detachment, particularly if nursing follows the medical model of professional status.

By contrast, a study by Martin, Arnold, and Parker (1988:340) shows that gender differences do play a role in how male and female doctors communicate with patients. Perhaps this is because medical schools do not place heavy emphasis on patient interviewing, and female patients therefore default to the less-directed communication style that is used predominantly by females in American society. Women's styles of speech are typically less obtrusive; men are more likely to interrupt women than vice versa, and women are more likely to allow such interruptions. The conflicting **paradigm** to this less directed communication style of women is that physicians are socialized to dominate the physician–patient interaction. The physician is to control the flow and topics of conversation. Female physicians tend to integrate these two models of communication by being more egalitarian in their relationships with patients, more respectful, and more responsive to patients' psychosocial issues (Martin, Arnold, and Parker, 1988).

The successful communication skills of female physicians is supported by Dickinson and Pearson (1979b). In their 1976 study of over 1000 physicians they found that female physicians related better to dying patients and their families than did male physicians. A 1986 follow-up of this study (Dickinson and Tournier, 1993b) showed even more striking differences between males and females after a decade of practicing medicine. Perhaps the traditional "feminine characteristics" of gentleness, expressiveness, responsiveness, and kindness help to explain these differences.

Martin, Arnold, and Parker (1988), in studying gender and medical socialization, reported that medical students regard female faculty physicians with clinical responsibility for patients to be "more sensitive, more altruistic, and less egoistic" than males; nurses believe that female physicians are more "humanistic" and have greater "technical" skill in communicating with patients; and patients also perceive female physicians as more humanistic, more empathic, and better listeners. If more physicians and other medical personnel were to display these "human qualities" with greater frequency, patients might receive more help and support in their dying.

Awareness Contexts of Dying

Whether male or female, nurse or physician, communication with terminally ill patients is of utmost importance. Barney Glaser and Anselm Strauss (1965) present four awareness contexts in interacting with a dying patient. They define the **awareness context** as what each interacting person knows of the patient's defined status, along with the recognition of the others' awareness of his or her own definition. The awareness contexts are: closed, suspicion, mutual pretense, and open.

Closed awareness is usually the first context. In order to maintain the patient's trust, and yet keep him or her unaware of the terminal condition, the staff may construct a fictional future biography. If the patient has not been told the truth, or has been "told" but did not want to hear, this often places an additional burden on the nursing staff in working with the patient on an 8-hour shift. Since the physician often directs the medical team, nurses are sometimes forced to work in a closed awareness context regardless of their own view. Since most patients are able to recognize death-related situational and spatial clues, this context tends to be unstable and the patient usually moves to suspicion or full awareness contexts.

Suspicion awareness is a contest for control between the patient and medical staff. The patient suspects that he or she is dying but receives no verification from the staff. Nurses must use teamwork to refute this challenge.

Mutual pretense often follows and requires subtle interaction with both patient and staff "acting correctly" to maintain the pretense that the patient is not approaching death. A game continues to be played whereby everyone "acts" as if they know nothing about the terminal condition of the patient.

If mutual pretense is not sustained, *open awareness* follows where the patient and everyone else knows the patient is dying. This is the context found in hospice programs (see Chapter 7). Ambiguities may develop in this context, however. The patient is obligated not to commit suicide and to die "properly." Dying "properly" is difficult, however. Nurses and other medical staff expect "proper" dying, but the patient usually knows no model to follow, notes Robert Blauner (1966). If the patient is dying in an unacceptable manner, then difficulties are faced when trying to negotiate for things from the staff.

Ashley-Cameron and Dickinson (1979) found that nurses working with dying patients seem to be comfortable in a closed awareness context. Since nurses spend more time with patients in the hospital than do physicians, a closed awareness context may produce a more comfortable setting for the nurse. A recent study in England, however, produced a very different finding regarding awareness contexts. Open awareness was preferred in a study of 548 physicians and nurses (Seale, 1991). Eighty-one percent of these British practitioners said they found it easier to work with dying patients if the patients were aware of their terminal condition. Perhaps the openness of the 1990s and/or the difference in cultures is reflected in these seemingly contradictory findings over different time periods.

John Stephenson (1985:78) states that dying is a human activity that is carried out in a normative manner. The individual learns the meaning of death and what are considered to be proper or "good" ways of dying from the larger society. One hopes to die what one's society considers a good death.

Though there is no good role model to follow in dying, perhaps the late Senator Hubert H. Humphrey of Minnesota came close by maintaining some control over final events in his life. Even in his dying, he kept a most positive attitude and frequently made telephone calls to individuals to wish them well and to greet them.

Calling former President Richard M. Nixon, for whom many in Humphrey's position would have had limited affection, to wish him a happy birthday epitomizes Humphrey's behavior during the final days of his illness. Since an **appropriate death** is generally consistent with past personality patterns, Senator Humphrey died as he had lived.

The concept of an appropriate death has been suggested as an alternative goal for those working with the dying (Hooyman and Kiyak, 1988:449). An appropriate death means that the individual has died as he or she wished to die. The individual maintained as much control over dying as possible in order to make it meaningful. Although an appropriate death is usually only partially obtained, those working with the dying can assist them in exerting such control.

Anne Hawkins (1990), in an article on pathographies about dying, notes various "constructions of death" in the literature. Simone de Beauvoir's model of death (1965) describes her mother's death from cancer as "an easy death," one in which suffering was avoided. Herbert Conley (1979) describes death as one's "finest hour" if it is accepted as a part of life, with avoidance of self-pity, concentration on the needs of others, and maintainance of dignity and self-composure. Conley's description of death fits Elisabeth Kübler-Ross's concept in *Death: The Final Stage of Growth* (1975). Lael Wertenbaker (1957) offers the model of a "heroic death," a "manly" death in which pain is endured as a test of bravery, courage, and heroism.

Whether a nurse or a physician, the ability to cope with terminally ill patients does not come easily. Society has not prepared one for such interaction. Some obviously react better than others. Working with AIDS patients may be especially difficult due to the fear attached to acquiring AIDS. The key to good relations with dying patients is personally coming to grips with death. One should also have good communication skills. If only the dying patient could be viewed as a person—not the "lung cancer" case in Room 314—and treated as a human being, certainly the trauma of the dying process could be eased. In the end medical personnel, the patient, and the family would benefit.

Dying as Deviance in the Medical Setting

One's treatment of the terminally ill patient may well be a product of socialization into the medical profession. The medical profession's attitudes toward patients, in particular the dying patient, are functional to the reinforcement of the view of "the physician as healer" and to maintaining order in the medical subculture.

The dying patient is a deviant in the medical subculture because death poses a threat to the image of the "physician as healer" (see Alban L. Wheeler, 1973, for an excellent discussion of dying as deviance—the source from which much of this section was taken). I remember submitting a manuscript on physicians' attitudes toward terminally ill patients to a medical journal a few years ago and the editor writing back, stating that dying patients cannot be called deviants.

Death also creates embarrassing and emotionally upsetting disruptions in the scientific objectivity of the medical social system. Thus, the disruption caused by death in the medical social system, if not controlled, could lead to a great deal of conflict.

Labeling Theory

A major school of thought explaining deviance is **labeling theory.** This perspective does not focus on the act or actor, but rather on the audience observing them. When a person is labeled deviant, that individual is stigmatized. Erving Goffman (1963) describes the stigmatized individual as a person who is reduced in the minds of others from a "whole and usual" person to a "tainted and discounted" one. Therefore, the key to the identification of deviance is found in the audiences labeling the individual or act as deviant. Thus, in analyzing the dying patient as deviant in the medical subculture, the medical audiences who interact with and participate in the labeling of the patient must be examined.

Regardless of whether or not the individual is responsible for the deviant label, the label-stigmatized individual is still discredited and is treated with less respect than other people. With such labeling, an entire interactional framework is created within which the "normals" relate to the "deviant." If indeed the dying patient is labeled "deviant," an individual with AIDS has a double deviant label—*dying with AIDS.*

Jerome Schofferman (1988) states that AIDS may be considered a socially unacceptable disease because common routes of infection are gay sexual activity and intravenous drug use. A former student of mine, currently suffering from AIDS, desired volunteer work at a funeral home because of his fascination with death. His request was denied. He later, rather jokingly, told me he did not know if the refusal came because he is gay or because he has AIDS. As Earl, Martindale, and Cohn (1992:36) report from their study of coping with HIV infection, *how* individuals become infected is frequently of more concern in the evaluation of positive adaptation than is the stage or progress of the ailment. Thus, whether the AIDS patient acquired the disease through sexual activity or intravenous drug use or through some other means, the stigma of deviance tends to apply.

According to Elliot Freidson (1972:236), when a person is labeled deviant, the stigma interferes with normal interaction. While individuals may not hold the deviant responsible for his or her stigma, they are nonetheless "embarrassed, upset or even revolted by it," says Freidson. Therefore, the assumption can be made that the deviant person elicits certain aversive attitudes from the audience with whom interaction occurs. These aversive attitudes may be strong enough to elicit attempts to manage them and to decrease aversion through avoidance behavior.

Deviance Results in Punishment

The primary reaction to deviance of any type is punishment of some sort. French sociologist Emile Durkheim (1961) observed that the primary purpose of punishment is not for the deviant himself or herself, but to affirm in the face of the offense the rule the offense would deny. Thus, one could suggest that illness is a rejection of the societal value of health or that the terminally ill patient to the physician is the antithesis of healing and getting well taught in medical school. For the AIDS patient, homophobia may be present in the community (Schofferman, 1988). The patient may feel extreme guilt or shame for being ill or may blame himself/herself for "getting what he/she deserved."

Characterizing the American deification of physical health, the hospital, and the physician, Robert Kavanaugh (1972:8) makes the following statement:

> Our universal deity, Physical Health, is the major god currently (worshipped). His demands for untold dollars in tribute are incessant. Every day it costs more to worship at his shrine (the hospital), yet the devout seem only too willing to scrape and to pay. They sit uncomplaining for endless hours in the offices of His high priests (physicians), and will purchase any drug or pill or lotion the priests prescribe, in any combination. In His shrine, the dying are excommunicated, the dead are damned.

The dying person can seldom assume normal role functioning, although he or she views the illness as undesirable and has tried to cooperate with medical personnel to get well. The dying person, therefore, is permanently cast into a deviant role due to the inability to respond to treatment and get well. According to the insert below, however, dying is really a normal state, not a deviant behavior.

DYING AS A NORMAL STATE

Dying must be considered as a normal state in and of itself. The process of dying is not extraordinarily different from the process of healthy normal living, for they coexist in the same world. It is the world of patienthood which is artificial. Modern medicine with its technology has created industrial complexes called hospitals. That environment is so artificial that creating normalization is essential.

Normalization of the life of the dying person is not the same as is normalization of the life of a patient. To be dying is normal and that is determined by the patient. In attempting normalization for the patient, the staff tries to keep the patient from slipping into an exaggerated state of patienthood. In normalization for the dying, the dying person must teach the staff that there is a normal process going on.

Hospitals are places in which dying could be allowed. There are many things patients need at times of their dying to make their time left more tolerable. There is room in hospitals to allow for the dying. Normalization is not really based on ethnic preferences, social patterns, and familial behavior. Normalization targets self-esteem, goal orientation, and abatement of loneliness. It generates a community that allows patients to continue to have full participation in human commerce.

The dying person redefines his or her community. The dying person is the high priest of his or her own temple. It is as if life has a holy of holies where only those initiated into that inner sanctum are allowed. It transcends the human construct of hospital and the secular state of patienthood. Hospitals will only be able to accommodate dying persons if the staff recognizes this transcendent element of the dying process. The current view of the human body as a machine that can be fixed without the spirit leaving the driver's seat makes it difficult to accommodate dying.

Adapted from Jan van Eys. "In My Opinion . . . Normalization While Dying." *Children's Health Care*, 1988, (Summer) 17:18–21.

THE AUTOPSY

A dissection and examination of a just-deceased patient is an **autopsy** (Clark and Springen, 1986). The **pathologist** performing the autopsy assumes a mechanical, physical cause for the death. A *complete autopsy* refers to an examination of the organs of the three major cavities of the body—the abdomen, chest, and the head. The pathologist makes a Y-shaped incision extending from each armpit to the center of the lower abdomen. Various internal organs are removed and weighed, and

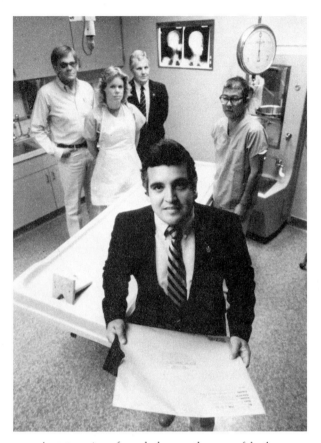

An autopsy is performed whenever the cause of death is uncertain. While the process is a mechanical procedure, the dignity of the patient should always be respected.

blood, urine, and other fluids are sampled. Much can be told from the size, color, and feel of various body parts. For example, an alcoholic's liver may be pale and shriveled, and a diseased heart is likely to be flabby and grossly enlarged.

Autopsies for natural deaths or deaths occurring among patients under the care of a physician are usually performed at the hospital where the death occurred and with the permission of the next of kin (*Journal of the American Medical Association,* 1988:2357). Traumatic or sudden, unexpected deaths or deaths due to external causes may be governed by local statutes that require an autopsy. Such an autopsy is either requested by a coroner (or medical examiner).

The purposes of an autopsy are noted by W. C. Roberts (1978):

1. serves as a check on the accuracy of the clinical diagnoses and histori-cal data
2. can be a check on the appropriateness of medical and surgical therapy
3. helps gather data on new and old diseases and surgical procedures
4. obtains information beneficial to the deceased's family
5. clarifies real or potential medicolegal deaths

The autopsy has ancient roots and has produced countless medical advances over time (Clark and Springen, 1986). The cumulative data gathered through autopsies have enabled physicians to treat or prevent a number of diseases. Post-mortems confirmed the link between cigarette smoking and lung cancer. They helped discover abnormalities involved in congenital heart defects, multiple sclero-sis, Alzheimer's disease, and viral infections in the brain that may cause dementia shown by some victims of AIDS. Perhaps the purpose of an autopsy is summed up by the statement on the entrance to the autopsy room at the Medical University of South Carolina: "This place is where death rejoices to come to the aid of life."

Despite the usefulness of autopsies, there has been a sharp decline in the num-ber of autopsies performed in the United States in recent years (Altman, 1988). In the mid 1940s half the patients who died in a hospital were dissected, while today only 13 percent are subjected to postmortems (Clark and Springen, 1986). Autopsy findings are believed to increase the reliability of death certificate data and therefore provide an essential check on the accuracy of diagnoses—although there may be legitimate disagreement between the attending physician and pathologist as to pre-cisely what killed the patient.

> "Doctor," complained the patient, "all the other physicians called in on my case seem to disagree with your diagnosis."
>
> "Yes, I know they do," said the doctor, "but the autopsy will prove that I'm right."

Physicians, hospital administrators, and families of the deceased have shown reduced interest in autopsies. Physicians in particular fear that an autopsy will uncover an error and thus spur malpractice suits (Clark and Springen, 1986). High-tech methods of diagnosis such as CAT scans have made some believe that postmortems are not necessary. Autopsies also cost hospitals $1000 to $3000 each and must be subsidized by general charges, since they are not directly covered by health insurance. In addition, physicians are reluctant to ask bereaved next of kin for permission to perform a procedure that many regard as upsetting and an invasion of privacy.

In the insert below, a college student discusses her observations of an autopsy and her emotional reactions to it. While it is difficult to generalize from one experience, it is possible that her first encounter with the autopsy is not unlike that of many first-year medical students.

AN AUTOPSY OBSERVED AND EXPERIENCED

We stepped into the autopsy room wondering what to expect. I was nervous for we had just been told that we might feel sick, and if we did we should leave the room so we would not faint and hurt ourselves. The sights and smells overwhelmed my senses. The mixed odors were of formaldehyde and old blood, and the air was thick with that scent. I was wondering how long I would last in this environment when we were offered surgical masks to wear. "I nearly fainted from the smell when I watched my first autopsy. Those masks help a little," said the resident who was working on the case. She was right about that.

The room was lined with stainless steel shelves and drawers. These contained countless preserved specimens from "interesting or unusual cases" to be studied in the future or used as references for curious medical students. Two large rectangular steel tables were in the center of the room. Each table had a gutter and tilted into a draining area leading to a sink. The water was always running to wash down the blood.

If what I've described so far is all there was, the room itself would not have been too bad. But there was more to the scene. On the top of one of the steel tables lay a large, naked, old, male body. That was my second shock (after the smell) and the major cause for my alarm. Fearing that I would pass out, I stood as far away from the tables and other people as I could. I took deep breaths and I stood with my legs spread apart for better balance, but I did not faint.

This man on the table seemed so vulnerable. I tried to think of him only as a body. Despite my efforts I began imagining myself in his position—a resident,

(continued)

a medical student, and an autopsy specialist cutting, probing, and making comments about my physical condition; other interested people coming into the room now and then to check out the progress; and six more students curiously watching the whole procedure. I did not like this situation, and I felt sympathy for the autopsy victim. Yet I was curious enough to stay and try to survive the whole autopsy.

When we had become accustomed to our surroundings, the resident told us about the "patient." This fifty-five year old white male had come to the hospital to get his foot treated. He had an ulcer (an open sore common to diabetics like himself) on his foot. "He was very lucky to have come in when he did, his foot ulcer was getting bad and it could have led to gangrene," said the resident. His accident happened as he was dressing to leave the hospital after getting treatment for the ulcer. He fell and broke his hip. His surgeon operated, making a large incision from the upper thigh to his waist. He replaced the joint and sent him into recovery. The surgeons thought he was doing well, but he died the next day (Hip operations are not usually life-threatening.).

This man had a good heart and did not smoke. He was not fat and he seemed to be in good health. What went wrong? The autopsy team was instructed to look for possible blood clots or other problems in the internal organ system.

When we began observing, the autopsy specialist was finishing the job of resuturing the long incision in the victim's hip. A blood clot the size of a big potato had been extracted. It was soft and jello-like and looked like a raw liver. When I asked, they told me that it was a small clot and that it was not the main reason for this poor man's death.

The next part of the autopsy process again unnerved me—and again I did not faint though I thought I would. The autopsy specialist made a huge Y-shaped incision from the lower abdomen to the lower chest branching out to the shoulders. The layer just below his skin was yellow and fatty, and the strong muscle layer was dark red. The upper layer peeled away from the muscle, but the muscle stuck tight to the ribs. The specialist then hacked through the muscle and ribs around the outside of the chest cavity with a curved pruning shears that had long handles for good leverage. Then he pulled away that layer to expose the heart and lungs.

The centrally located heart was at least as big as two of my fists. The lungs were located high in the chest region, starting at the top of the shoulders and going down only halfway to the lower ribs. They were pink and porous, and I wondered how such small organs could take in enough air for a man his size.

The heart, lungs, liver, and the rest of the smaller organs were then removed and put aside to be studied by the resident medical student, Kris. While Kris "breadsliced" (cut lengthwise at one-inch intervals to study the inside of the organ) the liver, lungs, and digestive system, the autopsy specialist started his electric saw; I wondered what he was planning to do with it. The noise was alarming. He cut a one-foot segment of the backbone out of the man's back and then cut that lengthwise down the middle. Then he extracted the spinal cord and laid it on the table for us to see. I touched it. The finger-thick cord was made up of hundreds of tiny nerves. To see and touch all of these incredible impulse messengers awed me.

The specialist was not done with the saw. While we were watching the dissection of the organs, the patient's scalp lay inside out over his face. I was glad that I could not see his face. The saw started again and cut away a portion of his skull at the back of his head. I looked inside the hole at the body's mastermind—the brain. The resident told me that the brain was too soft to cut right then, so they would store it in formaldehyde for several days until it "firmed up."

As we were examining the organs on another table, two more male medical students arrived. They planned to practice inserting a vein catheter. To practice they used our patient's leg veins. They worked at cutting a small hole and inserting the catheter tube (which drains out blood). They saw that there were some young, female observers in our group so they wanted to be noticed. They joked about how they were going to save him now. I was appalled at this crude behavior. I wondered how anyone could joke in a situation like this one. I tried to remind myself that it was a horrible place to work and that these students used humor to relieve their tensions and make their work more manageable.

(continued)

We had to leave soon after that incident. We thanked the resident and autopsy specialist and left the room. It was nice to take off the gloves, masks and aprons we had been wearing. Fresh air was welcome, too. But I began thinking about what I had seen that morning. I was upset by the whole situation: an innocent, older man suddenly dies, and with the loss of his life, he loses his identity and dignity. He was just a body for anatomical study. He was not a person, though he was still wearing his wedding ring.

As I contemplated this paradox, I thought again of the whole autopsy process, and was dismayed again. It had been so brutal. It was nothing like the delicate surgery I had expected. Since an autopsy must show every detail, huge incisions must be made. Nothing needs replacement, so little care is taken to keep the parts intact. This carelessness upset me.

I tried to sort everything out in my mind—the patient, the tragic accident, the brutal procedure, the stoic autopsy specialist, the helpful and concerned medical student (Kris), and the joking male medical students. All of this was too much for me to comprehend.

All that day and night, I kept smelling the autopsy odor in various places I went; I could not escape it! The next morning I wrote down my feelings in my journal concerning what I had seen and felt. I also talked with people about my frustrated emotions for several weeks. With the passing of time I can now talk about it, but sometimes I think about that old man.

Elizabeth Maxwell, college sophomore at St. Olaf College, after visiting a medical center during a health science internship experience.

CONCLUSION

Since the thought of dying is stressful, it seems appropriate that we be aware of dying and death. With more awareness, hopefully a greater acceptance of dying and death will result. Through a better understanding of death meanings, our coping with dying and death should be enhanced. It is difficult to relate to the dying if we ourselves have not been sensitized to our own death.

Traditionally, medical schools have had very limited offerings in death educa-tion. On-the-job training may only enforce one's anxieties about the dying. It is encouraging, however, that medical schools seem more concerned about the social and psychological aspects of their patients today. While death education does not constitute a significant place in current medical curricula, the situation is nonethe-less improving.

With dying patients being viewed as deviants in the medical subculture, the treatment of the dying is not always the most humane. After all, death is counter to what physicians learn in medical school. They take an oath to prolong life and relieve suffering—sometimes contradictory situations. To lose a patient is a failure.

We often play games in communicating with a dying patient. We know, the physician and nurse know, and the patient knows (probably whether told or not) when the condition is terminal, but we often exist in a closed awareness context. No one lets the other know that he or she knows. Death talk remains taboo.

SUMMARY

1. The meaning of dying depends on the social context in which it takes place.
2. Time, space, norm, role, value, self, and situational meanings are important components of the meaning of our dying.
3. One may go through stages in accepting his or her terminal self-meaning.
4. Physicians have limited education concerning issues of dying and death.
5. The dying patient is *viewed* as a deviant in the medical setting; thus the dying patient is *treated* accordingly. A typical reaction to deviance of any type is punishment.
6. Different awareness contexts exist between medical personnel, patients, and the patients' families.
7. Autopsies are sometimes performed after death to aid in determining the cause of death.
8. Differences in attitudes toward dying patients between physicians and nurses tend to be more a function of occupation than of gender.

DISCUSSION QUESTIONS

1. What does it mean to you to say that the meaning of dying will depend upon the social context in which the dying takes place?

2. Would you prefer to live with a person with a terminal disease or a person who is chemically dependent? Discuss the advantages and disadvantages of each.
3. How could steps be taken to overcome the diminished social and personal power of the hospital patient? Are such limitations on patients necessary for an orderly hospital?
4. Discuss the statement: The terminally ill eventually come to view death as a blessing.
5. You have just been told that you have inoperable cancer. Discuss how you think you would react. In what ways would you change your life?
6. If a patient's death represents a failure to a physician, how can medical schools assist in creating an attitude of acceptance of death as the final stage of growth?
7. List as many types of deviant individuals as you can. Do you include the dying patient as deviant? Why or why not?
8. Deviance may vary with time and place. What is meant by this statement?
9. Discuss Glaser and Strauss's four awareness contexts. Which do you think most often exists in a medical setting with a dying patient?

GLOSSARY

Appropriate Death: The person has died as he or she wished to die, generally consistent with past personality patterns.

Autopsy: A pathologist's medical examination of the organs of the body after death to determine the cause of death.

Awareness Context: What each interacting person knows of the others' defined status and the recognition of the others' awareness of his or her own definition.

Cadaver: A dead body. Human cadavers are used in medical schools for the purpose of dissection to learn the parts of the body.

Labeling Theory: The significance of how an act is viewed is on the audience observing rather than on the act itself or the actor.

Master Status: The status (position) most important in establishing an individual's social identity.

Norm: A plan of action or expected behavior pattern thought to be appropriate for a particular situation.

Palliative Care: To give the patient as pain-free a condition as possible.

Paradigm: A unifying concept embracing a set of shared general commitments to methodological techniques, research assumptions, and levels of analysis; a way of organizing bodies of knowledge produced by empirical research.

Pathologist: A physician who deals with the nature of disease, especially with the structural and functional changes caused by disease.

Role: Specified behavior expected for persons occupying specific social positions.

Sick Role: Characteristic behaviors a sick person adopts in accordance with the normative demands of the situation.

Situational Adjustment: The process by which an individual is "molded" by the group into which he or she is seeking acceptance; the person learns from the group how to continue successfully in a situation.

Socialization: The social process by which individuals are integrated into a social group by learning its values, goals, norms, and roles.

Societal Disengagement: A process whereby society withdraws from or no longer seeks the individual's efforts, as distinguished from *social disengagement* in which the individual withdraws from society.

REFERENCES

Altman, Lawrence K. 1988. "U.S. Moves to Improve Death Certificates." *New York Times,* October 18, p. 25.

Altman, Lawrence K. 1989. "Physicians Endorse More Humanities For Premed Students." *New York Times,* November 14, p. 22.

Ashley-Cameron, Sylvia, and George E. Dickinson. 1979. "Nurses' Attitudes Toward Working with Dying Patients." Unpublished paper presented at the Alpha Kappa Delta Research Symposium. Richmond, VA (February).

Atchley, Robert C. 1977. *The Social Forces in Later Life,* 2nd ed. Belmont, CA: Wadsworth Publishing Company.

Becker, Howard. 1964. "Personal Change in Adult Life." *Sociometry,* (March)27:40–53.

Black, D., D. Hardoff, and J. Nelki. 1989. "Educating Medical Students About Death and Dying." *Archives of Disease in Childhood,* 64:750–753.

Blauner, Robert. 1966. "Death and Social Structure." *Psychiatry,* 29:378–394.

Bugen, L. A. 1980. "Coping: Effects of Death Education." *Omega,* 11:175–183.

Campbell, Thomas W., Virginia Abernethy, and Gloria J. Waterhouse. 1984. "Do Death Attitudes of Nurses and Physicians Differ?" *Omega,* 14:43–49.

Charmaz, Kathy. 1980. *The Social Reality of Death.* Reading, MA: Addison-Wesley.

Clark, Matt, and Karen Springen. 1986. "The Demise of Autopsies." *Newsweek,* November 17, p. 61.

Coe, Rodney M. 1970. *Sociology of Medicine.* New York: McGraw-Hill.

Coffin, Margaret M. 1976. *Death in Early America.* New York: Elsevier/Nelson Books.

Conley, Herbert N. 1979. *Living and Dying Gracefully.* New York: Paulist Press.

de Beauvoir, Simone. 1965. *A Very Easy Death,* trans. P. O'Brien. New York: G.P. Putnam.

Dickinson, George E. 1985. "Changes in Death Education in U.S. Medical Schools During 1975–1985." *Journal of Medical Education,* (December)60:942–943.

Dickinson, George E. 1988. "Death Education for Physicians." *Journal of Medical Education,* (January)63:412.

Dickinson, George E., and Sylvia Ashley-Cameron. 1986. "Sex Role Socialization Versus Occupational Role Socialization: A Comparison of Female Physicians' and Female Nurses' Attitudes Toward Dying Patients." Unpublished paper presented at the Eastern Sociological Society's Annual Meeting. New York, NY (April 4–6).

Dickinson, George E. and Algene A. Pearson. 1979a. "Differences in Attitudes Toward Terminal Patients Among Selected Medical Specialties of Physicians." *Medical Care,* 17:682–685.

Dickinson, George E., and Algene A. Pearson. 1979b. "Sex Differences of Physicians in Relating to Dying Patients." *Journal of the American Medical Women's Association,* 34:45–47.

Dickinson, George E., and Algene A. Pearson. 1980–1981. "Death Education and Physicians' Attitudes Toward Dying Patients." *Omega,* 11:167–174.

Dickinson, George E., and Robert E. Tournier. 1993a. "A Decade Beyond Medical School: A Longitudinal Study of Physicians' Attitudes Toward Death and Terminally Ill Patients." Unpublished paper presented at the Southwestern Sociological Association Annual Meeting. New Orleans, LA (March 17–20).

Dickinson, George E., and Robert E. Tournier. 1993b. "A Longitudinal Study of Sex Differences in How Physicians Relate to Dying Patients." *Journal of the American Medical Women's Association,* 48(January–February):19–22.

Durand, Ronald P., George E. Dickinson, Edward D. Sumner, and Carol J. Lancaster. 1990. "Family Physicians' Attitudes Toward Death and the Terminally Ill Patient." *Family Practice Research Journal,* 9(Spring/Summer):123–129.

Durkheim, Emile. 1961. *Moral Education.* Glencoe, IL: The Free Press.

Earl, William L., C. J. Martindale, and David Cohn. 1992. "Adjustment: Denial in the Styles of Coping with HIV Infection." *Omega,* 24, 35–47.

Field, David, and Kevin Howells. 1986. "Medical Students' Self-Reported Worries About Aspects of Death and Dying." *Death Studies,* 10:147–154.

Frank, Arthur W. 1991. *At the Will of the Body: Reflections on Illness.* Boston: Houghton Mifflin Company.

Freidson, Elliot. 1972. *Profession of Medicine.* New York: Dodd Mead.

Garfield, Charles A. 1978. *Psychosocial Care of the Dying Patient.* New York: McGraw-Hill.

Gaspard, N. J. 1970. "The Family of the Patient with Long-Term Illness." *Nursing Clinics of North America,* 5:77–84.

Glaser, Barney, and Anselm Strauss. 1965. *Awareness of Dying.* Chicago: Aldine.

Goffman, Erving. 1963. *Stigma.* Englewood Cliffs, NJ: Prentice-Hall.

Goleman, Daniel. 1989. "Fear of Death Intensifies Moral Code, Scientists Find." *New York Times,* December 5, p. 19.

Gustafson, Elizabeth. 1972. "Dying: The Career of the Nursing Home Patient." *Journal of Health and Social Behavior,* 13:226–235.

Hafferty, Frederic W. 1991. *Into the Valley: Death and the Socialization of Medical Students.* New Haven: Yale University Press.

Hale, R. 1971. "Some Lessons on Dying." *Christian Century,* (September):1076–1079.

Hawkins, Anne H. 1990. "Constructing Death: Three Pathographies About Dying." *Omega,* 22:301–317.

Hooyman, Nancy R., and H. Asuman Kiyak. 1988. *Social Gerontology: A Multidisciplinary Perspective.* Boston: Allyn and Bacon.

Journal of the American Medical Association. 1988. "Autopsy Frequency—United States, 1980–1985." 259(April 22):2357–2362.

Kalish, Richard A. 1966. "Social Distance and the Dying." *Community Mental Health,* 11: 152–155.

Kamerman, Jack B. 1988. *Death in the Midst of Life: Social and Cultural Influences on Death, Grief and Mourning.* Englewood Cliffs, NJ: Prentice-Hall.

Kane, Anne C., and John D. Hogan. 1986. "Death Anxiety in Physicians: Defensive Style, Medical Specialty, and Exposure to Death." *Omega,* 16:11–22.

Kavanaugh, Robert E. 1972. *Facing Death.* Baltimore: Penguin Books.

Kellehear, Allan. 1990. *Dying of Cancer: The Final Year of Life.* Chur, Switzerland: Harwood Academic Publishers.

Klenow, D. J., and G. A. Youngs. 1987. "Changes in Doctor/Patient Communication of a Terminal Prognosis: A Selective Review and Critique." *Death Studies,* 11:263–277.

Kübler-Ross, Elisabeth. 1969. *On Death and Dying.* New York: Macmillan.

Kübler-Ross, Elisabeth. 1975. *Death: The Final Stage of Growth.* Englewood Cliffs, NJ: Prentice-Hall.

Leming, Michael R., Glenn M. Vernon, and Robert M. Gray. 1977. "The Dying Patient: A Symbolic Analysis." *International Journal of Symbology,* (July)8:77–86.

Leviton, Daniel. 1977. "The Scope of Death Education." *Death Education,* 1:41–56.

Marks, S. C., and S. L. Bertman. 1980. "Experiences with Learning about Death and Dying in the Undergraduate Anatomy Curriculum." *Journal of Medical Education,* 55:844–850.

Martin, Steven C., Robert M. Arnold, and Ruth M. Parker. 1988. "Gender and Socialization." *Journal of Health and Social Behavior,* 29(December):333–343.

Mermann, Alan C., Darlene B. Gunn, and George E. Dickinson. 1991. "Learning to Care for the Dying: A Survey of Medical Schools and a Model Course." *Academic Medicine,* 66(January):35–38.

Merton, Robert K., George G. Reader, and Patricia L. Kendall, (Eds). 1957. *The Student-Physician: Introductory Studies in the Sociology of Medical Education.* Cambridge: Harvard University Press.

Miles, M. S. 1980. "The Effects of a Course on Death and Grief on Nurses' Attitudes Toward Dying Patients and Death." *Death Education,* 4:245–251.

Nelson, W. A. 1980. "Clinical Teaching of Care for Terminally Ill in a Psychiatry Clerkship." *Journal of Medical Education,* 55:610–615.

Oken, D. 1961. "What to Tell Cancer Patients." *Journal of the American Medical Association,* 175:1120–1128.

Parsons, Talcott. 1951. *The Social System.* New York: The Free Press.

Pattison, E. Mansell. 1977. *The Experience of Dying.* Englewood Cliffs, NJ: Prentice-Hall.

Pine, Vanderlynn. 1975. "Institutionalized Communication About Death and Dying." *Journal of Thanatology,* 3:1–12.

Richardson, William C. 1992. "Educating Leaders Who Can Resolve the Health-Care Crisis." *The Chronicle of Higher Education,* June 3, B-1.

Roberts, W. C. 1978. "The Autopsy: Its Decline and a Suggestion for its Revival." *The New England Journal of Medicine,* (August 17)299:332–338.

Schofferman, Jerome. 1988. "Care of the AIDS Patient." *Death Studies,* 12:433–449.

Seale, C. 1991. "Communication and Awareness About Death: A Study of a Random Sample of Dying People." *Social Science and Medicine,* 32:943–952.

Seravalli, Egilde P. 1988. "The Dying Patient, the Physician, and the Fear of Death." *The New England Journal of Medicine,* 319:1728–1730.

Stephenson, John S. 1985. *Death, Grief, and Mourning.* New York: The Free Press.

Vernon, Glenn M. 1972. *Human Interaction.* New York: Ronald Press.

Wanzer, Sidney H., et. al. 1989. "The Physician's Responsibility Toward Hopelessly Ill Patients." *The New England Journal of Medicine,* 320:844–849.

Wertenbaker, Lael Tucker. 1957. *The Death of a Man.* New York: Random House.

Wheeler, Alban L. 1973. "The Dying Person: A Deviant in the Medical Subculture." Unpublished paper presented at the Southern Sociological Society Annual Meeting. Atlanta, GA (April).

SUGGESTED READINGS

Frank, Arthur. 1991. *At the Will of the Body: Reflections on Illness.* Boston: Houghton Mifflin Company. *Written by a medical sociologist who had a heart attack at 39 and cancer at 40, this book tells us how illness affects us and what it can teach us about life.*

Glaser, Barney, and Anselm Strauss. 1965. *Awareness of Dying.* Chicago: Aldine. *Uses the approach of awareness to deal with the practical and theoretical aspects of interaction between terminal patients, their families, and hospital personnel.*

Hafferty, Frederic W. 1991. *Into the Valley: Death and the Socialization of Medical Students.* New Haven: Yale University Press. *A sociologist using participant observation describes the experiences of a class of first-year medical students as they are exposed to dying patients and gross anatomy lab.*

Kellehear, Allan. 1990. *Dying of Cancer: The Final Year of Life.* Chur, Switzerland: Harwood Academic Publishers. *A sociological account of the social behavior and experiences of 100 individuals dying of cancer.*

Konner, Melvin. 1987. *Becoming a Doctor: A Journey of Initiation in Medical School.* New York: Penguin. *An anthropologist and physician, Konner takes the reader through hospital rounds, in various specialty areas and discusses encounters with death and with dying patients.*

Neale, Robert E. 1971. *The Art of Dying.* New York: Harper and Row. *Presents problems of dying by placing the reader in the role of the dying person.*

Rosen, Elliott J. 1990. *Families Facing Death: Family Dynamics of Terminal Illness.* New York: Lexington Books. *A family therapist provides guidance to the wide range of disciplines that interact with families facing death.*

Sudnow, David. 1967. *Passing On: The Social Organization of Dying.* Englewood Cliffs, NJ: Prentice-Hall. *Explores the sociological structure of certain aspects of death in hospital settings—both private and public.*

Chapter
7

The Hospice Approach: *Alternative Care for the Dying*

"I'm afraid of the pain." "I don't want to be alone when I'm dying." "I'm afraid of a long, protracted period of suffering." "I don't want to die in a hospital. Let me die at home." "I'm not afraid for myself, but I am worried about the effect of my death on those I love."

Frequent responses to the question: Does dying frighten you?

I N CHAPTER 1 we discovered that of the eight different types of death fears, the three areas of highest anxiety are the fear of pain, the fear of dependency, and the fear of isolation (Leming, 1979–1980). As the comments above reflect, it is the process of dying and not the event of death that causes the most concern for people in this country. This chapter is about the worldwide hospice movement that has developed as a response to fears related to the dying process and institutionalized ways in which death is typically handled in institutional settings. The three primary patient concerns that hospice care addresses specifically are the problems related to symptom and pain control, the apprehension caused by having others in control of one's life, and the anxiety about being alone at the time of death (Magno, 1990).

THE HISTORY OF THE HOSPICE MOVEMENT

Hospice should be thought of primarily as a concept of care—a way to provide humane and supportive care for dying patients and their families (Burns et al., 1989:65). Its philosophical origin comes out of teachings of Jesus found in the 25th chapter of Matthew when he encourages his followers with the following words:

> Then I, the King, shall say to those at my right, "Come, blessed of my Father, into the Kingdom prepared for you from the founding of the world. For I was hungry and you fed me; I was thirsty and you gave me water; I was a stranger and you invited me into your homes; naked and you clothed me; sick and in prison, and you visited me." . . . "Whenever you did these things for my brothers you were doing them for me!" (Matthew 25: 34–36, 40)

The words hospice, hospital, hostel, and hotel are all derived from the same Latin root *spitium*—which means host or guest. According to Kenneth Cohen (1979:15), "the first hospitals were actually an outgrowth of religion rather than of medicine." As early as the 4th century, Roman Emperor Julian expressed his concern about the emergence of the Christian movement. As a response to the Christian emphasis upon humanitarianism, Julian encouraged the priests of the ancient

Roman religion to "establish hospices (*xenodochia*) in every city and thereby not permit others to excel us in good deeds" (Phipps, 1988).

In medieval times the word hospice referred to a way-station for travelers needing assistance. Sandol Stoddard (1978) and William Phipps (1988) describe some of the early medieval hospices. Probably the most famous hospice in the world is the Hospice of Great Saint Bernard in the Alps. This hospice, founded over 1000 years ago, trains dogs to rescue travelers lost on the Alpine slopes. With the passing of time, the word hospice came to encompass houses maintained for the sick as well as the traveler.

With the passing of time and the secularization of the modern age, hospitals have come to be dominated by secular administrators and medical practitioners who have established the priority of providing medical cures for the acutely ill rather than caring for those who are incurable. In 1905, the Irish Sisters of Charity established St. Joseph's Hospice in Hackney (near London) to provide patient-centered care for the terminally ill. One-third of St. Joseph's Hospice's beds are for patients with a prognosis for living three months or less (Phipps 1988:96). According to the medical director of St. Joseph's Hospice, J. F. Hanratty, M.D., physicians find it difficult to care for patients whom they cannot cure and accept palliative medical skills and treatments as authentic medical protocol. It has not been uncommon to hear medical practitioners telling terminal patients, "There is nothing more I can do."

> At St. Joseph's "more" is done, and the "more" is sophisticated therapies to control, as much as possible, all of the patient's distressing symptoms. The practice at St. Joseph's Hospice is, first of all, to establish that the diagnosis is accurate and that death is not far distant. The management of terminal illness then requires a change of roles and attitude on the part of those caring for the patient. (Hanratty, cited by Carr, 1989:266)

St. Christopher's Hospice in London, England, played a pivotal role in the development of the modern hospice movement by disseminating the hospice concept of care of ministering to the spiritual and physical needs of dying patients. Opened in 1967, St. Christopher's was founded by Dr. Cicely Saunders, who began her career as a nurse and subsequently became a social worker. However, it was not until Dr. Saunders became a physician and obtained a grant to work with the Sisters of Charity at St. Joseph's Hospice for several years that she was able to provide international influence on the course of institutionalized health care for dying patients. Her achievements were recognized by Queen Elizabeth II in 1981 when she granted her the status of dame.

The first modern hospice program in the United States was the Connecticut Hospice, whose origin was directly related to that of St. Christopher's in London. In

THE UNIVERSAL PRAYER OF POPE CLEMENT XI

Teach me to realize that this world is passing,
that my true future is the happiness of heaven,
that life on earth is short,
and that life to come eternal.

Help me to prepare for death
with a proper fear of judgment,
but a greater trust in your goodness.

Lead me safely through death
to the endless joy of heaven.

Found in the Sacramentary and used by priests after they say Mass at St. Joseph's Hospice (cited by Carr, 1989:267).

1963, Dr. Cicely Saunders was invited to lecture in New Haven at the Yale University School of Medicine. Over the next several years, contacts between Dr. Saunders and personnel from the Yale Nursing and Medical Schools were frequent. Local leaders from various disciplines became involved in the development of a hospice in Connecticut, and their planning resulted in the establishment in 1971 of Hospice Inc., later changed to The Connecticut Hospice.

The original intent of the planning group was to build an inpatient facility similar to St. Christopher's. Funding proved to be a problem, however, and the group decided to inaugurate its home care program in 1974. To test the viability of home care, the National Cancer Institute provided funds for a 3-year demonstration project. As a result, an inpatient facility was eventually built with the help of both federal and state funds and opened in 1980 in New Branford, Connecticut.

After the inpatient facility was completed, The Connecticut Hospice, with the help of a foundation grant, organized a separate corporation—The Connecticut Hospice Institute for Education, Training, and Research, Inc. The institute offered special help to health-care leaders desiring to improve the quality of care to the terminally ill and their families. In 1981, the institute was merged with its founder and continues its educational work as a department of The Connecticut Hospice.

Since that beginning, the number of hospice programs throughout the United States has increased to over 1830 programs serving more than 210,000 patients annually. In 1978, National Hospice Organization (NHO) was formed to provide for coordination of hospice activities and to assure that quality standards of care would always be demonstrated by any program calling itself a hospice. Instrumental in working toward an accreditation procedure, the NHO also provides educational programs, technical assistance, publications, advocacy, and referral services to the general public. While it serves most of the nation's hospices and over 1830 professional members (National Hospice Organization, 1991), every state now also has its own hospice organization to promote education and standards of quality.

In 1991 the National Hospice Organization estimated that there are more than 20,000 people employed in hospice care across the country, the majority of whom work in Medicare-certified programs. On average these programs serve 150 patient-families per year. In serving these patients, more than 68,000 volunteers contributed over 5 million hours of their time each year.

THE NATURE OF THE CONTEMPORARY HOSPICE

While different types of hospice institutions exist, all hospice programs are unified by the general philosophy of patient care. Hospice is a specialized health-care program that serves patients with life-threatening illnesses. In 1991 approximately 84 percent of hospice patients in the United States had cancer, 4 percent had AIDS, 3 percent had cardiovascular diseases, and the remaining 9 percent had a variety of other diseases (National Hospice Organization, 1992). Nationally, the average number of days a hospice patient spends in hospice care is slightly less than 2 months (Bass, Garland, and Otto, 1985–1986). The majority of hospice services are delivered in the home, with inpatient care available as needed. In hospice, the *patient-family* is the unit of care. The primary goals of hospice care are to promote patient-family autonomy, assist patients in obtaining pain control and real quality of life before they die, and enable families of patients to receive supportive help during the dying process and in the bereavement period.

Pain Management

A hospice program is basically a medical program with physician direction and nurse coordination. Hospice leaders have discovered that patients cannot achieve quality of life unless physical pain and symptoms such as nausea, vomiting, dizziness, constipation, and shortness of breath are under control. A major emphasis of hospice, therefore, is pain and symptom management.

Traditional medical care is often based upon a "P.R.N." (Latin for *pro re nata*) approach, which means that medication is given "as the situation demands." In practice, this means that often a person must first hurt and ask for relief before the pain can be stopped. This procedure is responsible for much suffering among the terminally ill.

When Cicely Saunders first began working at St. Joseph's Hospice in 1958, she developed an alternative method of pain control that has become the standard of hospice care. She writes:

> Here [St. Joseph's], as elsewhere at that time, one saw people "earning their morphine," and it was wonderfully rewarding to introduce the simple and really obvious system of giving drugs to prevent pain happening—rather than to wait and give them once it had occurred. Here too there was the potential for developing ideas about the control of other symptoms, and also for looking at the other components of pain. But first of all I must salute the Sisters of St. Joseph's and the compassionate matter-of-factness of their dedicated care. Together we began to develop the appropriate way of caring, showing that there could be a place for scientific medicine and nursing. We could illustrate an alternative approach to the contrast between active treatment for an illness (as if to cure it were still possible) or some form of legalized euthanasia. (Saunders, 1992:20)

Hospice physicians believe that a patient should not hurt at all. Regular medication is, therefore, given in advance before the pain begins. The aim is to erase the memory of the pain that has been experienced and to deal with the fear of pain in the future. Pain medications are standardized to the needs of the patient. The aim is to control the pain and other symptoms without sedating the patient. Every symptom is treated as a separate illness, for only when each symptom is under control can a patient begin to find fullness and quality of life.

The hospice concept includes both home care and inpatient care. Ideally, hospice care represents a continuum that includes both forms of care when each is necessary. However, the major emphasis of hospice treatment is upon home care.

Home and Inpatient Care

Inpatient care usually becomes necessary for one of three reasons. The first is that in order to bring the patient's pain and symptoms under control, a stay of a few days in an inpatient facility may be necessary or helpful. The second is that the family taking care of the patient at home may become exhausted and need a few days rest while the patient is cared for elsewhere. The third reason is that home care is inappropriate at a given stage of the illness due to the patient's condition or home situation. It is hoped that upon admission to an inpatient facility, patients will be able to move back and forth from home care to inpatient care at various stages of the illness.

The Hospice Team

Hospice care is provided by an interdisciplinary team, with each discipline having something to contribute to the whole. All disciplines work together, each in its own area of expertise, and each interdisciplinary team includes several layers or levels of care. At the center of the team is the *patient and his or her family.* The hospice movement emphasizes the need for people to make their own decisions with the supportive help of health-care professionals and other trained persons. A vital part of the process is the *patient's own physician*—the professional who will continue to be in charge of the care of the patient and write medical orders when necessary.

The next layer of the team includes the hospice's professional caregiving staff. This consists first of *physicians,* required to direct medical care. *Nurses* comprise the next category. Registered nurses are responsible for coordinating the patient's care. Licensed practical nurses and nurses' aides are also included—especially in inpatient settings.

The *hospice social worker* constitutes an important part of the team. The social worker spends considerable time working with families, thus enabling family members to communicate with each other. While family members may be aware that the patient is dying, they may never have discussed it with each other or with the patient. The social worker also spends time in dealing with social problems, such as alcoholism and marriage problems, and in working with the children or grandchildren of patients. In modern society all too often children have been shielded from participation in events centering on the death of a family member.

Pastoral care is also a basic part of the team. A larger hospice may employ a *chaplain,* who will direct pastoral care to patients and their families, counsel other members of the caregiving team on spiritual issues, and try to involve clergy of the community in the care of their own people. In smaller hospice programs all of the care may be provided by local clergy who work closely with the hospice staff.

Financial counseling is a significant aspect of the hospice team. Because patients and families have often exhausted their financial resources at the time of care, attention is given to forms of third-party reimbursement, such as those provided by Medicare or private insurance companies, and to seeking other programs for which the patient may be eligible.

The next layer of the hospice team involves a variety of health-care professionals or other key leaders in the community whose help may be called upon during the illness. A *psychiatrist* or *psychologist* may be needed to provide expert counseling help. *Nurses, home health aides,* and *homemakers* employed by public health nursing agencies—such as visiting nurse associations—may be needed to provide special continuing health care or to share in the provision of patient care. *Physical* and/or *occupational therapists* may be needed to work with the patient to insure maximum daily functioning. Finally, the services of a *lawyer* and/or *funeral director* may be required to help the patient settle personal affairs and provide the needs of survivors after the death.

Artists are increasingly recognized as important members of the hospice team. The Connecticut Hospice pioneered the development of an arts program that considers the arts as a means to help patients find meaningful fulfillment during their

For many hospice patients, just having a volunteer attend to their physical appearance is an important aspect of patient-centered care.

last days. In many programs artists in such areas as metalwork, photography, pottery, drama, dance, and music work with patients interested in such self-expression.

Trained *volunteers* comprise an essential part of the hospice team. Medicare reimbursement is predicated on the requirement that volunteer time represent 80 percent of all patient care—no hospice can exist for long without a strong volunteer component. According to Chwee Lye Chng and Michael Ramsey (1984–1985:240), hospice volunteers are recruited from many groups: housewives, students, retired persons, and professionals such as social workers, psychologists, teachers, gerontologists, members of the clergy, and architects.

Many volunteers have lost loved ones and find that this experience provides them with an opportunity to serve others. Some volunteers are retired health-care professionals such as physicians or nurses. Others are nonprofessionals who are deeply interested in the needs of dying patients and their families. Each volunteer brings with him or her skills and experiences that can greatly enhance the life of the terminal patient (Chng and Ramsey, 1984–1985:240).

Before volunteers begin a hospice program's extensive training program, they are interviewed by the volunteer coordinator and may be asked to complete specially designed questionnaires that assess their feelings and sensitivity toward dying persons. Every hospice program has an initial volunteer training program and regular inservice training to maintain and update the volunteers' skills (National Hospice Organization, 1988).

Some volunteers work in patient-care tasks such as providing transportation, sitting with a patient to free family members to get out of the house for a while, carrying equipment, or providing bereavement counseling for family members after the death of the patient. However, according to Chng and Ramsey, hospice volunteers perform primarily three roles—companion/friend, advocate, and educator. In 1991 the average hospice received 3300 hours of service from volunteers. Nationwide, that translates into more than 5 million hospice volunteer hours—approximately two-thirds of which pertain directly to patient care (National Hospice Organization, 1991).

In a study of volunteers at the Mercy Hospital Hospice Care Program of Urbana, Illinois, Michael Patchner and Mark Finn (1987–1988:137) found that 93 percent of volunteers were female and that their average age was 39 years, with ages of volunteers ranging from 15 to 77 years. In all, 88 percent of the volunteers had experienced the death of a significant other, half of which were parents.

Eighty-six percent of the Mercy Hospice volunteers felt capable of performing all of their duties involved in hospice work and they were very satisfied with volunteering, but were most satisfied with assignments that involved direct contact with patients and families and palliative care work within the hospital. Volunteers were least satisfied with the following instrumental tasks: completing forms, attending volunteer meetings, and performing clerical duties. The primary reasons these volunteers were involved in hospice work were because the individuals felt that they had something to offer others and they wished to be of service to others (Patchner and Finn, 1987–1988:135–142).

The unpaid volunteer has the double benefit of being identified by the patient and family as being knowledgeable but without having the professional status that can create a social distance. In the hospice program where I volunteer, we refer to the companion/friend role as being a "competent presence" or "safe place." In being a stranger who provides a "listening ear," without emotional involvements or professional entanglements, the volunteer can support the patient and family members like no other participant in the social network of dying.

The volunteer also functions in an advocate role by acting on behalf of the dying patient and family. Sometimes patients and their loved ones are afraid to challenge or ask questions of physicians and other medical personnel. The volunteer, who has become a trusted friend and confidant, can often speak up for patients and their families and make their needs known to those responsible for their care. I once served as the primary volunteer for a male patient who was undermedicated. When the patient complained to his nurse regarding his pain, he was told to "brave it out." Knowing the medical system, I was able to contact the appropriate individuals, who were, indeed, able to have his pain medications reevaluated. The words of Chng and Ramsey (1984–1985:240) are good advice at this point:

> To be truly effective, the suggestions of the volunteer have to stem from knowledge and understanding of the intricate patient–family–institutional configurations. Under the careful guidance of professionals, the volunteer can serve a significant role as ancillary to professionals.

The final role served by volunteers is that of educator. Most individuals in our society have not had many personal experiences with death. The hospice volunteer can learn from each experience in working with dying patients and pass on insights that may be helpful to patients and families. The volunteer can help the dying and their loved ones understand that the dying process is usually complex, stressful,

One key to the success of the hospice movement is the level of volunteer involvement in patient care. In this photograph, a hospice volunteer offers the patient friendship, companionship, and the competent presence of a nonjudgmental listener.

and disordered. In addition, most patients and families have a strong need to have their feelings and experiences validated. Patients and families who have a difficult time understanding their feelings, emotions, and experiences during the dying process should be assured that they are "quite normal."

SHARING THE JOURNEY: A MINISTRY IN HOSPICE

Janet White

As a trained hospice volunteer, I provided vital non-clinical services such as transportation, companionship, respite care, and light housekeeping. My weekly visits also kept the patient and family in contact with the world beyond their own home, preserving the tie between them and the community, and preventing further isolation during the last phases of illness.

My first patient was like a grandfather to me. When I took my weekly turn in caring for Tom, I always received more than I gave. His attitude reflected an inner joy and peace, even though his frail body was wrecked by the perpetual coughing and shortness of breath that left him weaker every day.

"Please open the curtains," he would whisper first thing in the morning. "I want to see the sunshine."

His reply was always the same when I accomplished the task. "Thank you, my dear, that's grand." Oh, how he loved the sunshine. He reveled in each warming ray.

Although other family members, as well as doctors and nurses, did their best in taking care of his physical needs, the Lord knew he needed someone like me. I could listen and hold his almost transparent hand.

I often read the Bible to Tom, and we prayed together. We talked about heaven, where all sickness and pain, heartache and sorrow would no longer be our constant companion. This gave him courage and hope—something to look forward to beyond his feeble earthly existence. He knew his pain was only temporary and would end soon.

Tom loved music, and had sung in the church choir for most of his eighty-nine years. Sometimes I brought him Christian cassettes to listen to in the long hours alone. He played the "Hallelujah Chorus" again and again.

"Soon I'll be singing Hallelujah right to Jesus," he struggled to say with a weak smile. "I'll have a new voice and plenty of breath to praise the Lord."

After his funeral, I cried every time I heard that beloved classic, as I thought of Tom lying in the hospital bed in his living room. The brevity of life had helped both of us focus on what was truly important and of eternal value. I had shared Christ's love in a tangible way to a hurting person, acting as His hands extended to a dying world.

(continued)

Working as a hospice volunteer, I gained a sense of mission and fulfillment of God's purpose for my life. I now see care-giving and servanthood as a way of life for every Christian.

This verse became my daily prayer: "Lord make me to know my end, And what is the extent of my days, Let me know how transient I am" (Psalms 39:4).

Each Christian is God's gift to humankind, a treasure to be shared. We are blessed to be a blessing. We have a hope beyond death that we can share with others.

Jesus came not to be served, but to serve others. Sharing the journey of a dying man was how I followed my Lord's example of ministering to "one of the least of these."

The Lutheran Journal, 1992, vol. 60, no. 3, pp. 24–25.

Within the community at large, there are a number of influences at work that either assist with patient care or help to make it possible. *Family members* or *friends* are urged to participate in the patient's care as much as possible. When family members cannot provide as much care as may be needed at certain times, hospice personnel will try to meet the patient's needs by exploring all possible options to do so (National Hospice Organization, 1988). The patient-family support system is the most significant factor in the dying process for many patients, but elements of the system will also include numerous close or distant relatives, friends, neighbors, members of local churches, and/or other civic groups.

Hospice programs are dependent on a high degree of community interest and support. Bringing this about requires a planned program of public information. The concept of hospice must be sold to the medical community and to other members of the larger community. Specific activities require not only financial support (especially while the hospice program is developing), but a willingness to testify before regulatory agencies about the granting of hospice accreditation, Medicare certification, and/or approval to begin offering services to the people of the area.

Patient-Centered Care

One of the distinguishing features of the hospice concept of care is that, whenever possible, hospice enables patients to make decisions about how and where they want to live their lives. Patient-centered care is nonjudgmental, unconditional, and empowering.

One of the patients of the hospice program where I volunteer provides an example of this philosophy of care. This patient had adult children in town but lived as a single person with his dog. He had lung cancer and desired to die at home alone. He was also a smoker and heavy alcohol drinker. Our hospice program agreed to honor the patient's desires whenever it was possible. Therefore, a hospice nurse visited his house every 4 hours, and members of the police department checked in on the patient every hour from 10 P.M. to 7 A.M. The patient's pain was kept under control without sedation. A hospice volunteer (who also happened to be a licensed vocational nurse) visited the patient 2 to 3 times each day, and she, along with friends and family members, met the patient's requests for liquor and cigarettes. Visits from all members of the hospice team never lasted longer than 10 minutes. The patient died as he wanted—in his home, free from pain, and in control of his own care.

While not every member of the hospice team, or the patient's family, would have chosen to die as this patient did, everyone respected the patient's right to make decisions regarding his care. The hospice philosophy states that patients and their families have the right to participate in decisions concerning their care, and that they should not be judged because their decisions are contrary to the beliefs of their caregivers.

THE DYING PERSON'S BILL OF RIGHTS

I have the right to be treated as a living human being until I die.

I have the right to maintain a sense of hopefulness, however changing its focus may be.

I have the right to be cared for by those who can maintain a sense of hopefulness, however changing this might be.

I have the right to express my feelings and emotions about my approaching death in my own way.

I have the right to participate in decisions concerning my care.

I have the right to expect continuing medical and nursing attention even though "cure" goals must be changed to "comfort" goals.

I have the right not to die alone.

I have the right to be free from pain.

I have the right to have my questions answered honestly.

I have the right not to be deceived.

I have the right to have help from and for my family in accepting my death.

I have the right to die in peace and dignity.

I have the right to retain my individuality and not be judged for

(continued)

my decisions which may be contrary to the beliefs of others.

I have the right to expect that the sanctity of the human body will be respected after my death.

I have the right to be cared for by caring, sensitive, and knowledgeable people who will attempt to understand my needs and will be able to gain some satisfaction in helping me face my death.

Marilee Donovan and Sandra Pierce, *Cancer Care Nursing*. New York: Appleton Century Crofts, 1976, p. 33.

Bereavement Care

Since the family is part of the unit of care, the responsibility of the caregiving organization cannot arbitrarily stop when the patient dies. Hospice programs offer continuing bereavement follow-up to members of the patient's family for as long as may be appropriate. Some hospices have a **bereavement team,** consisting primarily of interdisciplinary volunteers, which follows up on all the families after the patient dies or on those family members for whom there is felt to be a major risk of serious problems developing later.

The bereavement team of The Connecticut Hospice illustrates this continued follow-up. The team consists of a number of persons who have previously served as volunteers within the organization. A considerable amount of time was spent by the team studying grief and how it could best aid people in the grieving process. When members feel that bereavement follow-up would be helpful to a family, a referral is made to the team. The team has found that many family members appreciate and need the opportunity to tell the story of the patient's illness to someone who has not previously heard it. Occasionally, a bereavement team member enters the picture while the patient is still alive.

Once the referral has been made, the team works out a care plan for the family, and a team member accepts the family as his or her own responsibility. The objective of bereavement care is to encourage the family to carry on its grieving process in an open and helpful manner. Hospice bereavement care has several goals (Boulder County Hospice, 1985):

1. to assess the normal grief response
2. to assess individual coping mechanisms and stress levels
3. to assess support systems
4. to set up additional support (groups, individual therapy, visits by team members) when needed
5. to identify individuals at high risk and make appropriate interventions
6. to make referrals for financial problems and medical care

Here, too, as in other aspects of hospice care, the art of listening is emphasized. Family members need someone willing to listen while they discuss their feelings. Bereavement team support may last for a year or more, although the team tries to encourage family members to stand on their own feet as soon as possible.

Persons Served by the Hospice

Hospice care knows no age restrictions, though two-thirds of the patients tend to be persons over 65 years of age—the remaining 32 percent were adults and 1 percent were children (National Hospice Organization, 1991). Most hospices provide care for patients suffering from any illness with a time-limited prognosis. According to David Bass, Neal Garland, and Melinda Otto (1985–1986:67):

> The "average" hospice patient is white, in his or her middle sixties, . . . is afflicted with a form of cancer and . . . is being taken care of by his or her spouse. The patients remain in the program for an average (mean) of forty-seven days. The profile of the "average" patient, while helpful in a number of ways, also conceals as much as it reveals. For example, while it is true that the average hospice patient is sixty-two years of age, there is a substantial segment of patients who are either much younger or older than this average. Further, evidence presented in our research suggests that younger-than-average patients have different experiences with hospice care (i.e., they remain in the program for a shorter period, receive fewer staff visits, and are more likely to die in a facility).

Patient eligibility criteria usually include a diagnosis of a terminal illness, a prognosis of 6 months or less, consent and cooperation of the patient's own physician, and a willingness to deal with the dying process in an open awareness context. Home care is often more viable when there is a relative (or friend) who can be a primary caregiver in the home and can assume responsibility for patient care when the latter is unable to provide care for himself or herself. Inpatient care usually requires that help is needed with pain or symptom control.

Special Aspects of Home Care

Since 65 percent of American hospice patients die at home (Lack and Buckingham, 1978), one of the questions frequently raised by family members is what to do if an emergency develops in the middle of the night or on a holiday. While many physicians and other health-care professionals do not make house calls, hospice personnel do. Home care for hospice patients is made viable by the fact that a physician and a nurse are on call 24 hours a day, 7 days a week. This gives patients and families confidence that they can manage at home.

Community physicians continue to be involved in the care of their patients, and usually remain primary caregivers, while the patient is receiving home care. Such community involvement relates the hospice program to the area in which it is located and tends to give hospice care greater visibility than is sometimes true of health-care programs.

In **inpatient care** the patient's own physician turns over the care of the patient to a hospice physician but must be willing to resume care if the patient is able to return home. Whereas traditional medical care in recent years has tended to concentrate care in specialized hospitals or in nursing homes, hospice care returns the focus to the family.

SIGNS OF APPROACHING DEATH AND WHAT TO DO TO ADD COMFORT

Hospice exists to support the family's desire to aid a loved one in dying in familiar surroundings. This time period is a very difficult one for families. The following was devised to help ease this time by alleviating some of the fears of the unknown. The information may help caregivers prepare for, anticipate, and understand symptoms as a patient approaches the final stages of life. It is important to note that some symptoms may appear at the same time and some may never appear.

Symptom: The hospice patient will tend to sleep more and more and may be difficult to awaken.
Action: Plan activities and communication at times when he or she seems more alert.

Symptom: You may notice your loved one having confusion about time, place, and identity of people.
Action: Remind your family member of the time, day, and who is with him or her.

Symptom: Loss of control of bowel and bladder may occur as death approaches, as the nervous system changes.
Action: Ask the hospice nurse for pads to place under the patient and for information on skin hygiene. Explore the possibility of a catheter for urine drainage.

Symptom: Arms and legs may become cool to touch and the underside of the body may become darker as circulation slows down.
Action: Use warm blankets to protect the patient from feeling cold. Do not use electric blankets, since tissue integrity is changing and there is danger of burns.

Symptom: Due to a decrease in oral intake, your loved one may not be able to cough up secretions. These secretions may collect in the back of the throat causing noisy breathing. This has been referred to as the "death rattle."
Action: Elevate the head of the bed (if using a hospital bed) or add extra pillows. Ice chips (if the patient can swallow) or a cool, moist washcloth to the mouth can relieve feeling of thirst. Positioning on a side may help.

Symptom: Hearing and vision responses may lessen as the nervous system slows.
Action: *Never* assume the patient cannot hear you. *Always* talk to the patient as if he or she could hear you.

Symptom: There may be restlessness, pulling at bed linens, having visions you cannot see.
Action: Stay calm, speak slowly and assuredly. Do not agree with inaccuracy to reality, but comfort with gentle reminders to time, place, and person.

Symptom: Your loved one will not take foods or fluids as the need for these decreases.
Action: Moisten mouth with a moist cloth. Clean oral cavity frequently. Keep lips wet with a lip moisturizer.

Symptom: You may notice irregular breathing patterns and there may be spaces of time of no breathing.
Action: Elevate the head by raising the bed or using pillows.

Symptom: If your loved one has a bladder catheter in place, you may notice a decreased amount of urine as kidney function slows.
Action: You may need to irrigate the tube to prevent blockage. If you have not been taught to do this, contact the hospice nurse.

Source: Hospice in the Home Program. Visiting Nurse Association of Los Angeles, Inc.

Special Aspects of Inpatient Care

Because the family is the unit of care within the inpatient hospice facility, sufficient space must exist for a large number of family members to congregate. In addition, such care requires a home-like environment—the aim is to make the facility as much like a home away from home as is possible. Patients are encouraged to bring with them favorite possessions such as pictures, a favorite chair, or plants.

The goal of an in-patient hospice facility is to provide a home-like environment where the patient and his or her family can appreciate the joys of social relationships.

No arbitrary visiting restrictions are placed on those wishing to see hospice patients. One may visit at any time of day or night. Visitors of any age, including young children, are not restricted in their visitation. Furthermore, family pets, such as dogs or cats, may come as well. The goal of an inpatient hospice facility is to provide a home-like environment where the patient and his or her family can appreciate the joys of social relationships.

The inpatient facility of The Connecticut Hospice in Branford illustrates the above principles. The family room is off-limits to staff and solely provided for the comfort of family members. Hospice care places considerable emphasis on the tastiness, attractiveness, and nutritional value of food prepared for patients. The Connecticut Hospice employs a gourmet chef with training in Paris to supervise its food preparation. Kitchens containing a refrigerator, a microwave oven, a stove, and a sink are also available for use by families. Washing machines are maintained for their use. Large living rooms with fireplaces are available. Ten four-bedded rooms for patients help develop social support systems among family groups. There are four single bedrooms, also. Spacious corridors next to patient rooms contain plants and areas for family gatherings. Beds may be moved around as desired—on a nice day these beds are often outside on patios. A commons room and chapel are used not only for religious services but for presentations by various kinds of artists. Operated by volunteers, a beauty parlor is available to help patients feel better about themselves. A preschool exists for 3- and 4-year-old children of staff, volunteers, and people in the community. When the patient dies, he or she is taken to a viewing room for the family members.

WITH END IN SIGHT, DANIEL RASMUSSEN CHOSE HOW TO DIE

Ann Nordby

In the spring of 1990, Daniel was diagnosed with astrocytoma grade 3, a deadly form of brain cancer. Surgeons removed most of the tumor right away, but because of the disease's characteristic offshoots into other parts of the brain, surgery was only a defensive measure to reduce pressure inside Daniel's head. Chemotherapy and radiation would only keep him comfortable and keep the disease from spreading quickly into other parts of his body.

Gordon Rasmussen remembers that the day his 36-year-old son was diagnosed, the doctor had trouble spitting out the words he wanted to say, that Daniel would die, probably within the next year or two. He kept talking about lifestyle.

"Daniel helped him," Gordon Rasmussen remembered. "He asked the doctor, 'What do you mean, lifestyle?'" When the doctor hestitated again, Daniel phrased the question differently.

"Have you ever had a patient with this disease before?" he asked. The doctor answered readily that he had. "What do they do?", Daniel probed further. The doctor responded that some patients continued working as long as they felt comfortable doing so. Others just gathered their assets and went on a world tour. Daniel then knew, his father remembered, that the doctor was telling him he was going to die.

During the next 66 weeks, the Rasmussens many times encountered people who were uncomfortable with the concept of death and its social side effects. They encountered others who enabled Daniel and the entire family to be together until the end, and to make choices about his treatment, death and funeral that made everyone as comfortable as possible.

Surgery enabled Daniel to stay in his south Minneapolis house through that first summer. But doctors found a second tumor in his brain that fall, just days before he was scheduled to leave on his fourth overseas USO tour, playing with a band called "Wizard."

Daniel's radiologist, the Rasmussens remembered, wanted him to start treatment on the tumor right away. Daniel asked whether his chances of survival would improve. When the doctor admitted they would remain the same, he decided there was no question that he would go on the tour.

Although the tumor was beginning to affect his left hand, the hand with which he made chord changes on the guitar, Daniel performed with the band

(continued)

through Greece, Turkey and Sicily. It was in Naples that he gave up and went home, this time to the house on Manitou Street [his parents' home].

By December, Daniel was beginning to have seizures. A Christmas Eve episode left him in a coma. A doctor presented the Rasmussens with a choice: an experimental drug that would either bring Daniel back to life or kill him. The family chose to take the risk, but only after making sure the comeback would be complete, and not just a life-prolonging measure. "If you can bring him back to be a vegetable, we don't want it," Gordon said they told the doctor.

The experimental injection worked a miracle, and Daniel was himself again, almost to the end.

During the winter and spring, Daniel lived with his parents. He periodically made trips to Fairview Southdale Hospital for chemotherapy and radiation, and to Northfield Hospital as needed. In between, local caregivers came and went from the house, making sure Daniel was bathed, fed and comfortable.

Home health aides cared for his physical needs. Physical Therapist Paul Prefontaine took a personal interest in Daniel, taking him for walks and pizza, and keeping Daniel mobile until June. "He is a magician," Gordon said.

Hospice workers cared more for the family's emotional needs. They spent time with Daniel and each of the family members talking about their feelings, plans and fears. They became friends, and supported the family in all their choices. Gordon said they not only responded well, but anticipated most problems before they happened. "I never felt intruded upon. We looked forward to seeing them. They were just good friends," Gordon said.

The Rasmussens say they were lucky in many ways. Daniel and the rest of the family were in agreement that his life would not be extended artificially. And they had the support of hospice workers and others as they made their non-traditional choices.

As the time of Daniel's death grew nearer, Gordon said, a couple of his older children came to him and suggested they take care of Daniel to the very end, not just in life, but in death, too.

At first, this idea was disturbing, even to Gordon, who as a retired minister, has seen death come many times. He said his children couldn't know that in death, the body's muscles let go, necessitating cleanup that isn't very pleasant. Most families today choose to leave that work to hospitals and funeral directors. "It's not like in the old movies, where the lady has the long, flowing blond hair," Gordon said.

But the siblings persisted, and Gordon and Charlotte eventually warmed to the idea. Gordon began building the box that would carry Daniel from his bed to the funeral home where he would be cremated. Gordon made the box from the tabletop on which Daniel's toy train set had been mounted and the handles from old hockey sticks.

He began visiting funeral directors to ask how to get a death certificate, how to transport the body and what equipment would be needed. Unfamiliar with the family's strong commitment and with Gordon's previous experience with dying and death, all but one discouraged him from what he was proposing. But that one gave Gordon the information he needed and became very helpful. The Rasmussens were able to borrow his covered pickup truck, as well as fill out much of the death certificate themselves.

When Daniel died on Aug. 26, 1991, his family cleaned him and dressed him in the running shorts he wore on a jog around Lake Harriet the night before he was diagnosed. Pastor Morris Wee presided over a private service. The only non-family member attending was Daniel's physical therapist and friend, Paul Prefontaine.

Daniel's family said good-bye to him individually and together. They laid him in the box and by chance, it was the grandchildren who fitted the screws into the box's lid. Around midnight, everyone drove to the funeral home.

Still feeling their task was unfinished, they hesitated to leave. Sensing their feeling, the funeral director offered to let them carry the box to the cremation oven. "We had been with him while he was suffering, so being with him now was not unusual," Gordon said.

Together, the entire family lifted the box and slid it into the steel door on the end of the fire brick oven. Their task accomplished, the Rasmussens got in their cars and went home.

Charlotte and Gordon say they realize the choices their family made during Daniel's illness are not for everyone. "I would never urge you to do it," Gordon said.

Charlotte added, "This is the way we wanted to do it, don't feel you have to handle it the same way."

In fact, Charlotte said, she isn't sure she would choose the same route if Gordon died. But the large family, the unanimity of their feelings, the support of Daniel's friends and professionals from Northfield Hospice and health care workers made it right for Daniel.

Charlotte's biggest concern was how Daniel's dying would affect the grandchildren, aged 11 through 18. Neither Charlotte and Gordon nor any of their children ever pushed the younger family members to be there when Daniel died or for the family service. They told them they could leave or stay away whenever they felt uncomfortable. But they never shied away from participating. "I thought, fine. They need to know that, too," Charlotte said.

Charlotte is on the board of Northfield Hospice. The local organization is one of more than 1,800 in the country. They provide support groups, medical care, psychological help and bereavement services. They are Medicare-certified and most of them are non-profit.

In Northfield, Hospice Director Kathie Harrington said about 9–10 patients are being served at any one time, the majority of them over age 65.

This is the tenth year of hospice in Northfield and during that time, Harrington said, the program has grown in numbers and in professional involvement.

(continued)

Rather than relying on volunteers as it did in the beginning, it has a paid staff. Dr. Robert Shannon is the hospice physician.

Although the Rasmussens' choices seem unusual, Charlotte notes "This is nothing new." For hundreds of years, human beings have taken care of their own sick family members. It is only in the past two or three generations that we have removed ourselves from it. The Rasmussens said the support of hospice made it possible not only to keep Daniel at home during his illness, but for Daniel and the others to choose how and where he would die.

Northfield News, Northfield, MN, November 27, 1992, pp. 1A and 5A.

MODELS OF INPATIENT HOSPICE CARE

Three models of inpatient hospice care exist: freestanding, hospital-based, and nursing home-based. A *freestanding hospice* is entirely independent—it works closely with other components of the health-care system, but employs its own staff and raises its own funds. The Connecticut Hospice, for example, is a 44–bed, free-standing inpatient facility and home-care program. In 1991, 47 percent of all NHO-affiliated hospice programs described their organizational type as independent, community-based programs (National Hospice Organization, 1992).

The second model is a *hospital-based hospice*. Twenty-six percent of all NHO affiliated hospice programs were hospital-based programs in 1991 (National Hospice Organization, 1992). The hospital-based model provides a unit for inpatient care within its physical plant. It provides for home care through the hospital's own home-care department by arrangements made with a local public health nursing agency or by its own staff employed for that purpose. The Northfield Hospice (Minnesota), where I serve as a volunteer, is an example of a hospital-based program.

The third model is the *nursing-home-based hospice* that also provides inpatient care when needed and arranges for home care in various ways. In 1991 nursing-home-based programs comprised 23 percent of all hospice programs (National Hospice Organization, 1992).

Hospice planning groups exist in virtually every major, and many smaller, cities across the United States. They range from discussion groups of interested citizens to fully developed freestanding hospice programs. Presently, there are more than 1700 hospice programs in the United States.

Paul M. DuBois (1980) describes several hospice programs. Calvary Hospital is classified as a chronic disease hospital with one-third of all deaths from cancer in New York City occurring there. Patients are admitted with a minimum of 3 weeks

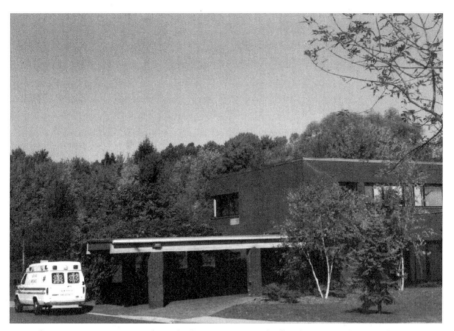

The Connecticut Hospice in Branford, Connecticut—the first hospice in the United States—is a facility for the terminally ill in their last few weeks of life. The emphasis is on care, not cure.

of life remaining and a maximum of around 6 weeks. Daily care at Calvary costs half that of a well-known, acute-care hospital for cancer patients nearby, but is approximately the same cost as some other less renowned nearby hospitals not focusing on dying patients. One primary physician is assigned to each patient. A well-organized recreation program includes trips for patients to nearby special events such as operas and plays. While the patients sleep in two constant-care units with 24 beds, day rooms are also provided for patient use.

Hospice-type features are found at St. Luke's Hospital in Manhattan, notes DuBois. The program began there in 1975, with a special hospice team working with five to ten patients scattered throughout the hospital. Patients are told they are hospice patients. They receive special privileges and extra attention from hospice staff (coordinator, two half-time nurses, half-time physician, half-time social worker, and additional assistance from chaplains and volunteers). Special privileges include extra visitors outside normal visiting hours, visits by children and even pets, and an apartment to enable visitors to stay overnight. Alcoholic beverages are allowed as determined by the primary physician.

Hospice Issues

Some have called the development of hospices a "people's movement." If the existing health-care programs in the community had been meeting the needs of the dying and supporting their families throughout the period of the illness and bereavement, hospices would not have been necessary. They originated in local communities, however, as the result of the desire of health-care professionals and civic leaders to provide better care. Many hospice leaders have seen their role as eventually working themselves out of their jobs as the principles of hospice care are absorbed by the health-care system. In the meantime, however, hospices pose a number of critical issues for health care in America. We will now examine some of them: the quality of life, the patient-family as the unit of care, cost, the training of professionals, and public attitudes.

Quality of Life

The hospice movement proclaims that every human being has an inherent right to live as fully and completely as possible up to the moment of death. Some traditional health care, emphasizing the curing of the patient at any cost, has ignored that right.

Many physicians have been trained, for example, to emphasize restoring the patient to health. Accordingly, many patients are subjected to a series of operations designed to prolong life, even though a cure is sometimes impossible, as in the case of a rapidly progressing cancer. Most hospice patients have had some surgery, chemotherapy, or radiation treatments. Some continue these even while they are hospice patients because of the pain-relieving nature of the treatments (radiation may reduce the size of a tumor and, therefore, reduce the discomfort). There comes a point, however, if quality of life is a goal, that one should refuse further surgery, seek ease of pain without curing, and attempt to live qualitatively rather than quantitatively. In hospice, cure goals for patients are changed to comfort goals, and every patient has a significant role in all health-care decisions.

Because of the emphasis on quality of life, hospices pay attention to many different facets of pain reduction, including but not limited to physical pain. Hospice medical professionals have spent considerable time in developing a variety of methods of pain control that subdue, not only what the patient describes as pain, but also the symptoms related to the illness.

Much of this emphasis on pain control has developed despite the practice by some professionals of sedating patients in pain. Quality of life cannot be achieved if the patient is "knocked out" or has become a "zombie." Physicians try to find the point at which the pain is managed, but before sedation occurs. Such pain management has necessitated considerable retraining of health-care leaders.

Hospice people also deal with social, psychological, financial, and spiritual pain. Terminally ill patients may experience social abandonment or personal isolation that comes when friends and acquaintances stop visiting them because of an inability to cope with issues of death, a lack of knowledge about what to say or do, or simply a lack of awareness of what the patients are experiencing. According to Chng and Ramsey (1984–1985), "in too many cases family members may inadvertently 'reject' the patient when confronted with the reality of death, while the professional staff may distance itself to avoid becoming too emotionally involved." It is ironic that the dying patient's need for social support and companionship is at a time when he or she may often be more alienated than at any other time in life.

Financial problems are also experienced by patients and their families, who face large hospital and medical bills at a time when family income may also be diminished. Finally, there is a spiritual pain that people experience when they seek answers to existential questions and ultimate meaning and purpose in the face of suffering. "Why did God allow this to happen to me?" and "Why do bad things happen to good people?" are questions frequently asked by patients and their families.

Hospice care makes the meeting of social, psychological, financial, and spiritual needs a major priority in patient care. By doing this, hospice provides an

THE MEANING OF PAIN

Sylvia A. Lack

Anxiety and depression are part of the chronic nature of pain. The patient is anxious about the pain returning; he or she is anxious because of the meaning of the pain. This is not the acute pain doctors are trained to deal with. It is not like the pain of a toothache or childbirth or appendicitis—pains which have a foreseeable end. Acute pain may serve a purpose by warning of a malfunction. Pain for the cancer patient has a sinister meaning. If I wake up in the morning with a stiff neck I assume I slept in a draft. The cancer patient wakes up in the morning with a stiff neck and assumes she has metastases. The degree of perceived pain is totally different in these two situations. One must take into account the anxiety that these patients are suffering, along with the chronic depression caused by chronic pain.

"Hospice: A Concept of Care in the Final Stage of Life." *Connecticut Medicine,* 1979, 43(6):369–370.

alternative to the health care found in most medical treatment centers. However, none of the social, psychological, financial, or spiritual needs of patients (or their families) can be met until all health-care professionals are comfortable with discussing death-related issues. If a physician, for example, is afraid of death or chooses to ignore it, it will be difficult for him or her to enable the patient to deal with the issues involved.

On another scale, the hospice movement emphasizes the importance of the *environment* in which quality of life can be experienced. The term environment refers to the home setting where provisions are made for the patient's needs. Much of the architecture, decor, and furnishings of most health-care facilities has been provided for the convenience of staff rather than for the needs of patients.

A critical question is what constitutes quality of life? What do people most want to accomplish before they die? What do they most want to do? When one of my hospice patients in Northfield, Minnesota, was asked that question, he said that he had always wanted to take a helicopter ride. With the help of the local NBC television station, we made this dream a reality. Like this patient, almost everyone has unfinished business in life. Some may wish to renew relationships with friends or family members. Others may desire to put their own affairs in order, to write their memoirs, to plant a garden, to watch the sunset, or to plan their own funeral service.

Robert Kavanaugh (1972) tells the story of Elaine, who, in her last months of life, studied for her real-estate license examination, passed the test, and with the help of her husband sold two houses. Thus, at age 37, Elaine found her first job while dying.

The Patient-Family as the Unit of Care

Traditional health care has concentrated on the patient and ignored the family. Perhaps many health-care workers would say, if given an opportunity to state their opinions confidentially, that they would prefer family members to stay away. Traditional ratios of physicians, nurses, social workers, or chaplains to those needing care have been based on an assumption that only the patients need attention. While hospice staff, to be sure, are not given the responsibility to meet physical needs of family members, they do have tremendous concern for the social, psychological, and spiritual needs of the family.

Hospices challenge the health-care system to provide an adequate ratio of professional staff members to patients. For example, in the state of Connecticut the public health code, in its regulations for hospice licensure, stipulates that at all hours of the day or night there must be at least one registered nurse for every six patients, and at least one nursing staff member (licensed practical nurse or nurse's aide and a registered nurse) for every three patients.

Family care, however, involves much more than numbers of staff. It requires that health-care workers know how to cope with the fears, worries, tears, and turmoil of family members; and when to speak, when not to speak, and what to say. It requires that they take time to listen, to determine how they may be most helpful.

Hospice care is costly care due to the number of staff people involved. It challenges society as a whole to give priority to such care because of the right of the dying to quality of life. A harried nurse in a traditional hospital setting, trying to meet the needs of perhaps a floor of patients at night, is not being granted the time required to sit with a dying patient for whom night is especially fearful. Neither does this nurse have the time to be of assistance to husbands, wives, or children struggling with grief.

The interdisciplinary team supports the staff person within each discipline by enabling resources of the entire team to come into play in meeting family needs. For example, a night-shift nurse asked questions relating to spiritual care might wish to give an answer at the time the question is asked. This nurse will, however, also have the resources of the chaplain to determine the best methods to meet patient needs. In hospice care the patient-family unit is involved in decision making. This poses crucial questions to caregivers who may be accustomed to making decisions and having everyone go along with what they have decided.

HOW TO LIVE WITH A LIFE-THREATENING ILLNESS

With the help of hospice you can:

1. Talk about the illness. If it is cancer, call it cancer. You can't make life normal again by trying to hide what is wrong.
2. Accept death as a part of life. It is.
3. Consider each day as another day of life, a gift from God to be enjoyed as fully as possible.
4. Realize that life never is going to be perfect. It wasn't before, and it won't be now.
5. Pray, if you wish. It isn't a sign of weakness, it is your strength.
6. Learn to live with your illness instead of considering yourself dying from it. We are all dying in some manner.
7. Put your friends and relatives at ease. If you don't want pity don't ask for it.
8. Make all practical arrangements for funeral, will, etc., and make certain your family understands them.

(continued)

9. Set new goals; realize your limitations. Sometimes the simple things of life become the most enjoyable.
10. Discuss your problems with your family, including your children if possible. After all, your problems are not individual ones.

Orville Kelly, *Make Each Day Count Newsletter.*

Cost of Hospice Care

No prospective hospice patient may be turned away because of lack of money. Hospice care is insured by the Medicare Hospice Benefit enacted in 1982, provided the hospice is Medicare certified. A hospice program must undergo a vigorous evaluation of the services it provides to become Medicare certified and agree to directly provide the following services: nursing care, medical social services, physician services, counseling, and volunteer services. As of 1992, more than two-thirds of all hospices were Medicare certified (National Hospice Organization, 1992). According to the National Hospice Organization, the daily, per-patient payment rates made to Medicare certified hospices (before adjustment for local wage adjustments) are:

Routine home care	$ 83.25
Continuous home care	$485.38
Inpatient respite care	$ 86.11
General inpatient care	$370.34

To the above payments there is an $11,551 annual per-patient program cap (this cap is computed on an aggregate basis for all Medicare patients in the hospice program). Furthermore, Medicare specifies that at least 80 percent of hospice care provided by a Certified Hospice Program must be provided in the home (National Hospice Organization, 1992). Additionally, hospice became an optional benefit under state Medicaid in 1986.

The General Electric Company was the first major employer in the United States to provide a hospice benefit for its employees. In 1989, a survey of 1500 corporations determined that 64 percent provide some form of hospice benefit for their employees (National Hospice Organization, 1989). Furthermore, the majority of private insurance companies offer a comprehensive hospice care benefit plan, and major medical insurance policies, provided through insurance companies and offered to employees as part of a benefit package, also underwrite hospice coverage in most instances. However, many hospice programs still rely on grants, donations, and memorials to meet the needs of their patients and families to provide services not covered by Medicare, Medicaid, and insurance reinbursements (National Hospice Organization, 1992).

Hospice leaders hope to make it possible for any person of any age suffering from a terminal illness to be eligible for the coverage of costs related to hospice care. They are also firm in their conviction that such care saves considerable money in the long run. Many patients currently hospitalized would not need hospitalization if hospice services were available for patients and families. A basic societal question is whether as Americans we believe enough in quality of life for the dying to be willing to make it possible.

Though hospice care requires a higher ratio of staff to patients than that usually provided in health-care programs, the cost is nonetheless lower than other forms of care. Because the majority of hospice patients are able to remain at home for much if not all of the illness, the costs of patient home care, when compared with any forms of inpatient care, are proportionately low. Due to the level of services provided, hospice inpatient care, however, will normally be higher than that provided in a nursing home, but lower than inpatient care in a general hospital setting.

Training Professionals

Most physicians, nurses, social workers, and clergy were trained in their respective fields of work without special attention to the needs of the dying. To rectify this problem, hospice programs in most states provide seminars and workshops that deal with the basic principles of hospice care. These programs not only train hospice leaders and volunteers in the specifics of hospice care, but also provide other health-care workers with the knowledge and skills to do a better job in their own settings regardless of whether or not they work in a hospice program.

Health-care decision-makers need to be encouraged to invest the time and money required for their staffs to better cope with the terminally ill and their families. Likewise, the curricula of schools of medicine, nursing, social work, and theology need to be revised in order to provide specialized training along the lines outlined in this chapter. (See Chapter 6 for a discussion of the status of thanatology curricula in health-care schools.)

Public Attitudes

The hospice movement began at a time when public consciousness of death and dying issues had reached an all-time high. It afforded an opportunity to do something tangible for other people, and many took advantage of the chance to volunteer for an active role. At the same time, increasing public awareness of death and dying gave rise to considerable publicity in the media. This helped provide public support when hearings were held by regulatory agencies relative to the granting of approval for hospice services.

Public attitudes toward care of the terminally ill and their families will play an increasingly important role in the future. These attitudes will help to determine whether health-care professionals will, in fact, broaden the scope of care to encompass the family and strengthen their skills in dealing with dying patients. Patients and families are, after all, consumers. In this age of consumer awareness it is becoming increasingly evident that those who purchase services can control to some extent the types of services available. Health-care professionals are increasingly responsible to desires of their clients. The most important factors causing caregivers to seek improvement of skills will be the desires of those they serve. At the same time, especially in areas of competition among hospitals, consumer awareness will play an important part in encouraging such institutions to humanize the care they give.

Many physicians, nurses, social workers, clergy, and other personnel at hospitals and nursing homes have heard about hospice care and have taken the initiative to secure specialized training and to incorporate the hospice philosophy into routine treatment of their patients. When any people's movement arises, an immediate question is whether it will become institutionalized to such an extent that the original spirit will be lost as it adjusts to the reality of regulation, control, and payments of costs. The hospice movement is currently at that juncture. There is every cause for encouragement that one of two things will happen: Either hospices will continue to provide the specialized care for dying patients, or the health-care system itself will change to incorporate many of the improvements represented by the hospice movement. Either outcome should result in the betterment of medical care for patients and their families.

EVALUATION OF HOSPICE PROGRAMS

While evaluations of hospice programs have not flooded the literature, some studies have taken a look at the hospice approach. An inhouse evaluation of The Connecticut Hospice (Lack and Buckingham 1978) reported less depression, anxiety, and hostility among terminally ill patients receiving home care as compared to others without these services. In addition, it was found that the overall social adjustment of family members was improved—individuals were better able to express thoughts and feelings with less distress.

Colin M. Parkes (1978) reports that only 8 percent of those who died at St. Christopher's Hospice in London suffered unrelieved pain; this compares with 20

A FEW RESERVATIONS CONCERNING THE HOSPICE MOVEMENT

Constance Holden

Some American doctors are cautious about the hospice idea. John C. Hisserich of the Cancer Center at the University of Southern California is eager to see the idea tried, but he warns that no scientific evaluation has been made of hospice care and that evidence of success is largely anecdotal. He also believes that hospice enthusiasts sometimes exhibit "a certain zealotry about the thing that may be necessary but that has the effect of turning off physicians who might otherwise be interested. . . ."

Perhaps the most serious reservations about efforts to sprout hospices in America come from Mel Krant, director of cancer programs at the new University of Massachusetts School of Medicine in Worcester. "My first reaction," he says, "is it's going to fail as an American idea. It will get into operation, but its intent will fail." The reason, he feels, is that hospices will simply add to the excessive fragmentation, overspecialization, and discontinuity in American medicine. A hospice will be the incarnation of yet another specialty—care of the dying—and will become "another discontinuous phenomenon" when what is needed is integration. Krant has high regard for the English hospices, but he fears that without the spirit of voluntarism and community feeling that exists in England, and without leaders as "utterly devoted" as Cicely Saunders, hospices will turn out looking like nursing homes. He also thinks hospices would help relieve hospitals and physicians of their true responsibilities, which should include more community involvement. Krant thinks it better that Americans develop their own indigenous models for incorporating hospice concepts.

Science, July 1976, vol. 193.

percent who died in hospitals and 28 percent who died at home. John Hinton (1979), in comparing the attitudes of terminally ill patients at a British hospice to those in hospital wards, noted that hospice patients appeared less depressed and anxious while preferring the more open type of communication environment available to them.

Janet Labus and Faye Dambrot (1985–1986) compared the experience of 28 cancer patients who died in an independent, voluntary, community-based hospice program with 29 nonhospice cancer patients who were treated in a small community hospital in Northeastern Ohio. While all of the nonhospice patients died in the hospital, 50 percent of the hospice patients died at home.

Furthermore, hospice patients at the time of admission were less likely to be ambulatory than hospital patients. According to Labus and Dambrot:

> The hospice group was younger, had more people living with them, and had been ill for a shorter period of time prior to hospice admission than the hospital group. Hospice patients spent more time in the hospice program after admission prior to death. The hospital patients spent fewer days in the hospital prior to death. Hospice patients were referred to other agencies significantly less frequently than hospital patients.

Labus and Dambrot concluded that this hospice program was succeeding in fulfilling the needs of their patients and in containing health-care costs through the multi-disciplinary team—only one outside referral had to be made, and 50 percent of the patients died at home. They argue that since the hospice group was on average 7 years younger (due to the requirement that a primary caregiver be available in the home), the hospice movement ought to consider ways in which their programs might be extended to groups presently excluded: the elderly and single terminal patients.

In the evaluation of hospice programs, another important concern is the effect of these programs upon professional caregivers. A study of hospice nurses conducted by Pamela Gray-Toft and James Anderson (1986–1987) sought to explain burnout and rapid turnover in the nursing staff. They found that hospice caregiving is significantly more stressful for nurses for the following reasons:

1. Traditional nurses often resent the special roles and treatment received by hospice nurses within institutional settings. Many hospital-based hospice nurses report feeling socially isolated from other hospital nurses.
2. Hospice nurses are often regarded by others as being "weird" or "different" because they choose to work with the dying.
3. The hospice concept of care creates increased (and often unrealistic) patient expectations; consequently, hospice nurses experience inordinate demands placed upon them by the patients and families with whom they work.
4. Because hospice often creates long-term relationships between dying patients, families, and nurses, nurses often experience strong feelings of loss and grief after the death of their patients. Many times hospice nurses are not provided an opportunity to grieve after a patient's death because of the demands of their other duties.

5. Hospice nurses are overexposed to death, which can sometimes contribute to a morbid view of life.

As a result of these findings Gray-Toft and Anderson created an experimental staff-support program for hospice nurses. Based on the initial success of this experiment, the group-support program has now expanded to include the professional contributions of a chaplain and medical social worker.

A prominent figure in the thanatology movement, Robert Kastenbaum (1981), notes that while hospice program evaluations tend to be encouraging, methodological flaws and limitations exist that are difficult to avoid. He notes three primary limitations to such evaluations: (1) High-quality research is difficult to conduct in such settings where the sensitivities of so many people must be considered; (2) Techniques for effective research into care of the terminally ill are at an infant stage of development; (3) Research and evaluation priorities generally fall way down on the list—improved care is the primary objective.

While Kastenbaum notes that many emerging reports on hospice are emphasizing the relative cost of hospice care as compared with traditional hospitalization, he hopes that the question of cost does not gain undue prominence. He is concerned that financial issues may warp our expectations and affect our ability to concentrate on the caring process itself.

It is the conclusion of Edward Crowther (1980) that the United States is not ready for the hospice. He notes that it is not a question of training or funding, but more of a problem of being unable or unwilling to change our attitudes toward proper care for a dying patient.

Crowther cites typical hospice development committee problems as power struggles, personal conflicts, and different opinions on approaches to take. The biggest stumbling block, however, seems to be attitudinal. He notes that the medical community remains to be convinced that current methods of treating the terminally ill must be changed. The dying cannot be treated in the same way as those who can expect to be cured. Physicians must learn the difference between the hospice goal of "care" and the traditional goal of "cure." The care concept admits that the patient is dying. Medical personnel must put their knowledge and efforts into relief of distressing symptoms and into human understanding. If this change in attitude does occur, Crowther believes that terminal care consistent with the ideals of the hospice movement can be provided in the United States.

This notion is supported by Dr. Josefina Magno (1990:117), the first executive director of the National Hospice Organization, when she claims that the biggest problem of the hospice movement in the 1990s is the lack of involvement of the medical profession. Physicians are most likely to wait to refer patients to hospice during the last few days of life when they are absolutely sure the patient is dying, rather than at the time of the terminal diagnosis when the hospice concept of care would be more beneficial to the patient-family.

AIDS: HOSPICE CHALLENGE FOR THE 1990S

The health-care challenge of the 1990s is the increasing numbers of patients with acquired immunodeficiency syndrome (AIDS) and AIDS-related complex (ARC). Unlike other terminal illnesses, AIDS is a communicable disease involving extremely labor-intensive care for patients who are often without family support systems. Furthermore, the physical, psycho-social, and emotional complexities of AIDS often require especially sensitive and humane approaches by health-care providers of every community.

Jeannee Parker Martin (1988), a member of a health-care team of the Visiting Nurses and Hospice of San Francisco, has written a significant article describing her hospice's treatment of AIDS/ARC patients in which she presents the special challenge to the hospice movement by the AIDS epidemic. In this article she exalts the appropriateness of the interdisciplinary team approach, which is basic to the hospice concept of care in meeting the special needs of persons with AIDS/ARC and persons significant in their lives. Yet it is crucial that professional caregivers and volunteers in hospice be trained to deal with the special needs of AIDS/ARC patients. Furthermore, hospice programs must review all policies and procedures,

CREATING A PLEASANT STOP ON THE JOURNEY TO DEATH

Timothy Egan

For the last four years, the designers of the Bailey-Boushay House have been wondering precisely how to create a large home in which somebody was going to die about every 30 hours.

Of course, it would need emergency equipment and the tools of hospitals and hospices, as well as places to cry and to say goodbye. But the designers wanted something more.

The Bailey-Boushay House represented one of the first opportunities in the country for people with the virus that causes AIDS to create a residence from the ground up. What emerged from hundreds of interviews was a single overwhelming sentiment: The place should be life-affirming, not reeking of death.

So when Seattle officials gave a tour of the $7 million residential complex today to the news media, they acted as if they were showing off a new museum or garden.

'Some Saving Grace'

It may very well turn out to be a model, not only for AIDS patients, but for chronically ill elderly people, said Dr. June Osborn, the chairwoman of the National Commission on AIDS.

"I've always said that if we do something like this right, we may be able to find some saving grace in this awful epidemic," said Dr. Osborn. "Our geriatric population is about to explode in the next few years, and housing is going to be the most critical need, as it is now for AIDS patients."

From the outside, the Bailey-Boushay House, named after two Seattle AIDS activists, looks more like a small European spa than an institution. Inside, there is a greenhouse on the third floor and solariums at the end of every hallway, and in every room there are wood armoires as well as a sofa for friends or relatives to stay overnight. Sun decks provide views of the Cascade Mountains, and artwork, some of it stunningly modern and bold, hangs from walls. There are beds for 35 residents, and day care space for another 35 adults.

For most of them, it will be the last place they call home.

"What this says to me is that I'm not going to end up on the street or in some sterile hospital room," said Kazas Jones, a founding board member of the Bailey-Boushay House who has AIDS.

Lower Costs, Too

But for all its gilded touches, the Bailey-Boushay House has attracted as much attention in the medical community for its costs as for its looks. Administrators say they can care for a patient for $200 a day—about one-third the cost of similar care in a regular nursing home or hospital. The extraneous costs of caring for people with a variety of illnesses are eliminated in the Bailey-Boushay House, where every chair, dinner table or bathing room was designed for the needs of AIDS patients.

"You can save a tremendous amount of money when you remove the diagnostic superstructure of a hospital," said Dr. Wayne C. McCormick, the associate medical director of the house.

Seattle does not have a big AIDS population; with 2,000 cases since the outbreak of the disease, Seattle has about 1 percent of the nation's total number of AIDS cases. But with the number of cases here expected to double by 1995, city officials say they are determined to get ahead of the disease.

Although there are numerous community homes for AIDS patients nationwide, officials here say the Bailey-Boushay House is the only newly built licensed care center in the United States designed for people with AIDS. Most of the building costs were paid for by private donors, more than 5,000 individuals and corporations, with city taxes contributing a portion. The residence will be run by Virginia Mason Medical Center, a nonprofit group with a hospital and clinics in the Pacific Northwest.

When plans to build the center were announced, neighboring residents and businesses were sharply opposed. The Madison Valley neighborhood is an

(continued)

older one, with expensive single-family homes, boutiques, small retail shops, restaurants and one of the city's most exclusive private schools all nearby.

Some residents of the neighborhood filed a lawsuit, trying to stop the project. But the suit has long since been dropped, and some of those home-owners who initially opposed the project have become silent donors.

As construction got underway, a huge banner was hung from a neighboring house, reading: "Welcome to my backyard."

"Part of what changed many peoples' minds was when they realized this was not going to look like a hospital wing, but that it would be more like the bagel and latte places in this neighborhood," said Bill Block, a resident who favored construction of the house.

The doors will open to the first residents some time in the spring, officials say. The center, which will be open to any AIDS patient in Seattle, is intended for someone who does not require intensive care, but has fully developed the symptoms of AIDS. Health insurance or Social Security benefits will cover patients' expenses.

Patients' Requests

In its small and big touches, the Bailey-Boushay House reflects the collective requests of AIDS patients who were interviewed in focus groups. For instance, chairs of solid maple frames and soft cushions meet all the regulations of nursing homes, and they are very easy to get in and out of. The meditation room is non-denominational, but has stained glass windows and broad, hand-carved wood benches.

In the greenhouse, patients can grow flowers, vegetables or other plants, just a few doors down from their rooms. "The greenhouse reflects the dream of horticultural therapy, the belief in the healing power of making things grow," said Christine Hurley, who is the administrator of the residence.

But growing plants may be offset by a more telling statistic: Officials say the average stay of a patient will be about 45 days.

"Somebody is going to die in this place every 30 hours," said Betsy Lieber-man, an official with the project. "So much money is spent on things like birthing rooms in hospitals, so we thought, 'Why not make it as nice as possible for a place where somebody will spend the last hours of their life?'"

New York Times, January 8, 1992, p. A10.

such as admission criteria and infection-control policies as they reach out to those infected with the AIDS virus. Finally, Martin concludes that from a societal point of view it is imperative that "home care and hospice services are available to all persons with AIDS/ARC and that when home care is no longer a viable alternative, other long-term care options are available."

CONCLUSION

As the American way of life has changed from a primary group orientation to a more secondary, impersonalized style, so has dying shifted from the home to the hospital or nursing home setting—away from kin and friends to a bureaucratized setting. The birth of the hospice movement in the United States might be considered a countermovement to this trend. As we seek out primary group relations in our secondary-oriented society, we seek to die in the setting of a familiar home rather than in the sterile environment of a hospital. Perhaps we are evidencing a return to a concern for each other—a dignity to dying may be on the horizon.

Hospice is a return to showing care and compassion. It is a revival of neighbors helping neighbors—a concept so often lost in our urbanized society. Hospice consists of professionals literally going the extra mile and coming to one's home when needed—medical personnel actually making house calls. Hospice, for example, encourages children under the age of 14 to be present with the terminally ill person rather than making them wait in the hospital lobby. Hospice is a grass-roots movement springing up in small communities, as well as larger urban settings, to provide better health care. To paraphrase the words of Robert Kavanaugh (1972:19), the hospice concept of care assists us to unearth, face, understand, and accept our true feelings about death and provide us with the opportunity for joyful living and dying as we choose. In short, hospice is a movement in America that transforms our impropriety at death into a celebration of life.

With federal money now covering some hospice expenses and with rigid government requirements for approval of hospice programs, it is important that every effort be made to prevent hospice programs from being strangled by the bureaucracy that financially assists patients—the bureaucracy that gives them little choice from dying in traditional hospital and nursing-home settings. Furthermore, hospice programs must continue to make the patient-family unit the central focus of its care and treat these clients in a nonjudgmental and unconditional manner, thus empowering them as autonomous human beings.

SUMMARY

1. Hospice is a specialized health-care program that serves patients with illnesses such as cancer during the last days of their lives.
2. Hospice care includes both home care and inpatient care.
3. The hospice interdisciplinary team includes the patient, family, physician, nurse, social worker, chaplain, trained volunteer, psychologist, physical therapist, and lawyer.

4. A homelike environment is provided for hospice inpatient care.
5. The first hospice program in the United States was The Connecticut Hospice, modeled after St. Christopher's in London.
6. The hospice movement demonstrates that every human being has an inherent right to live as fully and completely as possible up to the moment of death.
7. Hospice care emphasizes relief from physical, social, psychological, and spiritual pain.
8. While much of the cost of hospice care is covered by third-party reimbursements, Medicare, and/or Medicaid, no prospective hospice patient is turned away because of lack of money.
9. Presently 4 percent of hospice patients have the AIDS disease. Hospice programs provide a unique opportunity for AIDS patients because the care is humanistically based and the special needs for individualization often required by AIDS patients can be addressed within the hospice concept of care. However, the AIDS disease also provides special challenges for hospice programs.

DISCUSSION QUESTIONS

1. What is hospice care? How does it differ from the treatment given by most acute-care hospitals? Identify the major functions of a hospice program.
2. Trace the history of the hospice movement in the United States.
3. Discuss issues related to the family as a unit of care in hospice programs. How do hospices try to achieve quality of life for each of the "patients" they serve? How does the interdisciplinary hospice team concept help accomplish this?
4. What are some of the special aspects of inpatient and home care in hospice programs? What are some of the advantages of each of these approaches?
5. What, in your opinion, are the negative aspects of hospice care? How would you suggest they be rectified?
6. Do you feel that bereavement care should be offered to the families of the terminally ill even after their loved ones have died? Justify your answer in terms of medical, emotional, and financial considerations.
7. If you were terminally ill, would you consider entering a hospice? Explain your answer and refer to specific reasons such as cost, family burden, and imminent death.

8. Discuss the special opportunities and challenges in providing hospice services to AIDS patients.

GLOSSARY

Bereavement Team: An interdisciplinary group made up primarily of volunteers who follow up on families after the patient dies in order to encourage healthy grieving.

Hospice: A specialized health-care program that serves patients with illnesses such as cancer during the last days of their lives.

Inpatient Care: The type of institutionalized help required, for example, as the illness progresses, and which may be provided in a hospice facility.

REFERENCES

Bass, David M., T. Neal Garland, and Melinda E. Otto. 1985–1986. "Characteristics of Hospice Patients and their Caregivers." *Omega,* 16(1):51–68.

Boulder County Hospice. 1985. *Bereavement Care Manual.* Boulder, CO: Boulder County Hospice, Inc.

Burns, Nancy, Kim Carney, and Bob Brobst. 1989. "Hospice: A Design for Home Care for the Terminally Ill." *Holistic Nursing Practice,* 3(2):65–76.

Carr, William F. 1989. "Lead Me Safely Through Death." *America,* 160(11):264–267.

Chng, Chwee Lye, and Michael Kirby Ramsey. 1984–1985. "Volunteers and the Care of the Terminal Patient." *Omega,* 15(3):237–244.

Cohen, K. 1979. *Hospice, Prescription for Terminal Care.* Germantown, MD: Aspens Systems.

Crowther, C. Edward. 1980. "The Stalled Hospice Movement." *The New Physician,* pp. 26–28.

DuBois, Paul M. 1980. *The Hospice Way of Death.* New York: Human Sciences Press.

Gray-Toft, Pamela A., and James G. Anderson. 1986–1987. "Sources of Stress in Nursing Terminal Patients in a Hospice." *Omega,* 17(1):27–38.

Hinton, J. 1979. "Comparison of Places and Policies for Terminal Care." *Lancet,* pp. 29–32.

Kastenbaum, Robert J. 1981. *Death, Society, and Human Experience,* 2nd ed. St. Louis: Mosby.

Kavanaugh, Robert E. 1972. *Facing Death.* Baltimore: Penguin Books.

Labus, Janet G., and Faye H. Dambrot. 1985–1986, "Comparative Study of Terminally Ill Hospice and Hospital Patients." *Omega,* 16(3):225–232.

Lack, Sylvia A., and R. Buckingham. 1978. *First American Hospice: Three Years of Care.* New Haven, CT: Hospice, Inc.

Leming, Michael R. 1979–1980. "Religion and Death: A Test of Homans' Thesis." *Omega,* 10(4):347–364.

Magno, Josefina B. 1990. "The Hospice Concept of Care: Facing the 1990s." *Death Studies,* 14:3109–119.

Martin, Jeannee Parker. 1988. "Hospice and Home Care for Persons with AIDS/ARC: Meeting the Challenges and Ensuring Quality." *Death Studies,* 12:463–480.

National Hospice Organization. 1988. "The Basics of Hospice." Arlington, VA: National Hospice Organization.

National Hospice Organization. 1989. "Hospice Fact Sheet." Arlington, VA: National Hospice Organization.

National Hospice Organization. 1991. "Hospice Fact Sheet." Arlington, VA: National Hospice Organization.

National Hospice Organization. 1992. "1991 Annual Report." Arlington, VA: National Hospice Organization.

Parkes, Colin M. 1978. "Home or Hospital? Terminal Care As Seen by Surviving Spouses." *Journal of the Royal College of General Practice,* 28:19–30.

Patchner, Michael, and Mark Finn. 1987–1988. "Volunteers: The Life-Line of Hospice." *Omega,* 18(2):135–143.

Phipps, William E. 1988. "The Origin of Hospices/Hospitals." *Death Studies,* 12:91–99.

Saunders, Cicely. 1992. "The Evolution of the Hospices." *Free Inquiry,* (Winter):19–23.

Stoddard, Sandol. 1978. *The Hospice Movement: A Better Way of Caring for the Dying.* New York: Vintage.

SUGGESTED READINGS

Burns, Nancy, Kim Carney, and Bob Brobst. 1989. "Hospice: A Design for Home Care for the Terminally Ill." *Holistic Nursing Practice,* 3(2):65–76. / Carr, William F. 1989. "Lead Me Safely Through Death." *America,* 160(11):264–267. / Phipps, William E. 1988. "The Origin of Hospices/Hospitals." *Death Studies,* 12:91–99. / Saunders, Cicely. 1992. "The Evolution of the Hospices." *Free Inquiry,* (Winter):19–23. / Stoddard, Sandol. 1978. *The Hospice Movement: A Better Way of Caring for the Dying.* New York: Vintage. *Five great resources on the history of the hospice concept of care. They also provide a vivid description of the workings of the hospice programs, emphasizing how the patients and their families begin to help others.*

Death Education, 2 (1, 2), 1978. *Special issues on the hospice movement covering six models of hospice care found in the United States, England, and Canada.*

DuBois, Paul M. 1980. *The Hospice Way of Death.* New York: Human Sciences Press. *An overview of the hospice movement highlighting case studies of three hospices as well as the federal government's involvement.*

Koff, Theodore H. 1980. *Hospice: A Caring Community.* Cambridge, MA: Winthrop Publishers. *Delineates the practical and theoretical principles of the hospice and provides information on the administrative, developmental, and personal elements of hospice care.*

Lamberton, Robert. 1973. *Care of the Dying.* London: Priory Press, Ltd. / Saunders, Cicely. 1959. *Care of the Dying.* London: Macmillan. *Two early, influential works that explain the hospice philosophy and care for dying patients and their families.*

Martocchio, Benita C., and Karin Dufault. 1985. "Symposia on Hospice and Compassionate Care and the Dying Experience." *The Nursing Clinics of North America,* 20 (2), June. Philadelphia: Saunders. *The entire issue of this journal is dedicated to the hospice concept of care for dying patients. Sixteen essays cover a broad range of topics.*

National Hospice Organization, 1992, "1991 Annual Report"; 1991, "Hospice Fact Sheet"; 1988, "The Basics of Hospice." Arlington, VA: National Hospice Organization. *These pamphlets, along with other information regarding the hospice concept of care, are valuable resources that can be obtained without charge by contacting the National Hospice Organization, 1901 North Moore Street, Suite 901, Arlington, VA 22209, or calling (703) 243–5900.*

Chapter

8

Euthanasia and Biomedical Issues

It is silliness to live when to live is torment;
And then have we a prescription to die when death is our physician?

William Shakespeare
Othello

All substances are poisons; there is none which is not a poison.
The right dose differentiates a poison and a remedy.

Paracelsus

W
HAT IS EUTHANASIA? For many it means mercy killing; for others it means natural death without the so-called benefit of technologies related to life-extending, death-prolonging medical interventions. However, the etymology of the term reveals that **euthanasia** literally means "good death." Both definitions above, then, may qualify.

SANCTITY AND QUALITY OF LIFE

When most people think about a "good death," they usually do so within the context of their understanding of the meaning of life. What is life? When does life begin? When does life end? Is there a difference between biological life and human life as socially defined?

Occasionally you may read of a serious automobile accident whose survivor is said to be in a vegetative state. Has the patient died? Is the patient no longer human? Now consider the situation in which an individual is assaulted and put into an irreversible coma. Has the assailant committed murder or assault and battery? If this same patient is disconnected from life support or **intubation** (tube feeding) and dies, who caused the death—the person who committed the crime or the medical personnel who withdrew the life support or feeding device?

In general, people respond to such questions about medical conditions from one of two orientations concerning the meaning of life. The first perspective would emphasize the **sanctity of life**, while the second emphasizes a **quality of life**. Euthanasia from a sanctity-of-life perspective would contend that all *"natural"* life

BOY IN COMA UNHOOKED FROM LIFE SUPPORT; DOUBT CAST ON ASSAULT CASE

Doctors disconnected a life-support machine and let Craig Sieck, 15, die Tuesday despite doubt about what effect it will have on criminal charges against the youth accused of beating him.

Sieck had been in a coma since he was beaten and kicked in the head a week ago. James Sticka, 17, was charged with aggravated battery in connection with the beating. After tests on Sieck showed no brain activity, doctors said he had suffered "brain death."

"With another party involved, it could be a legal matter as to whether this party or the hospital was responsible for the death. The law in Illinois is not clear," hospital administrator John Imirie said.

Minneapolis Star and Tribune (UPI), March 15, 1978. Reprinted with permission of the Star Tribune.

has intrinsic meaning and should be appreciated as a divine gift. As a consequence, human beings have the obligation to enhance the quality of life as it may exist.

Hessel Bouma et al. note that the Hippocratic tradition in the medical profession recognizes that physicians' responsibility to terminally ill patients is to simply "mitigate their suffering while allowing them to die." Furthermore, the Hippocratic Oath, reacting against an earlier practice of actively and intentionally hastening the death of a terminal patient, forbids the giving of "a deadly drug" to dying patients (Bouma, Diekema, Langerak, Rottman, and Verhey, 1989:267–268).

The following two quotations illustrate the sanctity-of-life perspective.

> The sanctity of life approach is concerned about the quality of human life. The quality of all our lives suffers, it insists, unless every human life is considered inviolable because of the very fact of its existence. A dying patient's relationship to those about him symbolizes the relationship of all men to one another. To practice direct euthanasia, even at the request of the patient, is to weaken the claim of each one of us to the right to have others respect and not violate us. (Weber, 1981:49)

> No horror against life is impossible once we have allowed anyone but the Creator to usurp sovereignty over life. Whom the gods would destroy they first make mad. Legalized euthanasia (mercy killing) is such madness. (Morriss, 1987:149)

The quality-of-life perspective would hold that when life no longer has quality or meaning, death is preferable to life. The following statements by Claire Harrison, the central character in Brian Clark's play *Whose Life Is It Anyway?* (1981:73–74), illustrate this perspective:

Any reasonable definition of life must include the idea of its being self-supporting. I will spend the rest of my life in a hospital, but that while I am there, everything is geared just to keeping my brain active, with no possibility of it ever being able to direct anything. As far as I can see, that is an act of deliberate cruelty. . . .

The best part of my life was, I suppose, my work. The most valuable asset that I had for that was my imagination. It's just a shame that my mind wasn't paralyzed along with my body. Because my imagination—which was my most precious possession—has become my enemy. And it tortures me with thoughts of what might have been and of what might be to come. I can feel my mind slowly breaking up. . . .

I am filled with absolute outrage that you, who have no connection with me whatever, have the right to condemn me to a life of torment because you can't see the pain. There's no blood and there's no screaming so you can't see it. But if you saw a mutilated animal on the side of the road, you'd shoot it. Well, I'm only asking that you show me the same mercy you'd show an animal. But I'm not asking you to commit an act of violence, just take me somewhere and leave me. And if you don't, then, you come back here in five years and see what a piece of work you did today. . . .

Both sanctity-of-life and quality-of-life perspectives introduce ambiguous terms for those who must decide appropriate criteria for a "good death." Those who take a sanctity-of-life perspective must adequately define "natural" life. Should biological life, sustained by a respirator, be considered "natural"? How about life sustained by a feeding tube or intravenous glucose solution? When is it appropriate to reject medical intervention, and how can we determine when a "natural" death has taken place?

Ivan Illich (1976:207–208) illustrates this problem.

Today, the man best protected against setting the stage for his own dying is the sick person in critical condition. Society, acting through the medical system, decides when and after what indignities and mutilations he shall die. The medicalization of society has brought the epoch of natural death to an end. Western man has lost the right to preside at his act of dying. Health, or the autonomous power to cope, has been expropriated down to the last breath. Technical death has won its victory over dying. Mechanical death has conquered and destroyed all other deaths.

From a quality-of-life perspective, the concept of "quality" is even more difficult to define. Who should decide when life has quality? Quality is a relative term and its meaning often changes over the life cycle and as a result of social circumstance. I have little doubt that the quality of my life would diminish if I became paralyzed, blind, and/or deaf. However, many people with these disabilities experience a life of quality filled with purpose and meaning.

PASSIVE AND ACTIVE EUTHANASIA

There are two methods by which individuals try to facilitate a "good death"—passive and active euthanasia. **Passive euthanasia** involves a protocol whereby no action or medical intervention hastens death. Usually involving the removal of medical technology or the withholding of medical intervention, it is supported by people who affirm both sanctity-of-life and quality-of-life perspectives. In a 1985 Harris Poll, 85 percent of respondents endorsed a terminally ill patient's right to tell the doctor to stop trying to extend life. While not legally binding in some states, living wills provide a vehicle by which individuals make their intentions known concerning the withholding of medical treatment. Later in this chapter we will discuss the legal steps involved in the creation of living wills that assist family members in making decisions regarding the medical treatment of terminally ill patients.

ROUTINE CPR CAN ABUSE THE OLD AND SICK

Fazlur Rahman

Since cardiopulmonary resuscitation was introduced in 1960, it has saved countless lives. But we are in danger today of abusing this procedure. At some point, we must stop adding to the suffering of dying patients by pounding on their chests, possibly breaking bones, just to extend their lives by a few days or weeks.

CPR is performed routinely in hospitals, without regard to patients' chances of recovering to lead normal lives. Why try to revive with CPR a patient who has been sick for years with diabetes, hypertension, heart disease and kidney failure, and who has just had an operation for a perforated intestine? Why batter the sternum of a drastically debilitated, 85-year-old woman who is suffering from pneumonia? In terminal cases like these, the idea of beating on the chest of an old and sick person is morally and physically repugnant. Yet, for the lack of prior understandings between patients, families, and physicians, the procedure continues to be used indiscriminately.

Although some people will refuse as long as possible to let a loved one die, most families will abide by the medical decision on CPR. Trouble arises, however, when neither the terminal patient nor the doctor raises the subject of CPR soon enough. There is a vague hope that the problem may not have to be faced soon. Then, under the duress of the moment, it is hard for families to make a quick decision. So, the physician simply follows the routine of CPR.

What can we do to avoid this predicament?

First, we have to educate the public and professionals. An increasing number of patients are asking for a peaceful death. In time, I hope that this demand

(continued)

will become universal. Medical and nursing schools need to teach more about accepting death and dying.

Second, patients should sign living wills. Many states have enacted laws that recognize the terminally ill patient's right to refuse life-sustaining treatment. By court decisions, 12 states have acknowledged such a right.

Third, patients with incurable diseases should be tactfully approached by their families and physicians about the use of aggressive measures. While discussing the subject, one should not convey hopelessness; hope is an important part of medical care.

If the patient is opposed to resuscitation, the primary physician must write clearly on a patient's chart, "No CPR." Simply having an understanding with the nurses on the floor will not work. When a CPR code is activated by hospital monitors, doctors and nurses will rush to the victim. If the attending physician is not around and there are no instructions on the patient's record, confusion arises about what to do. In our lawyer-dominated society, hospitals have been forced to devise bureaucratic rules that may not have the patients' welfare foremost in mind. Moreover, once a patient is on the life-support system it is not easy to "pull the plug." Legal complexities will override ethical justifications. Thus, it is all the more important to decide ahead of time what steps are appropriate to revive incurable patients.

Minneapolis Star and Tribune, February 27, 1989, p. 9A. (Originally written for *The New York Times.*) Copyright 1989 by The New York Times Company. Reprinted by permission.

Some people have received the false impression that passive euthanasia is incompatible with a belief in the sanctity of life. The following statement by Pope Pius XII (1977: 283–284, 286) illustrates the Roman Catholic Church's belief in maintaining sanctity of life while affirming passive euthanasia.

Natural reason and Christian morals say that man (and whoever is entrusted with the task of taking care of his fellowman) has the right and the duty in case of serious illness to take the necessary treatment for the preservation of life and health. This duty that one has toward himself, toward God, toward the human community, and in most cases toward certain determined persons, derives from well ordered charity, from strict justice, as well as from devotion toward one's family.

But normally one is held to use only *ordinary means*—according to circumstances of persons, places, times, and culture—that is to say, means that do not involve any grave burden for oneself or another. A more strict obligation would be too burdensome for most men and would render the attainment of the higher, more important good too difficult. Life, health, all temporal activities are in fact subordinated to spiritual ends. Consequently, if it appears that the attempt to resuscitation constitutes in reality such a burden for the family that one cannot in all conscience impose it upon them, they can lawfully insist that the doctor should discontinue these attempts, and the doctor can lawfully comply.

Living Wills

A **living will** is a document that states that one does not want medical intervention if the technology or treatment that keeps one alive cannot offer a reasonable quality of life or hope for recovery (see sample below). Although only 9 percent of Americans have living wills, 38 states and the District of Columbia have laws saying that living wills are valid representations of a patient's wishes ("Specific Instructions Needed in Living Wills," 1989, p. 9F).

Despite a growing acceptance of living wills, the issue is still complicated by emotion and questions of when a will should be invoked. Many persons are

A LIVING WILL

To my family, my physician, my lawyer and all others whom it may concern:

Death is as much a reality as birth, growth, maturity, and old age. Death is the one certainty of life. If the time comes when I can no longer take part in decisions for my own future, let this statement stand as an expression of my wishes and directions, while I am still of sound mind.

If at such a time the situation should arise in which there is no reasonable expectation of my recovery from extreme physical or mental disability, I direct that I be allowed to die and not be kept alive by medications, artificial means or "heroic measures." I do, however, ask that medication be mercifully administered to me to alleviate suffering even though this may shorten my remaining life.

This statement is made after careful consideration and is in accordance with my strong convictions and beliefs. I want the wishes and directions here expressed carried out to the extent permitted by law. Insofar as they are not legally enforceable, I hope that those to whom this will is addressed will regard themselves as morally bound by these provisions.

Signed _____

Date _____

Witness _____

Witness _____

William E. Phipps, *Death: Confronting the Reality.* Atlanta, GA: John Knox Press, 1987.

reluctant to take steps leading to a patient's death, and some are willing to withhold further medical treatment, but do not want to disconnect existing life support ("Making a Living Will," 1985, p. 20).

If considering a living will, one should check to make certain that such a will is legal in the state of residence. After the will is drawn up, make several copies of it and share it with your physician, family members, and friends. Your attorney should also have a copy in his or her office. This is not something you should limit to one copy, lock up in your safety deposit box, and keep a big secret. Share the news.

In December 1991 the federal government created the Patient Self-Determination Act that requires most hospitals, nursing facilities, hospices, home health-care programs, and health maintenance organizations (HMOs) to inform patients at admission of their right to create "advance directives" relating to their care (see sample Directive to Physicians on p. 297). According to Ken Wibecan (1992), the two most common of these directives are the living will and the **durable power of attorney** for health care. The latter names a surrogate decisionmaker with legal authority to consent (or refuse consent) for medical treatment should the patient lack competency for making such decisions.

If one accepts the legitimacy of passive euthanasia as set forth in the living will, it is clear that the use of extraordinary measures is not required of terminal patients, members of their family, or attending physicians. However, differentiating between ordinary and extraordinary treatment is not an easy task. Gerald Kelly (cited by Bouma et al., 1989:274–275) defines these terms in the following manner: *Ordinary means* of preserving life are all medicines, treatments, and operations that offer a reasonable hope of benefit for the patient and that can be obtained and used without excessive expense, pain, and other inconveniences.

Extraordinary means of preserving life are all those medicines, treatments, and operations that cannot be obtained without excessive expense, pain, or other inconvenience, or that, if used, would not offer a reasonable hope of benefit.

These definitions introduce other ambiguous terms—"reasonable hope," "excessive expense," "excessive pain," and "excessive inconvenience." What is reasonable and excessive? Who among us can make decisions employing these highly relative concepts? Which of the following should society hold responsible to determine these matters: politicians, physicians, lawyers and judges, members of the community at large, and/or patients and their families?

Many within the medical community have operationalized **ordinary measures** to be any procedure that is "usual and customary" medical practice, and **extraordinary measures** to be those procedures that are exotic, innovative, and medically experimental. However, it is clear that this distinction provides us with little help because (1) technology has a way of imposing itself upon modern society in an amoral fashion and (2) what has been considered innovative and experimental becomes usual and customary with time. Consider the situation in which a Down's Syndrome infant starves to death because parents will not permit a physician to perform a simple operation that would allow food to be digested by the child. The fate of this Down's Syndrome infant is a classic example of what sociologists call **cultural lag**—a condition created by rapid medical technological development and relatively static definitions of biological life and death. Medical practice today can prolong life (or postpone death) without having precise definitions of a point at which meaningful living has stopped and death has occurred. This condition would be of little significance if medical science were unable to maintain some biological functioning of the individual with artificial means, but such is not the case. As Joseph Fletcher (1977:355) says, when the terminal patient "contemplates modern medicine's ability to prolong life, death itself is welcomed compared to the terrors of senility and protracted terminal treatment."

Furthermore, even if one were able to distinguish between ordinary and extraordinary treatments, would it be acceptable for patients (or someone acting on their behalf) to request the withdrawal of ordinary life support such as food and water? This is an issue that tends to divide persons who affirm a sanctity-of-life perspective and favor passive euthanasia.

1989 SUPREME COURT DECISION: CRUZAN V. DIRECTOR, MISSOURI DEPARTMENT OF HEALTH

Nancy Cruzan, the victim of a car crash, had been in a "persistent vegetative state" for six years. Her parents went to the Missouri state court to seek permission to have her feeding tube removed; the court refused. Missouri law required "clear and convincing" evidence of the patient's own wishes. Cruzan had told friends, in casual college chats, that she did not want to live "like a vegetable," but Missouri did not think that convincing enough.

The state, citing its "unqualified interest in life," set itself up as Cruzan's proxy and protector, deciding on her behalf that her best interest would be served by continuing to live. The U.S. Supreme Court narrowly ruled in Missouri's favor, and Cruzan lived until a county court judge ruled in December of 1990 (on new evidence of her wishes) that the tube should be disconnected.

Between 5,000 and 10,000 Americans are now being kept alive in circumstances, and with prognoses, much like Cruzan's.

The Economist, July 20, 1991, pp. 21–24. Copyright © 1991 The Economist Newspaper Group, Inc. Reprinted with permission.

If one can accept the legitimacy of passive euthanasia, Lowell Erdahl (1987: 143) raises the following questions:

> There are circumstances in which active euthanasia is more compassionate than passive. Is it, for example, more kind to cause death by dehydration and star-vation than it is to kill the patient by lethal injection? In both cases the motive and effect are exactly the same; only the method is different. Is it possible that in some cases the sin of omission (permitting death by dehydration and starvation) may be greater than the sin of commission (causing death by lethal injection)?

Active euthanasia requires a direct action to bring about death. There are two types of active euthanasia: **suicide** and **mercy killing.** Suicide is the voluntary act of taking one's own life. Those who favor active euthanasia prefer to use the term **self-deliverance** when a life of a terminally ill patient is terminated. However, they would reject the legitimacy of suicide for persons with clinical depression or other forms of psychological pain.

In a 1977 Cleveland, Ohio, study conducted by Mostafa Nagi and associates concerning Roman Catholic and Protestant clergy's attitudes toward euthanasia (1977–1978:159) it was discovered that 73 percent and 69 percent of Protestant and Catholic clergy respectively found passive euthanasia acceptable for patients who wanted to go home and die in peace surrounded by family members. However, only 18 percent of Protestant and 2 percent of Catholic clergy found active euthanasia acceptable.

In the United States, the Hemlock Society, founded in 1980, assists terminally ill individuals in the act of self-deliverance. In 1981 the Hemlock Society published a book written by its co-founder and director, Derek Humphry, entitled *Let Me Die Before I Wake: Hemlock's Book of Self-Deliverance for the Dying.* The first 10 chapters of this book provide detailed case studies of individuals (often with the assistance of family members and friends) who chose self-deliverance as an alternative to passive euthanasia. The remainder of the book provides a bibliography and an extended discussion of personal and legal issues related to the decision to take one's life.

A year earlier, the English counterpart of the Hemlock Society—**EXIT** (founded in 1935 as the British Voluntary Euthanasia Society)—published *A Guide to Self-Deliverance* (1980). This book is unique because it provides the reader with detailed instructions to successfully and painlessly commit suicide. In the United States this book would have been construed as an attempt to intentionally aid and/or solicit another to commit suicide—a felony in most states. Until 1991 when Derek Humphry published *Final Exit,* the Hemlock Society had not been willing to be explicit in providing such information to its members. However, with public sentiment turning more favorably toward active euthanasia, the Hemlock Society has taken a more active role in promoting self-deliverance. In addition to book sales, the Hemlock Society has raised as much as $500,000 in yearly membership fees. Humphry is paid an annual director's salary of $66,000 and heads a full-time staff of eleven (Gabriel, 1991:87). According to Trip Gabriel, the Hemlock Society plans to open offices around the country and to become even more active in political races. In 1991 the Hemlock Society was a strong advocate of Washington state's Initiative 119, contributing $313,000 in support of the bill that narrowly failed (Gabriel, 1991:46).

The Hemlock Society has been careful to differentiate suicide from self-deliverance, and self-deliverance from mercy killing. Suicide is often condemned socially and religiously as a selfish act or as an "overreaction of a disturbed mind." Suicide is considered by many as an irrational act that is a permanent solution to what is often a temporary problem. In contrast, self-deliverance should be considered a positive action taken to provide a permanent solution to long-term pain and suffering for the individual and his or her loved ones faced with a terminal condition. (Chapter 9 provides an extended treatment of suicide unrelated to terminal illness.)

Self-deliverance is a completely voluntary act on the part of the patient, while mercy killing involves other people's behavior that may or may not be sanctioned

DIRECTIVE TO PHYSICIANS

This directive is made this _____ day of _____ (month) _____ (year).

I, _____ being of sound mind, willfully and voluntarily make known my desire
   (a) ☐ That my life shall not be artificially prolonged and
   (b) ☐ That my life shall be ended with the aid of a physician
          under the circumstances set forth below, and do
          hereby declare:
1. If at any time I should have a terminal condition or illness certified to be terminal by two physicians, and they determine that
   my death will occur within six months,
   (a) ☐ I direct that life-sustaining procedures be withheld or
          withdrawn, and
   (b) ☐ I direct that my physician administer aid-in-dying in a
          humane and dignified manner. (You must initial (a) or
          (b) or both.)

(continued)

(c) ☐ **I have attached Special Instructions on a separate page to the directive.** (Initial if you have attached a separate page.)

The action taken under this paragraph shall be at the time of my own choosing if I am competent.

2. In the absence of my ability to give directions regarding the termination of my life, it is my intention that this directive shall be honored by my family, agent (described in paragraph 4), and physician(s) as the final expression of my legal right to

   (a) ☐ **Refuse medical or surgical treatment,** and

   (b) ☐ **To choose to die in a humane and dignified manner.**
   (You must initial (a) or (b) or both, and you must initial one box below.)

   ☐ If I am unable to give directions, I *do not* want my attorney-in-fact to request aid-in-dying.

   ☐ If I am unable to give directions, I *do* want my attorney-in-fact to ask my physician for aid-in-dying.

3. I understand that a terminal condition is one in which I am not likely to live for more than six months.

4. (a) I, _____
   do hereby designate and appoint _____ as my attorney-in-fact (agent) to make health-care decisions for me if I am in a coma or otherwise unable to decide for myself as authorized in this document. For the purpose of this document, "health-care decision" means consent, refusal of consent, or withdrawal of consent to any care, treatment, service, or procedure to maintain, diagnose, or treat an individual's physical or mental condition, or to administer aid-in-dying.

   (b) By this document I intend to create a Durable Power of Attorney for Health Care under The Oregon Death With Dignity Act and ORS Section 126.407. This power of attorney shall not be affected by my subsequent incapacity, except by revocation.

   (c) Subject to any limitations in this document, I hereby grant to my agent full power and authority to make health-care decisions for me to the same extent that I could make these decisions for myself if I had the capacity to do so. In exercising this authority, my agent shall make health-care decisions that are consistent with my desires as stated in this document or otherwise made known to my agent, including, but not limited to, my desires concerning obtaining, refusing, or withdrawing life-prolonging care, treatment, services and procedures, and administration of aid-in-dying.

5. This directive shall have no force or effect seven years from the date filled in above, unless I am incompetent to act on my own behalf and then it shall remain valid until my competency is restored.

6. I recognize that a physician's judgment is not always certain, and that medical science continues to make progress in extending life, but in spite of these facts, I nevertheless wish aid-in-dying rather than letting my terminal condition take its natural course.

7. My family has been informed of my request to die, their opinions have been taken into consideration, but the final decision remains mine, so long as I am competent.

8. The exact time of my death will be determined by me and my physician with my desire or my attorney-in-fact's instructions paramount.

I have given full consideration and understand the full import of this directive, and I am emotionally and mentally competent to make this directive. I accept the moral and legal responsibility for receiving aid-in-dying.

This directive will not be valid unless it is signed by two qualified witnesses who are present when you sign or acknowledge your signature. The witnesses must not be related to you by blood, marriage, or adoption; they must not be entitled to any part of your estate; and they must not include a physician or other person responsible for, or employed by anyone responsible for, your health care. If you have attached any additional pages to this form, you must date and sign each of the additional pages at the same time you date and sign this power of attorney.

Signed: _____

City, County, and State of Residence _____

(This document must be witnessed by two qualified adult witnesses. None of the following may be used as witnesses: (1) a health care provider who is involved in any way with the treatment of the declarant, (2) an employee of a health care provider who is involved in any way with the treatment of the declarant, (3) the operator of a community care facility where the declarant resides, (4) an employee of an operator of a community care facility who is involved in any way with the treatment of the declarant.)

The Oregon Death with Dignity Act, Oregon Revised Statutes, Chapter 97, 1990.

by the patient. In a 1985 Harris Poll, 61 percent of the respondents favored the patient's right to ask the doctor to "put him out of his misery." However, at the present time both suicide (self-deliverance) and mercy killing are illegal in the United States. Furthermore, U.S. laws do not distinguish between murder and mercy killing, and therefore mercy killing is predominantly treated as a criminal offense regardless of the motivations of individuals involved.

The Hemlock Society and EXIT wish to eliminate the stigma attached to self-killing and to extend to all individuals the right of active, rational, and voluntary euthanasia whenever the dying process only promises unrelieved pain and a life devoid of dignity, meaning, and purpose. The Hemlock Society has endorsed the 1990 Oregon Death with Dignity Act as a legal proposal to guarantee these rights.

The Legalization of Mercy Killing: The Dutch Experiment

In the Netherlands, physicians are allowed to perform mercy killing through lethal injections if the doctors follow a strict procedure established by the Dutch medical profession and sanctioned by the courts. In this procedure, the following conditions must be met (Diekstra, 1987:56):

1. The choice of suicide must be a free-will decision of the person and not made under pressure by others.
2. The wish to die can be an enduring one.
3. The person must be experiencing unbearable physical and/or emotional pain, and the improvement of this condition cannot reasonably be expected.
4. The person must not be mentally disturbed at the time of the decision to commit suicide.
5. The suicide should be carried out in such a way that harm is not caused to others.
6. The person who assists the suicide should be a qualified health professional, and only a medical doctor is allowed to administer the lethal drug.
7. The helper should never handle such cases entirely on his or her own, but should ask for professional consultation from colleagues (e.g., other medical colleagues and/or members of the clergy).
8. The assisted suicide would be fully documented, and the documents should be made available to the appropriate legal authorities.

Though this procedure is not codified as law, since 1972 the Dutch courts have established legal precedents that have made physician-assisted suicide fairly common. According to Paul Montgomery (1987), annually more than 6000 people in Holland commit suicide with medical assistance from physicians. Furthermore, the majority of Holland's AIDS (acquired immune deficiency syndrome) patients end their lives prematurely through medical intervention. Clearly, mercy killing has become socially sanctioned in a modern industrial nation. What are the effects of this precedent upon other European nations and the United States?

As early as 1973 a Gallup Poll was released in the United States that found that 53 percent of those interviewed said that physicians should have the *legal right* to painlessly end the life of a person with a terminal illness *if the patient and his family request it* (cited by Nagi et al., 1977–1978:155). More recently, in November of 1991, voters in the state of Washington considered Initiative 119, which proposed to expand the state's living-will law to include tube-feeding among the life-sustaining treatments that could be withdrawn from terminally ill patients and patients in persistent vegetative states. This bill, the first of its kind in the United States, would have also allowed terminally ill adults to seek physician-assisted suicide providing two doctors determined that the patient had less than 6 months to live. Although the initiative was supported by the Democratic Party, the Seattle Bar Association, the United Methodist Church in the Northwest, and several local chapters of the National Council of Jewish Women, it was not enacted into law in the populist state that was the first to liberalize abortion laws by popular vote in 1970 (Maples, 1991). Similarly, in the 1992 general election, the state of California failed to pass an initiative allowing physician-assisted suicide.

KEVORKIAN KILLING SPREE MAKES GOOD CASE AGAINST EUTHANASIA

Arthur Caplan

The body count continues to mount in Oakland County, Michigan. Jack Kevorkian, the 63-year-old retired pathologist who has made it his life's mission to bring death to the despondent, the mentally unstable and the severely disabled, has now helped kill four women in Michigan.

The latest "beneficiary" of his skills was Susan Williams, a 52-year-old resident of Clawson, Mich., a Detroit suburb, who was blind and severely disabled as a result of multiple sclerosis.

Geoffrey Fieger, Kevorkian's lawyer, originally denied that Kevorkian took any active role in causing Williams' death earlier this month. But he subsequently changed his tune. He now says it was Dr. Jack who purchased a canister

(continued)

of carbon monoxide gas, brought it to Susan Williams' home and counseled her about how to gas herself to death.

The authorities in Michigan seem unable to bring Kevorkian's serial euthanasia escapade to a halt. He has had his medical license suspended. And a Michigan judge did place him under a court order prohibiting him from using his suicide machine in the county after the death of his first client, Janet Adkins.

Oakland County prosecutors secured a grand jury indictment on two counts of murder in the deaths of two other women Kevorkian killed last October. But none of this legal activity has deflected the doctor from his self-appointed grisly mission. He continues to thumb his nose at Michigan's cops, judges and legislators while leaving a trail of disabled women's bodies in his wake.

The identity of his victims provides yet another reason for the state of Michigan to protect its residents from Dr. K. All four of Dr. Kevorkian's clients have been middle-aged women. Their ages: 54, 43, 58 and 52. None was terminally ill. All were despondent about facing a life of disability and impairment.

Why are Kevorkian's clients all women? Why are they all people with disabilities? Whatever one's views about the morality of assisted suicide and euthanasia, it is simply impossible to ignore the fact that Kevorkian's message of death has found its most receptive audience among older women who have or face the prospect of disability.

The women who have died with Kevorkian's help apparently believed that their lives had lost all value. What are those with disabilities to think when these women, their families, Kevorkian, his legal team and his myriad defenders constantly assert that life in a wheelchair, life without sight and life with pain is life without value? What should women make of the fact that Kevorkian accepts and promotes the idea that the only solution, the final solution, for women who see their lives as not worth living is death?

Euthanasia will soon replace abortion as the major source of moral contention and divisiveness on the American social agenda. In a society in which the ranks of the elderly are already exploding, where more and more people are kept alive by relying on medical technology and in which more and more people survive with devastating chronic illnesses such as AIDS, diabetes, Parkinson's disease, Alzheimer's and cystic fibrosis, issues of the managing of death will displace moral concerns about the management of birth.

Kevorkian's killing of the vulnerable and the frail, his belief that women who see their lives as lacking in value deserve immediate assistance when they say they wish to die, illustrates exactly what is morally wrong with the movement to legitimate active euthanasia and suicide. It is enormously tempting for society to respond to despair, vulnerability and disability with carbon monoxide or potassium chloride. It is cheap, clean and neat. It is also immoral.

The poor, the disabled and women have the most to lose from Kevorkian's campaign of "mercy." His brand of zealotry is precisely what would be unleashed on the weakest, most vulnerable members of society if his efforts to legitimate euthanasia and suicide are allowed to bear fruit.

Kevorkian himself provides the strongest case possible as to why the most vulnerable members of our society ought to fear the euthanasia movement. Look at who Kevorkian has helped to die and ask yourself whether he ought to be allowed to continue to "help" others.

"Kevorkian Killing Spree Makes Good Case Against Euthanasia." *Saint Paul Pioneer Press,* May 25, 1992, p. 13A.

The Slippery-Slope Argument

Persons who oppose active euthanasia often do so on the grounds of what they call the **slippery-slope-to-Auschwitz argument.** They would allege that the justification for withholding some treatments also justifies withholding any and all treatments from those whom society considers unworthy. It is further argued that if a society wishes to extend to any of its members the right to active euthanasia, none of its members is protected from being killed. Such was the case under Hitler when

Jack Kevorkian poses with Marcella Lawrence and Marguerite Tate at his attorney's office following a press conference concerning the passage of Michigan's new law banning assisted suicides. Both women took their lives with Kevorkian present just hours before Michigan's governor signed the bill into law.

German society's "unproductive," "defective," and "morally and mentally unfit"—Jews, homosexuals, and handicapped—were sent to Auschwitz and other places of confinement to be "euthanized" (murdered).

The slippery-slope argument asserts that society moves toward a disregard for human life in predictable steps. The first step is the acceptance of passive euthanasia when medical technology and surgical procedures are withheld from (or rejected by) chronically and/or terminally ill patients. The second step occurs when ordinary or customary procedures are withdrawn—such procedures would include food and water. We arrive at the third step when society accepts the legitimacy of suicide (self-deliverance). The fourth step is when these "rights" are extended to nonterminal patients such as quadriplegics. In the fifth step, the medical system will assist patients in self-deliverance or active euthanasia (as is presently the situation in Holland), believing that the incurably ill deserve the same "humane" treatment as that accorded to a beloved animal that is "put to sleep." All of these provisions are extended to the nonterminally ill and/or persons acting on their behalf in the sixth step. Finally, we arrive at the seventh step—"Auschwitz"—when society is willing to accord these "privileges" to the unwilling, incompetent, and/or undesirable.

To prevent society from reaching such a level of desensitization, people who embrace the "slippery-slope" argument argue that no type of euthanasia should be considered socially acceptable—in other words, to be safe, societies should "stay off the slope entirely!"

While one might disagree with the inevitability of these steps to lead toward a rejection of the sanctity of human life, we may acknowledge that the noble intentions of those who favor active euthanasia do not in themselves justify a public policy allowing mercy killing, nor will they counteract the potential abuse to which euthanasia can be put by those whose motives may be self-serving (Bouma et al., 1989:301).

Without a doubt, even so-called "voluntary" actions can be unduly influenced by social pressures. Consider the case of an elderly nursing home resident who realizes that the cost of her care depletes financial resources that might be used to support an able-bodied spouse or to bequeath to other family members. When one defines oneself as a burden to society, is euthanasia (even self-deliverance) truly a voluntary choice? In the words of Erdahl (1987:145):

> As costs of care increase, individuals in specific circumstances and society as a whole will be strongly tempted to sell out both compassion and responsible reverence for life in exchange for economic considerations. If the day comes when euthanasia is established as an economic policy, we will have ceased to be either fully moral or fully human.

DUTCH PARLIAMENT APPROVES LAW PERMITTING EUTHANASIA

Marlise Simons

Herbert Cohen who has a family practice, holds that doctors should be allowed to end the lives of their patients in certain cases. For more than 10 years in the village of Capelle, he said, he has brought on the end for some people and helped others kill themselves to relieve their suffering.

Dr. Karel Gunning, a family doctor in nearby Rotterdam, calls this murder. He did so again today after the Dutch Parliament approved by a 91 to 45 vote a law that sanctioned euthanasia under strict conditions, after two decades of tormented national debate.

"Today the Netherlands abolished the Hippocratic Oath," Dr. Gunning said. "Killing is not part of medicine. I regret to say that we are becoming a barbaric nation."

Growing Public Support

A Government-backed study says that Dr. Gunning belongs to the 11 percent of Dutch doctors who said they would refuse to practice euthanasia. Dr. Cohen is on the side of public and medical sentiment in the Netherlands and even lectures about euthanasia at police academies.

Both men have been very outspoken on the complex legal, ethical and moral questions of when and how doctors may actively bring on death.

Under the new law, euthanasia and help in suicide, by applying a lethal drug, while technically still illegal is permitted if doctors follow strict medical and ethical rules.

The rules, though not written into the law, state that the request for euthanasia and suicide must come from a patient who is doing so voluntarily, who is mentally competent, has a hopeless disease without prospect for improvement and is undergoing unbearable physical or mental suffering. The doctor may proceed only after consulting another experienced doctor and must then report the death and its circumstances to the city coroner.

Dr. Cohen says he has cooperated with his patients' request to die because "we need a counterweight for the enormous technology of present medicine."

"We are talking mostly about older people who in other times would have died from their condition," he said. "If we can keep people alive but give them a life that is no life, we must be consistent and give them the choice to end it."

The 62-year-old doctor said he was willing to discuss his actions in an interview because "I am used to reporting them" to the health authorities.

(continued)

Openness, he said, is essential for him and for the patient. "I need to discuss the case with others," he said. "It gives the patient the chance to take leave openly of his children, his grandchildren, a nurse, a household help, perhaps neighbors, the people in his world."

Makes Mourning Easier

Saying goodbye is painful, but it can be of great benefit, the doctor said. "It is dignified to say, 'I'm leaving.' It creates moments of great intimacy between people." He has become convinced that it makes the mourning process easier.

Dr. Cohen said his views have all been part of a learning process. "I've made all sorts of mistakes," he said. "Once I did not tell a nurse who came the next morning to find the patient dead. She came to me outraged. 'How could you not let me say goodbye,' she said. 'I cared for him for three months.' "

In his practice of 2,500 people, euthanasia does not happen often, he explained, because a request to die requires "an independent-minded person," someone who is willing to fight for that right.

"It may take 10 conversations or more before I am convinced," Dr. Cohen said. "Once it took three years. When we start talking, the patient may already have struggled for a long time with the idea, but I'm just beginning."

In Dr. Cohen's experience the main motive for requesting death is not only a question of physical suffering. "Generally, personal dignity plays an important role," he said. "People don't want to live on machines, someone may be half paralyzed, incontinent. This can be harder to bear than pain. Everyone has a different threshold of what is bearable."

To Dr. Gunning, who is the former president of the League of Dutch Physicians, a pro-life doctors group, it is society's, not the patient's, responsibility to solve this. He argues that it is up to doctors to make pain bearable, to care for people so that they do not feel embarrassed or burdensome.

"If people's feelings, their self-respect, suffers, the solution is better care, to change our attitude, not agreeing that they should die."

He said that in hospices in Britain, where he has studied, care has been such that people who on arrival said they wanted to die often changed their minds and wanted to hold on. He insisted that the Netherlands organize a better hospice network.

"The great danger is that here we may get into a euthanasia mentality," he said. "Our society is moving very quickly from birth control to death control."

Number of Deaths Rises

A Government-backed study said there were 2,300 deaths by voluntary euthanasia in 1990 and about 400 cases of doctor-assisted suicide. The figures represented about 2 percent of all deaths in the Netherlands that year.

Doctors reported practicing 440 cases of voluntary euthanasia in 1990 but in 1992 the number rose to 1,318. Legal and medical experts say the increase is the result of more open discussion of the issue and a clearer agreement on the rules that protect doctors from prosecution.

But the Government was troubled by the study's finding that in 1,000 other cases, a patient's life was ended by euthanasia without an explicit recent request.

In most of these cases, the patient had only days or hours to live, was often in great pain, and was either in coma or not fully conscious. In more than half the cases the patient had earlier talked about euthanasia to the doctor or others. In six cases, newborn babies were involved.

The Royal Dutch Medical Association, which has generally been pro-euthanasia said these findings had shocked many doctors and most of them outright condemned euthanasia without an explicit and clear request by the patient.

New York Times International, February 10, 1993, p. A5.

EUTHANASIA: THE DUTCH RULES

Voluntary Nature. The request for euthanasia must be made "entirely of the patient's own free will" and not under pressure from others.

Weighing Alternatives. The patient must be well informed and must be able to consider the alternatives.

Certain Decision. The patient must have a "lasting longing for death." Requests made on impulse or based on temporary depression cannot be considered.

Unacceptable Suffering. The patient must experience his or her suffering as perpetual, unbearable and hopeless. The physician must be reasonably able to conclude that the suffering experienced is unbearable.

Consultation. The doctor must consult at least one colleague who has faced the question of euthanasia before.

Reporting. A documented written report must be drawn up stating the history of the patient's illness and declaring that the rules have been met.

Source: Associated Press.

WHERE DEATH COMES NORMALLY

The scenery from the taxi window fits perfectly onto the familiar London palette: A gray, green, and brown cityscape marks the route to the collection of medical buildings known as St. Christopher's. St. Christopher's was the first modern hospice. It was opened 21 years ago to give more than tender, loving care to the dying; it promised to give medically skillful loving care.

I have come here because we read and hear so much about two alternatives for the terminally ill: suffering and suicide, merciless medicine and mercy killing. Many in America now believe that medicine is more concerned with prolonging life than preventing pain.

The beacon of the modern hospice movement offers a very different mode. A place where medicine and humanity can ease the way to death without technological heroism or its horror stories. A place where death is allowed its normalcy.

The hospice doesn't artificially prolong life, nor does it shorten life. Indeed, Dr. Tom West, director of St. Christopher's, makes clear distinctions between the hospice and euthanasia movements. "The pro-euthanasia community feels that if you can't cure a patient with cancer and can't control the symptoms, you should offer the patient a chance of opting out of life. Hospice is saying you *can* control symptoms and, having controlled symptoms, it is amazing to see how much use patients and families make of that extra time. I have seen so many situations that it makes me sweat to think I might have cut the life short." West adds his own beliefs into the equation carefully: "I happen to think we are not meant to shorten our time. I also happen to think we are not meant to suffer." The widespread perception of these as the only choices comes, he believes, out of mainstream medicine's ignorance about pain-killing drugs and from the reluctance of doctors to use them. "Every patient that every doctor has is going to die. But if you look at the curriculum of medical schools, symptom control is just not there." If he has a goal, it would be to carry the message of hospice, particularly about the control of pain, back into the world of mainstream medicine. To see the line between hospice medicine and traditional medicine blurred.

Unfortunately, today the glare of publicity is regularly focused on a patient who faced a choice between prolonging suffering and cutting life short. It's focused on a husband or wife who faced the options of merciless medicine or mercy killing. But hospice has been learning and teaching that there's a third and a better way.

Adapted from Ellen Goodman, *The Boston Globe*, 1988. The Boston Globe Newspaper Company/Washington Post Writers Group. Reprinted with permission.

ORGAN DONATIONS

Human organ transplants have long been cloaked in a special aura of mystery, and sometimes fear, linked to religious concerns about the sanctity of the body and even to frightening fictional stories like that of Frankenstein (Malcolm, 1986:8). Because of the sensitive nature of the topic, human organ transplants have not been widely discussed by society.

In many urban areas today kidney foundations, eye banks, and transplant centers will supply donor cards and arrange for transplants when death occurs. There are many kinds of tissues or organs used for transplantation including eye, skin, bone, tendon, bone marrow, kidney, liver, pancreas, blood vessel, lung, and heart. While some of these transplant operations are still in the areas of research, techniques are constantly improving.

The first modern human organ transplant was a kidney transplant in 1950 in Chicago (Cooper and Lanza, 1984:1). The first liver transplant was performed in 1963 in Denver (Ezell, Anspaugh, and Oaks, 1987:178). Transplantation received especially wide coverage in the media with the transplantation of the first human heart by Christiaan Barnard in South Africa in 1967. There is an increasing tendency today for individuals to donate their organs and tissues upon death to the living. By 1984, transferring human organs into other bodies was occurring over

DON WRIGHT/THE MIAMI NEWS

THE RECYCLED MAN

Joel L. Swerdlow

Consider this scenario: Dan Smith is injured in a boating accident. Physicians certify that his brain has quit functioning. Although medical equipment can maintain his heartbeat, he is dead. A nurse enters his Social Security number into a computer and the screen flashes "Universal Donor." The display notes that Dan's wife had approved his decision (and signed up herself).

The hospital calls the local organ and tissue center, and late that evening doctors remove Dan's pancreas, liver, kidneys, lungs, and heart. They also take more than 70 kinds of tissue—corneas, skin, bones, ligaments and tendons, veins and middle ears—with procedures so careful that the family can still have an open-casket funeral the next day.

Within 24 hours, elements of Dan's body are used to release two kidney patients from the rigors of dialysis. His heart saves a 40–year-old father of two. His lungs give life to a steelworker and a grandmother. His liver saves a college student and his pancreas is transplanted to a young diabetic.

In the next few days, he gives hearing to one child and eyesight to two others. His skin helps two burned firefighters. Other tissues aid in reconstructive surgery. Some of his bones are freeze-dried for dental and other use; some tissues are assigned to research labs.

Computer networks help allocate the material, allowing physicians to find a proper match (hip and knee bones, for example, are cut to fit specific patients) and all transplant results are fed into a data bank shared by clinicians and researchers.

The collective value of these procedures runs to millions of dollars. The lives saved and suffering relieved are priceless. Yet the cost of Dan's tissues and organs is zero. All were donated.

This is no futuristic daydream. Each of the medical techniques and communication technologies described above exists today.

The Washington Post, June 25, 1989, p. 3B. Excerpted from Matching Needs, Saving Lives, published by the Annenberg Washington Program of Northwestern University.

100 times a day in the United States (Malcolm, 1986:8). There were 24,000 eyes or corneas transplanted, 6968 kidneys, 346 hearts, 308 livers, 87 pancreases, and 30 heart-lung combinations.

The National Conference on Uniform Laws developed the Uniform Anatomical Gift Act to help answer questions concerning transplantations, and all 50 states had adopted the act with slight variations by 1971 (Ezell, Anspaugh, and Oaks, 1987:181). The act advocates that a person be over 18 years of age to donate part or

UNIFORM DONOR CARD

UNIFORM DONOR CARD of _name of donor_. In the hope that I may help others, I hereby make this anatomical gift, if medically acceptable, to take effect upon my death. The words and marks below indicate my desires.

I give: a. _____ any needed organs or parts
b. _____ only the following organs or parts _specify the organs(s) or parts(s)_ for the purposes of transplantation, therapy, medical research or education:
c. _____ my body for anatomical study if needed

Signed by the donor and the following two witnesses in the presence of each other:

_____   _____
Signature of donor   Date of birth of donor

_____   _____
Date signed   City and State

_____   _____
Witness   Witness

all of his or her body upon death. If the body or body part has not been donated prior to death, a family member may do so, with permission based on the priority of the relationship. The priority is as follows: spouse, adult son or daughter, parents, adult sibling, legal guardian, or another party responsible for disposition of the body.

Various problems affect human transplantations. Whether or not the donor and donee tissues are compatible can be a problem. There is often a chronic shortage of donors, thus sometimes producing a difficult decision in selecting among potential recipients. A lack of a legal definition of death in some states prevents surgeons from removing healthy organs when brain activity has stopped, but the heart and lungs are still functioning. A lack of a nationwide communications network to coordinate information presents a problem for human transplantations.

BABY WITHOUT BRAIN DIES; ORGANS NO LONGER FIT TO TRANSPLANT

The short life of Theresa Ann Campo Pearson ended Monday, just 10 days after she was born without a fully formed brain. But the troubling issues that the tiny anencephalic infant's life raised live on.

By the time of her death, her major organs had deteriorated and were no longer viable for transplants, said Les Olson, director of organ procurement for the University of Miami. The corneas of her eyes were saved, and would be given "to another tiny baby," Olson said.

The 4-pound baby died Monday afternoon at Broward General Medical Center in Fort Lauderdale, Fla., about 19 hours after she was removed from a ventilator that briefly had sustained her when her vital organs began to fail. Her parents, Laura Campo and Justin Pearson, were at her side, doctors said. The cause of death was listed as cardiac and respiratory failure.

"It was very peaceful, the baby just sort of slipped away," said Dr. Brian Udell, director of the medical center's neonatology unit. "At the end, they got to hold her and kiss her."

Since the infant's birth by Caesarean section March 21, her parents had been battling for legal permission to have her heart, lungs, kidneys and liver removed so they could be transplanted to other children who might need them. But two state courts ruled that state law prevented taking vital organs from any-one who was not brain dead.

Attorney Scott Mager had argued the law didn't apply.

"How can you have cessation of brain activity when you don't have a brain?" he asked.

Late Monday the Florida Supreme Court agreed to hear the couple's appeal. But by then it was too late.

In fact, doctors said, it was too late for Theresa Ann within days of conception. She was anencephalic, born with nothing but the nub of a brain stem—enough to provide her only with breath and a heartbeat. She had no brain, no top to her skull, no feeling or cognition and no hope, said Udell.

Most anencephalics are stillborn. Of those born alive, the vast majority die within minutes. But Theresa Ann lived unaided by mechanical support for eight days.

"Theresa's legacy is that now, hopefully, people in this country will under-stand what brain death is," Olson said. "Organ donation is the only loving thing to come out of the death. But the only candidates for organ donation are those cases where the patients are kept alive artificially. She was not a suitable donor."

Anti-abortion activists, who opposed efforts to take vital organs before the baby died, staged a demonstration outside the hospital Monday.

"We are not here to point accusatory fingers of judgment," said the Rev. Patrick Mahoney. "We are here to reach with hands of hope."

"Baby Theresa was a gift from God. . . . She was not created by God for

spare parts," said one demonstrator, Eddie Soblotne of Coral Springs.
    Susan Clarke, the baby's maternal grandmother, saw it differently.
    "Taking one and helping two, three, five—that's pro-life," she said.
    She said the family would continue to press for a change in the law.
    "We will go on from here to help the children . . . the families. You don't
stop in midstream," she said hours before the baby died.
    Dr. Wayne DiGiacomo, who delivered the baby, praised Laura Campo.
    "She's a brave woman to have this decision to carry the fight to this level, to
have her child live on through other children," he said.

Saint Paul Pioneer Press, March 31, 1991, vol. 143, no. 339, pp. 1A and 8A.

Another problem is the question of who will pay for expensive transplantation procedures. A few public insurers have recently decided in favor of coverage for heart and liver transplants. Kidney transplants have been covered since 1973 under Medicare's end-stage renal disease program. Though the costs of solid organ transplants are expensive, the benefits are substantial when one considers that they may be life-saving. Average estimated total first-year costs of solid organ transplant procedures are $95,000 for heart transplants, $35,000 for kidney transplants, $130,000 for liver transplants, and $35,000 for pancreas transplants (Ezell, Anspaugh, and Oaks, 1987:185).

As more and more transplants are desired to make living more comfortable or to prolong life, and if insurance does not cover many of the operations, who receives organ and tissue transplantations may be limited to those who can afford such surgery. A sort of survival of the fittest behavior may then result regarding transplantations. Thus, this sensitive topic may become even more touchy. Related to these issues is the potential problem of the wealthy of the society having the ability to secure organs from those who are poor. If poor people do not have enough money to feed themselves, and they only need one kidney to survive, what would prevent them from selling a kidney for $50,000 or more to a dying rich person. Presently this is not possible in the United States (even though some recipients are giving financial consideration to the survivors of donors for "funeral expenses"), but this ethical nightmare is a reality in other nations of the world, and with a global economy, wealthy Americans will become involved.

PUBLIC POLICY

Until this section we have primarily taken a social exchange perspective on biomedical issues. We have analyzed euthanasia and organ transplants from a cost-

EGYPT'S DOCTORS IMPOSE KIDNEY TRANSPLANT CURBS

Chris Hedges

CAIRO—In an effort to end the sale of human organs by the country's poor, Egyptian doctors have announced a ban on all kidney transplants from living donors that are not done between relatives.

The ban, to take effect in July, was established by the Egyptian society of kidney specialists. It applies to all of Egypt's doctors. The society is moving to set up an organ bank and for the first time begin to transplant kidneys from cadavers, rather than live donors.

"By July we want to replace this kidney trade with a kidney bank," said Dr. Rashad Barsoum, Secretary General of the Egyptian society of kidney specialists.

Egypt, like India and other third-world countries, does a brisk business in the sale of organs, primarily kidneys, especially to wealthy Persian Gulf Arabs who come to one of Cairo's six kidney transplant centers. The transplant centers do about 350 operations a year.

Foreigners who want to buy Egyptian kidneys must come to Egypt because there are no provisions here for the preservation of transplant organs. Patients and donors are wheeled into the operating theater at the same time.

While other countries in the Arab world have transplant centers, few have the vast numbers of poor who are willing to sell their organs.

Private laboratories often act as brokerage houses, sending out recruiters to the slums of Cairo to entice prospective donors in for tissue tests. Patients needing kidneys go to the laboratories, where they are matched with a donor and sold an organ. Kidneys sell for $10,000 to $15,000. Dr. Barsoum said he has even heard of auctions with the organ going to the highest bidder.

"We have stooped to a low point with this business," Dr. Barsoum said.

The sale of organs evolved into an organized business in 1987, 11 years after the first kidney transplant took place in Egypt, medical authorities say. Doctors, too, have been criticized for profiting from the buying and selling of organs.

The doctors' union banned live-donor transplants from Egyptians to foreigners in 1987 and prohibited newspaper advertisements in which kidneys were sought.

But the moves did little to affect the trade, which seemed to grow as the country's medical establishment was able to handle more patients.

"I could foresee an international market developing in this area," Dr. Barsoum said.

The ban will put more pressure on the country's medical centers, which already cannot cope with the large numbers of kidney failures. About 10,000 of the 56 million Egyptians suffer kidney failure annually, three times the rate in the West. Only 2,000 of those patients are able to receive kidney dialysis treatment because of the high cost and the shortage of equipment.

Setting up an organ bank will also take time, since it can only be accomplished through an act of Parliament. While medical authorities have managed to get the backing of Muslim leaders, and even the head of the Coptic Christian community, they must change the Constitution, which stipulated that the dead must be buried immediately, in accordance with Islamic law.

Muslim authorities, while allowing the procedure, insist that organs can only be taken from cadavers if the deceased agreed in advance to the donation. The clerics have long held that the sale of organs violates Islamic law.

The New York Times International, January 23, 1992.

benefit point of view and assumed that the individual (or small group of people) is the appropriate unit of analysis. In the final section of this chapter we will analyze American public policy in dealing with the health needs of critically ill persons.

Many Americans assume that health care should be a guaranteed right of all citizens who desire and can afford to pay for it. For those unable to pay, the government provides basic health care through Medicaid, federally assisted payments to the poor. While passive euthanasia would affirm the right of those who choose to reject medical intervention, many believe that those who wish to live have a legitimate claim on the resources of society in providing the medical assistance necessary for living. According to *The Economist* (1991):

> The terminally ill now account for 20 to 30 percent of hospital expenditures, yet no amount of money is going to make them better. Doctors tend to shy away from principles of "utility" and cost worthiness. Instead, they argue a principle of "justice."

Yet, with annual medical care costing more than $600 billion and with heightened concerns for fiscal responsibility and cost containment, Americans are beginning to question universal access to health care for all citizens. This reevaluation of public policy is motivated by a utilitarian concern for distributive justice.

Utilitarianism is the belief that social policy should be directed at providing the greatest good (maximum benefits) for the greatest number of people. If it costs more than a million dollars to provide an artificial heart for one patient to live 3 months in a hospital, it is believed that the same amount of money might be more appropriately spent on prenatal care for 10,000 women. Furthermore, in the United States approximately 50 percent of the medical expenditures that an individual will incur during his or her lifetime will be for medical services delivered in the final 6 months of life. Since all of us are involved to some extent in paying for these medical costs (either through government subsidy or health insurance premiums), it is easy to question whether or not these expenditures are a worthwhile investment for such a limited return.

These types of cost-benefit analyses de-emphasize the health needs of particular individuals in favor of the health needs of the entire society. Garrett Hardin (1985:21), professor of ecology at the University of California at Santa Barbara, presents this argument with the following statement: "Easy access to health care is exhausting America's medical resources." According to Hardin, whenever meeting medical needs becomes an obligation of the entire community, utilization will always benefit individuals, while costs will be shared by all members of the system. Therefore, individuals can never be expected to limit their use, and health-care costs will naturally rise to a place where the system will collapse—the end of health care to all. He asks:

> Should the artificial heart be considered an inalienable right of any needy patient? Should the public at large pay the extra cost of saving premature babies? What is to be gained by extending the lives of comatose patients a few more years?

Is it better to spend money to save the life of one premature infant or to provide prenatal care for 10,000 women?

It is clear that our society faces a grave danger: as medical technology advances and we spend more and more for less and less, we edge ever closer to what might be called the tragedy of the medical commons. . . . A tragic end can be prevented only by saying NO! But what should we limit? The kinds of defects and malfunctions eligible for treatment? The age beyond which a patient may not be treated with heroic medicine? These are good candidates. Every point in our medical and legal systems seems to be biased in favor of compassion. At some point compassion must yield to principle.

Former Governor Richard Lamm raised this same type of lifeboat ethic philosophy in considering the health needs of Colorado's poor.

According to Dr. John Kitzhaber (cited by Robinson, 1989:4–5), a physician and the president of the Oregon State Senate,

We spend over $50 billion a year on people in the last six months of their lives, while closing pediatric clinics. We spend over $3 billion a year on intensive care for newborn babies, while denying prenatal care to hundreds of thousands of expectant women. Every dollar spent on health care is one that can't be spent on schools, roads, or a cleaner environment. In the last ten years many states have changed eligibility requirements that have removed more than 800,000 American women and children from Medicaid. Presently Medicaid covers only 38 percent of the nation's poor, while ten years ago it provided benefits for 64 percent.

Dr. Daniel Callahan, director of the Hastings Center, has advocated that persons over 80 be ineligible for Medicare reimbursements for cancer surgery, intensive care, and heart bypass surgery. Callahan (cited by Robinson, 1989:5) says:

As a nation, we must set a hard line against the endless prolongation of life. We must direct our medical energies only to the relief of pain and suffering in the elderly, and to help them prepare for a graceful death after a full life.

CONCLUSION

As a society we are confronting difficult decisions and problems caused by modern medicine's successes, not failures. One of those problems is that when we are faced with medical decisions for ourselves and those who are significant to us we may act in ways that when applied to an entire society would be imprudent or counterproductive. Yet, to make these decisions a matter of personal choice, determined solely by the financial resources of those making the decisions, would be unjust from a societal (or global) point of view.

We have obviously come to a point where very tough health-care decisions must be made. Many of these are personal and family decisions—how long do we wish to extend the dying process for ourselves and those we love? Other decisions will involve the welfare of the entire society and will require us to make choices between extending terminal care to those whose time is diminished and investing resources to prevent the more able-bodied from becoming ill. From a personal perspective, we will always find it difficult to withhold treatment from anyone. From a national perspective, we must always support health-care policies that will benefit most of our citizens without inflicting pain and suffering on any.

SUMMARY

1. Euthanasia, or "good death," must be defined within the context of one's understanding of the meaning of life.

2. Euthanasia from a sanctity-of-life perspective would contend that all "natural" life has intrinsic meaning and should be appreciated as a divine gift. As a consequence, human beings have the obligation to enhance the quality of life as it may exist.

3. Euthanasia from a quality-of-life perspective would hold that when life no longer has "quality," death is preferable to living a life devoid of meaning.

4. There are two methods by which individuals try to facilitate a "good death"—passive and active euthanasia. Passive euthanasia involves a protocol whereby no action or medical intervention hastens death. Passive euthanasia usually involves the removal of medical technology or the refusal of medical intervention. Passive euthanasia is supported by people who affirm both sanctity of life and quality of life perspectives.

5. Active euthanasia requires a direct action to bring about death. There are two types of active euthanasia: *suicide* and *mercy killing*.

6. Suicide is the voluntary act of taking one's own life. Those who favor active euthanasia prefer to use the term "self-deliverance" when a life of a terminally ill patient is terminated. Self-deliverance should be considered a positive action taken to provide a permanent solution to the long-term pain and suffering for the individual and his or her loved ones faced with a terminal condition.

7. Self-deliverance is a completely voluntary act on the part of the patient; mercy killing involves other people's behavior, which may or may not be sanctioned by the patient. At the present time both suicide (self-deliverance) and mercy killing are illegal in the United States.

8. Courts in the Netherlands have set legal precedents that have made physician-assisted suicide fairly common.

9. Persons opposing active euthanasia often do so with the "slippery-slope-to-Auschwitz" argument. They allege that the justification for withholding some treatments also justifies withholding any and all treatments from those whom society considers unworthy. The slippery-slope argument asserts that society moves towards a disregard for human life in predictable steps.

10. Because of the sensitive nature of the topic, human organ transplants have not been widely discussed in society. There are difficult decisions that need to be made as to what qualifies a person to be eligible for a transplant.

DISCUSSION QUESTIONS

1. Compare and contrast sanctity-of-life and quality-of-life perspectives on euthanasia. What are the limitations of each perspective?

2. Compare and contrast passive and active euthanasia. What are the difficulties of implementing each of these approaches for current social policy dealing with health care for the terminally ill?

3. What are the difficulties in defining the following terms:
   a. Natural death
   b. Quality of life
   c. Ordinary and extraordinary medical interventions
   d. Usual and customary medical procedures
   e. Excessive expense and reasonable benefit

4. If your parent were dying from an extremely painful and incurable form of cancer and decided that life was not worth living, what role would you be willing to play in assisting him or her in self-deliverance? Would you be unwilling to assist your parent? If not, what actions would you take in discouraging your parent's action?

5. Provide arguments for and against the removal of food and water from a terminal patient in a coma.

6. Provide arguments favoring and disagreeing with national legislation legitimizing mercy killing.

7. What is a living will and a durable power of attorney? How do they differ? What is the benefit of having one over the other?

8. Discuss some of the problems affecting human transplantations from a societal and personal point of view.

9. Should the society make eligible only those persons who can afford a transplant, or should the potential societal contribution of the individual be taken into account? Are there some medical procedures that should never be financed by insurance benefits or governmental funds because they are too expensive?

GLOSSARY

Active Euthanasia: A direct action that causes death in accordance with the stated or implied wishes of the terminal patient. There are two types of active euthanasia: *suicide* and *mercy killing*.

Cultural Lag: A situation in which some parts of culture change more slowly than others. A typical situation is that technology changes faster than the values of the culture.

Durable Power of Attorney: A document that ascribes to a surrogate decisionmaker the legal authority to consent (or refuse consent) for medical treatment should the patient lack competency for making such decisions.

Euthanasia: Literally, a "good" death.

EXIT: The British society that promotes euthanasia.

Extraordinary Measures: All those medicines, treatments, and operations that cannot be obtained without excessive expense, pain, or other inconvenience, or that, if used, would not offer a reasonable hope of benefit.

Intubation: A procedure whereby the patient is fed through a tube placed in the stomach.

Living Will: A document that states that one does not want medical intervention if the technology or treatment that keeps one alive cannot offer a reasonable quality of life or hope for recovery.

Mercy Killing: Ending the life of a terminal patient in accordance with that person's stated or implied wishes.

Ordinary Measures: All medicines, treatments, and operations that offer a reasonable hope of benefit for the patient and that can be obtained and used without excessive expense, pain, or other inconvenience.

Passive Euthanasia: The withholding of treatment, which, in effect, hastens death.

Quality of Life: The perspective that when life no longer has *quality,* death is preferable to living a life devoid of meaning.

Sanctity of Life: The perspective that all *natural* life has intrinsic meaning and should be appreciated as a divine gift. As a consequence, human beings have the obligation to enhance the quality of life as it may exist.

Self-Deliverance: A rational and voluntary act of taking one's life; an alternative to the terms *suicide* and *mercy killing.*

Slippery-Slope-to-Auschwitz Argument: The belief that if a society wishes to extend to any of its members the right to active euthanasia, none of its members is protected from being killed. Auschwitz was the German concentration camp where people were killed during World War II.

Suicide: A voluntary act of taking one's life.

Utilitarianism: The principle of evaluation based upon the goal of providing the greatest good (maximum benefits) for the greatest number of people.

REFERENCES

Bouma, Hessel, Douglas Diekema, Edward Langerak, Theodore Rottman, and Allen Verhey. 1989. *Christian Faith, Health, and Medical Practice.* Grand Rapids, MI: Eerdmans.

Clark, Brian. 1981. *Whose Life Is It Anyway?* Chicago: The Dramatic Publishing Company.

Cooper, D.K., and R.T. Lanza, 1984. *Heart Transplants: The Present Status of Orthotopic and Heterotopic Health Transportation.* Boston: MTP Press.

Diekstra, Rene F. W. 1987. "Suicide Should Not Always Be Prevented." In *Death and Dying: Opposing Viewpoints,* Janelle Rohr (Ed.). St. Paul, MN: Greenhaven Press.

The Economist, 1991, "Euthanasia: What Is the "Good Death?" July 20, pp. 21–24.

Erdahl, Lowell. 1987. "Euthanasia Is Sometimes Justified." In *Death and Dying: Opposing Viewpoints,* Janelle Rohr (Ed.). St. Paul, MN: Greenhaven Press.

EXIT. 1980. *A Guide to Self-Deliverance.* London: EXIT.

Ezell, Gene, David J. Anspaugh, and Judy Oaks. 1987. *Dying and Death: From a Health and Sociological Perspective.* Scottsdale, AZ: Gorsuch Scarisbrick Publishers.

Fletcher, Joseph. 1977. "Ethics and Euthanasia." In *Death, Dying, and Euthanasia,* Dennis J. Horan and David Mall (Eds.). Washington, DC: University Publications of America.

Gabriel, Trip. 1991. "A Fight to the Death." *New York Times Magazine,* December 8, pp. 46–88.

Hardin, Garrett. 1985. "Crisis on the Commons." *The Sciences,* (September–October):21–25.

Hemlock Society. 1981. "The Hemlock Manifesto." Los Angeles, CA: The Hemlock Society.

Humphry, Derek. 1982. *Let Me Die Before I Wake: Hemlock's Book of Self-Deliverance for the Dying.* Los Angeles, CA: The Hemlock Society.

Illich, Ivan. 1976. *Medical Nemesis: The Expropriation of Health.* New York: Pantheon.

"Making a Living Will." 1985. *The New York Times.* November 23, p. 20.

Malcolm, Andrew H. 1986. "Taboo to Commonplace: Transplants Now Routine." *The New York Times,* February 15, p. 8.

Maples, Pam. 1991. "Washington to Vote on Legalizing Suicide." *Hartford Courant,* p. A17.

Montgomery, Paul. 1987. "In Holland, the Promise of an Easy Death." *Minneapolis Star and Tribune,* September 2, p. 15A.

Morriss, Frank. 1987. "Euthanasia Is Never Justified." In *Death and Dying: Opposing Viewpoints,* Janelle Rohr (Ed.). St. Paul, MN: Greenhaven Press.

Nagi, Mostafa H., M. D. Puch, and Neil G. Lazerine. 1977–1978. "Attitudes of Catholic and Protestant Clergy Toward Euthanasia." *Omega,* 8(2):153–164.

Pope Pius XII. 1977. "The Prolongation of Life: An Address of Pope Pius XII to an International Congress of Anesthesiologists." In *Death, Dying, and Euthanasia,* Dennis J. Horan and David Mall (Eds.). Washington, DC: University Publications of America.

Robinson, Donald. 1989. "Who Should Receive Medical Aid?" *Parade Magazine,* May 28, pp. 4–5.

"Specific Instructions Needed in Living Wills." 1989. *The Times Picayune,* New Orleans, LA., August 27, p. 9F.

Weber, Leonard J. 1981. "The Case against Euthanasia." In *Problems of Death: Opposing Viewpoints,* David Bender (Ed.). St. Paul, MN: Greenhaven Press.

Wibecan, Ken. 1992. "How Can I Be Sure My Living Will Is Honored?" *Modern Maturity,* vol. 35 (August–September), p. 73.

SUGGESTED READINGS

Bouma, Hessel, Douglas Diekema, Edward Langerak, Theodore Rottman, and Allen Verhey. 1989. *Christian Faith, Health, and Medical Practice.* Grand Rapids, MI: Eerdmans. *This book deals with biomedical issues from multidisciplinary and Christian points of view.*

Callahan, Daniel. 1987. *Setting Limits: Medical Goals in an Aging Society.* New York: Simon and Schuster. *Interesting food for thought about decisions regarding the elderly when financial resources are limited.*

Dickinson, George E., Michael R. Leming, and Alan C. Mermann (Eds.). 1992. *Annual Editions: Dying, Death, and Bereavement.* Guilford, Connecticut: Dushkin Publishing Group. *This reader contains a section dealing with ethical issues related to dying and death with seven articles on the following topics: euthanasia, the right to die controversy, physician-assisted dying, active euthanasia, natural death, and organ transplantation.*

Horan, Dennis J., and David Mall (Eds.). 1977. *Death, Dying, and Euthanasia.* Washington, DC: University Publications of America. / Rohr, Janelle (Ed.). 1987. *Death and Dying: Opposing Viewpoints.* St. Paul, MN: Greenhaven Press. / Weir, Robert F. (Ed.). 1986. *Ethical Issues in Death and Dying.* New York: Columbia University Press. *Three excellent anthologies on biomedical issues.*

Humphry, Derek. 1991. *Final Exit: The Practicalities of Self-Deliverance and Assisted Suicide for the Dying.* Eugene, OR: The Hemlock Society. / Humphry, Derek. 1981. *Let Me Die Before I Wake: Hemlock's Book of Self-Deliverance for the Dying.* Los Angeles: The Hemlock Society. *These books published by The Hemlock Society present a number of case studies of terminally ill individuals who choose self-deliverance (often with the assistance of family members and friends) as an alternative to passive euthanasia. They also provide methods for self-deliverance, a bibliography, and an extended discussion of personal and legal issues related to the decision to take one's life.*

Quill, Timothy E. 1991. "Open Letter: My Patient's Suicide." *Harper's,* May, pp. 32–34. *Article dealing with self-deliverance and physician-assisted suicide from a physician's point of view, within the context of a personal relationship growing out of a clinical experience.*

Chapter
9

Suicide

*Suicide is a permanent answer to a
temporary set of problems.*

NBC Evening News
March 12, 1987

*There are times in life when we would
like to die temporarily.*

Mark Twain

THOUGH SUICIDE HAS been around for as long as recorded history, the word "suicide" is of relatively recent origin. The word "suicide" is not in the Bible—or in the pamphlet by John Donne (1644) on self-homicide. The *Oxford Dictionary* states that "suicide" was first used in English in 1651 and is derived from the modern Latin "suicidium," which stems from the Latin pronoun for "self" and the verb "to kill" (Farberow, 1975). Though the word "suicide" was not used, the earliest recorded suicides in Western culture were the deaths of Samson and Saul around 1000 B.C. (Stillion and McDowell, 1991:327). Two other Old Testament individuals who took their own lives were Abimilech and Achitophel. Probably one of the more famous suicides was Socrates' drinking the hemlock.

Historically, attitudes toward suicide have been somewhat mixed. Early societies sometimes forced certain members into committing suicide for ritual purposes: Suicide was occasionally expected of the wives and slaves of husbands or masters who had died, as an expression of fidelity and duty. In the ancient Roman empire, suicide was socially acceptable until slaves started to practice it. Since the suicide of slaves caused a severe financial loss, however, suicide was declared a crime against the state (McGuire and Ely, 1984). Modern Judaism, while officially regarding suicide as a sin, rests upon a long tradition of honoring "heroic" suicides to avoid slavery, rape, or being forced into idol worship (Curran, 1987). From early times to the present, the Roman Catholic Church has denied Catholic ritual and burial to one who takes his or her own life (*Codex Jurix Canonici,* 1918). For Japanese kamikaze pilots in World War II, suicide represented the "great death." The Chinese regarded suicide as acceptable and honorable, particularly for defeated generals or deposed rulers (Ingram and Ellis, 1992). The New Testament records only the suicide of Judas Iscariot, but in no way is this act condemned in the scriptures (Alvarez, 1971).

Attitudes toward suicide changed radically when St. Augustine, drawing heavily from the philosophy of Plato and Aristotle, laid down rules against suicide that became the basis for Christian doctrine throughout the succeeding centuries. Societal opposition to suicide in Christian communities continued throughout the Middle Ages, until the Renaissance broadened thinking on the subject. Public and private opinion, however, remained far from unanimous. Even today in the United States, attempted suicide is considered a felony in nine states: Alabama, Kentucky, New Jersey, North and South Carolina, North and South Dakota, Oklahoma, and Washington (Curran, 1987).

Traditionally, suicide has been morally proscribed by Western culture. Calhoun and Allen (1991) note that surveys have suggested that the families in which a suicide has occurred are expected to feel shame, and individuals who commit suicide have been viewed as "crazy," mentally ill, and psychologically stressed. Yet when respondents were asked to evaluate individuals they knew who had been bereaved by suicide, the negative stigma was less. Knowing the individual may buffer the degree of negative social reactions. In addition to the negative feelings, surviving relatives of suicide victims are thought to be more grief stricken because their loved one willfully took his or her own life (Ingram and Ellis, 1992). Calhoun and Allen conclude that while recent data indicate that society rejects suicide less today under some specific conditions, such as a terminal illness, suicide continues to be viewed as an undesirable and abnormal act. Since suicide is still socially unacceptable, the family may lack the support systems normally available to those grieving other kinds of death—a traumatic loss is suffered, and the taboo act generates feelings of disapproval and shame (Dunn and Morrish-Vidners, 1987).

The difficulty of the stigma attached to a suicide for family members is pointed out in a study by Gibson, Range, and Anderson (1987). A vignette about the death (from either suicide or a rare disease) of an 11-year-old boy who came from either a single-parent home or a two-parent home was provided to 120 high school juniors and seniors. The suicide victim and his family were perceived more negatively than their rare disease counterparts, but knowledge that the parents were divorced did not interact with the cause of death to affect the respondents' impressions. A study by Range and Goggin (1990) also found that people respond more negatively to the victim and the bereaved family if the death is by suicide rather than by viral illness.

The general attitude of the public toward suicide remains confused and sometimes contradictory (Ingram and Ellis, 1992:33). Extreme views on suicide range

Doonesbury

BY GARRY TRUDEAU

©1986 REPRINTED WITH PERMISSION OF UNIVERSAL PRESS SYNDICATE

from total acceptance to total rejection of the right of an individual to commit suicide. At the heart of the debate is the question of whether people should be allowed to die without interference.

The meaning of suicide continues to be problematic. If we accept the definition of suicide as "any death resulting either from a deliberate act of self-destruction or from inaction when it is known that inaction will have fatal consequences" (Theodorson and Theodorson, 1969:427), we could possibly classify the following persons as engaging in suicidal behavior:

1. A person who smokes cigarettes, knowing that the Surgeon General has determined that smoking is an important cause of lung cancer.
2. A race car driver who drives even though he or she knows that in any given race there is a good chance that someone will be killed.
3. A person who takes a bottle of sleeping pills, hoping to draw attention to oneself and personal problems.
4. A person who takes an overdose of a prescribed drug.
5. A person who continues to eat fatty foods after having suffered a heart attack.
6. A person in the advanced stages of cancer who refuses chemotherapy or surgery.
7. A person who overeats (or undereats) to the extreme that personal health is directly affected.
8. A person with high blood pressure who refuses to take medication, control food intake, or exercise.
9. A person who mixes alcohol and drugs.

Probably, most of us would not consider the above list of actions as suicidal behaviors. Rather, we would be concerned with the intent of the person in question as to whether or not he or she was trying to kill him or herself. In classifying deaths as suicides, it is difficult to determine the motivations of a person no longer living.

There is a qualitative difference between a suicide gesture and a completed suicide. Suicide gestures are motivated by a need for aid and support from others, while completed suicides are acts of resignation. At this point, we have a problem of tautology—suicide gestures that mistakenly end in death are classified as intentional suicides, and unsuccessful suicide attempts are considered suicide gestures. In addition, suicides are sometimes classified as accidents or natural deaths as a favor to family members or as a method of "providing a more positive view" of the deceased. Thus, there are deaths resulting from intentional acts of self-destruction recorded as "natural deaths," and there are suicidal gestures accidentally ending in death being classified as suicide. Obviously, there are problems in compiling suicide statistics!

In recent years suicide has attracted increasing interest as a large-scale social phenomenon (Battin, 1982). Awareness of the problem of suicide has caused both increased scrutiny of the phenomenon by sociologists, psychologists, and researchers in other disciplines, and increased efforts to reduce its incidence by physicians, counselors, social workers, and the police. In fact, Lindsay Prior (1989:11) notes that during most of this century, the study of death was limited to the study of suicide, and that, in turn, was the study of social causation. Efforts to seek causes and to reduce the frequency of suicide work together. Suicide research centers and suicide-prevention services have developed in recent years, and the literature on suicide has increased significantly. Even a "cookbook" on ways to commit suicide entitled *Suicide, Its Use, History, Technique and Current Interest* by Guillon and Bonniec came out in France in 1982 and soon worked its way to the United States. In 1991 Derek Humphry's *Final Exit,* which tells people how to commit suicide, rose to Number 1 on the *New York Times* best-seller list. Though it failed to pass by a fairly narrow margin, Initiative 119 on the ballot in Washington in the fall of 1991 would have allowed terminally ill adults to seek a physician's help in committing suicide. A similar referendum failed in California in November of 1992. As mentioned in Chapter 1, Dr. Jack Kevorkian's "suicide machine" in the self-assisted deaths of individuals in Michigan beginning in 1990 continued to make headlines. The Michigan legislature, however, passed a law banning physician-assisted suicides in March, 1993. Thus, the topic of suicide is certainly attracting attention in the 1990s. As noted in the insert below, the cost of suicide in the United States today is staggering and also worthy of note.

In the United States, more than 28,000 individuals commit suicide each year—1 person every 20 minutes (Mayo Clinic, 1985). The number of reported suicides represents only 10 or 15 percent of the people attempting suicide. Typically, the

HUMAN COST FIGURED FOR HOMICIDE, SUICIDE

Suicide and homicide result in more premature loss of life for Americans each year than anything but accidents, AIDS, cancer and heart disease. The United States reported 19,796 homicides and 29,286 suicides in 1984. Those intentional killings took from their victims more than 1.2 million "years of potential life" they would have had if they had lived to be 65, according to the National Centers for Disease Control (CDC).

The average suicide occurred at age 43; the average homicide killed a 34-year-old. White males had the highest rate of life lost to suicide, followed by males of other non-black minorities, then black males and white females. Black men, however, had the highest rate of life lost to homicide, followed by black women, non-white males of other minorities and white males.

The Atlanta-based CDC said the statistics "emphasize the urgent need for efforts to prevent premature mortality from suicide among white males and from homicide among black males." Firearms accounted for most of the life lost to both suicide (57 percent) and homicide (61 percent). The CDC called for programs to prevent injuries and deaths from guns.

The CDC studies the loss of "potential life" to gauge the most serious causes of premature death in the United States. Age 65 is used merely as a statistical benchmark; the national life expectancy is actually higher than that. Accidents, the leading cause of premature death, account for about 2.2 million years of potential life lost in the United States each year.

Adapted from the *News and Courier*, Charleston, SC, August 21, 1987, p. 13A.

suicide rate for males peaks during adolescence and the elderly years, whereas the rate for females shows a gradual increase from young ages until ages 45 to 50, after which the rate gradually declines (McCall, 1991:43) Suicide obviously is a major concern in the United States today.

THEORETICAL PERSPECTIVES ON SUICIDE

Sociological Perspective

The most significant contribution on suicide by sociologists has been the sociological perspective itself—the insistence on seeing suicidal actions as in some way the result of social factors (Douglas, 1967:158). Suicidal persons construct their meanings of suicide and motivations for committing it out of collective values upon which the social structure rests. What constitutes suicide and why it happens at all are both understood through the meanings conferred on it by various persons. Thus, meanings of suicide arise out of what people think, feel, and do about it rather than what is simply given in the act. What people think, feel, and do about acts defined as suicide are intertwined with larger social values and meanings (Charmaz, 1980:234).

A comprehensive sociological theory of self-destruction was proposed in 1897 by the noted French sociologist Emile Durkheim entitled *Suicide: A Study in Sociology* (1951). The most frequent interpretation of Durkheim's *Suicide* by American sociologists involves the following propositions (Douglas, 1967:39–40):

1. The structural factors cause certain degrees and certain patterns of social interaction.
2. The degrees and patterns of social interaction then cause a certain degree of "social integration."
3. "Social integration," defined as either states of individuals or as a state of the society, is then defined as the "strength of the individual's ties to society."
4. The "strength of ties" is then defined either in terms of egoism, altruism, and anomie or else the "strength of ties" is hypothesized to be the cause of the given degrees of egoism, altruism, and anomie.
5. Egoism is defined as a relative lack of social or collective activity that gives meaning and object to life; altruism is defined as a relatively great amount of social activity; and anomie is defined as a relative lack of social activity that acts to constrain the individual's passions which, without constraint, increase "infinitely."
6. And, finally, the given balance of the degrees of egoism, altruism, and anomie is hypothesized to be the cause of the given suicide rate of the given society.

Thus, the three types of Durkheim's suicide noted above are related to his conception of social integration. Two recent time-series analyses of sociological and economic variables accounting for suicide rates in the United States give somewhat mixed findings to Durkheim's theory. One study of the United States from 1940 to 1984 by Bijou Yang (1992) concluded that economic growth appeared to lower male suicide rates, but increase that of females. This means that the suicide rates did not increase during the economic booms and busts as predicted by Durkheim. The impact depended on the social group involved. Durkheim had posited that since economic prosperity and depression bring about less social integration and less social regulation than normal economic situations, the suicide rate rises accordingly. Another time-series study by Yang, Lester, and Yang (1992) of the United States from 1952 to 1984 revealed that the economic variables of gross national product per capita and the unemployment rate contributed significantly to the suicide rate as did the social variables of divorce rate and female participation in the labor force. Thus, social processes that have been presumed to decrease social integration appear to be associated with a higher suicide rate.

Durkheim's main point was that although we think of suicide as a supremely individual and personal act, it also has a social and non-individual aspect. For example, different types of society produce different rates of suicide. **Egoistic suicide** occurs when the person is inadequately integrated into the society, such as intellectuals or persons whose talents or stations in life place them in a special category (a celebrity or star), and are therefore less likely to be linked to society in conventional ways. **Altruistic suicide** happens when the individual is overly integrated into the society (an exaggerated concern for the community) and is willing to die for the group, like kamikaze pilots of World War II or terrorists of today. **Anomic suicide** results from the lack of regulation of the individual when the norms governing existence no longer control that individual (feels let down by the failure of social institutions), such as a business person committing suicide after a stock market crash or one suddenly losing his or her job.

As Talcott Parsons (1949) interpreted *Suicide,* Durkheim considered altruistic suicide to be largely the result of the external forces of group structure, whereas egoistic suicide was more a result of the internal forces of the "collective conscience," and anomic suicide was seen as almost entirely the result of the internal forces of the "collective conscience."

A fourth type of suicide, called **fatalistic,** was introduced by Durkheim and has recently received more attention. This type suggests that one may feel overcontrolled by society and oppressed by its extremely strict rules and rigid red tape. In fatalistic suicide, one dies in despair of being able to make it in a society allowing little opportunity for satisfaction or individual fulfillment. Both the altruistic and the fatalistic suicide involve excessive control of the individual by society (Kastenbaum, 1986:205–206). Extreme examples of such control would be living in slavery or under totalitarian rule.

Dramaturgical Perspective

Derived from the general approach of symbolic interactionism, the **dramaturgical perspective** highlights the construction of action and its context by using the metaphor of the drama to explain behavior. Such an approach is not unlike the "psychological autopsy," which is a procedure for the reconstruction of suicidal death through interviews with survivors (Beskow and Asgard, 1990:307). Rather than inquiring into the definition of the situation, the dramaturgical analyst emphasizes the definition of the situation that seems apparent in the event. When someone commits suicide, this approach would look at how family members acted afterwards and would assess the meaning of the death to the family as it is visible in what they actually do, rather than what they might say about it to an interviewer. This approach tends to take nonverbal behavior into account.

A dramaturgical approach does not accept the social determinist view that social forces motivate the individual to act, but believes that motives are invoked by social actors as a way of explaining or accounting for past actions. (Charmaz, 1980:26–31). Behavior is analyzed from the standpoint of the observer (etic approach) rather than on the subjective meanings of participants (emic approach). While the dramaturgical analyst emphasizes action, the symbolic interactionist emphasizes intention. Both perspectives lead to an examination of meanings derived from interaction.

A good example of the dramaturgical approach is the film entitled "But Jack Was a Good Driver." In this film Jack, a high school student, has died in a single-car accident. As his two friends walk away from the cemetery, they begin to recall recent events involving Jack. As they describe the actions of Jack in recent weeks, he had flunked a chemistry exam, broken up with his girlfriend, given his tape collection away, and acted in ways out of the ordinary for Jack. They conclude that Jack's "accident" was more likely a suicide, since his actions of recent weeks showed some signs of suicide. The observers (Jack's friends) viewed the actions of the actor (Jack)—the dramaturgical approach.

Existentialist Perspective

Existentialist philosophy acknowledges that human existence is finite and that we all must face death. One must assume responsibility for his or her own actions and must be responsible for moral choices and actions. An emphasis is placed on the anticipation of death and the effects of that anticipation on everyday life, thus causing one to come to an understanding of how death and life are linked. From an existentialist view, it is conceivable that the confrontation with death during a suicidal crisis may cause suicidal individuals to sense their aloneness and personal responsibility for their experience. Thus, the choice of death may be fully akin to the choice of life, both the result of reflection. Death through suicide or any other means is not the enemy that it is in other perspectives (Charmaz, 1980:242).

Existentialism is linked with the phenomenological method of inquiry. This approach starts with an examination of the point of view of the experiencing person—from an emic perspective. Experience is studied from the inside—from what it appears to be to the involved person. What is dying to those who are experiencing it? This method tries to study the phenomenon directly and to discover how it is constituted. In studying attempted suicide, one would conduct interviews with persons having attempted suicide to determine what they were thinking during their crisis. By comparing patterns one can determine parallels between the suicidal experiences of these individuals (Charmaz, 1980:51–56).

Alienation

An individual may feel alienated if he or she does not feel in control of a situation. **Alienation** is a state of consciousness resulting from a concrete relationship between human beings and their products. Karl Marx noted that laborers are separated or alienated from nature itself, capitalism separated workers from each other,

This woman contemplates suicide as a solution to her feelings of alienation and social isolation. Her suicide gesture elicits a response from another to indicate the meaningfulness of her life.

and capitalism produced a separation of the workers from their work. The realization of human potential and creativity is prevented, according to Marx. Thus, alienation results in a loss of self or a lack of self-realization. ·

A sense of powerlessness may result, leading to hopelessness over time, then a feeling of helplessness (Charmaz, 1980:260). Individuals may not be wholly aware of their alienation and may feel frustrated, worthless, dependent, and powerless without connecting their feelings to the social structure. A worker on an assembly line, for example, performing the same task over and over again for 8 hours, is more likely to feel alienated than would a craftsperson who takes a raw material in hand and creates a finished product. Such feelings are likely to be intensified by the individuals' acceptance that they reflect who they are and what they may become. Such assessments may lead to feelings of hopelessness. Alienation may, therefore, lead to suicide.

As noted from the above-selected theoretical perspectives on suicide, the "whys" of suicide are not always easy to explain. For the survivors of a completed suicide, guilt is often associated with the event. The individuals may feel that they have contributed to the suicide: "If only" they had acted differently, this may not have happened.

SOCIAL FACTORS, SIGNS, AND METHODS OF SUICIDE

Social Factors of Suicide

The relationship between suicide and variables associated with suicide is not simple and easily understood. Nonetheless, some of the variables associated with suicide include age, gender, marital status, and socioeconomic level (Kastenbaum and Aisenberg, 1976:252–71). As noted elsewhere in this chapter, suicide is rare in childhood, rises sharply during adolescence and early adulthood, and peaks with persons in the age group from 75 to 84 years. Suicide could be described as a masculine type of behavior since males have a higher rate of completed suicides than females. A study (Taylor, 1990) conducted by Cornell University Medical School revealed that men infected with AIDS were 36 times more likely than average males to commit suicide. The same study also found that AIDS patients were far more likely to choose to end their lives than were men with other fatal diseases. Indeed, a study of 44 terminally ill patients (Brown, et al. 1986) concluded that patients with a terminal illness who are not mentally ill are no more likely than the general population to wish for premature death.

Regarding marital status, the suicide rate is lower for the married than for those never married, and highest for the widowed, divorced, and separated. Individuals with children commit suicide less than childless persons. These data on marital and parental status fit Durkheim's theory that suicide is a function of social integration.

Suicide rates tend to be highest at both extremes of the socioeconomic ladder. Certain professions such as physicians, dentists, and lawyers tend to be particularly suicide-prone, while the suicide rates of teachers and clergy are rather low.

There is also a difference in suicide rates between blacks and whites. Suicide rates among blacks are substantially lower than among whites—4.6 blacks versus 11.3 whites per 100,000 population annually (deCantanzaro, 1981). The suicide rate for Native Americans has been reported to be greater than the national average; however, rates have been found to vary greatly from reservation to reservation (Ellis and Range, 1989). Suicide among Native Americans tends to be more frequently alcohol-related, and violent methods (firearms and hanging) are more commonly used than in the mainstream United States population (May, 1990:200).

More suicides occur in heterogeneous urban areas than in more homogeneous rural areas. Nostalgic times like the Christmas season and "renewal of life" times like spring are the most frequent times of year for suicides, with fewest suicides committed in the summer. Suicides occur most often around the weekend on Saturday and Monday, the end and beginning of the routine workweek, but peak on Monday (Maldonado and Kraus, 1991:185). Protestant faiths have higher rates than Catholics, but the Jewish faith has the highest rate (Oaks and Ezell, 1993:217). Contrary to popular belief, suicide occurrence does not vary by lunar phase (Maldonado and Kraus, 1991:186).

Signs of Suicide

People who commit suicide tend to talk about their attempt prior to the act. One should be taken seriously if he or she repeatedly talks of killing oneself. Other than outright stating, "I am going to kill myself," other more subtle verbal clues might include such statements as "I'm not the person I used to be," "You would be better off without me," "I can't stand it anymore," "Life has lost its meaning for me," and "Nobody needs me anymore."

Behavioral clues might include giving away valued personal possessions, getting one's house in order as if ready for departure, unexplained frequent crying, changes in daily behavior like beginning to take long walks at night, poor sleeping habits, loss of appetite, inability to concentrate, a sudden change in appearance, a sudden shift in the quality of school work, and suddenly withdrawing from various organizations. The following factors tend to describe an individual at high risk of committing suicide: lethal weapon readily available, history of prior suicide attempts, detailed suicide plan, feelings of hopelessness and helplessness, problems in school, work, in relationships, or finances, severe personal loss such as health problems or bereavement, and alcohol or drug abuse (Oaks and Ezell, 1993:215).

Methods of Committing Suicide

Listed in decreasing order of frequency are the ways of committing suicide in the United States: firearms (especially handguns), overdose on drugs, cutting and stabbing, jumping from high places, toxic gas inhalation, hanging, and drowning (Ezell, Anspaugh, and Oaks, 1987:165). While women *attempt* suicide more often, men more often *complete* suicide. Since men are more likely to use firearms in suicide attempts and women more likely to use drugs, the method chosen obviously contributes to the higher "success" rate of males in suicide.

HOW YOU CAN HELP IN A SUICIDAL CRISIS

1. *Recognize the clues to suicide.* Look for signs of hopelessness and helplessness. Listen for suicide threats and words of warning. Notice if the person becomes withdrawn and isolated.

2. *Trust your own judgment.* If you believe someone is in danger of suicide, act on your beliefs. Don't ignore the signs of suicide.

3. *Tell others.* Share knowledge with parents, friends, teachers, employers, or other people who might help. If you have to betray a secret to save a life, do it. Don't worry about breaking a confidence if someone's suicidal plans are revealed to you.

4. *Stay with a suicidal person.* Don't leave a suicidal person alone if you think there is immediate danger. Stay until help arrives or the crisis has passed.

5. *Listen.* Encourage a suicidal person to talk. Don't give false reassurances that "everything will be okay." Listen and sympathize with what the person says.

6. *Urge professional help.* Offer to make an appointment for and go with the person for professional help, if that is what it takes. Call your community Hotline or crisis number for suggestions.

7. *Be supportive.* Show the person that you care. Help to make the person feel worthwhile and wanted.

From *Too Young to Die: Youth and Suicide* by Francine Klagsbrun. Copyright © by Francine Klagsbrun. Reprinted with permission of Houghton Mifflin Company.

CHILDHOOD SUICIDAL BEHAVIOR

Suicidal deaths are virtually nonexistent before age 5 and are rare in the age group of 5 to 9 years. Indeed, very little research on suicidal children under the age of 5 can be found, perhaps because early infancy research does not focus, in the main, on suicide (McGuire and Ely, 1984:21). The policy of the U.S. Division of Vital Statistics is to not even report the deaths of children under age 8 as suicides, regardless of what data may have been entered on a given death certificate—"other," "unknown," and "unspecified causes" are the classifications used for these deaths. Suicide is similarly uncommon in the cohort of children between the ages of 10 and 14 (Smith, 1985:103).

Adults prefer to believe that children do not commit suicide, notes Israel Orbach (1988). It seems inconceivable that children could become so desperate at their young age that they could choose death over life. Adults may also have the false perception that childhood is a carefree, happy time. Perhaps these perceptions account for the unique conclusion of a U.S. county coroner who stated that any death of a child under 14 should be regarded as accidental, even when a suicide note is left behind (Orbach, 1988:23).

As with many suicides, child suicides are easily mistaken as accidents. The causes of death themselves involve an element of chance: traffic accidents (sometimes running into traffic), falls (jumps?) from high places, fatalities in handling guns, or drowning (Orbach, 1988:25). The fact that young children do not write suicide notes compounds this difficulty, for notes are one chief category of evidence that coroners use to verify suicide (McGuire and Ely, 1984:19).

The role of family seems to play a major part in suicide attempts of children. A study of 8- to 13-year-old psychiatric inpatients and suicide attempts (Asarnow and Carlson, 1988) found strong support for a link between suicide attempts in children and perceptions of low family support. Likewise, in another study (Garfinkel, Froese, and Hood, 1982) of 505 children and adolescents who made 605 attempts to commit suicide and were admitted to an emergency room (as compared to a matched control group by sex and similar age of another 505 persons admitted) concluded that family disintegration played a significant part in these families where suicides were attempted.

Though the suicide rate among children is not high, a study of junior high school children (Domino, Domino, and Berry, 1987) indicated that over 20 percent have "seriously thought about suicide," and a slightly higher percentage have personally known someone who committed suicide. The Suicide Prevention Center of Los Angeles, in its work with children and adolescents in crisis (Peck, 1980), estimates that 50 percent of the deaths reported as accidents in the groups they studied are, in reality, unreported suicides. Thus, the state of reporting suicides and attempts of children and adolescents is filled with inconsistencies, confusion, and concealment.

ADOLESCENT SUICIDAL BEHAVIOR

The age group beginning with age 15 marks a noticeable shift in suicide rates. For example, every 90 minutes one teenager in the United States will take his or her own life, while every 9 minutes a teenager will make an attempt to kill himself or herself (Coleman, 1987:1). Adolescent and young-adult suicide is not unique to contemporary times, but the significance of the problem has recently emerged in the United States, especially since 1960. In recent years, cluster suicides (discussed later in this chapter) have certainly called attention of the media to suicide and have caused parents and educational personnel to be even more aware of suicides.

The suicide rates for adolescents, aged 15 to 24, increased approximately 250 percent from 1950 to 1980 (Osgood and McIntosh, 1986). The suicide rate for this age group in 1960 was 5.2 per 100,000. By 1980, however, the rate was 12.3 per

This young man has cut his wrist in a suicide gesture. His problems are now compounded by the fact that he must live with the stigma of a failed suicide attempt.

100,000 persons in this age group. These numbers could reflect a greater willingness today to report a death as a suicide. The taboo nature of identifying suicide is not as significant today as in 1960. Suicide is now the third leading cause of death in this age group (following accidents and homicides), and is the second leading cause of death among persons aged 15 to 19 years (U.S. Vital Statistics, 1981). Since 1980, however, the number of deaths by suicide among teenagers has begun to level off, possibly because of a decline in the use of mind-altering drugs and an increase in attention to children at risk of taking their own lives (Brody, 1987:16).

Accidents and homicides are viewed by many researchers as disguised suicides (Coleman, 1987:1). Many drug overdoses, fatal automobile accidents, and related self-destructive eating and alcoholic disorders are uncounted teen suicides. Thus, the total number of adolescent suicides may be greater than reported. The most commonly identified correlates of suicidal behaviors include depressive symptoms, social problems, family disorganization and problems, life stress, and poor problem-solving skills, notes Carol Garrison (1989:129). Overall, identity crises and mood fluctuations are significant psychological risk factors for suicide among adolescents, according to Stillion and McDowell (1991:343).

Geographically, Nevada is first in youth suicides, and New Mexico is second. In taking their own lives, boys tend to use violent means such as guns and hanging, though girls seem to be turning to violent means also (Brozan, 1986). Perhaps by using violent means, these adolescents are suggesting that they indeed are serious about their attempts. It is more than a "cry for help." Warning signs of suicide in adolescence include self-mutilation (for example, tatooing oneself with a penknife), changes in habits, truancy, behavior that implies preparation for death (for example, giving away valuable possessions), and poor school performance (Stillion and McDowell, 1991:345).

Suicides of individuals within the early stages of life are especially difficult to understand, since they are just growing up and beginning to launch out into the world. On the other hand, with the frustrations of adolescence, being expected to "act like an adult" yet at times being "not old enough" for certain behaviors, it is no wonder that the suicide rate in this age group is so high. Suicide becomes an available solution to one's problems. When stress is experienced, a constricted view of future possibilities and a momentary fix on present escapes may hold sway. Impulsive action and limited alternative problem-solving may make suicidal fantasies turn to suicidal behaviors. As noted at the beginning of this chapter, suicide is an answer (though permanent) to a set of temporary problems. The problem is gone, but so is life.

The letter below (Berman, 1986:151), written by a 17-year-old who took his life, apparently indicates that death was the solution to this adolescent's dilemmas of life. He lived with various problems but tended to keep his pain mostly to him-self.

Dear Mom, Dad, and everyone else,

I'm sorry for what I've done, but I love you all and I always will, for eternity. Please, please, please don't blame it on yourselves. It was all my fault and not yours or anyone else's. If I didn't do this now, I would have done it later anyway. We all die some day, I just died sooner.

Love,

John

After John's body was found, people began to piece together his life filled with the inevitable "if only's." This reconstruction of an interpretation after the event of sui-cide follows the dramaturgical approach, as discussed earlier.

Daniel Bell (1977) found that college students viewed suicidal peers as "cow-ardly, sick, unpleasant, and disreputable" and were much more negative in their attitudes toward peers who attempted suicide and lived than toward those who completed suicide. Thus, in the eyes of one's college-aged peers, the individual is better off not to fail in his/her efforts to commit suicide. The following shares some findings of colleges in the United States regarding suicide among college students.

WHAT COLLEGES HAVE LEARNED ABOUT SUICIDE

Daniel Goleman

All new students at the University of California, Los Angeles, receive in their registration packet a six-page pamphlet on suicide. Among other things, they are urged to watch for fellow students who exhibit certain warning signs: people who are chronically depressed and hint that they won't be around long, for example, or who give away prized possessions. The booklet lists eight phone numbers for students to call, from the campus counseling center to the university police.

U.C.L.A.'s effort is typical of the reaction at many colleges and universities to the rise in suicides among American youths in the last 30 years. From 1981 to 1983, the rate was about 8.7 per 100,000 youths, compared with 6.9 in 1973. Sometimes, they occur in clusters. This month, three students from the same Omaha high school committed suicide.

A school's role in preventing the deaths of despondent students is com-plicated by the question of liability. "Say a student who is seeing a college

(continued)

counselor threatens suicide and has a plan, but the therapist does not take the threat seriously," said Gary Pavela, a professor at the University of Maryland Law School, "if the student commits suicide, then both the college and the counselor could be held liable." Leighton Whitaker, a Swarthmore College psychologist who advises college officials on suicides, explained it another way: "A college is under a legal obligation to assess and refer for proper treatment any suicidal student who comes to their attention."

A turning point in colleges' attention to the problem came in 1967, when Congress made it illegal to discriminate against the handicapped, including the emotionally handicapped, in admitting students. This has meant that applicants cannot be asked about psychiatric problems and that a larger number of troubled students may find their way to campuses, Dr. Whitaker said.

In any case, psychologists say, the college community is well-suited to helping troubled young people and preventing suicides. The close contact among students and faculty members heightens the probability of spotting those at risk. Many campuses hold special classes for resident assistants, the students who supervise dormitories. At U.C.L.A., for example, they are instructed to watch for certain danger signs, such as weeping for no apparent reason, drawing back from friends or suffering social or academic crises.

"The resident assistants are told to err on the side of safety," said Morris Holland, an assistant vice chancellor for student development.

"The numbers of suicides here vary greatly from year to year," he continued. "Over the last five years, it has been between one and five each year, in a campus of 35,000 students. It happens rarely, but we're prepared when it does."

There are about 50 threats for every successful suicide among students, Dr. Whitaker said. And while threats are far more common among college women than among men, men are three to four times more likely to succeed in killing themselves—an imbalance that is also true for the population at large. "Women are more able to cry out for help with their emotional needs than are men," Dr. Whitaker said. "Twice as many women students as men seek help from college counselors. The higher risk is the silent and isolated college man who does not turn to anyone for help."

At Indiana University in Bloomington, resident assistants are warned not to challenge a student who threatens suicide, analyze motives or try to handle the situation themselves. "It's sometimes useful to find a small piece of the problem that can be dealt with positively, such as getting an 'incomplete' on a course the student is worrying about," said Nancy Stockton, a campus psychologist. Students who seem to be at serious risk are often asked to take health leaves and get psychological help, in which case their grades for the last term—which are frequently low—are removed from their transcript. A condition for the student's return may be a letter from a psychotherapist.

"A suicide arouses immense anxiety among everyone who knew the student, as well as a great deal of guilt," said Ben Lieber, dean of students at

Amherst College and formerly a dean at Columbia University. "Everyone thinks that if only they had done something else it wouldn't have happened. It helps to be as open as possible with them about the circumstances of the suicide, to let them know how common attempts are and generally to treat it as something that is not shameful, but is genuinely tragic."

The New York Times, February 23, 1986.

Since adolescents are caught between childhood and adulthood, the often intense and conflictual task of separating from the world of family can be more difficult when family dynamics interfere with the child's move toward self-sufficiency (Berman, 1986:157). Parents of suicidal adolescents have been found to experience more overt conflict, threats of separation and divorce, and loss of a parent occurring prior to the child's 12th year. Suicidal adolescents report receiving little affection, hold negative views of their parents, describe time spent in their family as unenjoyable, have deficient problem-solving skills, tend to have more prevalent use of drugs and alcohol, and see themselves as different from their parents. Suicidal behavior in childhood appears to be more closely associated with family turmoil and stress than is suicidal behavior in later life.

Active peer involvement may be the support one needs to discourage suicide behavior. Being involved with peers is negatively correlated with a depressive mood in adolescence. Suicidal adolescents tend to show greater withdrawal from, and less involvement with, the school milieu. On the other hand, suicidal adolescents tend to have more frequent and serious problems with peers, to be more interpersonally sensitive, and to be less likely to have a close confidant (Berman, 1986:159). Adolescents are especially vulnerable to rejections from their peer group (Rich et al., 1991). Since adolescents are highly suggestible individuals, suicidal adolescents are highly vulnerable to influence since they often lack reinforcing role models and may be low in self-esteem and ego strength. Thus, suicidal behavior by one may lead to an epidemic of followers.

THE MEDIA AND SUICIDE CLUSTERS

A **suicide cluster** refers to an excessive number of suicides occurring in close temporal and geographic proximity because this most closely approximates the concept of an "outbreak" in a particular community (Gould, Wallenstein, and Davidson, 1989:17). Philip May (1990), in compiling a bibliography on suicide among Native Americans, concluded that suicide clusters among particular groups of youths tend to take on epidemic form in many Native American communities. Suicide clusters among teenagers have been noted in the media, and imitation is generally cited as the cause. Madelyn Gould and David Shaffer (1986) studied the variation in the numbers of suicides and attempted suicides by teenagers in the greater New York area 2 weeks before and 2 weeks after 4 fictional films were broadcast on television in the fall and winter of 1984 and 1985. The number of attempts in the period after the broadcasts was significantly greater than the number before the broadcasts, leading the researchers to conclude that some teenage suicides are imitative.

Another study by David Phillips and Lundie Carstensen (1986) examined the relation between 38 nationally televised news or feature stories about suicide from 1973 to 1979 and the fluctuation of the rate of suicide among American teenagers before and after these stories. The observed number of suicides by teenagers from within 7 days after these broadcasts was significantly greater than the number expected. The more networks carrying a story on suicide, the greater was the increase in suicides thereafter. Teenage suicides increased more than adult suicides after stories about suicide. An extensive review of suicide clusters by Gould, Wallenstein, and Davidson (1989) confirms that temporal and geographic clustering of suicides occur, that they appear to be multidetermined, and that they appear to be primarily a phenomenon of youth. Imitation and identification are factors hypothesized to increase the likelihood of cluster suicides.

Though the above findings certainly suggest a correlation between media viewings on suicide and increased suicide clusters among adolescents, this is not to suggest that such media exposure "causes" an overall increased rate of suicides. Indeed, viewers previously thinking of suicide might be persuaded one way or the other after watching television programs on suicide. However, for nonsuicidal persons as a group, the impact may be somewhat different. For example, in exposing university students to films on suicide and violence, one study (Biblarz, Biblarz, Pilgrim, and Baldree, 1991:382) concluded that there was no reason to believe that nonsuicidal young people as a group will view suicide in a more positive light as a result of watching movies with suicidal or violent content. However, exposure to suicide films appears to have increased viewers' arousal levels significantly, if only temporarily.

Studies of the effect of the media on suicide have neglected the audience receptivity to suicide stories, notes Steven Stack (1992). Thus, Stack set out to test the thesis from symbolic interaction theory that the degree of media influence is contingent on audience receptivity. He developed a taxonomy of stories from the Great

Depression using the years 1933 to 1939 (1933 being the first year for which suicide data was collected for the nation as a whole). Stack hypothesized that the economic context of the nation's worst economic depression of the 20th century would increase the effect of the media on suicide—the economic collapse would promote a suicidal mood of depression, disrupted family organization, and other psychosocial processes thought to underlie suicide risk. However, there was no overall impact of suicide stories on suicide. The only significant relationship found by Stack to be associated with increases in the suicide rate was publicized stories about suicides by political heroes.

SUICIDE AND THE ELDERLY

The suicide rate of persons aged 65 and over has been increasing only since 1981 in the post–World War II period. In the three decades before 1980, the elderly suicide rate exhibited a decreasing trend and declined 42 percent between 1950 and 1980 (Osgood and McIntosh, 1986). Some sociologists and psychologists have proposed that the increased suicide rate among the elderly may be due to technological advances that extend the lives of the elderly and result in intolerable quality of life and/or medical treatments of ailing older patients that result in the depletion of family savings (Tolchin, 1989).

Age by itself does not *cause* suicidality. The person most vulnerable to suicide in the United States, however, is a white male between the ages of 75 and 84. The traditional, assertive, achievement-oriented role of a typical middle-aged male may not be as adaptable to the retirement situation as the traditionally more passive, nurturant role assumed by a typical middle-aged woman. Thus, the greater change in behavior and self-esteem necessitated in the older man may create more stress and depression if he is unable to find satisfaction in this new situation. A greater potential for suicidal behavior results (Aiken, 1982:114).

Gender and Suicide in the Elderly

Since gender is one of the most important predictors of suicide in the elderly, Silvia Canetto (1992) has addressed the question of why older women are less suicidal than older men. She suggests that women are less likely to die of suicide because they are more likely to seek professional help. Suicidal behavior in the elderly has been attributed to poverty, yet older women are more likely to be poor but less likely to be suicidal than older men. Canetto surmises that for many women, limited access to financial resources has been a longstanding problem, while for many men financial worries are less common until retirement. Thus, financial difficulties for older men may be a new experience.

Though living alone is frequently assumed to be a precipitant of suicidal behavior among the elderly, older women are more likely to live alone than older men. However, living alone may be more normative for older women, and older men living alone tend to be more isolated than older women living alone, concludes Canetto.

Though widowhood is a predictor of suicide in both women and men, the effect seems to be stronger for men than for women. Silvia Canetto observes that older men are more likely to depend on their wives for emotional support than the reverse situation, since older women appear to have more emotional connections with friends than do older men. Older men depend on their wives for their personal care and the running of the home. Losing a spouse may thus disrupt social support and emotional functioning more for a man than for a woman.

Danger Signals and Methods of Suicide

The *threat* of suicide is uncommon in the aged—they simply kill themselves, and their attempts rarely fail. When an elderly person makes an attempt at suicide, he or she usually has a profound death wish, and thus selects ways and means that are likely to result in the fulfillment of that wish. Recent studies have revealed that suicide is rarely an impulsive act unheralded by any warning signs, but as a rule is an event that can be anticipated. It has been estimated that 75 percent of elderly individuals contemplating suicide consult their physicians only shortly before committing the act (Achte, 1988:63).

Kalle Achte states that loneliness is the great tragedy of aging. Old age has been called "the era of losses" (Achte, 1988:58). After each loss, an elderly person has to try to pull him/herself together and adjust in order to be able to retain psychological equilibrium. If there is no possibility of communication with other people, loneliness can become extremely distressing for the older individual.

Robert Kastenbaum (1992:2) agrees that the reduced likelihood of open and substantive communication contributes to the possibility of suicide in the elderly. Kastenbaum notes that the following tend to reduce communication channels for the elderly: (1) living alone reduces the opportunities to express and explain suicidal intent to a caring person; (2) residing in a low-income, transient urban area tends to make a person socially invisible; (3) the depressive state often associated with suicidality frequently has the effect of reducing communication; and (4) the fact that most suicides in old age are committed by men suggests that reluctance to seek help may be strongest among those elders who are at greatest risk.

Though some danger signals for suicide among the elderly have already been noted, a listing of all such signals would include depression, withdrawal, bereavement (especially within the last year), isolation, expectation of death from some cause, retirement, loss of independence, physical illness, desire and rational decision to protect survivors from financial disaster, philosophical decision (no more pleasure or purpose in life), decreased self-esteem, and organic mental deterioration (Eddy and Alles, 1983:169–71).

Frequent methods used by the elderly to kill themselves are guns, drugs, hanging, and jumping. More subtle means such as not eating, not taking medication, drinking too much, delaying medical treatment, or taking physical risks are also used (Oaks and Ezell, 1993:226). Sometimes the elderly will "give up" psychologically, and this triggers biological changes that increase potential for disease.

Robert Kastenbaum (1986:196) notes other findings about suicide in later life: (1) Most elderly people do *not* have suicidal thoughts. (2) When suicidal intentions exist, the probability of a completed act of self-destruction is higher than at other ages. (3) Suicidality is less frequent among married older people who stay in touch with their children and relatives and have not had a suicide or an attempt in their family. (4) The suicidal older person is more depressed and sees self-destruction as an acceptable action.

Joseph Richman (1992) says that there is a great publicity campaign in favor of the view that suicide is a rational response to growing old. Though many elderly suicidal persons have severe problems in accepting their age, many of them have revealed similar problems in self-acceptance throughout their lives, and many felt "old" at age 15, notes Richman. The decision to commit suicide does not arise overnight; it is part of a lengthy process during which the significance of the individual's entire existence has been called into question. In working with over 800 suicidal persons, many of whom were elderly, ill, and some of them terminal, Richman (1992:134) says, "I can state unequivocally that suicide is not a rational response to aging." As the next section of the book discusses, however, rational suicide may be the answer for some individuals.

RATIONAL SUICIDE

There have been times in history when misery was so common and the outlook so bleak that suicide probably seemed a serious option. The Mark Twain quote at the beginning of the chapter suggests that there are times in life when we would like to die temporarily. The Judeo-Christian tradition, however, has generally advocated life and strongly urged that life not be disposed of no matter the temptations. For the elderly, to decide to take one's life tends to be a more rational or philosophical

AFTER 60 YEARS OF MARRIAGE, COUPLE DECIDES TO LEAVE WORLD TOGETHER

Julia Saunders, 81, had her hair done. Her husband, Cecil, 85, collected the mail one final time and paused to chat with a neighbor. Inside their mobile home, they carefully laid out a navy blazer and a powder-blue dress.

After lunch, the Saunders drove to a rural corner of Lee County and parked. As cows grazed in the summer heat, the couple talked. Then Cecil Saunders shot his wife of 60 years in the heart and turned the gun on himself.

Near the clothes they had chosen to be buried in, the couple had left a note:

"Dear children, this we know will be a terrible shock and embarrassment. But as we see it, it is one solution to the problem of growing old. We greatly appreciate your willingness to try to take care of us.

After being married for 60 years, it only makes sense for us to leave this world together because we loved each other so much."

On the floorboard of the car, Cecil and Julia Saunders had placed typewritten funeral instructions and the telephone numbers of their son and daughter.

Then they consummated their suicide pact, becoming two of the more than 4,000 elderly Americans authorities say will commit suicide this year.

"What struck all of us was how considerate, how thoughtful they were to all concerned about killing themselves," said Sheriff's Sergeant Richard Chard, who investigated the August 19 murder-suicide. "They didn't want to impose or be a bother to anyone. Not even in dying."

Julia's dimming eyesight, heart congestion and a stroke had driven Cecil to place his wife in a nursing home earlier this year. But she became hysterical over what she said was poor care there, and Cecil brought her home, said neighbors at the mobile home park where the couple had lived since 1974.

"You never saw him without her," said Vera Whittimore, 67. "If there ever was true love, they had it. I think they were just tired of living and couldn't wait for God to take them."

The Saunders had hot dogs and beans for lunch, then drove their Caprice to pastureland 5½ miles from their mobile home, parking on the grassy shoulder.

As thunderstorms rumbled in the distance, they talked.

"I can picture in my mind them sitting there," Chard said. "Maybe they spoke about how things were when they were young. Then he leaned over and gave her a farewell kiss."

The bodies were found by workers from nearby Owl Creek Boat Works, who called police.

In Philadelphia, a police officer stood by as the Saunders' son, Robert, 57, was told of his parents' death. His parents wanted no tears shed over their decision to die. The note they left for Robert and his sister, Evelyn, 51, ended with a wish:

"Don't grieve because we had a very good life and saw our two children turn out to be such fine persons. Love, Mother and Father."

Minneapolis Star-Tribune, October 4, 1983, p. 12A.

decision. Elderly individuals and others today seem to be asking if life is to be valued under all conditions because it has intrinsic value or if the value of life is relative to the circumstances. The preceding article, describing the Saunders' final days, suggests that the value of life for them *was* relative to the circumstances.

While suicide is usually treated as the product of mental illness or a desperate cry for help used by someone who does not really want to die, suicide can be considered a rational act. **Rational suicide** is presumably suicide in which the individual is not insane, in which the decision is reached in unimpaired, undeceived fashion, and in which the choice made is not a bad thing for that individual to do (Battin, 1982). Certainly one could argue that the Saunders' behavior in the insert above was a rational homicide/suicide. Jacques Choron's assertion (1972: 96–97) that "rational" implies "not only that there is no psychiatric disorder but also that the reasoning of the suicidal person is in no way impaired and that his motives would seem justifiable, or at least 'understandable,' by the majority of his contemporaries in the same culture or social group" seems to fit the case of the Saunders.

Richard Brandt (1986:339) notes that the person contemplating suicide is obviously making a choice between future world courses—the future world course that includes his or her demise an hour or so from now and several possible ones that contain his or her demise at a later point. While one cannot have precise knowledge about many features of the latter group, it is certain that they will all end with death sooner or later. The basic question for the person to answer to determine the best (or rational) choice is: which would be chosen under conditions of optimal use of information, when all personal desires are taken into account? It is not just a question of what is preferred now.

Certainly one's desires, aversions, and preferences may change after a short while. When one is in a state of despair, nothing but the thing he or she cannot have—rejection of a love or dismissal from a job—may seem desirable. The passage of time is likely to reverse all this. So if one acts on the preferences of today alone, when the emotion of despair seems more than one can stand, death might seem preferable to life. But if one allows for the preferences of the weeks and years ahead, when many goals might be enjoyable and attractive, life might be found to be preferable to death. Thus, Brandt is suggesting that a future world course might well be different from that of the hour.

Brandt further suggests that one must take into account the infirmities of one's "sensing" machinery. Knowing that the machinery is out of order will not tell one what results it would give if it were working. Thus the best recourse might be to refrain from making any decision in a stressful frame of mind. If decisions have to be made, one must recall past reactions, in a normal frame of mind, to outcomes like those under assessment. The future world course obviously did not look "enjoyable and attractive" to the Saunders after 80 years of life. A similar unattractive future lay ahead for a woman named Diane (below).

MY PATIENT'S SUICIDE

Dr. Timothy E. Quill

Diane was feeling tired and had a rash. Her hematocrit was 22, and her white-cell count was 4.3 with some metamyelocytes and unusual white cells. I called Diane and told her it might be serious. When she pressed for the possibilities, I reluctantly opened the door to leukemia. Hearing the word seemed to make it exist. "Oh, shit!" she said. "Don't tell me that." I thought, I wish I didn't have to.

Diane was raised in an alcoholic family and had felt alone for much of her life. She had vaginal cancer as a young woman, and had struggled with depression and her own alcoholism for most of her adult life. I had come to know, respect, and admire her over the previous eight years as she confronted and gradually overcame these problems. During the previous three and a half years, she had abstained from alcohol and had established much deeper connections with her husband, her college-age son, and several friends. Her business and artistic work were blossoming. She felt she was living fully for the first time.

Unfortunately, a bone-marrow biopsy confirmed the worst: acute myelomonocytic leukemia. In the face of this tragedy, I looked for signs of hope. This is an area of medicine in which technological intervention has been successful, with long-term cures occurring 25 percent of the time. As I probed the costs of these cures, I learned about induction chemotherapy (three weeks in the hospital, probable infections, and hair loss; 75 percent of patients respond, 25 percent do not). Those who respond are then given consolidation chemotherapy (with similar side effects; another 25 percent die, thus a net of 50 percent survive). For those still alive to have a reasonable chance of long-term survival, they must undergo bone-marrow transplants (hospitalization for two months, a whole-body irradiation—with complete killing of the bone marrow—infectious complications; 50 percent of this group survive, or 25 percent of the original group). Though hematologists may argue over the exact percentage of people who will benefit from therapy, they don't argue about the outcome of not having any treatment—certain death in days, weeks, or months.

Believing that delay was dangerous, the hospital's oncologist broke that news to Diane and made plans to begin induction chemotherapy that afternoon. When I saw her soon after, she was enraged at his presumption that she would want treatment and devastated by the finality of the diagnosis. All she wanted to do was go home and be with her family. She had no further questions about treatment and, in fact, had decided that she wanted none. Together we lamented her tragedy. I felt the need to make sure that she and her husband understood that there was some risk in delaying, that the problem would not go away, and that we needed to keep considering the options over the next several days.

Two days later Diane, her husband, and her son came to see me. They had talked at length about the problem and the options. She remained very clear about her wish not to undergo chemotherapy and to live whatever time she had left outside of the hospital. Her family wished she would choose treatment but accepted her decision. She articulated very clearly that it was she who would be experiencing all the side effects of treatment and that one-in-four odds were not good enough for her to undergo so toxic a course of therapy. I had her repeat her understanding of the treatment, the odds, and the consequences of forego-ing treatment. I clarified a few misunderstandings, but she had a remarkable grasp of the options and implications.

I have long been an advocate of the idea that an informed patient should have the right to choose or refuse treatment, and to die with as much control and dignity as possible. Yet there was something that disturbed me about Diane's decision to give up a 25 percent chance of long-term survival in favor of almost certain death. Diane and I met several times that week to discuss her sit-uation, and I gradually came to understand the decision from her perspective. We arranged for home hospice care, and left the door open for her to change her mind.

Just as I was adjusting to her decision, she opened up another area that fur-ther complicated my feelings. It was extraordinarily important to Diane to maintain her dignity during the time remaining to her. When this was no longer possible, she clearly wanted to die. She had known of people lingering in what was called "relative comfort," and she wanted no part of it. We spoke at length about her wish. Though I felt it was perfectly legitimate, I also knew that it was outside of the realm of currently accepted medical practice and that it was more than I could offer or promise. I told Diane that information that might be help-ful was available from the Hemlock Society.

(continued)

A week later she phoned me with a request for barbiturates for sleep. Since I knew that this was an essential ingredient in a Hemlock Society suicide, I asked her to come to the office to talk things over. She was more than willing to protect me by participating in a superficial conversation about her insomnia, but it was important to me to know how she planned to use the drugs and to be sure that she was not in despair or overwhelmed in a way that might color her judgment. In our discussion, it was apparent that she was having trouble sleeping, but it was also evident that the security of having enough barbiturates available to commit suicide, if and when the time came, would give her the peace of mind she needed to live fully in the present. She was not despondent and, in fact, was making deep, personal connections with her family and close friends. I made sure that she knew how to use the barbiturates for sleep, and how to use them to commit suicide. We agreed to meet regularly, and she promised to meet with me before taking her life. I wrote the prescriptions with an uneasy feeling about the boundaries I was exploring—spiritual, legal, professional, and personal. Yet I also felt strongly that I was making it possible for her to get the most out of the time she had left.

The next several months were very intense and important for Diane. Her son did not return to college, and the two were able to say much that had not been said earlier. Her husband worked at home so that he and Diane could spend more time together. Unfortunately, bone weakness, fatigue, and fevers began to dominate Diane's life. Although the hospice workers, family members, and I tried our best to minimize her suffering and promote comfort, it was clear that the end was approaching. Diane's immediate future held what she feared the most: increasing discomfort, dependence, and hard choices between pain and sedation. She called her closest friends and asked them to visit her to say good-bye, telling them that she was leaving soon. As we had agreed, she let me know as well. When we met, it was clear that she knew what she was doing, that she was sad and frightened to be leaving but that she would be even more terrified to stay and suffer.

Two days later her husband called to say that Diane had died. She had said her final good-byes to her husband and son that morning, and had asked them to leave her alone for an hour. After an hour, which must have seemed like an eternity, they found her on the couch, very still and covered by her favorite shawl. They called me for advice about how to proceed. When I arrived at their house we talked about what a remarkable person she had been. They seemed to have no doubts about the course she had chosen, or about their cooperation, although the unfairness of her illness and the death were overwhelming to us all.

I called the medical examiner to inform him that a hospice patient had died. When asked about the cause of death, I said acute leukemia. He said that was fine and that we should call a funeral director. Although acute leukemia was the truth, it was not the whole story. But any mention of suicide would probably have brought an ambulance, efforts at resuscitation, and a police investigation. Diane would have become a "coroner's case," and the decisions to perform an autopsy would have been made at the discretion of the medical examiner. The family or I could have been subjected to criminal prosecution; I could have been subjected to a professional review. Although I truly believe that the family and I gave her the best care possible, allowing her to define her limits and directions, I am not sure the law, society, or the medical profession would agree.

Diane taught me about the range of help I can provide people if I know them well and if I allow them to express what they really want. She taught me about taking charge and facing tragedy squarely when it strikes. She taught me about life, death, and honesty, and that I can take small risks for people I really know and care about.

"Death and Dignity: A Case of Individualized Decision Making." *Harpers Magazine*, May 1991, pp. 32–34. Originally published in *The New England Journal of Medicine*, March 7, 1991, vol. 324.

Individuals opposed to suicide outright would argue that a person does not have the right to commit suicide regardless of the circumstances. Others believe certain circumstances may be so unbearable that it is understandable why one commits suicide, but this should be an individual act and not one encouraged by society or the legal system, note Ellen Ingram and John Ellis (1992:35) in their review of literature on suicidal behavior. Opponents with extreme views argue that life should be preserved regardless of circumstances even in the case of a terminal illness. They would argue that suicide is an ambivalent act and that every person who wants to die also wants to live. Such a view suggests that suicidal thoughts are only temporary and through intervention the crisis often passes (Ingram and Ellis, 1992). Not only may the thoughts be temporary, but the quote at the beginning of the chapter reminds us that "suicide is a *permanent* answer to a *temporary* set of problems."

CONCLUSION

Just what constitutes a suicide is not clear today. Many persons display "suicidal behavior" by constantly taking risks and gambling with their lives; yet if death results from such behavior, it is often classified as "accidental" or "natural." Sociologists argue that suicidal persons construct their meanings of suicide and motivations for committing it out of collective values upon which the social structure rests. Meanings of suicide arise out of what people think, feel, and do.

Suicidal persons are more likely to be adolescents or very elderly, male, and not married. Though age by itself does not *cause* suicidality, the person most vulnerable to suicide is a white male between the ages of 75 and 84. Suicidal persons tend to talk about the attempt prior to the act and often display observable signs of suicide. Males are perhaps more "successful" at completing suicide than females because they tend to use a more lethal weapon—firearms. For suicidal persons, this act becomes an easy "solution" to their problems—a permanent answer to a temporary set of problems. Suicide can be a rational act, and one does not have to be "insane" to take one's own life.

A FEW WORDS ON SUICIDE: DON'T TRY IT!

A few months ago, I tried to commit suicide. The reason I did this was that I could no longer find happiness within me. I know that sorrow and pain are parts of life, but so are joy and laughter. I wasn't getting enough of the happiness that should be in everyone's life. I felt that, no matter how hard I tried to be a good, kind, thoughtful person, I failed. My best just wasn't good enough for people. This was making me miserable, and a miserable person is a burden to others. I didn't want to live the rest of my life feeling the way I was feeling, so I decided to end it all and find out what my Lord thought of me. It was wrong. I know that society thinks it's wrong. That's why, when I made the decision to commit suicide, I really wanted to die. Having to survive and face the music, so to speak, seemed worse than death itself.

I'm hoping now, though, that you won't make me feel as though I should be ashamed of myself. You see, I'm really glad to be alive, and I even believe I have a bright future. Someday I might even have children, and I don't want them to think badly of me. I know they won't if you don't.

I've learned to be stronger: I've done this by becoming a little more selfish. But that is necessary, or else you'll lose yourself to others and become their puppet. I've learned to make demands of others. The big one I'm making now is that you just keep giving me affection.

Sincerely,

Don't Try Suicide

Boston Globe, July 7, 1981, p. B13.

In the event that one does not take the advice of the preceding letter and suicide is completed, some suggestions for dealing with the aftermath of suicide are presented here:

1. Be available to the survivors by taking the initiative to help. Do not hesitate to visit them, even if you do not know what to say. Just being present shows that you care.
2. Discourage guilt feelings. Suicide tends to result from long-term feelings, thus the grievers should not blame themselves with the "if only" feelings.
3. Be truthful and honest at all times.
4. Discourage self-pity and encourage the individual to become involved in activities.
5. Encourage the griever to express his or her real feelings. Help guide the individual toward thinking ahead to the future.

SUMMARY

1. Suicide has been around for as long as recorded history.
2. Suicide has historically been viewed in different ways in different places. Even today the general attitude toward suicide remains confused and sometimes contradictory.
3. The meaning of suicide is problematic. Suicide research centers have evolved in recent years to address the complex issues of suicide.
4. In the late 1800s, French sociologist Emile Durkheim noted that suicide is related to one's degree of social integration. Different types of society produce different suicide types: egoistic, altruistic, anomic, and fatalistic.
5. The dramaturgical approach to suicide uses the drama or action to explain the behavior.
6. The existentialist perspective on suicide may view the choice of death as like the choice of life, both the result of reflection, and not see death as "the enemy."
7. If one feels alienated and powerless, suicide may appear to be a solution.
8. Though age by itself does not *cause* suicidality, the person most vulnerable to suicide in the United States is a white male between the ages of 75 and 84.

9. People who commit suicide tend to talk about their attempt prior to the act.
10. The most frequent method of completed suicide is firearms.
11. Suicidal deaths are virtually nonexistent prior to age 5 and are rare between 5 and 9 years. Adults prefer to believe that children do not commit suicide.
12. Rational suicide suggests that a person does not have to be mentally ill to take his or her own life.
13. The media has contributed to clusters of suicides by teenagers, according to some researchers.
14. Social factors tend to be associated with suicide: age, gender, marital status, and socioeconomic level.

DISCUSSION QUESTIONS

1. Discuss why the meaning of suicide continues to be problematic today.
2. Give examples of Durkheim's four types of suicide.
3. How does the dramaturgical approach view suicide?
4. How does an existentialist philosophy perspective explain suicide?
5. Describe signs of suicide. What should you do if you observe some of these signs in a friend?
6. Discuss why the suicide rate tends to be high among adolescents and the elderly.
7. Rational suicide implies that one does not have to be mentally ill to take his or her own life. Discuss whether you feel that one can be "sane" and take his or her own life.
8. Discuss your reaction to Julia and Cecil Saunders' deaths.

GLOSSARY

Alienation: One does not feel in control and does not feel a part of a situation, often resulting in a lack of self-realization and a feeling of powerlessness and hopelessness.

Altruistic Suicide: The individual is overly integrated into society and willing to die for the group.

Anomic Suicide: Results from a lack of regulation of the individual when the norms governing existence no longer control that individual.

Dramaturgical Perspective: Highlights the construction of action by using the metaphor of the drama to explain behavior.

Egoistic Suicide: The person is inadequately integrated into the society.

Existentialist Philosophy: The choice of death may be like the choice of life; death is not the enemy as viewed by some perspectives.

Fatalistic Suicide: Too much control by society may lead to feelings of oppression under extremely strict rules.

Rational Suicide: Suicide in which the individual is not insane and is aware of what he or she is doing.

Suicide Cluster: An excessive number of suicides occurring in close temporal and geographic proximity.

REFERENCES

Achte, Kalle. 1988. "Suicidal Tendencies in the Elderly." *Suicide and Life-Threatening Behavior,* 18(Spring):55–65.

Aiken, Lewis R. 1982. *Later Life,* 2nd ed. New York: Holt, Rinehart and Winston.

Alvarez, A. 1971. *The Savage God: A Study of Suicide.* London: Weidenfeld and Nicolson.

Asarnow, Joan Rosenbaum, and Gabrielle Carlson. 1988. "Suicide Attempts in Preadolescent Child Inpatients." *Suicide and Life-Threatening Behavior,* 18(Summer):129–136.

Battin, Margaret P. 1982. *Ethical Issues in Suicide.* Englewood Cliffs, NJ: Prentice-Hall.

Bell, Daniel. 1977. "Sex and Chronicity as Variables Affecting Attitudes of Undergraduates Towards Peers with Suicidal Behaviors." *Dissertation Abstracts International,* 38:3380B.

Berman, Alan L. 1986. "Helping Suicidal Adolescents: Needs and Responses." In *Adolescence and Death,* Charles A. Corr and Joan N. McNeil (Eds.) New York: Springer Publishing Company.

Beskow, Jan, and Ulf Asgard. 1990. "Psychological Autopsies: Methods and Ethics." *Suicide and Life-Threatening Behavior,* 20(Winter):307–323.

Biblarz, Arturo, Dolores Noonan Biblarz, Mary Pilgrim, and Brent F. Baldree. 1991. "Media Influence on Attitudes Toward Suicide." *Suicide and Life-Threatening Behavior,* 21(Winter):374–384.

Brandt, Richard B. 1986. "The Morality and Rationality of Suicide." In *Ethical Issues in Death and Dying,* 2nd ed., Robert F. Weir (Ed.) . New York: Columbia University Press.

Brody, Jane E. 1987. "Child Suicides: Common Causes." *The New York Times,* March 3, p. 16.

Brown, James H., Paul Henteleff, Samia Barakat, and Cheryl J. Rowe. 1986. "Is It Normal for Terminally Ill Patients to Desire Death?" *American Journal of Psychiatry,* 143 (February):208–211.

Brozan, Nadine. 1986. "Adolescent Suicides: The Grim Statistics." *The New York Times,* January 13, p. 16.

Calhoun, Lawrence G., and Breon G. Allen. 1991. "Social Reactions to the Survivor of a Suicide in the Family: A Review of the Literature." *Omega,* 23:95–107.

Canetto, Silvia Sara. 1992. "Gender and Suicide in the Elderly." *Suicide and Life-Threatening Behavior,* 22(Spring):80–97.

Charmaz, Kathy. 1980. *The Social Reality of Death.* Reading, MA: Addison Wesley Publishing Company.

Choron, Jacques. 1972. *Suicide.* New York: Charles Scribner's Sons.

Codex Juris Canonici. 1918. Rome, Italy: Polyglot Press.

Coleman, Loren. 1987. *Suicide Clusters.* Boston: Faber and Faber, Inc.

Curran, David K. 1987. *Adolescent Suicidal Behavior.* Washington, DC: Hemisphere Publishing Company.

deCatanzaro, D. 1981. *Suicide and Self-Damaging Behavior: A Sociobiological Perspective.* New York: Academic Press.

Domino, George, Valerie Domino, and Travis Berry. 1987. "Children's Attitudes Toward Suicide." *Omega,* 17:279–287.

Donne, John. 1930. *Biathanatos,* (reprint of 1st ed., 1644). New York: Facsimile Text Society.

Douglas, Jack D. 1967. *The Social Meanings of Suicide.* Princeton, NJ: Princeton University Press.

Dunn, Robert G., and Donna Morrish-Vidners. 1987. "The Psychological and Social Experience of Suicide Survivors." *Omega,* 18:175–186.

Durkheim, Emile. 1951. *Suicide: A Study in Sociology* (reprint of 1st ed., 1987) New York: Free Press.

Eddy, James M., and Wesley F. Alles. 1983. *Death Education.* St. Louis, MO: C.V. Mosby Company.

Ellis, Jon B., and Lillian M. Range. 1989. "Characteristics of Suicidal Individuals: A Review." *Death Studies,* 13:485–500.

Ezell, Gene, David J. Anspaugh, and Judy Oaks. 1987. *Death and Dying: From a Health and Sociological Perspective.* Scottsdale, AZ: Gorsuch Scarisbrick.

Farberow, Norman L. 1975. *Suicide in Different Cultures.* Baltimore, MD: University Park Press.

Garfinkel, Barry D., Art Froese, and Jane Hood. 1982. "Suicide Attempts in Children and Adolescents." *American Journal of Psychiatry,* 139(October):1257–1261.

Garrison, Carol Z. 1989. "The Study of Suicidal Behavior in the Schools." *Suicide and Life-Threatening Behavior,* 19(Spring):120–130.

Gibson, J. A., L. M. Range, and H. N. Anderson. 1987. "Adolescents' Attitudes Toward Suicide: Does Knowledge that the Parents Are Divorced Make a Difference?" *Journal of Divorce,* 163–167.

Gould, Madelyn S., Sylvan Wallenstein, and Lucy Davidson. 1989. "Suicide Clusters: A Critical Review." *Suicide and Life-Threatening Behavior,* 19(Spring):17–29.

Gould, Madelyn S., and David Shaffer. 1986. "The Impact of Suicide in Television Movies." *The New England Journal of Medicine,* vol. 315, (September 11):690–694.

Guillon, Claude, and Yves LeBonniec. 1982. *Suicide, Its Use, History, Technique and Current Interest.* Paris, France: Editions Alain Moreais.

Ingram, Ellen, and Jon B. Ellis. 1992. "Attitudes Toward Suicidal Behavior: A Review of the Literature." *Death Studies,* 16:31–43.

Kastenbaum, Robert J. 1986. *Death, Society and Human Experience,* 3rd ed. Columbus, Ohio: Charles E. Merrill Publishing Company.

Kastenbaum, Robert. 1992. "Death, Suicide and the Older Adult." *Suicide and Life-Threatening Behavior,* 22(Spring):1–14.

Kastenbaum, Robert, and Ruth Aisenberg. 1976. *The Psychology of Death.* New York: Springer Publishing Company.

Maldonado, George, and Jess F. Kraus. 1991. "Variation in Suicide Occurrence by Time of Day, Day of the Week, Month, and Lunar Phase." *Suicide and Life-Threatening Behavior,* 21:174–187.

May, Philip A. 1990. "A Bibliography on Suicide and Suicide Attempts Among American Indians and Alaska Natives." *Omega,* 21:199–214.

Mayo Clinic. 1985. "Suicide in America." *Mayo Clinic Health Letters* (September).

McCall, Patricia L. 1991. "Adolescent and Elderly White Male Suicide Trends: Evidence of Changing Well-Being?" *Journal of Gerontology,* 46(1):43–51.

McGuire, Donald J., and Margot Ely. 1984. "Childhood Suicide." *Child Welfare,* 63 (January/February):17–26.

Oaks, Judy, and Gene Ezell. 1993. *Dying and Death: Caring, Coping, Understanding,* 2nd ed. Scottsdale, AZ: Gorsuch Scarisbrick Publishers.

Orbach, Israel. 1988. *Children Who Don't Want to Live: Understanding and Treating the Suicidal Child.* San Francisco: Jossey-Bass Inc., Publishers.

Osgood, Nancy J., and John L. McIntosh. 1986. *Suicide and the Elderly: An Annotated Bibliography and Review.* New York: Greenwood Press.

Parsons, Talcott. 1949. *The Structure of Social Action.* New York: The Free Press.

Peck, M. 1980. *Recent Trends in Suicide among Young People.* Los Angeles: Institute for Studies of Destructive Behaviors.

Phillips, David P., and Lundie L. Carstensen. 1986. "Clustering of Teenage Suicides after Television News Stories about Suicide." *The New England Journal of Medicine,* vol. 315, (September 11):685–689.

Prior, Lindsay. 1989. *The Social Organization of Death: Medical Discourse and Social Practices in Belfast.* New York: St. Martin's Press.

Range, Lillian M., and William C. Goggin. 1990. "Reactions to Suicide: Does Age of the Victim Make a Difference?" *Death Studies,* 14:269–275.

Rich, Charles L., Gary M. Warsradt, Robert A. Nemiroff, Richard C. Fowler, and Deborah Young. 1991. "Suicide, Stressors, and the Life Cycle." *American Journal of Psychiatry,* 148 (April):524–527.

Richman, Joseph. 1992. "A Rational Approach to Suicide." *Suicide and Life-Threatening Behavior,* 22(Spring):130–141.

Smith, Walter J. 1985. *Dying in the Human Life Cycle.* New York: Holt, Rinehart and Winston.

Stack, Steven. 1992. "The Effect of the Media on Suicide: The Great Depression." *Suicide and Life-Threatening Behavior,* 22(Summer):255–267.

Stillion, Judith M., and Eugene E. McDowell. 1991. "Examining Suicide From a Life Span Perspective." *Death Studies,* 15:327–354.

Taylor, Greg W. 1990. "AIDS Mercy Killings." *Macleans,* 103(July 16):14.

Theodorson, George A., and Achilles G. Theodorson. 1969. *Modern Dictionary of Sociology.* New York: Thomas Y. Crowell Company.

Tolchin, Martin. 1989. "When Long Life Is Too Much: Suicide Rises among Elderly." *The New York Times,* July 19, p. 1.

Yang, Bijou. 1992. "The Economy and Suicide: A Time-Series Study of the U.S.A." *American Journal of Economics and Sociology,* 51(January):87–99.

Yang, Bijou, David Lester, and Chung-Hsin Yang. 1992. "Sociological and Economic Theories of Suicide: A Comparison of the U.S.A. and Taiwan." *Social Science and Medicine,* 34:333–334.

SUGGESTED READINGS

Corr, Charles A., and Joan N. McNeil. 1986. *Adolescence and Death.* New York: Springer Publishing Company. *An anthology covering numerous issues on adolescence and death, this book devotes one section to helping suicidal adolescents and the survivors of suicide.*

Culver, Charles M. 1990. *Ethics at the Bedside.* Hanover, NH: University Press of New England. *Several scenarios in this anthology reveal how moral decisions are made in modern hospitals.*

Curran, David K. 1987. *Adolescent Suicidal Behavior.* Washington, DC: Hemisphere Publishing Corporation. *Based on the premise that suicidal adolescents are significantly disturbed and historically troubled individuals, much of this book on adolescent suicidal behavior in America is devoted to suicide attempts rather than completed suicides.*

Davis, John M., and Jonathan Sandoval. 1991. *Suicidal Youth: School-Based Intervention and Prevention.* San Francisco: Jossey-Bass Inc., Publishers. *Brings information on youth suicides together and formulates it to present theoretical and clinical approaches that can be used for intervention and prevention strategies for potentially suicidal adolescents.*

Johnson, S. W., and L. J. Maile. 1987. *Suicide and the Schools: A Handbook for Prevention, Intervention, and Rehabilitation.* Springfield, IL: Charles C. Thomas Publisher. *A good reference for school personnel in working with students in a school setting.*

Lester, David, 1993. *The Cruelest Death: The Enigma of Adolescent Suicide.* Philadelphia: The Charles Press. *Prevention strategies for working with suicidal adolescents for both professionals and laypersons are presented.*

Orbach, Israel. 1988. *Children Who Don't Want to Die: Understanding and Treating the Suicidal Child.* San Francisco: Jossey-Bass Inc., Publishers. *Integrates current theoretical, empirical, and clinical knowledge about different manifestations of child suicide and uses case histories of suicidal children and their families as illustrations.*

Rohr, Janelle. 1987. *Death and Dying: Opposing Viewpoints.* St. Paul, MN: Greenhaven Press. *Has a good section on the pros and cons of suicide.*

Weir, Robert F. 1986. *Ethical Issues in Death and Dying,* 2nd ed. New York: Columbia University Press. *While this anthology is broader in scope than suicide, nonetheless a large segment of the book is devoted to ethical issues surrounding suicide.*

Part Four
Understanding the Bereavement Process

Chapter

10

The Anthropology
of Death Ritual

Some children love to watch the cremations.

The skull is usually the last thing to be burned. Sometimes it collapses with a loud pop, like a balloon bursting. When that happens, the children clap their hands.

Alexander Campbell
The Heart of India

DEATH IS AN event occurring in all societies, yet it evokes an incredible variety of responses. At the moment of death, survivors in some societies remain rather calm, others cry, while others mutilate their own bodies. Some societies officially mourn for months, yet others complete the ritual within hours. Family involvement in preparation of the corpse for the funeral ritual exists in many societies while others call professional funeral directors to handle the job.

The variety of responses to death is further noted by Richard Huntington and Peter Metcalf in *Celebrations of Death: The Anthropology of Mortuary Ritual* (1979:1). They state that corpses are burned or buried, with or without animal or human sacrifice; they are preserved by smoking, embalming, or pickling; they are eaten—raw, cooked, or rotten; they are ritually exposed as dead or decaying flesh or simply abandoned; or they are dismembered and treated in a variety of these ways. Funerals are times for avoiding people or holding parties, for weeping or laughing, or for fighting or having sexual orgies.

In most non-Western societies, death is not seen as one event, but as a process whereby the deceased is slowly transferred from the land of the living to the land of the dead (Helman, 1985). The process is illustrated by rituals marking biological death, followed by rituals of mourning, and then rituals of social death. The person is often viewed as a soul in limbo during rituals of mourning, though he/she is still a partial member of the society (Sweeting and Gilhooly, 1992). For the Kota people of South India, for example, a person is not socially dead until after the dry funeral, the second funeral for the deceased held annually and lasting 11 days (Mandelbaum, 1959).

The structural-functional perspectives of sociologist Emile Durkheim (1915) and anthropologists Bronislaw Malinowski (1948) and A.R. Radcliffe-Brown (1964) reduce the ritual process into an equilibrium-producing system. Death rituals are emphasized as mechanisms that recreate social solidarity. Since society is assumed to be a smoothly running machine, death "disrupts" a society's assumed smooth operation. Rituals of death help to restore order to that which has been disrupted. Strength is gained by individuals from the ritual affirmations of the community, and they are then able to continue their lives with the restoration of a smoothly running society. Thus, functionalists deduce that ritual is the key to a stable society living in equilibrium (Kozak, 1991).

For some, the burial ground can serve as a symbolic representation of the social order (Bloch and Parry, 1982:34). For example, among the Merina, after death one returns "home" to the tomb, representing a regrouping of the dead—a central symbol of the culture and an underlying joy of the second funeral. By the entry of the new corpses into the collective mausoleum, the tomb and the reunited dead within it represent the undivided and enduring descent group and become the source of blessings and the fertility of the future. The force of this symbol of the tomb as the representation of the eternal undivided group can only be sustained by down-playing the individuality of the corpses that enter it.

SOCIETAL MANAGEMENT OF DEATH-RELATED EMOTIONS

Though they vary significantly, all societies seem to have some social mechanism for managing death-related emotions and reconstructing family interaction patterns modified by death. These customs are passed down from generation to generation and are an integral part of a society's way of coping with a major event like death.

The study of death rituals is a positive endeavor. Regardless of whether societal customs call for festive or restrained behavior, the issue of death throws into relief the most important cultural values by which people live their lives and evaluate their experiences (Huntington and Metcalf, 1979). Life becomes transparent against the background of death, and fundamental social and cultural issues are revealed.

Anthropologists do not claim to have a special understanding of the mystery of death, but they can recount the collective wisdom of many cultures. The entire web of human social interrelations is founded on many invisible and indirect meanings that are bestowed on various individuals (Cuzzort and King, 1980:55). While we cannot actually see a mourner or a mortician, we can observe those who occupy such statuses. Until we are informed that they occupy such statuses (and are expected to behave accordingly), however, we cannot respond in an appropriate way.

The anthropologist is concerned as a scientist with the meanings that different events have for different societies. As Kellehear (1990:10) notes, anthropology has given modern sociological analysis a rich source of **ethnographic** description for comparative purposes, thus providing some basis for a general, cross-cultural analysis of the multifaceted and complex responses to death. A true understanding of various rituals and activities results from an immersion in the culture. While the anthropologist cannot determine what is in the mind of the person acting, similar events observed over time can result in some understanding of the behavior within that context. Marvin Harris (1974:4) states that human life is not merely random or

THE AMERICAN WAKE OF IRELAND

Nineteenth-century Irish emigrants to the United States were mainly peasants who lived a harsh life. Coming to America between 1820 and 1920 represented hope for the Irish but was also viewed as a symbolic form of death: families were separated temporarily and permanently. Like when someone died, when one left for America they held a wake for the individual—sometimes called a live wake, parting spree, convoy, or farewell supper. The American wake, referred to as early as 1830, was recognized throughout Ireland by the end of 1850, but almost completely disappeared by the decade after World War I.

Much overlap existed in rituals between an actual wake for the dead and an American wake. Both involved public participation allowing the family and community to grieve over their loss. Attendance reaffirmed family and group ties and was a mixture of grief and gaiety. Both an Irish funeral and an American wake drew very large crowds (in the Irish language the same word can be used interchangeably for both funeral and multitude). Though sad, one could actually rejoice at the departed's rebirth to a new state: death and emigration freed one forever from the stark hopelessness of poverty. Music, singing, dancing, and wake games were usually a part of the affair. Gifts were often brought to the wake, except for the years following the Great Famine when offerings were meager.

Though the merriment at wakes for the dead or the emigrant may seem disrespectful, they actually demonstrated the strong belief that the physically or symbolically dead would continue to exist more happily elsewhere. The American wake, like the Irish funeral, reiterated the significance of transitional times for the Irish, whether changes in the seasons or major life changes such as birth, death, and emigration. Public involvement in funerary rituals avows the passing from one status to another. A funeral also mirrors the values and expectations of a group. The Irish wake, reflecting Irish life and Irish death customs, was unique to Ireland.

Adapted from Eileen Metress, "The American Wake of Ireland: Symbolic Death Ritual." *Omega*, 1990, 21:147–153.

capricious. Since one does not expect dreamers to explain their dreams, life-stylers should not be expected to explain their lifestyles. Through careful observation over time, however, one can come to a better understanding of why people do what they do.

WHY STUDY CROSS-CULTURAL DEATH RITUALS?

Why should a student of death and dying become familiar with the death customs of other cultures? Our culture is characterized all too often by **ethnocentrism** —we tend to think that our way is the superior way. Just because another society's customs differ from our own does not mean they are wrong. In comparing different death-related customs, the similarities between cultures are often greater than the differences. As you read this chapter, note the many parallels existing between our death customs and those of others.

Being familiar with cross-cultural death customs should help to better understand the American concept of death. To blame a supernatural or a physician or someone else for one's death is functional in both literate and nonliterate societies—an explanation for the death and a scapegoat to relieve one's guilt feelings. While some nonliterate groups might attribute a death to the ghost of a deceased ancestor, a literate group might blame medical personnel.

We should also study death cross-culturally because of linkages of diseases around the world. AIDS, for example, in less than a decade has become a truly global pandemic (Feldman, 1990:2). Though the origin of AIDS is unknown, we do know that AIDS is rapidly emerging with major implications for the future vitality of humanity. In southwestern and northern Uganda in east Africa, half of all adults under 50 are HIV-positive. In Zambia in Africa one-fourth of adult men and women between 20 and 50 years of age are HIV-positive (Feldman, 1990:3). In the United States, AIDS is as devastating as it has become in parts of Europe, Africa, Asia, and Latin America.

Cross-cultural studies of death reveal that most societies seem to have a concept of soul and immortality. For some, a belief in a soul concept explains what happens in sleep and after death. For others, the belief in souls explains how the supernatural world becomes populated (Tylor, 1873). Much of the ritual performed at death is related to the soul and an appeasement of the beings in the spiritual world. This spiritual dimension of death plays a significant role in the social structure of societies that hold such beliefs.

Studying death cross-culturally reminds us of other similarities such as beliefs in ghosts. Souls of the dead become ghosts for many groups. Ghosts may take up residence. After a short period of wandering, however, ghosts may cease to exist. Some have conversations with ghosts and make offerings to them. This is sometimes referred to as the "cult of the dead" (Taylor, 1980). These ghosts are not worshipped but simply maintain a relationship with a spirit that acts as a guide and protector and confers power. To have a guardian spirit is a positive experience in some societies. For others, like Navajo and Apache Native Americans, ghosts are responsible for sickness and death and are to be avoided (Cox and Fundis, 1992). Ghosts are not unique to nonliterate cultures, however, but seem to also "exist" in literate societies. Many sane, sober individuals in the United States have had "encounters" with ghosts.

This chapter will present various death rituals and discuss the functions of such activities. In no way are these various cultures representative of all. Some

DEATH AND DYING IN AFRICAN-AMERICAN TRADITIONS

The African-American contemporary reactions to death are closely connected and deeply rooted in the traditional African tradition, yet are tempered by the American sociocultural experience. Funeral customs have evolved over centuries and reflect a tradition rich in cultural symbolism. To be an African-American in the United States is to be part of a history told in terms of contact with death. For in the era of slavery, death or other forms of personal loss could come at any time or age and often at the whim of someone else. This history is reflected in artistic expression in music, spirituals, poetry, novels, drama, and visual arts. These various art forms mirror the attitudes of African-Americans toward death. A consistent theme of death is often connected to a sense of solace in a theology and belief in an afterlife and promise of a better life.

Not unlike other Protestant groups in the United States, most African-American Protestant churches have no formally prescribed funeral ritual dictated by church hierarchy. Local church custom is followed. African-American funerals represent an attempt for dignity and esteem often denied in the dominant culture. Mourners are likely to depend upon the church and the community for support during bereavement. The African-American funeral is indeed a primary ritual and a focal occasion with a big social gathering after the funeral and the closest thing to a family reunion that might ever take place (a latent function of a funeral, as will be discussed later in this chapter).

Adapted from Ronald K. Barrett, "Psychocultural Influences on African-American Attitudes toward Death, Dying and Funeral Rites." In *Personal Care in an Impersonal World*, John Morgan (Ed.). Amityville, NY: Baywood Publishing Company, 1992.

examples may appear bizarre to the reader, but keep in mind that our own death rituals may appear strange to persons from other cultures.

DEATH AS A RITE OF PASSAGE

Death is a transition, but only the last in a long chain of transitions, according to Richard Huntington and Peter Metcalf (1979:93). The moment of death is related not only to the process of afterlife, but to the process of living, aging, and producing progeny. Death relates to life—to the recent life of the deceased and to the life he or she has procreated and now leaves behind. There is an eternity of sorts on either side of the line that divides the quick from the dead. Life continues generation after generation, and in many societies it is this continuity that is focused upon and enhanced during the rituals surrounding a death. To ease this continuity and soften the shock of death, euphemisms are often used, as was discussed in Chapter 3. Traditional African customs, for example, regard it as impolite to state bluntly that someone is dead. "Good breeding" is reflected by referring to the death of someone in euphemistic terms (Barrett, 1992).

One of the best-known accounts of death as one of a series of such **rites of passage** through the life cycle comes from Van Gennep (1909/1960) in his treatment of funerals. He had expected that the element of separation would be more marked in funerals than other rites of passage, but his evidence demonstrated that it is the transitional or the liminal that dominates mortuary ritual and symbolism. Van Gennep (1909:164) noted social status aspects of ritual and mourning:

> The length of the period (of mourning) increases with the closeness of the social tie to the deceased and with higher social standing of the dead person. If the dead man was a chief, the suspension affects the entire society.

However, persons for whom no rites are performed

> are the most dangerous dead. They would like to be reincorporated into the world of the living and since they cannot be, they behave like hostile strangers toward it. They lack the means to subsistence which the other dead find in their own world and consequently must obtain them at the expense of the living.

Individuals are often considered to be composed of several components, each of which may have a different fate after death (Palgi and Abramovitch, 1984:117). The purpose of the destruction of the corpse, whether through cremation, burial, or decomposition, is to separate the components—the various bodies and souls.

For the Lugbara of Uganda (Middleton, 1965) when people die, they cease to be "people of the world outside" and become "people who have died" or "people in the earth." Death marks the beginning of an elaborate rite of passage as a dead man has relations with both living and dead kin.

THE RITUAL OF MOURNING AT DEATH

Ritual can be defined as "the symbolic affirmation of values by means of culturally standardized utterances and actions" (Taylor, 1980:198). People in all societies are inclined to symbolize culturally defined feelings in conventional ways. Ritual behavior is an effective means of expressing or reinforcing these important sentiments and helps make death less socially disruptive and less difficult for individuals to bear (Haviland, 1991:577).

Rituals differ from other behavior in that they are formal—stylized, repetitive, and stereotyped (Rappaport, 1974). Rituals are performed in special places and occur at set times and include liturgical orders—words and actions set forth previously by someone.

Functions of rituals include validation and reinforcement of values, reassurance and feelings of security in the face of psychological disturbances, reinforcement of

This Japanese funeral emphasizes the social status of the man who has died. The living honor the dead and thereby create a symbolic community consisting of their ancestors and living members of their families.

group ties, aiding status change by acquainting persons with their new roles, relief of psychological tensions, and restabilization of patterns of interaction disturbed by a crisis (Taylor, 1980). Ritual can also have negative functions by causing tensions.

Whereas death rituals in the United States are generally subdued and rather gloomy affairs, some societies engage in rather spirited activities. The Bara people in Madagascar, for example, engage in "drunken revelry" at a funeral—rum is consumed, sexual activities occur, dancing takes place, and contests involving cattle occur (Huntington and Metcalf, 1979). Among the Cubeo of South America, simulated and actual ritual coitus is part of the mourning ritual (Goldman, 1979). The dances, ritual, dramatic performances, and the sexual license have the purpose of transforming grief and anger from a death into joy.

CUTTIN' THE BODY LOOSE: DANCING IN DEFIANCE OF DEATH IN NEW ORLEANS

Kalamu ya Salaam

"They gon cut the body loose!"

One short brother with a mustache was running up and down the funeral procession explaining that they wasn't going to have to go all the way to the cemetery on account of they was going to cut the body loose. This meant that the hearse would keep on going and the band and the second liners and the rest of the procession was going to dance on back to some tavern not too far away.

"They gon cut the body loose, y'all."

The marshal, out in front of the hearse, was draped in a blue-black suit that was a little too big and too long but was all the better to dance with. He wore yellow socks and brown shoes as a crazy combination of his own. After the body was cut loose, the steps he invented were amazing contortions of knees, shins, and flying feet. He executed those moves with the straightest, most nonchalant, don't-give-a-damn look I have ever seen on anybody's face what was doing as much work as he was doing under this merciless hot sun. He had somebody by him fanning and wiping his face after every series of grief-inspired movements. He looked so sad to be dancing so hard and making so many others of us smile as we watched him. We tried to imitate some of his easier and more obvious moves but couldn't. He was the coolest person in that street marching toward a tavern two or three blocks away under a 2:30 p.m. New Orleans summer sun. The coolest.

So we stood in a line and the second liners were shouting, "open it up, open it up," meaning for the people in front to get out the way so the hearse

(continued)

could pass with the body. After the hearse was gone we turned the corner and danced down to the bar.

Like a sudden urge to regurgitate and with the intensity of an ejaculation, an explosive sound erupted from the crowd under the hot New Orleans sun. People spontaneously answered the traditional call of the second line trumpet.

"Are you still alive?"

"YEAH!"

"Do we like to live?"

"YEAH!"

"Do you want to dance?"

"YEAH!"

"Well damn it, let's go!"

The trumpeter was taunting us now, and the older people were jumping from their front porches as we passed them, and they were answering that blaring hot high taunt with unmistakable fires blazing in their 60-year-old black eyes. They too danced as we passed them. They did the dances of their lives, the dances they used to celebrate how old they had become and what they had seen getting to their whatever number years. The dances they used to defy death.

Nowhere else in this country do people dance in the streets after someone has died. Nowhere else is the warm smell of cold beer on tap a fitting conclusion for the funeral of a friend. Nowhere else is death so pointedly belittled. One of us dying is only a small matter, an occasion for the rest of us to make music and dance. Nothing keeps us contained. With this spirit and this music in us, black people will never die, never die, never.

We were all ecstatic. We could see the bar. We knew it was ending, we knew we were almost there and defiantly we danced harder anyway. We hollered back even that much louder at the trumpeter as he squeezed out the last brassy blasts his lungs could throw forth. The end of the funeral was near, just as the end of life was near for some of us but it did not matter. When we get there, we'll get there.

Utne Reader, September/October, 1991, pp. 78–79.

The Display of Emotions

An examination of ethnographic data from 78 societies (Rosenblatt, Walsh, and Jackson, 1976) to identify the essence of universal grief behavior showed that it is a near universal that death is associated with emotionality and that the most usual expression among the bereaved is crying. The study further concluded that, if there are gender differences in emotions during bereavement, the women tend to cry and self-mutilate more than men. The men tend to direct anger and aggression away from self. One of the traditional theories suggested to explain gender differences in emotional expression was that it may be easier to socialize women than men to be overtly nonaggressive; thus crying may represent a female expression of aggression. Another explanation was the belief that women will be more affected by the loss from a death because of their stronger attachments through their role as mothers. On the other hand, women may not experience death more strongly, but they may simply be used as the person symbolizing publicly, in burdensome or self-injuring ways, the loss that all experienced. The analysis of data from these 78 societies concludes that the kind of data needed to "explain" the emotional difference by gender is lacking.

Paul Rosenblatt and colleagues (1976) note that most societies have developed mechanisms to control the anger of the bereaved and channel it along nondestructive paths. Ritual specialists help to minimize anger leading to disruptive social behavior. In a country so deritualized as the United States, funeral directors may provide a positive role in developing sets of norms for mourning behavior.

The expression of emotions ranges from complete abstinence to amplified wailing, notes Effie Bendann's *Death Customs: An Analytical Study of Burial Rites* (1930). She states that after a death the aborigines of Australia and Melanesia indulge in the most exaggerated forms of weeping and wailing. They display other manifestations of emotional excitement seemingly because of grief for the departed. At the end of a certain designated time period, however, they cease with metronomic precision and the would-be mourners indulge in laughter and other forms of amusement.

An outgoing display of emotions is found among the Kapauku Papuans of West New Guinea (Pospisil, 1963). Their ritual at death requires the relatives of the deceased to give a formal expression of their grief as soon as the soul leaves the body. They weep, eat ashes, cut off their fingers, tear their garments and net carrying bags, and smear their faces and bodies with mud, ashes, or yellow clay. A loud sing-song lamentation follows.

As noted above, mourning often falls most heavily on the women. For example, women among the Cheyenne Indians cut off their long hair and gash their foreheads as the blood flows (Hoebel, 1960). If the deceased was killed by enemies, they slash their legs until caked with dried blood. Mourning gives the women their own masochistic outlet. Cheyenne men, on the other hand, simply let down their hair in mourning and do not bother to lacerate themselves. In traditional African funerals (Barrett, 1992) women tend to wail, while men sing and dance; men are not to cry in front of women because they would appear weak before the very group they are to protect.

The Dinka women of the Sudan (Deng, 1972) cut their leather skirts and cover their bodies with dirt and ashes for as long as a year. Widows among the Swazi in Africa (Kuper, 1963) shave their heads and remain "in darkness" for three years before given the duty of continuing the **lineage** for the deceased through the

levirate, or required marriage with her husband's brother. Mourning imposed on the Swazi husband is less conspicuous and shorter than on the wife.

Somewhat less dramatic than the previous examples, the Huichol of Mexico (Weigand and Weigand, 1991:62–65) display a "great deal of crying and wailing" at the actual moment of death. This subsides during the preparation of the corpse but resumes again at the funeral site. However, Huichol women who have suffered the death of a mother or a child often express their loss by suicidal gestures—the stated goal of such behavior is to accompany the deceased. In reality, however, these gestures seldom result in suicide, according to Weigand.

In the United States some funeral directors have noted that occasionally individuals "carry on to the point of fainting" but catch themselves before completely passing out. If such behavior is expected within a subculture, some will comply. However, a more stoic approach appears to be normative in the United States. For example, the response of Jacqueline Kennedy when President John F. Kennedy was assassinated in Dallas in 1963 was praised by the media as "holding up well." Her reaction was probably one of shock more than bravery. In the 19th century, Italian immigrants to the United States actually hired mourners for funerals, a custom from the Old World (Cowell, 1986:79).

Types of Weeping

One could argue that people display the outward emotion of crying at the time of death because they are sad. Perhaps it is not as simple as that. Anthropologist A. R. Radcliffe-Brown (1964) notes two types of weeping. There is reciprocal ritual weeping to affirm the existence of a social bond between two or more persons. It is an occasion for affirming social ties. Although participants may not actually feel these sentiments that bind them, participation in various rites will strengthen whatever positive feelings they do have. The second type of ceremonial weeping, where one cries over the remains of a significant other, expresses the continued sentiment of attachment despite the severing of this social bond.

Richard Huntington and Peter Metcalf (1979) observe that Radcliffe-Brown was strongly influenced by the French sociologist Emile Durkheim. Durkheim (1954) argued that the emotions developed are feelings of sorrow and anger and are made stronger by participation in the burial rite, while Radcliffe-Brown claimed that those participating in ceremonial weeping come to feel emotion that is not sorrow but togetherness. What Durkheim finds significant is the way other members of society feel moral pressure to put their behavior in harmony with the feelings of the truly bereaved. Even if one feels no direct sorrow, weeping and suffering may result. Thus, to say that one weeps because of sadness may be too simplistic.

In conclusion, cross-cultural studies of the ritual of mourning at death reveal that a double standard prevails among some cultures—different "scripts" for different genders. Women in many societies, including the United States, are expected to display more of their emotions than men. Mourning rituals also tend to last for a set period of time in many societies.

ATTITUDES TOWARD DEATH

In some societies death is viewed as a continuation of life, simply in a different form. For example, the traditional African attitude towards death is "positive and accepting and comprehensively integrated into the totality of life"; death becomes a prolongation of life (Barrett, 1992). Death may be accepted by some as a natural part of life—the "final stage of growth" as Elisabeth Kübler-Ross notes. Yet for others, death is the end of everything. For example, the Navaho Indians (Habenstein and Lamers, 1963) have no belief in a glorious immortality for the soul and believe that death is the end of everything good. Likewise, the Semai of Malaya (Dentan, 1968) talk about life after death, but most admit they do not believe in it. Thus,

The feast of the dead in Peru demonstrates the belief in the continuity of relationships between the living and the dead.

DECORATION DAY: CELEBRATING KIN IN THE BLUE RIDGE MOUNTAINS

Doris Wiseman Boulton

Deep in the balsam groves of the Blue Ridge Mountains, time moves reluctantly. Old folk customs linger like the thick mists that creep in at twilight and huddle in the coves until the rising sun nudges them over the horizon.

TV dishes may scar the hillsides and unpicturesque mobile homes line up next to the chestnut bark cottages of another generation, but even in the midst of 20th-century clatter some hardy mountain people continue to live their traditions, celebrations, and superstitions in much the same way they always have. Old ways and rituals are still important to the life of family and community. A keen example of this is the survival of the family graveyard decoration day.

There is hardly a summer Sunday in any area that is not some family's decoration day. Perhaps this tradition has its roots in the outdoor communions and field preachings of 17th-century Scotland; no one knows for sure. Whatever its beginnings, decoration day has survived as a time to renew ties of kinship and friendship, share a meal, and honor the dead.

Each festival day falls on its own established Sunday—the first Sunday of June, for instance, or the last Sunday of July—and is referred to by its ancestral name. There is a Houston Decoration Day, a Pitman Decoration Day, and as many decorations as there are descendants of the pioneer families. These are family graveyards and not churchyards, so there may or may not be a church nearby. On decoration day the preacher and singers situate themselves in a visible spot and begin to preach and sing as people arrive with baskets of fresh flowers and food. The graves are soon heaped with a blaze of color, and care is taken that no grave is slighted.

A long row of tables is set up adjacent to the graveyard. Family members, no matter how extended, are expected to come bearing food and flowers. Friends bring flowers but no food. Both friends and family arriving from a distance are greeted so enthusiastically the preacher may have to shout to be heard. Each family has developed its own liturgy over the years, and each decoration day has a personality of its own.

When I was a child, my favorite decoration fell in early September when chinquapins were ripe and the late summer days were fading into harvest. We were always invited to the Woody family decoration. I remember this last decoration of summer as a mournful celebration in which laughter and handshakes were often punctuated by the sudden onset of tears, especially if the conversation moved into the past.

But the Woody decoration had a beautiful ritual built into the day's structure that was unique. Just as the preacher concluded his remarks for the day and just before the women left the graveyard to set out the stacks of fruit pies and platters of chicken, the family patriarch stood to speak.

"Now, dear friends, we are going to have our living decoration. Tell someone you love them, what they mean to you, while they can still hear you. Tell
them today!"

The singers started to sing again, and everyone joined in the minor wails of
"Give Me My Roses While I Live." Old men, young men, women and children
milled among the tombstones pinning blossoms on one another's lapels and col-
lars. At the singers' discretion the singing stopped. Tears dried as abruptly as
they had begun and we all went to lunch.

Utne Reader, September/October, 1991, pp. 81–82.

attitudes toward death are partly reflected in beliefs about what happens after
death.

In our own culture, a popular belief is that the dead and the living are separated from each other. Yet, like many cultures, we periodically pay respect to the
dead through All Saints Day and Memorial Day (Decoration Day). For example,
people in New Orleans still throng cemeteries on All Saints Day (Marcus, 1988).
Burial places bloom with white and yellow chrysanthemums, and family tombs are
scrubbed and whitewashed as in the past. A century ago in New Orleans on All

HOPI ATTITUDES TOWARD DEATH

W. H. Oswalt

The Hopi Indians viewed life and death as a phase of a recurrent cycle.
Death was an important change in individual status because it represented an
altered state for the person involved. The Hopi believed that a duality of being
existed in each person—a soul and a body expressed as a "breath-body." A person dying on earth literally was reborn in the afterworld. Corpses were washed
and given new names before burial. The breath-body's pattern of existence
would supposedly be the same in the domain of the dead as it had been on
earth—when it died in the afterworld, it would be reborn on earth.

During their elaborate ceremonies, the Hopi performed specific rites for
making the desires of the living known to the dead. Thus, the living solicited
the active aid of the dead. The dead returned symbolically to earth at given
times through katchina performers (masked and costumed individuals who
impersonated spirits of the dead).

From *Life Cycles and Lifeways.* Palo Alto, CA: Mayfield Publishing Company, 1986, p. 174.

The traditional funeral for the Igbo of Nigeria includes
males dancing to celebrate the life of the deceased.

Saints Day crowds poured into cemeteries from dawn to dusk. Families gathered for picnics, entertained friends, and told stories about the dead. Even today, All Saints Day remains a holiday for New Orleans municipal employees.

The continuity between the living and the dead is elaborated in ideas of reincarnation and in other ways found in non-Western as well as Western societies. For example, many Japanese today think that a person's spirit belongs to the same family and the same local community before and after death (Nagamine, 1988:67). A person's spirit gradually fades away from its family as time goes on. The Japanese do not clearly distinguish the dead from the living and seem to recognize the continuity between life and death.

The Igbo in Nigeria (Uchendu, 1965) believe that death is important for join-ing the ancestors. Without death, there would be no population increase in the ancestral households and thus no change in social status for the living Igbo. The lineage system is continued among the dead. Thus the world of the "dead" is a world full of activities.

The Ulithi of Micronesia are not morbid or defeated by death, according to William A. Lessa (1966). Their rituals afford them some victories and their mythol-ogy provides a hope for a happy life in another realm. Though their gods are some-what distant, they assure that the world has an enduring structure and their ancestral ghosts stand by to give more immediate aid when merited. Thus after expressing their bereavement, rather than retreating, they spring back into their normal work and enjoyment of life.

For the Dunsun of North Borneo, few events focus more on the beliefs and acts concerned with the non-natural world than the death of a family member (Williams, 1965:39). Death is considered a difficult topic of which everyone is fear-ful of talking, yet it must be prepared for since it causes great changes.

The Abkhasians on the coast of the Black Sea (Benet, 1974) view death as irra-tional and unjust. The one occasion when outbursts of feeling are permitted is at a funeral—wailing and scratching at one's flesh are permitted.

ABKHASIANS—THE LONG-LIVING PEOPLE

Over 125,000 native Abkhasians live mostly in rural areas on the coast of the Black Sea in Abkhasia, a country about half the size of New Jersey. These people do not have a phrase for "old people." Those over one hundred years of age are called "long-living people." Most of the aged work regularly performing light household tasks, working in the orchards and gardens, and caring for the animals.

These long-living people seem to enjoy fairly good health in their "old age." Close to 40 percent of the aged men (over 90) and 30 percent of aged women have good vision—do not need glasses for any sort of work. Nearly half have "reasonably good hearing." Most have their own teeth, and their posture is unusually erect.

Why do these people live so long? First, they have no retirement status but simply decrease their expected work load as they grow older. Second, they do not set deadlines for themselves; thus, no sense of urgency is accepted in emer-gencies.

Third, overeating is considered dangerous, and fat people are regarded as sick. When eating, they take small bites and chew slowly, thus insuring proper

(continued)

digestion. Leftovers are not eaten. Milk and vegetables make up 74 percent of their diet. The aged average 1900 calories per day—500 less than the U.S. National Academy of Science recommends for those over 55. They do not use refined sugars, and drink water and honey before retiring in the evening. A fermented drink (like buttermilk) with a high food value and useful for intestinal disorders is drunk. They eat a lot of fruit. Meat is eaten only once or twice per week. They usually cook without salt or spices. A dry red wine not fortified with sugar and with a low alcohol content is drunk. Few of them smoke, and they do not drink coffee or tea. Their main meal is at lunch (between 2 and 3 p.m.), and their supper is light. Between meals they eat fruit or drink a glass of fermented milk. They have a relaxed mood at mealtimes and eat slowly.

Fourth, stress is avoided by reducing competition. Fifth, they exercise daily. Sixth, their behavior is fairly uniform and predictable. Seventh, moderation is practiced in everything they do.

Though some social scientists question the longevity of the Abkhasians, they do seem to have their act together regarding health habits. Much of the above is advice we have often heard but failed to put into practice. Perhaps we should adhere to some of the Abkhasians' practices. Who knows, we might even live longer—if that is a goal to be sought.

Adapted from Sula Benet, *Abkhasians: The Long-Living People of the Caucasus*. New York: Holt, Rinehart and Winston, 1974.

CUSTOMS AT DEATH

As will be discussed in Chapter 12, a professional is called upon in the United States to prepare the body for final disposition, since we are a very specialized society with a high division of labor. The funeral director takes the body away and returns it later for viewing. The kin and friends in the United States normally play no significant role in handling the corpse. Compared with most societies, we are unique in the level of professional specialization relative to the preparation of the corpse and the actual disposal of the body. Most of the cultures discussed in this section encourage families and friends to become very involved in preparing the corpse for its final disposition.

Norms Prior to Death

Some societies have specific norms just prior to the death. It is important in many societies, including the United States, that one be with the dying person at the time of death. So often it is said, "If only I had gotten there a few minutes earlier . . ." A visit prior to death allows one to say goodbye. Among the Dunsun of

North Borneo (Williams, 1965), relatives come to witness the death. The dying person is propped up and held from behind. When the body grows cold, the social fact of death is recognized by announcing "he exists no more" or "someone has gone far away."

The Salish Indians of the Northwest United States (Habenstein and Lamers, 1963) leave the dying person alone with an aged man who neither receives pay nor is expected to have any special qualifications for the task. One near death must confess his or her misdeeds to this person. The confession is to prevent the ghost from roaming the places in life frequented by the dying person.

The Ik of Uganda (Turnbull, 1972) place the dying person in the fetal position since death for them represents a "celestial rebirth." The Magars of Nepal (Hitchcock, 1966) purify a dying person by giving him or her water that has been touched with gold.

The Maori of New Zealand (Mead, 1991:49) have a ceremony just before the person dies to send the spirit of the dying away while the person is still alive and conscious of what is happening. Once the spirit is gone, the individual may be medically dead but, in a Maori sense, is not wholly dead yet. Now that the person is a corpse, ceremonies begin and a space is set aside in the meeting house for the corpse to lie in an open coffin.

Having a cultural framework prescribing proper behavior at the time of death provides an established order and perhaps gives comfort to the bereaved. These behavioral norms give survivors something to do during the dying process and immediately thereafter, thus facilitating the coping abilities of the bereaved.

Handling the Corpse

Cleaning the Body

Family members' preparation of the body for final disposition, especially cleaning the body, is very evident in some societies. For the Bornu of Nigeria (Cohen, 1967) family members are required to wash the body, wrap it in a white cloth, place it on a **bier**, and take it to the burial ground. Similarly, the Semai in Malaya (Dentan, 1968) have the housemates bathe the corpse and sprinkle it with perfume or sweet-smelling herbs to mask the odor of decay. They then wrap the body in swaddling.

The Mapuche Indians of Chile (Faron, 1968) sometimes smoke the body, then wash and dress it in the person's best clothes, lay it out on a bier in the house, and place the body in a pine coffin. Among some groups in South Thailand (Fraser, 1966), the body is held and bathed with water specifically purified with herbs and clay. The corpse is then rinsed and dried and all orifices plugged with cotton.

FUNERAL HOME PROPOSED FOR SPECIAL RITUALS OF INDIANS

Mike Kaszuba

The strange odyssey of Steve Perion, the man who wants to open a funeral home in Minneapolis for American Indians, has already taken him to the State Capitol posing for pictures with Gov. Rudy Perpich and to City Hall looking for money.

He has impressed politicians with his business acumen and collected a stack of letters praising his sensitivity from people he hardly knows. "His particular expertise in and commitment to serving the funeral needs of the American (Indian) community here would fill a desperate need," says Minneapolis DFLer [Democratic Farm Labor Party] Rep. Karen Clark, who acknowledges she barely knows him.

Perion has huddled with financial analysts and come away with a polished business plan for success based on death—60 indigent Indian deaths a year will mean $15,600 in gross profits.

So goes the balancing act for Perion, a Chippewa Indian who admits he has no money of his own. Entering an arena where many Indian families can't afford even the simplest of funerals, he is trying not to be viewed as an opportunist. But Perion, who claims his will be the first funeral home for Indians in urban America, is quickly enlisting support by promising the city's large Indian community a perspective other funeral homes can't match and promising financiers a steady cash flow from county welfare payments for indigent deaths.

"The issue is sensitivity," said the Rev. James Notebaart, director of the Catholic Indian Ministries in south Minneapolis. "It's really a clash of cultures—the urban economic life and culture and the (Indian) tradition of living off the land and living without dollars. . . . The business of burying the dead costs money and there's often a clash there."

As Perion moves to bridge the two worlds using a yellow Ford station wagon as a hearse, the task also can be tiring. That point was driven home only last week as Perion coordinated a wake for a 38-year-old Sioux woman who died in Duluth. Between Tuesday and Friday, Perion had gone to Duluth to get the body; used a Richfield funeral home to prepare it for burial and then had overseen a 24–hour wake at the American Indian Center on Franklin Avenue in Minneapolis.

Then there was a 10–hour drive with the coffin to Belcourt, N.D., for another wake and burial. In between, there was the haggling by phone with a North Dakota funeral home that wanted a consulting fee of nearly $400. And finally, there were arrangements with the family to place a hatchet in the coffin—an Indian custom to ward off evil spirits—and to put tobacco between the body's fingers to feed the spirits.

Perion's fee, excluding the price of the poplar wood coffin: $927. "It's really amazing. When I get through with a funeral, I'm exhausted," he said.

It is that commitment that has won Perion friends. "I see a pretty big need," said Philip Gleason, co-owner of Gleason Mortuary in Richfield where Perion uses space for embalming. "The white man does not understand the Indian and his traditions. . . . (Perion's) all set to go, you might say, if he can come up with a building."

Perion's financial plan, written with the help of economic development experts, lists start-up costs of $100,245—more than half of which would go to buy a four-wheel-drive funeral coach and two new Buicks. Regarding the size of the building he'll need, Perion said: "The square footage is based on how many Indians will die in the first year—how many will die in Minneapolis and St. Paul, and how many calls I'll get out of that."

But he also stresses the sensitivity he will bring to the role. He advertises his familiarity with the water drum ceremony, during which an Indian elder wraps an animal hide around a canister of water that symbolizes the purification of the spiritual world. Perion talks also of the star quilt burial rite, in which a large quilt with a star in the middle hangs behind the casket during the wake and is often then used to wrap the body before burial.

And he talks of the pain of burying his own people.

His most heart-wrenching Indian funeral? That, says Perion, might be the time the family of an Indian infant who had died wanted to wrap the body in a blanket just before the casket was closed. But when the family began wailing and wouldn't let the body go, Perion finally found himself having to pry the body from them. "I'll never do that again," he said.

Others agree the uniqueness of Indian burials can make them challenging. "They have evening wakes that last the entire (night)," said Les Rosecke, a funeral director at Albin Funeral Chapel in south Minneapolis. The funeral home, which Rosecke said handles an estimated 35 Indian burials a year, is considered to have the largest number of Indian funerals locally. Of a funeral home for Indians, he said: "We certainly would cooperate with them."

As Perion searches for money and a funeral home, the supports continue to roll in. "I tell ya', I think it would be a marvelous idea if it works," said Mary Williams, a funeral director in Duluth who once worked with Perion. "It's a culture that's very unique to itself—different rituals, different time considerations. (Steve's) very much involved in tribal activities."

Minneapolis Star Tribune, October 9, 1989. Reprinted with permission of the Star Tribune, Minneapolis-St. Paul.

In the French West Indies (Horowitz, 1967) the neighbors wash the body with rum and force a liter or more of strong rum down the throat as a temporary preservative before dressing and placing the body on a bed. Rather than use a strong drink like rum, the Zinacantecos of Mexico (Vogt, 1970) pour water into the mouth of the deceased about every half hour "to relieve thirst" while the grave is being dug.

Other Customs Regarding the Corpse

In addition to cleaning the corpse, many groups spend time decorating the body. For example, the Tiwi of Australia (Hart and Pilling, 1960) wrap the body in bark. The Qemant of Ethiopia (Gamst, 1969) wrap the body in a piece of white cloth and cover it with a mat of woven grass. Tewa Indians in Arizona (Dozier, 1966) bury a woman in her wedding outfit and wrap a man in a blanket for burial. The Hopi Indians wrap a man in buckskin and a woman in her wedding blanket, bury them in the clothes they were wearing at the time of death, and do not wash or prepare the body other than to wash and tie back the hair (Cox and Fundis, 1992). After cleaning the body, the Ulithi in Micronesia (Lessa, 1966) cover it with a tuberous plant and decorate the head and hands with flower garlands. The Navajo in the Southwestern United States (Cox and Fundis, 1992) bathe the corpse, then dress it in fine clothes and put the right moccasin on the left foot and the left on the right foot.

Not all groups are interested in decorating the corpse. For example, the custom of Anglo-Canadians in and around Toronto, Canada, and in suburban London, England (Ramsden, 1991:38), is to remove the corpse from the company of the living immediately following death. The corpse is never to be seen by them again. It is disposed of as quickly as is practical in a way that precludes any suggestion of further involvement by the deceased. The complete avoidance of the corpse also precludes any opportunity to note changes in the individual following death, thus reinforcing the perception of the Anglo-Canadians that death is a static state. They wish to get across the idea that the dead are physically and socially immediately gone. From the moment of death, the physical condition of the body is of no consequence with the exception that it must be permanently removed from the world of the living just as the dead person must be banished from social relations. The event of death is perceived as an instantaneous occurrence and marks a distinct boundary between a state of being alive and a state of being dead.

The Huichol of Mexico (Weigand and Weigand, 1991:62) handle the corpse with a great deal of respect and care. A singer/curer who is usually closely related to the deceased supervises the preparation of the corpse for burial or placement in a cave: Clothing is changed, personal items are arranged to accompany the body, and the individual's hands and face are washed with water. Most adults aid in the preparation, unless "emotional collapse prevents such activity." However, most people are rather calm during these preparations.

The Konyak Nagar in India (Furer-Haimendorf, 1969) place the corpse on a bier. Six days after the funeral, the head is removed from the body, and the skull is placed in an urn hollowed from a block of sandstone. For three years the skull is given portions of food and beer whenever the kinsmen celebrate a feast.

Bronislaw Malinowski (1929) reports that the Trobriand Islanders continually handle the remains throughout the death ritual. The body is **exhumed** (removed from its grave or tomb) twice and cut up. Some of the bones are peeled out of the carcass, handled and given to different individuals.

Among the Yanomamo Indians of Venezuela and Brazil (Chagnon, 1983), the body of one dying in an epidemic is placed on a tree platform and allowed to decay. After several months, an elderly man is appointed to strip the remaining decayed flesh from the bones, which are then cremated. Under normal circumstances, the body of a deceased Yanomamo is burned, the ashes are mixed with boiled plantain soup, and are eaten at a feast. This **endocannibalism** is supposed to put the warriors in an appropriate frame of rage prior to going out to kill the enemy. Such behavior is considered a supreme form of displaying friendship and solidarity for the Yanomamo.

THE YANOMAMO

Approximately 12,000 Yanomamo Indians live in Venezuela and Brazil in villages ranging in size from 40 to 250 inhabitants. Being horticulturalists, the Yanomamo grow 85 percent of their food. They occasionally enjoy the delicacies of caterpillars, roasted spiders, and armadillos.

The Yanomamo are a very aggressive and fierce people living in a state of chronic warfare and believing it is the "nature of men to fight." Because they define themselves as fierce, they act accordingly. The "fierceness" of the Yano-mamo is exemplified by their gruesome methods of infanticide and abortion, their raiding parties where men are killed and women raped and captured as wives, their games of chest pounding, side slapping, club pounding and ax fights played at village feasts, their chopping on their wives with machetes to "show their love," and 24 percent of adult males dying in warfare.

Women's status among the Yanomamo is not high. They perform the bulk of the garden work, while men do the initial heavier ground-breaking duties with their digging sticks. Almost daily, the men lie in their hammocks getting high on hallucinogenic drugs. The drugs are taken from the bark of the ebene tree and shot into their nostrils in a powdery form. Though side effects of the drug are vomiting, runny nose, and watery eyes, the men have contact with the

(continued)

deceased ancestors while under the drug's influence. Husbands beat their wives, and brothers will trade their sisters to other groups of brothers for wives for themselves.

Competition and aggressiveness are certainly prevalent in the United States, especially among the middle class. We too are a somewhat fierce people. We have a reputation of high crime and violence and of cutthroat economics. While not like the Yanomamo, the United States would likely fall closer to the Yanomamo on a continuum with aggressive behavior at one end and passive behavior at the other.

Adapted from Napoleon A. Chagnon, *Yanomamo: The Fierce People,* 3rd ed. New York: Holt, Rinehart and Winston, 1983.

It seems significant in most societies that the body be cleaned and steps taken to assure a tolerable odor prior to final disposition. A reverence for the body also seems prevalent. As in the United States, it is important in many other societies that the deceased "look good" to the mourners.

The body is not exhumed to take various parts home in the United States, but some individuals have been known to keep the **cremains** (remains from cremation) in a vase in the home or to carry them around in their purse. Others take photographs of the deceased or collect important reminders to be placed in scrapbooks or albums. According to Judy Tatelbaum (1980), keepsakes like photographs, clippings, and stories about the deceased can provide a satisfying memorial later on. Fearing that we will be unable to remember the deceased distinctly enough, we desire a "piece" of the person we loved.

BURIAL RITES

As noted in Chapter 5, Bronislaw Malinowski (1948) stressed the roles of religion and magic as a means of reducing death anxiety and fears. A. R. Radcliffe-Brown (1965) argued for a different interpretation, suggesting that rites may contribute to death anxiety and insecurity. These are simply different explanations for the same rites. Conrad Kottak (1982) notes that for one raised within the cultural tradition of a particular culture, performance of the rite does relieve anxiety—it is the socially approved means of doing so. On the other hand, anxiety may result *because* the rite exists. A common stress may be produced by participation in the rite, thus enhancing the social solidarity of the participants.

BURIAL RITES OF RUSSIAN IMMIGRANTS IN OREGON

Richard A. Morris

Members of the Russian Old Believer community which settled in Oregon since 1964 represent an eminently traditional group with ancient Slavic roots. Their way of life is fashioned after a mid-17th century religious ethic of the Old Orthodox Russian Church. Death is a "village" affair, and all turn their attention to it, when it happens. They rather rapidly do what they consider necessary to lay the body to rest, rarely taking more than 24 hours.

When death occurs, the body is washed and dressed in a white, loosely based cloth. The body is then placed inside the casket with the arms crossed on the chest and the hands formed into the sign of the cross in the old style: the first two fingers are extended and the thumb is joined with the third and fourth fingers. The service occurs in the living room of the home, where the casket has been placed.

Another service is held at the grave site. In addition to final prayers, the grave is circled three times in a clockwise direction. The immediate kin give their final farewell as they take their last look and sometimes give a kiss to the deceased. After the lid is placed on the casket, it is lowered into the ground. The grave is then filled by the closest kin, followed by distant kin, and then others, all of whom throw three handfuls of dirt onto the casket.

The graves are lined up in an easterly direction. At the foot of each grave stands an eight-ended Orthodox cross, thus, at sunrise, the shadow of the cross is cast onto the grave, superimposed on the deceased in proper perspective. At the Second Coming, when the dead are called from the grave, the deceased will simply rise up to stand next to their crosses and face the East, from whence they believe Christ will come. After the burial, those in attendance return to the home of the deceased for a dinner which has been set to commemorate the dead.

From "Po Starykovsky (The Old People's Way): End of Life Attitudes and Customs in Two Traditional Russian Communities." In *Coping with the Final Tragedy: Cultural Variation in Dying and Grieving*, David R. Counts and Dorothy A. Counts (Eds.). Amityville, NY: Baywood Publishing Company, Inc., 1991, pp. 91–112.

Functions

The term *function* refers to the extent to which some part or process of a social system contributes to the maintenance of that system. Function means the extent to which a given activity promotes or interferes with the maintenance of a system (Cuzzort and King, 1980:172). Robert Merton (1957) distinguished between two forms of social function. **Manifest functions** are objective consequences for the person, subgroup, or social system that contribute to its adjustment and were so intended. **Latent functions** are consequences that contribute to adjustment but were not so intended. Manifest functions are the official explanations of a given action (such as, going to a funeral to pay respects to the deceased and to let the survivors know that you care). Latent functions are the sociological explanations (for instance, a funeral really becomes a family reunion). Ronald Barrett (1992) notes that African-American funerals are indeed "a primary ritual and a focal occasion with a big social gathering after the funeral and the closest thing to a family reunion that might ever take place."

Rather than leave all corpses to environmental elements, an event like a burial rite obviously has some positive consequences for the survivors of the deceased. Burial rite functions can be enumerated as follows. First, burial rites are the reaffirmation of group structure and social cohesiveness of the individuals suffering loss. Second, they give meaning and sanction to the separation of the dead person from the living. Third, burial rites help effect the transition of the soul to another, otherworldly realm. Fourth, they assist in the incorporation of the spirit to its new existence. Fifth, according to Melvin Williams (1981), for middle-class Americans in Pittsburgh, Pennsylvania, a funeral may establish, validate, and reinforce social status, whereas for the lower class, funerals tend to be rites of intensification and solidarity, putting aside feuds and squabbles for the moment.

To assure that the spirit will be reborn again, some societies go to great lengths. For example, the Dunsun of North Borneo (Williams, 1965) kill animals to accompany the deceased on the trip to the land of the dead. The Ulithi in Micronesia (Lessa, 1966) place a loincloth and a gingerlike plant in the right arm of the deceased so that gifts can be presented to the custodian at the entrance of the world. For the Zinacantecos of Mexico (Vogt, 1970), a chicken head is put in a bowl of broth beside the head of the corpse. The chicken allegedly leads the "inner soul" of the deceased. A black dog then carries the "soul" across the river.

Though not the common practice, an 18-year-old woman in India recently rested the head of her dead husband on her lap, sat on his funeral **pyre** (a combustible pile for burning a corpse) and was burned alive (Salamat, 1987). No one could stop her from committing **sati,** the most noble act of loyalty a widow can perform for her husband who, in the Hindu religion, is supposed to be considered a god by his wife. A widow cannot remarry and is treated as an evil omen and an economic liability. If she chooses to live, she has to remain barefoot, sleep on the floor, and can never go out of the house, for she would be slandered if seen talking to a man. Some would argue she is better off dead. Prior to this recent act in 1987, however, sati had not been performed in this community since early in the 20th century.

As is also true for the Zinacantecos of Mexico (as noted earlier), a chicken is used in the burial rite of the Yoruba in Southwestern Nigeria (Bascom, 1969). A man with a live chicken precedes the carrier of the corpse, plucking out feathers and leaving them along the trail for the soul of the deceased to follow back to town. Upon reaching the town gate, the chicken is killed by striking its head against the ground. The blood and feathers are then placed in the grave so that others will not die. A second chicken is killed and its blood put in the grave so the soul of the deceased will not bother the surviving relatives.

Soul houses are built in some parts of Appalachia (Gaines, 1981) to provide protection for the deceased from evil spirits, wild animals, grave robbers, and other unwelcome visitors. These little houses are placed directly over the grave. Some are box-shaped concrete slabs while others have rooftop structures. The more elaborate of the soul houses are miniature homes with actual tin roofs, gutters, drainpipes, carpets, furniture, and various objects dear to the deceased. The following passage further discusses customs of burial in Appalachian and non-Appalachian Kentucky.

BURIAL RITES IN APPALACHIAN AND NON-APPALACHIAN KENTUCKY

In the latter part of the 18th century in Kentucky the responsibility for the care of the sick and dying and the disposal of the dead fell primarily on the family unit. The body was usually buried as soon as the women could prepare the corpse and the men could dig the grave. Coffins were seldom used, due to the unavailability of suitable lumber, but the body could be somewhat protected by constructing a rock cairn.

In the early to mid-19th century, numerous full-time mortuary roles were introduced in non-Appalachian Kentucky—professional casketmakers, tombstone carvers, and funeral directors. Though the dying continued to be cared for at home, hospitals and homes for the aged were beginning to be built. It was customary to visit the dying individual "for a last moment" if death was imminent. When death occurred, funeral invitations were published in the newspapers and were carried to friends and neighbors and posted on public notice boards. Services were often held in the home of the deceased.

After the Civil War and up until 1910, in Appalachian Kentucky the body was prepared by friends and neighbors who washed it and applied lotions to retard mortification. The eyelids were shut and weighted with coins, and the mouth was closed with a bandage around the head and jaw. The corpse was dressed and placed in the coffin or laid out on planks for visitation. All ages participated in preparations and mourning. After 1910, funeral directors from

(continued)

non-Appalachian Kentucky (Lexington and the Bluegrass area) solicited the mountaineer's business in local papers. As noted in the discussion above, it was during the early 20th century that gravehouses were occasionally erected over the burial plots.

From 1930 onward, funeral customs slowly changed as the services of professionals became more widely available to Appalachian Kentucky. Funeral practices in the 1930s and 1940s became similar to those used elsewhere in the United States, except for more isolated counties where local residents continued to prepare corpses and monuments for a nominal fee. Today, however, the pattern that emerges of death and dying practices in Appalachian and non-Appalachian Kentucky is one of similarity in customs.

From Thomas F. Garrity and James Wyss, "Death, Funeral and Bereavement Practices in Appalachian and Non-Appalachian Kentucky." *Omega*, 1976, 7:211–227.

For the Cree in the province of Quebec in Canada (Preston and Preston, 1991:143–144) it is important not to delay the burial. Delay may interfere with the forthcoming journey of the deceased and result in intense expression of grief for the bereaved. Thus, the Cree respond quickly in preparing the body for burial.

In summary, burial rites serve the functions of maintaining relations with ancestral spirits, reaffirming social solidarity, and restoring group structures dismembered by death. As Gerry Cox and Ronald Fundis (1992) sum up so well in their discussion of Native American burial practices, "If nothing else is known, it is that tribal groups did not abandon their dead. They provided them with ceremony and disposal." Indeed, a lot of ceremony and a way of disposing of the dead tend to go hand in hand with death among different cultures. These burial rites not only reaffirm group structure but enhance social cohesiveness. Even with the death of pets, a way of disposing of the remains can be important, as illustrated in the article on Japan on the next page.

Variations

As expressions of mourning vary with cultures, different burial rites tend to be widespread among societies. The depth of the burial area, the place of disposal, and the importance of the status of the deceased are examined here.

In the old days of the Wild West in the United States, one was buried "six feet under with his boots on." It is true that graves were six feet deep in earlier periods of United States history, but today graves are less than six feet deep—typically around four and a half feet in depth with 18 inches of dirt above the top of the

A GOOD FRIEND UP IN SMOKE

Tom Torok

The death of a pet can be especially devastating for most Japanese. Most don't have a garden where they can lay the departed critters to rest. A cemetery plot could cost more than a Toyota. So typically when Fido passes on, folks just wait for trash night, stuff him in the can and bid him a fond farewell.

"A pet is a member of the family," Hideki Arasawa said. "You shouldn't just throw them in the rubbish—you should treat them like a human being."

Arasawa's firm has an alternative to trash night. The company manufactures a mobile pet crematorium that lets owners give their cats, dogs and birds a fitting send-off—right in front of their homes.

One firm using the vans charges $275 to cremate a 15-to-17 pound dog. Cats, rabbits and birds, which use less fuel, cost $196. The firm, The Dog's Friend, conducts funerals that closely mimic human send-offs. As an added bonus, the temperature of the furnace is closely controlled, to leave the bones intact.

"If people just send their pet off somewhere for cremation they're left with an unsettled feeling," said Takayuki Sato, who runs the Tokyo branch. "If they can actually see it with their own eyes and then put the bones in a jar, they feel extremely satisfied."

Adapted from the *Philadelphia Inquirer,* June 28, 1992, p. 3A.

casket/vault. With sealed, heavier caskets today—often placed within a steel or concrete vault—it is not necessary to place the body so deep in the ground, as was the case with an unsealed pine box of an earlier period.

The Kalingas of the Philippines (Dozier, 1967) bury adults in six-feet deep and three-feet wide graves. The Mardudjara aborigines of Australia (Tonkinson, 1978) dig a rectangular hole about three feet deep, line the bottom with leafy bushes and small logs, then place the body inside. Similarly, the Semai of Malaya (Dentan, 1968) dig the grave two to three feet deep. In death as in life, gender differences exist: Among the Abkhasians near the Black Sea (Benet, 1974), women are buried 10 centimeters deeper than men.

Some societies keep the corpses in or near the home of the deceased (Chapter 12 describes a corpse kept in a home in Louisville, Kentucky). The Yoruba of Nigeria (Bascom, 1969), for example, dig the grave in the room of the deceased. An adult man among the Lugbara of Uganda (Middleton, 1965) is buried inside his

This Buddhist funeral in Ceylon demonstrates the communal nature of the special care taken in preparing the body for final disposition.

first wife's hut in the center of the floor. The Swazi of Africa (Kuper, 1963) bury a woman on the outskirts of her husband's home.

One's rank or status in the community or village may determine how the corpse is treated or the final disposition of the remains. For example, a deceased Buddhist common person in Thailand (Leming and Premchit, 1992) will be cleaned, dressed, and placed in a casket. For the bodies of high-status Buddhist individuals, however, the body will be embalmed, then bathed and dressed with new clothes. The face will be covered with gold leaves prior to placing the body in the casket. Cremation follows in the Buddhist tradition as the final form of disposition. The Barabaig of Tanzania (Klima, 1970) place women and children out in the surrounding bush where they are consumed by the hyena. Only certain male and female elders will receive a burial. The following insert about the Kapauku Papuans further details the importance of one's position in the community determining how and where burial or final disposition will occur.

Thus, in death as in life, one's social status determines how one is treated. Whether buried or left to the elements is often determined by gender, age, standing

BURIAL RITES AMONG THE KAPAUKU PAPUANS

Leopold Pospisil

Among the Kapauku Papuans of West New Guinea, burial rites are determined by the deceased's status and cause of the death. The simplest burial is given to a drowned man whose body is laid flat on the bank of the river and protected by a fence erected around it. The body is then abandoned to the elements. Very young children and individuals not particularly liked and considered unimportant are completely interred. Children, women, and the elderly who were unimportant but loved are tied with vines into a squatting position and semi-interred with the head above ground. A dome-shaped structure of branches and soil is then constructed to protect the head.

A respected and loved adult male among the Kapauku Papuans receives a tree burial. Tied in a squatting position, the corpse is placed in a tree house with a small window in front. Corpses of important individuals, who are feared by their relatives, and of women who died in childbirth require a special type of burial. Their bodies are placed in the squatting position on a special raised scaffold constructed in the house where death occurred. The house is then sealed and abandoned.

The most elaborate burial among the Kapauku Papuans is given to a rich headman. A special hut is built on high stilts, the body is tied in a squatting position, and a pointed pole is driven through the rectum, abdomen, chest cavity and neck with its pointed end supporting the base of the skull. The body is then placed in the dead house with the face appearing in the front window of the structure. The body is pierced several times with arrows to allow the body fluids to drain away. Years later, the skull of the respected man may be cleaned and awarded a second honor of being placed on a pole driven into the ground near the house of the surviving relatives.

From *The Kapauku Papuans of West New Guinea.* New York: Holt, Rinehart and Winston, 1963.

in the community, and cause of death. If buried in the ground, even the depth of burial may vary by one's social position.

CONCLUSION

As discussed in Chapter 2, dying is more than a biological process. One does not die in a vacuum but in a social milieu. An act of dying has an influence on others because it is a shared experience. The sharing mechanism is death-related meanings composed of symbols.

Since death meanings are socially constructed, patterns of "correct" or "incorrect" behavior related to dying and death will largely be determined within the social setting in which it occurs. Death-related behavior of the dying person and of those relating to him or her is in response to meaning, relative to the audience and the situation. As noted, death-related behavior is shared, symboled, and situated.

Because death generally disrupts established interaction networks, shared "scripts" aid in providing socially acceptable behavior for the bereaved. Such scripts are essential because they prevent societal breakdowns while providing social continuity. Burial rituals are important in assuring social cohesion at the time of family dismemberment through death. Since death is a family crisis (see Dickinson and Fritz, 1981), appropriate networks for coping must be culturally well grounded.

Death-related meanings are socially created and transmitted. Through participant observation, small children learn from others how to respond to death. If children are sheltered from such situations, their socialization will be thwarted. As noted in this chapter, family involvement plays an important role in most societies as individuals prepare for death, as they prepare the corpse for final disposition, and in burial rituals that follow. Therefore, whether death rituals involve killing a chicken, scraping the meat from the bones of the corpse, crying quietly, wailing loudly, mutilating one's own body, or burning or burying the corpse, all bereavement behavior has three interconnected characteristics—it is shared, symboled, and situated.

SUMMARY

1. Anthropologists are concerned with the meanings that different events, such as death, have for different cultures.
2. Customs for caring for the dying prior to death assist both the dying individual and the survivors in coping with the impending death.
3. Death for some is viewed as the end, while for others it is viewed as a continuation of life in a different form.
4. While mourning rituals tend to be commonplace with different cultures, the prescribed behavior is affected by the social status and gender of the individuals involved.
5. Some social groups mourn for a few hours after death while others mourn for months or years.
6. The depth of burial often varies by the gender and socioeconomic status of the deceased.

7. Burial rituals serve the functions of appeasing the ancestral spirits and the soul of the deceased, bringing the kin together, reinforcing social status, and restoring the social structure.

8. In most societies, the body of the deceased is cleaned and prepared for burial. Some groups even keep parts of the body for ornamental or special purposes.

9. Being familiar with cross-cultural death customs should help to better understand the American concept of death.

DISCUSSION QUESTIONS

1. Why is it important to learn about bereavement patterns in other cultures?

2. Cite as many death custom similarities between other cultures and the United States as you can. Cite death custom differences between other cultures and the United States.

3. What is your own concept of "soul"? How is your concept of soul similar to and different from some other cultures' soul concept? How does a concept of "soul" relate to death?

4. Drawing on your own knowledge of United States culture, discuss any behavior patterns toward the dying just prior to death. How do these customs compare to those cited in this chapter?

5. Describe mourning rituals commonly found in the United States. Mourning rituals may differ by region of the country or ethnicity. Discuss these differences.

6. It is suggested that an explanation of crying at the time of death may be rather complex. Discuss the reasons for crying over a death.

7. A professional generally prepares the corpse for final disposition in the United States, but this is not universally true. Discuss the importance of the family being involved in preparing the body for final disposition.

8. In death, as in life, gender discrimination occurs. Discuss with a local funeral director the differences in funerals for males and females. Do you notice discrepancies in grave markings (such as, size of the stone and length of epitaphs) between males and females?

9. Unlike many societies where squatting occurs, in the United States we basically give birth and bury in a horizontal position. Why do you

suppose the United States has a "laid-back" approach from the womb to the tomb? Can you cite advantages and disadvantages to horizontal burials?

10. What are some of the functions of burial rites in this chapter?

Glossary

Bier: A framework upon which the corpse and/or casket is placed for viewing and/or carrying.

Cremains: That which is left after cremation.

Endocannibalism: The Yanomamo Indian practice of eating the ashes of the deceased in order to charge a warrior up prior to going into battle and to display friendship and solidarity.

Ethnocentrism: Literally means "culture-centeredness." The belief that one's own culture is superior to others.

Ethnography: The systematic description of a culture based on firsthand observation.

Exhume: To remove a corpse from its place of burial.

Latent Function: Consequences of behavior that were not intended (for example, a funeral brings the family together usually in an amiable way).

Levirate: A marriage rule whereby a widow marries her deceased husband's brother or, in some societies, at least has sexual intercourse in hopes of providing heirs.

Lineage: A group of relatives who trace their descent unilineally from a common ancestor.

Manifest Function: Consequences of behavior that are intended and overt (such as, going to a funeral to pay respects to the deceased).

Pyre: A combustible pile (usually of wood) for burning a corpse at a funeral rite.

Rites of Passage: Ceremonies centering around transitions in life from one status to another (including baptism, marriage ceremony, and funeral).

Ritual: The symbolic affirmation of values by means of culturally standardized utterances and actions.

Sati: A controversial practice rarely exercised in some segments of India where the widow throws herself on the funeral pyre of her deceased husband. This "most noble act of loyalty" makes her a goddess who is worshipped at her cremation site.

REFERENCES

Barrett, Ronald K. 1992. "Psychocultural Influences on African-American Attitudes toward Death, Dying and Funeral Rites. " In *Personal Care in an Impersonal World,* John Morgan (Ed.). Amityville, NY: Baywood Publishing Company.

Bascom, William. 1969. *The Yoruba of Southwestern Nigeria.* New York: Holt, Rinehart and Winston.

Bendann, Effie. 1930. *Death Customs: An Analytical Study of Burial Rites.* New York: Alfred A. Knopf.

Benet, Sula. 1974. *Abkhasians: The Long-Living People of Caucasus.* New York: Holt, Rinehart and Winston.

Bloch, Maurice, and Jonathan Parry. 1982. *Death and the Regeneration of Life.* Cambridge: Cambridge University Press.

Chagnon, Napoleon A. 1983. *Yanomamo: The Fierce People,* 3rd ed. New York: Holt, Rinehart and Winston.

Cohen, Ronald. 1967. *The Kanuri of Bornu.* New York: Holt, Rinehart and Winston.

Cowell, Daniel David. 1986. "Funerals, Family, and Forefathers: A View of Italian-American Funeral Practices." *Omega,* 16:69–86.

Cox, Gerry R., and Ronald J. Fundis. 1992. "Native American Burial Practices." In *Personal Care in an Impersonal World,* John Morgan (Ed.). Amityville, NY: Baywood Publishing Company.

Cuzzort, Ray P., and Edith W. King. 1980. *Twentieth Century Social Thought,* 3rd ed. New York: Holt, Rinehart and Winston.

Deng, Francis M. 1972. *The Dinka of the Sudan.* New York: Holt, Rinehart and Winston.

Dentan, Robert K. 1968. *The Semai: A Non-Violent People of Malaya.* New York: Holt, Rinehart and Winston.

Dickinson, George E., and Judy L. Fritz. 1981. "Death in the Family." *Journal of Family Issues,* (September 2):379–384.

Dozier, Edward P. 1966. *Hano: A Tewa Indian Community in Arizona.* New York: Holt, Rinehart and Winston.

Dozier, Edward P. 1967. *The Kalinga of Northern Luzon, Philippines.* New York: Holt, Rinehart and Winston.

Durkheim, Emile. 1915. *The Elementary Forms of Religious Life.* New York: Free Press.

Durkheim, Emile. 1954. *The Elementary Forms of the Religious Life.* New York: The Free Press.

Faron, Louis C. 1968. *The Mapuche Indians of Chile.* New York: Holt, Rinehart and Winston.

Feldman, Douglas A. 1990. *Culture and Aids.* New York: Praeger.

Fraser, Thomas M., Jr. 1966. *Fishermen of South Thailand: The Malay Villagers.* New York: Holt, Rinehart and Winston.

Furer-Haimendorf, Christoph Von. 1969. *The Konyak Nagar: An Indian Frontier Tribe.* New York: Holt, Rinehart and Winston.

Gaines, Judith. 1981. "Appalachia Comes Alive in Studying Tombstones." *Louisville Courier Journal,* Louisville, KY, November 1, p. 5.

Gamst, Frederick C. 1969. *The Qemant: A Pagan-Hebraic Peasantry of Ethiopia.* New York: Holt, Rinehart and Winston.

Goldman, I. 1979. *The Cubeo: Indians of the Northwest Amazon.* Urbana, IL: University of Illinois Press.

Habenstein, Robert W., and William M. Lamers. 1963. *Funeral Customs the World Over.* Milwaukee: Bulfin Printers, Inc.

Harris, Marvin. 1974. *Cows, Pigs, Wars and Witches.* New York: Vintage Books.

Hart, C. W. M., and Arnold R. Pilling. 1960. *The Tiwi of North Australia.* New York: Holt, Rinehart and Winston.

Haviland, William A. 1991. *Anthropology,* 6th ed. Fort Worth, TX: Holt, Rinehart and Winston.

Helman, C. 1985. *Culture, Health, and Illness.* Bristol, UK: Wright.

Hitchcock, John T. 1966. *The Magars of Manyan Hill.* New York: Holt, Rinehart and Winston.

Hoebel, E. Adamson. 1960. *The Cheyennes: Indians of the Great Plains.* New York: Holt, Rinehart and Winston.

Horowitz, Michael M. 1967. *Morne-Paysan: Peasant Village in Martinique.* New York: Holt, Rinehart and Winston.

Huntington, Richard, and Peter Metcalf. 1979. *Celebrations of Death: The Anthropology of Mortuary Ritual.* Cambridge: Cambridge University Press.

Kellehear, Allan. 1990. *Dying of Cancer: The Final Year of Life.* Chur, Switzerland: Harwood Academic Publishers.

Klima, George J. 1970. *The Barabaig: East African Cattle-Herders.* New York: Holt, Rinehart and Winston.

Kottak, Conrad P. 1982. *Cultural Anthropology,* 3rd ed. New York: Random House.

Kozak, David L. 1991. "Dying Badly: Violent Death and Religious Change Among the Tohono O'Odham." *Omega,* 23:207–216.

Kuper, Hilda. 1963. *The Swazi: A South African Kingdom.* New York: Holt, Rinehart and Winston.

Leming, Michael R., and Sommai Premchit. 1992. "Funeral Customs in Thailand." In *Personal Care in an Impersonal World,* John Morgan (Ed.). Amityville, NY: Baywood Publishing Company.

Lessa, William A. 1966. *Ulithi: A Micronesian Design for Living.* New York: Holt, Rinehart and Winston.

Malinowski, Bronislaw. 1929. *The Sexual Life of Savages.* New York: Harcourt, Brace and World.

Malinowski, Bronislaw. 1948. *Magic, Science and Religion, and Other Essays.* Boston: Beacon Press.

Mandelbaum, D. 1959. "Social Uses of Funeral Rites." In *The Meaning of Death,* H. Feifel (Ed.). New York: McGraw Hill.

Marcus, Frances Frank. 1988. "An Invitation to Become the Life of the Cemetery." *The New York Times,* November 1, p. 8.

Mead, Hirini Moko. 1991. "Sleep, Sleep, Sleep; Farewell, Farewell, Farewell. Maori Ideas About Death." In *Coping With the Final Tragedy: Cultural Variation in Dying and Grieving,* David R. Counts and Dorothy A. Counts (Eds.). Amityville, NY: Baywood Publishing Company.

Merton, Robert K. 1957. *Social Theory and Social Structure,* rev. ed. New York: The Free Press.

Middleton, John. 1965. *The Lugbara of Uganda.* New York: Holt, Rinehart and Winston.

Nagamine, Takahiko. 1988. "Attitudes Toward Death in Rural Areas of Japan." *Death Studies,* 12:61–68.

Palgi, Phyllis, and Henry Abramovitch. 1984. "Death: A Cross-Cultural Perspective." *Annual Review of Anthropology,* 13:385–417.

Pospisil, Leopold. 1963. *The Kapauku Papuans of West New Guinea.* New York: Holt, Rinehart and Winston.

Preston, Richard J., and Sarah C. Preston. 1991. "Death and Grieving Among Northern Forest Hunters: An East Cree Example." In *Coping with the Final Tragedy: Cultural Variation in Dying and Grieving,* David R. Counts and Dorothy A. Counts (Eds.). Amityville, NY: Baywood Publishing Company.

Radcliffe-Brown, A. R. 1964. *The Andaman Islanders.* New York: The Free Press.

Radcliffe-Brown, A. R. 1965. *Structure and Function in Primitive Society.* New York: The Free Press.

Ramsden, Peter G. 1991. "Alice in the Afterlife: A Glimpse in the Mirror." In *Coping with the Final Tragedy: Cultural Variation in Dying and Grieving,* David R. Counts and Dorothy A. Counts (Eds.). Amityville, NY: Baywood Publishing Company.

Rappaport, Roy A. 1974. "Obvious Aspects of Ritual." *Cambridge Anthropology,* 2:2–60.

Rosenblatt, P. C., R. Walsh, and A. Jackson. 1976. *Grief and Mourning in Cross Cultural Perspective.* New Haven, CT: Human Relations Area Files Press.

Salamat, Ail. 1987. "A Young Widow Burns in Her Bridal Clothes." *Far Eastern Economic Review,* 138:54–55.

Sweeting, Helen N., and Mary L. M. Gilhooly. 1992. "Doctor, Am I Dead? A Review of Social Death in Modern Societies." *Omega,* 24:251–269.

Tatelbaum, Judy. 1980. *The Courage to Grieve.* New York: Lippincott and Crowell Publishers.

Taylor, Robert B. 1980. *Cultural Ways,* 3rd ed. Boston: Allyn and Bacon.

Tonkinson, Robert. 1978. *The Mardudjara Aborigines.* New York: Holt, Rinehart and Winston.

Turnbull, Colin M. 1972. *The Mountain People.* New York: Simon and Schuster.

Tylor, E. B. 1873. *Primitive Culture.* London: John Murray.

Uchendu, Victor C. 1965. *The Igbo of Southeast Nigeria.* New York: Holt, Rinehart and Winston.

Van Gennep, A. 1960. *The Rites of Passage,* trans. M.B. Vizedom and G.L. Caffee (orig. *Les Rites de Passage, 1909).* Chicago: University of Chicago Press.

Vogt, Evon Z. 1970. *The Zinacantecos of Mexico: A Modern Maya Way of Life.* New York: Holt, Rinehart and Winston.

Weigand, Celia Garcia, and Paul C. Weigand. 1991. "Death and Mourning Among the Huicholes of Western Mexico." In *Coping with the Final Tragedy: Cultural Variation in Dying and Grieving,* David R. Counts and Dorothy A. Counts (Eds.). Amityville, NY: Baywood Publishing Company.

Williams, Melvin D. 1981. *On the Street Where I Lived.* New York: Holt, Rinehart and Winston.

Williams, Thomas R. 1965. *The Dunsun: A North Borneo Society.* New York: Holt, Rinehart and Winston.

SUGGESTED READINGS

Barber, Paul. 1988. *Vampires, Burial, and Death: Folklore and Reality.* New Haven, CT: Yale University Press. *This book is about how people in preindustrial cultures look at the processes and phenomena associated with death and the dissolution of the body.*

Bendann, Effie. 1930. *Death Customs: An Analytical Study of Burial Rites.* New York: Alfred A. Knopf. *A thorough anthropological analysis of death customs including an analysis of burial rites, causes of death, attitudes toward the corpse, mourning, and beliefs in the afterlife.*

Blackburn, Stuart H. 1988. *Singing of Birth and Death.* Philadelphia: University of Pennsylvania Press. *Based on data gathered in India, the author takes the reader through translated performances sung in different bow song festivals from birth to death.*

Bloch, Maurice, and Jonathan Parry. 1982. *Death and the Regeneration of Life.* Cambridge: Cambridge University Press. *This anthology focuses on the significance of symbols of fertility and rebirth in funeral rituals from China, India, New Guinea, Latin America, and Africa.*

Counts, David R., and Dorothy A. Counts, Eds. 1991. *Coping with the Final Tragedy: Cultural Variation in Dying and Grieving.* Amityville, NY: Baywood Publishing Company. *An anthology that discusses death and grieving in various parts of the world.*

Habenstein, Robert W., and William M. Lamers. 1963. *Funeral Customs the World Over.* Milwaukee, WI: Bulfin Printers, Inc. *A review of the cultures of the world especially significant to assist in cross-cultural study of the various practices of funerals in all cultures.*

Huntington, Richard, and Peter Metcalf. 1992. *Celebrations of Death: The Anthropology of Mortuary Ritual,* 2nd ed. Cambridge: Cambridge University Press. *An anthropological analysis of dying and death including universals and culture, death as transition, and the royal corpse and the body politic.*

Irish, Donald P., Kathleen F. Lundquist, and Vivian Jenkins Nelson. 1993. *Ethnic Variations in Dying, Death and Grief.* Washington, DC: Taylor and Francis. *An anthology that discusses dying, death, and grief in the following groups: African Americans, Mexican Americans, Hmong, Native Americans, Jews, Buddhists, Islamics, Quakers, and Unitarians.*

Metcalf, Peter. 1982. *A Borneo Journey Into Death.* Philadelphia: University of Pennsylvania Press. *This ethnographical approach to dying and death includes the topics of the soul, celebrating the ancestors, and the cosmology of the ancestral spirits.*

McGuire, Randall H. 1992. *Death, Society, and Ideology in a Hohokam Community.* Boulder, CO: Westview Press. *An archaeologist explores the nature of Hohokam social organization in the prehistory of southern Arizona.*

Stannard, David E. 1977. *The Puritan Way of Death.* New York: Oxford University Press. *A portrayal of death in the Western tradition including discussions of death, childhood, and burial.*

Strocchia, Sharon T. 1992. *Death and Ritual in Renaissance Florence.* Baltimore, MD: Johns Hopkins University Press. *An historian shows how death rites in Renaissance Florence reflected Florence's quick rise to commercial wealth in the 14th century and steady progress toward power in the 15th and 16th centuries.*

Chapter

11

The History
of Bereavement
and Burial
Practices in
American Culture

As long as the cemetery is being filled with a fresh stream of the recently dead,
it stays symbolically a live and vital emblem, telling the living of the meaning
of life and death.

W. Lloyd Warner
The Living and the Dead

THIS CHAPTER TRACES the development of bereavement practices in America from the Puritans to the present. As death bereaves family members, friends, and more distant relatives, the survivors generally follow established rituals to care for the corpse, to reaffirm the solidarity of important groups, to create a new status for the dead person, and to comfort each other in such a way that they can eventually resume their roles in society. These rituals were established in time and come to us from the past. Therefore, we need an historical explanation to fully understand them.

We deal with historical explanations every day, but we seldom consider what constitutes an historical explanation. Historians mainly determine chronology and context in order to demonstrate causation and coincidence in human affairs. We begin with chronology in order to determine the order in which events or processes occurred. This in itself has a certain explanatory value; for example, it is useful to know that discovery of the germ theory of disease preceded the widespread use of embalming in America. Too often, however, history begins and ends with chronology, and students are stuck with memorizing names and dates. History also explores the context of events to help explain them. For example, it is easier to understand the development of the funeral parlor if we see it in the context of developments in the domestic parlor.

Sometimes, historians can use chronology and context to determine causation. Knowing, for example that rural cemeteries preceded the public parks movement in America, we might conclude that cemetery reforms caused the parks movement. More frequently, however, chronology and context allow us only to identify coincidences (events or processes that occurred during the same period of time). Especially in social and cultural history, this chronicle of coincidences is crucial because people think analogically as much as they think logically. They do not isolate problems or ideas when they are faced with them; instead their whole range of prior experience affects their decision. In evaluating embalming, for example, few people treated the preservation of the corpse as a discrete issue. Instead, it coincided with other issues such as the importance of appearances in a consumer culture, the sanitary movement, the germ theory of disease, the privacy of the home, a stress on the "natural," a respect for surgery and surgeons, and the need to delay many funerals for distant relatives to return home.

Likewise, history shows that bereavement is but one part of a social construction of reality that changes through time. Bereavement practices are virtually inseparable from prescriptions for dying and descriptions of death, just as the whole American way of death is inseparable from the American way of life. Therefore, this chapter explains how changes in the American way of life brought changes in the American way of death and bereavement. It traces the historical roots of our bereavement practices so that we can begin to trace the routes of future change.

LIVING DEATH, 1600–1830

Between 1600 and 1830, death was a living part of the American experience. Most people in this primarily agricultural period were well acquainted with death. In New England towns, for example, if people escaped death in their own homes, they still heard the toll of the funeral bell, encountered the funeral procession winding through the streets, or saw the stark *memento mori* of the graveyard. Even more, death was highlighted by the intellectual and emotional framework of the Reformed Tradition.

The Reformed Tradition

The Reformed Tradition was the one part of the Protestant Reformation that most influenced colonial Americans. Although most colonists followed the beliefs of the Reformers, the New England Puritans made the most convincing synthesis of their ideas and attitudes. In their view, a sovereign God ruled over an earth inhabited by depraved people. God displayed his sovereignty in "special providences" in which He intervened in the natural or social world. One such providence was death.

Because of original sin and their own sinfulness, Puritans knew they deserved death and damnation. They also celebrated, however, the fact that God freely elected a select few for salvation. Therefore, they approached death with an amazing ambivalence. They believed that "the last Enemy was Death; and God had made that a friend too" (Sewall, 1973:1, 599). Death was an enemy for several reasons: It was painful, a punishment for sin, a possible prelude to everlasting hellfire, and meant separation from loved ones. Death was a friend, however, because it ended the pain and the earthly pilgrimage of the deceased, served as a "sanctified affliction" (Geddes, 1981:31)—either confirming a saint's faith or converting a sinner—

When death was viewed as a part of life, the body of the deceased was laid out in the home and friends of the bereaved visited to offer their condolences.

and could open the gates to Heaven. Indeed, it was both a friendly enemy and a fearful friend.

Unlike modern thanatologists, the Puritans encouraged each other to fear death. They increasingly used that strong human emotion to rouse people from their psychological and spiritual security. Puritans knew that they would die, but not *when* they would die, or if they were among the elect. Therefore, they admonished themselves and each other to be constantly prepared for death. "It will do you no hurt. You will Dy not One Minute the sooner for it," argued Cotton Mather, "and being fit to Dy, you will be the more Fit to Live" (Geddes, 1981:64–65). Over and over again, they prayed, "Lord, help me to redeem the time!" Like modern thanatologists, they felt an awareness of death could improve the quality of their lives, and that they had a role to play in the work of God's redemption. Indeed, for them, dying, death, and bereavement were opportunities to glorify God by demonstrating human dependence on divine providence.

The deathbed was the final place of preparation. Dying Puritans received visitors who wanted to help provide "a lift toward heaven." Unlike Catholics, who relied on the sacramental rite of Extreme Unction, the Puritans focused on the state of the dying person's soul and mind. They prayed together, read the Bible, and urged active acceptance of the will of God.

In the same way, "the funeral was another opportunity for the bereaved to turn affliction into spiritual growth through resignation to, and joyful acceptance of, the will of God" (Geddes, 1981:104). Most Puritan deaths occurred at home. The family sent out for midwife-nurses to care for the corpse, ordered a coffin, and notified friends and relatives not already present. Puritans considered the corpse a mere shell of the soul. They simply washed it, wrapped it in a shroud, and placed it in the coffin. They embalmed bodies only to transport them to other towns for burial, or to prevent an offensive stench in hot weather.

Friends and relatives visited the home to console and congratulate the bereaved. They brought gifts of food to allow the survivors to mourn and to prepare the funeral. In this way, as in their own participation in the funeral, they reaffirmed the solidarity of the covenanted community. The funeral itself usually took place within a few days of death, and it followed the simple guidelines of the 1644 Westminster Confession: "When any person departeth this life, let the dead body, upon the day of Buriall, be decently attended from the house to the place appointed for publique Buriall, and there immediately interred, without any ceremony" (Geddes, 1981: 110–124).

Pallbearers, ministers, and civil officials were commonly invited to a funeral with a gift of gloves. Wealthier families might also bestow scarves and/or memorial rings, and give gloves to anyone who marched in the procession. These items were the common symbols of mourning in a colonial society, but more elaborate mourning apparel was also available. The tolling of the town bell announced the onset of a funeral, and participants gathered at the home for prayer and the procession.

Puritans prayed not for the soul of the deceased but for the comfort and instruction of the living. They believed that judgment occurred at death and that the dead were beyond human aid, so they prayed to reaffirm their faith and to glorify their God. For example, upon the death of his 2-year-old daughter, Samuel Sewall had his surviving children read passages from the Bible. John read Ecclesiastes 3 on the acceptance of the seasons of life, Elizabeth read Revelation 22 on the theme of hope, Hannah read Psalm 38 on the mercy of God, and young Samuel asked for God's comfort in Psalm 102 (Sewall, 1973:1, 364). In addition to prayers, Puritans might also read an **elegy,** which generally depicted the dead person as a saint freed from the world and entering eternal bliss. Such elegies confirmed the new, separate status of the deceased, helping to bring grief under control, and provided a good example for structuring life after bereavement. Sometimes a copy of the elegy was pinned to the coffin or hearse for the funeral procession (Geddes, 1981:130–131).

The mourners walked from the home to the graveyard, where the men of the family, or the **sexton,** had opened a grave. They carried the coffin on a bier, covered with a black cloth "pall"—both of which were the property of the town instead of the church, as was the custom in England. During the procession, mourners were supposed to "apply themselves to meditations and conferences suitable to the occasion." At the gravesite, the pallbearers lowered the coffin into the earth, and the grave was refilled (Geddes, 1981:111, 133–135).

After the burial, the mourners returned home where they shared food, drink, prayers, and comforting words. The family thanked the pallbearers and participants, and sometimes gave additional presents. They might also request the minister to deliver a funeral sermon, which would occur not on the day of burial, but at the next regular meeting of the congregation. Sometimes families had such sermons and/or the elegies published and distributed to friends as *memento mori*. At a later date, the family might also erect a marker over the grave to proclaim the imminence of death or God's promise of salvation. Such markers near the much-frequented meetinghouse were another way of maintaining the vitality of death in early American culture (Geddes, 1981:139–140; Ludwig, 1966).

The Puritan funeral was the primary social institution for channeling the grief of survivors. It provided for the disposition of the body and the acknowledgment of the absence of the deceased. It drew the community together for mutual comfort, and it allowed mourners to honor the dead, to express their sorrow at separation, and to demonstrate their acceptance of God's will. After the funeral, Puritans expected mourners to return to their calling and to resume their life's work. They did not approve elaborate or extended mourning of the sort that became customary in the 19th century because it undermined the cheerful resignation to God's will that was essential to the Puritan experience.

Reforming the Reformed Tradition

In 1802, Nathaniel Emmons delivered a magnificent funeral sermon called "Death without Order." In it, he reviewed the Puritan orthodoxy about death, observing that "in relation to God, death is perfectly regular; but this regularity he has seen proper to conceal from the view of men." Emmons saw the uncertainty of death as a demonstration of God's sovereignty and human dependence, and as a way of teaching people "the importance and propriety of being constantly prepared for it." However, he also saw that, despite the fact of death's disorder, multitudes of Americans had resolved "to observe order in preparing to meet it" (Emmons, 1842:3, 29–38). Between the 1730s and the 1830s, such orderly Americans were influenced by the Enlightenment, the American Revolution, Unitarianism, and Evangelicalism—and all of these were influenced by an underlying market revolution. These movements slowly but surely reformed the Reformed Tradition and gave Americans an eclectic tradition from which to fashion new beliefs and behavior about dying, death, and bereavement.

The Enlightenment replaced the Puritans' providential God with a First Cause who designed the universe to operate by orderly and observable natural laws, and it replaced depraved dependent Puritans with Enlightened, rational people. Enlightened people, therefore, viewed death not as a time of judgment, but as a natural occurrence. They looked for a serene and stoic death and a simple, emotionally controlled funeral. Because Enlightened ideas were exchanged almost entirely among the educated classes of the Eastern seaboard, they had little immediate impact on American bereavement practices. In conjunction with the social forces of the American Revolution, however, the Enlightenment eventually affected American society.

In most areas of America, a basically Puritan way of death persisted until the 19th century, especially in rural areas where religion remained the focus of life. The increasing specialization and commercialization of life, however, eventually shaped death customs, too. During the 18th century, economic, geographic, and population growth began to produce cities, social stratification and diversity, political dissent, and cultural controversy. Anxiety over the ideology of opportunistic individualism that produced many of these internal conflicts combined with extended imperial control to produce a Revolution that reinforced Enlightenment ideas of rationality and activity. The Revolution "acted as an inspirational model of human beings' power to alter their own lives, to think new thoughts, to act on the best ideas of humanity, to liberate themselves from the dead weight of the past" (Gross, 1976:191). As a newly independent people pursued life, liberty, and happiness, they no longer depended on God's will; instead they made their own plans— plans that did not include death as a fact of life.

In religious developments, both Unitarianism and Evangelicalism accepted the enhanced view of human nature and human agency. The Unitarian gospel of "capitalism, theism, liberalism, and optimism" appealed especially to the commercial and professional classes of Boston—America's cultural capital in the 19th century (Howe, 1970:21). The Unitarians, however, were influential far beyond their numbers. Many people in other denominations accepted their progressive optimism— which derived from conceptions of a beneficent God. Unitarians were viewed by others as being basically good people whose lives were the best evidence of their religiosity, and they were admired for their rational approach to religion. Almost all Americans accepted the mid-19th-century rural cemetery reform that began in Brahmin Boston.

Outside of Boston, more Americans were affected by revivalistic Evangelicalism than by Unitarianism. The Second Great Awakening of American Evangelicalism began in the 1790s as a response to the Enlightenment and grew throughout the 19th century. Evangelicals stressed the Bible, a conversion experience, and a Christian life (and death). They preached God's persuasiveness more than His arbitrary power, His moral government rather than the ideas of predestination and election, and willful sinfulness more than innate depravity. Therefore, although Evangelicals generally approached death from a Puritan position, they believed that God offered salvation, and people could take it if they willed. Consequently, evangelicalism offered assurance to the saved, even as it heightened the anxiety of the unregenerate. With the idealization of home and family, this could account for the abundant literature on the death of children, as parents agonized over an ailing child "hoping all the while that death would terminate its sufferings, and fearing that something worse would be the result." After 1850, however, the romanticization of childhood overcame ideas of infant damnation, provided more assurance to worried parents, and tipped the delicate balance of evangelical belief from anxiety to assurance. By

During the early part of the 19th century, Americans socialized their children to view dying as a natural process to be accepted by all members of the family.

that time, however, Evangelicalism had begun to be affected by sentimentalism, scientific naturalism, and liberal theology, as well as the social and institutional developments of the dying of death.

THE DYING OF DEATH, 1830–1945

Between 1830 and 1945, the ideas and institutions with which Americans approached death changed in a process that an English author of 1899 called "The Dying of Death." This process brought "the practical disappearance of the thought of death as an influence bearing upon practical life" ("The Dying of Death," 1899:364–365), and the tactical appearance of funeral institutions designed to keep death out of sight and out of mind.

The Rise of the Middle Class

Both ideas and institutions were the product of a new American middle-class, a group of people trying to distinguish themselves from the European aristocracy and from the American common people. Alexis de Tocqueville saw the middle-class as "an innumerable multitude of men almost alike, who, without being exactly rich or poor, possess sufficient property to desire the maintenance of order" (de Tocqueville, 1945:2, 145); contemporary historians see them as substantial property owners, professionals, businessmen and merchants, shopkeepers and skilled artisans, commercial farmers, and their families. They possessed property, but their property (and the hope of increasing it) also possessed them, intensifying their fear of death. For the acquisitive member of the middle-class, "the recollection of death is a constant spur. . . . Besides the good things that he possesses, he every instant fancies a thousand others that death will prevent him from trying if he does not try them soon." Therefore, the middle-class wanted death with order.

One strategy for achieving death with order was the ideology of separate spheres. In the course of the 19th century, middle-class people separated management from labor, men's work from the home, and women's work from men's. They also tried to separate death from life, both intellectually and institutionally. Increasingly, specialists (either medical or clerical or academic) revised ideas of death, while other specialists segregated the funeral from the home, and the cemetery from the city.

Both separation and specialization were strategies of control, an increasingly important idea in Victorian society. Nineteenth-century Americans worked for self-control, social control, and control over nature. They saw self-control as the key to character, and sexual control as the key to marriage. In separating their homes from their shops, they tried to control both spheres of their lives. The home would be a controlled environment for reproduction and **socialization,** while the workplace would be a controlled environment for increased production and time-discipline. Schools served as a transition from one controlled environment to another, while asylums provided controlled environments for societal deviants. Science and technology attempted to make the whole continent a controlled environment. Therefore, it should not surprise us that the same class that practiced birth control should also devise forms of death control (Hale, 1971:25; Howe, 1970:304; Rosenberg, 1973:137).

Intellectual Influences

In the process of the dying of death, the most important intellectual influences were Romanticism, sentimentalism, scientific naturalism, and liberal religion.

Romanticism

Romanticism was an intellectual response to the rationality and uniformity of the Enlightenment. Romantics discarded the Enlightenment idea of God as First Cause of a mechanistic universe operating according to predictable natural cycles. Instead, they emphasized the emotional and intuitive communion with the Oversoul (or Cosmos) in a mysteriously organic nature. Asher B. Durand depicted the essential correspondence of God, nature, and humanity in his painting *Kindred Spirits* (1849). It shows painter Thomas Cole and poet William Cullen Bryant in a beautiful natural setting, kindred to each other, to nature, and to the spirit that informed them all.

Such Romantic naturalism converted death from an untimely, unnatural event into a natural, conclusive communion with nature. In Romantic poetry, such as Bryant's "Thanatopsis" or "A Forest Hymn," death was swallowed up in the teeming life of the landscape. Such soothing conceptions of natural death encouraged people to accept their demise. At the same time, such Romantic ideas influenced the inception of rural cemeteries, which institutionalized Romantic naturalism, even as they provided the consolations of Mother Nature to mourners.

Sentimentalism

The Romantic emphasis on emotions led to simple sentimentalism, which was "part of the self-evasion of a society committed to laissez-faire industrial expansion and disturbed by its consequences" (Douglas, 1977). As Americans began to experience the hard-headed rationalism of the Industrial Revolution, they began to create counterpoints to the "railroad principle" of American life. These counterpoints included the conventions of romantic love, the cult of true womanhood, the idealization of childhood, the home as "haven in a heartless world," residential suburbs, and an "emotional revolution" that bound family members with ties of intimacy. Domestic intimacy heightened the sense of loss upon the death of a "loved one," and required public outlets for the expression of private grief (Douglas, 1977: 12–13, 200–226).

For most of the 19th century, the main outlet for the grief of sentimentalism was the **ritual** of mourning, including the funeral, but also extending beyond it. This ritual differed markedly from the simple Puritan rite as mourners immersed themselves in grief to become, through their expressive (and often excessive) emotions, the central feature of the ritual. It allowed many members of the middle-class (especially the women, who were supposed to be creatures of the "heart") to indulge in grief as "therapeutic self-indulgence." Like other forms of sentimentality, the sentimental mourning ritual counterpointed "the real world" because it forced all mourners to consider the power of personal connections in their lives. It turned people from life to death, from the practical to the ceremonial, from the ordinary to the extraordinary, and from the banal to the beautiful (Taylor, 1980:39–48).

Belief in the beauty of death and the funeral was new to the 19th century as the middle-class used its aesthetic awareness to beautify corpses, door badges, caskets, casket backdrops, hearses, horses, funeral music, cemeteries, monuments, mourning costume, and death itself. In the process, they made death so artistic that it almost became artificial, and, therefore, less fearful. At the same time, concerned with an etiquette of proper social relations, people used the beauty of the funeral to preserve appearances among their middle-class peers. Finally, the middle-class called for "taste" and "refinement" in funerals as mourning rituals served to distinguish them from the common folk (Farrell, 1980:110–111).

Especially around the mid-1800s, the tastefully refined middle-class funeral was a dark and formal affair. After death, which still generally occurred in the home, the family either cleaned and dressed the deceased, or, if possible, hired an undertaker to care for the corpse. If they had secured an undertaker, he would place a black badge over the doorbell or door knocker to indicate the presence of mourning and to isolate the intimate family from the unwanted intrusions of everyday life. The family would also close window shades and drapes. Sometimes they draped black crepe over pictures, mirrors, and other places throughout the house (Habenstein and Lamers, 1962:389–444).

By the time of the funeral, family members had swathed themselves in black mourning garb that symbolized the intimacy of relationship to the deceased and the depth of grief. After the funeral, custom encouraged the continued expression of grief, as widows were expected to spend a year in "deep" mourning, and a year in "second" mourning. For the first year, a bereaved woman wore dull black clothes, matched by appropriately somber accessories. In the second year, she gradually

During the latter part of the 19th century, mourners were expected to dress the part. In this picture, pallbearers wore mourning clothes, black sashes and badges, and dark hats.

lightened her appearance by using a variety of materials in somewhat varying colors. Widowers and children were supposed to follow a similar regimen, but in practice, women bore the burden of 19th-century mourning. Social contact and correspondence followed similar rules, with widened social participation or narrowed black borders on stationery as indicators of different stages of mourning.

The funeral ceremony itself reflected and affected the somber atmosphere in which it occurred. In the mid-1800s, people were invited to funerals with hand-delivered printed cards. By the end of the century, the **obituary** began to serve as a funeral notice, and the telephone allowed people to deliver their own invitations without leaving the house of mourning. Once invited, people generally came to the house, offered condolences to the bereaved family, viewed the corpse, and sat in chairs arranged in the parlor by the undertaker. Sometimes, however, the funeral took place in church, in which case people would process from the home to the church. In either place, services were generally extended affairs in which ministers counter-balanced fears of death, decay, and damnation with hopes of regeneration and resurrection. Funerals might include music and hymns, but the central feature of the ceremony was the sermon, which combined an elegy with exhortations for repentance and renewal. This gloomy funeral was not, however, the only type of sentimental funeral. As the 19th century proceeded, a more hopeful sentimentality entered funeral services as middle-class religious liberalism began to domesticate death (Habenstein and Lamers, 1962:389–444; Hillerman, 1980:101; Stannard, 1980:26).

After the funeral, the procession continued to the cemetery, which was, as we shall see, beautified in order to belie the presence of death. There, the body was interred, and people returned home, not like the Puritans to resume their life's work, but like Victorians to extend their expressions of emotional grief. Mourning garb was one symbol of such sorrow, but mourning portraits and consolation literature were other ways to prolong the period of lamentation.

In the early 19th century, embroidered or painted mourning pictures flourished as a form of memorialization. These pictures often showed stylized graveyard scenes including such standard features as the weeping willow, the gravestone and **epitaph** (tombstone inscription) of the deceased, the mourners, and a *memento mori*. These remained popular until the 1830s, when printed memorials with spaces for names and dates came into vogue. During the middle third of the century, posthumous mourning portraiture also flourished, depicting the deceased with conventional symbols of mortality like the broken shaft or roses held with blooms downward. These paintings were drawn from the corpse, and they expressed "the desire for the restoration of the dead through art." All of these forms of mourning art provided icons for the bereaved to contemplate as a part of the extended mourning ritual (Lloyd, 1980:71–89).

Consolation literature allowed people to share their grief without sharing it with people they knew. It showed mourners that they were not alone in the house of sorrow, and it showed them the emotional and moral benefits of their heartache. Consolation literature included obituary poems and memoirs, mourner's manuals, prayer guidebooks, hymns, and books about heaven. Such writings inflated the importance of dying and the dead by every possible means; they sponsored elaborate methods of burial and commemoration, communication with the next world, and microscopic viewings of a sentimentalized afterlife. Books like *Agnes and the Key of Her Little Coffin* (1857) or *Stepping Heavenward* (1869) or *The Empty Crib: The Memorial of Little Georgie* (1873) all featured and championed the ideal of "the sensitized mourner" (Douglas, 1977:240–249).

To the modern mind, these sentimental expressions of grief may seem forced, overdone, or even false. Such attitudes, however, tell more about us than about our Victorian ancestors. Nineteenth-century Americans "mourned well" because they gave themselves symbols, rituals, and time in which to work out their feelings. We do not understand this because of important intervening historical forces, one of which was scientific naturalism.

Scientific Naturalism

If sentimentality was one way of controlling the hard fact of death, scientific naturalism was another. Although it systemized the hard-headed rationalism that sentimentalism tried to smother, it contributed to the dying of death, as the middle-class used the "laws" of science like they used the "customs" of etiquette to legitimize their cultural values.

"What strikes the historian," writes Burton J. Bledstein, "is the totality of the mid-Victorian impulse to contain the life experiences of the individual from life to death by isolating them as science." Another instance of the ideology of separate spheres, the rise of science in the last half of the 19th century allowed Americans to invoke authority for "those scientific plausibilities which fitted most conveniently into their social needs and presuppositions" (Bledstein, 1976:55). An integral part of the social construction of reality, science isolated the mystery of death as "a matter of fact," and interpreted that fact in order to reduce the impact of death on practical life.

Scientific naturalists insisted first that death was "natural, a product of natural causes, the same as any other natural phenomenon, and that these causes are bound to the fixed, and as we believe beneficent, laws of the universe" (Johnson, 1896:77). Their insistence on the "natural" quality of death complemented the natural death of Romanticism, but the scientific fact of death eliminated providential intervention and the possibility of death as punishment.

Consequently, scientific naturalists insisted that death was painless, and that all people could eventually attain an "easy," natural death at an advanced age. Pain, which (like fear) was an important part of the Puritan world, lost its cultural relevance in the 19th century. With the discovery of ether in the 1840s and the coining of the word *painkiller* in the 1850s, Americans applied physical and mental anaesthetics to kill the pain of death ("Pain, Life, and Death"). Magazine articles constantly stressed "the modern belief that the process [of dying] is easy," as easy and "as painless as falling asleep" ("The Fear of Death," 1912:21). In so doing, they eliminated a major reason for people to think seriously about death.

Other scientific and medical innovations persuaded many Americans that death might be postponed or prevented. Even before the demographic transition, they began to treat death as an occurrence of old age, an idea that encouraged people to postpone or pre-empt preparation for death. In addition, some prominent medical researchers asserted that even old age was a curable congenital disease and asked "Why Not Live Forever?" Indeed, when Elie Metchnikoff, the head of the

Pasteur Institute in Paris, claimed that cultured milk products could combat the "autointoxication" of old age, Americans immediately began to buy yogurt and buttermilk. Especially between 1900 and 1920, the prestige of science convinced many Americans that individual physical immortality might be imminent (Farrell, 1980:60–61).

Other scientific naturalists admitted individual mortality, but promoted a species immortality whereby "we are immortal if we but form a sturdy link in the great chain of life." Influenced by Darwin's idea of natural selection, these scientists viewed death as "an inevitable corollary to the advancement of the species" (Hutchinson, 1893:637). Therefore, they advised Americans not to take death personally, but to accept it as part of human progress. This species perspective did not prevent individuals from dying, but it did turn their attention from death and the deceased to survivors and posterity. As we shall see, this species perspective of death and immortality was institutionalized in "life" insurance.

By itself, scientific naturalism had almost no impact on American bereavement practices. In conjunction with religious liberalism and the culture of professionalism, however, scientific naturalism did affect changes in funeral service.

Liberal Religion

Religious liberals tried to reconcile new scientific knowledge with traditional religious interpretations of death. Between 1850 and 1930, liberals like Henry Ward Beecher and Phillips Brooks enunciated "the attitudes and values of a new urban middle-class" (Clark, 1978:3). They combined scientific naturalism, higher Biblical criticism, Romantic idealism, and sentimentality in order to show the place of evolution in God's plan, the place of death in evolution, and the progress of life through death to an exalted immortality. In addition, changing ideas of death and immortality brought them into the arena of funeral reform.

Henry Ward Beecher was the most popular and influential of liberal clergymen. His pulpit at the Plymouth Congregational Church of Brooklyn Heights gave him opportunities for public speaking and publication, and he became a "symbol for a middle-class America" (Clark, 1978). He rejected the Evangelicalism of his youth, and preached instead a gospel of divine immanence, natural law, and human hope. He accepted scientific naturalism and wrote an article for the first issue of the *Popular Science Monthly*. He believed that God acted primarily in the world through natural laws and that people responded naturally to God by electing their own salvation. Eventually, he even rejected the doctrine of everlasting punishment in hell.

Beecher viewed death as the first step up toward heaven, as God's call to "Come home!" "I would not, for the world, bring up a child to have that horror of death which hung over my own childhood," claimed Beecher, because "the thought of death was to me awful beyond description" (Beecher, 1859:194–195). Instead, he wanted people to see that "a funeral is the nearest place to heaven," and that sorrow was inappropriate. He suggested:

> When friends have gone out from us joyously, we should go with them to the grave, not singing mournful psalms, but scattering flowers. Christians are wrong to walk in black, and sprinkle the ground with tears, at the very time when they should walk in white, and illumine the way by smiles and radiant hope. The disciples found angels at the grave of Him they loved; and we should always find them too, but that our eyes are too full of tears for seeing. (Beecher, 1858:189)

At his own funeral in 1887, Beecher's family reversed the somber formality of the Victorian funeral by making sure that "no emblem of parting or sorrow was there, but the symbols of love, and faith, and hope, the glad tokens of eternal reward, such as befitted his life, his death, and his fame" (Handford, 1887:47–49). On a practical, pastoral level, other ministers counseled people to follow Beecher's example. They celebrated death as a passage to eternal life, not as a moment of judgment. They tried to soothe survivors instead of promoting self-examination or preparation for death. They worked with funeral directors to effect funeral reforms. In 1913, Lyman Abbott recalled the achievements of liberal funeral reform:

> We have done much to Christianize our farewells to those who have gone before us into the next stages of life. We no longer darken the rooms that now more than ever need the light and warmth of the sun; we no longer close the windows as if to shut out Nature at the moment when we are about to give back to Mother Earth all that was mortal in the earthly career now finished; we no longer shroud the house in black, we make it sweet with flowers; for the hymns of grief we are fast substituting the hymns of victory; for words charged with a sense of loss we listen to words that hold wide the door of hope and faith; and on the memorials which we place where they lie who have vanished from our sight we no longer carve the skull and crossbones, the hourglass and the scythe—we recall some trait or quality of achievement that survives the body and commemorates the spirit.

Such changes, thought Abbott, helped people "to think of life as one and indivisible, of immortality as our possession, here and now, of death as normal change in an eternal process of growth" ("There Are No Dead," 1913:979–980).

By defining death as part of evolutionary progress propelled by an immanent and merciful God, liberals allowed bereaved Americans to approach death optimistically. This new definition of death derived from ideas of Romanticism, scientific naturalism, and religious liberalism. Together with the institutional innovations of cemetery superintendents, life insurance agents, and funeral directors, these ideas caused the dying of death in America.

Institutional Influences

Like religious liberalism, cemetery reform derived from Romantic naturalism, middle-class family sentimentality, and scientific concerns. In 1895, a writer in *American Gardening* wrote that "the modern garden cemetery like the modern religious impulse seeks to assuage the cheerlessness and the sternness of life and to substitute the free and gracious charity of One who came to rob death of its hideousness" ("Extracts," 1895:108). By the 1830s, many physicians had begun to worry about the possible health hazards of city graveyards. By the same time, commercial development had raised the price of land on which graveyards were located, and Romantic ideas of landscape architecture had begun to affect the aesthetically oriented members of the middle class. Also, space limitations of city graveyards prevented the possibility of family plots, and many of the burial places had become overcrowded, unkempt, and unsightly.

Rural Cemeteries

The solution to these problems was the rural cemetery, a landscaped garden in a suburban setting. In 1831, Mount Auburn Cemetery was founded four miles west of Boston, and its success stimulated the spread of such cemeteries all over the country. In rural cemeteries, family plots averaging 300 square feet were nestled among trees and shrubs upon the slopes of soft hills or on the shores of little lakes. Paths curled throughout the grounds, passing lots enclosed by stone coping or wrought iron fences and surmounted by a monument of some sort. Such cemeteries were invented to bury bodies and to ease the grief of survivors; to bring people into communion with God, with Nature, and with deceased family and friends, and to teach them important lessons of life; to surround bereavement with beauty and to divert the attention of survivors from death to the setting of burial; and to display "taste" and "refinement" and to reinforce the class stratification of the status quo (Bender, 1973:196–211; French, 1975:69–91; Rotundo, 1973:231–242).

The founders of Mount Auburn were liberal Unitarian reformers, progressive professionals and businesspeople who considered the cemetery in the context of social developments of their day. They equated the family with the garden and imagined both as a counterpoint to a society of accumulation. In the same way that upper-middle-class families moved to suburbs where curved roads and greenery contrasted with the grid-block plan of the cities and offered space to raise a family, they moved from the "cities of the dead" to rural cemeteries that offered space to "plant" a family.

During this period of "the discovery of the asylum," social deviants were located in restorative rural settings that would rehabilitate people away from the contaminating influence of urban life. Like insane asylums, orphanages, and penitentiaries, many of these reformers saw the cemetery as an "asylum" from urban ills. In the cemetery, "the weary and worn citizen" was also rehabilitated. Cleaveland (1847:13–14, 26) noted:

> Ever since he entered these greenwood shades, he has sensibly been getting farther and farther from strife, from business, and care. . . . A short half-hour ago, he was in the midst of a discordant Babel; he was one of the hurrying, jostling crowd; he was encompassed by the whirl and fever of artificial life. Now he stands alone in Nature's inner court—in her silent, solemn sanctuary. Her holiest influences are all around him.

The rehabilitation of the rural cemetery paralleled the philosophy of education found in the common school. Like the new compulsory schools, rural cemeteries responded to middle-class fears of mobilization of the masses in the Age of Jackson. Educational reformers like Horace Mann both reflected and affected cemetery proponents in their belief that "sentiment is the great conservative principle of society," and that "instincts of patriotism, local attachment, family affection, human sympathy, reverence for truth, age, valor, and wisdom . . . constitute the latent force of civil society" (Tuckerman, 1856:338–342).

Like these other reforms of antebellum society, rural cemeteries "took the public mind by storm." Cities and towns throughout the United States established rural cemeteries, and people flocked to visit them. In New York, Baltimore, and Philadelphia, Andrew Jackson Downing estimated that over 30,000 people a year toured the rural cemeteries. Consequently, he wondered whether they might not also visit landscaped gardens without graves. In articles like "Public Cemeteries and Public Gardens" and "The New York Park," Downing (1921:28–40, 374) advanced the idea that would eventuate in New York's Central Park and in a new direction for cemetery development.

The new direction was the lawn-park cemetery emphasizing a new aesthetic— efficiency—and the absence of death. By the end of the century, members of the Association of American Cemetery Superintendents routinely wrote in journals like *Park and Cemetery* that "a cemetery should be a beautiful park. While there are still some who say 'a cemetery should be a cemetery,' . . . the great majority have come to believe in the idea of beauty" (Simonds, 1919:59). This new aesthetic emphasized the open meadows of the beautiful style over the irregular hill-and-dale outcroppings of the picturesque style and the irregular outcroppings of obelisks and monuments in the unregulated rural cemetery. This aesthetic coincided with considerations of efficiency as the uncluttered landscape required less upkeep than the enclosures and elaborate monuments of the rural cemetery. Finally, this aesthetic buried death beneath the beauty of the design. Andrew Jackson Downing

(1921:59) had said that "the development of the beautiful is the end and aim of all other fine arts. . . . And we attain it by the removal or concealment of everything uncouth or discordant." The cemetery superintendents practiced what Downing preached. "Today cemetery making is an art," said one superintendent in 1910, "and gradually all things that suggest death, sorrow, or pain are being eliminated" (Hare, 1910:41).

Cemetery superintendents eliminated suggestions of death by banning lot enclosures and grave mounds, and by encouraging fewer gravestones and fewer inscriptions. They banned lot enclosures (fencing or stone coping) because they broke up the unified landscape, blocked the path of the lawn mower, and signified a "selfish and exclusive," possessive individualism. While grave mounds obstructed the view and the lawn mower, they also reminded people of death. Without them, a cemetery lot would evoke "none of the gruesomeness which is invariably associated with cemetery lots. . . . *No grave mounds are used, so save the headstones, there is nothing to suggest the presence of Death*" (Smith, 1910:539).

FOREST LAWN

Song by Tom Paxton

Oh, lay me down in Forest Lawn in a silver casket,
Put golden flowers over my head in a silver basket.
Let the drum and bugle corps blow taps while cannons roar,
Let sixteen liveried employees pass out souvenirs from the funeral store.
I want to go simply when I go, and they'll give me a simple fun'ral there, I know.
With a casket lined in fleece,
And fireworks spelling out "rest in peace."
Oh, take me when I'm gone to Forest Lawn.

Oh, lay me down in Forest Lawn—they understand there.
They have a heavenly choir and a military band there.
Just put me in their care, and I'll find my comfort there, with sixteen planes
in last salute, dropping a cross in a parachute.
I want to go simply when I go, they'll give me a simple fun'ral there, I know.
With a hundred strolling strings.
And topless dancers in golden wings,
Oh, take me when I'm gone to Forest Lawn.

(continued)

Oh come, come, come, come,
Come to the church in the wildwood,
Kindly leave a contribution in the pail.
Be as simple and as trusting as a child would
And we'll sell you a church in the dale.

To find a simple resting place is my desire,
To lay me down with a smiling face comes a little bit higher.
My likeness done in brass will stand in plastic grass,
And weights and hidden springs will tip its hat to the mourners filing past.
I want to go simply when I go.
And they'll give me a simple fun'ral there, I know.
I'll sleep beneath the sand, with piped in tapes of Billy Graham.
Oh, take me when I'm gone to Forest Lawn.
Rock of Ages, cleft for me, for a slightly higher fee.
Oh, take me when I'm gone to Forest Lawn.

Some superintendents did not want to save the headstones either, proposing instead "a cemetery where there is no monument, only landscape" (*Association*, 1889:59). Most superintendents favored sunken stones at the site of the grave. Howard Evarts Weed (1912:94), author of the influential *Modern Park Cemeteries,* argued that "with the headstones showing above the surface we have the old grave-yard scene, but buried in the ground they do not appear in the landscape picture and we then have a park-like effect." Some superintendents zoned the cemetery to permit monuments only on large "monument lots." This allowed the superinten-dent, like a realtor, to charge premium prices for such lots and for prime locations for corner lots or hillside or lakeside property. This **social stratification** of the cemetery allowed for the social mobility of the dead, as ambitious dead people moved to better "neighborhoods" as their survivors saw fit. Where they could not ban or limit the number of monuments, superintendents tried to make them as unobtrusive as possible, preferring horizontal monuments to the earlier upright markers, and preferring sorted inexpressive inscriptions to the poetic epitaphs of earlier times. They wanted to replace the *memento mori* of earlier stones with "for-getfulness" as they buried death with the dead (Farrell, 1980:122–127).

GRAVE REMARKS

I'll Write My Own Epitaph Before I Leave, Thank You

Epitaphs are footnotes chiseled on tombstones.

They are parting shots taken at or by the deceased. They can be patriotic, poetic, profound or pathetic. They can be wise, witty or just weird. They can glorify, be grievous or gruesome.

Few of them have summed up a person's attitude toward life as well as one found in a Georgia cemetery:

I told you I was sick!

Perhaps the most famous epitaph is one credited to W. C. Fields, written for himself:

On the whole I'd rather be in Philadelphia.

But Fields' epitaph was not used and his tombstone in Forest Lawn (Glendale, California) contains only his vital statistics. Here are some others.

Epitaph from Kilmurry Churchyard, Ireland:

This stone was raised to Sarah Ford.
Not Sarah's virtues to record,
For they're well known to all the town,
No Lord, it was raised to keep her down.

From Streatham Churchyard, England:

Here lies Elizabeth, my wife for 47 years, and this is the first damn thing
she ever did to oblige me.

Epitaph on one of three tombstones in a family burial plot in Niagara Falls, Ontario:

Here I lie between two of the best women in the world; my wives. But I
have requested my relatives to tip me a little toward Tillie.

In a Falkirk, England, cemetery:

At rest beneath this slab of stone
Lies stingy Jimmy Wyatt;
He died one morning just at ten,
And saved a dinner by it.

(continued)

Here's one from Boot Hill, Dodge City, Kansas, that reflects a popular epitaph theme:

Here lies the body of Mannie,
They put him here to stay;
He lived the life of Riley
While Riley was away.

From Burlington Churchyard, Mass.,

Sacred to the memory of Anthony Drake
Who died for peace and quietness sake,
His wife was constantly scolding and scoffin',
So he sought repose in a twelve-dollar coffin.

Railroad conductor Charles B. Gunn's tombstone in Colorado Springs, Colo., contains these words:

Papa—Did you wind your watch?

And in a Moultrie, Ga., cemetery:

Here lies the father of twenty-nine
He would have had more but he didn't have time.

From Burlington, Mass., again:

Here lies the body of Susan Lowder
Who burst while drinking Seidlitz powder;
Called from the world to her heavenly rest
She should have waited till it effervesced.

On a hanged sheep-stealer from Bletchley, Bucks, England:

Here lies the body of Thomas Kemp
Who lived by wool and died by hemp.

Abraham Newland, a lonely London Banker, who wrote his own epitaph:

Beneath this stone old Abraham lies;
Nobody laughs, and nobody cries.
Where he has gone, and how he fares,
Nobody knows and nobody cares.

In a Thurmont, Md., cemetery:

Here lies an atheist—All dressed up and no place to go.

And in a Stowe, Vt., cemetery:

I was somebody. Who is no business of yours.

An infant's epitaph in a Plymouth, Mass., cemetery:

Since I have been so quickly done for
I wonder what I was begun for.

In a Uniontown, Pa., cemetery:

Here lies the body of Jonathan Blake;
Stepped on the gas instead of the brake.

Written by a widow on her adulterous husband's tombstone in an Atlanta, Ga., cemetery:

Gone. But not forgiven.

Similarly, a Middlesex, England, widow put this on the gravestone of her wandering husband:

At last I know where he is at night!

An "old maid's" epitaph in Scranton, Pa.:

No hits, no runs, no heirs.

At Cripple Creek, Colo., an epitaph to a man who died by accident:

Within this grave there lies poor Andy;
Bit by a snake no whiskey handy.

Another one from Cripple Creek:

Here lies the bones of a man named Zeke,
Second-fastest draw in Cripple Creek.

Near Atlanta, Ga., a cemetery hosts this unique epitaph:

Due to lack of ground in this cemetery,
two bodies are buried in this one plot.
One of them was a politician, the other
was an honest man.

An English epitaph over the grave of Sir John Strange, a lawyer:

Here lies an honest lawyer, and that is Strange.

Epitaph to Joseph Crump, a musician:

Once ruddy, and plump
But now a pale lump
Beneath this same hump
Lies honest Joe Crump

(continued)

> *What, tho' by Death's thump*
> *He's laid on his rump*
> *Yet up he shall jump*
> *When he hears the last triumph.*
>
> An 1890 epitaph of Arthur C. Hormans of Cleveland, Ohio, puts this in startlingly clear perspective:
>
> *Once again I wasn't. Then I was. Now I ain't again.*

Excerpt from "Grave Remarks" from *The People's Almanac* by David Wallechinsky and Irving Wallace. Copyright 1975 by David Wallechinsky and Irving Wallace. Reprinted by permission of Doubleday and Co., Inc.

Superintendents tried to structure cemetery services "to mitigate the harshness and cruelty of death and its attendant details and ceremonies" (Seavoy, 1906:488) and to provide a sort of grief therapy for bereaved individuals. They encouraged private, family funerals, and they tried to remove or conceal the uncouth and discordant aspects of interment. They carted the dirt away from the grave, or they hid it beneath cloth, flowers, or evergreens. They lined the grave with cloth to make it look like a little room. They suggested changes in religious services, and they escorted mourners away from the grave before filling it in order to avoid the finality of death. In all of these services, "everything that tends to remove the gloomy thoughts is done. . . . The friends cannot but leave the sacred spot with better, nobler thoughts, freed from the gloom and terror that otherwise would possess them" (Hay, 1900:46).

Life Insurance

A second institutional innovation, life insurance, tried to exorcise the anxiety and financial insecurity that would otherwise possess people contemplating death. Established about the same time as rural cemeteries, life insurance flourished after 1850. In 1850, 48 companies held policies valued at $97 million; by 1920, 335 companies recorded 65 million policies worth $40 billion. Life insurance contributed to "the practical disappearance of the thought of death as an influence bearing upon practical life," and thus it contributed to the dying of death (U.S. Bureau of the Census, 1975:1050–1059).

Life insurance emerged from the same historical context as rural cemeteries and funeral reform; it assumed the uniformity and continuity of death as a natural occurrence. Life insurance depended on the science of statistics and on a species perspective of death and immortality that focused attention, not on the life of the individual policyholder, but on the lives of beneficiaries. Like the rural cemetery, it

LIFE INSURANCE

The middle-class American value of planning ahead for the future is exemplified by the fact that the majority of Americans have life insurance. Life insurance is to protect one's dependents and to give the insured a feeling of security in knowing that his or her dependents will have some coverage in the event of death.

The amount of life insurance needed is related to the number of dependents one has. For example, if one is the primary provider in a family consisting of three small children, he or she would have a greater need for life insurance than a single person with no dependents. If the primary provider were to die, these dependents would have some financial coverage at least for the time being. At the time of death, the added burden of the loss of income is not needed.

If one's only purpose for life insurance is to provide for one's dependents, **term life insurance** is probably the best choice. Term life insurance tends to have the lowest premiums for the greatest amount of coverage. Group policies, such as those provided by one's place of employment, tend to have lower premiums than policies obtained outside of a group. Term life insurance is for a specific number of years, such as five or ten, with premiums going up as one ages. "My suggestion is to start with term, but if there is a permanent insurance need, convert to a good universal life policy," says Andrew Gross, a financial planner in Washington, DC (Smith, 1988:154).

Today, however, life insurance for many individuals is more than security for one's dependents. Some policies, universal life policies, for example, are a form of tax-deferred investment from which one can also borrow. Thus, one can have coverage in the event of death and can have the opportunity to build cash assets at the same time. These insurance policies are called **whole life** from which, for a set premium, one receives life insurance and a savings fund. **Universal life insurance** is more flexible, has investment opportunities, and allows one to raise or reduce premiums and the amount of coverage on one's life. **Variable life insurance** does not allow for the premium or minimum coverage on one's life to change, but one can switch the savings from among money-markets or various forms of stock.

It is advisable to shop around and compare the benefits of the different life insurance programs. Premiums vary considerably for the same coverage. Be cautious of high-powered salespersons trying to sell coverage not needed. Become informed about life insurance by talking with knowledgeable consumers or by reading consumer magazines before purchasing any life insurance. Comparison shopping should pay off.

was praised for its educational benefits as it taught lessons of self-reliance, fore-thought, thrift, discipline, and (very) delayed gratification. For these reasons, clergymen like Henry Ward Beecher endorsed the system of life insurance, responding to critics that in effect, God helps those who help themselves. Also, life insurance accentuated the importance of the family, as did Romantic sentimentalism and the family plot of the rural cemetery. Finally, life insurance provided families with money to pay for elaborate funerals, a fact that affected both the development of funeral service and of the history of bereavement.

Funeral Services

Like burial service, funeral service also changed between 1850 and 1920. Because "the growing wealth and prosperity of our country has caused people to demand something more in accordance with their surroundings" (Benjamin, 1882:3), and because funeral directors cultivated a "steadily advancing appreciation of the aesthetics of society" ("Funeral Directors," 1883:3), the new funeral would be, like the 19th-century cemetery, a work of art. As cemetery superintendents used their art to hide the uncouth and discordant aspects of death, so did funeral directors use "the varied improvements in (their) art . . . to conceal much that is forbidding in (their) calling" ("Funeral Directors," 1882:5). As cemetery superintendents institutionalized "the modern religious impulse" to "assuage the cheerlessness and sternness of life," the funeral director worked to "adopt some philosophy or some new customs and ideals that will make death less of a tragedy" ("The Ideas of a Plain Country Woman," 1913.42).

The demand for a new funeral service came from the American middle class, but it was created and supplied by casket manufacturers and funeral directors. The National Funeral Directors Association was founded in 1882 in Rochester, New York, the home of the Stein Casket Manufacturing Company. The association's official journal was *The Casket,* founded and funded for several years by the Stein Company. As this suggests, the first widespread innovation in funeral service was the casket, a stylish container for the corpse. Before 1850, most Americans were laid to rest in a coffin, a six-sided box that was constructed to order by the local cabinet-maker. By 1927 "the old wedge-shaped coffin [was] obsolete. A great variety of styles and grades of caskets [were] available in the trade, ranging from a cheap, cloth-covered pine box to the expensive cast-bronze sarcophagus" (Gebhart, 1927:8). The rectangular shape of the new caskets complemented the artwork in concealing the uncouth corpse. In applying for a casket patent in 1849, A. C. Barstow explained:

> The burial cases formerly used were adapted in shape nearly to the form of
> the human body, that is they tapered from the shoulders to the head, and from the

shoulders to the feet. Presently, in order to obviate in some degree the disagreeable sensations produced by a coffin on many minds, the casket, or square form has been adopted. (Habenstein and Lamers, 1962:270, 251–310)

The adoption of the word *casket* also accelerated the dying of death, as the word had previously denoted a container for something precious, like jewels.

Accepting the associated idea of the preciousness of the body, Americans decided that a dead-looking corpse looked out of place in an elaborate silk-lined casket. Rather than remove the casket, they decided to stylize the body. Originally a way of preserving bodies for shipment home from Civil War battlefields or western cities, embalming soon became a way of preserving appearances. Responding to the germ theory of disease and the public health movement, funeral directors attempted to gain professional status by emphasizing the disinfectant qualities of embalming. Most funeral directors, however, wanted simply "to retain and improve the complexion" so that the corpse would look "as natural as though [it] were alive" (Hohenschuh, 1921:82, 88). To do this, they began to cosmetize the corpse, and to clothe and position the body naturally. They replaced the traditional shroud with street clothes, and they tried "to lay out the body so that there will be as little suggestion of death as possible." By 1920, they succeeded so well that a Boston undertaker supposedly advertised (Dowd, 1921:53):

For composing the features,	$1
For giving the features a look of quiet resignation,	$2
For giving the features the appearance of Christian hope and contentment,	$5

Bereavement practices were affected by the change from coffin to casket and by the "restorative art" of the embalmer; they were also changed by the movement of the funeral from the domestic parlor to the funeral parlor. As they began banishing death from their homes to hospitals, they started moving the funeral from the family parlor to a specialized funeral parlor. After the Civil War, middle-class Americans began to exclude the formal parlor from their homes and to replace it with a "living room." At the same time, funeral directors wanted full control of the corpse and the funeral. The ease and efficiency of directing funerals in a funeral home made them more profitable. In spite of these benefits, the transition to the funeral parlor was slow, extending well into the 20th century (Farrell, 1980:172–177).

Both in the domestic parlor and in the funeral parlor, the procedure of the turn-of-the-century funeral changed. In conjunction with the reform forces of religious liberalism, funeral directors began to redirect funerals to be shorter, more secular, and more soothing. They shortened the service by trying to revise the long sermon with its exhortations of repentance and renewal. Although some clerics resisted, funeral directors wanted the sermon redirected from theology to psychology, from preaching to grief therapy, and from the state of survivors' souls to the state of their emotions. The funeral director took care of all the details of the funeral and performed as much as a stage manager as a mortician. "Really it is much the same," wrote one director, "I work for effect—for consoling and soothing effect" ("The Man Nobody Envies," 1914:68–71).

After 1880, funeral directors used their arts and the culture of professionalism to effect a massive change in the American way of bereavement. Professionalism was part of the middle-class strategy of specialization. It required education in an area of expertise and an ethic or service, and it provided autonomy and income for its practitioners. The American undertaker sought professional status because it would help him to become "enough of an *authority* to convince his clients, without offense, that there are better methods than are prescribed by custom" (Hohenschuh, 1921:9). Etiquette books reinforced this culture of professionalism by advising readers that "the arrangements for the funeral are usually left to the undertaker, who best knows how to proceed" (Wells, 1887:303). To the middle-class people who feared death anyway, this established a situation in which the public passively accepted changes in funeral service suggested by funeral directors (Hohenschuh, 1921:9; Wells, 1887:303).

Indeed, restraint and passivity became the watchwords of 20th-century bereavement. If the funeral director was a stage manager, then the family was the audience, responding to the drama in prescribed ways in the hopes of achieving a catharsis of death. Instead of the expressive grief of the sentimental funeral, the family was expected to contain and control their emotions and to meet death stoically. At the turn of the century, some religious liberals saw grief as lack of faith in the imminence of immortality. Others reacted to the central place of the mourners in the mournful Victorian funeral and charged that "over-much grief would seem mere selfishness" (Mayo, 1916:6). Over and over again, writers proclaimed that "the deepest grief is the quiet kind" (Sargent, 1888:51). An 1890s etiquette book suggested that "we can better show our affection to the dead by fulfilling our duties to the living, than by giving ourselves up to uncontrolled grief" (Pike and Armstrong, 1980:125). Portraying grief as a selfish ploy to stop the ongoing business of life, these reformers called for controlled and private grief. In the long run, they predicted the modern practice of grief therapy in which grief is seen as a disorder by people who still want death with order (Mayo, 1916:6; Pike and Armstrong, 1980:125; Sargent, 1888:51).

With this new ideal of grief, Americans reduced their symbolic expressions of sorrow—mourning wear, for example, which declined after World War I—because extended grief offended others who preferred to live for life. In concealing mourning, Americans reversed the 19th-century tradition that *required* good mourning. Like cemetery superintendents and funeral directors, Americans in general began to conceal the uncouth and discordant emotion of grief. Thus, modern grief isolates the mourners and forces them to discover their own private mourning ritual. It dictates the appearance of control and the dying of death (Hillerman, 1980:104–105; Oxley, 1887:608–614).

THE DISPLAY OF THE DEAD

Truly, we need to do away with some of the false ideas of Death which are shown in so many gruesome ways at funerals, and strive to give the young a different and truer idea of what the passing away of a soul means. The awfulness of some funerals is nothing short of criminal, especially as it affects the minds of the young. If there is work cut out for the minister of today, it is the enlightenment of his people on the subject of death and the funeral. But the minister must, first of all, imbibe a wholesome lesson of self-restraint for himself, and abolish the fulsome and tiresome eulogy which is the bane of so many funerals. He must learn for himself, and teach to his people, the beauty and solemnity of the brief service as prescribed by his church and attempt nothing more, and he must also relentlessly oppose the tendency which exists to turn the modern funeral, especially in the country, into a picnic. The present outpouring of a heterogeneous mass of folk from every point of the countryside is a farce that cannot be too soon abolished. A funeral is essentially a time for the meeting of the family and relatives and the closest friends, and the fewer the number of outsiders present the better. Nor is there anything quite so barbarous as the present custom at so many funerals of "viewing the remains" by a motley collection of folk, many of whom never even knew the dead in life, or, if they did, never thought enough of him to come and see him. The vulgar curiosity that prompts "a last look" at the loved one cannot be too severely denounced. Only second to it is the pretentious line of vehicles that "escorts the remains to the grave" and the mental calibre of a community that bases the popularity of a man on the number of carriages that follow him to the grave!

If there is a crying need of the gospel of simplicity it is in connection with funerals. It seems inconceivable that Death should be made the occasion for display, and yet this is true of scores of funerals. The flowers, including those fearful conceptions of the ignorant florist, such as "Gates Ajar"; the quality of casket and even of the raiment of the dead, the "crowd" at the "obsequies," the number of carriages in the "cortege"—oh, oh, "what fools these mortals be," to say naught of the wicked and wanton waste of much-needed money. It is difficult to conceive that a national love of display should have become so deep-rooted as to lead to the very edge of the grave!

Ladies' Home Journal, September 1903. Courtesy *Ladies' Home Journal* magazine.

The modern bereavement practices described proceeded from a simple desire to make death as painless for survivors as for the deceased. It came from a widespread cultural attempt "not to mention trouble or grief or sickness or sin, but to treat them as if they do not exist, and speak only of the sweet and pleasant things of life" ("The Ideas of a Plain Country Woman," 1913:42). This dying of death came from the desire of the middle-class for control—of self, society, and the environment. It ended exactly where de Tocqueville (1945:2, 4) predicted:

> As they perceive that they succeed in resolving without resistance all the little difficulties their practical life presents, [the Americans] readily conclude that everything in the world can be explained, and that nothing in it transcends the limits of the understanding. Thus they fall to denying what they cannot comprehend.

Denying and disguising death, middle-class Americans achieved, on the surface at least, the dying of death.

THE RESURRECTION OF DEATH, 1945 TO THE PRESENT

Although Americans sought a death sentence for death, the judge granted only life imprisonment. Consequently, although death had disappeared from the streets, Americans worried that this hardened killer might escape. After World War II, some Americans suggested instead that death had been rehabilitated, and like 19th-century "resurrectionists," they began to resurrect death. Presently Americans are deciding between the dying of death and "living with dying."

The Atomic Age

On August 6, 1945, the United States dropped a single atomic bomb on the Japanese city of Hiroshima. It exploded in the air, with a heat flash that inflamed clothing within a half-mile radius and trees up to a mile and a half. The shock wave followed soon after, rupturing internal organs. Finally, the blast blew bodies at 500 to 1000 miles per hour through the flaming, rubble-filled air. The bomb destroyed everything within 8000 feet, killed at least 70,000 people, and destroyed or damaged 98 percent of Hiroshima's buildings. The effects of atomic radiation have disfigured or killed thousands more, and the whole world bears the psychological scars of the blast.

President Truman announced the explosion:

> It is an atomic bomb. It is a harnessing of the basic power of the universe. . . .
> What has been done is the greatest achievement of organized science in history.

One of the scientists, Albert Einstein, responded "Ach! The world is not ready for it." Within a year, Einstein argued that "the unleashed power of the atom has changed everything save our modes of thinking, and we thus drift toward unparalleled catastrophe."

The atomic bomb and the arms race did, however, begin to change our mode of thinking about death. In a prescient 1947 article on the social effects of the Bomb, Lewis Mumford predicted that, in the Atomic Age,

> Life is now reduced to purely existentialist terms: existence towards death. The classic other worldly religions undergo a revival; but even more quack religions and astrology, with pretensions to scientific certainty, flourish; [so do] new cults. The young who grow up in this world are completely demoralized: they characterize themselves as the generation that drew a blank. The belief in continuity, the sense of a future that holds promises, disappears; the certainty of sudden obliteration cuts across every long-term plan, and every activity is more or less reduced to the life-span of a single day, on the assumption that it may be the last day. . . . Suicide becomes more frequent . . . and the taking of drugs to produce either exhilaration or sleep becomes practically universal. . . .
>
> These conditions—as unfamiliar to the experience of the race as the atom bomb itself—must lead to grave psychological disruptions. We can posit the familiar forms of these regressive actions: escape in fantasy would be one; purposeless sexual promiscuity would be another; narcotic indulgence would be a third.
>
> Not a single life [will yet have] been lost in atomic warfare; nevertheless death has spread everywhere in the cold violence of anticipation. (Mumford, 1947:9–20, 29–30)

"For the first time in six centuries," says Edwin Shneidman (1973:189), "a generation has been born and raised in a thanatological context, concerned with the imminent possibility of the death of the person, the death of humanity, the death of the universe, and, by necessary extension, the death of God." "The bomb," said philosopher William Barrett (1958:65), "reveals the dreadful and total contingency of human existence. Existentialism is the philosophy of the atomic age." Indeed, the Bomb did lead many postwar people to the philosophy of existentialism, which began with the reality of death, worked through anxiety and alienation, and culminated with individuals condemned to the freedom to undertake responsible action in the world. Like the "God Is Dead" theology of the 1960s, atomic existentialism returned Americans to the basic fact of death.

The threat of "megadeath" has also taken the traditional future away from young people. Twenty-eight percent of high school seniors in 1975 to 1978 believed that "nuclear or biological annihilation will probably be the fate of all mankind in my lifetime." Even younger children are aware of the Bomb, and many are pessimistic about the possibilities of preventing a nuclear war. "Others report deep despair, a sense of living totally for today, anger at adults for appearing impotent to do anything, and varying degrees of ability to commit to a future or to invest

"Wouldn't you know it! Now the Hendersons have the bomb."

in their own personal capacity to do anything about one." This affects not only the way that children live their lives, but the way they deal with death. "What happens to the child's concept of death and capacity to cope with death in a rational way," asks one researcher, "when death ceases becoming an end state of the growth process, or an incidental accidental happening, but rather becomes a catastrophic threat for all humans by our own doing?" (Greenwald and Zeitlin, 1987:21, 30–31).

The apocalyptic possibility of nuclear megadeath reminded many people of the fragility of life and the uncertainty of existence—ideas that the Puritans could surely appreciate. Because the historical context was different, however—now people could plan their own extinction—the effects were different. Instead of experiencing death in life as an incentive for righteousness, people experience the "death in life" that comes from psychic numbing. In psychic numbing, we block our capacity to feel as strongly about other aspects of everyday life. In extreme cases, we become emotionally dead; in most cases, we are merely schizophrenic, ignoring the threat of the Bomb, and consequently ignorant of the ways we might try to reduce the threat (Lifton and Falk, 1982:103–106).

LATE NIGHT THOUGHTS ON LISTENING TO MAHLER'S NINTH SYMPHONY

Lewis Thomas

I cannot listen to Mahler's Ninth Symphony with anything like the old melancholy mixed with the high pleasure I used to take from this music. There was a time, not long ago, when what I heard, especially in the final movement, was an open acknowledgement of death and at the same time a quiet celebration of the tranquility connected to the process. I took this music as a metaphor for reassurance, confirming my own strong hunch that the dying of every living creature, the most natural of all experiences, has to be a peaceful experience. I rely on nature. The long passages on all the strings at the end, as close as music can come to expressing silence itself, I used to hear as Mahler's idea of leave-taking at its best. But always, I have heard this music as a solitary, private listener, thinking about death.

Now I hear it differently. I cannot listen to the last movement of the Mahler Ninth without the door-smashing intrusion of a huge new thought: death everywhere, the dying of everything, the end of humanity. The easy sadness expressed with such gentleness and delicacy by that repeated phrase on faded strings, over and over again, no longer comes to me as old, familiar news of the cycle of living and dying. All through the last notes my mind swarms with images of a world in which the thermonuclear bombs have begun to explode, in New York and San Francisco, in Moscow and Leningrad, in Paris, in Paris, in Paris. In Oxford and Cambridge, in Edinburgh. I cannot push away the thought of a cloud of radioactivity drifting along the Engadin, from the Moloja Pass to Ftan, killing off the part of the Earth I love more than any other part.

I am old enough by this time to be used to the notion of dying, saddened by the glimpse when it has occurred but only transiently knocked down, able to regain my feet quickly at the thought of continuity, any day. I have acquired and held in affection until very recently another sideline of an idea which serves me well at dark times: the life of the Earth is the same as the life of an organism: the great round being possesses a mind: the mind contains an infinite number of thoughts and memories: when I reach my time I may find myself still hanging

(continued)

around in some sort of midair, one of those small thoughts, drawn back into the memory of the Earth: in that peculiar sense I will be alive.

Now all that has changed. I cannot think that way anymore. Not while those things are still in place, aimed everywhere, ready for launching.

This is a bad enough thing for the people in my generation. We can put up with it, I suppose, since we must. We are moving along anyway, like it or not. I can even set aside my private fancy about hanging around, in midair.

What I cannot imagine, what I cannot put up with, the thought that keeps grinding its way into my mind, making the Mahler into a hideous noise close to killing me, is what it would be like to be young. How do the young stand it? How can they keep their sanity? If I were very young, sixteen or seventeen years old, I think I would begin, perhaps very slowly and imperceptibly, to go crazy.

There is a short passage near the very end of the Mahler in which the almost vanishing violins, all engaged in a sustained backward glance, are edged aside for a few bars by the cellos. Those lower notes pick up fragments from the first movement, as though prepared to begin everything all over again, and then the cellos subside and disappear, like an exhalation. I used to hear this as a wonderful few seconds of encouragement: we'll be back, we're still here, keep going, keep going.

Now, with a pamphlet in front of me on a corner of my desk, published by the Congressional Office of Technology Assessment, entitled "MX Basing," an analysis of all the alternative strategies for placement and protection of hundreds of these missiles, each capable of creating artificial suns to vaporize a hundred Hiroshimas, collectively capable of destroying the life of any continent, I cannot hear the same Mahler. Now, those cellos sound in my mind like the opening of all the hatches and the instant before ignition.

If I were sixteen or seventeen years old, I would not feel the cracking of my own brain, but I would know for sure that the whole world was coming unhinged. I can remember with some clarity what it was like to be sixteen. I had discovered the Brahms symphonies. I knew that there was something going on in the late Beethoven quartets that I would have to figure out, and I knew that there was plenty of time ahead for all the figuring I would ever have to do. I had never heard of Mahler. I was in no hurry. I was a college sophomore and had decided that Wallace Stevens and I possessed a comprehensive understanding of everything needed for a life. The years stretched away forever ahead, forever. My great-great grandfather had come from Wales, leaving his signature in the family Bible on the same page that carried, a century later, my father's signature. It never crossed my mind to wonder about the 21st century; it was just there, given, somewhere in the sure distance.

The man on television, Sunday midday, middle-aged and solid, nice-looking chap, all the facts at his fingertips, more dependable looking than most high-school principals, is talking about civilian defense, his responsibility in Washington. It can make an enormous difference, he is saying. Instead of the outright death of eighty million American citizens in twenty minutes, he says, we can, by careful planning and practice, get that number down to only forty million, maybe even twenty. The thing to do, he says, is to evacuate the cities quickly and have everyone get under shelter in the countryside. That way we can recover, and meanwhile we will have retaliated, incinerating all of Soviet society, he says. What about radioactive fallout, he is asked. Well, he says. Anyway, he says, if the Russians know they can only destroy forty million, this will deter them. Of course, he adds, they have the capacity to kill all two-hundred-and-twenty million of us if they were to try real hard, but they know we can do the same to them. If the figure is only forty million, this will deter them, not worth the trouble, not worth the risk. Eighty million would be another matter, we should guard ourselves against losing that many all at once, he says.

If I were sixteen or seventeen years old and had to listen to that, or read things like that, I would want to give up listening and reading. I would begin thinking up new kinds of sounds, different from any music heard before, and I would be twisting and turning to rid myself of human language.

From *Late Night Thoughts on Listening to Mahler's Ninth Symphony.* Copyright © 1982 by Lewis Thomas. Reprinted by permission of Viking Penguin, a division of Penguin Books USA Inc.

The threat of the end of the world had taken away some of the traditional consolations of the dying and bereaved, including three cultural conceptions of immortality: biosocial (immortality through reproduction); natural (immortality through the continuity of Nature); and creative (immortality through creative endeavors). It has forced people to reconsider their faith in the future, or to place their faith fully in spiritual immortality, a choice that is difficult in a secular society (Fulton and Gottesman, 1981).

AT A COUNTRY FUNERAL

Wendell Berry

Now the old ways that have brought us
farther than we remember sink out of sight
as under the treading of many strangers
ignorant of landmarks. Only once in a while
they are cast clear again upon the mind
as at a country funeral where, amid the soft
lights and hothouse flowers, the expensive
solemnity of experts, notes of a polite musician,

(continued)

persist the usages of old neighborhood.
Friends and kinsmen come and stand and speak,
knowing the extremity they have come to,
one of their own bearing to the earth the last
of his light, his darkness the sun's definitive mark.
They stand and think as they stood and thought
when even the gods were different.
And the organ music, though decorous
as for somebody else's grief, has its source
in the outcry of pain and hope in log churches,
and on naked hillsides by the open grave,
eastward in mountain passes, in tidelands,
and across the sea. How long a time?
Rock of Ages, cleft for me, let me hide my
self in Thee. They came, once in time,
in simple loyalty to their dead, and returned
to the world. The fields and the work
remained to be returned to. Now the entrance
of one of the old ones into the Rock
too often means a lifework perished from the land
without inheritor, and the field goes wild
and the house sits and stares. Or it passes
at cash value into the hands of strangers.
Now the old dead wait in the open coffin
for the blood kin to gather, come home
for one last time, to hear old men
whose tongues bear an essential topography
speak memories doomed to die.
But our memory of ourselves, hard earned,
is one of the land's seeds, as a seed
is the memory of the life of its kind in its place,
to pass on into life the knowledge
of what has died. What we owe the future is not a
new start, for we can only begin
with what has happened. We owe the future
the past, the long knowledge
that is the potency of time to come.
That makes of a man's grave a rich furrow.
The community of knowing in common is the seed
of our life in this place. There is not only
no better possibility, there is no
other, except for chaos and darkness,
the terrible ground of the only possible

new start. And so as the old die and the young
depart, where shall a man go who keeps
the memories of the dead, except home
again, as one would go back after a burial,
faithful to the fields, lest the dead die
a second and more final death.

From *The Country of Marriage,* copyright © 1971 by Wendell Berry, reprinted by permission of Harcourt Brace Jovanovich, Inc.

CONCLUSION

This historical approach to death has gone full circle from living death, to the dying of death, to the resurrection of death. This change of attitude has taken place over a 400-year period. One of the real assets of history is its ability to demonstrate causation and coincidence in human affairs by determining chronology and context.

In this chapter we have discussed bereavement and burial practices in the United States from the early beginnings of European settlement. While European influences were obviously present in this development, a "breaking away" from the European aristocracy is evidenced by middle-class Americans in the 1830s. Certainly various "isms" played significant roles in the shaping of American bereavement and burial practices. An historical perspective blends the various influences on the development of American death customs as we know them today.

With the developing of cemeteries, building of funeral homes, and the establishing of life insurance companies, certain needs of Americans have been fulfilled. Security comes from the sheer orderliness and structure of these "institutions." One should know what to "expect" from these services, and payment turns the responsibility over to the professionals. We Americans differ significantly from nonliterate societies where such functions are completed within the kin network. However, paying someone else to perform a service fits middle-class Americans' specialization and division of labor.

It is important that the consumer stay well informed about burial practices and insurance in our society through staying abreast of various funeral home regulations and different life insurance offerings. It is also significant with the threat of nuclear war that the public be well-informed and actively involved in seeking peace and avoiding such a war. Perhaps this recent "resurrection of death" in an atomic age will be history behind us that will not continue into the future.

SUMMARY

1. Historians mainly determine chronology and context in order to demonstrate causation and coincidence in human affairs.
2. Rural Americans between 1600 and 1930 were well acquainted with death; it was commonplace.
3. The Reformed Tradition of the Protestant Reformation stressed that death and damnation were deserved, but God had elected a select few for salvation. Thus, death was approached with ambivalence.
4. Death was feared by the Puritans, who prayed not for the soul of the deceased but for the comfort and instruction of the living. The funeral was the main social institution for channeling the grief of Puritan survivors.
5. The Enlightenment replaced depraved dependent Puritans with rational people who viewed death as a natural occurrence rather than a time of judgment. Unitarianism and Evangelicalism accepted this view of human nature.
6. Between 1830 and 1945, as a middle-class America emerged, "the dying of death" occurred as funeral institutions designed to keep death out of sight and mind appeared.
7. Important intellectual influences on "the dying of death" were romanticism, sentimentalism, scientific naturalism, and liberal religion.
8. At the middle of the 19th century, the rural cemetery evolved—a landscaped garden in a suburban setting. Life insurance was established at this time to remove anxiety and financial insecurity.
9. Death was resurrected after 1945 with the ushering in of the atomic age.

DISCUSSION QUESTIONS

1. Describe and discuss the Puritan view of death. Describe the procedures and atmosphere surrounding the typical Puritan funeral.
2. How did the Enlightenment affect the Reformed Tradition of funerals and view of death?
3. Discuss influences of the following on the "Dying of Death": romanticism, sentimentalism, scientific naturalism, and liberal theology.
4. What are the influences of the following occupations upon the "Dying of Death": life insurance agents, cemetery superintendents, and funeral directors.

5. Describe and explain the reforms that have taken place over the years in the construction and maintenance of the cemetery.
6. What effect has the dropping of the atom bomb had on American death conceptions?
7. Describe the changes that have taken place with regard to the role of the family in the funeral process.

GLOSSARY

Elegy: A song or poem expressing sorrow, especially for one who is dead.

Epitaph: An inscription, often on a tombstone, in memory of a deceased person.

Obituary: Notice of a death, usually with a brief biography.

Ritual: A behavioral form prescribed by custom or law, often associated with religion.

Sexton: A church custodian charged with the upkeep of the church and parish buildings and grounds.

Socialization: The learning process through which an individual is taught to be accepted in his or her society.

Social Stratification: A ranking of social status (position) in groups; upper, middle, and lower classes are basically distinguished in the U.S. social class system, for example, while India's stratification is a caste system.

Term Life Insurance: A type of insurance policy covering the insured for a fixed period of time (five, ten, twenty or so years). Premiums are usually lower for a greater amount of coverage than for other types of life insurance.

Universal Life Insurance: A policy that is flexible and allows one to raise or reduce premiums and the amount of coverage on one's life.

Variable Life Insurance: A type of insurance that does not allow for the premium or minimum coverage on one's life to change but allows one to switch the savings from among money-markets or various forms of stock.

Whole Life Insurance: A type of insurance in which, for a set annual premium, one receives life insurance coverage and, at the same time, invests one's money.

REFERENCES

Abbott, Lyman. 1913. "There Are No Dead." *Outlook*, 104 (August 30):979–980.

Association of American Cemetery Superintendents. 1889. 3, p. 59.

Barrett, William. 1958. *Irrational Man: A Study in Existential Philosophy*. New York: Doubleday.

Beecher, Henry Ward. 1858. *Life Thoughts*. Boston: Phillips, Sampson.

Beecher, Henry Ward. 1859. *Notes from Plymouth Pulpit*. New York: Derby and Jackson.

Bender, Thomas. 1973. "The 'Rural Cemetery' Movement." *New England Quarterly*, 47 (June):196–211.

Benjamin, Charles L. 1882. "Essay." *The Casket*, 7(February):2.

Bledstein, Burton J. 1976. *The Culture of Professionalism: The Middle Class and the Development of Higher Education in America*. New York: Norton.

Clark, Jr., Clifford E. 1978. *Henry Ward Beecher: Spokesman for a Middle-Class America*. Urbana, IL: University of Illinois Press.

Cleaveland, Nehemiah. 1847. *Green-Wood Illustrated*. New York: R. Martin.

de Tocqueville, Alexis. 1945. *Democracy in America* (Originally published 1835.) New York: Vintage Books.

Douglas, Ann. 1977. *The Feminization of American Culture*. New York: Knopf.

Dowd, Quincy L. 1921. *Funeral Management and Costs: A World-Survey of Burial and Cremation*. Chicago: University of Chicago Press.

Downing, Andrew Jackson. 1921. *Landscape Gardening*, 10th ed. New York: Wiley.

"The Dying of Death." 1899. *Review of Reviews*, 20(September):364–365.

Emmons, Nathaniel. 1842. "Death without Order." In *The Works of Nathaniel Emmons*, 3, Jacob Ide (Ed.). Boston: Crocker and Brewster.

"Extracts." 1895. *Park and Cemetery*, 5(August):108.

Farrell, James J. 1980. *Inventing the American Way of Death, 1830–1920*. Philadelphia: Temple University Press.

"The Fear of Death." 1912. *Harper's Weekly*, 56(October 5):21.

French, Stanley. 1975. "The Establishment of Mount Auburn and the 'Rural Cemetery' Movement." In *Death in America*. Philadelphia: University of Pennsylvania Press.

Fulton, Robert, and David J. Gottesman. 1981. "Loss, Social Change and the Prospect of Mourning." Unpublished paper.

"Funeral Directors." 1883. *The Casket*, 8(June).

Gebhart, John C. 1927. *The Reasons for Present-Day Funeral Costs*. Unpublished.

Geddes, Gordon. 1981. *Welcome Joy: Death in Puritan New England*. Ann Arbor, MI: U.M.I. Research Press.

Greenwald, David S., and Steven J. Zeitlin. 1987. *No Reason to Talk About It: Families Confront the Nuclear Taboo*. New York: W. W. Norton.

Gross, Robert A. 1976. *The Minutemen and Their World*. New York: Hill and Wang.

Habenstein, Robert W., and William M. Lamers. 1962. "The Pattern of Late 19th Century Funerals." *The History of American Funeral Directing*. Milwaukee: Bulfin.

Hale, Nathan G. 1971. *The Origin and Foundations of the Psychoanalytic Movement in the United States, 1876–1918*. New York: Oxford University Press.

Handford, Thomas W. (Ed.) 1887. *Beecher: Christian Philosopher, Pulpit Orator, Patriot and Philanthropist*. Chicago: Donahue, Henneberry.

Hare, Sidney J. 1910. "The Cemetery Beautiful." *Association of American Cemetery Superintendents,* 24:41.

Hay, Mrs. E. E. 1900. "Influence of Our Surroundings." *Association of American Cemetery Superintendents,* 14:46.

Hillerman, Barbara. 1980. "Chrysallis of Gloom: Nineteenth Century Mourning Costume." In *A Time to Mourn: Expressions of Grief in Nineteenth Century America,* Martha V. Pike and Janice Gray Armstrong (Eds.). Stony Brook, NY: The Museums at Stony Brook.

Hohenschuh, W. P. 1921. *The Modern Funeral: Its Management.* Chicago: Trade Periodical Company.

Howe, Daniel Walker. 1970. *The Unitarian Conscience: Harvard University Press, 1805–1861.* Cambridge: Harvard University Press.

Hutchinson, Woods. 1893. "Death As a Factor in Progress." *North American Review,* 156(May):637.

"The Ideas of a Plain Country Woman." 1913. *Ladies Home Journal,* 30(April):42.

Johnson, J. B. 1896. "A More Rational View of Death." *Proceedings of the Association of American Cemetery Superintendents.* Association of American Cemetery Superintendents, 10:77.

Lifton, Robert Jay, and Richard Falk. 1982. *Indefensible Weapons: The Political and Psychological Case Against Nuclearism.* New York: Harper and Row.

Lloyd, Phoebe. 1980. "Posthumous Mourning Portraiture." In *A Time to Mourn: Expressions of Grief in Nineteenth Century America,* Martha V. Pike and Janice Gray Armstrong (Eds.). Stony Brook, NY: The Museums at Stony Brook.

Ludwig, Allen. 1966. *Graven Images: New England Stonecarving and its Symbols.* Middletown, CT: Wesleyan University Press.

"The Man Nobody Envies: An Account of the Experiences of an Undertaker." 1914. *American Magazine,* 77(June):68–71.

Mayo, Wyndham R. 1916. "Address." *Association of American Cemetery Superintendents,* 2:51.

Mumford, Lewis. 1947. "Atom Bomb: Social Effects." *Air Affairs,* 1(March):370–382. Reprinted as "Assumptions and Predictions," in *In the Name of Sanity,* 1954. New York: Norton, pp. 10–33.

Oxley, J. MacDonald. 1887. "The Reproach of Mourning." *Forum,* 2(February):608–614.

Pike, Martha V., and Janice Gray Armstrong (Eds.). 1980. *A Time to Mourn: Expressions of Grief in Nineteenth Century America.* Stony Brook, NY: The Museums at Stony Brook.

Rosenberg, Charles E. 1973. "Sexuality, Class, and Role in Nineteenth Century America." *American Quarterly,* 25(May):137.

Rotundo, Barbara. 1973. "The Rural Cemetery Movement." *Essex Institute Historical Collections,* 109(July):231–242.

Sargent, A. H. 1888. "Country Cemeteries." *Association of American Cemetery Superintendents,* 2:51.

Seavoy, Mr. 1906. "Twentieth Century Methods." *Park and Cemetery,* 15(February):488.

Sewall, Samuel. 1973. *The Diary of Samuel Sewall,* M. Halsey Thomas (Ed.). 2 vol. New York: Farrar, Straus and Giroux.

Shneidman, Edwin. 1973. "Megadeath: Children of the Nuclear Family." *Deaths of Man.* Baltimore: Penguin Books.

Simonds, O. C. 1919. "Review of Progress in Cemetery Design and Development with Suggestions for the Future." *Association of American Cemetery Superintendents,* 24:41.

Smith, Bayley. 1910. "An Outdoor Room on a Cemetery Lot." *Country Life in America,* 17(March):539.

Smith, Marguerite T. 1988. "Why You Might Go for a Cash-Value Policy." *Money,* December, pp. 153–161.

Stannard, David E. 1980. "Where All Our Steps Are Tending: Death in the American Context." In *A Time to Mourn: Expressions of Grief in Nineteenth Century America,* Martha V. Pike and Janice Gray Armstrong (Eds.). Stony Brook, NY: The Museums at Stony Brook.

Taylor, Lawrence. 1980. "Symbolic Death: An Anthropological View of Mourning Ritual in the Nineteenth Century." In *A Time to Mourn: Expressions of Grief in Nineteenth Century America,* Martha V. Pike and Janice Gray Armstrong (Eds.). Stony Brook, NY: The Museums at Stony Brook.

Tuckerman, Henry. 1856. "The Law of Burial and the Sentiment of Death." *Christian Examiner,* 61(November):338–342.

U.S. Bureau of the Census. 1975. *Historical Statistics of the United States, Colonial Times to 1970,* pp. 1050–1059. Washington, DC: Department of Commerce, Bureau of the Census.

Warner, W. Lloyd. 1959. *The Living and the Dead.* New Haven: Yale University Press.

Weed, Howard Evarts. 1912. *Modern Park Cemeteries.* Chicago: R. J. Haight.

Wells, Richard A. 1887. *Decorum: A Practical Treatise on Etiquette and Dress of the Best American Society.* Springfield, MA: King, Richardson.

SUGGESTED READINGS

Bailey, Brian. 1987. *Churchyards of England and Wales.* Bristol, GB: WBC Printers. *Discusses the origin and history of churchyards, legends surrounding them, and traditions and rituals. Includes over a hundred photographs and drawings.*

Farrell, James. 1980. *Inventing the American Way of Death, 1830–1920.* Philadelphia: Temple University Press. *Examines the transformation from the Puritan Way of Death to the American Way of Death. Includes intellectual and institutional changes, and concludes with a case study of how such changes affected a single county.*

Geddes, Gordon. 1981. *Welcome Joy: Death in Puritan New England.* Ann Arbor, MI: U.M.I. Research Press. *Good descriptive study, rich in detail. Particularly good on the Puritan funeral and bereavement.*

Habenstein, Robert, and William Lamers. 1962. *The History of American Funeral Directing.* Milwaukee: Bulfin. *Prepared for the National Funeral Directors Association, this detailed study is a good history of the development of the profession.*

Jackson, Charles O. (Ed.) 1977. *Passing: the Vision of Death in America.* Westport, CT: Greenwood Press. *A collection of classic essays on death in America, a few of which have been superseded by more recent work in the area.*

Pike, Martha, and Janice Gray Armstrong (Eds.). 1980. *A Time to Mourn: Expressions of Grief in Nineteenth Century America.* Stony Brook, NY: The Museums at Stony Brook. *A beautifully illustrated collection of excellent essays, a must for anyone who wants to see and feel the grief of 19th-century America.*

Sloane, David Charles. 1991. *The Last Great Necessity: Cemeteries in American History.* Baltimore: Johns Hopkins University Press. *Explores changing attitudes about cemeteries as well as changing landscapes. Describes many of America's most famous cemeteries.*

Stannard, David (Ed.). 1975. *Death in America.* Philadelphia: University of Pennsylvania Press. *The December 1974 special issue of* American Quarterly, *with an added essay on the cemetery as a cultural institution, by Stanley French.*

Chapter
12

The Funeral: Expression of Contemporary American Bereavement

*You must express your grief at the loss of a loved one and then you must go on.
The eyes of the dead must be gently closed and the eyes of the living must be
gently opened.*

Jan Brugler
Indian Lake, Ohio, high school student

MOST ANTHROPOLOGISTS agree that there has been no civilization discovered and studied that has not in some form given social recognition of death through a process involving activities, rites, and rituals associated with the final disposition of the deceased's body. This process varies greatly from culture to culture, but the basic elements of the recognition of the death—a rite or ritual and the final disposition of the body—have their counterparts in every culture. As we concluded in Chapter 10, funeral rituals allow individuals of every culture to maintain relations with ancestors, while uniting family members, reinforcing social status, fostering group cohesiveness, and restoring the social structure of the society.

SOCIAL AND CULTURAL ROOTS OF AMERICAN FUNERAL TRADITIONS

In contemporary American culture, the process of final disposition of the body should be studied within its cultural and historical context. As we discovered in Chapter 10, it is wrong to believe that the funeral is either unique to Western culture, or has been invented or created by it. To bury the dead is a common social practice. The methods to accomplish burial, and the meanings associated with it, are culturally determined.

This process requires the involvement of a functionary, who may be a professional, tradesperson, religious leader, servant, or even a member of the family. The functionary in each society is closely associated with the folkways and mores of the culture and its philosophical approach to life and death.

The Hebrew scripture reveals in the 50th chapter of Genesis (verse 2) that physicians embalmed the body of Jacob, the father of Joseph. This is followed by a detailed description of the funeral and burial. The historian Herodotus records embalming preparation as early as circa 484 B.C. These two documents and archaeological discoveries of earlier cultures give evidence of the disposition of the dead.

The most elaborate and famous burial customs were those of the Egyptians.

It is often stated that Egypt had a secret process for the preservation of the dead. The Egyptian embalming process, however, is fully described in several sources. There is perhaps no ancient culture that provides more evidence of its burial procedures than the great number of Egyptian mummies available for observation and study.

The Egyptians believed that the soul made a journey following death. According to their beliefs, this journey took approximately 3000 years followed by the soul's returning to the body it had left. This belief required the preservation of the body so that the soul, upon its return, would have a final destination. In addition to

DEATH IN ANCIENT EGYPT

A. J. Spencer

The earliest burials known in Egypt date to a period well before 3000 B.C. and display evidence, through funerary gifts in the graves, of a belief of continued existence after death. The earliest graves were very simple affairs consisting of shallow circular or oval pits in the ground where the body was placed in a fetal position. The introduction of methods to protect the body from the filling of the pit was motivated by a desire to improve the conditions for the dead.

During the middle and late Predynastic Period (before 3100 B.C.) the practice of wrapping the body in animal skins gradually gave way to other forms of protection, particularly the use of basket trays upon which the body was laid

(continued)

out. Wooden coffins, made of rough planks joined by dowels, became common by the end of the Predynastic Period (circa 3200 B.C.). By the beginning of the Fourth Dynasty (2613 B.C.), a significant number of burials occurred in which the body was placed in a coffin in a fully extended position.

The main advance in Predynastic tomb design (before 3100 B.C.) was the gradual introduction of wood-roofed graves, thus creating an underground chamber within which the coffin could be placed and separated from the sand. The pits were often lined with mud-plaster or wood therefore providing an additional barrier between the body and the ground. An important consequence of the added separation between the body and the filling of the grave, however, was the loss of the natural preservative effects of direct contact with the dry sand which served to preserve some of the soft tissues through rapid drying.

Wrapped bodies of the first three dynasties were not truly mummified, since no treatment other than the use of linen bandages and resin was employed. By the Fourth Dynasty, however, evidence was found of deliberate attempts to inhibit decomposition by removal of the soft internal organs from the body—accomplished by means of an incision in the side of the abdomen. Removal of the liver, intestines, and stomach improved the chances of securing good preservation because the emptied body-cavity could be dried more rapidly. The removed organs were deposited in a safe place in the tomb in order for the body of the deceased to be complete once more in the netherworld.

Bandages soaked in resin were carefully molded to the shape of the body in order to reproduce the features, particularly in the face and the genital organs. As the resin dried, it consolidated the linen wrapping in position, preserving the appearance of the body for as long as it remained undisturbed. The corpse itself decomposed very rapidly within this linen shell, leaving the innermost wrappings in close contact with the skeleton.

An important factor in the development of the Egyptian tomb was the necessity to provide storage space for the items of funerary equipment considered essential for continued use by the deceased in the hereafter. A significant part of the material provided for the dead took the form of actual offerings of food and drink—required for the "very survival" of the deceased before enjoying all the other possessions in the tomb. Because of the need to provide offerings of food at the tomb, the tomb had to combine the function of a burial-place with that of a mortuary chapel in which the priests could officiate.

The Egyptians believed there were two main spiritual forms of the deceased. The Ka was supposed to dwell in the tomb in the mummified body. The Ba was usually represented as a human-headed bird, which left the body at the time of death, and was free to travel in the tomb during the daytime but returned to dwell in the mummy at night. The Predynastic cultures may have believed that continued existence after death resembled earthly life, also a popular belief in later times.

Death in Ancient Egypt. New York: Penguin Books, 1982.

the embalming procedures, the Egyptians attempted to exclude air and moisture from the body by the liberal use of wrappings, oils, and gums. They also practiced elaborate encasement and burial of the remains. Such attempts at body preservation were obviously effective as evidenced by the many specimens still in existence today.

In many cultures the religious beliefs of the people influence their funeral and burial practices. Such was the case on the European continent during the medieval period of the feudal estates. Each landholder or lord was responsible for the people who worked for him and were members of the lord's extended family. These lords had a chaplain or religious person as a part of their staff, and they became responsible for the care and burial of the dead.

In the structure of the Christian church, priests were assigned to certain duties during specified hours. It is suggested that our use of the word *sexton* today comes from the practice of assigning the priest in charge of the sixth hour (in Latin, *sex*) with the burial of the dead and the supervision of the churchyard or cemetery.

As Western civilization developed and progressed, there is evidence that many of the functionaries were anatomists, doctors, or artists. Each profession wanted to preserve the human body to further its own interests and offered to do so in return for the availability of bodies for study and research. Still in existence today are anatomical plates that Leonardo daVinci drew from his observations of human specimens.

With the advent of the discovery of the circulatory system of the body, circa 1600, and the possibility of diffusion of preserving chemicals through that system, more sophisticated methods of embalming the body were developed. Dr. Hunter of England and Dr. Gannal of France, independently of each other, furthered the process in the early 1600s. In France, this work coincided with the advent of the bubonic plague. During this period of time, extensive attempts were made to preserve the bodies of the dead to protect the health of those who survived the plague.

Historically, through a considerable period of time, the pattern of mortuary behavior in any society is subject to change, although basic death beliefs remain fundamentally unchanged. The roots of American funeral behavior extend back in a direct line several thousand years to early Judeo-Christian beliefs as to the nature of God, man, and the hereafter, and, in turn, these beliefs and practices were influenced to some extent by even earlier beliefs and practices.

Robert W. Habenstein and William M. Lamers, *The History of American Funeral Directing.* Milwaukee: Bulfin, 1962.

EARLY AMERICAN FUNERAL PRACTICES

During the colonization of America, early evidence exists of the care and burial of the dead. There is, however, no evidence of any attempt at body preservation, even though the body was bathed and dressed prior to burial. This was usually done by nurses, midwives, or members of the family. It was not until the time of the Civil War that embalming was promoted to temporarily preserve the body for return to the soldier's home. Some reports credit this practice to a military doctor by the name of Thomas Holmes. It was not until the late 1800s and early 1900s that states began to promote the practice of embalming to protect the public's health. With the advent of the practice of embalming, laws were soon passed to regulate both the practice and the practitioner.

The current practitioner of the funeral profession evolved from the artisan or cabinetmaker (invariably a man who built the casket as part of his trade) and the livery owner (who provided the special vehicles needed at the time of the funeral—particularly the hearse and special buggies for the family). As the public came to expect the services associated with the casket and transportation, persons began to specialize in providing these services, and the funeral functionary of today evolved as a provider of these services.

With the development of contemporary funeral practices over the past 90 years, it is interesting to observe the kind of facilities evolving to provide these services. It was not customary to hold funerals in the church in colonial America. The Puritans gave little importance to the funeral and seemed only to demand proper and reverent disposition of the dead by burial. Almost without exception, death occurred in the home. It was, therefore, expected that the dead would be bathed,

NEW FUNERAL OPTION FOR THOSE IN A RUSH

Isabel Wilkerson

The convenience and high technology of drive-through banks and hamburger places have come to the funeral world. A Chicago funeral home has set up a drive-through service with cameras and a sound system that let on-the-go visitors pay their respects, sign the funeral register and view the remains of the loved one round the clock without ever leaving the car.

Carloads of working people pressed for time, as well as bus loads of senior citizens confined to wheelchairs, have paraded through the drive-in at Gatling's Funeral Home on the city's South Side to see the images of embalmed friends and relatives on a television screen covered by a white canopy that is lit up at night.

The owner, Lafayette Gatling, a former construction worker who says he used to feel uncomfortable himself paying his respects in soiled work clothes, added the drive-through service two years ago. "The working person doesn't have time to come in," Mr. Gatling said. "They want to see the body but they don't want to have to wait. I always thought there should be some way they could see the body any time they want."

The procedure goes something like this: Visitors, cautioned to drive through slowly, ride to a speakerphone and push a button for service. An attendant in a control room asks whom they wish to see. "I would like to view the remains of John Doe," the visitor says into the speakerphone. "You may proceed," the attendant says, using controls to turn on the lights and cameras over the body of the deceased lying in one of the rooms.

The motorist then signs the register, conveniently tucked underneath the speakerphone, and drives a couple of feet to the viewing area where a head shot of the loved one in a coffin instantly appears on a 25-inch screen. The picture lasts three seconds, but visitors can push a button to request to see the loved one over and over again, and some stare at the screen for half an hour. When the car moves on, the next in line takes its place.

The feature has been a hit with visitors, who are used to ordering hamburgers and fries from a drive-through, a comparison that Mr. Gatling finds insulting. "We're dealing with remains here—I wouldn't compare that with food," Mr. Gatling said. "The only thing similar is the speaker system."

Drive-up windows displaying a single coffin came on the scene briefly several years ago at a few funeral homes in Florida and California, but there have been none using the complex system of relays, switches and timers needed to accommodate requests to see as many as a dozen bodies as the Gatling Funeral Home allows.

Mr. Gatling is now seeking a patent for the system. And he is planning bigger and better things for his funeral home, which already sells flowers and sympathy cards for mourners who forgot theirs and holds weddings in the main chapel on off-days. In addition to adding more chapels and parlors, he plans to make videotapes of the remains and the funeral services, which he hopes to sell to the bereaved.

Others worry about what all this convenience could do to the funeral business. "You could have the curious going through and checking out who happens to be laid out today," said W. Timothy Simms, president-elect of the Illinois Funeral Directors Association. "It lends a circus atmosphere to the services. It seems we're in a changing world."

Bernard Beck, an associate professor of sociology at Northwestern University, agreed, saying: "There seems to be no end to the need to save time. There has been a loosening of our communal ties. Still this is a way of putting in an appearance."

dressed, put in a casket, and laid out (viewed) in the home. The funeral rite was either in the home or at the gravesite. When the first practitioners began to specialize in the burial of the dead, they continued to use the home for this purpose. They often would acquire a large house in the community and convert it to use as a "funeral home." It should be noted that the word *home* was associated with this facility, and today is still the most commonly used term to describe funeral facilities.

It was only natural that with specialization, special facilities would be developed for the funeral ceremony. The influence of the family and the church is readily seen in that most facilities try to provide both a home-like atmosphere for the gathering of the community and a chapel-like atmosphere for the funeral service. If the family chooses not to use a church for the funeral service, the funeral home provides a similar setting. Approximately 50 percent of the funerals are currently held in churches, and the remaining 50 percent are held in funeral homes or cemetery chapels (National Funeral Directors Association, 1986). The Department of Commerce of the United States Government estimates that approximately 23,500 funeral homes serve the families of the approximately 2.1 million annual deaths (NFDA, 1991).

THE DECLINE OF MOURNING

A decade ago, anthropologist Geoffrey Gorer wrote a much reprinted article on "the pornography of death." Gorer's point, also made by German theologian Helmuth Thielicke, is that death is coming to have the same position in modern life and literature that sex had in Victorian times. Some support for the theory is provided by the popular movie *The Loved One*, which turns death into a slapstick dirty joke.

Is grief going underground? People want briefer funeral services, says Dr. Quentin Hand, an ordained Methodist minister who teaches at the theological school of Georgia's Emory University. "No one wants a eulogy any more—they often ask me not to even mention Mother or Father." Even those much scolded death-deniers, the undertakers, seem to sense that something is missing. Dean Robert Lehr of the Gupton Jones College of Mortuary Science in Dallas says that whereas students used to study only embalming, they now go in heavily for "grief psychology and grief counseling." Explains Lehr: "There are only 16 quarter hours in embalming now and 76 in other areas. We're in a transition period."

The outward signs of mourning—veils and widow's weeds, black hat and armbands, crepe-hung doorways—are going the way of the hearse pulled by plumed horses. There is almost no social censure against remarrying a few months after bereavement in what one psychiatrist calls "the Elizabeth Taylorish way" (referring to her statement six months after husband Mike Todd was killed in a plane crash: "Mike is dead now, and I am alive"). Many psychologists who have no quarrel with the life-must-continue attitude are dubious about the decline in expression of grief. Psychology Professor Harry W. Martin of Texas Southwestern Medical School deplores the "slick, smooth operation of easing the corpse out, but saying no to weeping and wailing and expressing grief and loneliness. What effect does this have on us psychologically? It may mean that we have to mourn covertly, by subterfuge—perhaps in various degrees of depression, perhaps in mad flights of activity, perhaps in booze." In his book, *Death, Grief and Mourning*, anthropologist Gorer warns that abandonment of the traditional forms of mourning results in "callousness, irrational preoccupation with and fear of death, and vandalism."

Whether or not such conclusions are justified, the take-it-in-stride attitude can make things difficult. Gorer cites his brother's widow, a New Englander, whose emotional reticence, combined with that of her British friends, led her to eschew any outward signs of mourning. As a result, "she let herself be, almost literally, eaten up with grief, sinking into a deep and long-lasting depression." Many a widow invited to a party "to take her mind off things" has embarrassed herself and her hostess by a flood of tears at the height of the festivities. On occasion, Gorer himself "refused invitations to cocktail parties, explaining that I was mourning; people responded to this statement with shocked embarrassment, as if I had voiced some appalling obscenity."

Funerals seem ever harder to get to in a high-pressure, computerized way of life. But the social repression of grief goes against the experience of the human race. Mourning is one of the traditional "rites of passage" through which families and tribes can rid themselves of their dead and return to normal living. Black funeral parades, Greek klama (ritual weeping), Irish wakes each in their own way fulfills this function. Orthodox Jewish families are supposed to "sit *shiv'ah*"; for seven days after the burial they stay home, wearing some symbol of a "shredded garment," such as a piece of torn cloth, and keeping an unkempt appearance. Friends bring food as a symbol of the inability of the bereaved to concern themselves with practical affairs. For eleven months sons are enjoined to say the prayers for the dead in the synagogue twice a day.

By no means all observers agree that the decline of such demanding customs is a bad thing. The old rituals, while a comfort and release for some, could be a burden to others. And grief expressed in private can be more meaningful than the external forms. London psychiatrist Dr. David Stafford-Clark thinks that the new attitude toward death should be considered in the context of "the way the whole structure of life has changed since World War II, particularly the very different attitude toward the future which has arisen. It is a much more expectant attitude—an uncertain one, but not necessarily a more negative one."

"On Death as a Constant Companion," *Time Magazine*, November 12, 1965. Copyright 1965 Time Inc. Reprinted by permission.

The Contemporary American Funeral

Most people use the words *death, grief,* and *bereavement* confusedly, which can lead to difficulty in communication. The words are closely interrelated, but each has a specific content or meaning. As discussed in Chapter 1, death is that point in time when life ceases to exist. *Death* is an event. It can be attached to a certain day, hour, and minute. *Grief* is an emotion, a very powerful emotion. It is triggered or stimulated by death. Although one can have anticipatory grief prior to the death of a significant other, grief is an emotional response to death. *Bereavement* is the state of having lost a significant other to death. Alternative processes—such as denial, avoidance, and defiance—have been shown by psychologists and psychiatrists to be only aberrations of the grief process and, as such, are not viable means of grief resolution.

The ultimate method of final disposition of the body should be determined by the persons in bereavement. Those charged with these decisions will be guided by their personal values and by the norms of the culture in which they live.

With over two-thirds of American deaths occurring in hospitals or institutions for the care of the sick and infirm, the contemporary process of body disposition begins at the time of death when the body is removed from the institutional setting. Most frequently the body is taken to a funeral home. There, the body is bathed, embalmed, and dressed. It is then placed in a casket selected by the family. Typically, arrangements are made for the ceremony, assuming a ceremony is to follow. The funeral director, in consultation with the family, will determine the type, time, place, and day of the ceremony. In most instances, the public rite or ceremony will have a religious content (Pine, 1971). The procedure described above is followed in approximately 75 percent of funerals. Alternatives to this procedure will be examined later in this chapter.

Following this ceremony, final **disposition** of the body is made by either earth burial (78 percent), cremation (17 percent), or entombment (5 percent). (These percentages are approximate national averages and will vary by geographical

REPRINTED BY PERMISSION OF JOHNNY HART AND NAS, INC.

region.) The bereavement process will then be followed by a period of postfuneral adjustment for the family.

HOW THE FUNERAL MEETS THE NEEDS OF THE BEREAVED

Paul Irion (1956) has described the following needs of the bereaved: reality, expression of grief, social support, and meaningful context to the death. For Irion, the funeral is an experience of significant personal value insofar as it meets the religious, social, and psychological needs of the mourners. Each of these dimensions is necessary to return bereaved individuals to everyday living and, in the process, resolve their grief.

The *psychological* focus of the funeral is based on the fact that grief is an emotion. Edgar Jackson (1963) has indicated that grief is the other side of the coin of love. He contends that if a person has never loved the deceased—had an emotional investment of some type and degree—he or she will not grieve upon death. Evidence of this can easily be demonstrated by the number of deaths that we hear, see, or read about daily that do not have an impact on us unless we have some kind of emotional involvement with those deceased persons. We can read of 78 deaths in a plane crash and not grieve over any of them unless we personally knew one or more of the individuals killed. Exceptions to the above might include the death of a celebrity or public figure, when people experience a sense of grief even though there has never been any personal contact.

In his original work on the symptomatology of grief, Erich Lindemann (1944) stressed this concept of grief and its importance as a step in the resolution of grief. He defines how the emotion of grief must support the reality and finality of death. As long as the finality of death is avoided, Lindemann believes grief resolution is impeded. For this reason, he strongly recommends that the bereaved persons view the dead. When the living confront the dead, all of the intellectualization and avoidance techniques break down. When we can say, "He or she is dead, I am alone, and from this day forward my life will be forever different," we have broken through the devices of denial and avoidance and have accepted the reality of death. It is only at this point that we can begin to withdraw the emotional capital that we have invested in the deceased and seek to create new relationships with the living.

On the other hand, viewing the corpse can be very traumatic for some. Most people are not accustomed to seeing a cold body and a significant other stretched out with eyes closed. Indeed, for some this scene may remain in their memories for a lifetime. Thus, they remember the cold corpse, not the warm, responsive person. Whether or not to view the body is not a cut-and-dried issue. Many factors should be taken into account when this decision is made.

Grief resolution is especially important for family members, but others are affected also—the neighbors, the business community in some instances, the religious community in most instances, the health-care community, and the circle of friends and associates (many of whom may be unknown to the family). All of these groups will grieve to some extent the death of their relationship with the deceased. Thus, many people are affected by the death. These affected persons will seek not only a means of expressing their grief over the death but also a network of support to help cope with their grief.

Sociologically, the funeral is a social event that brings the chief mourners and the members of society into a confrontation with death. The funeral becomes a vehicle to bring persons of all walks of life and degrees of relationship to the deceased together in one place for expression and support. It is for this reason that in our contemporary culture the funeral becomes an occasion to which no one is invited but all may come. This was not always the case, and some cultures make the funeral ceremony an "invitation only" experience. It is perhaps for this reason that private funerals (restricted only to the family or a special list of persons) have all but disappeared in our culture. (The possible exception to this statement is the funeral for a celebrity—where participation for the general public is limited to media coverage.)

At a time when emotions are strong, it is important that human interaction and social support become a high priority. A funeral can provide this atmosphere. To grieve alone can be devastating because it becomes necessary for that lone person to absorb all of the feelings into him- or herself. It has often been said that "joy shared is joy increased"; surely grief shared will be grief diminished. People need each other at times when they have intense emotional experiences.

A funeral is in essence a one-time kind of "support group" to undergird and support those grieving persons. A funeral provides a conducive social environment for mourning. We may either go to the funeral home to visit with the bereaved or for the purpose of working through our own feelings of grief. Most of us have had the experience of finding it difficult for the first time to discuss the death with a member of the family. We seek the proper atmosphere, time, or place. It is during the funeral, the wake, the shiv'ah, or the visitation with the bereaved where we are provided the opportunity to express our condolences and sympathy comfortably.

Anger and guilt are often deeply felt at the time of death and will surface in words and actions. They are permitted within the funeral atmosphere as honest and candid expressions of grief, when at other times, they might bring criticism and reprimand. The funeral atmosphere says in essence "You are okay, I am okay; we have some strong feelings, and now is the time to express and share them for the benefit of all." Silence, talking, touching, feeling, and all means of sharing can be expressed without the fear of it being inappropriate.

Another function of the funeral is to provide a *theological* or *philosophical* perspective to facilitate grieving and provide a context of meaning in which to place one of life's most significant experiences. For the majority of Americans, the funeral is a religious rite or ceremony (Pine, 1971). For those who do not possess a religious creed or orientation, death will find definition or expression in the context of the values that the deceased and the grievers find important. Theologically or philosophically, the funeral functions as an attempt to bring meaning to the death and life of the deceased individual. For the religiously oriented person, it will perhaps contain a belief or understanding of an afterlife. For others, it may be seen only as an end of biological life and the beginning of symbolic immortality caused by the effects of one's life on the lives of others. The funeral should be planned in order to give meaning to whichever value context is significant for the bereaved.

"Why?" is one of the most often asked questions at the moment of death or upon being told that someone we know has died. Though it cannot provide the final answer to this question, the funeral can place death within a context of meaning that is significant to those who mourn. If it is religious in context, the theology, creed, and articles of faith confessed by the mourners will give them comfort and assurance as to the meaning of death. Others who have developed a personally meaningful philosophy of life and death will seek to place the death in that philosophical context.

Cultural expectations require that we typically dispose of the dead with ceremony and dignity. The funeral can also ascribe importance to the remains of the dead.

The Needs of Children and Their Attendance at Funerals

For children, as well as their adult counterparts, the funeral ceremony can be an experience of value and significance. At a very early age, children are interested in any type of family reunion, party, or celebration. To be excluded from the funeral may create questions and doubts in the mind of children as to why they are not permitted to be a part of an important family activity.

Another consideration in denying the child an opportunity to participate in post-death activities is what goes through the child's mind when such participation is denied. Children deal with other difficult situations in life, and when denied this opportunity, many will fantasize. Research suggests that these fantasies may be negative, destructive, and at times more traumatic than the situation from which the child is excluded.

Children also should not be excluded from activities prior to the funeral service. They should be permitted to attend the visitation, wake, or shiv'ah. (In some situations it would be wise to permit children to confront the deceased prior to the public visitation.) It is obvious that children should not be forced into this type of confrontation, but, by the same token, children who are curious and desire to be involved should not be denied the opportunity.

Children will react at their own emotional levels, and the questions they ask will usually be asked at their level of comprehension. Two important rules follow: Never lie to the child, and do not overanswer the child's question.

At the time of the funeral, parents have two concerns about their children's behavior at funerals. The first is that they are worried that the child will have difficulty observing the grief of others—particularly if the child has never seen an adult loved one cry. The second is that parents themselves become confused when the child's emotional reactions may be different from their own. If the child is told of a death and responds by saying "Oh, can I go out and play?" the parent may interpret this as denial or a suppressed negative reaction to the death. Such a reaction can increase emotional concern on the part of the parent. However, if the child's response is viewed as only a first reaction, and the child is provided with loving, caring, and supportive attention, the child will ordinarily progress into an emotional resolution of the death.

The final reasons for involving children in post-death activities are related to the strength and support that they give other grievers. They often provide positive evidence of the fact that life goes on. In other instances, having been an important part of the life of the deceased, their presence is symbolic testimony to the immortality of the deceased. Furthermore, it is not at all unusual for a child to change the atmosphere surrounding bereavement from one of depression and sadness to one of laughter, verbalization, and celebration. Many times the child does this through his or her normal behavior, without any understanding of the kind of contribution being made.

CHILDREN AND FUNERALS

William Lamers

Before the visit to the funeral home children should be told that they will have a chance to see grandma, if they desire. They should be told that she is no longer breathing, that she is not just "asleep"; that she is no longer alive. They might be told that she does not look exactly the way she used to, but that this is all right; that it is easier to say "goodbye" if it is possible to see the person and be certain that they appear calm and at peace. They should be told that they may have questions, some of which will be hard to answer.

Children, depending on their age, will react differently to viewing the deceased. Children between five and ten years of age seem to ask many questions; they tend to be more open than adolescents. Older children usually experience and express stronger emotions than younger children. They need assurance that this, too, is all right. Children need assurance that they may have questions even after this last "goodbye" visit and that every attempt will be made to help find the answers.

The same sort of approach is indicated when preparing a child for attendance at a funeral or for a visit to the cemetery. In general, it is easier to include children in the entire course of the funeral than to exclude them from part or all of the activities and then try to deal with their subsequent inability to understand what happened at the funeral.

In order to be most supportive of their children when a friend or family member has died, parents should be told that it is natural for children to want to be included in funeral activities. They should be advised that advance preparations, some explanation and time for questions will provide children with the support and understanding needed for respectful involvement. Parents should be told that children are welcome to come to the funeral home, that staff will be pleased to assist the parents in this work, and that children should be invited to attend and even participate in funeral service activities.

Parents should be told to invite and encourage children to be part of the funeral service—but not to force them or coerce them into participating. If the parents are having a difficult time because of the death, the children can be brought to services in the care of a close friend or relative with whom they are comfortable. If there is some concern that the children might have a difficult time at the funeral, it is best to encourage attendance and, at the same time, see that supportive people are available to them.

"Helping the Child to Grieve." In *Children and Death*, Gary H. Paterson (Ed.). London, Ontario: King's College Press, 1986, pp. 105–120.

THE AMERICAN PRACTICE OF FUNERAL SERVICE

Education and Licensure

Earlier in this chapter we indicated that with the evolution of the funeral there likewise has been an evolution of a funeral functionary. Our contemporary American culture refers to that functionary as a funeral director. One hundred years ago this functionary was a "layer out of the dead," often a member of the family who physically and emotionally could perform the necessary tasks of bathing the body, closing the eyes and mouth, and dressing the body. It was not unusual for a midwife or other person who provided nursing-like services in the community to be called on to assist the family. Early advertisements indicate that nurses did offer such services.

The advent of the cabinetmaker and livery person has been discussed, and out of this transition evolved the funeral director. As early as the 1890s, the various states began to enact legislation to protect the public's health by licensing embalmers. The early licenses directed their attention to the embalming process, and it was not until the decades of the 1920s and 1930s that licensing agencies began to regulate the other aspects of the funeral and the operation of funeral homes.

> Clarence Darrow, discussing an ancestor reported to have been an undertaker, said: "One could imagine a more pleasant means of livelihood, but, almost any trade is bearable if the customers are sure."

The rationale for this licensure was based upon the felt need to protect the public, primarily in the financial area. However, regulations also addressed themselves to the conduct of the funeral where the cause of death was due to a contagious disease. Another issue of public health protection was the transportation of the dead from the place of death to the location of final disposition. Public health authorities claim that the regulation of the treatment of the dead has significantly contributed to the advanced standard of health of our country.

Based on these concepts, the licensing agencies most often charged with responsibility to regulate the funeral industry have been the various state boards of health. In some states, special boards were established for the regulation and enforcement procedures.

Licensure has been reserved to the individual states and includes three basic licenses. A license as an *embalmer* permits a person to legally remove the dead from the place of death and prepare the body through the process of embalming for viewing and funeralization. All states require persons who function in this regard to be licensed. A second license, to practice as a *funeral director,* permits the holder to arrange the legal details of the funeral, including the preparation of the death certificate and counseling with the family to arrange, plan, and implement the kind of funeral desired for the deceased. A third license is one that permits the licensee to practice *mortuary science*—an all-inclusive specialty that covers the practices of both embalming and funeral directing.

A few states have a license for a funeral director, a license that may be held by only one person in each firm (usually the owner or manager) and that serves to give the licensing agency control over all of the practitioners within that firm. A greater number of states have created a funeral home license or permit that is required to be issued to each funeral home and permits the state to close the funeral home by the withdrawal of the license without taking action against the licensees employed by that firm. In addition to every state requiring embalmers to be licensed, 49 states and the District of Columbia require practitioners to be licensed as funeral directors. The exact number of states requiring funeral home licenses or permits is hard to determine inasmuch as some are required by law, some by regulation, and some by local ordinance. Approximately one-half of the states have some requirement that governs the operation of a funeral home.

The qualifications for licensure deal basically with age, citizenship, and specific education. As of 1990 (with the exception of Colorado, which has no current basic educational requirements for embalmer's and funeral director's licenses), all states require a high school education and professional preparation in mortuary college. In addition, 8 states require 1 academic year of college in addition to the professional preparation, and 21 states require 2 academic years of college in addition to the professional preparation. Following the academic training, and in some instances before academic training is begun, all states require an internship or apprenticeship period. This varies from 1 to 3 years. The variance is directly related to the amount of college and professional training required. Upon the completion of academic and internship or apprenticeship requirements, applicants for licensure are required by all states to successfully pass a qualifying examination prior to the issuance of the license to practice. As of 1990, 14 states mandate continuing education to renew the license to practice. There is also an Academy of Professional Funeral Service Practice that provides a voluntary program of continuing education.

According to the U.S. Bureau of Labor Statistics (National Funeral Directors Association, 1991) there are approximately 23,500 funeral homes in the United States with 45,000 licensed personnel and 89,000 funeral service and crematory personnel. Approximately 5 percent of the licensees in the United States are women. However, in the last decade, the number of women entering colleges of funeral service education and becoming licensed has greatly increased. In 1991, the latest year for which statistics are available, 26 percent of the 1500 graduates from the 40 accredited schools of mortuary science in the United States were women. In 1976, only 8 percent of graduates were women (Goldman, 1993:A8).

In a recent survey of funeral home establishments conducted by the Federated Funeral Directors of America (1992), it was determined that in 1991 the average salaries for full time, licensed personnel ranged from $28,500 per year in communities of less than 25,000 population to $31,300 in communities above 100,000 population.

Should Funeral Directors Professionalize?

Raymond DeVries

Like many other occupations, funeral directors would like to be thought of as professionals. Should we as consumers support the attempts of funeral directors to become more professional?

Our first response to this question is, "Yes, of course." But let's not be so hasty. We must first consider what it is that makes an ordinary job a "profession." How do we distinguish a profession from a regular job? One way is to list the features or traits of occupations commonly accepted as professions. If asked which occupations are professions, most of us would answer: Physician, lawyer, minister. What sets these occupations apart? They are characterized by:

1. a specialized body of knowledge
2. a long period of training
3. an orientation toward service rather than profit
4. a commonly accepted code of ethics
5. legal recognition (most often through licensure)
6. a professional association

Implicit in this definition is the assumption that professionals have the best interest of the public in mind. After all, they submit to a long period of training, look forward to serving others, abide by a code of ethics, and police themselves through their professional associations. All occupations should become professions!

But this is not the only way to define a profession. Others look more cynically on the role of professions in society. George Bernard Shaw said, "Professions are a conspiracy against the laity." What did he mean? Shaw's comment hints at an alternative definition of the professions, a definition that suggests that there is just *one* distinguishing characteristic of the professions: power. Professions are those occupations that have accumulated enough power to control the definition and substance of their work. For example, this view contends that physicians are professionals by virtue of their complete control of matters of health. Through their associations they control the number and training of doctors, they limit the practices of competitors (e.g., chiropractors, nurse-practitioners), they set rates of reimbursement for health care. Adherents to this view point out that professionals in fact incapacitate us: they limit our choices, make us feel unable to help ourselves, encourage dependency.

> Should funeral directors become more professional? Not all would agree. Funeral directors subscribe to the first definition and assert that professionals can better attend to the needs of the public. Followers of the second definition conclude that the move toward professionalization would limit competition, drive prices up, and, by promoting dependency, make us less able to deal with death.

Raymond DeVries, Associate Professor, Saint Olaf College, Northfield, MN.

The Role of the Funeral Director

Rabbi Earl Grollman (1972) describes the role of the funeral director as that of a caretaker, caregiver, and gatekeeper. He indicates that the etymology of the word *undertaker* is based upon the activities of the early undertaker who "undertook" to do for people at the time of death those things that were crucial in meeting their bereavement needs. The funeral director, from the perspective of the community, was viewed as a secular gatekeeper between the living and the dead.

John Brantner (1973), elaborating upon the caregiver role, emphasizes that the funeral director is a crisis intervenor. Support for this idea can be documented in the vast amount of literature on the counseling role of crisis intervenors, who are not clinical practitioners by training, but to whom the public turns in crisis.

The funeral director will serve families by determining their needs and responding to them (Raether and Slater, 1974). This service will include, but not be limited to, the funeral (or its alternative) that they will plan and implement together. As a licensee of the state, the funeral director will handle the details requiring the death to be properly recorded and will file permits for transportation and final disposition of the body. The funeral director will serve as a liaison with other professionals working with the family medical personnel, clergy, lawyers, cemetery personnel, and, when necessary, law enforcement officials.

According to the National Funeral Directors Association (NFDA, 1991), 85 percent of funeral homes are family-owned and average 59 years in operation in the same community. The average funeral home arranges 160 funerals a year and has 1.6 locations (NFDA, 1991).

Body Preparation

While the Egyptian process of embalming required 70 days to perform, body preparation today is completed within a few hours and is more effective and acceptable. Body preparation may be as simple as bathing the body, closing the eyes and mouth, and dressing the body for final disposition (placement or disposal). This procedure, infrequently selected, is utilized by families who wish direct disposition. Later in this chapter we will discuss direct disposition where this procedure may be an acceptable and a logical choice.

Nationally, it is estimated that four out of five bodies are embalmed before final disposition. **Embalming,** by definition, is the replacement of normal body fluids with preserving chemicals. This process is accomplished by using the vascular system of the body to both remove the body fluids and suffuse the body with preserving chemicals. The arterial system is used to introduce the chemicals into the body, and the venous system is used to remove the body fluids. This intravascular exchange is accomplished by using an embalming machine. The machine can best be described as an artificial heart outside of the body that produces the pressure necessary to accomplish the exchange of fluids. This, together with procedures to remove the contents of the hollow viscera from the body organs, constitutes the embalming procedure.

In addition to the embalming procedure and the thorough bathing of the body, cosmetic procedures are used to restore a more normal color to the face and hands. When death occurs, the pigments of the skin, which give the body its normal tone and color, no longer function. It is for this reason that creams, liquids, and/or sprays are used to restore color.

The question "Why embalm or cosmetize the dead body?" is based on the assumption that one of the needs of the family is the reality of death; thus the body should be left in its most deathlike appearance. Those who have seen a person die (especially if the dying process was painful, prolonged, and emaciating) know that the condition of the body at the time of death can be very repulsive. Many people cannot accept this condition. It is for this reason that contemporary funeral directors embalm and cosmetize the body.

Another reason for embalming is the mobility of the American population. Viewing, which is practiced in over 75 percent of the funerals today involving earth burial and 22 percent of cremation services (Dawson et al., 1990), often requires more than a bathing and dressing of the body. Due to the time involved, embalming is necessary to accomplish a temporary preservation of the body to permit the gathering of the family, which may take as long as 2 or 3 days. If the body were to remain unembalmed for this length of time, the distasteful effects of decomposition would create a significant problem for grievers.

Though arguments have been presented favoring embalming, it may not always be necessary or desired. Embalming is not required in all states. In many states, for example, if the body is disposed of within 72 hours, is not transported on a common carrier or across state lines, and/or the person did not die of a contagious disease, embalming is not required. If a body is to be cremated and no public viewing is held, embalming would *not* be necessary. Many consumers just assume that embalming should or must occur.

A frequently asked question is, "If a body is embalmed, how long will it last?" There is no simple answer to this question. It is for that reason that funeral directors talk in terms of temporary preservation. Most families are interested in a preservation that will permit them to view the body, have a visitation, and allow the body to be present for the funeral. Beyond that, they are not concerned with the lasting effects of embalming.

Final Disposition

Earlier in this chapter we indicated three forms of final disposition and their approximated utilization. According to a study by Randall Cottrell and associates (1984), persons choosing earth burial are more likely to do so for religious reasons and for family considerations or social acceptability, while those selecting cremation do so for economic, simplicity, or altruistic concerns.

Earth burial as a method of final disposition is by far the most widely used in the United States. It is involved in approximately 78 percent of all the 2.1 million annual American deaths. Almost without exception, earth burial is accomplished within established cemeteries. In some instances, earth burial can be made outside of a cemetery if the landowner where the interment is to be made and the health officer of jurisdiction grant their permission. By law, cemeteries have the right to establish reasonable rules and regulations to be observed by those arranging for burial in them. A person does not purchase property within a cemetery, but rather purchases the "right to interment" in a specific location within that cemetery. Most cemeteries require that the casket be placed in some kind of outer receptacle or burial **vault**. The cemetery will also control how the grave can be marked with monuments or grave markers.

Cremation is the next most common method of final disposition. In the last decade the number of cremations has nearly doubled, and in 1991, nationally, 17 percent of deaths involved cremation. Nevada leads the nation with 52 cremations per 100 deaths, followed by Hawaii with 50 percent and California with more than 40 percent. States with the fewest cremations are Mississippi (1.8 percent) and Alabama (2.7 percent) (Associated Press, 1992). In a 1992 study of 1000 Americans conducted by the Funeral and Memorial Information Council (1992:8), it was discovered that 37 percent of respondents over the age of 30 said that they would choose cremation for themselves, while 32 percent said they would choose it for a loved one. Some predict that by the year 2000 cremation will account for

The columbarium provides families with an additional option for body disposition. Approximately 17 percent of the 2.2 million annual deaths use cremation as the method of final disposition.

approximately one-fourth of all methods of final disposition in the United States (Associated Press, 1992).

Asked why they were likely to choose cremation for themselves or a loved one, the respondents in the study conducted by the Funeral and Memorial Information Council gave the following explanations:

19 percent said it saves land
18 percent said it saves money
13 percent said they did not like to think of the body in the earth
8 percent thought it "was convenient"

Until recently, the **crematory** was generally located within the cemetery. With the increase of cremation as an option for final disposition, however, some funeral homes have now installed crematories. Cremation is accomplished by the use of either extreme heat or direct flame. In either instance, the actual process of reducing the casket (or alternative container) and the body to "ashes" takes approximately 2 hours. After the cremation, the residue of cremated remains is collected, put in an **urn** or box, and then disposed of according to the wishes of the family. The cremains may be buried in the earth, scattered in an appropriate or significant place, placed in a **niche** in a **columbarium** (a special room in a cemetery), or placed in some churches where cremains may be memorialized.

One might assume that cremation would be the least expensive form of final disposition because the typical cost of a simple "no-frills" cremation is approximately 40 percent of the cost of the traditional funeral service with burial (Lino, 1990). However, a cremation service may be as simple or as elaborate as family members wish. It is entirely possible to spend *more* money on a funeral involving cremation if plans include a "traditional funeral" involving a review of a casketed body and the cremated remains are to be put in an urn and placed in a niche in a columbarium.

A TRUE DIE-HARD FAN: HE'LL ATTEND GAME IN URN

Les Boatwright's death won't keep him from going to the Super Bowl today. He'll be there in a small brass urn. Boatwright, 75, died of a heart attack Monday, clutching two Super Bowl tickets as he prepared to place a bet with his bookie, said Boatwright's widow, Midge.

His two sons will take the urn carrying the ashes of the San Jose, California, resident to the Big Game between the San Francisco 49ers and the Cincinnati Bengals, Mrs. Boatwright said. "I told the boys, 'Do it for your daddy,'" she said. Boatwright's 33–year-old son Todd, flew to south Florida with his father's ashes early yesterday. His brother Marc, 37, arrived earlier.

Associated Press, *Arizona Daily Star,* Tucson, AZ., January 22, 1989, p. E3.

Entombment is the least practiced of final disposition options. It consists of placing the body (contained within a casket) in a special building designed for this purpose. Cemeteries offer large buildings (**mausoleums**) as an alternative to earth burial or cremation. In some instances, families may purchase the right to interment in a cemetery, and on the designated space build a private or family mausoleum that will hold as few as one or two bodies or as many as 12 to 16. Both types of mausoleums must be specifically constructed and designed in such a way as to provide lasting disposition for the body. Most states and/or cemeteries regulate the specifications and construction of the mausoleum.

FATHER KEEPS SON'S MEMORY ALIVE WITH CORPSE IN HOME

William Sneed's son died November 8 of injuries suffered in an auto accident. He won't be buried. Instead, Sneed said, the body will remain in a casket with a clear plastic top in a room off the family kitchen.

"There are three especially painful moments one goes through at the death of a loved one," Sneed said. "The first is at the news of the death, the second when you see the body in the casket at the funeral home, and the third and most difficult is when you have to turn away from the grave site and know you'll never see that person again. We simply decided not to go through that last step."

Sneed obtained a burial permit naming himself custodian of the body of his son, William B. Sneed III, 29. The permit names the place of entombment as the Sneed Family Mausoleum—the room off the kitchen.

There is no law in Louisville, Kentucky, that requires burial below ground. Sneed said the decision to keep the body of his son at home really began eight years ago.

"At first, it was like a joke, just between the three of us (himself, his daughter and his son)," he said. "But after talking about it for a while, it got serious. We decided then—I don't remember how long ago it was—that whichever one of us was the first to go, the other two would take care of everything like this."

Sneed said he plans to remodel the interior of his home to accommodate a small chapel at the rear, and the body will be placed there.

Adapted from Associated Press, *Minneapolis Tribune,* November 20, 1975.

ALTERNATIVES TO THE FUNERAL

People often ask if there are alternatives to the traditional funeral. Three alternatives exist: immediate disposition of the body of the deceased, the bequest of the deceased to a medical institution for anatomical study and research, and the memorial service. Each of these alternatives is defined and discussed below.

Immediate disposition occurs when the deceased is removed from the place of death to the place of cremation or earth burial without any ceremony; proper certificates are filed and permits received in the interim. In these instances, the family is not present, usually does not view the deceased after death, and is not concerned with any further type of memorialization. It is immediate in that it is accomplished as quickly after death as is possible. In this situation the body will not likely be embalmed, and the only preparation will consist of bathing and washing the body. The 1985 National Funeral Directors Association (NFDA) survey of members found that approximately 5 percent of all deaths involved immediate disposition. The frequency of this procedure differs by region of the country—it is performed most in the South Central part of the United States (approximately 7 percent of cases) and least in New England and the Mountain States (less than 1 percent of cases).

Body-bequest programs have become more well known in the last four decades and permit the deceased (prior to death) or the family (after the death) to donate the body to a medical institution. A compendium of body donation information (National Funeral Directors Association, 1981) indicates that, when the family desires, 75 percent of the donee institutions permit a funeral to be held prior to the delivery of the body to the institution for study or research. Some medical schools will pay the cost of transporting the body to the medical school, while others will not. With regard to expenses, this is the least expensive way of disposition of the body, especially if a memorial service is conducted without the body present. The compendium also indicates that in almost every instance the family may request that either the residue of the body or the cremated remains be returned when it is of no further benefit to the donee. In those instances where the family does not desire to have the body or the cremated remains returned, the donee institution will arrange for cremation and/or earth burial—oftentimes with an appropriate ceremony. People who are considering donating their bodies should be aware of the fact that at the time of death the donee institution may not have the need of a body. If this does happen, the family will have to find another institution or make other arrangements for the disposition of the body. The 1985 NFDA survey found that anatomical gifts account for less than 1 percent of all deaths.

To some, body donation may not appear to be an alternative to the funeral (especially when a ceremony is held prior to the delivery of the bequested body), but inasmuch as the procedure is different from the most common methods of disposition, it may be considered as an alternative. According to the National Funeral Directors Association, approximately 7000 such donations are made each year out of 2,099,000 deaths.

The *memorial service* is defined as a service without the body present. It is true that every funeral is a memorial service—inasmuch as it is in memory of someone—but a memorial service, by our definition, is an alternative to the typical funeral. It may be conducted on the day of the death, within two or three days of the death, or sometimes as much as weeks or months following the death. The content of the service places little or no emphasis on the death. Instead, it often is a service of acclamation of philosophical concepts. Religious or nonreligious in content, these services can meet the needs of the bereaved.

Organizations exist for consumers called **memorial societies.** Such an example is in Ithaca, New York. The by-laws of this particular nonprofit and nonsectarian organization establish the following as purposes of their society:

1. To promote the dignity, simplicity, and spiritual values of funeral rites and memorial services.
2. To facilitate simple disposal of deceased persons at reasonable costs, but with adequate allowances to funeral directors for high-quality services.
3. To increase the opportunity for each person to determine the type of funeral or memorial service he or she desires.
4. To aid its members and promote their interests in achieving the foregoing.

Thus, such a memorial society would help educate consumers regarding death prior to the actual death of a significant other and present options for final disposition of the body. Likewise, many funeral directors today serve as valuable resource persons by sharing information regarding death with various community groups.

FUNERAL, FINAL DISPOSITION, AND RELATED EXPENSES

Charges made by a funeral home ordinarily involve the services of the professional staff, the use of the funeral home facilities and equipment, transportation, and the casket or other alternate container. In addition, most funeral homes provide burial vaults or other types of outer enclosures for the casket and ancillary items that may be purchased from the funeral director—clothing, register books, acknowledgment cards, and Stars of David, crucifixes, or crosses.

The other major cost of the funeral is the cemetery charges—either for the purchase of cemetery property for the right to interment therein, for mausoleum space, or for an urn for the cremated remains (in some instances, charges will include a space in a columbarium for the urn). Most families will also select, in one form or another, a monument or marker to identify the grave or other place of final disposition.

A final category of expenses incurred by the family is money sometimes advanced by the funeral home at the request of, and as an accommodation to, the

In addition to providing a service to families in bereavement, funeral directors sell burial merchandise to their customers. Typically the cost of such merchandise comprises approximately 25 percent of the total amount collected by funeral directors.

family. Such cash advances might include, but are not limited to, the following: charges for opening and closing the grave, crematory costs, honoraria for clergy and musicians, obituary notices, flowers, and transportation costs in addition to the transportation ordinarily furnished by the funeral home.

In a recent survey by the Federated Funeral Directors of America of 192,000 funerals conducted in 1991, it was determined that the average cost for an adult funeral in the United States was $3,507.19. This cost did not include grave or cremation expenses, the cost of a vault, clothing, or extra service requirements, nor cash advances (including minister, florist, and musicians). In 1991 the operating expenses for a regular adult funeral were $2597.69, the average casket cost was $606.04, and profit reported was $303.46—8.65 percent of sales. In 1981, the typical firm's profit was 13.17 percent; thus in 10 years, profits in the funeral industry have declined by more than half. In 1991 (Federated Funeral Directors of America, 1991) the average expenses of $3507.19 for an adult funeral were broken down in the following manner (these figures do not include cemetery charges and cash advances to ministers, florists, and musicians).

Personnel (owner salaries, employee salaries,
retirement plan, payroll taxes, insurance,
professional services) $1209.51

Cost of facilities (rent allowance/rent, depreciation,
heat-water-light, insurance/general maintenance
and repairs, taxes, telephone, leased music,
interest expense) $789.55

Automotive equipment (depreciation and insurance,
automotive expenses, livery expense, leased
autos) $213.11

Promotion (advertising, business contributions,
convention/meeting, organization dues,
subscriptions, business promotion,
meals/entertainment) $146.72

Supplies (preparation room supplies, misc.
funeral supplies) $74.69

Business services (legal services,
postage, office supplies,
consultants, accounting) $86.49

Casket cost $606.04

After-sale expenses (bad debts and discounts) $66.90

Sundry (sundry expenses, tips and gratuities,
laundry and cleaning, freight, travel) $10.72

Profit $303.46

Total cost of average adult funeral $3507.19

In a 1986 survey of National Funeral Directors Association members (1986:5) it was determined that nationally, for every dollar taken in by affiliated funeral homes, money was distributed in the following manner:

32 cents for salaries and benefits
25 cents for merchandise (caskets, vaults, etc.)
21 cents for other operating expenses
13 cents for facilities
9 cents for before-tax profits

The 1986 NFDA financial survey provides us with a number of other important findings. First, the data suggest that funeral service is a competitive industry. When the cost of an average funeral is compared, the difference between the highest and the lowest prices charged vary less than $600 regardless of demographic category (region of the country, number of families served, number of facilities operated, or metro/rural location) (NFDA, 1986:1).

Second, approximately 70 percent of firms operate only one funeral home facility and another 20 percent operate two facilities (NFDA, 1986:40). Third, on average, 56 percent of all funeral home assets are owned by the funeral home—

funeral directors appear to be more willing to leave their assets within the company than other service professionals (NFDA, 1986:4).

Finally, the average funeral service firm's actual return on net worth is approximately 8 percent. This relatively low return on equity makes funeral service (like other capital-intensive industries) a very difficult one to enter as a new entrepreneur. For the new entrant, the price of land and buildings would result in higher operating expenses to perform the same service as a more established funeral home (NFDA, 1986:1).

Until 1984 there were basically three ways that a funeral home charged for its services and merchandise selected by the family. The first was the unit method of pricing. In this procedure, all of the costs involved with the funeral home providing the services (including the staff, the facilities, the automotive equipment, and the casket) were included in a single charge. In making a selection under this procedure, the family looked at a "bottom line" figure to which only other charges paid by the funeral home (such as, a vault, additional burial merchandise, cash advances) might be added.

The second method was referred to as the bi-unit or tri-unit pricing system. The bi-unit procedure was to make separate charges for professional services and the casket, and the tri-unit procedure was to separate charges made for professional services, the use of facilities, and the casket selected. This system enabled families to understand the charges for the three basic components making up funeral costs.

A third method of presenting costs was referred to as either functional, multi-unit or **itemization.** (There is an interchange of the use of these terms. However, they usually refer to the same basic procedure.) In this method of pricing, each and every item of service, facility, and transportation was shown as a separate item together with its related cost. With this method there was usually a minimum of 8 to 10 items listed, and the family decided in each instance whether or not that item would become a part of the funeral service. In 1984 the Federal Trade Commission (FTC) mandated that all American funeral homes itemize their fees and that consumers have access to pricing information over the phone.

A major advantage of itemization is the opportunity to provide family members greater flexibility in arranging a funeral and the ability to control costs. The family should have the freedom to decline those items that they do not want, and a proper allowance should be made for such items that are not used. For example, one may ask to see "the pine box"—usually a cloth-covered wood casket or a pressed wood container. These caskets are relatively inexpensive and may or may not be in the display room. If the body is to be transported a great distance to the gravesite or crematorium, perhaps the funeral director's van or station wagon could be used rather than the expensive hearse. Similarly, the consumer should have the right to

"He'd rest a lot better with thirty per cent off."

choose among types of **vault liners.** The greatest advantage of the process of itemization is that one can look carefully at the itemized services and obtain the most adequate services at the best price.

There are two major disadvantages of the FTC policy requiring funeral homes to give prices over the phone and to itemize funeral expenses. The first is that when consumers receive prices over the phone it is difficult to make accurate price comparisons. One firm can say that they sell an oak casket for $1200, and another will price a different oak casket at $3200. It is entirely possible that the price–quality ratio is better for the more expensive casket. A helpful analogy might be to imagine calling two import automobile dealerships, Yugo and Mercedes, to ask each "How much do cars cost in your dealership?" The only way one can make accurate price comparisons is to personally inspect both products carefully. The same is true for the funeral industry. Families are better served when they can make careful comparisons between the costs of services provided by funeral firms prior to the death of a significant other. Most people do not wait until the car breaks down before they shop for a new one. Furthermore, if they did find themselves in this situation, they would not purchase a car over the telephone.

The second disadvantage of the FTC ruling regarding the itemization of funeral expenses is that itemization did not uniformly result in decreasing expenses to families. Prior to the 1984 ruling, many funeral firms included some merchandise and services as part of the standard funeral. With itemization, funeral directors could provide justification to raise the cost for funeral services. The analogy of restaurant pricing may be appropriate at this point—it is often less expensive to order a complete meal than to order food a la carte.

President Roosevelt left detailed instructions for his funeral and burial, should he die while President. He directed that the funeral service be simple, that the casket be plain and of wood, that there be no embalming of the body or sealing of the casket and that his grave have no lining.

These instructions were found in a private safe days after his burial, too late to be considered. Consequently, Franklin D. Roosevelt's remains were embalmed, sealed in a copper coffin and placed in a cement vault.

Consumer Survival Kit, The Last Rights: Funerals. Owings Mills, MD: Maryland Center for Public Broadcasting, 1977.

NEW TRENDS IN FUNERAL SERVICE

The newest trends in funeral service are to cultivate new business by courting the living with special services. Included in these services are working with the public in preneed funeral planning, providing after-care for survivors, and assisting community and religious organizations in providing death education for the public. All of these efforts can be thought of as an extension of past efforts at marketing and advertising, but the funeral industry has made concerted efforts to make these strategies effective in a very competitive industry where, in the past 10 years, no-frills cremation services have increased significantly and corporate profits have declined by more than half—as a percent of sales, from 13.17 percent in 1981 to 8.65 percent in 1991 (Federated Funeral Directors of America, 1992).

Preneed Funerals: A "New" Trend in Planning Funerals

One of the more controversial issues today in funeral service is the trend toward **preneed funerals. Prearranging** is the process of arranging funerals in advance of need. This process can include the selection of merchandise, planning the service, determining method of review and final disposition, and the selection of persons to be involved in the funeral. In addition to prearranging, **prefunding,** or the legal commitment of money to pay for the funeral service, is also common. This is usually accomplished through *insurance* or a *trust*. Preneed is a generic term that refers to both processes of prearranging and prefunding (Hocker, 1987: 1–2).

According to a 1983 national survey conducted by the National Research and Information Center (Will, 1988:366), 9.2 percent of the American public have made prearrangements for their funerals, and another 62 percent feel that they should make funeral prearrangements with a funeral director. Presently, approximately one million people a year prearrange their funerals, compared to 22,000 in 1960 (Anderson, 1991). The AARP expects the annual number of Americans who will prearrange their funerals to increase to five million persons by the year 2000. According to James Will (1988:367) and William Hocker (1987:4–11), the reasons consumers prearrange and/or prefund funerals are the following:

1. To provide a forum for death-related discussions that is not profoundly affected by the grief that naturally accompanies the event of death.
2. To make one's funeral preferences known to one's survivors may assure that survivors will not select a type of funeral that differs from the one desired.
3. To provide an opportunity to personalize the funeral.
4. To plan one's funeral can be one of the last pieces of unfinished business one can accomplish for one's survivors. This action can provide the dying with peace of mind.
5. To give individuals an opportunity to get the most for their money through comparison shopping at a time when they are not faced with urgent need or overwhelmed by grief.
6. To unburden loved ones of the obligation of having to plan and pay for a funeral.
7. To protect an estate from funeral expenses in the future.
8. To assure that funds are available in the future for the type of funeral that is desired.

The problem with preneed funerals from the perspective of consumers and funeral service professionals is that a potential exists for consumer fraud. There have been some consumers who have bought and paid for funerals from unethical funeral salespersons (some licensed and others not) and later found at the time of death that either the firm was no longer in business, the money had not been put in a trust account, and/or the deceased had moved to a location not served by the firm. For these reasons Thomas D. Bischoff (cited by Kelly, 1987:32), Senior Vice-President of the Prearranged Funeral Division of Service Corporation International (the largest chain of funeral homes in the United States and the world), has made the following recommendation:

> We, as funeral service professionals, must encourage that everything be done to minimize these eventualities. We would again suggest that an insurance-funded prearranged funeral program is the best safeguard that the funeral director and the consumer have. Insurance companies are very tightly and closely regulated and are required to maintain sufficient funds on hand to meet requirements. An insurance-funded prearranged funeral program has very little potential for mismanagement or fraud and as such should become the standard for the industry.

Ultimately, consumers must protect themselves against fraudulent entrepreneurs and dishonest "get-rich-quick" salespersons. Insurance-funded prearranged funeral programs are important potential safeguards, but the words of Robert W. Ninker (cited by Kelly, 1987:32), Executive Director of the Illinois Funeral Directors Association, should also be heeded.

> The best protection a buyer can have is to purchase from a funeral director with a long history of success, after asking and understanding that this person is licensed and, in fact, trusts his funeral funds. . . . The buyer should also check references with acquaintances. That is about as much certainty as there is in life. Of course, if the buyer responds to door-to-door sellers or boiler room operations, he is his own victim! No one can protect someone from his own fool-like actions.

NOW YOUR LOVED ONE CAN BE A TV STAR

James Anderson

Videotaped tributes to the dead are increasingly popular. For up to $125, National Music Service of Spokane, Washington, guarantees shipment of a Video Tribute with photographs of the deceased, natural scenery and songs from a 3,000-song playlist within 48 hours.

A typical six-minute tribute opens with a sunrise and features pictures of the deceased, places he or she lived and liked to visit, and closes with a sunset. Quotations for favorite authors or religious works can be screened.

Company president Merrill Womach, who sings on many of the tracks, said his firm has prepared 50,000 such tributes.

"It's what a funeral service should be all about," Womach said. "When you take pictures and put them to beautiful music you can tell what that person's life was about."

Womach acknowledged many people aren't comfortable with the idea. "There is resistance to having a television set at a funeral chapel. People look at

(continued)

it and say, 'I don't know,' " he said. But many like it so much they order their own tributes ahead of time.

Wulff Family Mortuaries in St. Paul reports that of the 525 funerals held at its funeral homes last year, nearly two-thirds of the families ordered videotapes. "It makes it very personal for the family," says owner Greg Wulff (Scott and Dolan, 1991).

"Funeral Industry, Seeking New Business, Courts the Living with Special Services." Associated Press, *New York Times*, May 27, 1991, p. B1.

After-Care: The Future Business Is to Be Found in Today's Customers

The funeral industry has always known that 80 percent of its business is with families served in the past. However, after-care is one method to increase the likelihood of getting repeat business. The newest trend in funeral service is to provide extensive after-care services and products for widows and widowers. Among these services and products are grief therapy, bereavement support groups, video tributes, and even greeting cards sent to survivors to mark the anniversary of death or the deceased's birthday (Scott and Dolan, 1991).

An example of such after-care efforts can be found at the Bradshaw Family of Funeral Homes in the Twin Cities (Minnesota) and the work of Paul Johnson. Mr. Johnson taught sociology and death-and-dying courses at Bethel College (St. Paul) for 10 years, until he resigned in 1985 to become the bereavement services director at the Twin Cities chain of seven funeral homes. Johnson's work requires that he be involved in service plans of all deaths where problematic grieving is likely—the death of a child, accidental death, homicide, suicide, and death from AIDS. Johnson also contacts the surviving spouse or other family members a few weeks after the funeral to "hear their concerns about their own particular situation." Johnson recommends grief support groups and provides families with information about the grieving process. Johnson also puts on bereavement workshops for the public, sponsored by the funeral home, and edits *Caregivers Quarterly* — a newsletter that is distributed without charge to 800 clergy in the Twin Cities Area.

Many other funeral homes in the United States, such as the John McAlister Funeral Home in Charleston, South Carolina, and the Carbon Funeral Home in Windsor Locks, Connecticut, are offering grief counseling and support groups for their clients. In the 1970s the Carbon Funeral Home created its support group called "Begin Again." Begin Again meets weekly and sponsors seminars on a wide range of topics including financial management, car maintenance, and occupational re-entry. They even have meetings whose primary function is entertainment—featuring magicians and ventriloquists during their programs (Anderson, 1991).

Other funeral establishments are sponsoring tree-planting ceremonies and annual memorial observances as a service to the families of the deceased. In Chicago, the Blake-Lamb Funeral Home even provides free limousine services for weddings in the family of the deceased (Scott and Dolan, 1991). Another optional service sponsored by the Fitzgerald and Son Funeral Home of Rockford, Illinois, is the annual "Walk to Remember" for families mourning stillbirths, miscarriages, and early infant death. During the walk, participants plant a tree in a public park, scrawl their babies' names on paper, and put them next to the tree (Anderson, 1991).

CONCLUSION

Grief is the emotional working through of a significant loss. The funeral is a part of the grief process in contemporary America.

In our discussion, we have described funerals and their alternatives within a cultural and historical perspective. In the United States an evolutionary, not a revolutionary, process has occurred. Americans did not invent the funeral or the funeral functionary. However, contemporary Americans have found an expression for their bereavement.

SUMMARY

1. To understand contemporary funerals conducted in the United States, one must understand the American cultural and historical context.
2. Embalming, a process as old as 484 B.C., was introduced in France and England in the 1600s and in the United States during the Civil War. Presently four out of five American bodies are embalmed.
3. The contemporary role of funeral director has evolved from the occupations of cabinetmaker and livery owner.
4. Presently there are approximately 23,500 funeral homes in the United States serving the families of the approximately 2.1 million annual deaths.
5. Associated with the contemporary American funeral, final disposition of the body is made by either earth burial (78 percent), cremation (17 percent), or entombment (5 percent). These percentages are approximate national averages and vary by region of the country.
6. The funeral is designed to meet the psychological, sociological, and theological or philosophical needs of bereaved persons.
7. A person does not purchase property within a cemetery, but purchases the right to interment in a specific location within that cemetery.

8. Alternatives to funerals exist, including immediate disposition, body donation, and memorial services.
9. Funeral bills have been presented to customers utilizing the following pricing systems: unit pricing, bi- or tri-unit pricing, and itemization. The latter is mandated in all states by the Federal Trade Commission. In 1991 the cost of the average adult funeral was $3507.19.
10. Children should not be excluded from participating in funerals. To do so might have adverse effects on the child's emotional well-being and impede his or her bereavement.

DISCUSSION QUESTIONS

1. Describe how the funeral process can assist in coping with grief and facilitate the bereavement process.
2. Distinguish between grief, bereavement, and the funeral process.
3. Describe and compare each of the following processes: burial, cremation, and entombment.
4. Based on Irion's concept of psychological needs of the bereaved, explain how funerals can meet various needs of those involved.
5. Discuss the factors affecting post-death costs and the expenses related to funerals and final disposition.
6. Discuss the psychological, sociological, and theological–philosophical aspects of the funeral process. How do each of these aspects facilitate the resolution of grief?
7. What would you include in your own obituary if you were to write it?
8. What would be your choice of final disposition of your body? Why would you choose this method, and what effects might this choice have upon your survivors (if any)?
9. What is the difference among preneed, prefunding, and prearranging funerals? What are the advantages and disadvantages of preneed funeral arrangements?

GLOSSARY

Cremation: The reduction of human remains by means of heat or direct flame. The cremated remains are called cremains or ashes and weigh between 6 and 8 pounds. "Ashes" is a very poor description of the cremated remains because they are actually processed bone fragments and calcium residue that have the appearance of crushed rock or pumice.

Crematory: An establishment in which cremation takes place.

Columbarium: A building or wall for above-ground accommodation of cremated remains.

Disposition: Final placement or disposal of a dead person.

Embalming: A process that temporarily preserves the deceased by means of displacing body fluids with preserving chemicals.

Entombment: Opening and closing of a crypt, including the placement and sealing of a casket within.

Itemization: A method of pricing a funeral in which every item of service, facility, and transportation is listed with its related cost. A service presently mandated by the Federal Trade Commission.

Mausoleum: A building or wall for above-ground accommodation of a casket.

Memorial Society: A group of people joined together to obtain dignity, simplicity, and economy in funeral arrangements through advanced planning.

Niche: A chamber in a columbarium into which an urn is placed.

Prearranging: The process of arranging funerals in advance of need. This process can include selecting merchandise, planning the service, determining method of review and final disposition, and selecting of persons to be involved in the funeral.

Prefunding: Legally committing money to pay for the funeral service.

Preneed Funerals: A generic term that refers to both processes of prearranging and prefunding funerals.

Urn: A container for cremated remains.

Vault or Grave Liner: A concrete or metal container into which a casket or urn is placed for ground burial. Its function is to prevent the ground from settling.

REFERENCES

Associated Press. 1992. "Percentage of Cremations Increases in Palmetto State." 1989. *Charleston Post and Courier,* May 26, p. B6.

Brantner, John P. 1973. "Crisis Intervenor." Paper presented at the Ninth Annual Funeral Service Management Seminar, National Funeral Directors Association. Scottsdale, AZ (January).

Cottrell, Randall R., James M. Eddy, Wesley F. Alles, and Richard W. St. Pierre. 1984. "An Analysis of College Students' Attitudes and Beliefs Concerning Body Disposal." *Death Education,* 8:113–122.

Dawson, Grace. D., John F. Santos, and David C. Burdick. 1990. "Differences in Final Arrangements Between Burial and Cremation as the Method of Body Disposition." *Omega,* 21(2):129–146.

Federated Funeral Directors of America. 1992. *1991 Facts on Funeral Costs,* P. O. Box 19244, Springfield, IL 62744.

Funeral and Memorial Information Council. 1992. "The Funeral and Memorial Information Council Conduct Study." *Canadian Funeral Director,* (March):8.

Goldman, Ari L. 1993. "Increasingly, Funeral Business Gets Female Touch." *The New York Times,* February 15, p. A8.

Grollman, Earl A. 1972. Commencement Address, Department of Mortuary Science, University of Minnesota, Minneapolis, MN (May).

Hocker, William V. 1987. "Financial and Psychosocial Aspects of Planning and Funding Funeral Services in Advance as Related to Estate Planning and Life-Threatening Illness." Unpublished article distributed by the National Funeral Directors Association.

Irion, Paul E. 1956. *The Funeral: An Experience of Value.* Milwaukee: National Funeral Directors Association.

Jackson, Edgar N. 1963. *For the Living.* Des Moines, IA: Channel Press.

Kelly, Thomas E. 1987. "Predict Preneed Vital to Financial Future." *The American Funeral Director,* (February):3169.

Lindemann, Erich. 1944. "Symptomatology and Management of Acute Grief." *American Journal of Psychiatry,* 101, (September):141–148.

Lino, Mark. 1990. "The $3,800 Farewell." *American Demographics* (July), p. 8.

National Funeral Directors Association. 1981. "Body Donation: A Compendium of Facts Compiled as an Interprofessional Source Book." Produced by the College of Health Sciences (University of Minnesota) and the National Funeral Directors Association.

National Funeral Directors Association. 1986. *Financial Operations Survey for Fiscal 1985.* Milwaukee, WI: NFDA.

National Funeral Directors Association. 1991. *Fact Sheet for 1991.* Milwaukee, WI: NFDA.

Pine, Vanderlyn R. 1971. *Findings of the Professional Census,* (June) Milwaukee: National Funeral Directors Association.

Raether, Howard C., and Robert C. Slater. 1974. *Facing Death as an Experience of Life.* Milwaukee: National Funeral Directors Association.

Scott, Carley R., and Carrie Dolan. 1991. "Funeral Homes Hope to Attract Business by Offering Services after the Service." *Wall Street Journal,* April 11, p. B1.

Will, James. 1988. "Preneed: The Trend Toward Prearranged Funerals." In *The Funeral Director's Practice Management Handbook,* Howard Raether (Ed.) Englewood Cliffs, NJ: Prentice-Hall.

SUGGESTED READINGS

American Association of Retired Persons. 1989. *AARP Product Report: Pre-Paying Your Funeral?*, vol. 1, no. 2; and *AARP Product Report: Funeral Goods and Services*, vol. 1, no. 3. *A report by the American Association of Retired Persons for consumers on prepaying and preplanning conventional funerals, burials, and alternatives including cremation, direct burial, and body donation.*

Habenstein, Robert W., and William M. Lamers. 1962. *The History of American Funeral Directing*. Milwaukee: Bulfin. *An excellent source for the study, review, and analysis of the history of funeral directing in the American culture from its introduction in colonial times to present.*

Irion, Paul F. 1966. *The Funeral: Vestige or Value?* Nashville: Abingdon Press. / Irion, Paul E. 1968. *Cremation.* Philadelphia: Fortress Press. / Irion, Paul E. 1971. *Humanistic Funeral Service.* Baltimore: Waverly Press. *This series of books gives the serious student an excellent background in the whole area of grief and bereavement as well as their relation to the funeral.*

Pine, Vanderlyn R. 1975. *Caretaker of the Dead.* New York: Irvington Publishers. *An excellent source to discover the ways in which a society views death and cares for its dead. It is written from both a funeral director's and a sociologist's analytical perspective. Pine is not only a licensed funeral service practitioner but also a professor of sociology at New Paltz University in New York.*

Raether, Howard C. 1988. *The Funeral Director's Practice Management Handbook.* Englewood Cliffs, NJ: Prentice-Hall. *A valuable resource on the internal workings of funeral service in America.*

Chapter
13

The Bereavement Process

Only people who avoid love can avoid grief. The point is to learn from it and remain vulnerable to love.

John Brantner
From J. William Worden, *Grief Counseling and Grief Therapy*

I F AT THE conclusion of the funeral service grief work were finished, the process of reintegration of the bereaved into society would be completed. The funeral service and the final disposition of the dead, however, mark only the end of public mourning; private mourning continues for some time.

THE BEREAVEMENT ROLE

In earlier chapters we discussed bereavement behavior within historical and cross-cultural perspectives. We have given a general description of the norms and cultural patterns that prescribe proper conduct for the bereaved within American society. When we apply these bereavement norms to particular persons occupying statuses within a group or social situation, we are talking about the **bereavement role.**

In discussing the adaptation to the crisis of becoming ill, Talcott Parsons (1951:426–437) describes the *sick role* as being composed of two rights and two obligations. The first right is for the sick person to be exempted from "normal" social responsibilities. The extent to which one is exempted is contingent upon the nature and severity of the illness. The second right is to be taken care of and to become dependent on others as one attempts to return to normal social functioning. In exchange for these rights, the sick person must express a desire to "want to get better" and must seek technically competent help.

J. D. Robson (1977) suggests that behavior related to the death of a significant other (spouse, parent, etc.) is similar to illness behavior patterns. At the onset of death, the bereaved are exempted from their normal social responsibilities. Depending on the nature and the degree of relationship with the deceased, the bereaved are awarded time away from employment in much the same way as they are given sick leaves—spouses and children may be given a week, while close friends and relatives may only be given time to attend the funeral.

The bereaved are also allowed to become dependent on others for social and emotional support and for assistance with tasks related to the requirements of normal, daily living. In offering this type of support, neighbors and friends call on survivors with gifts of food, flowers, and other expressions of sympathy. This custom led Robert Kavanaugh's younger brother to ask if "dead people ate meatloaf and chocolate cake" (Kavanaugh, 1972:32).

In exchange for these privileges created by the death of a loved one, those adopting the bereavement role are not only required to seek technically competent help from funeral directors and clergy members, but are expected to return as soon as possible to normal social responsibilities. The bereavement role is considered a temporary one, and it is imperative that all role occupants do whatever necessary to relinquish it within a reasonable period of time. Time extensions are usually granted to spouse and children, but there is a general American value judgment that normal grieving should be completed by the first anniversary of the death.

American folk wisdom would contend that "time heals"—with the intensity of the grief experienced diminishing over time. According to Paul Rosenblatt (1983), however, a more accurate picture of mourning would point out that the time intervals between intense experiences of grief increase with the passing of time. Furthermore, in analyzing 19th-century diaries, Rosenblatt discovered that it was quite common to experience periods of mourning for losses that occurred many years earlier. What is abnormal behavior, from the perspective of the American bereavement role, is the preoccupation with the death of the loved one and refusing to make attempts to return to normal social functioning. Examples of deviant behavior of this type would include the following:

1. Malingering in the bereavement role and memorializing the deceased by refusing to dispose of articles of clothing, personal effects, and living as if one expected the dead to reappear.
2. Rejecting attempts from others who offer social and emotional support, refusing to seek professional counseling, and taking up permanent residence in "Pity City."
3. Rejecting public funeral rituals and requesting that the funeral functionaries merely pick up the body and dispose of it through cremation without any public acknowledgment of the death that has occurred.
4. Engaging in aberrant behavior such as heavy drug or alcohol usage.
5. Rushing into major life changes such as a hasty remarriage or moving to a new home.

Behaviors such as these may be sanctioned by others through social avoidance, ostracism, and criticism. As a consequence, most people are not only encouraged but forced to move through the grieving process.

A WEDNESDAY AFTERNOON

Jane Soli

The hot, humid air of August enveloped us in the crowded car. Sig drove. The Air Force had flown him home from Tahiti. Behind him sat Karen, her arm around Johanna. Peter sat on the other side looking vacantly out the window. Tina sat between Sig and me. The handle of my black purse felt as moist as my sweaty palms. My dress stuck to the skin of my back. How lucky it was that Harmar's Fashion Shop had a black linen dress, size 12. The yellow dotted Swiss I sewed for summer best would not be appropriate today.

The procession crept down Division Street. The neon sign at the Rock County Bank flashed 94 degrees and 3:06. Behind the plate glass of The River Inn, businessmen shook dice for their afternoon coffee. Lois Palmer came out of Hanson's Variety Store carrying a lamp shade.

We turned the corner at the lumberyard, crossed the wagon bridge, then, over the tracks and up the hill. Once in the country the long line of cars moved a little faster. After the turn at Benson's farm the gravel road narrowed. I could see the cemetery.

Why did you die, Dan? Did you have to die when the children were so young? You were lean and fit, physically active, no apparent health problems. You were fine when you went to bed, but I heard your death rattle; a small cough, I thought. You were dead when I came to bed five minutes later.

Is there any money? Will Karen be able to finish her last year of college? How about Peter—he's only seventeen. And then Johanna and Tina, thirteen and eleven. At least Sig is out of school. Such problems. Such a loss. How will I ever manage?

Two things came back to me during those early days of worry, fear, and grief. I recalled twenty years of bridge games with Judy and Elmer and the late-night discussions of death and funerals as we ate brownies and drank coffee. We spoke of our own deaths and our personal wishes. Dan, always the most vocal, stated again and again, "Don't spend any money on me when I am dead," and "Give me a military funeral." There was not a man in the USA more proud to be a Marine than Dan Soli. To hear him tell it, the Marines fought World War II single-handedly. Though he was 33 and the others in boot camp were 18, he was a member of the United States Marine Corps and never mind if the recruits called him "Grandpa."

With Dan's wishes uppermost in my mind, the children and I had the gruesome task of selecting a casket at the Anderson Brothers Mortuary. A basement room displayed a dozen or more for my choice. Mr. Anderson, ever solicitous, hovered over me giving the cost in a hushed voice—$2500, $3000, or, if we wanted the best, it would be $5000. Together we returned to the main floor for my decision. I asked, "What is your cheapest casket?"

"We have a pine box for county paupers at $50," he answered.

"What is your next price?"

"There is a casket we use for servicemen. It is made of wood and covered with grey velour. The flag would go over it. That sells for $100."

"I'll take it," I said quickly. In my mind I was doing rapid arithmetic. Twenty-five hundred dollars would pay for Karen's last year of college.

The entire tenor of our meeting changed. The solicitousness ended. The Anderson brothers conferred in the hallway and practically rushed us out of there.

Dan's wish was fulfilled in that regard; we would spend minimum money. A call to the Veterans of Foreign Wars would insure the military funeral.

The hearse turned into the City Cemetery; we followed. Behind our blue Chevy were twenty more vehicles. To the right I saw the Erickson family plot with remnants of Memorial Day decorations: white plastic crosses with letters in gold—"Mother," "Father," "Sister." We passed the graves of my grandparents, my infant brother, my father.

About one hundred yards into the cemetery the procession came to a stop. I saw the fake grass surrounding the open grave over by the fence. Close by stood the caretaker's tool shed with a barrel for refuse in front. Someone had lettered a crude sign above the barrel. It said, "Rubbage." The grave diggers stood behind the tool shed waiting to complete their job.

As the casket moved from the hearse to the waiting pallbearers, the honor guard, smart in their black uniforms, aligned themselves on either side of the men carrying the casket and accompanied them to the gravesite.

The children and I left the car to follow. Tina cried, "I'm too young to be without a father," and clung to me. I had vowed to remain dry-eyed. My silly little purse held a lawn hanky—no Kleenex, no billfold, no lipstick. I would not open that purse.

Friends and relatives surrounded the grave as Pastor Jensen gave the committal service. Somehow the next part took me by surprise. Two of the honor guards stepped forward and together removed the American flag from the casket. With ceremony they folded it in the traditional way and presented it to me—the widow.

The two uniformed men rejoined the honor guard and they all stepped back from the mourners. At the command of the captain they fired a twenty-one gun salute.

At that point Peter moved away from the family, raised his trumpet and blew Taps for his dad. Sweet, melancholy notes rose plaintively over the gathered crowd. From the other side of the hill came the faraway echo. My heart ached with the pain of that moment.

The worst of the day was over. Everyone returned to the basement of the Lutheran Church for sandwiches, cake, and coffee. The Ladies Aid was famous for their "funeral sandwiches," made from ground pork and beef, and each lady brought her special cake. The choices of cake on the plate seemed endless.

(continued)

People sat around the tables, enjoying the food and visiting. Many expressed their condolences to me. My food remained untouched.

As we were leaving, Alice Overbeck came over to me, reached for my hand and said, "Too bad your husband died, but you'll get over it."

She was wrong; I didn't get over it.

I cry when I hear Taps.

Jane A. Soli is the retired secretary to the academic dean of Saint Olaf College, Northfield, MN.

DISENFRANCHISED GRIEF

Like other aspects of death-related behavior, grief is socially constructed—people grieve only when they feel it appropriate. Social scripts are provided for grievers, and social support is given to those who are recognized as having experienced loss and act in accordance to the norms. However, not all loss is openly acknowledged, socially sanctioned, and publicly shared. Kenneth Doka (1989) uses the term **disenfranchised grief** when referring to phenomena of this type.

According to Doka (1989) there are four types of situations that lead to disenfranchised grief. The first situation is one in which the *relationship to the deceased is not socially recognized.* Examples of this type of disenfranchised grief would include nontraditional relationships—such as extramarital affairs, heterosexual cohabitations, and homosexual relationships (Doka, 1987 and Thornton et al., 1991:356). If outsiders are unaware that a relationship exists and the bereaved are unable to publicly acknowledge their loss, they will not receive social support for their grief and their bereavement will be problematic.

A second type of disenfranchised grief will occur when *the loss is not acknowledged by others* as being genuine loss. An abortion or miscarriage is often deemed to be of lesser significance because the mother never had the opportunity to develop a face-to-face relationship with the child (Thornton et al., 1991). In the case of abortion, it is assumed that since the pregnancy was unwanted, grieving is unnecessary. According to Idell Kesselman (1990:241), whatever one's position on abortion, "we must acknowledge that at least one death occurs—in addition to the fetus, there is often the death of youth, of innocence, of dreams, and of illusion." Kesselman maintains that women who have had an abortion need to express "unresolved feelings of loss" and deal with "issues of 'death, loss and separation.' " Kesselman concludes that grief therapy must be a necessary part of abortion counseling.

Two different examples of unacknowledged losses are the death of a companion pet and the death of a former spouse. According to Avery Weisman (1990–

1991:241), the loss of a companion animal is often accompanied by intense grief and mourning but is seldom recognized by others as an important and authentic occasion for bereavement. Likewise, the death of a former spouse is rarely thought of as a legitimate loss because most people believe that grief work should be completed shortly after the divorce.

Related to the unacknowledged loss is the third type of disenfranchised grief, in which *the grievers are unrecognized.* The death of an adolescent peer or friend is rarely openly acknowledged and socially sanctioned. One of the reasons wakes and visitation services often attract larger audiences than do funerals is that employers are increasingly unwilling to provide employees with released time from work to attend a funeral of a person who is not a family member (Sklar and Hartley, 1990). Other unrecognized grievers are young children, the mentally incompetent and/or retarded, and elderly adults. In each of these cases the bereavement needs of individuals are also often ignored by most social audiences (Sklar and Hartley, 1990; Kloeppel and Hollins, 1989).

The final type of disenfranchised grief occurs when *the death is not socially sanctioned,* as in the case of a death occurring in the act of a crime, or when death is caused by suicide, AIDS, or autoerotic asphyxia (Thornton et al., 1989; Ness and Pheffer, 1990; Murphy and Perry, 1988). When people feel ambivalent, awkward, and/or uncomfortable about the cause of the death, they are generally unable or unwilling to provide the social support needed by the bereaved.

According to Kenneth Doka (1989), whenever disenfranchised grief occurs, the experience of grief is intensified while the normal sources of social support are lacking. Disenfranchised grievers are usually barred from contact with the deceased during the dying process. They are also frequently excluded from funeral rituals as well as care and support systems that may assist them in their bereavement. Finally, they may often experience many practical and legal difficulties after the death of their loved one. All of these circumstances intensify the problematic nature of bereavement for disenfranchised grievers.

THE GRIEVING PROCESS

In Chapter 12 we defined *grief* as a very powerful emotion that is often triggered or stimulated by death. Thomas Attig makes an important distinction between grief and the grieving process. While grief is an emotion that engenders feelings of helplessness and passivity, the process of *grieving* is a more complex coping process that presents challenges and opportunities for the griever and requires energy to be invested, tasks to be undertaken, and choices to be made (Attig, 1991:387).

Most people believe that grieving is a disease-like and debilitating process that renders the individual passive and helpless. According to Attig (1991:389):

> It is misleading and dangerous to mistake grief for the whole of the experience of the bereaved. It is misleading because the experience is far more complex, entailing diverse emotional, physical, intellectual, spiritual, and social impacts. It is dangerous because it is precisely this aspect of the experience of the bereaved that is potentially the most frustrating and debilitating.

Death ascribes to the griever a passive social position in the bereavement role. Grief is an emotion over which the individual has no control. However, understanding that grieving is an active coping process can restore to the griever a sense of autonomy where the process is permeated with choice and where there are many areas over which the griever does have some control. Attig helps us to understand the active nature of the grieving process by emphasizing some of the choices that confront those who grieve.

MAKING CHOICES IS PART OF THE ACTIVE GRIEVING PROCESS

Thomas Attig

The bereaved can choose whether to indulge in the paralyzing grief emotion or to struggle against what tempts them in it. This fundamental choice may require a kind of hope beyond hope or a faith rooted in convictions that support and sustain the very capacity to affirm life and its meaningfulness. The bereaved can choose their own timing and pacing in undertaking the [bereavement] tasks and define their own styles in addressing them. They can choose to attack the tasks and challenges vigorously, investing much time and energy in their grief work, or they can choose to go slowly, allowing themselves frequent respite from the rigors of the process.

They can choose the focus of their attention. They can choose whether and how to interact with the body of the deceased. They can choose which of their physical surroundings now permeated with new significance they are willing to encounter, what they have need to witness or interest in witnessing, and the like. They can choose to visit or to stay away from places of significance. They can choose to keep, discard, or postpone until later decisions about what is to be done with physical effects, pictures, mementos, and other objects that have significant relation to the deceased. They can choose alternative means of effectively expressing the emotions they experience of the new meanings they discern. They can choose to actively participate in social responses to the death such as the funeral or merely to witness the participations of others. They can choose to do or say what is meaningful to them either in private or together with others. They can choose at times to withdraw from others and at other times to reach out for support or comfort. They can choose to find means to building a new and dynamic relation with the deceased, giving shape to their lives in part through continuing, albeit transformed, interaction with the story of the life now ended.

Viewing grieving as an active coping process offers the bereaved some understanding of the possible objectives of and even fruits of their labors. Beyond restored emotional equilibrium, renewed motivation for engaging in everyday life, and revived hope for the future, the bereaved can experience their grieving as life enhancing in yielding increased feelings of strength and security in their own person, deepened self-understanding and self-esteem, enhanced capacities to understand and respond sensitively to others, improved critical perspective on personal relationships, and enriched perspectives of reality and the human condition. Emphasizing the active and potentially life-enhancing character of the coping process motivates the bereaved to invest the energy required for change and life transformation.

"The Importance of Conceiving of Grief as an Active Process." In *Death Studies*, vol. 15. Washington, DC: Taylor and Francis, 1991, pp. 390–392.

COPING WITH GRIEF

The grieving process, like the dying process, is essentially a series of behaviors and attitudes related to coping with the stressful situation of changing the status of a relationship. As discussed in Chapter 6, many have attempted to understand coping with dying as a series of universal, mutually exclusive, and linear stages. However, since most will acknowledge that not all people will progress through the stages in the same manner, we will list a number of coping strategies used as people attempt to resolve the pain caused by the loss of a significant relationship.

Robert Kavanaugh (1972) identifies the following seven behaviors and feelings as part of the coping process: shock and denial, disorganization, volatile emotions, guilt, loss and loneliness, relief, and reestablishment. It is not difficult to see similarities between these behaviors and Kübler-Ross's five stages (denial, anger, bargaining, depression, and acceptance) of the dying process. According to Kavanaugh (1972:123), "these seven stages do not subscribe to the logic of the head as much as to the irrational tugs of the heart—the logic of need and permission."

Shock and Denial

Even when a significant other is expected to die, at the time of death there is often a sense in which the death is not real. For most of us our first response is "no, this can't be true." With time our experience of shock diminishes, but we find new ways to deny the reality of death.

Some believe that denial is dysfunctional behavior for those in bereavement. However, denial is not only a common experience among the newly bereaved, but also serves positive functions in the process of adaptation. The main function of denial is to provide the bereaved with a "temporary safe place" from the ugly realities of a social world that only offers loneliness and pain.

With time the meaning of loss tends to expand, and it may be impossible for one to deal with all of the social meanings of death at once. For example, if my wife dies, not only do I lose my spouse, I lose my best friend, my sexual partner, the mother of my children, a source of income, the person who writes the Christmas cards, and so on. Denial can protect me from some of the magnitude of this social loss, which may be unbearable at one point in time. With denial, I can work through different aspects of my loss over time.

Disorganization

Disorganization is that stage in the bereavement process in which one may feel totally out of touch with the reality of everyday life. Some go through the three-day time period just prior to the funeral as if on "automatic pilot" or "in a daze." Nothing normal "makes sense," and an individual may feel that life has no inherent meaning. For some, death is perceived as preferable to life, which appears to be devoid of meaning.

This emotional response is also a normal experience for the newly bereaved. Confusion is normal for those whose social world has been disorganized through death. When my father died, my mother not only lost all those things one loses with a death of a spouse, but she also lost her care-giving role—a social role and master status that had defined her identity in the five years my father lived with cancer. It is only natural to experience confusion and social disorganization when one's social identity has been destroyed.

Volatile Reactions

Whenever one's identity and social order face the possibility of destruction, there is a natural tendency to feel angry, frustrated, helpless, and/or hurt. The volatile reactions of terror, hatred, resentment, and jealousy are often experienced as emotional manifestations of these feelings. Grieving humans are sometimes more successful at masking their feelings in socially acceptable behaviors than other animals, whose instincts cause them to go into a fit of rage when their order is threatened by external forces. However apparently dissimilar, the internal emotional experience is similar.

In working with bereaved persons over the past 15 years, I have observed that the following become objects of volatile grief reactions: God, medical personnel, funeral directors, other family members, in-laws, friends who have not experienced death in their families, and/or even the person who has died. I have always found it interesting to watch mild-mannered individuals transformed into raging and resentful persons when grieving. Some of these people have experienced physical symptoms such as migraine headaches, ulcers, neuropathy, and colitis as a result of repressing these intense emotions.

Guilt

Guilt is similar to the emotional reactions discussed above. Guilt is anger and resentment turned in on oneself and often results in self-deprecation and depression. Typically manifested in statements like "If only . . . ," "I should have . . . ," "I could have . . . ," and "Maybe I did the wrong thing," guilt is a normal part of the bereavement process.

From a sociological perspective, guilt can become a social mechanism to resolve the **dissonance** others feel when unable to explain why someone else's loved one has died. Rather than view death as something that can happen at any time to any one, friends can **blame the victim** of bereavement, and believe that the survivor was in some way responsible for the death—"if he had been a better parent, the child might not have been hit by the car," or "if I had been married to him I might also have committed suicide," or "no wonder he died of a heart attack, her cooking would give anyone high cholesterol." Therefore, bereaved persons are sometimes encouraged to feel guilt because they are subtly sanctioned by others' reactions.

Loss and Loneliness

As we discussed earlier, loss and loneliness are the other side of denial. Their full sense never becomes obvious at once; rather each day without the deceased helps us to recognize how much we needed and depended upon that person. Social situations in which we expected them always to be present seem different now that they are gone. Holiday celebrations are also diminished by their absence. In fact, for some, most of life takes on a "something's missing" feeling. This feeling was captured in the 1960s love song "End of the World."

Why does the world go on turning?
Why must the sea rush to shore?
Don't they know it's the end of the world
'Cause you don't love me anymore?

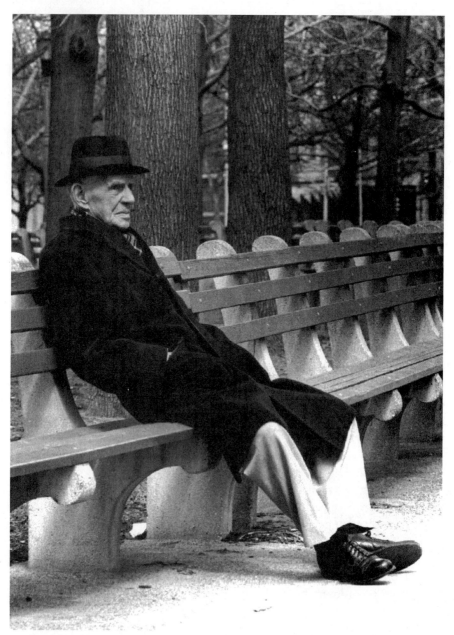

Of all the emotions related to the bereavement process, grief, loss, and loneliness are usually the most intensely experienced feelings.

Loss and loneliness are often transformed into depression and sadness fed by feelings of self-pity. According to Kavanaugh (1972:118), this effect is magnified by the fact that the dead loved-one grows out of focus in memory—"an elf becomes a giant, a sinner becomes a saint because the grieving heart needs giants and saints to fill an expanding void." Even a formerly undesirable spouse, such as an alcoholic, is missed in a way that few can understand unless his or her own heart is involved. This is a time in the grieving process when anybody is better than nobody, and being alone only adds to the curse of loss and loneliness (Kavanaugh, 1972:118).

Those who try to escape this experience will either turn to denial in an attempt to reject their feelings of loss or they will try to find surrogates—new friends at a bar, a quick remarriage, or a new pet. This escape can never be permanent, however, because loss and loneliness are a necessary part of the bereavement experience. According to Kavanaugh (1972:119), the "ultimate goal in conquering loneliness" is to build a new independence or to find a new and equally viable relationship.

Relief

The experience of relief in the midst of the bereavement process may seem odd for some and add to their feelings of guilt. My mother found relief in the fact that my father's battle with cancer had ended, even though this end provided her with new problems. I have observed a friend's relief six months after her husband died. This older friend of mine was the wife of a minister, and her whole life before he died was his ministry. With time, as she built a new world of social involvements and relationships of which he was not a part, she discovered a new independent person in herself that she perceived was a better person than she had ever been.

While relief can give rise to feelings of guilt, like denial, it can also be experienced as a "safe place" from the pain, loss, and loneliness that are endured when one is grieving. According to Kavanaugh (1972:121):

> The feeling of relief does not imply any criticism for the love we lost. Instead, it is a reflection of our need for ever deeper love, our quest for someone or something always better, our search for the infinite, that best and perfect love religious people name as God.

Reestablishment

As one moves toward reestablishment of a life without the deceased, it is obvious that the process involves extensive adjustment and time, especially if the relationship was meaningful. It is likely that one may have feelings of loneliness, guilt, and disorganization at the same time, and that just when one may experience a sense of relief, something will happen to trigger a denial of the death. What facilitates bereavement and adjustment is to fully experience each of these feelings as normal and realize that it is hope (holding the person together in fantasy at first) that will provide the survivor with the promise of a new life filled with order, purpose, and meaning.

Reestablishment never arrives all at once. Rather, it is a goal that one realizes has been achieved long after it has occurred. In some ways it is similar to Dorothy's realization at the end of "The Wizard of Oz"—she had always possessed the magic that could return her to Kansas. And, like Dorothy, we have to experience our loss before we really appreciate the joy of investing our lives again in new relationships.

DON'T REDUCE MY GRIEF TO SOMETHING LOGICAL AND UNIVERSAL

Stephanie Ericsson

Grief discriminates against no one. It kills. Maims. And cripples. It is the ashes from which the phoenix rises, and the mettle of rebirth. It returns life to the living dead. It teaches that there is nothing absolutely true, or untrue. It assures the living that we know nothing for certain. It humbles. It shrouds. It blackens. It enlightens.

Grief will make a new person out of you, if it doesn't kill you in the making. People say "How are you?" and they have that look in their faces again. And I look at them like they're crazy. I think, how do you think I am? I'm not strong enough for talk. A woman said to me, in a comforting tone of conspiracy, "My mother had breast cancer and lost her right breast. . . ." "Oh," I say, "that's awful. . . ." and wonder if that is supposed to be some sort of comparison. A tit, a husband—same thing? Strange how people want to join you in your intensity, your epiphany, by trying to relate—grabbing at straws of a so-called "like" experience while simultaneously they are repulsed by the agony. They see you on the street, driving by and pretending they don't see you. Shit, we all have our stuff to deal with. I suppose it's hard enough dealing with your own.

I can't tell them to shut up, not because I'm not rude by nature (it takes too much energy to be polite) but because I am afraid they'll go away. One more abandonment. "I lost my father two years ago. . . ." and I think, schmuck, that's supposed to happen, it's a natural part of becoming adult—children are supposed to outlive their parents. Did you lose the only other person in the world who would love your child the way you do? Did you lose the person you held all night, who slept next to you, warmed your bed so much you didn't need an extra blanket in the winter? Do you know how many blankets it takes to replace a husband? Did you lose the person who would worry about bills with you?

Screw in a light bulb when you were busy with the baby? Don't reduce this experience to something logical, universal. Even if it is, I walk alone amongst the dead; it's my death, my pain. Don't pretend you know it, like you know batting averages. Don't sacrilege all over my crucifixion.

"The Agony of Grief." *Utne Reader,* September/October, 1991, pp. 75–78.

THE FOUR TASKS OF MOURNING

In 1982, J. William Worden published *Grief Counseling and Grief Therapy,* which summarized the research conclusions of a National Institutes of Health study called the Omega Project (occasionally referred to as the Harvard Bereavement Study). Two of the more significant findings of this research, displaying the active nature of the grieving process, are that mourning is necessary for all persons who

Visiting the grave of a loved one can provide the bereaved with an opportunity to accept the reality of the loss and experience the pain of grief.

have experienced a loss through death, and that four tasks of mourning must be accomplished before mourning can be completed and reestablishment can take place.

According to Worden (1982:10), unfinished grief tasks can impair further growth and development of the individual. Furthermore, the necessity of these tasks suggests that those in bereavement *must* attend to "grief work" because successful grief resolution is not automatic, as Kavanaugh's (1972) stages might imply. Each bereaved person must accomplish four necessary tasks: (1) accept the reality of the loss, (2) experience the pain of grief, (3) adjust to an environment in which the deceased is missing, and (4) withdraw emotional energy and reinvest it in another relationship (Worden, 1982).

Accept the Reality of the Loss

Especially in situations where death is unexpected and/or the deceased lived far away, it is difficult to conceptualize the reality of the loss. The first task of mourning is to overcome the natural denial response, realize that the person is dead and will not return.

There are many ways in which bereaved persons can facilitate the actualization of death. The traditional methods are to view the body, attend the funeral and committal services, and visit the final place of disposition. The following is a partial list of additional activities that can assist in making death real for grieving persons.

1. view the body at the place of death before preparation by the funeral director
2. talk about the deceased and the circumstances surrounding the death
3. view photographs and personal effects associated with the deceased
4. distribute the possessions of the deceased among relatives and friends

Experience the Pain of Grief

Part of coming to grips with the reality of death is experiencing the emotional and physical pain caused by the loss. Many people in the denial stage of grieving attempt to avoid pain by choosing to reject the emotions and feelings they are experiencing. Some do this by avoiding places and circumstances that remind them of the deceased. I know of one widow who quit playing golf and stopped eating at a particular restaurant because these were activities that she had enjoyed with her husband. Another widow found it extremely painful to be with her dead husband's twin, even though he and her sister-in-law were her most supportive friends.

J. William Worden (1982:13–14) cites the following case study to illustrate the performance of this task of mourning:

One young woman minimized her loss by believing her brother was out of his dark place and into a better place after his suicide. This might have been true, but it kept her from feeling her intense anger at him for leaving her. In treatment, when she first allowed herself to feel anger, she said, "I'm angry with his behavior and not him!" Finally she was able to acknowledge this anger directly.

The problem with the avoidance strategy is that it is impossible to escape the pain associated with mourning. According to Bowlby (cited by Worden, 1982:14), "Sooner or later, some of those who avoid all conscious grieving, break down—usually with some form of depression." Tears can afford cleansing for wounds created by loss, and fully experiencing the pain ultimately provides wonderful relief to those who suffer, while eliminating long-term chronic grief.

Adjust to an Environment in Which the Deceased Is Missing

The third task, practical in nature, requires the griever to take on some of the social roles performed by the deceased, or find others who will. According to Worden (1982:15), the aborting of this task is to become helpless by refusing to develop the skills necessary in daily living and ultimately withdrawing from life.

I knew a woman who refused to adjust to the social environment in which she found herself after the death of her husband. He was her business partner, as well as her best and only friend. After 30 years of marriage, they had no children, and she had no close relatives. She had never learned to drive a car. Her entire social world had been controlled by her former husband. Three weeks after his funeral she went into the basement and committed suicide.

The alternative to social withdrawal is to assume new social roles by taking on additional responsibilities. Extended families who always gathered at Grandma's house for Thanksgiving will be tempted to have a number of small Thanksgiving dinners after her death. The members of this family may believe that "no one can take Grandma's place." While this may be true, members of the extended family will grieve better if someone else is willing to do Grandma's work, enabling the entire family to come together for Thanksgiving. Not to do so will cause double pain—the family will not gather, and Grandma will still be missed.

Withdraw Emotional Energy and Reinvest It in Another Relationship

The final task of mourning is a difficult one for many because they feel disloyal or unfaithful in withdrawing emotional energy from their dead loved one. One of my family members once said that she could never love another man after her husband died. My twice-widowed aunt responded, "I once felt like that, but I now consider myself to be fortunate to have been married to two of the best men in the world."

Other people find themselves unable to reinvest in new relationships because they are unwilling to experience again the pain caused by loss. The quotation from John Brantner at the beginning of this chapter provides perspective on this problem: "Only people who avoid love can avoid grief. The point is to learn from it and remain vulnerable to love."

However, those who are able to withdraw emotional energy and reinvest it in other relationships find the possibility of a newly established social life. Kavanaugh (1972:122–123) depicts this situation well with the following description.

> At this point fantasies fade into constructive efforts to reach out and build anew. The phone is answered more quickly, the door as well, and meetings seem important, invitations are treasured and any social gathering becomes an opportunity rather than a curse. Mementos of the past are put away for occasional family gatherings. New clothes and new places promise dreams instead of only fears. Old friends are important for encouragement and permission to rebuild one's life. New friends can offer realistic opportunities for coming out from under the grieving mantle. With newly acquired friends, one is not a widow, widower, or survivor—just a person. Life begins again at the point of new friendships. All the rest is of yesterday, buried, unimportant to the now and tomorrow.

ASSISTING THE BEREAVED

In his book *Bereavement: Studies of Grief in Adult Life,* Colin Parkes (1972:161) notes that the funeral often precedes the "peak of the pangs" of grief that tends to be reached in the second week of bereavement. The face put on for the funeral can no longer be maintained, and a need exists for the bereaved to be freed to grieve. The most valued person at this time is the one making few demands on the bereaved, quietly completing household tasks, and accepting the bereaved person's vented anguish and anger—some of which may be directed against the helper.

It is important to recognize that the bereaved person has painful and difficult tasks to perform that cannot be avoided or rushed. The best assistance one can offer those in grieving is to encourage them to attend to the four tasks of mourning described earlier.

One can help the bereaved come to grips with the reality of the death by talking about the deceased and encouraging them to conceptualize the loss they are experiencing. Parkes observes that it is often reassuring to the bereaved person when others show they are not afraid to express feelings of sadness. Such expressions make the bereaved person feel understood and reduce a sense of isolation. How people grieve will vary; the important thing is for feelings to emerge into consciousness. How they appear on the surface may be of secondary importance.

It is not uncommon for one approaching a newly bereaved person to be unsure as to how to react. Parkes suggests that while a conventional expression of sympathy can probably not be avoided, pity is the last thing the bereaved person wants. Pity makes one into an object—the bereaved person somehow becomes pitiful. Pity puts the bereaved person at a distance from, and in an inferior position to, the intended comforter. Parkes maintains it is best to get conventional verbal expressions of sympathy over as soon as possible and to speak from the heart or not at all. There is not *a* proper thing to say at this time; a trite formula serves only to widen the gap between the two persons.

The encounter between the bereaved and the visitor may not seem satisfactory, since the helper cannot bring back the deceased and the bereaved person cannot gratify the helper by seeming helped. Bereaved people do, however, appreciate the visits and expressions of sympathy paid by others. These tributes to the dead confirm to the mourner the belief that the deceased is worth all the pain. The bereaved are also reassured that they are not alone and feel less insecure.

The Hallmark Card Company sells its products with the slogan, "When you care enough to send the very best, send a Hallmark." While sending a card is one way to validate the loss of the bereaved and assist them in their grieving, if you really care enough to send the very best, a personal visit or hand-written letter should be favored over merely sending a card. On the other hand, if one finds it impossible to communicate a personal expression of sympathy, a card is preferable to doing nothing. Following are seven helpful suggestions for expressing condolence.

THE ART OF CONDOLENCE

Based upon their studying thousands of condolence letters and analyzing their structure, Leonard and Hillary Zunin (1991) share seven components that provide the writer with a practical, simple, and clear outline for sharing his or her thoughts. Though all seven components need not be included in every letter of condolence, keeping them in mind will provide an effective guide for sharing thoughts in such a letter. The components include:

1. *Acknowledge the loss.* Mention the deceased by name and indicate how you learned about the death. It is very acceptable to relate personal shock and dismay at hearing such news and such an acknowledgement sets the tone for your letter.
2. *Express your sympathy.* Share your sorrow in an honest and sincere fashion. In so doing you are showing that you care and

(continued)

relate in some way to the difficult situation they are facing. Do not hesitate to use the words died or death in your comments.

3. *Note special qualities of the deceased.* As you reflect upon the individual who has died, think about those characteristics you valued most in that person and share them in your letter. These may be specific attributes, personality characteristics, or other qualities. Sharing these with the bereaved help them realize that their loved one was appreciated by others.

4. *Recount a memory about the deceased.* At the time of a death, memories we have of the deceased person are a most valued possession and something which can never be too great a supply. Because the bereaved often have difficulty keeping those memories in the forefront of their thoughts, your sharing of memories will be very gratefully received. Feel free to recall humorous incidents as they can be very beneficial at this time.

5. *Note special qualities of the bereaved.* Grieving people also need to be reminded of their personal strengths and other positive qualities—those characteristics which will help them through this difficult time. By reminding them of the qualities you have observed in them, you will be encouraging them to use these qualities to their advantage at this time.

6. *Offer assistance.* Offering help need not be part of a condolence letter, but if help is offered, it should be for a specific thing. An open-ended offer of help places the burden for determining what that help will be on the bereaved, and they have enough burdens already. Making an offer to do something specific and then doing it is a most welcome extension of yourself.

7. *Close with a thoughtful word or phrase.* The final words in your letter of condolence are especially important and should reflect your true feelings. Flowery or elaborate phrases do not help. Honest expressions of your thoughts and feelings communicate best.

From Paul V. Johnson, "Book Review of *The Art of Condolence* by Leonard M. Zunin and Hilary Stanton Zunin." *Caregivers Quarterly*, 6, 3(Fall 1991):3–4.

While many bereaved people are frightened and surprised by the intensity of their emotions, reassurance that they are not going mad and that this is a perfectly natural behavior can be an important contribution of the helper (Parkes, 1972:164–165). On the other hand, absence of grief in a situation where expected, excessive guilt feelings or anger, or lasting physical symptoms should be taken as signs that all is not going well. These persons may require special help, and the caregiver should not hesitate to advise the bereaved to get additional help if the caregiver is uncertain about the course of events.

SUPPORT GROUPS FOR THE BEREAVED

Support groups empower persons to cope with social crisis and loss in a de-alienating environment. According to Louis La Grand (1991:212), the power of support groups lies in the "introduction of new ways of looking at one's problems and the development of belief systems that enhance the twin attributes of self-determination and interdependence, all of this accruing in a socially secure setting."

The grieving process often socially isolates the bereaved by marginalizing them from normal patterns of social interaction. Bereavement self-help groups, by their very nature, challenge the assumption that grievers are unique by confronting them with a group of caring people who understand their experience of loss and are willing to practice patterns of coping that reduce feelings of despair and depression (La Grand, 1991:212).

Some of the national support groups for grievers would include The Compassionate Friends, Candlelighters, Empty Arms, Begin Again, Widow to Widow Program, The Omega Project, Parents Without Partners, and various hospice programs and/or hospital grief therapy groups.

GRIEVERS KNOW BEST

We lost the eldest of our three sons nearly two years ago when he fell from the roof of a building. Keith was only 21 years old. Sometimes I wonder if everyone he knew has forgotten him because his name is never mentioned. I suppose they think they're being kind and don't want to upset me by reminding me that Keith is dead. Believe me, there is never a minute of the day that I am not aware that my son is dead. No one needs to be afraid of "reminding" me. *How I would love to talk about the son I lost with someone who knew him.*

I lost my beloved husband over a year ago and when his birthday came around, not a soul mentioned it to me. I spent the day alone—weeping because nobody wanted to risk "stirring up my emotions." It hurt me more wondering if everyone who had known him had forgotten that he had ever lived. Or perhaps they didn't know how much he meant to me. A grieving person *wants* to talk about the one he or she lost. So what if it does bring on a flood of tears? The tears are there anyway, waiting to be shed.

Abigail Van Buren (Dear Abby), *Minneapolis Star-Tribune*, January 3, 1989. Copyright Universal Press Syndicate.

GRIEVING PARENTS AND THE LOSS OF AN INFANT

Adaptation to the death of a loved one is always difficult. However, the death of a child is typically regarded as the most difficult of all deaths. As we discussed in Chapter 3, the death of a child goes against the natural order—parents are supposed to die before their children. Furthermore, the death of a child symbolically threatens the family's hope for a future.

In order to conceptualize the nature of loss involved in the death of a child, we should remember that the relationship of a parent with a child begins long before birth (Raphael, 1983:230–231). For each parent, from the time of conception, the child becomes a source of fantasy—the imagined child he or she will become. These hoped-for extensions of self are very common among expectant parents. As the pregnancy progresses, the fantasy relationship with this imagined child intensifies with the selection of the name for the baby, the rehearsal for parenting, the fantasies shared with others, and finally the birth of the child. With the death of a newborn or a stillbirth, the bubble of one's fantasy world is suddenly burst.

The death of an infant places severe strains on parents and members of the family—a sense of loss that will likely persist over a number of years. Studies show (Nicol, Tompkins, Campbell, and Syme, 1986) that up to one-third of mothers experience a marked deterioration in their health and well-being after the loss of an infant. The death of a child also has dysfunctional consequences for family systems. William Worden (1982:101) reports the results of a study at Stanford University Hospital in which 70 percent of the parents whose children had died of leukemia were divorced within 2 years following the death. Another study by Nixon and Pearn (1977) reported that 7 of 29 couples separated following the deaths of their children. In a more recent study by Reiko Schwab (1992) concerned with the effects of a child's death on the marital relationship, it was discovered that there is an increase in general irritability between spouses and a loss of communication and sexual intimacy following the death of a child.

Longitudinal studies of grieving parents demonstrate that the experience of grief does not go away with time, rather its focus changes. According to McClowry, Davies, May, Kulenkamp, and Martinson (1987), even after 9 years, parents are still experiencing significant pain and loss—which the researchers refer to as "an empty space." This "empty space" feeling takes on three recurring patterns of grieving. The first is "getting over it." In this pattern the grievers do what they can to get back to life as usual and accept death matter-of-factly.

The second way of dealing with the empty space is to "fill the emptiness" by keeping busy. Some parents attend grief groups, others immerse themselves in work, become more religious, increase their food or alcohol intake, or become involved as volunteers in organizations such as Candlelighters (a support group for parents of children with cancer), Compassionate Friends or Empty Arms (two support groups for bereaved parents). Other parents attempt to replace the dead child with another by getting pregnant or through adoption.

The third theme in the experience of the empty space is described as "keeping the connection." In this pattern of grieving, parents attempt to integrate this pain and loss into their lives (McClowry et al., 1987):

> Although most of the grievers who were "keeping the connection" expressed satisfaction with their present lives, they continue to reserve a small part of themselves for the loss of a special relationship which they view as irreplaceable.

Mourning the death of a fetus or newborn baby differs from mourning the death of another loved one (Furman, 1978). Mourning is a dual process of detachment from the loved one that is moderated by identification. The bereaved take into themselves aspects of the deceased, but because a fetus or newborn has not lived long enough as a separate person, the parents have little to take into themselves of their baby. Thus, they suffer detachment without identification. Parents must readjust their self-image with the knowledge that the baby will never again be part of them.

Support from Health-Care Professionals

To assist the parents with their adjustment, it is important they receive support from those around them. In a study of 130 parents who had experienced a **perinatal death,** Judith Murray and Victor Callan (1988:242) discovered that a consistent predictor of better adjustment was the parent's level of satisfaction with the comfort and support provided by physicians, nurses, and other hospital staff. Parents who were pleased with the level of support they received from medical personnel were also less depressed and had higher levels of self-esteem and psychological well-being. Furthermore, emotional support from partners, family, and hospital staff was linked to fewer grief reactions and better overall adjustment. Therefore, support from others can go a long way to facilitate parental bereavement at the death of a child.

Hospital-based intervention is especially necessary and helpful to parents experiencing the death of a newborn or a stillbirth, and medical personnel are in a unique position to assist parents in their grief (Davis, Stewart, and Harmon, 1988:242). However, while the majority (70 percent) of bereaved parents wish to discuss their concerns with their physician (Clyman et al., 1979), 50 percent of parents received no physician follow-up, and many others had no contact with their physicians until a regularly scheduled postpartum check (Rowe et al., 1978). Thus, while parents seem to desire medical personnel to acknowledge their feelings of shock, guilt, and grief, such wishes do not seem to be fulfilled in many instances.

Part of the emotional support needed by parents involves encouraging them to accept the reality of death, express their feelings of loss, and then validating these feelings. Communication and understanding by the medical staff will serve as a great source of support and comfort. By being available, medical personnel can help to reduce the isolation parents often feel at this difficult time. Since grief is a necessary process, whenever bereavement is facilitated, the parents become subject to a lower risk for psychological and physical disturbances.

Table 13.1 identifies various ways in which professionals can contribute to the adjustment of grieving parents.

Parental Involvement with Professional Helpers: Perinatal Deaths

The death of a fetus or newborn infant is stressful not only for parents and siblings, but also for all people who are involved with the child. Increasingly, parents are being included in the direct care of critically ill children until the time of death and following. Familiarity with the types of procedures and decisions that parents may face at the death of their child is essential. Most bereaved parents will learn about hospital procedures and how to share in decision making only when they are faced with such a situation.

The nursing procedures are fairly clear, and nurses are instructed to respond in ways that can help in the socioemotional adjustments. The nurse notifies a nursing-social worker counselor at the time of admission concerning the fetal death or infant trauma. Even baptism is offered by some hospitals, where it may be done by anyone in the absence of a chaplain. The pastoral care department of a hospital is notified, as is the communications department, so that accurate information is available to others.

In the case of stillbirths, fetal deaths, and infant deaths, the parents may be given the option to see and hold their infant, to learn the baby's gender, and to decide on an autopsy and funeral arrangements. The medical staff explains what the parents can expect the baby to look like. Believing that the age of siblings is the major factor in determining their involvement in these settings, Furman (1978:217) notes:

> Adolescents should decide for themselves. Elementary grade children are helped by attending a service but not helped by seeing a malformed dead body. Children under school age are particularly not helped by seeing their dead brother or sister, but they are sometimes helped by being in the company of the parents at the time of the funeral.

The extent of individual involvement depends upon the preference of individual family members.

Table 13.1   Behaviors of Professionals Identified to Be Helpful by Grieving Parents

HELPFUL BEHAVIORS	PRIMARY RESPONSIBILITY FOR THIS BEHAVIOR
1. Informs the parents immediately of the condition of the baby.	Doctor
2. Expresses feelings over the baby's death with consoling words to parents.	Doctor/Nurse
3. Provides as much factual information surrounding the baby's death as is available.	Doctor/Nurse
4. Describes the appearance of the baby in factual and tender terms before bringing the baby to them.	Doctor/Nurse
5. Encourages parents to see and hold the baby and stays with them while they initially examine the baby.	Doctor/Nurse
6. Touches parents affectionately and appropriately; words are not always necessary.	Doctor/Nurse
7. Encourages parents to grieve openly.	Doctor/Nurse
8. Acknowledges the baby's death at first contact with parents and daily thereafter; does not act like death has not occurred.	Doctor/Nurse
9. Spends extra time with the parents to provide time to review the events surrounding the baby's death.	Doctor/Nurse

Patricia Estok and Ann Lehman, "Perinatal Death: Grief Support for Families." *Birth* (March 1983) 10:1, p. 19. By permission of Blackwell Scientific Publications, Inc.

The nurses' responsibility includes attaching identification bands to wrist and ankle, measuring the weight, length, and head circumference, taking footprints and possibly a handprint, and completing standard forms. These forms might include a fetal death certificate, an authorization for autopsy, and a record of the death for the receptionist. Medical photographs may be taken by the medical photographer of a full front and back view, as well as close-ups of any abnormalities. These are used by physicians to describe the infant's medical condition. The nurse is also encouraged to take nonmedical photographs that include the infant in a blanket, unclothed, a close-up of the face, and the parents holding the child if they so desire. These pictures are given to the counselor and later to the parents.

The dead infant is wrapped in a blanket, labeled, and taken to the morgue. In the case of a fetus, the body is sent to pathology with a surgical pathology lab slip.

The physician may request that the placenta be included in the case of spontaneous abortions or fetal deaths. Genetic studies may also be requested; these might include a cord blood sample, a placenta sample, fresh tissue such as gonadal tissue or connective tissue around the kidneys, skin sample, and a complete genetic study that is sent to the state laboratory. The nurse then completes a checklist for assisting parents experiencing perinatal deaths, and she or he may, if procedure calls for it, place an identifier by the name tag at the entrance to the mother's room.

Hospitals with a special program to help the survivors of fetal and infant deaths provide nursing, medical, social work, and/or pastoral counselors who may assist the surviving parents and siblings. Time is taken to explain and help in the following matters: (1) autopsies and hospital procedures after death; (2) funeral or cremation options (arrangements for the disposition of the body are required in most states if the fetus was at least 20 weeks); (3) the nature and expression of grief and mourning; (4) coping with the reactions of friends and relatives; (5) other children in dealing with the death of their brother or sister; and (6) decisions regarding another pregnancy. Monthly meetings of bereaved parents can be established to provide a setting for sharing and learning about grief. These experiences of sharing with other parents allow for reality-based comparisons and for active support of other parents whose loss is also great.

While this list of hospital procedures is by no means complete, it does, however, outline what parents of spontaneous abortion, stillbirth, fetal death, or neonatal death may encounter. The attitudes and responses of physicians, nurses, and others may vary greatly. At times, for example, the helpers are in need of socioemotional support along with parents and siblings. Many hospitals, on the other hand, have not dealt with the special needs of families experiencing perinatal deaths. While these practices are becoming more common around the country, one should not be surprised if a nurse or physician appears stunned at the request of a parent to spend some time with the body of their child. We can only hope that the human values of medical care will prevail over bureaucratic values as the welfare of the whole person is taken into account in the medical arena. This can be accomplished most effectively if parents are provided with accurate information, encouraged to ask questions, given plenty of time to make decisions, and given opportunities to share their experience in parental bereavement with others.

THE DEATH OF PETS: A SPECIAL KIND OF GRIEVING

According to Jack Kamerman (1988:112), the death of pets represents an opportunity to study attitudes and behaviors toward human death. Such a loss often represents a child's first experience with death, and the stance taken by parents influences a child's attitude toward human death encountered later on. For example, in a study of college students recalling their first childhood experience with death (Dickinson, 1992:171), a pet was involved for 28 percent of the students—birds, cats, chickens, cows, dogs, fish, mice, toads, rabbits, pigs, hamsters, gerbils, and turtles.

Sociological issues are clarified by examining the death of pets, such as the process by which human traits are attributed to animals. For many individuals, a pet is a significant member of the family. People talk to pets and care for them as if they were their children. Pets often live with a family as many years as children live at home prior to leaving for college or emancipation. Pets can make people feel needed, can relieve loneliness, and can serve as friends and companions. Such a death is a traumatic experience for family members. As would occur for any other member of the family, the resulting dismemberment leaves a big void.

Unlike the person losing a friend or relative who receives outpourings of sympathy and support, one who loses a pet often receives ridicule for overreacting, for being foolishly emotional, and expressing grief over the death of an animal (Brody, 1985). There has not traditionally been a funeral or an acceptable time of mourning or standard words of comfort for friends to speak on the death of a pet. This leads to the problem of disenfranchised grief as discussed earlier in the chapter.

Grief, however, is a natural response to the loss of any significant object, person, or circumstance. Such attachments can be made to any pet—a rat, a guinea pig, a bird, or a fish—providing the animal provides emotional gratification. To a child, for whom a pet offers the most secure and certain acceptance, the loss can be especially painful.

Many individuals go through an agonizing separation when they lose a pet. Their symptoms are very similar to those experienced within the process of bereavement for a significant other. As with the death of a person, when a pet dies suddenly, as in an accident, guilt is a common reaction. Putting an animal to sleep may also leave one with a feeling of guilt.

In discussing bereavement counseling for persons who had lost companion animals, Avery Weisman (1990–1991) discovered that clients were reluctant to tell others of their bereavement, but within the therapy group they spoke freely and with relief when they received acceptance and respect for their bereavement. According to Weisman (1990–1991:243–244):

> Clients felt that their grief was both exceptionally strong and abnormally tenacious, and they wept accordingly, as if confessing something unmentionable. Most people apologized for crying. One client hesitantly said, "I've actually mourned more than I did for my father."

Discussion of pet bereavement enables individuals to share their own feelings of grief, fear, and loss. Weisman's (1990–1991) work with bereaved pet owners suggests

HOSPITAL LETS DOG VISIT DYING WOMAN

Hospital officials made an exception to policy and allowed Sunny, a collie who was a woman's constant companion for eleven years, to lie at the foot of her bed as the woman was dying of cancer. Sunny curled up beside the 63-year-old Jeanette Dahl at Metropolitan Medical Center in Minneapolis on Friday, occasionally licking her arm and putting a paw in her hand. Ms. Dahl responded by squeezing the dog's paw.

The dog was taken out of the room late Friday when Ms. Dahl began having breathing problems. She died at 4 p.m. Saturday. As Ms. Dahl's condition deteriorated, Sunny refused to budge from the bed. "She was much more intent about staying on the bed than she was this morning," said Ms. Dahl's niece. As the woman's breathing became more erratic, the dog became nervous and was taken home.

Ms. Dahl had raised Sunny since the dog was a puppy, and the two were virtually inseparable. The hospital usually does not allow pets to visit patients but agreed to make an exception in this case.

Adapted from the *Lexington Herald-Leader*, Lexington, KY, January 7, 1985, p. C8. Reprinted with permission of the *Lexington Herald-Leader*.

that there were many similarities in grieving to that found in human death—preoccupation was common, people reported mistaking shadows and sounds for their lost pet, guilt and ambivalence were experienced, and there were also corresponding feelings of loneliness and emptiness in the grieving process.

Pets in the Lives of the Elderly

Companion-animal visits sponsored by community volunteers to nursing homes offer residents opportunities for conversation, sensory stimulation, tactile warmth, and ongoing relationships with others (Savishinsky, 1988:143). The effectiveness of these visits derives in part from the symbolic meanings (fears, hopes, values, and identities) that people attribute to pet animals.

According to Hiroko Akiyama, Joseph Holtzman, and William Britz (1986–1987), companion animals are valuable assets to grieving widows, particularly elderly widows, because they provide a reason to live and care while supplying entertainment, unconditional love, and companionship. Furthermore, owners of companion pets experience less incidence of depression and psychogenic symptoms than nonowners during the period of bereavement.

People project onto their pets, and onto their animals' deaths, some of the qualities of human kinship (Savishinsky, 1988:142). This phenomenon is supported by Avery Weisman's (1990–1991) studies of a number of grief groups for persons losing companion animals. He made the following observation:

> I was somewhat surprised to hear that they had special ways of communicating with the pet. For example, some clients regularly talked over the day's happenings when they came home and felt that their cat or dog actually understood, and perhaps they did. There was strong silent communication, as well, as if the relationship was both unique and secret. A few spoke about a certain look or empathic eye contact.

Having a Pet "Put to Sleep"

Like other professionals dealing with issues related to dying and death, veterinarians are also concerned about discussing euthanasia and giving bad news to pet owners (Edney, 1988). Fears and anxieties experienced by the clinician wanting to succeed in curing the pet's illness make it difficult for the veterinarian breaking the bad news. A prime fear is that the owner will blame the veterinarian for the animal's illness. If veterinarians can understand that blaming the professional is a normal grief reaction, they can learn to depersonalize this reaction.

When contemplating having an animal put to sleep, Herbert Nieburg and Arlene Fischer (1982) suggest asking the owner whether the pet can do the things it once enjoyed, whether there is more pain or more pleasure in its life, whether the animal has become bad-tempered and snappish as a result of old age or illness, whether it has lost control of its bodily functions, and whether one can afford the expense and time involved in keeping a sick pet alive. Whatever the final decision, this is not an easy choice for an individual to make.

For those who do make the decision to euthanize their pet, at first there is a feeling of regret for having given permission for euthanasia, despite illness, invalidism, or senescence (Weisman, 1990–1991). According to Weisman this should not be interpreted as an indictment of euthanasia but rather an expression of how guilty owners felt about invoking their power of life and death over their beloved companion.

Disposal of Pets after Death

When a pet dies, many people arrange for disposal through their veterinarians or the local sanitation department. Though many people today may not choose to bury their pets, there are about 500 pet cemeteries in the United States used by 2 percent of pet owners (News and Courier, 1987). The choice of pet caskets runs the gamut from simple fiberglass caskets ranging from $45 to $150, depending on size, to an actual child's casket. Casket, plot, and perpetual care average $300, but a body bag and temporary marker can be purchased for about half that amount

*The grave of a pet indicates the meaningful relationship
that existed between the pet and its owner.*

(Langley, 1987). Markers for grave sites come in bronze and granite. In addition to
the pet's name and dates for birth and death, markers often bear an affectionate
word from the owner, an engraving of the dog's face, or a photo of the pet embedded in the bronze or granite. The box at the top of the next page, however,
shows that the cost of pet burials for the military is bothering certain officials.

Cremation is another alternative to dispose of one's deceased pet, whether by
communal cremation or *separate cremation*. The former is less expensive and involves
cremation in groups, with ashes distributed according to the law. Separate cremation allows the remains to be placed in an urn. Costs of communal cremation by a
pet cremation service in South Carolina, for example, range from $40 to $75 depending on the size of the animal, and separate cremation costs range from $60 to $125.

The final disposition of pets is of such concern that the following was proposed

BASE PET CEMETERIES TO LOSE ARMY FUNDING

The Army, facing shrinking budgets and skeptical Capitol Hill overseers, has promised to stop spending taxpayer funds to build and maintain pet cemeteries. The rhubarb over Rover's remains ended recently when the House Armed Services Committee, which had questioned a $16,674 pet burial plot at Fort Gordon, Georgia, last year, published an Army statement halting the practice.

"Army policy regarding pet cemeteries has been reviewed, and new guidance is being issued to installations," the Army statement said. "The policy does not permit new pet cemeteries, and the use of (government) funds for maintenance and repair of cemeteries is prohibited." Existing pet cemeteries will be maintained by volunteers—or restored to their natural state—and Army personnel will be encouraged to use "commercial incineration" instead.

Adapted from the Associated Press, *News and Courier,* Charleston, SC, March 17, 1989, p. 6A.

to the American Animal Hospital Association by the Professional Animal Disposal Advisory Council (Cooke, 1988):

> The recognition of the importance of the human/companion-animal bond as it relates to the veterinary profession has mandated changes in methods of disposing of pet animal carcasses. Recent legal decisions make it especially important to provide pet owners with a complete description of their options. In view of the fact pet owners view the final disposition of their pets in terms of human reference, it is important the attending veterinarian avoid the responsibility of providing the disposal options whenever possible. Pet disposal services should be turned over to outside contractors whenever possible, in order to avoid implications that veterinarians are purveyors of these services.

Suggestions by the Professional Animal Disposal Advisory Council include:

1. acceptable methods of pet disposition, such as burial or cremation when available, or the use of landfills
2. outline of suggested disposition procedures and a full-disclosure consent form, signed by the client, and used in all hospitals to relieve the veterinarian of future legal ramifications
3. sealing of the body in a sturdy plastic bag sufficient in size and strength to contain the entire pet and its body fluids
4. proper identification of the body and storage in a freezer
5. identification of pets known to have diseases contagious to human beings and/or other pets

CONCLUSION

In this chapter we have discussed the grieving process, bereavement roles, normal adaptations to experiences of loss, the four tasks of mourning, and special grieving issues related to the loss of children and pets. We have attempted to demonstrate that the bereaved *must* attend to grief work because successful grief resolution is not automatic. This grief work refers to Worden's (1982) four necessary tasks of bereavement: accepting the reality of the loss, experiencing the pain of grief, adjusting to an environment in which the deceased is missing, and withdrawing emotional energy and reinvesting it in other relationships.

Grievers need support and assistance in the bereavement process. One can help the bereaved come to grips with the reality of the death by talking about the deceased and encouraging survivors to conceptualize the loss they are experiencing. It is often reassuring to the bereaved person when others show they are not afraid to express feelings of sadness. Such expressions make the bereaved person

"Sometimes a cute card just isn't appropriate, Jane."

feel understood and reduce a sense of isolation. Many well-meaning friends find it difficult to find proper words to say. Unfortunately, their discomfort often causes them to do nothing. Even trite words are better than no words at all. One well-known slogan says, "When you care enough to send the very best, send a Hall-mark." When comforting bereaved friends, however, a better personal slogan might be, "When you care enough to send the very best, send yourself." At this time, the very best we have to offer is our own caring presence.

Summary

1. The bereavement role is a temporary role that gives one the right to be exempted from normal social responsibilities and to become dependent upon others.
2. Abnormal bereavement behavior is preoccupation with the death of the loved one and refusal to attempt return to normal social functioning.
3. Disenfranchised grief involves loss that cannot be openly acknowledged, socially sanctioned, and publicly shared. There are four circumstances that lead to disenfranchasied grief: 1) where the relationship to the deceased is not socially recognized; 2) situations when the loss is not acknowledged by others as being genuine loss; 3) circumstances where the grievers are unrecognized; and 4) occurrences when the death is not socially sanctioned.
4. The grieving process is similar to the dying process in that it is a series of behaviors and attitudes related to coping with the stressful situation of changing the status of a relationship. The grieving process need not be passive because the bereaved can make a number of decisions as they attempt to cope with their loss.
5. It is important in grieving to let feelings emerge into consciousness and not be afraid to express feelings of sadness.
6. It is not uncommon to be unsure as to how to act around a newly bereaved person.
7. Rather than suggesting that "time heals," an accurate description of the mourning process would point out that the time intervals between intense experiences of grief increase with the passing of time.
8. There are seven behaviors and feelings that are part of the normal bereavement process: shock and denial, disorganization, volatile emotions, guilt, loss and loneliness, relief, and reestablishment.
9. All persons who have experienced a loss through death will need to attend to the four necessary tasks of grief work before mourning can

be completed and reestablishment can take place. These tasks involve accepting the reality of the loss, experiencing the pain of grief, adjusting to an environment in which the deceased is missing, and withdrawing emotional energy and reinvesting it in other relationships.

10. Mourning the death of a fetus or newborn baby differs from mourning the death of another loved one because parents must suffer detachment without identification.

11. The death of a pet often represents a child's first experience with death, and the stance taken by parents influences a child's attitude toward human death encountered later on.

12. Many individuals go through an agonizing separation when they lose a pet. Their symptoms are very similar to those experienced within the process of bereavement for a significant other. However, unlike those losing a friend or relative who receive outpourings of sympathy and support, those who lose a pet often receive ridicule for overreacting, for being foolishly emotional, and for expressing grief over the death of an animal.

Discussion Questions

1. How can one avoid "deviant" or "abnormal" behavior regarding the bereavement role? What are some functions of defining bereavement roles as "deviant" or "abnormal?"

2. What is the relation between time and the feelings of grief experienced within the bereavement process?

3. Discuss how the seven stages of grieving over one's death can also be applied to losses through divorce, moving from one place to another, or the amputation of an arm or leg.

4. If grief is a feeling that is imposed upon the individual through loss, how can grieving be conceived of as being an active process for those who are bereaved?

5. What are the unique problems faced by those whose grief is disenfranchised? What are the different types of disenfranchised grief?

6. Describe the four necessary tasks of mourning. What are some of the practical steps one can take to accomplish each of these tasks?

7. What does Parkes mean by the statement: "The funeral often precedes the 'peak of the pangs'"? How can one assist friends in bereavement?

8. What are the special problems encountered in the death of a child and in a perinatal death?

9. Explain how suggestions related to medical procedures involved in perinatal deaths might better help parents cope with the death of children.

10. What are some of the signs of aberrant bereavement? What could you do to assist people experiencing abnormal grief symptoms?

11. In what ways are deaths of pets and deaths of significant others similar with regard to the bereavement process? What are some special problems related to the death of a pet?

GLOSSARY

Bereavement Role: Behavioral expectations for the bereaved, structured around specific rights and duties.

Blaming the Victim: A strategy developed by individuals to relieve the dissonance experienced when innocent people suffer loss.

Disenfranchised Grief: Loss that cannot be openly acknowledged, socially sanctioned, and publicly shared.

Dissonance: An inconsistency in beliefs and values relative to a particular social situation that causes personal discomfort or tension for the individuals involved.

Perinatal Death: The death of a child during or around its birth.

REFERENCES

Akiyama, Hiroko, Joseph M. Holtzman, and William E. Britz. 1986–1987. "Pet Ownership and Health Status during Bereavement." *Omega,* 17(2):187–193.

Attig, Thomas. 1991. "The Importance of Conceiving of Grief as an Active Process." *Death Studies,* 15:385–393.

Brody, Jane E. 1985. "Loss of a Pet Often Agonizing for Owners." *The News and Courier,* Charleston, SC, October 27, p. 14E.

Clyman, Ronald I., Charlotte Green, Cynthia Mikkelsen, Jane Rowe, and Linda Ataide. 1979. "Do Parents Utilize Physician Followup after the Death of Their Newborn?" *Pediatrics,* 64:655–667.

Cooke, David C. 1988. "Animal Disposal: Fact and Fiction." In *Euthanasia of the Companion Animal,* William J. Kay et al. (Eds.). Philadelphia: The Charles Press.

Davis, Deborah L., Marguerite Stewart, and Robert J. Harmon. 1988. "Perinatal Loss: Providing Emotional Support for Bereaved Parents." *Birth,* 14(December):242–246.

Dickinson, George E. 1992. "First Childhood Death Experiences" *Omega,* 25(2):169–182.

Doka, Kenneth J. 1987. "Silent Sorrow: Grief and the Loss of Significant Others." *Death Studies,* 11:441–449.

Doka, Kenneth J. 1989. *Disenfranchised Grief.* Lexington, MA: Lexington Books.

Edney, Andrew T. B. 1988. "Breaking the News: The Problems and Some Answers." In *Euthanasia of the Companion Animal,* William J. Kay et al., (Eds.). Philadelphia: The Charles Press.

Furman, E. 1978. "The Death of a Newborn: Care of the Parents." *Birth Family Journal,* 5:214.

Kamerman, Jack B. 1988. *Death in the Midst of Life.* Englewood Cliffs, NJ: Prentice-Hall.

Kavanaugh, Robert E. 1972. *Facing Death.* Baltimore: Penguin Books.

Kesselman, Idell. 1990. "Grief and Loss: Issues for Abortion." *Omega,* 21 (3):241–247.

Kloeppel, D. A. and S. Hollins. 1989. Double Handicap: Mental Retardation and Death in the Family." *Death Studies,* 13:31–38.

LaGrand, Louis E. 1991. "United We Cope: Support Groups for the Dying and Bereaved." *Death Studies,* 15:207–230.

Langley, Lynne. 1987. "Pet Cemeteries First Stop on Way to Hound Dog Heaven." *News and Courier,* Charleston, SC, September 13, p. 1D.

McClowry, S. G., E. B. Davies, K. A. May, E. J. Kulenkamp, and I. M. Martinson. 1987. "The Empty Space Phenomenon: The Process of Grief in the Bereaved Family." *Death Studies,* 11:361–374.

Murphy, Sister Patrice and Kathleen Perry. 1988. "Hidden Grievers." *Death Studies,* 12:451–462.

Murray, Judith, and Victor J. Callan. 1988. "Predicting Adjustment to Perinatal Death." *British Journal of Medical Psychology,* 61:237–244.

Ness, David E. and Cynthia R. Pheffer. 1990. "Sequelae of Bereavement Resulting From Suicide." *American Journal of Psychiatry,* 147, 3(March): 279–285.

News and Courier 1987. "Pet's Death Can Be as Grievous as Person's." Charleston, SC, March, p. 7A.

Nicol, M. T., J. R. Tompkins, N. A. Campbell, and G. J. Syme, 1986. "Maternal Grieving Response after Perinatal Death." *The Medical Journal of Australia,* 144:287–289.

Nieburg, Herbert A., and Arlene Fischer. 1982. *Pet Loss.* New York: Harper and Row.

Nixon, J., and J. Pearn, 1977. "Emotional Sequelae of Parents and Sibs Following the Drowning or Near-Drowning of a Child." *Australian and New Zealand Journal of Psychiatry,* 11:265–269.

Parkes, Colin M. 1972. *Bereavement: Studies of Grief in Adult Life.* New York: International Universities Press.

Parsons, Talcott. 1951. *The Social System.* Glencoe, IL: The Free Press.

Raphael, Beverly. 1983. *The Anatomy of Bereavement.* New York: Basic Books.

Robson, J. D. 1977. "Sick Role and Bereavement Role: Toward a Theoretical Synthesis of Two Ideal Types." In *A Time to Die,* Glenn M. Vernon (Ed.). Washington, DC: University Press of America.

Rosenblatt, Paul. 1983. *Bitter, Bitter Tears.* Minneapolis: University of Minnesota Press.

Rowe, Jane, Ronald Clyman, Charlotte Green, Cynthia Mikkelsen, Jeannette Haight, and Linda Ataide. 1978. "Followup of Families Who Experience a Perinatal Death." *Pediatrics,* 62:166–170.

Savishinsky, Joel S. 1988. "The Meanings of Loss: Human and Pet Death in the Lives of the Elderly." In *Euthanasia of the Companion Animal: The Impact on Pet Owners, Veternarians, and Society,* William J. Kay et al. (Eds.). Philadelphia: The Charles Press.

Schwab, Reiko. 1992. "Effects of a Child's Death on the Marital Relationship: A Preliminary Study." *Death Studies,* 16(2):141–154.

Sklar, Fred and Shirley F. Hartley. 1990. "Close Friends and Survivors: Bereavement Patterns in a 'Hidden' Population." *Omega,* 21(2):103–112.

Thorton, Gordon, Katherine D. Wittemore, and Donald U. Robertson. 1989. "Evaluation of People Bereaved by Suicide." *Death Studies,* 13:119–126.

Thorton, Gordon, Donald U. Robertson, and Mary Lou Mlecko. 1991. "Disenfranchised Grief and Evaluations of Social Support by College Students." *Death Studies,* 15:355–362.

Weisman, Avery D. 1990–1991. "Bereavement and Companion Animals." *Omega,* 22(4):241–248.

Worden, J. William. 1982. *Grief Counseling and Grief Therapy: A Handbook for the Mental Health Practitioner.* New York: Springer Publishing Company.

Zunin, Leonard M. and Hilary Stanton Zunin. 1991. *The Art of Condolence.* New York: Harper Collins.

SUGGESTED READINGS

Attig, Thomas. 1991. "The Importance of Conceiving of Grief as an Active Process." *Death Studies,* 15:385–393. *A very helpful article in assisting the bereaved to become active agents in their grieving process.*

Doka, Kenneth J. 1989. *Disenfranchised Grief.* Lexington, MA: Lexington Books. *A very helpful book for identifying "hidden" grievers and for expanding one's understanding of the grieving process.*

Grollman, Earl. 1982. *What Helped Me When My Loved One Died.* Boston: Beacon Press. *Collection of personal stories of parents, wives, husbands, children, and friends.*

Kay, William J., Susan P. Cohen, Herbert A. Nieburg, Carole E. Fudin, Ross E. Grey, Austin H. Kutscher, and Mohamed M. Osman (Eds.). 1988. *Euthanasia of the Companion Animal: The Impact on Pet Owners, Veterinarians, and Society.* Philadelphia: The Charles Press. *An anthology of recent studies on relating to the death of pets and the effect of dying and death of pets on humans.*

Lattanzi-Licht, Marcia E., Jane M. Kirschling, and Steven Flemming. 1990. *Bereavement Care: A New Look at Hospice and Community Based Services.* Binghamton, NY: The Haworth Press. *This book addresses the importance of delivery of bereavement care and services in a hospice setting. The book examines the grieving process and distinguishes grief from clinical depression. The book is helpful for mental health professionals, social workers, chaplains, nursing personnel, and volunteers who work with the bereaved.*

Manning, D. 1984. *Don't Take My Grief Away from Me.* Hereford, TX: In-Sight Books. *Assistance for the bereaved in how to respond to "unhelpful friends."*

Rando, Therese A. 1993. *Treatment of Complicated Mourning.* Champaign, IL: Research Press. *A comprehensive coverage of loss and grief written by a noted clinical psychologist.*

Raphael, Beverly. 1983. *The Anatomy of Bereavement.* New York: Basic Books. *An encyclopedia-like reference book on human grief and bereavement.*

Worden, J. William. 1991. *Grief Counseling and Grief Therapy: A Handbook for the Mental Health Practitioner,* 2nd ed. New York: Springer Publishing Company. *A very practical reference guide for the professional and lay grief counselor.*

Zunin, Leonard M., and Hilary Stanton Zunin. 1991. *The Art of Condolence.* New York: Harper Collins. *A book that will provide the reader with concrete skills in assisting the bereaved.*

Copyrights and Acknowledgments

Index

A

AARP. *See* American Association of Retired Persons (AARP)
Abbott, Allen, 107
Abbott, Lyman, 420
Abkhasians, 381–382, 393
Abortion, 494
Abramovitch, Henry, 371
Academy of Professional Funeral Service Practice, 465
Acceptance, as stage of dying, 217, 497
Achte, Kalle, 346
Acquired immunodeficiency syndrome. *See* AIDS
Active euthanasia, 296–308
Acute diseases, 34
Adams, Cecil, 16
Adams, David, 92
Adkins, Janet, 302
Adler, Alfred, 122
Adolescence
    black adolescents, 125
    death themes in rock music, 126–128
    definition of, 123
    helping adolescents cope with death, 128–129
    identity crisis in, 124–126
    perinatal deaths and, 512
    suicide during, 330–343, 344
Adulthood
    introduction to, 120–130
    middle-aged adulthood, 134–137
    older adulthood, 137–147
    young adulthood, 131–133
Africa. *See also names of specific countries*
    AIDS in, 369
    attitudes toward death in, 381
    burial rites in, 391, 393–394
    euphemisms for death in, 371

handling the corpse in, 383
    Swazi of, 375–376, 394
After-care services, 482–483
Afterlife. *See* Immortality
Afterlife experiences by clinically dead, 191–196
Age
    AIDS and, 133
    life expectancy by, 31–33
    suicide and, 330, 335, 354
Aging. *See* Older adulthood
Agnes and the Key of Her Little Coffin, 417
AIDS
    athletes with, 6
    deviance and, 228–229
    disenfranchised grief and, 495
    fear of, 211, 227
    gays and, 132–133, 228–229
    as global pandemic, 369
    hospice and, 278–280
    labeling theory and, 228–229
    media portrayal of, 6, 8
    mercy killing and, 301
    statistics on, 132–133, 249
    suicide and, 335
AIDS-related complex (ARC), 278
Aisenberg, R., 137, 335
Akiyama, Hiroko, 516
Albert, Edward, 8
Alcor Life Extension Foundation, 18
Alienation, 334–335
Alioto, Angela, 18
All Saints Day, 370–380
Allen, Breon G., 327
Allen, Woody, 7, 186
Alles, Wesley F., 347
Altman, Lawrence K., 222, 232
Altruistic suicide, 332
AMA. *See* American Medical Association (AMA)
Amenta, M., 146
American Animal Hospital

Association, 519
American Association of Retired Persons (AARP), 141, 480
American Bar Association, 14
American Cancer Society, 211
American Cryonics Society, 18–19
American Medical Association (AMA), 14, 207
American Psychological Review, The, 52
American Sociological Review, The, 52
American Way of Death, The (Mitford), 10
Anderson, H. N., 327
Anderson, James, 277, 480, 481–482
Anger
    funeral and, 460
    during mourning, 374–375
    of siblings of dying child, 92
    as stage of dying, 216, 217, 497
    of young adults who are dying, 131
Anglo-Canadians, 386
Animal deaths, 82, 97, 99, 393, 494–495, 514–519
Anomic grief, 113
Anomic suicide, 332
Anomie, 157
Anspaugh, David J., 310, 313, 337
Anthropology of death ritual
    attitudes toward death, 377–382
    burial rites, 388–395
    cleaning the body, 383, 385–386
    customs at death, 382–388
    death as rite of passage, 371–372
    death meanings and, 395–396
    display of emotions during

mourning, 374–377
handling the corpse,
    383–388
norms prior to death,
    382–383
rationale for study of cross-
    cultural death
    rituals, 360–371
ritual of mourning at
    death, 372–377
societal management of
    death-related emotions,
    367–369
types of weeping, 376–377
Anxiety. *See also* Death anxiety
    pain and, 269
    religious ritual observance
    and, 64–66, 388
Apaches, 370
Apnea monitor, 112
Appalachia, burial rites in,
    391–392
Appropriate death, 227
ARC. *See* AIDS-related com-
    plex (ARC)
Aristotle, 36, 327
Armbruster, W. A., 62–63
Armstrong, Janice Gray, 432
Arnold, Robert M., 225
Artists, on hospice team,
    251–252
Asarnow, Joan Rosenbaum,
    338
Asgard, Ulf, 333
Ashe, Arthur, 8
Ashley-Cameron, Sylvia, 224,
    226
Associated Press, 469, 470
Association of American
    Medical Colleges, 222
Atchley, Robert C., 212
Atomic Age, 434–441
Atomic bomb, 434–435
Attig, Thomas, 127–128,
    495–497
Attitudes
    cross-cultural attitudes
    toward death, 377–382
    on suicide, 297, 326–329
Atwater, P. M., 196
Augustine, St., 156, 327
Australia, 386, 393
Autopsy, 230–236
    psychological autopsy,
    332–333
Awareness contexts, of dying,
    225–227
Ayer, Margaret, 180

B

Ba, 452
Baez, Joan, 127
Baldree, Brent F., 344
Bara people, 373
Barabaig, 394
Bargaining, as stage of dying,
    216, 217, 497
Baring-Gould, William S., 107
Barrett, Ronald K., 370, 371,
    375, 377, 390
Barrett, William, 435
Barstow, A. C., 430–431
Bascom, William, 391, 393
Bass, David M., 249, 259
Bass, M., 112
Battin, Margaret P., 329, 349
Beatles, 127
Beauvoir, Simone de, 227
Beck, Bernard, 455
Becker, Ernest, 10, 122–123
Becker, Howard, 219, 224
Beckwith, J. B., 109
Bedding, and infant deaths,
    111
Bedford, James, 16
Beecher, Henry K., 14
Beecher, Henry Ward,
    410–420, 430
Begin Again, 509
Behaviorists, 123
Bell, Daniel, 341
Bendann, Effie, 375
Bender, Tomas, 421
Benet, Sula, 381–382, 393
Benjamin, Charles L., 430
Bereavement. *See also* Grief
    anthropological perspec-
    tives on, 372–377
    assisting the bereaved,
    506–509
    Atomic Age and, 434–441
    bereavement role, 490–494
    consolation literataure and,
    417
    coping with grief, 497–503
    decline of, 456–457
    definition of, 458
    disenfranchised grief,
    494–495
    display of emotions during
    mourning, 374–377
    from 1830 to 1945,
    413–434
    Enlightenment and,
    410–411
    Evangelicalism and,
    412–413

funeral and needs of the
    bereaved, 450–463
grieving process, 495–497
historical perspectives on,
    406–441
hospice and, 258–259
Islam's approach to, 174
in Judaism, 168–169
liberal religion and,
    410–420
life insurance and,
    428–430
mourning pictures and,
    417
from 1945 to present,
    434–441
of parents at loss of infant,
    510–514
of parents at Sudden Infant
    Death Syndrome,
    112–113
of parents of dying chil-
    dren, 80–91
pet death and, 514–519
Puritans and, 407–410
reforming the Reformed
    Tradition, 410–413
and rise of middle class,
    413–414
Romanticism and, 414
and rural cemeteries in
    19th and early 20th
    centuries, 421–428
scientific naturalism and,
    418–419
sentimentalism and,
    414–418
of siblings of dying chil-
    dren, 91–93
from 1600 to 1830,
    407–413
social status aspects of
    mourning, 371
as spirited activities,
    373–374
stages of grieving process,
    497–503
support groups for the
    bereaved, 509,
    510–511
tasks of mourning,
    503–506
types of weeping, 376–377
Unitarianism and, 411,
    421
women's apparel during
    19th century, 415–416
Bereavement: Studies of Grief in

Adult Life (Parkes), 506
Bereavement self-help groups, 509, 510–511
Bereavement team, 258
Berger, Peter, 156–157
Berman, Alan L., 340, 343
Berry, Travis, 338
Berry, Wendell, 430–441
Bertman, S. L., 220
Beskow, Jan, 333
Biblarz, Arturo, 344
Biblarz, Dolores Noonan, 344
Bible, 108–109, 130, 166, 160–170, 246, 326, 327, 408, 409, 412, 450
Bier, 383
Big Chill, The, 126
Bill of Rights, of dying person, 257–258
Biological process of dying, 46–48
Biomedical issues
    organ donations, 308–315
    public policy on, 315–317
Biosocial immortality, 437
Birckhead, John, 15
Bischoff, Thomas D., 480–481
Bishop, Katherine, 18–19
Black, D., 218, 221
Blacks
    adolescents in black communities, 125
    AIDS and, 132, 133
    death ritual for, 370
    suicide of, 336
Blame the victim, 499
Blau, Peter, 63
Blauner, Robert, 226
Bledstein, Burton J., 418
Bloch, Maurice, 367
Block, Bill, 280
Blue Ridge Mountains, Decoration Day in, 378–379
Bluebond-Langner, Myra, 86, 88, 92
Boatwright, Les, 471
Body. *See* Corpse
Body-bequest programs, 473
Booth, John Wilkes, 189
Bordewich, Fergus M., 7, 9
Bornu, 383
Boulton, Doris Wiseman, 378–379
Bouma, Hessel, 289, 294, 307
Bowlby, John, 94, 505
Boyle, Joan M., 207
Brahma, 176

Brahmins, 179
Brain death, 13–16
Brandt, Richard, 340–350
Brantner, John, 104–105, 467, 506
Brazil, 387–388
Bremner, Linda, 87
Britz, William, 516
Brody, J. A., 137
Brody, Jane E., 340, 515
Brooks, Phillips, 419
Brown, James H., 335
Brown, Willie, 18
Brozan, Nadine, 340
Brugler, Jan, 450
Bryant, William Cullen, 414
Buckingham, R., 259, 274
Buddhism, 170–184, 394
Bugen, L. A., 222
Bureau of Labor Statistics, 465
Burial rites. *See also* Cemeteries; Funerals
    anthropological perspectives on, 388–395
    in Appalachian and non-Appalachian Kentucky, 391–392
    in Buddhism, 394
    in Christianity, 171–172
    in 18th and early 19th centuries, 424, 428
    functions of, 380–392
    of indigent infants, 83–85
    in Islam, 173–174
    in Judaism, 166–168
    of Kapauku Papuans, 394, 395
    for pets, 517–519
    of Puritans, 400–410
    rural cemeteries in 19th and early 20th centuries, 421–428
    of Russian immigrants in Oregon, 389
    statistics on, 458, 469
    variations in, 392–395
Burns, Nancy, 246
Butler, Robert, 140, 143
Buursma, Bruce, 89
Byron, George Gordon Lord, 189

C

Cadavers, 219
Calhoun, Lawrence G., 327
Callahan, Daniel, 317
Callan, Victor, 511
Campbell, Alexander, 366

Campbell, N. A., 510
Campbell, Thomas, 224
Campo, Laura, 312–313
Canada, 386, 392
Cancer
    brain cancer, 263–266
    children with, 86–88
    fear of, 211
    lung cancer, 232, 256–257
    pain and, 269
    physicians' communication of prognosis to patients with, 207–209
    suicide and, 350–353
Candlelighters, 509, 510
Canetto, Silvia, 345–346
Canning, Ray R., 195
Caplan, Arthur, 301–303
Cardwell, Jerry D., 67
Carlson, Gabrielle, 338
Carmaz, Kathy, 55–59
Carr, William F., 248
Carse, J., 166
Carstensen, Lundie, 344
Casket, The, 430
Caskets, 430–431, 477–478
Catholics, 169, 172, 189, 195, 292–293, 296, 326, 336, 408
Causation, in historical explanations, 406–407
CDC. *See* Centers for Disease Control (CDC)
Celebrations of Death: Anthropology of Mortuary Ritual (Huntington and Metcalf), 366
Cemeteries. *See also* Burial rites
    for pets, 517–519
    rules and regulations of, 469
    rural cemeteries in 19th and early 20th centuries, 421–428
    social stratification of, 424
    in Victorian period, 417
Census Bureau, 428
Centers for Disease Control (CDC), 330
Chagnon, Napoleon A., 387–388
Charmaz, Kathy, 196, 217, 331, 333, 334, 335
Chevra Kadisha, 167
Chevra Kevod Hamet, 167–168
Cheyenne Indians, 375
Children

ages birth to age 3, 100–101
ages 3 to 5, 101–103
ages 6 to 10, 103–108
animal deaths and, 82
with cancer, 86–88
communication about death with, 93–99, 113–114
death concepts and, 82–83
dying children, 85–88
and euphemisms in explaining death to, 95–97
funerals and, 461–463
honesty and openness in explaining death to, 94–95
hospice and, 281
parents' grief at infant's death, 510–514
parents of dying child, 80–91
perinatal deaths and, 512, 513
and pet death, 514–519
showing emotion when talking about death, 97–99
siblings of dying child, 91–39
Sudden Infant Death Syndrome, 108–112
suicide of, 338–339
understanding of death, 90–108
Children's Hospice International, 88
Chile, 383
Chiriboga, David, 132
Chng, Chwee Lye, 252, 253, 254, 269
Choron, Jacques, 349
Christianity
humanitarianism and, 246–247
interpretation of death by, 160–172
martyrs in, 187
and priests' duties concerning burial, 453
suicide and, 326–327, 336
Chronic diseases, 34, 36
Cigarette smoking. See Smoking
Clark, Brian, 280–290
Clark, Clifford E., Jr., 419
Clark, Karen, 384

Clark, Matt, 230, 232
Clarke, Susan, 312
Cleaning the body, 383, 385–386
Cleaveland, Nehemiah, 422
Clement XI, Pope, 248
Clergy, on hospice team, 251
Closed awareness, 225–226
Cluster suicides, 339, 341, 343–345
Clyman, Ronald I., 511
Cnattinguius, Sven, 109
Cockerham, William C., 30
Codex Jurix Cononici, 326
Coe, Rodney, 210
Coffin, Margaret M., 219
Cognitive development, 101
Cohen, Herbert, 304–305
Cohen, Kenneth, 246
Cohen, Ronald, 383
Cohen, Susan R., 113
Cohn, David, 229
Cole, Thomas, 414
Coleman, Loren, 339, 340
Collins, Randall, 67
Columbarium, 471
Coma, 289
Commerce Department, 456
Communication
and awareness contexts of dying, 225–227
with children about death, 93–99, 113–114
of female physicians, 225
physicians' communication with dying patients, 215, 224–225
by physicians of prognosis of illness, 207–209
Compassionate Friends, 90, 509, 511
Condolence, 506–509
Conflict theory, 58–61
Conley, Herbert, 227
Conrad, Joseph, 189
Consolation literataure, 417
Contract murder, cost of, 37
Cook, Emily Williams, 194
Cook, J. A., 91
Cooke, David C., 519
Cooper, D. K., 309
Cope, L., 109
Cope, Lewis, 14
Coping
adolescence and coping with death, 128–129
with American way of dying, 34–36

with grief, 497–503
Coroner, 231
Coroners' deputies, 55–58
Corpse. See also Burial; Funerals
body preparation in funeral homes, 467–469
cleaning the body, 383, 385–386
destruction of, 371
disposition of, 458–459, 460–472
handling of, 383–388
viewing of, 459, 468
Costs
of funerals and final disposition, 474–479
of hospice, 272–273
for medical care, 315–317
of organ transplants, 313
Cotton, C. Randy, 83
Cottrell, Randall, 469
Counts, David R., 13
Counts, Dorothy A., 13
Cowell, Daniel David, 376
Cox, Gerry R., 370, 386, 392
CPR, 291–292
Crandall, Richard C., 14, 144
Creative immortality, 439
Cree, 392
Cremains, 388
Cremation
acceptance of, 50
in Buddhism, 182, 183–184, 394
in Hinduism, 178
of pets, 393, 518
reasons for, 470–471
statistics on, 458, 460–470
Crematory, 471
Crib death. See Sudden Infant Death Syndrome (SIDS)
Cross-cultural perspectives. See Anthropology of death ritual
Crowther, Edward, 277
Crump, Joseph, 427
Cruzan, Nancy, 295
Cruzan v. Director, Missouri Department of Health, 295
Crying. See also Emotions
during mourning, 374–377
types of weeping, 376–377

Cryonics, 16–19
Cubeo, 373
Cultural lag, 295
Cummins, V. A., 9
Cunnington, L., 136
Curran, David K., 326
Curvilinear, 162
Customs at death, 382–388
Cuzzort, Ray P., 367, 389

D

Da Vinci, Leonardo, 453
Dahl, Jeanette, 516
Dailey, Ann A., 88
Dambrot, Faye, 275
Darrow, Clarence, 464
Darwin, Charles, 419
Darwin, Mike, 18, 19
Dattel, Andrew R., 22
Davidson, Lucy, 343, 344
Davies, E. B., 510
Davis, Deborah L., 511
Dawson, Grace D., 468
De Tocqueville, Alexis, 413, 434
Death. *See also* Anthropology of death ritual; Dying; Fear of death; Historical approach to death; Social meaning of dying and death; Thanatology
    American definitions of, 13–16
    children's understanding of, 90–108
    conflicting meanings on, 68–69
    coping with American way of dying, 34–36
    cross-cultural attitudes toward, 377–382
    current interest in, 4–11
    definition of, 11–16, 458
    denial of, 16–20, 122–123
    due to chronic versus acute diseases, 34–36
    etiology of, 28–30
    euphemisms for, 16, 95–97
    explaining death to children, 93–99
    historical perspectives on, 406–441
    international definitions of, 12–13
    as marginal situation, 157
    media and, 6–8
    mortality statistics, 27–34
    rationale for increased interest in, 4–6
    religious interpretations of, 156–184
    as rite of passage, 371–372
    social meaning of, 46–73
    temporal interpretations of, 184–191
Death: The Final Stage of Growth (Kübler-Ross), 227
Death announcements, by coroners' deputies, 55–58
Death anxiety
    in adolescence, 125, 126–128
    as basic problem of meaning, 122–123
    content of fears, 21–23
    Leming Death Fear Scale, 22, 24–27
    and older adulthood, 141–144
    origin of, 100
    of physicians, 223
    Puritans and, 408
    religion and, 160–165
Death Customs: An Analytical Study of Burial Rites (Bendann), 375
Death Education, 10
Death education
    current status of, 8–10
    for hospice staff and volunteers, 273
    in medical schools, 11, 220–223, 237
Death fears. *See* Death anxiety
Death, Grief, and Mourning (Gorer), 457
Death ritual. *See also* Bereavement; Burial rites; Funerals; Wakes
    anthropology of, 366–396
    burial rites, 388–395
    cleaning the body, 383, 385–386
    cross-cultural attitudes toward death, 377–382
    customs at death, 382–388
    death meanings and, 395–396
    display of emotions during mourning, 374–377
    handling the corpse, 383–388
    mourning at death, 372–377
    norms prior to death, 382–383
    purposes of, 366–367
    rationale for study of cross-cultural death rituals, 360–371
    sentimentalism and, 415–418
    and societal management of death-related emotions, 367–369
    as spirited activities, 373–374
    types of weeping, 376–377
Death Studies, 10, 52
DeCantanzaro, D., 336
Decoration Day, 378–379
Deeb, Larry C., 108, 109
Definitions of death, 11–16, 458
DeFrain, John D., 108, 109, 112, 113
DeJong, Gordon, 162
Deng, Francis M., 375
Denial
    of death, 16–20, 122–123
    evidence of denial of death, 16–20
    as stage of dying, 216, 497
    as stage of grieving, 497–498
Denial of Death, The (Becker), 10, 122–123
Dentan, Robert K., 377, 383, 393
Depression
    pain and, 269
    as stage of dying, 216, 217, 497
Desert Storm, 5–6
Deveau, Eleanor, 92
Developmental approach
    adolescence, 123–129
    adulthood, 120–146
    childhood, 90–108
    definition of, 123
    limitations of, 120–130
    middle-aged adulthood, 134–137
    older adulthood, 137–147
    psychologists on, 122–123
    young adulthood, 131–133
Deviance
    dying as, 228–229, 237
    labeling theory and,

228–229
punishment and, 229
DeVries, Raymond, 466–467
Dharma, 176
Diamond, Neil, 127
Dickinson, George E., 10, 11,
    82, 94, 96, 97, 98,
    208, 220–226, 396, 515
Diekema, Douglas, 289
Diekstra, Rene F. W., 300
DiGiacomo, Wayne, 312–313
Dinka, 375
Dion, 127
Disenfranchised grief,
    494–495
Disorganization, as stage of
    grieving, 498
Disposition
    final disposition of body,
        458–459, 460–472
    immediate disposition,
        472–473
    of pets, 517–519
Dissection of cadavers, 219
Dissonance, 499
Divorce, 91, 495–496, 510
Doctors. *See* Physicians
Doe, Baby Jane, 5
Doka, Kenneth, 494, 495
Dolan, Carrie, 482, 483
Domino, George, 338
Domino, Valerie, 338
Donations of organs. *See*
    Organ donations
Donne, John, 326
Douglas, Ann, 414, 415
Douglas, Jack D., 330, 331
Douglas, Joan D., 134, 135
Dowd, Quincy L., 431
Downing, Andrew Jackson,
    422–423
Down's Syndrome, 295
Dozier, Edward P., 386, 393
Dramaturgical perspective, of
    suicide, 332–333
DuBois, Paul M., 266, 267
Dumont, Richard, 4, 16, 141
Dunn, Robert G., 327
Dunsun, 381, 382–383, 390
Durable power of attorney,
    294
Durand, Asher B., 414
Durand, Ronald P., 222
Durkheim, Emile, 53–54,
    164–165, 229, 331–
    332, 336, 366, 376
Dyad, 46
Dying. *See also* Death; Hospice

assumptions about, 71
awareness contexts of,
    225–227
Bill of Rights of dying
    person, 257–258
as biological versus social
    process, 46–48
by chronic versus acute
    diseases, 34–36
coping with American way
    of, 34–36
death meanings and their
    effects on, 206–218
as deviance in medical
    setting, 228–229, 237
how to live with life-
    threatening illness,
    271–272
labeling theory and,
    228–229
norm and role meanings
    of, 211–213
as normal state, 230
object and self-meanings
    of, 213–218
palliative care of, 222
pets for dying patients,
    516
physicians and the dying
    patient, 207–209, 215,
    218–223
as process, 206–237
relating to dying patients,
    217, 223–227
signs of approaching
    death, 260–261
social meaning of, 46–73
social situation meanings
    of, 218
space meanings of,
    200–211
stages of, 216–218, 497
time meanings and,
    206–209
value meanings of, 213
Dying children
    information provided to,
        85–86
    parents of, 80–91
    siblings of, 91–93
    support for, 86–88
Dysfunctional, 160

E

Earl, William L., 229
Eberstein, I. W., 108, 109
Eddy, James M., 347
Edney, Andrew T. B., 517

Education, of funeral directors,
    463–467. *See also*
    Death education
EEG. *See* Electroencephalo-
    gram (EEG)
Egan, Timothy, 278–280
Ego psychologists, 122
Egoistic suicide, 332
Egypt
    death ritual in ancient
        Egypt, 451–453, 467
    kidney transplants in,
        313–314
Eickelman, Dale F., 174
Einstein, Albert, 434–435
Elderhostel, 4, 140
Elderly. *See* Older adulthood
Electroencephalogram (EEG),
    15
Elegy, 409, 417
*Elementary Forms of Religious
    Life* (Durkheim), 164
Ellis, John, 353
Ellis, Jon B., 327
Ely, Margot, 326, 338
Embalmer, licensure for, 464
Embalming, 431, 450–451,
    453, 454, 467–469
Emmons, Nathaniel, 410
Emotions. *See also* Anger; Grief
    display of, during mourning,
        374–377
    funerals and, 450–461
    in grieving process,
        497–503
    showing emotion when
        talking with children
        about death, 97–99
    societal management of
        death-related emotions,
        367–369
Empirical, 48–49
Empty Arms, 509, 511
*Empty Crib: The Memorial of
    Little Georgie*, 417
End, The, 216
Endocannibalism, 387
Enlightenment, 410–411
Entombment, 458, 471–472
Epitaph, 417, 425–428
Erdahl, Lowell, 307
Ericsson, Stephanie, 502–503
Erikson, Erik, 100, 130, 134,
    140, 143, 214
Ernst, Linda, 108, 112
Espin, Oliva, 126
Estok, Patricia, 513
Ethiopia, Qemant in, 386

Ethnicity. *See* Blacks; Hispanics; Native Americans; Race
Ethnocentrism, 369
Ethnographic, 368
Etiology
  of death, 28–30
  of religion, 156
  of Sudden Infant Death Syndrome (SIDS), 100–112
Eulogy, 456
Euphemisms, 16, 95–97, 371
Euthanasia
  active euthanasia, 296–308
  Catholics' view of, 292–293, 296
  definition of, 288
  Kevorkian and, 301–303
  legalization of, in Netherlands, 300–301, 305–307
  living wills and, 293–300
  passive euthanasia, 291–296
  of pets, 517
  and sanctity and quality of life, 288–290
  slippery-slope-to-Auschwitz argument against, 303–308
Evangelicalism, 412–413
Exhume, 387
Existentialism, 333–334, 436
EXIT, 296, 300
Extraordinary measures of preserving life, 294–295
Extreme Unction, 408
Ezell, Gene, 310, 313, 336, 337, 347

F

Faces of Death, The, 126
Faircloth, Bill, 187
Falk, Richard, 437
Family members, and hospice, 250, 256, 270–271. *See also* Parents; Siblings
Family property, division of, 60–61
"Family Ties," 147
Farberow, Norman L., 326
Faron, Louis C., 383
Farrell, James J., 415, 419, 424, 431
Fatalistic suicide, 332
Faulkner, Joseph, 162

Fear
  of AIDS patients, 211
  of cancer patients, 211
  of pain, 269
Fear of death
  in adolescence, 125, 126–128
  as basic problem of meaning, 122–123
  content of fears, 21–23
  gender and, 22, 24
  Leming Death Fear Scale, 22, 24–27
  origin of, 100
  of physicians, 223
  Puritans and, 408
  reasons for, 20–21
  religion and, 160–165
  socialization to, 126–128
Fear of nothingness, 190
Federal Trade Commission (FTC), 477–479
Federated Funeral Directors of America, 465, 475
Federowicz, Michael, 18
Feelings. *See* Emotions
Feifel, Herman, 10, 123
Feldman, Douglas A., 369
Fetal deaths. *See* Perinatal deaths
Fieger, Geoffrey, 301–302
Field, David, 222
Fields, W. C., 425
Films, 7, 126, 216
Final Exit (Humphry), 296, 329
Financial counseling, in hospice, 251
Finn, Mark, 253
Fischer, Arlene, 517
Fletcher, Joseph, 295
Flynn, Charles P., 191, 196
Former spouse, death of, 494–495
Foss, Dennis C., 4, 16, 141
Fox, Sandra, 93
Frank, Arthur, 215
Fraser, Thomas M., Jr., 383
Frederick, Lynn M., 11
Freestanding hospice, 266
Freidson, Elliot, 229
French, Stanley, 421
French West Indies, 385
Freud, Sigmund, 122, 130
Friends, and hospice, 256
Fritz, Judy L., 396
Froese, Art, 338
FTC. *See* Federal Trade Com-

mission (FTC)
Fulton, Robert, 7, 8, 134, 140, 439
Functions
  of burial rites, 380–392
  latent functions, 390
  manifest functions, 380–390
Fundis, Ronald J., 370, 386, 392
Funeral and Memorial Information Council, 469, 470
Funeral directors
  body preparation by, 467–469
  and denial of death, 20
  education and licensure of, 463–467
  historical perspectives on, 430–432, 463–464
  on hospice team, 251
  in 19th and early 20th centuries, 430–432
  role of, 467–469
  salaries for, 465–466
Funeral homes
  after-care services of, 482–483
  for American Indians, 384–385
  contemporary services of, 458
  costs of, 474–479
  and denial of death, 20
  in 19th and early 20th centuries, 430–432
  statistics on, 456, 465, 467
Funerals
  alternatives to, 472–474
  Buddhist funeral, 180–184
  children and, 461–463
  Christian funeral, 171–172
  contemporary American funeral, 458–459
  costs of, 474–479
  drive-through service for, 454–455
  early American funeral practices, 454–457
  Hindu funeral, 178–179
  Islamic funeral, 174
  Jewish funeral, 167–168
  and liberal religion in 19th and early 20th centuries, 420
  and needs of the bereaved, 450–463

new trends in, 470–483
philosophical perspective
on, 461
planning of, 470–482
prearrangements and
prefunding for,
470–482
preneed funerals, 470–482
psychological focus of,
450–460
Puritans and, 400–410
and sentimentalism from
1830 to 1945,
415–417
social and cultural roots of,
450–453
sociological focus of, 460
statistics on, 480
theological perspective on,
461
in U.S. during 19th and
early 20th centuries,
430–434
Van Gennep on, 371
Furer-Haimendorf, Christoph
Von, 387
Furman, E., 511, 512

G

Gabriel, Trip, 297
Gaines, Judith, 391
Gamarekian, Barbara, 88
Gamst, Frederick C., 386
Gannal, Dr., 453
Garfield, Charles A., 217
Garfinkel, Barry D., 338
Garland, Judy, 187
Garland, T. Neal, 249, 259
Garrison, Carol, 340
Garrity, Thomas F., 391–392
Gaspard, N. J., 212
Gatling, Lafayette, 455
Gays
    AIDS and, 132–133,
        228–229
    disenfranchised grief and,
        494
Gebhart, John C., 430
Geddes, Gordon, 407, 408,
    409, 410
Gender
    burial rites and, 393–395
    death fears and, 22, 24
    display of emotions during
        mourning, 374–377
    life expectancy by sex,
        31–34
    of physicians versus pro-

fessional role in relat-
    ing to dying patients,
    224–225
sex ratio, 30, 33
suicide and, 330, 337,
    342, 345–346
General Electric Company, 272
Geriatrics, 142, 143–144
Gerontologist, The, 52
Gerontologists, 144
Gervais, K. G., 12
Ghosts, 360–370, 381
Gibson, J. A., 327
Gibson, Richard, 104–107
Gilhooly, Mary L. M., 137, 366
Gillon, Raanan, 15
Ginsburg, Herbert, 101, 123
Glaser, Barney, 207, 225
Glass, L., 112
Gleason, Philip, 385
Glock, Charles, 162
God. See Religion
"God Is Dead" theology, 435
Goethe, 137
Goffman, Erving, 21, 228
Goggin, William C., 327
Goldman, Ari L., 465
Goldman, I., 373
Goleman, Daniel, 213,
    341–343
Goodenow, Carl, 126
Goodman, Ellen, 307–308
Goodman, Rabbi Arnold M.,
    167–168
Gordon, A. K., 9
Gordon, Audrey, 123, 126,
    128
Gorer, Geoffrey, 10, 456, 457
Gottesman, David J., 439
Gould, Madelyn S., 343, 344
Graham, Elizabeth, 84
Graveyard decoration day,
    378–379
Gray, Robert M., 206
Gray-Toft, Pamela A., 277
Greenwald, Davaid S., 436
Greer, Rosie, 99
Grief. See also Bereavement
    anomic grief, 113
    compared with grieving
        process, 495–497
    coping with, 497–503
    definition of, 458, 483,
        495
    disenfranchised grief,
        494–495
    funerals and, 450–461
    pain of, 502–505

pet death and, 515
symptomatology of, 459
Grief Counseling and Grief
    Therapy (Worden), 503
Grief Observed, A (Lewis),
    170–171
Grief therapy, 424, 432,
    482–483, 509
Grollman, Rabbi Earl, 97, 122,
    467
Gross, Andrew, 429
Gross, Robert A., 411
Guide to Self-Deliverance, A
    (EXIT), 296
Guillon, Claude, 329
Guilt, as stage of grieving, 499
Gunn, Charles B., 426
Gunn, Darlene B., 220, 221
Gunning, Karel, 304–306
Guru, 179
Gustafson, Elizabeth, 217

H

Habenstein, Robert W., 174,
    176, 178, 179,
    183–184, 377, 383,
    415, 417, 431, 453
Hafferty, Frederic, 219, 220
Haglund, Bengt, 109, 377
Hale, Nathan G., 414
Hale, R., 200–210
Haley, Alex, 11
Hall, G. S., 82
Hall, Geoffrey, 107
Hall, Kenneth F., 82
Hallmark Card Company, 507,
    521
Hand, Quentin, 456
Handford, Thomas W., 420
Handley-Taylor, Geoffrey, 107
Hanratty, J. F., 247
Hardin, Garrett, 316–317
Hardoff, D., 218, 221
Hare, Sidney J., 423
Harmon, Robert J., 511
Harrington, Kathie, 265
Harris, Marvin, 368
Hart, C. W. M., 386
Hartley, Shirley F., 495
Harvard Bereavement Study,
    503–504
Harvard Medical School, 14
Haviland, William A., 372
Hawkins, Anne, 227
Hay, Mrs. E. E., 428
Health professionals. See
    Nurses; Physicians
Heart defect, and infant

deaths, 110
Hedges, Chris, 313–314
Helman, C., 366
Hemlock Society, 296–297, 300, 351
Hernandez, Andreas Santiago, 37
Herodotus, 450
Heroes, 180–191, 326
Hill, C. T., 61
Hillerman, Barbara, 417, 433
Hinduism, 175–179
Hinker, Fred, 126
Hinton, John, 275
Hispanics, 132, 133
Hisserich, John C., 275
Historical approach to death
    Atomic Age, and, 434–441
    causation in historical explanations, 406–407
    from 1830 to 1945, 413–434
    Enlightenment, 410–411
    Evangelicalism, 412–413
    funeral services, 420–434
    liberal religion in 19th and 20th centuries, 410–420
    life insurance, 428–430
    from 1945 to present, 434–441
    Puritans, 407–410
    Reformed Tradition, 407–410
    reforming the Reformed Tradition, 410–413
    rise of middle class, 413–414
    Romanticism, 414
    rural cemeteries, 421–428
    scientific naturalism, 418–419
    sentimentalism, 414–418
    from 1600 to 1830, 407–413
    social and cultural roots of American funeral traditions, 450–453
    Unitarianism, 411, 421
Hitchcock, John T., 383
Hitler, Adolf, 303–304
HIV, 6, 133, 229, 369
Hocker, William V., 480
Hoebel, E. Adamson, 375
Hogan, John, 223
Hohenschuh, W. P., 431, 432
Holden, Constance, 275–276
Holland, Morris, 342

Hollins, S., 495
Holtzman, Joseph, 516
Homans, George C., 50–51, 52, 64–66, 160, 161–162
Home care, of the dying, 250, 250–261
Home health aides, 251
Homemakers, 251
Homes, Thomas, 454
Homicide, 330
Homosexuality. See Gays
Hood, Jane, 338
Hooyman, Nancy R., 227
Hopi Indians, 379, 386
Hormans, Arthur C., 428
Horowitz, Michael M., 385
Hospice
    AIDS and, 278–280
    bereavement care and, 258–259
    children and, 281
    cost of, 272–273
    definition of, 246
    eligibility for, 259
    evaluation of, 274–278
    freestanding hospice, 266
    goals of, 249, 281
    history of, 246–249
    home care by, 250, 250–261
    hospital-based hospice, 266
    and how to live with life-threatening illness, 271–272
    inpatient care by, 250, 260, 261–263, 266–267, 307–308
    issues of, 268–274
    models of inpatient care, 266–267
    nature of contemporary hospice, 240–266
    nursing-home-based hospice, 266
    pain management and, 240–250
    patient-centered care in, 256–257
    patient-family as unit of care, 250, 270–271
    public attitudes toward, 273–274
    quality of life and, 268–270
    and signs of approaching death, 260–261

statistics on, 249
team approach in, 250–256, 271
training professionals for, 273
volunteers in, 252–256
Hospital-based hospice, 266
Hospitals. See Institutional settings
Hostler, Sharon L., 100, 103
Howe, Daniel Walker, 411, 414
Howells, Kevin, 222
Huggins, Charles, 218–219, 220
Huichol, 376, 386
Human Group, The (Homans), 65
Human immunodeficiency virus. See HIV
Human Organization, 52
Humanistic approach, 123
Humphry, Derek, 296–297, 329
Humphry, Hubert H., 226–227
Hunter, Dr., 453
Huntington, Richard, 366, 367, 371, 373, 376
Hutchinson, Woods, 419
Hyner, Gerald C., 30

I

Identity crisis, in adolescence, 124–126
Igbo, 381
Ik, 383
Illich, Ivan, 290
Immediate disposition, 472–473
Immortality
    and afterlife experiences by clinically dead, 191–196
    biosocial immortality, 439
    Buddhism on, 170–180
    Christianity on, 160–170
    creative immortality, 439
    fading of, 180–190
    of heroes, 180–191
    Hinduism on, 176–178
    Islam on, 172–173
    Judaism on, 166
    meaning immortality, 47
    natural immortality, 439
    and relative death meanings in society, 187–189

species immortality and scientific naturalism, 419
symboled immortality, 47
symbolic immortality, 185–187
India, 366, 387, 390
Indians. See Native Americans
Infants
  burial of, 83–85
  deaths of, 12–13, 84
  effects of other's death on, 100
  parents' grief at death of, 108–112, 510–514
  perinatal deaths of, 511–514
  Sudden Infant Death Syndrome, 108–112
Ingram, Ellen, 327, 353
Inheritance, 60–61
Inpatient hospice care, 250, 260, 261–263, 266–267
Institutional settings. See also Hospice
  control of resources in, 210
  for dying, 200–211
  for elderly, 144, 146
  and normalization of dying, 230
  restriction on mobility in, 210
  statistics on deaths in, 458
  stripping process in, 210
  support for parents after perinatal death, 511–515
Insurance. See Life insurance
International Association for Near-Death Studies (NIANDS), 191
Intersubjectivity, 195
Intubation, 288
Ionesco, Eugene, 190
Irion, Paul, 459
Irish immigrants, 368
ISAS, 67
Islam, 172–174
Itemization, 477–479

J
Jackson, A., 374
Jackson, Edgar, 459
Jacques, Elliott, 136
Jakub, Deanne K., 109, 112, 113
Japanese, 380, 393

Jasper, Jackson H., 15
Jews. See Judaism
Johnson, Earvin "Magic," 6
Johnson, J. B., 418
Johnson, Paul V., 482, 508
Johnson, Skip, 191, 196
Jones, Kazas, 279
Joseph, Jenny, 145, 146
Journal of Abnormal and Social Psychology, The, 52
Journal of Near-Death Studies, 191
Journal of Social Psychology, The, 52
Journals, 10, 52, 430
Judaism, 166–169, 186, 326, 336, 450
Judas Iscariot, 327
Julian, Emperor, 246–247
Jung, Carl, 134, 136

K
Ka, 452
Kaliai, 13
Kalingas, 393
Kalish, Richard, 141, 143, 146, 223
Kamerman, Jack, 224, 514
Kane, Anne, 223
Kapauku Papuans, 375, 394–395
Karma, 176
Kass, Leon, 13
Kastenbaum, Robert, 82, 124–125, 137, 141, 143, 277, 332, 335, 346, 347
Kaszuba, Mike, 384–385
Kavanaugh, Robert, 85, 86, 93–94, 147, 163, 164, 184, 217, 229, 270, 491, 497, 501, 504, 506
Keats, John, 189
Keifer, Lorraine, 37
Keith, P., 142
Kellehear, Allan, 58, 143, 217, 367
Kelly, Gerald, 294
Kelly, Orville, 211, 271–272
Kelly, Thomas E., 480–481
Kemp, James, 111
Kendall, Patricia L., 220
Kennedy, Jacqueline, 376
Kennedy, John F., 376
Kentucky, burial rites in, 391–392
Kesselman, Idell, 494

Kevorkian, Jack, 5, 301–303, 329
Kidney transplants, 313–314
Kindred Spirits (Durand), 414
King, Edith W., 367, 389
King, Rodney, 6
Kitzhaber, John, 317
Kiyak, H. Asuman, 227
Klagsbrun, F., 337
Klass, D., 9, 91
Klenow, D. J., 207
Kletti, Ray, 191
Klima, George J., 394
Kloeppel, D. A., 495
Knapp, Ronald, 89
Knight, Bernard, 109
Knobel, Peter S., 166, 168
Konyak Nagar, 387
Koocher, Gerald P., 93, 125
Kota people, 366
Kotch, Jonathan B., 113
Kottak, Conrad, 388
Kozak, David L., 367
Krant, Mel, 276
Kraus, Jess F., 336
Kravath, R. E., 112
Krous, Henry, 111
Kübler-Ross, Elisabeth, 10, 11, 208, 211–212, 215, 216–218, 227, 377, 497
Kulenkamp, E. J., 510
Kuper, Hilda, 375, 394
Kushner, Rabbi Harold, 88, 96
Kutner, Lawrence, 135

L
La Grand, Louis, 509
Labeling theory, 228–229
Labus, Janet, 275
Lack, Sylvia A., 259, 269, 274
Lamers, William M., 174, 176, 178, 179, 183–184, 377, 383, 415, 417, 431, 453, 462–463
Lamm, Richard, 317
Lancaster, Carol J., 222
Langerak, Edward, 289
Langley, Lynne, 518
Lanza, R. T., 309
Lawyer, on hospice team, 251
LeBonniec, Yves, 329
Lee, Brian C., 15
Leggard, Bruce, 83
Lehman, Ann, 513
Lehr, Robert, 456
Leming, John H., 188
Leming, Michael R., 22, 66,

Leming, Michael R., (continued)
72, 141, 143, 145,
162, 164, 206, 246,
394
Leming Death Fear Scale, 22,
24–27
Lenin, V. I., 188
Lessa, William A., 381, 386
Lester, David, 332
Let Me Die Before I Wake
(Humphrey), 296
Levinson, Daniel, 132
Levirate marriage, 186, 376
Leviton, Daniel, 9, 222
Lewis, C. S., 170–171
Liberal religion, 410–420
Licensure, of funeral directors,
463–467
Lieber, Ben, 342–343
Life, monetary value of, 37
Life after Life (Moody), 191
Life expectance, 28–30, 35
Life insurance, 428–430
Life review, 140, 143
LifeShare of the Carolinas, 187
Lifton, Robert J., 47, 125, 185,
437
Lindemann, Erich, 459
Lineage, 375
Living wills, 293–300
Lloyd, Phoebe, 417
Loneliness, as stage of griev-
ing, 490–501
Lonetto, Richard, 103
Long, J. Bruce, 173
Longitudinal studies, 130
Loss, as stage of grieving,
490–501, 504
Loved One, The, 456
Lowenthal, Marjorie F., 132
Ludwig, Allen, 410
Lugbara, 371–372, 393–394
Lund, Dale A., 141, 143
Lyons, Christine, 95, 97, 104

M

Madagascar, 373
Magars, 383
Mager, Scott, 312
Magno, Josefina B., 246, 277
Mahayana, 179
Mahler, Gustav, 437–439
Mahoney, Patrick, 312
"Make Each Day Count," 211
Malaya, 377, 383, 393
Malcolm, Andrew H., 309,
310
Maldonado, George, 336

Malinowski, Bronislaw, 64–66,
150–161, 163, 366,
387, 388
Mandelbaum, D., 366
Mandell, F., 112
Manifest functions, 380–390
Mann, Horace, 422
Mann, Thomas, 189
Man's Concern with Death
(Toynbee), 131
Mao Tse-Tung, 188
Maori, 383
Maples, Pam, 301
Mapuche Indians, 383
Marcus, Frances Frank, 379
Marcuse, Herbert, 58
Mardudjara aborigines, 393
Marginal situations, 157
Marital status, and suicide,
335–336
Marks, S. C., 220
Marriage. See Levirate marriage
Martin, Douglas, 83–85
Martin, Harry W., 457
Martin, Jeannee Parker, 278,
280
Martin, Steven C., 225
Martindale, C. J., 229
Martinson, I. M., 510
Martyrs, 187
Marx, Karl, 188, 334–335
Master status, 216
Mather, Cotton, 408
Mausoleums, 471–472
Maxwell, Elizabeth, 233–236
May, K. A., 510
May, Philip A., 336, 343–344
Mayo, Wyndham R., 432
Mayo Clinic, 329
McBrien, Richard P., 169
McCall, Patricia L., 330
McCarthy, Abigail, 141, 143
McClain, M., 112
McClean-Rice, Nicholas, 194
McClowry, S. G., 510, 511
McCormick, Wayne C., 279
McCown, Darlene, 92
McDowell, Eugene E., 326,
340
McGee, Julie, 90
McGuire, Dawn, 11
McGuire, Donald J., 326, 338
McIntosh, John L., 339, 345
McKenzie, Sheila C., 143
McLean, Don, 127
McNeil, Joan N., 129
Mead, Hirini Moko, 383
Meaning

conflicting death-related
meanings, 68–69
creation and change of,
40–50
death meanings and their
effects on the dying
process, 206–218
norm and role meanings of
dying, 211–213
object and self-meanings of
dying, 213–218
relative death meanings in
society, 187–189
religious interpretations of
death, 164–184
religious-meaning systems,
158–159
social nature of, 48–49
social situation meanings
of dying, 218
space meanings of dying,
200–211
temporal interpretations of
death, 184–191
time meanings and the
dying process,
206–209
value meanings of dying,
213
Meaning immortality, 47
Meaning of Death, The (Feifel),
10, 123
Media
AIDS and, 8
portrayal of death on, 6–8,
100, 104–105, 126
suicide clusters and,
343–345
Medicaid, 272, 273, 315
Medical schools
death education in, 11,
220–223, 237
socialization in, 210–220
Medicare Hospice Benefit, 272
Melby, Christopher L., 30
Memento mori, 410
Memorial Day, 379
Memorial services, 172,
473–474
Memorial societies, 474
Mendoza, Betty L., 109, 112,
113
Mercy killing, 296–297,
300–301, 304–306,
307.
See also Euthanasia
Merina, 367
Mermann, Alan C., 220, 221

Merton, Robert K., 220, 389
Metcalf, Peter, 366, 367, 371, 373, 376
Metchnikoff, Elie, 418–419
Metress, Eileen, 368
Mexico
 Huichol in, 376, 386
 Zinacantecos in, 386, 390, 391
Micronesia, 381, 386, 390
Middle class, rise of, 413–414
Middle-aged adulthood
 beginning of, 134
 and beginning of panic, 134–136
 characteristics of, 134
 personal growth during, 134, 136–137
 philosophical outlook of, 136
Middleton, John, 371, 393
Miles, M. S., 222
Millay, Edna St. Vincent, 97
Miller, Kyle E., 15
Miller, M. David, 126
Minorities. See Blacks; Hispanics; Native Americans; Race
Mitford, Jessica, 10
Modena, Rabbi Leona, 166
Modern Park Cemeteries (Weed), 424
Moksha, 176
Montagu, Ashley, 30, 99
Montgomery, Paul, 301
Moody, Raymond A., Jr., 191–193, 195
Mores, 50
Mormons, 195
Morris, Richard A., 389
Morrish-Vidners, Donna, 327
Mortality statistics, 27–34
Mortuary science, licensure for, 464
Moss, Miriam S., 142
Moss, Sidney Z., 142
Mother Goose, 104–107
Mourning. See Bereavement
Mourning pictures, 417
Movies. See Films
Mumfurd, Lewis, 435
Mummies, 451, 452, 453
Munnichs, J. A. A., 143
Murphy, Sister Patrice, 495
Murray, Judith, 511
Music, death themes in, 126–128
Mutual pretense, 226

N

Nagamine, Takahiko, 380
Nagi, Mostafa, 296, 301
Nagy, Maria, 101, 103
Nam, Charles B., 108, 109
Nardi, Peter, 8
National Endowment for the Humanities, 7
National Funeral Directors Association (NFDA), 430, 456, 465, 467, 473, 476–477
National Hospice Organization (NHO), 248–249, 253, 256, 259, 266, 272, 277
National Institute of Aging, 143
National Research and Information Center, 480
Native Americans
 attitudes toward death, 377, 379
 customs at death, 383
 customs regarding the corpse, 386
 emotions displayed during mourning, 375
 funeral homes for, 384–385
 ghosts and, 370
 suicide of, 336, 344
Natural immortality, 437, 439
Naturalism, scientific, 418–419
Navajo Indians, 370, 377, 386
NDE. See Near-death experiences (NDE)
Near-death experiences (NDE), 191–196
Neimeyer, Robert A., 22
Nelki, J., 218, 221
Nelson, Tom, 209
Nelson, W. A., 221
Nepal, 383
Ness, David E., 495
Netherlands, legalization of mercy killing in, 300–301, 304–306, 307
Neugarten, Bernice L., 135, 137
New Orleans, 373–374, 370–380
New Zealand, 383
NFDA. See National Funeral Directors Association (NFDA)

NHO. See National Hospice Organization (NHO)
NIANDS. See International Association for Near-Death Studies (NIANDS)
Niche, 471
Nicol, M. T., 510
Nieburg, Herbert, 517
Nigeria
 Bornu in, 383
 Igbo in, 381
 Yoruba in, 391, 393
Ninker, Robert W., 481
Nir, Yehuda, 86–88
Nirvana, 180
Nixon, J., 510
Nixon, Richard M., 227
Nordby, Ann, 263–266
Normalization, of dying, 230
Norman, William H., 143
Norms
 definition of, 211
 norm meanings of dying, 211–213
 prior to death, 382–383
North Borneo, 381, 382–383, 390
Notebaart, James, 384
Nothingness, fear of, 190
Noyes, Russell, Jr., 191
Nuclear Age, 434–441
Nurses
 and AIDS patients, 227
 and awareness contexts of dying, 225–227
 death education for, 11
 and dying patients, 211–212, 224–227
 hospice nurses, 251, 276–277
 perinatal death and, 511–515
Nursing-home-based hospice, 266
Nursing homes. See Institutional settings

O

Oaks, Judy, 310, 313, 336, 337, 347
Obituary, 416
Object meanings, of dying, 213–218
O'Brien, John M., 126
Occupational therapist, 251
O'Dea, Thomas, 157, 158–159
Oken, D., 207

Older adulthood
  death fears and, 141–144
  death taboo and, 140–141
  Erikson's final stage of life, 140
  overview of, 137–140
  pets for elderly, 516–517
  place of death for, 144–146
  suicide during, 345–349
  young-old versus old-old, 137, 139
Olson, E., 47, 185
Olson, Les, 311–312
Omega: The Journal of Death and Dying, 10, 52
Omega Project, 503–504, 509
On Death and Dying (Kübler-Ross), 10, 216
Open awareness, 226
Opper, Sylvia, 101, 123
Orbach, Israel, 82, 338
Ordinary measures, of preserving life, 294–295
Oregon
  Death with Dignity Act, 300
  Russian immigrants in, 389
Organ donations, 186–187, 309–315
Osborn, June, 279
Osgood, Nancy J., 339, 345
Oswald, Lee Harvey, 189
Oswalt, W. H., 379
Otto, Melinda E., 249, 259
Owen, Greg, 7, 8, 134, 140
Oxley, J. MacDonald, 433

P
Pain, meaning of, 269
Pain management, in hospices, 240–250
Palgi, Phyllis, 371
Palliative care, 222
Papua, New Guinea, 13
Paracelsus, 288
Paradigm, 52, 225
Pardue, Peter, 179, 180
Parents
  and children at funerals, 461–463
  of dying children, 80–91
  grief at loss of infant, 510–514
  of SIDS children, 112–113
  of suicidal adolescents, 343

  support from health-care professionals after perinatal death, 511–513
Parents Without Partners, 509
Parker, Kevin C. H., 101
Parker, Ruth M., 225
Parkes, Colin M., 274, 506–507, 508
Parry, Jonathan, 367
Parsons, Talcott, 212, 332, 490
Pascal, Blaise, 156
Passive euthanasia, 291–296
Pastoral care, in hospices, 251
Patchner, Michael, 253
Pathologist, 230
Patient Self-Determination Act, 294
Pattison, E. Mansell, 217
Pattison, E. Marshall, 131
Paul, Apostle, 160–170
Pavela, Gary, 342
Paxton, Tom, 423–424
Pearn, J., 510
Pearson, Algene A., 222, 225
Pearson, Theresa Ann Campo, 14, 311–313
Peay, Pythia, 191
Peck, M., 338
Pediatric oncologist, 88
Peplau, L. A., 61
Perinatal deaths, 511–514
Perion, Steve, 384–385
Perpich, Rudy, 384
Perry, Kathleen, 495
Perry, Paul, 191
Pet deaths, 82, 97, 99, 393, 494–495, 514–519
Pheffer, Cynthia R., 495
Philippines, 393
Phillips, David, 344
Phipps, William E., 247
Physical therapist, 251
Physicians
  active suicide and, 297–300
  and AIDS patients, 227
  and awareness contexts of dying, 225–227
  death education for, 11, 220–223, 237
  and dying as deviance, 228–229, 237
  and dying patients, 207–209, 215, 218–227
  gender versus professional

  role of, 224–225
  and home care of the dying, 295–260
  hospice physicians, 250, 260, 261–263
  hospices and, 251, 277–278
  perinatal death and, 511–515
  referrals for hospice care, 277–278
  situational adjustment of, 210–220, 224
  socialization of, 210–220
  and suicide of patient, 350–353
Piaget, Jean, 101, 123, 124
Pike, Martha V., 432
Pilgrim, Mary, 344
Pilling, Arnold R., 386
Pine, Vanderlyn R., 9, 224, 458, 461
Pius XII, Pope, 292–293
Plato, 327
Pollack, J. M., 22
Postmortem. *See* Autopsy
Pratt, Clara, 92
Prearranging, of funerals, 470–482
Prefunding, of funerals, 470–480
Premchit, Sommai, 394
Preneed funerals, 470–482
President's Commission for the Study of Ethical Problems in Medicine and Biomedical and Behavioral Research, 14
Presley, Elvis, 127
Preston, Richard J., 392
Preston, Sarah C., 392
Prior, Lindsay, 10, 12, 329
Professional Animal Disposal Advisory Council, 519
Professions, characteristics of, 466–467
Propositions, 51–52
Pryor, Richard, 207
Psychiatrist, on hospice team, 251
Psychoanalysis, 123. *See also* Freud, Sigmund
Psychological autopsy, 332–333
Psychologist, on hospice team, 251

Public policy, on biomedical issues, 315–317
Punishment, and deviance, 229
Puritans, 407–410
Purohita, 179
Pyre, 390

Q

Qaddish, 168, 169
Qemant, 386
Quality of life
  euthanasia and, 288–290
  hospice and, 268–270
Quill, Timothy E., 350–353
Quinlan, Karen Ann, 5
Qur'an, 172–174

R

Race. *See also* Blacks; Hispanics; Native Americans
  AIDS and, 132, 133
  life expectancy by, 31–33
  suicide and, 336
Radcliffe-Brown, A. R., 64–66, 160, 161, 162, 366, 376, 388
Raether, Howard C., 467
Rahman, Fazlur, 173, 174, 291–292
Rambachan, Anant, 176–177
Rambo movies, 126
Ramsden, Peter G., 386
Ramsey, Michael, 252, 253, 254, 269
Ramsey, Paul, 13
Rand, Irving, 19
Range, Lillian M., 83, 327
Raphael, Beverly, 510
Rappaport, Roy A., 372
Rasmussen, Daniel, 263–266
Rasmussen, Gordon, 263–266
Rational suicide, 347–353
Rawlings, Maurice, 191
Ray, James Earl, 189
Reader, George G., 220
Reagan, Ronald, 14, 37
Redditt, Carol A., 126
Reece, R. M., 112
Reestablishment, as stage of grieving, 501–502
Reformed Tradition, 407–410
Reid, Ed, 186–187
Reid, Eric, 186–187
Reid, Lucie, 139
Reincarnation, 176–177, 380
Relief, as stage of grieving, 501
Religion

afterlife experiences by clinically dead, 191–196
Buddhism, 170–184
Christianity, 160–172
compared with temporal interpretations of death, 184–191
death and origin of, 156–159
death fears and, 160–165
definition of, 196
as dysfunctional, 160
etiology of, 156
Evangelicalism, 412–413
functions of, 196–197
"God Is Dead" theology, 436
Hinduism, 175–179
interpretations of death by, 164–184
Islam, 172–174
Judaism, 166–169
liberal religion in 19th century, 410–420
Puritans, 407–410
and relative death meanings in society, 187–189
rituals of, and anxiety, 64–66, 388
suicide and, 336
and understanding of death, 150–164
Unitarianism, 411, 421
Religiosity, 162
Reynolds, Burt, 216
Reynolds, D. K., 141
Rich, Charles L., 343
Richardson, Virginia, 135
Richardson, William C., 222
Richman, Joseph, 347
Riley, Jack, 135
Rilke, Rainer Maria, 189
Ring, Kenneth, 191, 192, 195
Rites of passage, 371–372
Rituals. *See also* Death ritual
  definition of, 128, 372
  funeral rituals, 159
  religious rituals and anxiety, 64–66, 388
  sentimentalism and, 415
Ritzer, George, 52–53, 54, 61
Roberts, W. C., 232
Robinson, Donald, 317
Robinson, Joan, 7
Robson, J. D., 490
Rockefeller, John D., 188

Rodabough, Tillman, 195
Role disengagement, 212
Role meanings of dying, 211–213
Roles
  bereavement role, 490–494
  definition of, 211
  sick role, 212–213, 490
Rolling Stones, 128
Romanticism, 414
Roosevelt, Franklin D., 479
Rosecke, Les, 385
Rosenberg, Charles E., 414
Rosenblatt, Paul C., 374, 375, 491
Rosenthal, Nina R., 10
Rottman, Theodore, 289
Rotundo, Barbara, 421
Rowe, Jane, 511
Rubin, Z., 61
Rudner, Richard, 51
Rules of the Sociological Method (Durkheim), 53
Runyon, Damon, 186
Russian immigrants, 389

S

Sahler, Jane, 82
Salaam, Kalamu ya, 373–374
Salamat, Ail, 390
Salish Indians, 383
Samsara, 176
Sanctity of life, 288–290
Sanders, C. M., 89
Sands, Roberta, 136
Sargent, A. H., 432
Sati, 390
Saunders, Al, 84
Saunders, Cecil, 348–349
Saunders, Cicely, 247, 248, 250, 276
Saunders, Julia, 348–349
Savishinsky, Joel S., 516
Scaramelli, Thomas J., 143
Schachter, Sherry, 125
Schaefer, Dan, 95, 97, 104
Schneidman, Edwin, 436
Schofferman, Jerome, 228, 229
Schulz, Charles, 82
Schwab, Reiko, 89, 90, 91, 510
Science. *See also* Anthropology of death ritual; Sociology
  intersubjectivity in, 195
  sociology as, 51–53
Scientific naturalism, 418–419
Scott, Carley R., 482, 483
Scott, M., 140

Seale, C., 208
Seavoy, Mr., 424
Self-deliverance, 296–297, 300
Self-fulfilling prophecy, 48
Self-meanings, of dying, 213–218
Semai, 377, 383, 393
Senescence, 140, 214
Sentimentalism, 414–418
Seravalli, E. P., 209, 215
Sewall, Samuel, 407, 409
Sex. See Gender
Sex ratio, 30, 33
Sexton, 409, 453
Shaffer, David, 344
Shah, A. M., 175, 176
Shakespeare, William, 288
Shannon, Robert, 266
Shaw, George Bernard, 466
Shelley, Percy Bysshe, 188, 189
Shiv'ah, 168–169
Shock, as stage of grieving, 497–498
Shraddha, 179
Siblings
    of dying children, 91–93
    perinatal deaths and, 512, 513
Sick role, 212–213, 490
SIDS. See Sudden Infant Death Syndrome (SIDS)
Sieck, Craig, 289
Significant others, 50
Simon, Paul, 127
Simonds, O. C., 422
Simons, Marlise, 305–307
Sirhan, Sirhan, 189
Sisler, H., 142
Situational adjustment, 210–220, 224
Skinner, B. F., 20
Sklar, Fred, 495
Skynyrd, Lynyrd, 127
Slater, Robert C., 467
Slippery-slope-to-Auschwitz argument, 303–308
Smith, Bayley, 423
Smith, JoAnn Kelley, 47
Smith, Marguerite T., 429
Smith, Walter J., 338
Smoking
    lung cancer and, 232
    maternal smoking and infant death, 109
Sneed, William, 472
Soblotne, Eddie, 312
Social Behavior: Its Elementary

Forms (Homans), 65
Social definitionist paradigm, 61–72
    social exchange theory, 63–66
    symbolic interaction theory, 67–72
Social exchange theory, 63–66
Social factist paradigm, 53–61
    conflict theory, 58–61
    structural-functionalist theory, 54–58
Social factors, of suicide, 335–336
Social meaning of dying and death
    conflict theory, 58–61
    creating and changing meaning, 40–50
    labeling theory, 228–229
    reasons for use of sociological perspective, 72–73
    social definitionist paradigm, 61–72
    social exchange theory, 63–66
    social factist paradigm, 53–61
    social nature of meaning, 48–49
    sociological approach, 50–53
    structural-functionalist theory, 54–58
    symbolic interaction theory, 67–72
    versus biological process of dying, 46–48
Social nature of meaning, 48–49
Social situation meanings, of dying, 218
Social stratification, of cemeteries, 424
Social worker, on hospice team, 251
Socialization
    on death, 6
    to death fears in adolescence, 126–128
    of medical students, 210–220
    and rise of middle class, 414
Societal disengagement, 209
Sociology
    approach to understanding dying and death,

50–53
    conflict theory, 58–61
    definition of, 50–51
    of funerals, 460
    labeling theory, 228–229
    paradigms in, 52–53
    reasons for use of sociological perspective, 72–73
    as science, 51–53
    social definitionist paradigm, 61–72
    social exchange theory, 63–66
    social factist paradigm, 53–61
    structural-functionalist theory, 54–58
    of suicide, 330–332
    symbolic interaction theory, 67–72
Socrates, 142, 326
Soli, Jane, 492–494
Soul, 369, 379, 390. See also Immortality
Soul houses, 391
Sourkes, B., 92
South America
    Cubeo of, 373
    Yanomamö Indians in, 387–388
Southall, D. P., 109
Space meanings, of dying, 200–211
Species immortality, 419
Spencer, A. J., 451–452
Spinetta, J. J., 92
Springen, Karen, 230, 232
Srinivas, M. N., 175, 176
Stack, Steven, 344–345
Stafford-Clark, David, 457
Stalin, Joseph, 188
Stambrook, Michael, 101
Stannard, David E., 417
Stark, Rodney, 162
Stendahl, Krister, 190
Stephenson, John, 226
Stepping Heavenward, 417
Stevens, Wallace, 438
Stevenson, Ian, 201
Stewart, Marguerite, 511
Stillion, Judith M., 24, 142, 326, 340
Stockton, Nancy, 342
Stockwell, Edward G., 12
Stoddard, Sandol, 247
Strange, Sir John, 427
Strauss, Anselm, 207, 225
Stricherz, M., 136

Stripping, as process in institutional settings, 210
Structural-functionalist theory, 54–58
Suda, 375
Sudden Infant Death Syndrome (SIDS)
  etiology of, 100–112
  incidence of, 108–109
  parents of SIDS children, 112–113
Suicidal gestures, 329
Suicide. *See also* Euthanasia
  as active euthanasia, 296–297, 300
  of adolescents, 330–343, 344
  age and, 330, 335, 354
  AIDS and, 335
  alienation and, 334–335
  altruistic suicide, 332
  anomic suicide, 332
  Catholics' view of, 326
  of children, 338–339
  cluster suicides, 339, 341, 343–345
  of college students, 341–343
  dealing with aftermath of, 355
  definition of, 328
  disenfranchised grief and, 495
  dramaturgical perspective of, 332–333
  egoistic suicide, 332
  of elderly, 345–349
  existentialist perspective on, 333–334
  fatalistic suicide, 332
  gender and, 337, 342, 345–346
  historical perspectives on, 326–327
  how to help in suicidal crisis, 337
  as large-scale social phenomenon, 329
  marital status and, 335–336
  methods of committing, 337, 346–347
  professions and, 336
  public attitudes toward, 297, 326–329
  race and, 336, 344
  rational suicide, 347–353
  religion and, 336
  signs of, 336–337, 346–347
  social factors of, 335–336
  sociological perspective on, 330–332
  statistics on, 320–330, 330–340, 341, 345
  suicidal gestures versus, 329
  survivors' reactions to, 34
  theoretical perspectives on, 330–335
  time of year and time of week of, 336
  views of suicide survivor, 354
Suicide: A Study in Sociology (Durkheim), 331, 332
Suicide, Its Use, History, Technique and Current Interest (Guillon and LeBonniec), 329
Suicide clusters, 339, 341, 343–345
"Suicide machine," 5, 329
Sullivan, Andrew, 132
Sumner, Edward D., 11, 222
Support groups for the bereaved, 509, 510–511
Suspicion awareness, 226
Sussman, Marvin, 60
Swazi, 375–376, 394
Sweeting, Helen N., 137, 366
Swerdlow, Joel L., 310
Symboled immortality, 47
Symbolic immortality, 185–187
Symbolic interaction theory, 67–72
Symbols
  and death-related meanings, 395–396
  definition of, 67
  empirical nature of, 48–49
  social nature of meaning and, 48–49
  in symbolic interaction theory, 67
Syme, G. J., 510

T

T-3. *See* Triiodothyronine (T-3)
Taboos
  on death conversation, 16
  death taboo and the elderly, 140–141
  Elderhostel and, 4, 140
on suicide, 340
Tantrayana, 179
Tanzania, 394
Tatelbaum, Judy, 388
Taylor, Elizabeth, 456–457
Taylor, Greg W., 335
Taylor, Jacque, 108, 112
Taylor, Lawrence, 415
Taylor, Robert B., 370, 372, 373
Team approach, in hospices, 250–256, 271
Television, 7, 100, 104–105, 147
Temporal, 162
Temporal interpretations, of death, 184–191
Tennyson, Alfred Lord, 190
Term life insurance, 429
Terminally ill. *See* Dying
Tewa Indians, 386
Texas Chain Saw Massacre, The, 126
Thach, Bradley, 111
Thailand, 383, 394
Thanatology. *See also* Bereavement; Death; Dying
  courses in, 8–10
  definition of, 4
  as discipline, 8–10
  for health professionals, 11, 220–223, 237
  journals in, 10
  rationale for increased interest in, 4–6
Theodorson, Achilles G., 328
Theodorson, George A., 328
Theravada, 179
Thielicke, Helmuth, 456
Thin Lizzy, 128
Thomas, Lewis, 437–439
Thomas, W. I., 48, 61
Thornton, Gordon, 494, 495
Thurnher, Majda, 132
Time meanings, and the dying process, 206–209
Tiwi, 386
Tobin, S., 82
Todd, Mike, 457
Tolchin, Martin, 345
Tolstoy, Leo, 189
Tompkins, J. R., 510
Tonkinson, Robert, 393
Toolbox Murders, The, 126
Torok, Tom, 393
Tournier, Robert E., 208, 223
Toynbee, Arnold, 131
Transplant surgery, 186–187,

Transplant surgery, (continued) 300–315
Triiodothyronine (T-3), 112
Trobriand Islanders, 387
Truman, Harry, 434
Tuckerman, Henry, 422
Turnbull, Colin M., 96, 206–207, 383
Turner, Jonathan H., 65, 67
Twain, Mark, 326, 347
Tylor, E. B., 369

U

Uchendu, Victor C., 381
Uganda
    AIDS in, 369
    Ik of, 383
    Lugbara in, 393–394
    Lugbara of, 371–372
Ulithi, 381, 386, 390
Uniform Anatomical Gift Act, 310
Uniform Donor Card, 311
Unitarianism, 411, 421
United Nations, 12
Universal life insurance, 429
Urn, 471
Utilitarianism, 315–316

V

Valdes-Dapena, Maria A., 109
Value meanings, of dying, 213
Van Buren, Abigail, 509
Van Eys, Jan, 230
Van Gennep, A., 371
Variable life insurance, 429
Vault, 469
Vault liners, 478
Vedas, 175
Venezuela, 387–388
Venturism, 18
Verhey, Allen, 289
Vernon, Glenn M., 67, 68–69, 71, 184–185, 206
Verstehen, 61
Victorian period, 414–418

Video Tribute, 481–482
Viewing of corpse, 459, 468
Viney, Linda L., 133
Viral infections, 109, 112
Vogt, Evon Z., 386, 390
Volatile reactions, as stage of grieving, 498–499
Volunteers, on hospice team, 252–256
Vovelle, Michel, 10

W

Waechter, Eugenia, 86
Wagner, Randall, 211
Wakes, 172, 368
Walker, Barbara, 191, 195
Wallenstein, Sylvan, 343, 344
Walsh, Ken, 20
Walsh, R., 374
Wanzer, Sidney, 222
Ward, Joe, 90–91
Ward, S. L., 112
Warner, W. Lloyd, 46, 406
Wass, Hannelore, 126, 140–141, 142
Weber, Max, 61
Wee, Morris, 265
Weed, Howard Evarts, 424
Weeping. See Crying
Weigand, Celia Garcia, 376, 386
Weigand, Paul C., 376, 386
Weiner, Morris, 167
Weisman, Avery D., 143, 494–495, 515–516, 517
Wells, Richard A., 432
Wertenbaker, Lael, 272
West Indies, 385
West New Guinea, 375, 394–395
Wheeler, Alban L., 228
Whitaker, Leighton, 342
White, Janet, 255–256
White, Jerry, 19
Who, The, 127

Whole life insurance, 429
Whose Life Is It Anyway? (Clark), 280–290
Wibecan, Ken, 294
Widow to Widow Program, 509
Wilkerson, Isabel, 454–455
Will, conflict theory's approach to fairness of, 60–61
Will, James, 480
Williams, Thomas R., 390
Williams, Melvin, 390
Williams, Susan, 301–302
Williams, Thomas R., 381, 382
Wizard of Oz, The, 187, 502
Wolterstorff, Eric, 89
Womach, Merrill, 481–482
Worden, J. William, 503–505, 510, 520
World Health Organization, 12
Wulff, Greg, 482
Wyss, James, 391–392

Y

Yahrzeit, 169
Yalom, I., 101
Yang, Bijou, 331, 332
Yang, Chung-Hsin, 332
Yanomamö Indians, 387–388
Yoruba, 391, 393
Young adulthood
    AIDS and, 132–133
    as novice phase, 132
    remembering death in, 131
Youngner, S. J., 15
Youngs, G. A., 207

Z

Zambia, 369
Zeitlin, Steven J., 436
Zevon, Warren, 127–128
Zinacantecos, 386, 390, 391
Zinn, H. Jackson, 18, 19
Zunin, Hillary, 507–508

Learning Resources
Centre